HAMILTON COUNTY

A HISTORY OF

HAMILTON COUNTY

TENNESSEE

James W. Livingood

MEMPHIS STATE UNIVERSITY PRESS

To
Alma
and three young Hamiltonians,
Eric, Brent, and Kevin

Contents

Preface

As the last words of this narrative are written, it becomes only too clear that the study of Hamilton County's history has just begun. So much of the drama and adventure of the people who called the area home cannot be caught in the rush of time; so much of the impact of their contribution to our heritage cannot be truly measured or properly interpreted. Judgments have had to be made; certain things included, others left out. It is hoped that those readers whose interests are slighted or ignored will be tolerant of the problems of Clio, muse of history.

Change is the constant factor which marks all history. In certain eras change in Hamilton County was extremely slow, as illustrated by the evolution of prehistoric Indian events. At other moments it was most abrupt—called by some "deep change"—creating almost complete, unconnected transitions, as recorded in the Cherokee Removal, the Civil War, and the social revolt of the 1960s.

As measured by time, today's Hamiltonians are a new people. Only since 1819 have they made a direct contribution to the heritage of the county's pattern of life or the state of its technology. As typical American pioneers they bequeathed to the future an optimistic faith in themselves, a pragmatic knowledge, and a variety of hard-earned experiences.

But the story of the county cannot be constructed solely on the experiences of its residents. Local life, thought, and dreams have always been influenced by state, regional, and national affairs; so the history of the county becomes a miniature of the United States.

For aid and encouragement in preparing this study I wish to express gratitude to numerous people. To the librarians in the historical division of the Chattanooga-Hamilton County Bicentennial Library I am grateful for their courtesy and professional skill: Mrs. Clara W. Swann, Miss Judy Sketoe, Mrs. Marsha Broughton, Mrs. Pat Bennett, and Douglas Vandagriff. David Gray, a most knowledgeable local historian, Robert Elmore of the Convention and Visitors Bureau, and James Hunt of the Chamber of Commerce have my heartfelt appreciation. Mayor Charles Rose and his colleagues of the Chattanooga city government consistently extended their encouragement to me and the officials of both the old and new county government promoted the project with certain financial considerations to help meet the costs of research. Finally, the Chattanooga-Hamilton County Bicentennial Commission—Dr. Spencer J. McCallie, Jr., chairman; Floyd C. Delaney, James Hunt, John Stophel, Mayor Charles Rose, Judge Don Moore, C. C. Bond, Mrs. Z. Cartter Patten, John Popham, Robert Kirk Walker, and Rudolph H. Walldorf—adopted this volume as one of its projects and assisted in raising money to make the book available at a reasonable price. The commission earned the encouragement and assistance of the Chattanooga Chamber Foundation when it disbanded. To all, a sincere thank you.

1 September 1979   James W. Livingood

HAMILTON COUNTY

A County Is Created

ON 25 October 1819, the Tennessee General Assembly sitting in Murfreesboro approved legislation creating Hamilton County.[1] The lawmakers specifically stated that they chose the name "in honor and to perpetuate the memory of the late Alexander Hamilton, secretary of the treasury of the United States." It was an unusual selection, for the vast majority of voters in the Tennessee country supported the political ideals of Thomas Jefferson rather than those of Hamilton, who favored nationalistic unity and a strong federal government that subordinated state authority. Nevertheless, the small, slender former cabinet member who boasted elegant clothes and fine manners enjoyed considerable popularity as a founding father and as a political martyr whose career ended in 1804 at the age of forty-nine in a duel with Aaron Burr.

The establishment of county government represented a unique feature of the American political experiment. In no other corner of the world had anything like it been undertaken. Here, when an area became open for settlement, the local people gained the right to establish local government. By the authority of the state, the citizens received the vital privilege of providing for law and order and a seat of justice where deeds would be recorded, marriage licenses obtained, records assembled, taxes levied and paid, and justice meted out. It represented democracy at the grass roots.

Although novel in world political history, the process was neither new in the United States nor in the state of Tennessee. When Governor Joseph McMinn received the private act establishing Hamilton County, forty-one Tennessee counties had already experimented with the county process in their local political laboratories. And in the year 1819 six other counties—Hardin, McMinn, Monroe, Perry, Shelby, and Wayne—launched themselves along with the local county.[2]

The date of the creation of Hamilton County relates not to a pressing necessity for local government but rather to the federal government's acquisition of new Indian lands. In 1820 only 821 persons, including 16 free blacks and 39 slaves, resided in the area. They were clustered mainly in the Sale Creek section where they had cleared land and built homes under the jurisdiction of Rhea County. They did provide a working community, however, from which commissioners could be selected to decide on a county seat and launch a government. The legislature named Charles Gamble, Robert Patterson, and William Lauderdale for this responsible duty.[3]

Some nonresidents who held land claims within the limits of the new county had a special interest in its development. These absentee claimants, although they paid no taxes on their lands, could not utilize their potential until Indian land cessions were a reality. Interest in the land actually dated back to 1663 when the English king granted a charter for the colony of Carolina which extended westward beyond the mountains, included the future Hamilton County, and ran on to the Pacific Ocean. Some years later when the colony separated into North and South Carolina, the extent of the western claim was reduced; North Carolina, however, found herself with control over all of the Tennessee country under British supreme authority.

The American Revolution cost Great Britain her claim to the land; North Carolina now held independent, sovereign power, insisting that the Indians' claims were extinguished by the very fact that the Cherokees had participated in the war on the wrong and losing side. So her politicians and land speculators—often the same people—began a program of transferring land titles into private hands by the time the fighting stopped. They allocated millions of acres within the Tennessee country as military bonuses or generous bargains to individuals. Since no distinction was made as to whether the grants were located in territory open to frontier settlement or in Indian country, numerous tracts were registered in all parts of the Tennessee country including the land that later become Hamilton County.

One of the earliest signs of North Carolina's "prodigal generosity" was the registration of a large tract in the future Hamilton County in 1788 to Martin Armstrong and Stockley Donelson. Donelson, son of Colonel John Donelson and future brother-in-law of Andrew Jackson, and Armstrong were active surveyors. Working in the field with a sharp eye to future profits they received, partly in payment for their services, huge claims in many parts of the state.

The wording of this first Hamilton County land grant is typical:

> To all to whom these presents shall come, Greeting: Know ye that we, for and in consideration of the sum of ten pounds for every one hundred acres Hereby Granted, paid into our Treasury by Martin Armstrong and Stockley Donelson, have given and granted and by these presents do give and grant unto the said Martin Armstrong and Stockley Donelson a tract of land containing six hundred and forty acres lying and being in our County of Hawkins on the North side of the Tennessee River at the mouth of Deep Creek beginning at two ashes on a Rocky bluff near the mouth of a Spring branch, then up the river as it meanders to a stake, thence west three hundred and forty poles to a stake, thence South foure hundred and forty poles to a stake, thence East two hundred and forty poles to the Beginning as the plat hereunto annexed dothe appear, together with all the woods, waters, mines, minerals, heriditaments and appurtannances to the said land belonging or appertaining. To hold by the said Martin Armstrong and Stockley Donelson, their heirs and assigns forever, yielding and paying to us such sums of money yearly or otherwise as our General Assembly from time to time may direct. Provided always that the said Martin Armstrong and Stockley Donelson shall cause this grant to be registered in the Register's office of our County of Hawkins within twelve months from the date hereof, otherwise the same shall be void and of no effect.

Donelson got other grants, one with William Terrill for 5,000 acres including the mouth of Little Chickamauga Creek and another dated 1795 and comprising 20,000 acres specifically "but with the boundaries described to include 150,000 acres," part of which later lay in Marion County. The 20,000-acre tract extended from the mouth of North Chickamauga up that stream to the Cumberland Mountain or Walden Ridge and along that elevation to Richland Creek at the present site of Dayton and then along the creek and river to the beginning.

Some of the other grants included 640 acres to Landon Carter in 1789 and three grants, amounting to 2,400 acres, to Hugh McClung. John Hackett, another surveyor and attorney who had close ties with Stockley Donelson and his heirs, received a 1787 grant for 640 acres.

David Eagleton, David Stuart, Stephen Adair, John Medaris, and Moses McSpadden also had North Carolina grants.[4] Generally, the lands north of the Tennessee River, with the exception of the mountainous parts of Walden Ridge, were transferred to individual owners by the state of North Carolina before that state ceded its western lands to the United States in December 1789. Furthermore, North Carolina stipulated in the cession agreement that provisions the state had made for reserving lands for soldiers, for those who had made entries under her laws, and for occupants should remain in force.

Neither land claimant, speculator, or settler had any actual impact on the timing of the creation of Hamilton County. The pivotal point rested on the acquisition of Indian lands which had been the sole responsibility of the national government since 1785, when the United States finalized negotiations with the Cherokees in the Treaty of Hopewell. In November of that year the fledgling national government made a very lenient treaty which guaranteed the Cherokees sovereignty over their lands. This document nullified North Carolina's contention that the Revolutionary War voided the Indians' title to the land. North Carolina leaders protested vigorously in what became the first states' rights feud in the history of the republic.[5]

The United States made an effort to move settlers from Indian lands and to insist such lands were not open to frontier development. In 1796 when Tennessee gained its statehood, some three-fourths of the area of the state was Indian country. In many places whites drifted into the Cherokee territory; many "intruders," for example, pushed into the lower Sequatchie Valley and were ordered to move under a threat of military force. Few if any so-called intruders filtered into the future Hamilton County area, most likely because the Cherokee Agency on the Hiwassee River was located near enough to allow constant official surveillance.[6]

Tennessee officials were not a bit pleased with this situation. Placed between settlers and speculators, who insisted on expanding frontiers, and the federal government, which was pledged to a closed land policy, they endured constant pressure from all sides. Governors encouraged migration into the state to help neutralize the Cherokee claims, and whenever local governments were established after 1801, the state endowed them with extensive borders reaching far into the Indian country. Such shadowy borders which carried no legal authority represented a subterfuge for establishing future claims.

So between 1796 and 1801 the territory of future Hamilton County fell within the extended boundaries of Knox County. Then it was transferred in 1801 to the new county of Roane with Kingston as the county seat. A few years later, following the land purchase treaty of 1805, the Hamilton area was transferred to the newly created county of Rhea with official business transacted at Washington, later affectionately called Old Washington. However, during all this time, the Hamilton area was Indian country, closed to white settlement.

During these years, as Tennessee pressured the federal government to purchase more of the Indian lands and to promote the idea of total Indian removal from the area to lands beyond the Mississippi River, national authorities in turn reluctantly pressured the Cherokees to sell great chunks of their territory. New purchases in 1805 and 1806 made possible the creation of such counties as Bledsoe, Rhea, and Franklin, among others, and in 1817 the Jackson-McMinn Treaty opened the way for the establishment of Marion County. Within two years, on 27 February 1819, another large purchase resulted from negotiations known as the Calhoun Treaty. This agreement with the Cherokees called for their giving up the remainder of their lands in Tennessee north of the Tennessee River and all land on the south side of the Tennessee River north of the mouth of the Hiwassee River. All of this new acreage would be legally open to white settlement, with the exception of a few reservations specifically assigned to individual Cherokees who had lived there and made improvements on the land. Across southeastern Tennessee the Tennessee River south of the mouth of the Hiwassee River in 1819 marked the boundary between Cherokee territory and country populated by citizens of the United States.[7]

Before the year was out Tennessee created Hamilton County "southwest of Rhea and south and east of Bledsoe and Marion counties." In the typical loose language of the time the legislature described its boundaries. A selected section read: "Beginning at a point at the foot of Walden's Ridge of Cumberland mountain on the east side thereof; thence running to a point on the Tennessee river two and one half miles below the lower end of Jolly's island, so as to include Patrick Martin in the County of Hamilton . . . "[8]

Such vague directives coupled with the tasks of surveying a wilderness area led to many problems which meant lucrative business for a generation of lawyers. Trees, natural geographic features, and sites of tragedy often described the location of a boundary line. One such "call" describes a line as crossing a branch of Mountain Creek "at the place where Hugh Cunningham was drowned." Within two years the legislators acted "to settle" the new county boundaries. This time they stated:

> That the line running between the counties of Rhea and Hamilton, shall commence at a point one half mile below Blyth's ferry, and run across the valley to the mountain so as to run between the lands of Benjamin Jones and John Russell, thence up the foot of the said mountain to the line of said counties as now run and marked.
>
> That the dividing line between the counties of Hamilton and Marion shall be as follows, to wit: Beginning in the southeast corner of Bledsoe county thence along the extreme height of the mountain to the head of Suck creek, thence down said creek to the mouth thereof, thence due south to the southern boundary of the state.[9]

In this same era another boundary line was marked, creating problems which never went away entirely. Tennessee, believing it "would greatly tend to the prevention of disputes," sought Georgia's cooperation in a survey to locate the state line—the thirty-fifth parallel. Commissioners representing the two states met in May 1818 at the western end of the line, which was found to be two miles south of Nickajack. The spot, called Camak's Rock for the chief Georgia commissioner, marked the point where Georgia, Tennessee, and the future state of Alabama met.

The commissioners worked across wild, unbroken Indian country. Tennessee, pleased with the project, ratified the boundary as "the true dividing line between the states" and announced it would become the effective, legal border as soon as Georgia passed "a law similar." Georgia, on the other hand, had a map of the line recorded but never passed "a law similar."

Camak, believing the work of the surveying team faulty, made an unofficial second survey. He concluded that the original line was not the thirty-fifth parallel; he insisted it was too far south by approximately half a mile. To Camak, this meant that Georgia lost 50.51 square miles or over thirty-three thousand acres. But the border—which is also the southern boundary of Hamilton County—has remained where it was first drawn. Across the years arguments have boiled up over the matter; governors of Georgia, usually in jest, have claimed sovereignty over Chattanooga and dreamed of the tax money lost to Tennessee.[10]

The enabling legislation creating Hamilton County not only called for commissioners to select a temporary seat of justice "until otherwise provided by law" but also stated that courts of pleas and quarter-sessions and a circuit court should function "under the same rules, regulations and restrictions, and shall possess and exercise the same power and jurisdiction of said courts in other counties in this state." The sheriff was instructed to hold elections "on the first Thursday and Friday in March next" to select field officers for the militia, designated the Sixty-fourth Regiment attached to the Seventh Brigade.

Residents of the area immediately had the privilege of voting in local, state, and national elections. Along with Rhea and McMinn, Hamilton could elect one state representative; the same three together with Anderson, Roane, Morgan, Bledsoe, and Marion counties composed a state senatorial district.[11]

Locally, the people in this first election chose Charles Gamble for sheriff. He served until 1823. The Gambles, of Scotch-Irish descent, were typical residents. Their ancestors migrated to America, settling for a time in southeastern Pennsylvania before moving on down the great Philadelphia wagon road to Augusta County, Virginia. Members of the next generation pushed on to the southwest, taking up land in Knox County, but restless sons and daughters soon moved on. Charles acquired land on Sale Creek and moved to that corner of Rhea County in 1806. Upon the creation of Hamilton, he found himself within its jurisdiction and immediately assumed a role in public service in the family tradition.[12]

As the Cherokees from time to time agreed to the various land cession treaties, some moved west beyond the Mississippi River; others pushed southward into the vacant lands of northern Alabama and Georgia, to the growing consternation of the residents of those states. Claiming their state's sovereignty and honor to have been violated, Georgia officials pressured national authorities to get rid of the Cherokees. They insisted that the Indians were mere tenants, occupying land at the will of the state. Believing they could get no satisfaction from Washington, the Georgians decided to take matters into their own hands, and a law extending the jurisdiction of Georgia over the Cherokee territory went into effect on 1 June 1830. Cherokee law and custom were outlawed, contracts were deemed invalid, and public assemblies forbidden. The state took over Cherokee lands, homes, and improvements and distributed them by lottery to Georgia citizens. A demoralized nation of Cherokees recoiled into Tennessee.

Once Georgia extended her authority over the Cherokees, state officials urged her neighboring states to follow her example. Alabama did so at once. In Tennessee similar measures suffered defeat in the Tennessee Assembly in three different years. However, on 8 November

1833, upon recommendation of Governor William Carroll a measure was passed to extend the laws and jurisdiction of the state to its southern border "over that tract of country now in the occupancy of the Cherokee Indians." To facilitate this goal Tennessee counties immediately to the north of the Tennessee River received instructions to extend their limits on the southern shore to the state line.

For Hamilton County this 1833 law meant a major enlargement with extensive new boundaries, which the law described thus,

> . . . in addition to its present limits, the border line shall commence at the extreme height of the Raccoon mountain, at the point where the Marion County line terminates, running thence along the line dividing the States of Georgia and Tennessee, until it crosses White Oak mountain, continuing thence five miles to a point on said line and there terminating; thence running so as to strike the White Oak mountain two miles above Robinson's Gap, through which Wolf river creek runs, thence to the extreme height of said mountain to the Blythe's Ferry road at the place now occupied by Wilson Evans; thence along said road towards the Tennessee river, within two miles of William Blythe's; thence such a course to the Tennessee river as will leave William Blythe's plantation on the north side of said line, and strike the Tennessee river opposite the Rhea county line on the north bank of said river.

The "Surveyor General of the Hiwassee district" must have done a great deal of improvising as he carried out instructions to mark this and other county lines. Within a few years several modifications were legally made in the Marion-Hamilton line.

Although this law extended county boundaries, it represented only a shadow of things to come. Under its terms the Indians were to be exempt from taxation, road work, and military duty, and "shall be secured and protected in the free and unmolested enjoyment of their improvements and all personal property, according to the customs and usages of said Cherokee Indians." The act further stated that nothing should interfere with the Cherokee marriage customs and that Tennessee courts should not take jurisdiction of any criminal offense committed within the Indian country by any resident Cherokee "except for murder, rape and larceny." The Cherokees who had received reservations under the treaties of 1817 and 1819 and had become citizens of the United States were made subject to the laws of Tennessee.

This 1833 legislation also addressed the whites. It specifically stated, "nothing in this act contained, shall be construed to authorize any white man to settle within the limits of the lands in this State now within the occupancy of the Cherokee." In addition, "any entry or appropriation or occupancy of any of the land" continued to be illegal.[13]

Such deference to Cherokee rights and customs disappeared completely with the ratification of the Treaty of New Echota (the Removal Treaty) by the United States Senate on 23 May 1836. Cherokee opposition to its terms led to the tribe's forcible removal in 1838. All the while, between 1836 and 1838, whites filtered into the Indian territory south of the Tennessee River to gain early land claims; the area around Ross's Landing especially attracted early settlers. Hamilton County's jurisdiction now extended to all the area south of the Tennessee River.

Although acquired by the federal government, title to the Cherokee lands passed to Tennessee. On 18 October 1836, the General Assembly established what it termed a surveyor's district of all the acquired Cherokee territory known as the Ocoee District. Surveyors completed their work the next year and on 20 November 1837 the legislature provided a plan for the sale of land to individuals. It called for the opening of an entry taker's office at Cleveland "from and after" the first Monday in November 1838.

The complex initial stages of Hamilton County's history were then completed.

Almost twenty years later an unusual situation resulted in the temporary expansion of the county. Agitation from residents in parts of Marion and Bledsoe counties led to a movement to create Sequatchie County. When it appeared that a majority of the people concerned favored the idea, someone discovered that the state constitution of 1834 thwarted the plan. It restricted the taking of parts of an established county to form a new one in such ways as to block the Sequatchie scheme. Then state officials discovered an interesting constitutional loophole: the constitution had made no provision against taking parts of counties and attaching them to existing counties. The legislature accepted this interpretation and on 25 February 1856 attached the tenth civil district of Bledsoe and the first and second civil districts of Marion County to Hamilton County. Technically, this merger lasted only from 21 September to 9 December 1857, for it was generally understood that the arrangement was one of convenience and not to be permanent. On the latter date the General Assembly created Sequatchie County simply by detaching the three civil districts from Hamilton. So a constitutional fight was avoided although Sequatchie County had to face other problems before its legal status was fully determined.[14]

Immediately following the removal of the Cherokees, the county electorate voted on the site of the county seat. The decision on that

January date in 1840 called for moving the political center of the county from Dallas to Harrison, on the southern bank of the river. Thirty years later another referendum tested the will of the people regarding the location of the courthouse; this time Chattanooga won over Harrison. On 5 December 1870, in a funereal atmosphere, the last court convened at Harrison to appoint a new clerk and master and to direct the removal of records and files in a two-horse-drawn vehicle.

While Judge David M. Key supervised these proceedings, an attorney for the people of Harrison worked to get an injunction to prevent removal. A furious fight over the county seat ensued. The Harrison advocates charged fraud; they claimed that black women in large numbers, dressed as men, voted in Chattanooga to move the courthouse. Meanwhile the "carry all" with its freight of books and records unloaded at the new office and one phase of the struggle ended.

Now the Harrison supporters chose another approach. They worked for and succeeded in getting a new county established from fractions of Hamilton and Bradley counties. The act, passed 27 January 1871, named the new unit James County in honor of the Reverend Jesse J. James, father of Representative Elbert James, who had introduced the bill.

The legal boundaries for James County as set forth in the law were as follows:

> Beginning at the corner of Hamilton, Bradley, and Meigs county lines; thence running along and with said Meigs county line to the middle of the Tennessee River; thence down the middle of said river to the Dallas island, leaving the said Dallas island in the new county; thence continuing down the middle of said river to a point opposite the mouth of the Harrison Spring branch, where it enters into the said river below Harrison; from thence south-east of the residence of the late George House, on the East Tennessee and Georgia Railroad; thence south, southwest of the Georgia State line, at or near Blackwell's ford on Chicamauga [sic] Creek; thence with the Georgia State line to a point midway between Fayette Howard's residence in Bradley county, and the Hamilton County line; and thence north-west along Antioch Ridge across the old Alabama road, to T. C. Jones', leaving the said Jones in the new county; thence to the gap of Round Mountain; thence to Nathan Hinche's, leaving the said Hinche in the new county; and thence to the Hamilton county line at Johnson's Gap on White Oak Mountain; and thence with the Bradley county line to the beginning.[15]

The voters approved the establishment of the new county in January 1871. Then a new argument arose which was settled by a referendum on the location of the county seat. Harrison again lost; this time

Ooltewah gained the victory as the small railroad town defeated the small river community. The courthouse at Harrison was torn down, moved to Ooltewah, and the salvaged material used for the new James County court building. Sharp differences did not easily disappear, and some folks in the Harrison area apparently soon managed to get their lands transferred back into Hamilton.[16]

James County, affectionately known as "Jim," immediately began to harvest a crop of problems. School funds, highway moneys, and the daily expenses of running the county soon produced a great financial strain. As early as 1890 the state legislature moved to abolish the county. The state supreme court, however, declared unconstitutional the law designed to unite James and Hamilton counties. Although the constitution was silent about this type of consolidation procedure, the justices held that a legal requirement for approval of two-thirds of all qualified voters in the concerned territory in order to create a new county applied in this case. James County lived on with its troubles.

In 1913 the courthouse burned down; some who favored the abolition of the county thought this catastrophe and the resultant expense of erecting a new building would change minds in favor of a merger. Others cried arson and used bloodhounds in an effort to prove their point. One vocal opponent summed up his views: "Union with Hamilton County will resemble too strikingly the union which a boa-constrictor is fond of establishing between himself and a goat. After the union, it's all boa-constrictor. The goat has disappeared."

By 1919 James County experienced bankruptcy. The state legislature on 14 April again approved the abolition of the county. This time the act called for a referendum. Some echoes of discontent continued to be heard as the voting date neared; some insisted that the portion of James County that originally came from Bradley County should be returned to that unit. But the vast majority now desired to be associated with Hamilton. One wily fellow saw it as the case of the poor folk moving in with rich relatives.

The result of the 11 December voting was 953 for annexation, 78 against. Since the required two-thirds majority approved the merger, James County ceased to exist. The indebtedness of James County became the obligation of Hamilton, whose area increased by about fifty percent. Apparently only a few officeholders in James and their supporters tried to hold out against annexation. Hamilton County, on the other hand, seemed to welcome the "addition of an empire to its borders." A population of about fifty-three hundred living in an area of 285 square miles brought an added strength and geographic balance to the older county. Only a few Hamilton politicians, officeholders, and aspirants bemoaned the fact that the new residents were traditionally Republican.[17]

The merger of the two counties represents something very unusual on the American political scene. Despite the fact that many people have deplored the presence of many small, inefficient, and uneconomical counties across America, this geographic consolidation is declared the first in the country by *The Tennessee Blue Book*. It is the only merger in Tennessee's history and one of the very few cases in the United States.[18]

Except for minor but numerous border adjustments since 1919, the present limits of Hamilton County were established that December just 100 years after the county was created.

NOTES

1. William C. McIntyre and Thomas W. Graham, comp., *Private Acts of Hamilton County, Tennessee,* 2 vols. (Nashville: County Technical Assistance Service, University of Tennessee Institute for Public Service, 1974), 1:98–99.

2. For a summary presentation of factual data on Tennessee counties see Sophie and Paul Crane, *Tennessee Taproots* (Old Hickory, Tenn.: Earle-Shields Publishers, 1976).

3. McIntyre and Graham, *Private Acts*, 1:98.

4. Zella Armstrong, *History of Hamilton County and Chattanooga, Tennessee,* 2 vols. (Chattanooga: Lookout Publishing 1931), 1:88–92. In the wording of the Armstrong-Donelson land grant, Hawkins County refers to the county in North Carolina that had jurisdiction over this area at the time; Deep Creek, also known as Deep River or Mill Creek, is now called Possum Creek. The 20,000-acre Donelson grant refers to the mouth of North Chickamauga Creek on the Georgia boundary line, further confusing the issue. Donelson had another 5,000-acre grant south of this "Georgia line," later called the McIver Grant.

5. Merritt B. Pound, *Benjamin Hawkins: Indian Agent* (Athens, Ga.: University of Georgia Press, 1951), pp. 45–52.

6. Penelope Johnson Allen, "Leaves From the Family Tree," *Chattanooga Times,* 5 April 1936.

7. Ibid., 8 December 1935.

8. McIntyre and Graham, *Private Acts*, 1:98.

9. Ibid., p. 100.

10. E. Merton Coulter, "The Georgia-Tennessee Boundary Line," *Georgia Historical Quarterly* 35, no. 4 (December 1951): 269–306; Robert H. White, ed., *Messages of the Governors of Tennessee: 1796–1821*, 8 vols. (Nashville: Tennessee Historical Commission, 1952), 1:536–537. Some estimates state Georgia's loss to have been as much as sixty-eight square miles.

11. McIntyre and Graham, *Private Acts*, 1:98–99.

12. Allen, "Leaves," 3 December 1933.

13. Robert C. White, *Cherokee Indian Removal From the Lower Hiwassee Valley* (n.p.: Hiwassee River Watershed Development Association and Tennessee Valley Authority, 1973), p. 19; McIntyre and Graham, *Private Acts*, 1:101–103. The latter act of 17 February 1836, modfying the Marion-Hamilton county border, reads, "That the dividing line between the counties of Marion and Hamilton, on the south side of the Tennessee river, shall commence opposite the mouth of Lick creek, running the nearest direction to the extreme height of the Raccoon mountain, thence in a direction so as to strike the Georgia line wherein said line intersects the Lookout valley, leaving the Lookout valley in Hamilton county."

14. J. Leonard Raulston and James W. Livingood, *Sequatchie: A Story of the Southern Cumberlands* (Knoxville: University of Tennessee Press, 1974), pp. 91–92.

15. McIntyre and Graham, *Private Acts*, 1:54–55.

16. "James County" (Clipping file, Historical Section, Chattanooga-Hamilton County Bicentennial Library).

17. Ibid.; McIntyre and Graham, *Private Acts*, 1:106–107. Miscellaneous privately owned clippings include an address by Judge Lewis Shepherd on the history of county courthouses.

The last James County bonds were retired by Hamilton County in 1956.

18. *The Tennessee Blue Book*, 1947–1948, p. 287; Lee S. Greene, David H. Grubbs, and Victor C. Hobday, *Government in Tennessee*, 3rd ed. (Knoxville: University of Tennessee Press, 1975), pp. 227–228; Robert M. McBride, "Lost Counties of Tennessee," (East Tennessee Historical Society) *Publications* 38 (1966):11–15.

Following the James County merger an attempt to consolidate Meigs County with Hamilton County failed. There are instances of county consolidations in South Dakota and Virginia.

Among border areas added to Hamilton County were two mountain tracts along Suck Creek which chiefly made up the right-of-way for the Dixie Highway. These additions made in 1917 required that Hamilton County assume certain costs of construction of the highway, which Marion County—where the acreage was formerly located—was unable to assume. *Chattanooga Times*, 11, 12, 15 April 1917.

2

Natural Features

HAMILTON County comprises 587 square miles of territory and a population that is fourth largest of Tennessee counties. Lying at the extreme southern limits of the valley of East Tennessee, it has features typical of this geographic province. The valley is actually a portion of a great, complex "trough" extending from Pennsylvania southwestwardly into Alabama, which long served as a manageable route for restless migrants and their trade goods. Its relatively narrow proportions are framed by steep and rugged mountains.

The western limits of Hamilton County, uneven and isolated, rest on the shoulders of the Cumberland Plateau, while its eastern borders are defined by and in places drape over lesser ranges known locally as White Oak and Grindstone mountains and Lauderback Ridge. To the poetic Civil War correspondent, Benjamin Franklin Taylor, who wrote for the Chicago *Evening Journal*, this landscape as he viewed it in 1863 looked "as if the Titans had plowed and forgotten to harrow it."[1]

Dr. Thomas Walker, Virginia explorer, booster of the West and practicing physician, gave the name Cumberland to the plateau as well as to a great variety of other physical features including a Tennessee river and mountain gap. Designed as a tribute to a son of the British king,

George II, who used the title Duke of Cumberland, its origin soon was generally forgotten. This pleased many American Scots, who hated Cumberland for his unmerciful border warfare against their people. They cursed his name and for years some kept in use the old Indian name *Ouasioto* for the plateau.

The eastern edge of this section, straight and uniform, rises abruptly from the valley floor, "presenting a formidable, gray, rocky, cliff-lined rampart." Only rare gaps through the palisades invited travelers to undertake east-west passage. Known as the Allegheny or Cumberland Front, this escarpment is popularly known as Walden Ridge. Its name honors the deeds and daring of a "long hunter" of the 1760s who ventured out of Virginia into the Tennessee country—but not as far south as the future Hamilton County. His first name was Elisha; his surname has been variously spelled as Walden, Walling, Wallins, Walding, and Wallen. Walden Ridge, capped with sandstone, has an elevation of approximately two thousand feet; its soil is generally sandy, thin, and unproductive. Only the extreme southern tip, now called Signal Mountain, has attracted a concentrated population in the form of a Chattanooga suburb.

The deeply incised canyon of the Tennessee River separates Walden Ridge from mountains of a similar height and rugged character to the south. Raccoon Mountain, which is the northern extremity of Sand Mountain (with its local features known as Elder and Aetna mountains), along with Lookout Mountain, dominates this entire southwestern corner of the county. Only three miles of the northern end of Lookout are within Tennessee where an elevation of 2,126 feet and a unique shape make it a distinguished landmark. Early maps mark it with the Indian name Chatanuga, a Creek word meaning "rock that comes to a point"; in the Cherokee tongue the name, literally interpreted, means "mountains looking at each other."[2]

By the early 1800s the name Lookout Mountain seems to have been in general use. When the young minister, Elias Cornelius, visited the Brainerd Mission in 1817–18, he was deeply impressed by the natural beauty of the country. "The summit of Lookout Mountain," he wrote, "overlooks the whole country. And to those who can be delighted with the view of an interminable forest, penetrated by the windings of a bold river, interspersed with hundreds of verdant prairies, and broken by many ridges and mountains, [it] furnishes in the month of May a landscape which yields to few others, in extent, variety, or beauty."[3]

The original usage of the name Lookout Mountain is not known;

only colorful speculations explain reasons for its selection. Some say the mountain provided a high bastion from which to view the countryside—Cornelius noted this advantage. Others theorize that the name refers to a warning to early rivermen to watch out for the rough waters of the mountain gorge. Yet another explanation deals with desperadoes. Flatboatmen from upriver, keenly interested in marketing the farm produce of isolated East Tennessee, appeared on the river in increasing numbers despite navigation problems. Since they did not want to undertake a passage through the mountain canyon in the dusk of evening or later, they pulled their unwieldy crafts to shore at the mouth of Chattanooga or Lookout Valley creeks, located near the base of the mountain. Learning of this practice, outlaws began to make nightly raids on the boatmen. News of these attacks spread upriver and warnings circulated, such as, "When you pass Ross Landing look out for robbers." Romantics soon attached "lookout" to the mountain itself, thereby marking the entrance to turbulent waters.[4]

The eastern county borders follow White Oak Mountain on the north but reach eastward in the south beyond this range to include other areas such as Bauxite and Pine Hill ridges. White Oak is actually not a mountain but a prominent ridge with a minimum crest area. Like the Cumberlands it is steep, rough, rocky, and can be traversed only at a relatively few passes: Taliaferro Gap, Dead Man's or Ooltewah Gap, and Collegedale Gap. As White Oak Mountain drifts off into northern Georgia toward Ringgold, its name changes to Taylor's Ridge in honor of the Cherokee Richard Taylor, trader, interpreter, and member of the Cherokee National Council.

Immediately to the east through Ooltewah Gap rises another smaller elevation only a mile and a half long and a mile or so broad some 750 feet above the surrounding valley. Still given over today mainly to laurel and holly, oaks, gums and other trees, it carries the interesting name Grindstone Mountain. Some who view it from a distance say it got its name because the shape of its crown is like a giant grindstone. But its origin is far more prosaic: a pre–Civil War resident fashioned stones from the fine grade of sandstone found on the mountaintop which he peddled to neighboring farmers.[5]

Between the gray crags of the western heights and the eastern limits of the county lie numerous ridges, some with rocky spines and others mere mounds of chert. Prominent among them are Bakewell Mountain, Godsey Ridge, Gold Point Ridge, Stringer's Ridge (honoring Captain William Stringer), and Missionary Ridge.

A woman missionary traveling to Brainerd in 1821 found it necessary to go from Ross's Landing to the mission by carriage as "strangers in a dark forest." On crossing the ridge—named for the mission—she and her party were told that in spite of a pouring rain "the horse could not ascend, nor we be safe, unless we walked."[6] Today it is not necessary to walk, but three tunnels and a great interstate highway cut are required to get surface traffic into the bowl that defines the margins of downtown Chattanooga and causes so much concern for those who are troubled by the presence of air pollution.

The ridges differ more or less in shape of outline, height, and other features while they are at once remarkable for their general uniformity of character. Some are steep and have sharp crests notched with gaps; others have broad slopes and rounded contours. In addition, there are steep knobs standing alone or in groups; some are conical in shape while others present curious patterns. Practically all run in a general northeast-to-southwest direction.

The mountainous areas abound in springs, swift-flowing streams, cascades, and spectacular panoramic scenery. One spot was deemed worthy of description by a writer in 1842. He described the plunging waters of Falling Water in these words: "The stream pours down into a kind of basin below, formed by ledges of rock that lie all around; and the falling of the water produces a roaring and lumbering sound, that can be heard at a distance of six or seven miles, like the voice of distant, but continued thunder."[7]

The steep mountainsides, marked by ravines and rocky bluffs, are scalloped with cool, narrow coves. The lesser ridges and slopes of stubborn chert create a washboard appearance which has allowed real estate developers a wide choice of such landmark terms as hill, crest, height, highland, knob, glen, ridge, and cove.

The map of the county abounds in colorful place names often determined in part by geography. One cannot but be curious of their origin or fascinated by the reason for their usage. The map lists Checkerbox Ridge, McGill Gulf, Shingle Mill Hollow, Rattlesnake Hollow, Grasshopper Road, Stillhouse Branch, Joe Smith Hill, Skillet Gap, Owl Hollow, Summit Knobs, Bauxite Ridge, the Hellican, Green Shanty Hollow, Back Valley, Dead Man's Gap, Rabbit Valley, Pulltight Hollow (named for the extreme tenacity of the mud), Wolfpen Point, Chickamauga Gulch, and Hobo Bluff.

The Cherokees, imaginative mythmakers, had an explanation for the abundance of hills and valleys. Their "Genesis" story tells of the age when all the earth was flat, soft, and wet. The animals, gathered in Galunlati "beyond the arch," sent out birds to see if it was dry enough for the animals. Many failed. Then the Great Buzzard went forth; he flew everywhere. When he finally soared over the Cherokee country, he became very tired. His wings touched the soft earth and "wherever they struck the earth was a valley, and where they turned up again there was a mountain." The animals called the Great Buzzard back, fearing all the earth would be rough piles of dirt, "but the Cherokee country remains full of mountains to this day."[8]

In the rocks under the landscape lies a more scientific explanation of how the region emerged into what it is. The rocks act as a record or saga, whose chapters cover the billions of years before man, when the great natural upheavals of the past molded, destroyed, altered, and refashioned the earth's surface. The rocks tell of the pressure of minute marine organisms whose slowly accumulating skeletons helped create what volcanic and earthshaking action later remade under violent releases of pressure and energy.[9]

The geological timetable for the Hamilton County area reaches back to the Paleozoic era—perhaps 600 million years ago—but the oldest rock lies deeply buried and seems but a foundation for younger rock formations. Fossils in the limestone and shale of a later date serve as evidence of sea life which featured an abundance of marine fauna in the form of tiny organisms and shellfish. This section was only a part of a vast muddy-bottomed sea which later changed to become a shelflike platform. The shoreline, ever shifting, had the appearance of a great tidal flat bordering a shallow sea rich in aquatic life. The depositional features of rock and the nature of the fossils suggest a gradual filling up of this subsiding ocean basin.

Then later—some 455 million years ago—the eastern parts of North America shook with furious volcanic activity in the highlands. Dust and debris darkened Hamilton County skies as ashes settled into the ocean sea. Geologists find proof of this phenomenon in the thin, clay-rich layers of volcanic ash beds along the western, lower slopes of Missionary Ridge. One scientist writes, "With subsequent weathering the limestone directly beneath each ash bed was replaced by silica leached from the overlaying ash to form a bed of dark green chert. Because each layer was deposited everywhere at the same time, each bed provides an excellent time marker."

Meanwhile the sea advanced and retreated periodically; eventually it became so stagnant that it resembled a blanket of black mud spread over the land and naturally the number of organisms living there de-clined. This blanket resulted eventually in the development of the Chattanooga shale, so named in 1891 by C. W. Hayes, who studied an exposed area on the side of Cameron Hill.[10]

Gradually environmental changes produced a new shallow, warm, open sea. Limestone rich in fossils was deposited, but with continued fluctuations the carbonate sequence gave way to a shale overlaid by barrier sand bars, deltas, and channel sandstone. The ocean shores in this era were vast swamplands rich with ferns and scaly-barked trees and teeming with reptiles, snails, and amphibians. Tremendous quan-tities of plant debris were transformed into thick peat deposits and, under pressure, slowly changed into coal with rich deposits found on Walden Ridge and Lookout and Aetna mountains.

Time continued its slow pace. Some 230 million years ago the rock strata of the eastern United States underwent new disturbances. It proved to be a time of mountain building called the Appalachian orogeny. A great range of mountains, now known as the Older Appalachians, emerged massive and high. In the Hamilton County area, as elsewhere, great folds of rock fractured under tremendous tectonic pressure; the earth wrenched and twisted as the topography became distorted with up and down folds. Layers of rock shoved up over other formations. All, in turn, became subjected to the weathering forces of rain, wind, frost, and erosion. The debris-laden rivers carried their cargoes to this part of the lowlands and sea where they accu-mulated in layers of sand, clay, and limestone. As the soft parts washed away, the tall mountains shrank as in old age and nature carried its extra chert and rock westward, liberally depositing some in Hamilton County. These deposits in turn weathered into a nearly featureless plain, not much above sea level, through which large rivers continued to meander.

But still more geologic changes were to come. The entire region again went through a period of fold and uplift; a new landscape featuring valleys and ridges emerged. Then the higher portions eroded, exposing weaker, less resistant strata to the elements. Eventually everything was turned upside down. The eroded heights became the valleys and the valleys became the mountains and ridges in an operation the ge-ologists simply describe as "reversal topography." Today the exposed rock strata of Lookout Mountain or Walden Ridge are inclined upward toward former peaks. Lookout and Chattanooga valleys are the eroded floors or provinces of early heights.

The Tennessee River in its meandering course proved strong enough to retain its channel during the era of uplift, ever chewing away the elevated shores which restricted the river to the deep mountain canyon between the mountains. Once known as the "Narrows," this dramatic gash is now called the "Grand Canyon of the Tennessee."

Erosion was not limited to the surface features. As a result of the solvent action of underground water on limestone, a great number of caves and caverns were formed. As water seeped downward through the soil, solutions were created by rock containing calcium carbonate; this happened mainly near the upper boundary of the water table, and as the table lowered due to the slow uplift of the landscape, the cave systems grew into huge caverns with miles of winding passageways. The largest cavern systems are in the Mississippian Limestone in the Cumberland Plateau but a few small ones occur in the valley. The biggest in the county and that with the greatest historical interest is Lookout Mountain Cave.[11]

The Hamilton county area did escape direct consequences from the Ice Age with its glaciation effects. But the advance and retreat of the great ice masses southward to the Ohio River left their stamp on the local area. An intensification of frost action interspersed with tropical interludes, along with customary rains, eroded away the softer portions of the sandstone rock which caps Lookout Mountain, Walden Ridge, and parts of White Oak Mountain. Here large rocks and boulders of striking shapes and size dot the landscape, giving anyone with a lively mind the opportunity to visualize a rock city, rock castles, or spectacular fairylands.

A curious observer associated with the Brainerd Mission examined the "citadel of rocks" on Lookout Mountain and reported:[12]

> This is just at the top of the mountain, and is composed of rocks as high as houses of one, two, or three stories. It is so situated as to afford streets and lanes and to form many convenient shelters from the heat, rain and wind. Especially we noticed one apartment twelve by fifteen and six feet high in the highest place, arched over head and walled on each side by solid rock, except an opening for a door, and one or two places in the corners, which would serve for chimneys. This natural fortress was formerly inhabited by the Creeks. We saw where they hung their meat and where they prepared their lodgings. Here, after viewing for a moment the wonders of the Omnipotence, being retired from all the world, we bowed with adoration before Him, whose favor is compared to the shadow of a great rock in a weary land.

The natural beauty of the terrain compensates in a way for the fact that most of the rock of the area is of a sedimentary type and contains few valuable minerals other than bituminous coal, silica sand, clay, and shale.

Hamilton's cliff-crowned mountains with their rugged tangled slopes, the undulatory hills and ridges interspersed with narrow valleys, isolated coves, and rich bottomlands are well watered. The county is virtually bisected by the Tennessee River. This long wandering stream, sometimes referred to as a lady because of its many graceful curves, is more often thought of as an awkward rustic—forced to curl up like a tall man in a spare bed.

European explorers carried the banners of three monarchies along its shores, claiming the land and giving the river exotic names: Caskinampo, Casquinambaux, Hogohegee, Callamaco, Cussatees, Rivière des Cheroquis, and others.[13] At a comparatively late date it was christened the Tennessee, a name derived from that of a Cherokee Overhill town along the Little Tennessee River. The original word, believed to have been *Tanisi,* has come down to us in a score of different spellings. But actually it was not until 1889 that legal meaning was assigned to the name; the law then decreed the Tennessee River, despite all other usages, began at the junction of the north fork of the Holston with the main Holston River at Kingsport in Sullivan County. This settled the tale of the river for a brief time. Then in the 1930s the historic, contrary old river was drowned by engineers under a series of great lakes. A new river, managed by the Tennessee Valley Authority, replaced it on the map.

The very presence and character of the old river determined much of Hamilton County's history. Draining a vast area characterized by heavy rainfall and rapid runoff, the upper Tennessee River like most western streams had many shoals, reefs, and shifting bars of sand or gravel. Also, there were hidden ledges, an ever-changing channel, and stretches of swift current. During the course of the seasons a great difference in depth, resulting from the stream flow variation, created spring tides and summer shallows when the river was of "shirttail" depth. Furthermore, its circuitous course across the southeast, twisting in every compass direction, meant many added miles in a journey to its mouth at the Ohio River.

The above conditions created vexing situations for Indians, frontiersmen, or steamboat captains who used the river. They were mere annoyances compared to the problems caused by two notorious stretches of rough water which made downstream travel treacherous and regular upstream navigation almost impossible: In North Alabama they encountered the historic maelstrom called Muscle Shoals, and on the western border of Hamilton County extending downstream were the mountain waters where millions of years earlier the Tennessee River cut its way through the Cumberlands, abandoning a much simpler direct southern course to the Gulf of Mexico.

This latter site has been called the "Valley of the Whirlpool Rapids." At the place where the river left the valley of East Tennessee, it swept past the foot of Lookout, ever twisting and turning until it marked out the pattern of a moccasin print. On past Williams Island the waters moved into the eroded and chiseled canyon between Walden Ridge and Raccoon Mountain. The steep wooded slopes on both shores, rising a thousand feet or more above the water's edge, confined the river to a narrow channel where swift currents created whirls and eddies.

The turbulence began with the Tumbling Shoals, a wild roaring stretch of water in certain seasons 454 miles from the mouth of the river. About 2½ miles beyond was the Suck or "great whirlpool" where the untamed mountain stream, Suck Creek, often discharged vast quantities of rock, logs, and debris into the river. The channel narrowed; rocks jutted into the current, piling up the waters and increasing their velocity. Here the whirl was called the Suck, the old English term for whirlpool. The Cherokees called it the Kettle or Boiling Pot; the frontiersmen took these names and, to complete their household outfit, tagged the next three bad spots Pan, Skillet, and Pot. The Pot, described at certain depths as "wild and beautiful," was some 3½ miles downstream from the Suck. A mile beyond was the Skillet, actually a precipice in the path of the river where, in order to get over this "protrudent ledge the water boils and hisses in an angry manner." Finally there was the Pan. The entire distance—some 8½ miles—was commonly referred to as the Suck.

The first known use of the designation Suck appears in a report of a British army engineer in 1768–69 when that officer made an inventory of lands acquired by the British in the French and Indian War. He graphically described this section of the river: "Here is the suck at which place the River is about 60 yrds. over. The River for about 6 Miles Back is upw'd of a ¼ Mile over & Gradually diminishes. The Mountains gathering Lap over both sides of the River resembling a Brick Fortification."[14]

The area drew the attention of both the inquisitive and the scientifically minded. A late eighteenth-century English visitor wrote, "It is reckoned a greater curiosity than the bursting of the Potomack through the Blue ridge." Thomas Jefferson, who never saw the Suck, mentioned in his book, *Notes on the State of Virginia*, that it "takes in trunks of trees or boats, and throws them out again half a mile below."[15]

The Indians in their wonder stories called the place Untiguhi, meaning "pot-in-the-water."[16] A great doctor, Thunder, lived close by who had a son born "in the east" with scrofulous sores over his body. Following his mother's advice, the boy found Thunder at Untiguhi and got his promise to cure him. According to the Cherokee myth:

> There was a large pot in the corner and he told his wife to fill it with water and put it over the fire. When it was boiling, he put in some roots, then took the boy and put him in with them. He let it boil a long time until one would have thought that the flesh was boiled from the poor boy's bones, and then told his wife to take the pot and throw it into the river, boy and all. She did as she was told, and threw it into the water, and ever since there is an eddy there that we call Untiguhi, "Pot-in-the-water." A service tree and a calico bush grew on the bank above. A great cloud of steam came up and made streaks and blotches on their bark, and it has been so to this day. When the steam cleared away she looked over and saw the boy clinging to the roots of the service tree where they hung down into the water, but now his skin was all clean.

Another legend tells of the haunted whirlpool. The Cherokees told that the Suck operated on an intermittent timetable and boatmen kept constant vigil for signs of a coming eruption so that they could tie up and wait ashore until it quieted again. The story goes:

> It happened once that two men, going down the river in a canoe, as they came near this place saw the water circling rapidly ahead of them. They pulled up to the bank to wait until it became smooth again, but the whirlpool seemed to approach with wider and wider circles, until they were drawn into the vortex. They were thrown out of the canoe and carried down under the water, where one man was seized by a great fish and was never seen again. The other was taken round and round down to the very lowest center of the whirlpool, when another circle caught him and bore him outward and upward until he was finally thrown up again to the surface and floated out into the shallow water, whence he made his escape to shore. He told afterwards that when he reached the narrowest circle of the maelstrom the water seemed to open below him and he could look down as through the roof beams of a house, and there on the bottom of the river he had seen a great company of people, who looked up and beckoned to him to join them, but as they put up their hands to seize him the swift current caught him and took him out of their reach.

These strange and marvelous tales romanticized the terror of the valley of the whirlpool rapids but they did not diminish the trials, labors, and hardships of the river travelers. Generation after generation of rivermen puzzled over ways to remove the dangerous shoals and whirls. Not until the fall of 1913 did that "great company" of folks on the river bottom cease their efforts to lure others to join them. Then the impounded waters of Hales Bar Lock and Dam drowned out the bad waters; the "famous suck obliterated," screamed the headlines of a local newspaper.[17] It was the dawn of a new day and a new river.

The navigational limitations of the old river prevented it from developing into a great water highway for western migrants—in contrast to the Ohio River. Some who ventured west used the Tennessee, but Hamilton County and other sites along its course never became way stations for those who moved to the Middle West and beyond.

The barriers to navigation cut the river into three separate segments. Prehistoric Indians living in the valley developed different cultural traits along each sector of the river.[18] One wag concluded that the Tennessee River really was not a river; it was a liquid lie. In the steamboat days owners limited regular shipping schedules to a run within a section, for example, from Knoxville to Chattanooga or from Chattanooga to Decatur. This restricted use of the river did emphasize the relatively easy passage from Hamilton County on southward. The divide separating the valley of eastern Tennessee from the Deep South offered easy access in that direction. This gateway furnished a route for the early wheeled vehicular travel of the area and provided the passage used by the Union armies to split the Confederacy in 1864; for instance, General William T. Sherman led his troops through it to Atlanta and the sea.

Twenty years after Hales Bar Lock and Dam drowned the worst features of the mountain stretch of the river, the Tennessee Valley Authority undertook a complete transformation of the river and its valley. The 1930s marked the birth of a new river. Its march to the Ohio River became managed: its nine-foot channel provided smooth water for tugs and barges; its great lakes offered a new dimension to the life of the valley.

In Hamilton County this transformation began in January 1936 when construction on the $39.8 million Chickamauga Dam was started. The 5800-foot-long dam some 125 feet high above the foundation created a 58.9-mile-long lake with 810 miles of shoreline and an area of 35,400 acres. In 1964 a new dam in Marion County named Nickajack came under construction as a replacement for the old and leaky Hales Bar

Dam. This multipurpose facility, like the other mainstream dams, created a great lake 46.3 miles long with 192 miles of shoreline. The impounded waters backed into Hamilton County as far as Chickamauga Dam to cover 10,730 acres. Hamilton County found itself in the very heart of TVA country.[19]

The Tennessee River, as it sweeps into and through Hamilton County, gathers numerous tributaries to itself. Moving downstream, those on the right rise in the Cumberland Plateau and at certain seasons race over the side of Walden Ridge in torrents only to become wide, dry, or nearly dry boulder stream scars in the dry months of summer. Sale Creek is the northernmost; in 1779 militiamen from Virginia and northeastern Tennessee stopped here and auctioned among the men the booty taken in an Indian offensive, giving a historical basis for the stream's name. Next is Possum Creek, formerly referred to as Deep Creek, Deep River, and Mill Creek. Next is Soddy Creek, an Indian name appearing on old maps as Sauda Creek, which may have been a corruption of Chota, the name of the Cherokee's beloved town. Moving south, one comes to North Chickamauga Creek, Mountain Creek, Shoal Creek, Middle Creek, and Suck Creek.

Sale Creek, Big and Little Possum creeks, Soddy, and North Chickamauga with their branches all have cut deep gorges into the ridge and along their walls coal seams are exposed and were mined at an early date.

On the south, the tributaries flow through broader and more fertile valleys. They include Grasshopper Creek, Ware Branch, Wolftever and Long Savannah creeks, South Chickamauga Creek, Chattanooga Creek, and Lookout Creek, which the state declared navigable to the Georgia State line in 1837–38 in order to qualify for river improvement funds.

The Indian word Chickamauga is difficult to translate. J. P. Brown, who has long studied the subject, originally believed it to be a Creek word, Cukko-Micco, meaning "dwelling place of the war chief." Later he concluded that the original was the Cherokee, Tsi-gwa-amo-gi, meaning "Much Muddy or Red Waters," or "Much Big Waters, Red."[20] Some time after the Civil War an imaginative person coined the translation as "river of death."

The river and streams abounded in fish. At Brainerd Mission a fish trap in Chickamauga Creek netted forty fish altogether weighing 150 pounds one morning and 150 on another morning weighing from 5 to 10 pounds apiece. The missionaries reported that fish were caught at all seasons. Robert Cravens, who lived on Lookout Mountain in 1857, stopped with a guest at the mouth of Chattanooga Creek on his way home. Here Cravens kept a fish net; at the time it held a dozen good fish. They took a sixteen- to eighteen-inch salmon home for dinner and returned the net to the water, for "the fish kept better there than up at the house."[21]

A Union soldier entering the area in 1863 found North Chickamauga Creek "one of the cleanest streams I ever seen. The bottom is covered with very large round rocks and looks as if you could easily touch them with your hand when in reality the water is ten or twelve feet deep."[22]

The Union soldiers complained of the snakes which they found in tremendous numbers, reminiscent of the stories told by the very first settlers at Ross's Landing. When streets were first laid out in the village, they bordered on many low swampy areas in which reptiles were found in abundance. Some enterprising folks rendered rattlesnake oil by placing dead reptiles on the newlycut treestumps, leaving the rest of the process to solar energy. Small animals appear to have been just as plentiful as the reptiles, but no evidence was found of buffalo in this section after the arrival of permanent settlers. Elk, bear, catamounts, wolves, gray and red foxes, rabbits, squirrels, opossums, beaver, mink, and muskrats were hunted here.

The Indians had badly depleted the deer population, sending thousands of skins into the English trade channels, but at the time of the Cherokee removal, droves of deer were still to be found. So too were wild hogs, which in 1836 were said to have treed a boy. Wild turkey, grouse, partridges, small birds, and waterfowl were plentiful, but the passenger pigeon had already disappeared from the scene.

The flora was more diverse than the fauna. Ferns, lichens, mosses, vines, and shrubs grew in profusion. Robert Sparks Walker reported some years ago that more than 125 species of trees grew in the 130 acres of the Audubon Acres sanctuary. This list includes pines (short leafed, Virginia, and white), some ten varieties of oaks, many hickories, and several species of maples, gums, and oaks. In addition, hackberry, cherry, walnut, sourwood, persimmon, beech, ash, cedar, black locust, and dogwoods still flourish, among other varieties. But the once-popular native chestnuts are now gone.[23] In the same preserve lovers of wild flowers have counted 551 species growing.

In the crisp days of fall when light fogs often hang over the valleys, the deep color of the evergreens provides a vivid backdrop for the many hues of autumnal color. In the spring, as Cartter Patten has expressed it, "When you mix holly, hemlock, rhododendron and mountain laurel with the murmur of a mountain stream, you have Walden's Ridge at its peaceful best."[24]

NOTES

1. Louis M. Starr, *Bohemian Brigade: Civil War Newsmen in Action* (New York: Knopf, 1954), p. 269.

2. J. P. Brown, *Old Frontiers: The Story of the Cherokee Indians From Earliest Times to the Date of Their Removal to the West* (Kingsport, Tenn.: Southern Publishers, 1938), p. 528. Brown says the Creek meaning is "rock that comes to an end." Robert Sparks Walker, *Torchlights to the Cherokees: The Brainerd Mission* (New York: Macmillan, 1931), p. 60. The missionary Cornelius says that the Cherokee called the mountain "O-tullee-ton-tanna-ta-kunna-ee," meaning "mountains looking at each other."

3. Ibid., p. 218.

4. Harry M. Wiltse, "History of Chattanooga" 2 vols. (Typescript, Chattanooga-Hamilton County Bicentennial Library), 1:6.

5. Robert Sparks Walker, "Grindstone Mountain," *Chattanooga Times*, 26 January 1936.

6. Walker, *Torchlights*, p. 195.

7. J. W. M. Breazeale, *Life As It Is* . . . (Knoxville: James Williams, 1842), p. 120.

8. James Mooney, "Myths of the Cherokee," U.S., Bureau of American Ethnology, *Nineteenth Annual Report* (Washington, D.C., Government Printing Office, 1900), pt. 1, p. 239.

9. Robert L. Wilson, "Chattanooga and Geology" (Typescript, made available by courtesy of author).

10. A geological formation is given the name for the area in which it was first identified and studied.

11. The principal caves of the county are as listed by Thomas C. Barr, Jr., in *Caves of Tennessee*, Bulletin no. 64 (Nashville: State of Tennessee, Department of Conservation and Commerce, Division of Geology, 1961), pp. 244–253.

Cave Springs Cave: about four miles southeast of Daisy.

Chickamauga Cave: two and a half miles southwest of Daisy near mouth of Chickamauga Gulch.

Crystal Caves: two miles northwest of Wauhatchie at base of Raccoon Mountain. First called Tennessee Caverns; reopened in 1952 as Crystal Caves.

Harrison Bluff Caves: on shore of Chicakmauga Reservoir.

Havens Caves: at western base of White Oak Mountain just south of Mahan Gap.

Levi Cave: near mouth of Falling Water Gulch below Buzzard Point.

Lookout Mountain Cave: at north end of Lookout Mountain; original entrance opened near Nashville & Chattanooga railroad tunnel.

Mystery Falls: northeast end of Lookout Mountain, two-tenths of a mile southeast of Ruby Falls gatehouse.

Ruby Falls Cave: north end, Lookout Mountain.

Tumbling Shoals Cave: at base of Elder Mountain, also called Pitchfork or Airplane Cave.

Larry E. Mathews, *Descriptions of Tennessee Caves* (Nashville: State of Tennessee, Department of Conservation, Division of Geology, 1971, p. 50), lists five more Hamilton County caves:

Adams Cave: three-tenths of a mile south of junction of Highway 27 and Rhea County line.

Clay Cave: east slope of Lookout Mountain two hundred feet south of the Incline tracks.

Lee Highway Cave: Highway 41 southeast of junction with state highway.

Posey Cave: five-tenths of a mile south of Cooly Road and six-tenths of a mile west of Dividing Ridge.

"W" Road Cave: north-northwest of Mountain Creek School, west of hairpin turn on "W" Road, Signal Mountain.

12. Walker, *Torchlights,* p. 222.

13. Samuel Cole Williams, *Dawn of Tennessee Valley and Tennessee History* (Johnson City, Tenn.: Watauga Press, 1937), pp. 33–49; Thomas M. N. Lewis and Madeline Kneberg, *Hiwassee Island: An Archaeological Account of Four Tennessee Indian Peoples* (Knoxville: University of Tennessee Press, 1946), p. 13.

14. Nashville District, Corps of Engineers, *Engineers on the Twin Rivers: A History of the Nashville District Corps of Engineers, United States Army* (n.p., 1979), pp. 1–6; Samuel Cole Williams, *Early Travels in the Tennessee Country 1540–1800* (Johnson City, Tenn.: Watauga Press, 1928), p. 226. The engineer and mapmaker Thomas Hutchins also used the names Tennessee and Hiwassee for those two streams.

15. Gilbert E. Govan and James W. Livingood, *The Chattanooga Country,* 3d ed. (Knoxville: University of Tennessee Press, 1977), pp. 15–17; James W. Livingood, "The Valley of Whirlpool Rapids," *Perspective* 6, no. 1 (Fall 1975): 21–27.

16. Mooney, "Myths," pp. 312, 347.

17. *Chattanooga Times,* 23 October, 1913.

18. Thomas M. N. Lewis and Madeline Kneberg, *Tribes That Slumber* (Knoxville: University of Tennessee Press, 1958), p. 64.

19. *TVA Handbook*, rev. ed. (Knoxville: TVA Information Office, 1976), pp. 46–49.

20. Brown, *Old Frontiers*, p. 529; J. P. Brown, *Pioneers of Old Frontiers with Supplements: Pioneer Settlers of the Chattanooga Area* (by Penelope J. Allen) and *The Story of Another Pioneer: A Brief History of Pioneer Bank* (Chattanooga: Pioneer Bank, 1962), p. 6n.

21. Walker, *Torchlights*, p. 143; Mary Thomas Peacock, *The Circuit Rider and Those Who Followed* (Chattanooga: Hudson Printing, 1957), p. 81.

22. John W. Rowell, *Yankee Artillerymen: Through the Civil War With Eli Lilly's Indiana Battery* (Knoxville: University of Tennessee Press, 1975), p. 94. The trooper Henry Campbell added, "This valley aint to be compared with Sequatchie in regard to fertility or beauty."

23. Robert Sparks Walker, *As the Indians Left It: The Story of the Elise Chapin Wild Life Sanctuary and the Chattanooga Audubon Society* (Chattanooga: Hudson Printing, 1955), p. 55.

24. Cartter Patten, *Signal Mountain and Walden's Ridge* (n.p.: author, 1962), p. 121.

3

According to the Archaeologists

LONG before posted boundary line markers read, "This is Tennessee" or "This is Hamilton County," anonymous humans tramped the woodlands trails and used the waterways there. From the evidence we have of their doings—scattered fossils and artifacts—we actually know little of their story. Through the years, moreover, farmers more interested in corn than in potsherds and Indian bones, relic seekers with no regard for the methods of scientific inquiry, and people who find a queer satisfaction in vandalism contributed to the destruction of some of these meager records of the past.

Accepted theories maintain that the first people of North America originated in Asia. They migrated in different waves across a land bridge where the Bering Sea islands now exist and, over the centuries, scattered across much of the continent. They left no trace of their ethnic or linguistic background, of their clan or tribal association, or of their true identity.[1]

Our calendar of prehistoric peoples features long eras of cultural similarity which includes all the values, techniques, ideas, and beliefs of the generations whose life-style generally conformed to such cultural standards. Archaeologists, having no alternative, assign arbitrary names to these epochs: Paleo-, Archaic, Woodland, and Mississippian. Of course some variations developed in different sections of the country resulting from contacts with dissimilar cultures or from new knowledge gained by experience or accident. Again the archaeologists, in order to distinguish these features, use arbitrary terms, many of which refer to some modern landmark related to the site of professional excavations. Locally we have, as a consequence, cultural traits of the Hamilton People, of the Hiwassee Island Focus, and of the Dallas Indians. Each term reflects what was a level of culture over an extensive area, not one confined to a limited territory.

At least fifteen thousand years have passed since the first nomadic hunter ventured into the Hamilton County area. Akin to the Ice Age wanderers who first peopled the new world, he hunted great animals now extinct, mammoths, mastodons, giant sloths, saber-toothed tigers, and straight-horned bison. He camped where food appeared available but always moved on.

This rover had few worldly goods and traveled in small bands. Consequently, the fragmentary evidence of his occupancy is limited to projectile points and some stone tools such as choppers, scrapers, gravers, and knives. Hamilton County has yielded some fluted, pointed spear points and larger quantities of cutting and scraping tools, which belonged to some ancient inhabitants who stopped at possible Stone Age winter quarters such as the Le Croy site.

Eventually climatic changes caused the ice fields to recede and forests moved northward, supplying new and more varied resources. The great prehistoric beasts became extinct, but they were replaced by many species of large and small game. Nuts, fruits, and seeds ripened in abundance and fish and shellfish became plentiful. These conditions supported an expanding human population whose life became more sedentary than that of the Paleo-Indians. These people, known as Archaic Indians, became the area's first real settlers.

The new cultural era which had its inception in the Tennessee Valley at least eight thousand years ago began when this new wave of Asian immigrants replaced or possibly merged with the Paleo-Indians. For thousands of years they dominated the area. Their technology featured ground stone axes, cutting tools chipped from flint or similar stone, and flint weapon points. But a short spear tipped with stone and hurled with a throwing stick represented their most advanced achievement. Known as an *atlatl*, it lengthened the huntsman's range and increased the force of the projectile. Bone, shell, and animal teeth supplied the raw material for both tools and ornaments.

The Archaic Indian lived either in caves or crude huts so unsubstantial in construction that no evidence remains to suggest their size or pattern. Cooking was done outside over open fires. Each family appears to have been quite self-sufficient, with communities offering some protection and featuring common burial grounds. Although cemeteries were usually refuse heaps where bodies were interred along with pet dogs—the only domesticated animals—the treatment of the deceased implies a respect for the dead as well as the holding of certain primitive religious concepts.

Archaic sites are relatively common along the Tennessee River in this section. The best known is Russell Cave, near Bridgeport, Alabama. Archaeological excavations at the Nickajack Dam reservoir in Marion County and on Moccasin Bend reveal aboriginal occupation generally in accordance with the mainstream of the chronology of the southeastern United States.

The next great cultural era was given the name Woodland because it prevailed throughout the extensive eastern woodlands of the continent. The Woodland Indians, thought to be newcomers from Asia, pushed the Archaic peoples into isolated areas or absorbed them into their own revolutionary life pattern. They arrived in the Tennessee Valley possibly three thousand years ago and dominated the culture for the next two millennia.

Typifying a new or late Stone Age society, the Woodland Indians learned to manage nature by domesticating plants, thereby emancipating themselves from the uncertainties of wild-growing supplies. Corn became a central part of the menu, as well as a feature of ceremonial observances. Many new arts and crafts developed: the technique of the grindstone, the art of weaving, the making of pottery, and the use of the bow and arrow.

Pottery, one of the archaeologist's most useful research artifacts, is valuable when found either intact or in broken bits (sherds), revealing both technical achievement and artistic expression. The earliest pottery carried imprints of cords or coarsely woven fabric—the only evidence of textile work—impressed on the surface before vessels were fired. Later vessels often bore impressions made by carvings on wooden paddles. Most were limestone-tempered.

Cooking mostly over open fires, the Woodland woman also used an underground oven, a kettle-shaped pit in the ground, smaller at the top than at the bottom. Some vessels, bowls, and tubes were made of soapstone.

These people lived in small villages. Their dwellings, built by sticking small saplings into the ground which were bent together to form a dome, had bark or mat sides and were often no larger than ten feet in diameter at the base. Little is known of their personal possessions with the exception of beads, tobacco pipes, gorgets (ornamental collars), and jewelry made of animal teeth, marine shells, or bone.

Late in the era the Woodland people gave considerable attention to the burial of their dead in earthen mounds, thereby earning a reputation as "mound builders." Mounds of this type stood all along the Tennessee River across Hamilton County, at Williams Island, Moccasin Bend (from heel to toe), Chattanooga Island, Citico Creek, near the mouth of South Chickamauga Creek, Harrison Ferry, Dallas Island, Lovelady Landing, Igou Ferry, Hiwassee Island, and many other rural sites.[2]

Throughout eastern Tennessee these mound builders are usually called Hamilton Indians, named for the area where their culture had great influence. While the Woodland cultural pattern existed over a very wide area, there developed local variations in the use of raw materials. In the Tennessee Valley the Hamilton people differed from those living along the river in northern Alabama—the Copena people who treasured copper and galena items—as well as from those occupying the lower valley.

The Hamilton culture existed throughout the upper Tennessee Valley. Along the river banks and islands numerous reminders of this pre-Columbian life-style can be found, but one of the most spectacular centers was on Hiwassee Island. This island, at the mouth of the river by the same name, lies just north of the Hamilton County border. Prior to the TVA engineering projects, it contained 781 acres and measured approximately one mile by two miles in size. The area of Hiwassee Island and the bordering main shoreline represented an ideal location for aboriginal occupation with its abundance of fertile soil, game, fish, mollusks, wild plants, forest trees, and cane. This island played a long, continuous role in the local prehistoric saga.

Archaeologists, drawn to such an inviting site, have assembled an interesting record of the Hamilton people. Of course all things perishable are gone, such as these people's songs, music, clothing fashions, and oral traditions. But stone, shells, and pottery tell of the ancient life. Hamilton people lived in scattered households with apparently little fear of invaders and no special need for group protection. So they each went their own way with little dependence upon the settlement as a whole.

Their dwellings, apparently of light construction, have left no indication of their shape or size; only small refuse piles, or middens, mark their location. These circular middens, usually rich hunting ground for the archaeologist, actually contained only small amounts of cultural debris. But since they were composed mostly of clam shells, they do tell much about the important place of the mussel in the Hamilton diet.

The Hamilton people are best known for their burial mounds. The products of their labors can still be seen in many parts of the area, although TVA construction has drowned out many of them. The mounds, constructed as ceremonial burial centers, represented the one centralizing social force in the life-style of the era. Some measured fifty-five feet or more at the base and often rose eight to ten feet in height.

A central tomb usually made of logs formed the nucleus of a mound. A special interment such as this was a surface burial and marked the passing of an important personage. This grave, covered with earth or with a layer of mussel shells, later attracted other burials. As more bodies were added, the cemetery grew in size and gradually assumed the form of a mound.

Various articles, placed alongside the dead as aids for their existence in the spirit world, today serve as clues to the overall picture of the Woodland culture. In addition to an inventory of tools of stone, bone, and antler, the Hamilton graveyards contained tobacco pipes made of a variety of materials but usually created in simple, nondecorated style. More distinct as a local cultural hallmark were ponderous shell ornaments. Displaying masterful craftsmanship, the "massive, spirally shaped shell beads" represented a unique development in aboriginal jewelry. The Hamilton Indians of Hiwassee Island, along with others who lived along the river, especially on Williams Island and on Moccasin Bend, bequeathed not only elements of their ceremonialism to their successors but also their earthen mounds and deserted village sites.

About 1000 A.D. the Woodland culture gave way to another pattern, the Mississippian culture. As the name implies, its practitioners were people concentrated in the Mississippi River Valley. They moved into rather large permanent villages located on the most desirable spots, which frequently meant that Woodland peoples were pushed aside or were assimilated by the newcomers. In addition to living in Hiwassee Island settlements the Mississippian Indians, at one time or another during the seven hundred years they dominated the region, lived in villages on Dallas Island, in the Hixson area, at the mouth of Wolftever and Citico creeks, on Chattanooga and Williams islands, on Moccasin Bend, and at Audubon Acres on Chickamauga Creek. They are remembered for their temple mounds, the best known of which, although not the largest in Tennessee, are located in the Tennessee Valley northeast of Chattanooga.

The Mississippian people represented many unknown tribes and tongues; however, those living east of the Mississippi River appear to have been mainly of the Muskhogean language group. Theirs was a more sophisticated culture than their predecessors and their homes, built around a single, open court, gave a true sense of community. Pottery of various sizes and styles points up the versatility and creativity of their master craftsmen. The Mississippians hunting-and-gathering economy was well assisted by agriculture. Temples and civic buildings crowned earthen mounds, reflecting a widespread influence of traditions from Middle America, although without the latter's cut-stone and cement materials. The flat-topped temple mounds served not only for religious ceremonies but also as council chambers where leaders handed down civil decisions, declared war, or made peace. Unlike the Woodland Indians, the Mississippian people left no graves with treasures for the archaeologist to read; rather, it is believed, they either cremated their dead or stored their deceased in "bone houses."

The second Indian occupancy of Hiwassee Island came without much of a time interval; apparently the Hamilton people simply moved out and the Mississippian people moved in shortly thereafter. So typical was this new aspect of Mississippian culture that it is named the Hiwassee Island Component. It began between the eleventh and twelfth centuries and lasted some two hundred years, thus covering most of the temple mound period in Tennessee.

The town on Hiwassee Island clustered about an open court with its three important public structures. The first construction began on the surface but with some seven rebuildings on the same site it assumed an elevated form of about fifty-five feet. According to Lewis and Kneberg, "The settlements were protected by stockades, and constant rebuilding took place within the enclosed area. The important community buildings were usually erected upon clay foundations finished with stairways, ramps, platforms, and accessory buildings; at most sites there were adjacent buildings upon each level of the substructure. The majority of the buildings were rectangular, and the framework was composed of long slender saplings set vertically at close intervals in wall trenches."The roof was woven like a large basket and then thatched with grass. The walls were lathed with split cane and plastered with clay. Some structures were large enough to accommodate three hundred persons and were decorated with colorful mats and elaborate carvings.

Houses, built in the same manner, usually had small dimensions, twenty by twenty-five feet, or smaller. The large population required the development of intensive agricultural techniques; corn, beans, pumpkins, squash, and native sweet potatoes were principal crops. Distincitively designed and decorated pottery—bottles, jars, bowls, and large basins—complemented utilitarian, shallow "salt pans." Archaeological observations note that bear and deer were hunted in large numbers along with opossum, squirrel, rabbit, raccoon, fox, wildcat, beaver, turkey, and turtles; quantities of fish and shellfish were also consumed.

A later Mississippian cultural aspect bears the name Dallas. Following the Hiwassee Island era as the dominant pattern of the eastern Tennessee Valley, the Dallas people became the leaders in an evolving culture. They appear to have merged with the Hiwassee Island culture and assimilated many of their traits. However, it is believed that the Dallas people actually represented the arrival of the Creek Indians in the region before 1300 A.D.

Dallas activity centered on the eighty-four-acre Dallas Island, which today lies largely submerged beneath the water of TVA's Chickamauga Lake. A small portion of the original site is a "new" island at the Hamilton County Park. Here, in relative stability, an Indian metropolis flourished, beginning at a time estimated about 1450 A.D. During some periods of its prominence it occupied both banks of the river as well as the mile-long island.

The first settlement, on the river's eastern bank, featured a large temple mound similar to the architectural plans used on Hiwassee Island. Later, the Indians built a ceremonial center on the opposite shore. A third center, almost identical to that of the historic Creeks, ultimately completed the complex. Some interpreters associate Dallas with the Indian town of Chiaha described by scribes journeying with Hernando de Soto's expedition of discovery in 1540.[3]

In June of that year the bold conquistadors arrived from Tampa Bay in this area, where they noted they first found fenced villages. They rested with the Indians for a time before moving west to discover the Mississippi River, where de Soto met his death. A quarter of a century later other Spaniards, led by Juan Pardo, reached Chiaha. One of Pardo's party wrote in 1567 of the Indian village, "it is rich and broad land, a big place, surrounded by pretty rivers; around this place . . . are many small towns, all surrounded by rivers. There are leagues of fine land, of many grapes, of medlar trees; in fact it is an angelic land."[4]

Scholars differ as to the exact location of Chiaha: de Soto specialists have placed it on Burns Island in Marion County and students of Pardo conclude that it was on Williams Island. Others suggest that Dallas Island compares favorably with the stockaded villages found by the European explorers. More important than this debate is the fact that this section of the country fell under the jurisdiction of Spanish colonialism.

One of the characteristics of the Dallas culture was the community plan calling for "the compact, stockaded village type with the dwelling houses adjacent to a prominently located community center. Dallas council houses were usually built upon elevated foundations, and the desire to obtain height in these substructures seems to have been an important objective," conclude archaeologists Lewis and Kneberg.[5]

But Dallas culture consisted of more than temple mounds with their extensive religious and civic stockaded areas and rotunda-shaped buildings. In eastern Tennessee, centers like Hiwassee Island and Dallas became closely affiliated with the historic Creek Indians of the Muskhogean peoples as kinds of tribal provinces. They all shared the Mississippian culture and were involved in intertribal alliances or confederations. The name Creek, used by English traders, was not an Indian name. It represented a corruption of the name, Ocheese Creek Indians, representing a people who lived in Georgia along a stream by that name (the present Ocmulgee River). As time passed, it became popular to shorten the term to Creek, which eventually became the name used for members of the entire great confederacy.[6]

The Dallas Indians practiced entirely different burial customs from the Hiwassee Island Focus group. Graves, scattered widely throughout the villages, indicated that the dead were interred near their homes. They contained most of the deceased's worldly possessions as well as burial gifts to assist in meeting the hazards of the journey to another world. These artifacts reveal a very high standard of craftsmanship in working pottery, ceremonial flints, copper ornaments, and in carving and engraving shells.

Shellcraft became one of the high accomplishments of the Dallas people. "In addition to using several different varieties of small marine shells and fresh water pearls for beads," Lewis and Kneberg report, "they cut and shaped many large and small beads from large marine conches and fresh water species of clam."[7] Some bore incised designs, some featured cross designs or animal, human, or bird motifs. Shell ornaments were used as beads, legbands, belts, ear pins, and wrist cuffs. In addition to jewelry, shell ornaments and gorgets made up much of the burial tribute.

Village life centered around the square and its public buildings. Here the marine conch shell trade must have been a lively subject of discussion. Here people gathered in groups, for homes were generally very small and simple. The square also served as the site for local government, for talk of wilderness politics, and for ceremonials and festivals. Here the rituals, Middle American in tone and showing the Indian's esteem for the sacredness of fire and corn, were enacted in season. And nearby the "chunky yard" witnessed the Indians not only at play but also passionately involved in gambling over the game's outcome.

Shortly before the year 1700 a number of significant changes affected the area. Englishmen from the Atlantic coast at Charleston, South Carolina, and Frenchmen penetrating mid-America via the Mississippi River established shadowy claims over the Tennessee Valley with only disdain for Spain's earlier asserted title. Soon European trade goods became Indian necessities, and horses, trinkets, blankets, firearms, and ammunition, vital diplomatic devices.

Not many years later, about 1715, the powerful Cherokee Nation expelled all other Indians from Tennessee lands. The Cherokees, who called themselves "principal people," were of an Iroquois language group. They had migrated into the Southeast many centuries earlier and lived mainly in the Southern Appalachian valleys of Georgia, South Carolina, and North Carolina. Only one group of them, the Overhill Cherokees, living along the Little Tennessee, Hiwassee, and Tellico rivers, had villages in the Tennessee country. After the Creeks, Shawnees, and Yuchi Indians had been driven out, all of the western land except for that of the Overhill villages was unoccupied. It was a vast hunting ground, a kind of Indian no-man's-land. The temple mounds and public squares of Hiwassee and Dallas islands and other sites within Hamilton County fell into decay: the elements tore at their buildings, eroded the mounds, and encouraged the growth of a new blanket of vegetation.

Although no Indians actually lived in the area, the old trails continued to be widely used. For generations, wild beasts and humans had trod them. First engineered, it is claimed, by the buffalo, whose instinct singled out the most desirable river crossings and easiest grades, some of the traces became so worn as to be well below the neighboring terrain. The Indians traveled extensively by land on missions of pleasure, adventure, war, and business. Burial objects reveal trade items from the Atlantic Ocean to the Gulf of Mexico, from the Appalachian Mountains to the Great Lakes.

A number of major traces, all of which were fed by a network of lesser trails, used the gateway position of Hamilton County for both east-west and north-south travel. Many of them led to or from the Great Creek Crossing of the Tennessee River at Long Island near the present site of Bridgeport, Alabama, known as one of the major Indian river crossings in all of southeastern United States.

One of the most-traveled paths, drawing traffic from the East via the Chesapeake fork and the Midwest via the Ohio branch, was named the Great Indian Warpath. Crossing eastern Tennessee, it passed through present-day Cleveland and Ooltewah and crossed Chickamauga Creek in the Brainerd area. It then ran to Citico Creek and on to the towns of Running Water and Nickajack in the river gorge on its way to the Creek Crossing.

An eastern spur of the Black Fox Trail, which went westward from Rattlesnake Springs in Bradley County, served this area as did the Sequatchie Trail, which ran through the Sequatchie Valley. Another way, called the Chickamauga Path, brought the traveler from northern Georgia through Chattanooga northward to Kentucky along the top of Cumberland Plateau through such spots as Beersheba Springs.

A more important route out of north Georgia carries the cumbersome name, the Tennessee River, Ohio, and Great Lakes Trail. At the southern end it connected with a major network of paths from all parts of the south. It continued on to the Hamilton County area where, consolidating with other routes, it headed northward on the north side of the Tennessee River east of the base of Walden Ridge. It touched on Hiwassee Island and joined other main trails going northward into Kentucky and beyond.

One other major route led from Middle Tennesse via the Creek

Crossing through the Chattanooga passes and on into the south on its way to Florida. This trace bore the name Cisco and St. Augustine Trail, while portions of it in the Tennessee country were known as the Nickajack Trace. These trails and the waterways of the region clearly pointed to a day when Indians would again settle in the region.[8]

In 1735 the trader James Adair estimated that the Cherokees numbered as many as seventeen thousand; their extensive and vaguely defined land claim, judged to be forty thousand square miles, was called the "key to Carolina" because it controlled the back door to that colony. The Indians, described as well built, of moderate stature and olive coloring, shaved their heads "tho many of the old people have it [hair] plucked out by the roots, except a patch on the hind part of the head, about twice the bigness of a crown-piece, which is ornamented with beads, feathers, wampum, stained deers' hair, and such like baubles . . . "[9]

From the time of the first appearance of the French and English in the Cherokee country, the Indians became pawns in Europe's seventeenth-century brand of colonialism. Increasingly dependent on British trade goods which were cheaper and more readily available, they sent thousands of furs and deerskins to Charleston, South Carolina, a thriving hub of the southern Indian trade.

Carolina soon dispatched traders to the Cherokee villages. They learned the geography of the area, became interpretors, served as an important link in the trade, and represented the Crown as an informal diplomatic corps. A number settled with the Cherokees. They married Indian women, and in accordance with Cherokee tradition, became full-fledged members of the tribe. Most came from Scotland. These men had an uncanny ability as traders and possessed a relaxed talent for "going native." Many of them and the mixed-blood generation they sired gained the high esteem and trust of the tribesmen.

Peripheral effects of the eighteenth-century Anglo-French wars of empire immediately were felt in the Cherokee country. French policy challenged the dominant position of the English, reaching a climax in the French and Indian War of 1754–63. On the Little Tennessee River the English built their westernmost American fort, Fort Loudoun. Here under the Union Jack they hoped to control the region, retain Cherokee support, and dilute the effectiveness of French intrigue. But cordial relations with the Cherokees collapsed in a series of inept dealings with the Indians on the part of frontiersmen and British representatives alike. On 7 August 1760, Fort Loudoun surrendered to the Cherokees.

The Indians at once sent victory messages to the French at New Orleans inviting them to take possession of the conquered fort. Although the war was going badly for them at the time, the French dispatched riverboats loaded with stores and gifts for the long journey. After days of toil they reached the canyon of the Tennessee River, where they were unable to ascend the strong currents of the Suck:

> . . . they were luckily stopped in their mischievous career, by a deep and dangerous cataract; the waters of which rolled down with a prodigious rapidity, dashed against the opposite rocks, and from thence rushed off with impetuous violence, on a quarter-angled course. It appeared so shocking and unsurmountable to the monsieurs, that after staying there a considerable time, in the vain expectation of seeing some of their friends, necessity forced them to return back to New Orleans, about 2600 computed miles, to their inconsolable disappointment.[10]

Shadowy evidence of the Frenchmen's failure exists. Old maps show an "Old French Store," possibly located on Williams Island or nearby, which some scholars explain as the temporary outpost of this French expedition.

By 1763 the war ended with a peace treaty giving the English sovereignty over all of the eastern portion of the continent. The English immediately adopted a new policy: to regulate the Indian trade and restrict colonial settlement to the Atlantic seaboard east of the mountains. The Cherokees again accepted British sovereignty, especially appreciating the appointment of Colonel John Stuart, whom they regarded as a true friend, as Indian agent for the Southern District.

The Cherokees, now completely dependent on English trade goods, guns, and ammunition, saw a renewal of the activity of the Carolina traders. One of the newcomers was John McDonald. This young Scot had arrived in Charleston, South Carolina, in 1766 at the age of nineteen and immediately became associated with the Cherokee trade. His employers soon sent him to the Tennessee country where he did business with the villages along the Little Tennessee River. McDonald married Anna Shorey, mixed-breed daughter of trader William Shorey and his Cherokee wife Ghi-goo-ie, and according to custom became a member of the Cherokee tribe.[11]

In 1770 the McDonalds moved to South Chickamauga Creek where the Great Indian Warpath crossed that stream. Here, far removed from any Indian settlement, John McDonald ran a trading post. At the same

time the McDonalds may have constructed the first room of the house
in Rossville Gap later known as the John Ross House. McDonald also
received from John Stuart, the British superintendent, a commission
as an agent for the British government. So in 1770 McDonald became
the first European to settle in the territory of Hamilton County and
the first businessman of the district.

Meanwhile other whites used the peace to spy out the lands west
of the Appalachian Mountains. Frontiersmen called Long Hunters (including Elisha Walden for whom the Cumberland Front was named)
roamed far and wide. The natural resources, fertile soil, and abundant
game pleased them; by 1769 permanent settlers moved into the region
called Watauga. They defiantly ignored the English policy of a closed
Indian frontier.

In contrast to settlers who occupied but a few acres, North Carolina
speculators planned in terms of millions of acres. A group under the
leadership of Judge Richard Henderson organized the Transylvania
Company for this purpose. In March 1775 at Sycamore Shoals they
negotiated a treaty with the Cherokees for some twenty million acres,
also illegal from the British point of view.

One of the lesser chiefs from the small town of Great Island of the
Little Tennessee River, muscular, pock-marked Dragging Canoe, vigorously opposed the sale. He blamed the older people of his tribe for
signing away the Nation's birthright. He warned that more land conces-
sions would be demanded and that "finally the whole country, which
the Cherokee and their fathers had so long occupied, will be demanded,
and the remnant of *Ani-Yunwiya*, 'The Real People,' once so great and
formidable, will be compelled to seek refuge in some distant wilderness."

Dragging Canoe represented a new generation of Cherokees for
whom he spoke in forceful, impassioned terms, but the chaotic conditions existing on the eve of the American Revolution complicated all
relationships. Most Tennesseans of the time favored independence;
the Cherokees, resentful of frontiersmen's pressure for land, supported
the British. During the summer of 1776 the Indians carried out a
determined invasion of the East Tennessee settlements in which
Dragging Canoe played a prominent role. He and his Indian warriors
lost; the colonists immediately retaliated. Superior power overawed
the Cherokees, who sent their older chief to again seek overtures of
peace, but Dragging Canoe refused to participate.

In the spring of 1777 the defiant Canoe and his followers seceded
from the Overhill Cherokee towns. By trail and river they left their

homes at Settico, Great Island, Tellico, Toquo, and Chilhowie. Among the important warriors they counted Willenawah, Bloody Fellow, Hanging Maw, Kitegiska, Young Tassel (later called John Watts), Lying Fish, the Buck, and Little Owl. These were the people who would challenge the settlers and fight for their homeland at any cost.

As a new homesite from which to carry on resistance, they chose the area close by the trading post of John McDonald on South Chickamauga Creek. Those from Great Island led by Dragging Canoe settled at the old Creek village site of Chickamauga, several miles from the mouth of the creek. Little Owl, the brother of the Canoe, selected a spot on the creek just inside the present Tennessee-Georgia border.

The Indians from Settico located at the north of a stream they named Settico Creek (later called Citico) while those from Toquo also gave their new village the name of their earlier village.[12]

As the months passed, other Cherokee warriors joined the groups as did militant Creeks and other tribesmen. The people of the settled frontier soon realized that there was little possibility "of a lasting peace with them at Chuckemogo." Dragging Canoe's resolve continued strong; those Cherokees who sold land he regarded as traitors and rogues. By the end of 1778 he ranked as the most powerful chieftain in the Old Southwest with a following of more than one thousand braves. This splinter tribe, having seceded from the Cherokee Nation, received the name Chickamauga. They brought the American Revolution directly to the area of Hamilton County.

NOTES

1. Material concerning the prehistoric era is based on the following: Clarence B. Moore, *Aboriginal Sites on Tennessee River* (Philadelphia: n.p., 1915); reprint *Journal of the Academy of Natural Sciences of Philadelphia* (1915); 354–396; and the following books by Thomas M. N. Lewis and Madeline Kneberg: *Tribes That Slumber* (Knoxville: University of Tennessee Press, 1958); *Hiwassee Island: An Archaeological Account of Four Tennessee Indian Peoples* (Knoxville: University of Tennessee Press, 1946); *The Prehistory of the Chickamauga Basin in Tennessee* (Knoxville: Division of Anthropology, University of Tennessee Press, 1941). Clarence Moore in 1914 and 1915 was one of the first persons to carry out a systematic program of exploration along the Tennessee River. Most of the archaeological work was not undertaken until

the beginning of the work by TVA when the Authority and University of Tennessee combined forces to make studies prior to impounding the waters.

2. Moore, *Aboriginal Sites*, pp. 354–396.

3. John R. Swanton, *Final Report of the United States de Soto Expedition Commission* (Washington, D.C.: Government Printing Office, 1939), pp. 139, 190, 191, 201, 202, 208; J. W. M. Breazeale, *Life As It Is* . . . (Knoxville: James Williams, 1842), p. 232. Breazeale, writing four years after Cherokee removal, reports special fortifications at the town of Dallas. Here, he wrote,

> There is an entrenchment, running out from the bank of the river, then in a direction down the river, and then to the river again, including an area of about seven acres. Before the land was cleared and the entrenchment included within a farm, the ditch was about six or seven feet deep; and the gateway or passage out, on the back line from the river, was apparent. The ditch was cut in an angular line, the lines of the angles being about twenty feet in length, so as to prevent the raking of the ditch; which proves beyond doubt, that it was not only cut by a people understanding the modes of civilized warfare, but that it was intended as a defence against a people possessing the knowledge and use of fire-arms. Within the entrenchment are several large mounds, on one of which was standing, at the first settling of the country by the white people, very large forest trees, which, from their appearance, must have been at least four hundred years old. On the south side of the river, both below and above this fortification, are found the ruins of ancient towns.

4. Stanley J. Folmsbee and Madeline L. Kneberg, eds., and Gerald W. Wade, trans., "Journal of the Juan Pardo Expedition, 1566–1567," (East Tennessee Historical Society), *Publications* (1965), pp. 106–21.

5. Lewis and Kneberg, *Chickamauga Basin*, p. 12.

6. Lewis and Kneberg, *Tribes That Slumber*, pp. 93–94.

7. Lewis and Kneberg, *Chickamauga Basin*, p. 15.

8. William E. Myer, *Indian Trails of the Southeast* (Nashville: Blue and Gray Press, 1971), pp. 15–31, 103–110, 112–116 (originally published in U.S., Bureau of American Ethnology, *Forty-Second Annual Report*, 1928).

9. James Adair, *History of the American Indians*, ed. Samuel Cole Williams (Johnson City, Tenn.: Watauga Press, 1930), p. 238; Henry Timberlake, *Lieutenant Henry Timberlake's Memoirs, 1756–1765*, ed. Samuel Cole Williams (Johnson City, Tenn.: Watauga Press, 1927), pp. 75–77.

10. Adair, *American Indians*, p. 287.

11. Penelope Johnson Allen, "Leaves From the Family Tree," *Chattanooga Times*, 2 February 1936. William Shorey, an interpreter, died enroute to England in 1762; he was traveling with Henry Timberlake and three Cherokees who were being escorted on a visit to George III.

12. J. P. Brown, *Old Frontiers: The Story of the Cherokee Indians From Earliest Times to the Date of Their Removal to the West* (Kingsport, Tenn.: Southern Publishers, 1938), pp. 163–164.

4

The Chickamaugas

GOVERNOR Patrick Henry of the new state of Virginia showed deep concern over conditions on the frontier in early 1779. He knew that a British military campaign against the South had won Savannah and pressed on toward Augusta in Georgia. He also had information that Tories and Indians planned an offensive against the backcountry. Addressing his colleague Governor Richard Caswell, he asked the assistance of North Carolina in a campaign against the Chickamauga towns before the aggressive Dragging Canoe could launch an offensive.[1]

Henry reminded Caswell that the Chickamaugas—sometimes referred to as the Lower Cherokees—brought death and destruction to the exposed frontiers of both states. They drove off cattle and horses, burned cabins, and terrified and massacred the settlers. Their weapons and ammunition came through British agents and suppliers in Florida and encouragement poured forth from American supporters of the Crown. The Chickamaugas were active opponents of the American war for independence. Moreover, Henry advanced another reason for destroying Chickamauga power; he pointed out to the North Carolina governor the need to open navigation on the Tennessee River, "in which your state, as well as ours, seems deeply interested, which is rendered unsafe and impracticable as long as these banditti go unpunished."

James Robertson, serving as American agent to the Cherokees, also advised the North Carolina governor to chastise the "Chickamoggy" Indians, suggesting that pioneer militiamen would be willing to fight "at their own expense."

Little time was lost in arranging a joint campaign under the command of Colonel Evan Shelby, the operator of a busy trading post at Sapling Grove (Bristol). Men gathered on the banks of the Holston River at Long Island and at the mouth of Big Creek to build boats. They planned to use the river to invade Dragging Canoe's stronghold; in their crude craft the men of Tennessee's first "navy" set out on 10 April 1779. According to instructions, Shelby, upon reaching the Little Tennessee River, sent dispatches to the Overhill Cherokees informing them of the impending assault. The spring "tide" hurried the boats onward to the mouth of South Chickamauga Creek and the troops, numbering between six and nine hundred men, prepared for action on Hamilton County soil.

An Indian fisherman, found asleep at his nets, was taken prisoner and with him as a guide the soldiers waded through flooded canebrakes to the main Chickamauga town. They soon discovered many of the warriors had previously set out for British headquarters at Savannah while others, along with the women and children, fled to the cover of the forests during a brief engagement in which four Indians fell.

Shelby spent two weeks destroying the Chickamauga towns in a typical "scorched earth" campaign. He burned eleven villages without opposition. The trade establishment of John McDonald attracted special attention: British war supplies and McDonald's collection of pelts and deerskins were confiscated. Any horses found were also seized as part of the campaign booty.

Some members of the invasion force under Colonel John Montgomery again took to their boats, floating on down the Tennessee River to join George Rogers Clark in his major campaign to wrestle the Illinois country from the British. Meanwhile Shelby and his followers crossed the Tennessee River, destroyed their own boats, and started homeward by land on the Tennessee River, Ohio, and Great Lakes Trail. On the banks of a small creek Shelby stopped and held an auction of the captured goods and horses. Since that April day in 1779 this stream has carried the name Sale Creek.

At first it appeared that Shelby's foray into the Hamilton County

territory resulted in complete success for the American cause. Only
two men had died and their deaths occurred on the homeward journey.
The destruction of the Chickamauga towns had importance too, for
British success, running at high tide east of the mountains, focused
special attention on this rear-guard phase of the war.

On closer examination, however, this naval campagin against
Dragging Canoe represented success without victory. The manpower
losses of the Indians were slight; destroyed spring crops could be
replanted and the burnt villages soon rebuilt. As Dragging Canoe's
people reorganized, the sight of the debris of their former homes
kindled within them a spirit of revenge. British agents soon reappeared
along Chickamauga Creek and new Tory associates joined Indian recruits, reoccupying old town sites, while fresh supplies arrived by pack
train from Pensacola.

Although Montgomery with 150 men successfully made the trip from
Chickamauga to the old Northwest via the Tennessee River to become
a potent force in the military plans of Clark, the offensive against the
Indians did not result in making river travel any safer. Shelby not only
failed to eliminate the "banditti" but the stretches of bad water, not
mentioned by the Virginia governor, still existed.

Before the Chickamauga Indians moved to the Hamilton County
area, a few settlers ventured to use the Tennessee River, but it never
became a major thoroughfare to the west. In 1768 a party of emigrants
passed downstream on the free currents bound for land in newly acquired West Florida. Others may have soon followed but none left
records until 1779. That year, fragmentary evidence indicates, a group
of some two hundred voyagers in forty boats passed Muscle Shoals on
their way to the Illinois country.

About the time that Evan Shelby's militiamen returned to their
homes in upper East Tennessee, Richard Henderson, James Robertson,
and John Donelson created a lot of talk throughout the Tennessee
country. They laid plans to start a new settlement in the Cumberland
River valley. Scouting parties reported an exciting future because the
region possessed great salt licks, fertile soil, and abundant game. James
Robertson, with a small band of men and boys, journeyed by
Cumberland Gap and across Kentucky with horses, cows, and sheep
to the new settlement at Nashborough. The rest of the party with their
household belongings decided to use the rivers: the Tennessee, the
Ohio, and the Cumberland. The wandering spirit of the pioneers and
their avid search for land were blunted neither by the unfriendly

mountains nor the dense wilderness separating eastern Tennessee from the Cumberland area. Nor were these bold adventurers deterred by the fact that the American Revolution was in mid-course and that Dragging Canoe's veterans watched the Tennessee River for every opportunity of revenge.

The river trip, destined to be one of the great sagas of Tennessee history, began in late December 1779.[2] Colonel John Donelson, master of the flagship *Adventure*, led the flotilla of thirty to forty boats, crowded with possibly three hundred persons, including slaves. Mrs. James Robertson, and her five children, and the Donelsons, including their young daughter Rachel (who later married Andrew Jackson), sailed on the *Adventure*. Delayed at the outset for about two months by the extremely cold winter, they went into temporary winter quarters until the end of February.

Ten days later the crude boats faced a "high sea" as they came to the "uppermost Chickamogga Town, which was then evacuated" and made an early camp. Here Mrs. Ephraim Peyton, whose husband had gone overland, gave birth to the first recorded white baby in Hamilton County's annals.

Wednesday, 8 March, the pioneers started their passage through the Chattanooga area and into the mountain gorge. They passed by Citico, by then reoccupied by the Chickamaugas, and soon noticed warriors in the war colors of black and red. The Indians followed in canoes, making gestures of friendship—which were mere ruses to induce the travelers into ambush. As Donelson guided the flotilla close to the shore at Moccasin Bend, one young man on board died from an Indian bullet fired from cover among the cane brakes.

Thomas Stuart's party with family and friends numbering twenty-eight people sailed in the rear of the fleet by prearranged plan as a self-imposed quarantine because smallpox had broken out among them. The Indians noticed their helpless plight and intercepted them. They killed or captured all on board while "their cries were distinctly heard by those boats in the rear."

Dragging Canoe's followers continued to torment the voyagers from the river banks as the little fleet headed for the worrysome Suck, about which some on board had previously heard. Torn between watching out for the strong currents and jagged boulders and the savages, they plunged into the turbulent waters. A canoe loaded with personal possessions attached to a large boat overturned. When the party landed on the north bank to give aid in an effort to recover the canoe's cargo,

Indians from the cliffs above opened fire from concealed vantage points. Those who had landed raced back to the boats and immediately pushed off. Shot continued to pour down from the river bluffs, wounding four on board.

The boat of Jonathan Jennings ran onto a large rock at the Suck and became partly immersed. No one could come to the aid of those aboard. Chickamaugas concentrated their attention on this disabled craft, subjecting it to harassing fire. Jennings, an excellent marksman, held them off while directing his wife, a grown son, a young man, and two blacks to cast the cargo into the river to lighten the boat. Soon after starting their task three of the men, either wounded or scared, jumped from the boat and tried to swim ashore. The black was shot. The Indians captured the other two; they ransomed young Jennings later and burned the other fellow at the stake.

Mrs. Jennings, her daughter Mrs. Peyton, and the black woman finally jumped into the water to push the boat off the boulder. Mrs. Peyton, just a day after childbirth, suffered from exposure; her mother nearly lost her life when the boat suddenly jerked free of the rock into the swift current. The infant, according to the log kept by the master of the flagship, "was unfortunately killed in the hurry & confusion consequent upon such a disaster." Three days later the Jennings craft caught up with the other boats.

Many other members of the flotilla performed heroic deeds. Four suffered wounds on Abel Gower's boat; near panic followed. A young woman, Nancy Gower, then seized the tiller. Although shot through the thigh, she kept to her post until other passengers discovered the blood soaking through her clothes.

For weeks they journeyed on, not reaching their destination at the Big Salt Lick until 24 April. Hours of exhausting drudgery, unending toil, and dreadful fear became prime ingredients in fashioning the new community on the Cumberland. But there was no peace. Dragging Canoe and his Chickamaugas harbored a special hatred toward the Middle Tennessee frontiersmen. No sooner had fields been planted on the Cumberland than small bands of braves attacked the settlements, drove off the livestock, and massacred relentlessly.

The Canoe realized that his villages along Chickamauga Creek and east of Lookout Mountain could not be defended. Understanding the fundamentals of military strategy, he led his warriors and their families on a second trek to sites for new towns. This time he chose locations west of Lookout Mountain along the rough waters of the canyon, where his people built five towns. Running Water Town on the Tennessee River some twelve miles beyond the Suck became Dragging Canoe's headquarters. Here John McDonald and his family moved and he continued to serve as an agent for the British. Three miles to the west stood Nickajack Town on the south bank. The next town sprang up on Long Island near present-day Bridgeport, and some ten miles distant on a small creek they built Crow Town, which was about thirty miles from the Suck. In the narrow valley of Lookout Creek they erected Lookout Mountain Town in the vicinity of present-day Trenton, Georgia.

Collectively these Chickamauga towns were known as the Five Lower Towns. They occupied a natural bastion guarded by the steep shoulders of Lookout Mountain and Walden Ridge to the east and by the turbulent whirls and sucks of the mountain stretch of the river. On downstream was the famed Creek Crossing of the Tennessee where major trails formed a junction point. The territory of Hamilton County would no longer be the center of Chickamauga life. However, Chickamaugas continued to occupy some of the villages east of Lookout Mountain and any expedition from the Watauga settlements of East Tennessee and beyond had to cross the future acres of the county to approach the lair of Dragging Canoe.[3]

The rapid growth of frontier clearings and the undying hatred of the Canoe for Americans produced continuous Chickamauga raids. Colonel John Sevier now headed the over-mountain militiamen. As colonel he decided when to campaign, what Indians to chastise, and how to deal with the defeated tribesmen.

The Chickamaugas, wily foes, deliberately passed through and idled about the Overhill towns of the more peaceful Cherokees in order to throw suspicion on them. Sevier, in his early operations, limited his assaults to the villages of these upper Cherokees, systematically destroying homes and food caches. Finally in 1782, fresh Chickamauga forays became so numerous and savage that the state government of North Carolina authorized an offensive against their towns, "all the males therein to be killed, and the females captured for exchange; supplies captured to be divided among the soldiers participating."

After many changes in plans the campaign finally got under way in mid-September with a reduced quota of 250 transmountain men under Sevier. The governor of North Carolina authorized expenses to be borne by "Continental credit," giving the operation official Revolutionary War status.

The soldiers, stopping at the Overhill towns to make sure they would not be exposed to an attack from the rear, pushed on with an Indian guide. The guide, a smooth-talking, mixed-blood, variously called John Watts or Young Tassel, actually was a loyal supporter of the Canoe and had no intention of guiding Sevier to the Five Lower Towns. The troops did arrive at the original Chickamauga towns and burned Bull Town, Settico, Vann's, Chickamauga, and Tuskegee village. Food and supplies were destroyed.

While Tuskegee, located on Williams Island, came under the torch, defiant warriors taunted Sevier's men from the cliffs of Lookout Mountain. The frontiersmen answered the challenge. On the boulder-strewn slopes of the mountain they fought a brief but spirited action. Rifle fire and shouts echoed across the valley as contestants on both sides fought from behind rocks and trees. Soon the Chickamaugas slipped away and Sevier's men withdrew to continue their campaign in the Coosa River area of north Georgia. The indecisive action on Lookout Mountain occurred on 20 September 1782—some eleven months after the British surrender at Yorktown—and is recorded as the last battle of the American Revolution.

With the war over, an era of almost 250 years when Spanish, French, and English banners proclaimed European control over the area came to a close. North Carolina now claimed the Tennessee country, and her politicians and speculators immediately carved up the region into land parcels turned over to individuals as private property. A rush of new settlers pushed the frontier westward.

But the Five Lower Towns had not been touched and their war aims remained unchanged. For a brief period, supplies from the British via Detroit kept them in war matériel. Then Spain undertook to be the supplier and John McDonald, who still lived at Lookout Mountain Town, became a Spanish agent. The Iberian monarchy held Florida and the land west of the Mississippi as a result of the 1783 peace arrangements and was determined to protect its possessions from the aggressive, expansionist frontiersmen. One way to achieve the success of this policy was to keep the Indians stirred up. The young American government, weak, inexperienced, and far from the Spanish borderlands, attempted to avoid conflict with both the Europeans and the tribesmen.

The United States government struck a conciliatory note with the Cherokees in 1785 when it negotiated the treaty of Hopewell with them. Despite vigorous protests by North Carolina, the federal authorities assumed control of Indian policy, made the Cherokees wards of the central administration, and promised not to take their lands. In fact, the United States actually moved pioneers off Indian territory.

Needless to say, the frontiersmen did not approve. Their violations of the treaty infuriated the Indians, who had accepted the good intentions of the new government. From Dragging Canoe's towns war parties struck at the Cumberland for scalps and horses; they harassed the frontiers of eastern Tennessee and carried their silent assaults into Virginia. And they continued to limit the use of the Tennessee River.

In 1785 a trader, one Francis Mayberry, made a trip to carry merchandise to the Chickasaw country. With him traveled a young helper, an orphan, who had recently arrived in the United States from Sutherlandshire, Scotland. Near Lookout Mountain a band of Chickamaugas stopped their craft; the Indians discovered not only interesting trade goods on board but also a chieftain whom they considered hostile.

Disagreeing over the fate of their prisoners, the Indians called on John McDonald for advice, for he was regarded as the most powerful man in the area. The fresh strong brogue of youthful Daniel Ross certainly must have appealed to the shrewd, intelligent veteran Scot. Ross's life was spared. He was encouraged to stay among the Chickamaugas and soon set himself up in business at Setecoe, a small village in Lookout Valley. In 1787 Ross married Mollie McDonald, the seventeen-year-old daughter of John and Anna Shorey McDonald.

In keeping with Cherokee tradition Daniel Ross was made a fullfledged member of the Cherokee Nation. In 1788 the McDonald and Ross families moved their homes to Turkeytown (near Center, Alabama) where on 3 October 1790, the third child and oldest son of Daniel and Mollie Ross was born. The infant, named John Ross, was destined to became the leader of his people; his father lived with the Indians forty-five years, raising a family of nine children.[4]

Another river party failed to find the good fortune of Daniel Ross. In May 1788 Colonel James Brown sailed on a large boat with two-inch oak plank placed around the gunwales and carrying a small swivel gun. Brown, a Revolutionary War veteran, planned to take up land in Middle Tennessee as a military bonus and chose the route followed earlier by John Donelson. On board the craft loaded with household goods traveled the colonel's wife, four sons, three daughters, five young men, and a black woman.

At Tuskegee Island Town they encountered Indians who alerted comrades on down the river to attack the boat. They massacred eight of the men and made Mrs. Brown, her three daughters, and two younger sons prisoners. Young Joseph Brown lived as a captive at Nickajack for a year in the life-style of the Indians before being exchanged. During these days he learned much about the Chickamauga towns and later acted as a scout, guiding a frontier army into the Indian stronghold.

No complete record of river travel exists. Some parties did use the Tennessee to get to new western homes as did the Hardeman family in about 1786.[5] Chickamaugas, however, controlled the use of the waterway so thoroughly that the United States in 1791 included a provision in the treaty of Holston guaranteeing "free" navigation. Dragging Canoe never signed this treaty and refused to recognize its terms. He let it be known that those who used the Tennessee did so at their own risk.

The Canoe and his followers reached the zenith of their power about 1788–89. An elderly chieftain, Old Tassel, who had long been friendly to the Americans as a leader of the Overhill Cherokees, fell, treacherously murdered under a flag of truce. As a result new recruits poured into the Lower Towns. The center of government moved from Chota on the Little Tennessee River to Ustanali on the Coosewatie River in Georgia. Small bands of warriors lay in ambush along the trails, at fords and river portages, and in the mountain passes. It was the time of the scalping knife and the firebrand.

In 1788 Joseph Martin served North Carolina both as brigadier general of militia and Indian agent to the Cherokees; Sevier's activity as leader of the independent state of Franklin naturally resulted in Sevier's following his own Cherokee policy. Martin, a veteran of the border, had years of experience with the Indians. Never anxious to use the tomahawk, he believed in attempting to solve problems with diplomacy. Actually, many of the people of the border considered him suspect, for he lived at times with the Indians and married Betsy Ward, daughter of the famed "beloved woman" of the Cherokees, Nancy Ward.

As matters on the frontier disintegrated into a chaotic state and danger of a major Indian war seemed imminent, Martin had no choice other than to strike against Dragging Canoe. He assembled some five hundred men at White's Fort (Knoxville): three days in the saddle brought them to the Hiwassee River and a night march of twenty miles was undertaken to bring them close to Lookout Mountain. The troops pushed on at a gallop but found the Indian town at the base of the

mountain freshly evacuated. Disappointed, they realized that they had
not come upon the Chickamaugas unaware.

It was late evening. Camp arrangements for the night were completed. Some volunteers, however, pushed for immediate action to
secure some of the mountain passes. Martin approved, and about one
hundred moved out along the trail over the bench of the mountain.
As the soldiers strung out single file, they rode amid boulders and
trees directly into a well-concealed ambush. With this unexpected
assault the horsemen wheeled and in confusion raced for camp in the
growing darkness. That night Indian drums beat constantly as the
Chickamaugas rallied their braves for further action.

Early next morning a small company moved forward from camp
about half a mile from the mountain to reconnoiter the same pass.
Secluded Indians again surprised the militiamen, firing on them from
the ambush used the previous evening. Again the frontiersmen beat
a hasty retreat. Martin, on hearing the rifle fire, ordered his force
forward, fearing the advance party was surrounded. At the mountain
they dismounted and led their horses along the trail. This time the
Chickamaugas attacked from a different place of concealment. Eight
soldiers received wounds, three of which were fatal.

The frontiersmen returned the fire, gathered up their fallen comrades, and beat a disorganized retreat. Martin tried to rally them, but
most refused to continue the fight. Some, who claimed Martin was too
friendly with the Indians, accused him of betraying his own men.

The Chickamaugas lost but two warriors. Their victory was complete.
They had turned aside a well-armed force and again had slammed shut
the eastern gateway to the Five Lower Towns. Excited by their success,
the Chickamaugas sent new raiding parties along the frontier.

Dragging Canoe had reached the summit of his career. Militant
tribesmen including Creeks and Shawnee moved in and out of the
Lower Towns. The youthful Tecumseh spent time with them in the
lower Sequatchie Valley. Stolen horses and slaves along with prisoners
added to the confusion in the villages. Warriors with fascinating names
made the bastion their headquarters. Among the leading citizens of
the area were Bloody Fellow, the Breath, Doublehead, John Watts,
Fool Warrior, Kitegiska, the Glass, Richard Justice, Cotetoy, Bench,
Turtle-at-Home, Middlestriker, Pumpkin Boy, the Boot, the Crier, and
Tatlanta.

On 28 February 1792, Dragging Canoe attended a great victory party
where the eagle tail dance was held in his honor. The following day

the Canoe died. At Running Water Town the widely acclaimed chieftain was buried; his body rests today, it is believed, under the waters of Nickajack Lake. He had always stood firm as a patriot who would not sell or barter away the hills and valleys of his people.

The Chickamaugas selected John Watts as Dragging Canoe's successor. A mixed-blood (his father was a white trader and his mother a sister of Old Tassel), Watts was an able organizer, great orator, and skilled diplomat. He used the title of colonel, which had been bestowed on him by the Spanish, who continued to supply the Chickamaugas with war goods.

By this time major changes had occurred in Tennessee that were fated to have a fundamental impact on Hamilton County affairs. The state of North Carolina ceded the Tennessee country, which had received the status of a federal territory, to the national government. President George Washington inherited the Chickamauga problem and named William Blount territorial governor and superintendent of Indian affairs. New settlers continued to pour into the region after establishing home places in the Indian country in defiance of existing treaties. A new agreement, the treaty of Holston, was arrived at on 2 July 1791, to establish "perpetual peace and friendship" with the Cherokees. In addition to its emphasis on the free navigation of the Tennessee River it guaranteed the Indians all their land not already ceded. This treaty, to aid the Cherokees "to become Herdsmen and cultivators," pledged to furnish them with assistance.[6]

The Chickamaugas did not take part in the treaty negotiations. Although the federal government emphasized that there should be no offensive military campaigns against the Indians, the people of the border continued to insist that the only way to neutralize the Chickamauga threat was with "fear and not love."

In 1794 the Indian problem received top priority on the part of the territorial house of representatives which went so far as to give some members leaves of absence to "go on a scout against the Indians." The federal government remained adamant: there should be no offensive campaign. Finally frontiersmen in the Cumberland area supported by Kentucky recruits organized an expedition under Major James Ore. Guided by Joseph Brown, the former prisoner of the Chickamaugas, they crossed the Cumberland Plateau, descended the Sewanee Mountain, arriving at the Tennessee River near the mouth of Battle Creek on the night of 11 September 1794. By entering the Chickamaugas' stronghold by the back door, they completely surprised the Indians.

Running Water and Nickajack towns lay in ruins and many of the Chickamaugas were killed or captured. The spirit of Indian resistance was broken. Moreover, the men of Ore found evidence that Spain, because of her involvement in the French Revolutionary wars, could no longer furnish supplies to Watts and his followers.

That fall a colorful group of Chickamaugas and Cherokees met with Governor Blount at the Tellico Blockhouse across the Little Tennessee River from the ruins of old Fort Loudoun. They gathered for peace talks; they arranged for an exchange of prisoners and dealt with the touchy subject of stolen horses and slaves. But more importantly the agreement signaled the return of the splinter tribe, the Chickamaugas, to the Cherokee Nation. Blount smoked the peace pipe with John Watts and with Hanging Maw, the old Cherokee leader.[7]

At the confluence of the Clinch and Tennessee rivers the United States built the garrison station Southwest Point in the fall of 1792. When the blockhouses and stockade were completed, a company of light horse patrolled the area; later regiments of United States infantry from Detroit moved in. The garrison's strategic location commanded the gateway road passage over the Cumberlands to the west as well as the Tennessee River. Soon the hamlet called Kingston sprang up nearby where traders, politicians, speculators, and travelers tarried. Here the young John Ross was sent to clerk in a store and learn about the mercantile business. The leading Cherokees called at the garrison—Doublehead, the Glass, and Bloody Fellow. Indian traders stopped by on business, including John D. Chisholm, Daniel Ross, and Sam Riley. From the agency the annuities for the Cherokees were distributed. All business from the Hamilton County area was conducted here.[8]

In midsummer 1801 Return Jonathan Meigs arrived at Southwest Point. This newcomer, who had passed his sixtieth birthday, carried a letter of appointment signed by President Thomas Jefferson to the dual posts of Cherokee Indian agent and agent of the War Department in Tennessee. Connecticut-born Meigs, a Revolutionary War patriot, had earned the rank of colonel. At the close of the struggle he settled at Marietta, Ohio, taking an active role in the settlement of that area.

For twenty-two years Meigs served as a liaison between the whites and the Cherokees. Until 1807 his headquarters were at Southwest Point; in that year the agency moved to the Hiwassee Garrison at the mouth of the Hiwassee River in order to be nearer the Nation. Completely without personal ambition, Meigs displayed a deep sympathy for the Cherokees, whom he helped guide along the path toward

American values. He distributed farm implements and household utensils, arbitrated disputes, ordered intruders off Indian lands, negotiated treaties, and helped maintain law and order. He early gained the respect and loyalty of the Cherokees, who gave him the name "White Path."[9]

One of Meigs's first decisions concerned the appointment of a subagent to reside among the Cherokees to whom they could "apply for immediate advice & [who could] attend personally their councils." On the recommendation of a prominent Cherokee the colonel selected Major William Lewis Lovely for the post. This Irish-born subagent apparently possessed great ability in getting along with the natives, who appreciated his ready wit. Early in 1802 Major Lovely with his family moved by river to the area near the mouth of Lookout Creek and became the first official of the United States government to make his residence in Hamilton County. The spot selected for his home was a small Indian village with its few huts and blacksmith shop called Brownsville, located near the foot of Lookout Mountain, where the subagent lived until 1804. During Lovely's stay in the area Gasper Vaught, a German millwright living in East Tennessee, built a grist mill near the post to be used for the benefit of the Cherokees, for which Vaught received $300 in pay.[10]

In this period the federal government pressed for the opening of roads through the Cherokee Nation to connect the white settlements of eastern and middle Tennessee with coastal Georgia communities. Many of the Cherokees opposed this idea, believing that roads would only bring more whites among them. This resistance, however, gradually disappeared as a result of the efforts of Lovely and Meigs and the acceptance of the plan by the prominent mixed-blood trader, plantation owner, and political leader, Chief James Vann of Spring Place, Georgia.

In the treaty of 25 October 1805, the Cherokees formally agreed to the plan and two roads soon crossed the Nation. The states of Tennessee and Georgia provided funds, and the Cherokees organized a turnpike company to provide maintenance and establish a schedule of tolls and ferry charges.

From Augusta, Georgia, a road led around the southern shoulder of the Appalachian Mountains to Spring Place. Here the two Cherokee roads began. One, generally called the Federal Road, led northward to the Tellico Blockhouse and to Southwest Point where it connected with routes to Knoxville. The other took a northwestward course to

Stone's River where it connected with a road to Nashville. This way is usually called the Georgia Road.

The original Georgia Road ran from Spring Place across Lookout Mountain to Lookout Mountain Town (Trenton, Georgia) and on to Nickajack Town where it crossed the Tennessee River at the ferry operated by Turtle-at-Home. From the ferry it wound up the valley of Battle Creek, following the old trail on to the Cumberland Plateau. Shortly after its completion, an alternate route from Nickajack came around the end of Lookout Mountain and through the Rossville Gap to Spring Place.

This latter route across a portion of southern Hamilton County was the first vehicular road in the region. Along it passed large wagons drawn by four oxen loaded with flour, hides, whiskey, beeswax, and other country produce. Riders on horseback going at a "fox trot" could travel forty miles a day. Much more slowly moved the herds of horses, mules, cattle, and hogs from the Cumberland Valley or Kentucky on their way south. One who used the road reported five hundred to two thousand swine in a drove. And great flocks of turkeys also made their way to market in care of wranglers. Taverns, also called stands, with stables and fenced lots soon appeared at strategic spots to care for man and beast.[11]

On the stretch of the road across the future Hamilton County, mixed-blood businessmen took advantage of the economic opportunities offered by the road. About 1803 John Brown built a two-story log tavern where the road met the trail from the north which crossed the Tennessee River at the ferry also run by Brown. In addition to these activities, Brown had a reputation as the most skilled river pilot in the area, an able blacksmith, and canny horse trader.[12]

Daniel Ross, after having lived in different places in the Nation, moved to Chattanooga Creek about 1800 near the eastern base of Lookout Mountain on the important trail where the Georgia Road opened a few years later. His lands and home served as a center of social activity as well as a business hub and appeared on old maps, marked "Ross." Following his death, his heirs, Joseph and Jean Coody, carried on with the farm and ran the deerskin tannery and the mill. Later, at the time of Cherokee removal, the appraiser of Cherokee property described the home as "one of the best, well-framed houses, one and one-half stories high with good useful buildings such as negro cabins, stables, corn-cribs, etc., mill house, an excellent one indeed, the tan-yard of the best kind, etc." In addition he listed two large orchards.[13]

About the same time, John McDonald and his family moved back to Poplar Springs in the Missionary Ridge gap about three miles east of his son-in-law. John Ross, a favorite grandson, made his home with the McDonalds after John's mother's death in 1808. Soon he directed much of the business from a 4½-story log building and also added to the home which he inherited.

Meanwhile Ross expanded his interests. For a short time he joined forces with Timothy, son of agent Meigs, in the firm of Meigs & Ross, located at the Hiwassee Garrison. After Meigs's death in 1815, Ross associated himself with his brother Lewis and began operations at Ross's Landing on the Tennessee River. Shipping on the river was carried on in connection with the general store in the gap.

The landing, located near the foot of Market Street in present-day Chattanooga, offered great potential, but it was far from being a pretentious enterprise. A missionary in 1817 wrote that it was a "kind of shanty for goods and a log hut for the ferryman. All, all the region within the sight of Lookout's summit was then a wilderness, with here and there an Indian cabin and 'truck-patch.' "

On 1 April 1817, the United States government opened a post office at the McDonald store; they called it Rossville and employed John Ross as postmaster. Semiweekly service by stage between Nashville and Augusta brought the mail to this office in the heart of the Cherokee Nation. Legend has it that twelve horses teamed together to haul the stage with its passengers and baggage over the saddle of Lookout Mountain. A stage stand where relays of horses were stationed stood on the west side of the mountain and the next one at McDonald's store.[14]

The roads opened a new era for the Hamilton County area. Those who wished to sensationalize history could imagine the crimes of robbery and murder committed upon drovers returning with heavy money bags at the isolated taverns. To those with a legal turn of mind the question of who had sovereign power in the Indian country became paramount. Economically, the Cherokees living along the roads generally prospered. One official reported, "In the Cherokee agency, the wheel, the loom, and the plough is in pretty general use, farming, manufacturing, and stock raising the topic of conversation among the men and women."[15]

The gateway to the Deep South had been opened.

NOTES

1. The 1779 campaign is reconstructed from J. P. Brown, *Old Frontiers: The Story of the Cherokee Indians From Earliest Times to the Date of their Removal to the West* (Kingsport, Tenn.: Southern Publishers, 1938), pp. 171–174; Samuel Cole Williams, *Tennessee During the Revolutionary War* (Knoxville: University of Tennessee Press, 1974), pp. 91–99; and James W. Livingood, "The American Revolution in the Tennessee Valley," *Tennessee Valley Perspective* 6, no. 4 (Summer 1976), pp. 5–10.

2. *Three Pioneer Tennessee Documents* (Nashville: Tennessee Historical Commission, 1964), pp. 1–10, contains "John Donelson's Journal."

3. *American State Papers, Indian Affairs* (Washington, D.C.: Gales and Seaton, 1832), 1:264; Clarence Edwin Carter, ed., *The Territorial Papers of the United States*, vol. 4, *The Territory South of the River Ohio: 1790–1796* (Washington, D.C.: Government Printing Office, 1936), p. 227. The Chickamaugas later developed another town called Willstown near the present town of Fort Payne, Alabama.

4. Penelope Johnson Allen, "Leaves From the Family Tree," *Chattanooga Times,* 9 January and 2 February 1936.

5. Nicholas Perkins Hardeman, *Wilderness Calling: The Hardeman Family in the American Westward Movement, 1750–1900* (Knoxville: University of Tennessee Press, 1977), pp. 9–10.

6. Carter, *Territorial Papers*, 4:60–65.

7. *American State Papers, Indian Affairs*, 1:536–38.

8. Allen, "Leaves," 30 September 1934.

9. Ibid., 28 January 1934; Henry Malone, "Return Jonathan Meigs: Indian Agent Extraordinary," (East Tennessee Historical Society) *Publications* 28 (1956): pp. 3–22. Meigs was born 17 December 1740, and died on 28 January 1823. A son, Return Jonathan Meigs, Jr., Yale University graduate, served as chief justice of the Ohio Supreme Court, U.S. senator, and governor of Ohio, 1810–14. In 1814 he was appointed postmaster general, serving under Presidents Madison and Monroe until 1823. A grandson, Return Jonathan III, worked with his grandfather at the Cherokee Agency. He studied law and became one of Tennessee's most distinguished lawyers. Another son, Timothy, born in 1782, came with his parents to make his home in Tennessee, serving as secretary and clerk for his father.

10. Allen, "Leaves," 25 April 1937.

11. J. N. Goff, "Retracing the Old Federal Road," *Emory University Quarterly* 6:159–171; W. J. Cotter, *My Autobiography* (Nashville: Methodist Publishing House, 1917), pp. 73–74.

12. Allen, "Leaves," 8 December 1935.

13. Ibid., 9 February 1936.

14. Ibid., 2 February 1936; Gilbert E. Govan and James W. Livingood, *The*

Chattanooga Country, 3d ed. (Knoxville: University of Tennessee Press, 1977), pp. 76–78.

15. James Mooney, "Myths of the Cherokee," in U.S., Bureau of American Ethnology, *Nineteenth Annual Report* (Washington, D.C., Government Printing Office, 1900), pt. 1, p. 82.

5

The Cherokees

ON 8 July 1817, three United States commissioners—Andrew Jackson, General David Meriwether of Georgia, and Governor Joseph McMinn of Tennessee—concluded an important treaty with the Cherokee Nation. Their negotiations, conducted at the agency located on the north side of the Hiwassee River, clearly illustrated the twin problems existing between the national government and the local Indians.

By the terms of the treaty the Cherokees ceded to the United States two land tracts of considerable size, a certain area within Georgia and Alabama and the southern section of the Sequatchie Valley. Other timely provisions stated the conditions under which Cherokees who wished to do so could move west of the Mississippi River. The government agreed to furnish flatboats for the journey and to reimburse the emigrants for valuable improvements left behind. As a token of rare generosity the United States promised poor Indians who would go west a rifle, ammunition, a blanket, and a brass kettle or a beaver trap. Those who migrated would receive land in the Arkansas or White River valley.[1]

The Cherokees, in turn, agreed to transfer to the United States at a later date lands east of the Mississippi equal to the proportion of the population that went west. So if one-half of the Nation's people moved, those remaining would give up one-half of their remaining lands. In addition to this complicated formula, the treaty contained another provision destined to cause many heartaches. It held that Indians living on land ceded by the treaty (or land which should later be ceded) would have the right to become citizens of the United States and to receive a reservation of one square mile of land within the territory ceded.

Many of the Cherokees bitterly opposed this treaty. Over the years they had been subjected to tremendous pressure to sell their homeland, beginning as early as 1721. Now so much territory had been given up that a major population shift had resulted. The center of the Nation drifted southward toward the Hamilton County area; large numbers moved into northern Georgia and Alabama. The political center gravitated to the Coosa River area in Georgia.

United States officials had no direct responsibility for this development. But by this time many of them sponsored the idea of complete removal from the eastern part of the country. The proponents of this concept, which was possibly first suggested by President Jefferson in 1803, rationalized that the Indians would be better off if resettled beyond the Mississippi River where they could live "forever." The governors of Tennessee took readily to this scheme.

Some Cherokees responded agreeably. An early migration led by Chief Bowl went west in 1794. After the major land cessions of 1805 and 1806, others followed in order to escape association with the white man and his broken promises. Agent Meigs encouraged migration; as early as 1809 he dispatched an inspection party composed of young John Ross and others to examine the western country at government expense. The resulting voluntary migration became a large enough movement to justify ordering agent Major Lovely to move his post and establish himself among the Arkansas Cherokees by 1813.[2]

Most of the Indians, however, opposed migration and the new treaty of 1817. Their resentment resulted in the signing of a memorial by numerous chiefs which they submitted in protest even before the treaty was concluded. In summary, it read, "Let us, therefore, remain where we are, in the land of our fathers, without further cessions of territory." Nevertheless the treaty was concluded, although opposition continued, led by Chief Pathkiller.

Meigs, on the other hand, encouraged groups to enroll for the westward migration. Governor McMinn went into the Indian country, praising the western paradise, and labored to persuade Cherokees to move.[3] An outstanding leader who agreed to go west was Ooloosteeskee, better known as John Jolly. Jolly most likely came into the area and acquired holdings and wealth when Dragging Canoe brought his Chickamaugas southward. He took possession of the old Hiwassee Island with its prehistoric treasures which was soon called Jolly's Island. For three years young Sam Houston lived with Jolly as a foster son; he became a member of the tribe and received the name Colonah (the Raven). Shortly thereafter, Jolly and a band of Indian families numbering 331 left in February 1818 for western homes; he was described thus: "being half an Indian, and dressed as a white man, I should scarcely have distinguished him from an American, except by his language. He was very plain, prudent, and unassuming in his dress and manners; a Franklin amongst his countrymen and affectionately called the 'beloved' father."[4]

Despite such migrations the majority of the Cherokees bitterly resisted the policy of removal. Like Dragging Canoe they strove to remain in their homeland, pinning their hopes to a vain expectation of justice from the government. Agent Meigs used every possible persuasive argument to meet their protests, vowing that he could not protect them from the encroachment of the surrounding whites. Eventually a small delegation of Cherokees went to Washington, D.C., where a new treaty, the Calhoun Treaty, was concluded on 27 February 1819 with the secretary of war.

This arrangement contained the same plan for reservations for qualified Cherokees found in the 1817 treaty and was designed to gain the support of leading members of the Nation. Some direct bribery of the eastern Cherokees who signed the treaty also took place. By its terms the Indians actually ceded more land: some six thousand square miles or about one-fourth of the territory held by the Nation in the east. For this they received no compensation; they were told that this arrangement was made to cover the value of lands in the West previously received.

The Tennessee lands involved in this transfer, called the Hiwassee Purchase, included the present counties of Monroe and McMinn and that part of Meigs County north of the Hiwassee River. It also took in that section of Hamilton County which lies north of the Tennessee River and paved the way for the formal creation of the county about eight months later. Cherokee land holdings within Tennessee had been reduced to that relatively small corner of the southeastern part of the state south of the Tennessee and Hiwassee rivers.[5]

Plans immediately followed to mark off the 640-acre reservations for those qualifying as industrious, capable persons. In Hamilton County six sites along the north shore of the Tennessee River were surveyed. The Cherokees who lived there had taken up the good river and creek bottom lands and had made improvements in substantial log cabins, barns, and needed outbuildings. All the recipients were mixed-bloods: David Fields, John Brown, William Brown, Richard Timberlake, James Brown, and Fox Taylor.[6]

David Fields's reservation was marked in January 1820 on the north side of the Tennessee River opposite Williams Island, covering a portion of the site of the old Indian village of Tuskegee Island Town. (Some of the land is now part of Baylor School.) Fields did not use the property for long, for the next year he migrated to Arkansas. He appointed Judge James Brown of the Cherokee Court to receive the "rent due from William Lauderdale for the mill and farm, just above the suck, granted to the said Fields by the United States." In 1825 Fields conveyed his holding to Judge Brown, who soon sold it along with his other Hamilton County property to James Smith, one of the early settlers in this section.

John Brown's reservation, situated just below Moccasin Bend on the north shore, was also surveyed in January 1820. It comprised his ferry on the road from Old Washington and his dwelling located on the south shore near the ferry landing. Here he operated a tavern which bore his name until the Cherokee removal. Brown, however, sold his reservation in 1830 to Ephraim and William Hixson for $5,500.

William Brown's holdings, a mile to the west of the mouth of North Chickamauga Creek, remained his property only a short time, for he sold it in 1821 to John Cornett.

A fourth reservation located along North Chickamauga Creek some distance from the mouth of the stream belonged to Richard Timberlake. This mixed-blood was a descendant of Lieutenant Henry Timberlake, who had visited the Cherokee country in 1762 and published a volume describing the native customs. By 1821 Timberlake sold his interests to James Brown and moved across the river into the Cherokee Nation.

Judge James Brown, a member of the Cherokee Court, had his home along North Chickamauga Creek where the public road from Old Washington to Brown's Ferry crossed Little Chickamauga Creek. Brown lived here at Long Pond Place for some time before it became his reservation. It continued to be his home until, like other reservation claimants, unpleasantness and altercations with incoming whites forced him to move to the Cherokee side of the river.

On the north bank of the river opposite an island called Oo-le-quah by the Cherokees (Dallas Island) the surveyors marked off the reservation of Fox Taylor on 25 October 1819. The Taylor family, descendants of Nancy Ward, held influential positions in the Nation. Fox transferred his reservation to his brother Richard, who served as an interpreter and prospered as trader and tavern keeper. Richard Taylor later sold the site and also the early settlement of Dallas to Asabel Rawlings, one of the county's early pioneers.

The scheme of allocating reservations led to misunderstandings and disputes so intense that all land involved lying north of the Tennessee River was soon given up by Cherokee owners. Governor McMinn claimed many reservations had been secured through "fraudulent and speculative motives," while the Cherokee owners claimed unbearable harassment on the part of white neighbors. More perplexing complications grew from the fact that the reservations were on lands granted years before by the state of North Carolina to individuals who could now claim them for the first time since the area was opened to settlers.[7]

In addition to the six reservations north of the Tennessee River, some of the Nation's leaders had reservations surveyed for themselves in the Cherokee country south of the river in order to establish claims to certain areas in the case of additional land cessions. Among these Cherokees were Richard Taylor, Daniel Ross, John McDonald, John Wilson, William McDaniel, William Blythe, and Samuel Gandy.

At the time Tennessee organized Hamilton County the eastern Cherokees had developed a life-style and attained a cultural standard superior to all other eastern Indians. The use of spinning wheel and loom led to the development of new skills in addition to the ancient crafts of basket making and pottery. Most Cherokees lived in log houses, a few in elaborate plantation homes. The young dressed like whites although many wore turbans. Many, especially those of mixed-blood ancestry, made good livings as tavern keepers, ferrymen, traders, livestockmen, farmers or artisans. Native craftsmen—tanners, saddlers, millers, blacksmiths, wheelwrights, and silversmiths—supplemented white workers brought to the Nation by the government to teach the natives. Large herds of cattle, horses, hogs, sheep, and goats were raised and farmers produced staple crops of wheat, corn, cotton, and tobacco. A census taken in 1825 in the eastern Nation listed 13,563 native Cherokees, 147 white men married into the Nation, 73 white women married into the Nation, and 1,277 Negro slaves. One year later it was said that within the Nation there were 22,000 cattle, 7,600 horses, 46,000 swine, 2,500 sheep, 762 looms, 2,488 spinning wheels, 172 wagons, 2,943 plows, 10 saw mills, 31 grist mills, 62 blacksmith shops, 8 cotton machines, and 18 schools.[8]

During the Creek War of 1812–13 at least five hundred Cherokees served under the American flag as troops under General Jackson, especially distinguishing themselves at Horseshoe Bend. Some proudly retained such military titles as major, afterward using them as given names. During the campaign Camp Ross, located near the mouth of Chattanooga Creek, served as a rendezvous for troops and as a marshaling area for supplies, some of which were Cherokee supplies.

In the fall of 1820 a more subtle form of progress unfolded in the adoption of a republican form of government for the Nation. It divided the Nation into eight districts, each of which was entitled to send four representatives to the Cherokee national legislature, which consisted of a national committee and a national council. Franchise privileges were limited to Cherokee citizens. Each district had a judge, a marshall, and a council house for semiannual meetings. Companies of "light horse" assisted in the execution of the law. Laws concerned with the collection of taxes and debts, road repairs, licenses to white persons doing business in the Nation, support of schools, regulation of liquor traffic, conduct of slaves, and crimes of theft and horse stealing illustrate the comprehensive nature of their political arrangements. The right of blood revenge—capital punishment—was taken from the seven clans and placed with the central administration. And finally, no individual could sell land to the whites without the consent of the national council; such negotiations were deemed treasonous and punishable by death.[9]

Lands south of the Tennessee River between Lookout Valley and Ooltewah Creek comprised the first district, known as the Chickamauga District. The first Mondays of May and September served as court days. The courthouse for the Chickamauga District, located at Crawfish Springs, also was the voting place for the third precinct of the district, which included the area of present Chattanooga.

Assistance and encouragement in the acceptance of the white man's civilization came about this time from an unexpected source. In the fall of 1816 at a council meeting at Turkeytown, Andrew Jackson presented a representative of the American Board of Commissioners for Foreign Missions to the Cherokee leaders present. Thirty-year-old

Cyrus Kingsbury, the advance agent of the board and a graduate of Brown University and Andover Seminary, pleaded for their endorsement of a mission and school his people wished to establish. The council approved, being especially receptive to the idea of instruction in English and the industrial arts as well as to the fact that at least some Cherokees would be given the opportunity for an education without cost.

The Cherokees knew of earlier missionary efforts. Although stationed beyond the borders of Hamilton County, a small group of Moravians at Spring Place had exerted a favorable influence since 1801. So too had the program of Gideon Blackburn, who was operating a mission and school on the Hiwassee River in 1804. During his total of five years with the Cherokees he opened a branch school and mission at Sale Creek and assisted with a school at the home of Daniel Ross in the Chattanooga area.

Kingsbury's proposed plan had certain great advantages over the modest earlier efforts. The interdenominational American Board (Congregationalist, Dutch Reformed, and Presbyterian in membership) had a proven, well-working organization. Moreover, on his way south from New England Kingsbury had stopped at Washington, D.C., and won the help of national authorities. President Madison not only gave his moral support but promised to provide a school building, a house for a teacher, tools for the farm, and equipment for a girls' school.

When the Cherokee councilmen approved Kingsbury's proposal, they appointed the Glass to go with the New England divine to select a site for the mission. They soon found what turned out to be an ideal spot: the cleared lands of John McDonald on South Chickamauga Creek directly across the stream from Dragging Canoe's old village of Chickamauga (the shopping area of present-day Brainerd Village and Eastgate). For $500 the mission acquired all buildings and improvements together with about twenty-five acres of cleared land.[10]

With the arrival of the first missionaries the school opened early in 1817 under the name Chickamauga Mission. It soon, however, became obvious that Chickamauga was an overworked word, and in May of the next year the board substituted the name Brainerd, honoring David Brainerd, an early New England missionary to the northeastern Indians. Engaged to the daughter of Jonathan Edwards, Brainerd had studied at Yale but was expelled for minor rule violations. Although he died in 1747 at the age of twenty-nine, he had achieved a fine reputation as a Presbyterian minister and writer.

Elias Cornelius, a Yale graduate and Congregationalist minister associated with the American Board, visited the mission and described its facilities in graphic detail:

The place where the institution stands is two miles north of the line that divides the State of Georgia from the State of Tennessee, on the southwest side of a small river, called Chick-a-mau-gah creek. On approaching it from the northeast, you come to the creek at the distance of fifty rods from the principal mission house. Immediately, you leave the woods, and crossing the stream, which is from four to six rods wide, you enter an area of cleared ground, on the right of which appear numerous buildings of various kinds and sizes. At the distance of a few steps stand a grist mill and a saw mill, turned by a canal three quarters of a mile in length, which conducts the water from a branch of the creek in the neighborhood. A little farther on, you come to a lane, on either side of which are several houses occupied by laborers and mechanics of various description. Following the lane, which runs across the cleared ground, you pass a large and commodious barn, with some other buildings, and are conducted directly in front of a row of houses, which forms the principal part of the settlement and makes a prominent appearance in the view of Brainerd.

Nearly in the center of the row is the mission house, two stories high, having a piazza its whole length, with a pleasant court yard in front of it. It is occupied by the superintendent and other missionaries. Behind it, and immediately connected with it, is the dining hall and kitchen for the establishment. On your right, and at the distance of a few feet, stands another building of two stories, which is used for the instruction of the girls. It is well finished, and was built by the particular direction of President James Monroe. . . . Many smaller buildings are ranged upon the right and left of these two, and afford convenient lodging places for the children, and other persons connected with the institution.

Passing onward, about thirty rods, to the end of the lane which has been mentioned, you come to the school house for the boys; which stands in the edge of the woods, and is large enough to accommodate one hundred scholars. On the Sabbath it is used also as a place of worship. The whole number of buildings belonging to the institution exceeds thirty. They are, most of them, however, constructed of logs, and make but a plain appearance.

The ground, on the south and east side of the lane (the direction of the lane is northeast and southwest), is divided into a garden, an orchard, and several other lots, which are neatly fenced in, and present a pleasant prospect in front of the mission house. In a corner of the orchard, next the schoolhouse, is the graveyard, where lie the bodies of those who have died at the institution . . .

The whole circumference of the ground which has been described may not, perhaps, include fifty acres, but being in the midst of a wilderness, whose deep forests appear on every side, it presents to the beholder a scene of cultivation and of active and cheerful life, which cannot but inspire him with pleasure.[11]

The spiritual leaders, teachers, and artisans who labored at Brainerd, some of whom were seminarians from Andover and Princeton, came mainly from New England and Pennsylvania. Prominent among them, in addition to Cyrus Kingsbury, were Samuel Worcester and his nephew Samuel Austin Worcester. Samuel Worcester, a 1795 graduate of Dartmouth who was largely responsible for the development of the missionary effort among the Cherokees, died at Brainerd on 7 June 1821.[12] Samuel Austin Worcester, an alumnus of the University of Vermont, to which institution he had walked more than seventy miles to register, arrived at Brainerd in the fall of 1825. The Cherokees gave him the name A-tse-nu-sti, a "messenger"; his service to the Indians terminated only with his death in 1859.[13]

The missionaries took great care to enter into their *Journal* the visits of Cherokee leaders, the Boot, Pathkiller, and Charles Hicks (one-time treasurer of the Nation). Also recorded was the marriage of the son of one of the superintendents, Milo Hoyt, to the daughter of Cherokee Major George Lowry, an active supporter of the mission.

The most distinguished guests at Brainerd were Governor McMinn and President James Monroe. Monroe and his party stopped by un-announced on 27 May 1819—the first presidential visit to the Hamilton County area. According to the mission journal, he was pleased with the progress of the Brainerd program. However, the president let his hosts know that a new building being constructed for girls was not good enough and recommended a more elaborate replacement, which the federal government would finance. Other later visitors noted that from eighty to more than one hundred students lived at the Brainerd Mission, some of whom went on for additional training at the American Board's school in Connecticut.

The pious missionaries faced perplexing problems at times, especially regarding the admission of certain students. One day a young twenty-one-year-old hunter, having walked all the way from North Carolina from the "most uncivilized part of the tribe," suddenly appeared at the mission garbed in very rough, untidy clothing. Although his rude appearance was discouraging, the missionary leaders reluctantly accepted John Arch as a student. He learned to read and write, became the chief interpreter at Brainerd, and for some seven years assisted the teachers before his untimely death in 1825. And to them also came for instruction the mixed-blood Catherine Brown, such a beautiful young squaw that the missionaries at first feared that her presence would disturb the whole school. She too proved their judgment sound in admitting her; she made such progress in English and in the understanding of Christianity that four years later she won an assignment to teach at one of the mission substations.

On Sundays whites, Indians, and blacks worshipped together at the nonsectarian church services at Brainerd. Many walked a score or more miles over rough country to be present. But the central mission could not meet all of the earnest demands of the Indians, so during the course of its history the Brainerd Mission developed ten additional mission stations scattered throughout the tristate area. For varying periods they functioned at Carmel, Creek Path, Hightower, Willstown, Haweis, Candy's Creek, New Echota, Amohee, Red Clay, and Running Water.

The favorable results at Brainerd undoubtedly influenced programs sponsored by other denominations. The Methodists especially became active with some of their efforts centered in the Hamilton County area. In the early 1820s Joseph Coody, who lived on a farm on Chattanooga Creek near the Daniel Ross place, encouraged the establishment of a school and mission at his home. Eventually this became the nucleus of the Upper Cherokee Mission to which the Reverend Nicholas Scales was assigned. By 1825 this station boasted a membership of eighty-one Indians and twenty Negroes. Indians served as "exhorters," interpreters, and licensed ministers.

Scales, according to tribal tradition, became a member of the Nation when he married Polly Coody, daughter of Joseph and Jane Ross Coody. Scales bought the Ross home in Rossville from his wife's uncle, Chief John Ross, and kept a store there as well as serving as the Rossville postmaster. Ross himself joined the Methodist Church although his wife and children were associated with the Moravians.[14]

The presence of educated men at Brainerd had an impact on the Nation far beyond the cultivated acres of the mission. When Samuel Austin Worcester, for instance, became aware of the discovery of the mixed-blood Sequoyah, he gave every encouragement possible to the perceptive Indian so amply endowed with curiosity, inventiveness, and determination.

Sequoyah grew up in the valley of East Tennessee. Born about 1760 and called George Gist by the whites, he earned fame for his talent as silversmith and artist. In trying to fathom the secret of the white man's superiority to the natives, he concluded that it rested on their ability to communicate with written messages. Sequoyah thereupon dedicated himself to the development of a Cherokee syllabary.

Ridicule and discouragement failed to divert him from years of frustrating effort. Eventually, without knowledge of spoken or written English, this mixed-blood scholar created eighty-six characters to represent sounds which could be combined into words. Like many of his fellow tribesmen, Sequoyah had moved west, but in 1821 he returned to his eastern homeland to submit his work to the Nation. The simplicity and adaptability of his syllabary made it possible for both the educated and the completely unschooled Cherokees to learn to read and write within a remarkably short time. In their cabins and along the open trails the Cherokees trained themselves with surprising success.

Through the influence of Dr. Worcester, Cherokee-language type was cast in Boston and a printing press acquired. The American Board underwrote the cost of this equipment for which the Cherokee Nation later fully reimbursed it.

The Cherokees, recognizing Sequoyah's extraordinary literary contribution, awarded him an annual pension of $300 for life and had a medal struck in his honor. In the presentation ceremony Chief John Ross commented, "The great good designed by the author of human existence in directing your genius to this happy discovery cannot be fully estimated—it is incalculable." The United States gave Sequoyah $500 in recognition of his achivement. Later his name was appropriately given to the great redwood trees of the Pacific coast (spelled Sequoia) and to the Sequoia National Park in California. The state of Oklahoma also paid tribute; it selected Sequoyah along with Will Rogers as its two representatives in Statuary Hall in Washington, D.C.[15]

With the encouragement of the staff at Brainerd, biblical translations, hymnals, religious tracts, as well as texts and the laws of the Cherokee Nation found their way into print. The Indians soon decided to publish a national bilingual newspaper. With Elias Boudinot, a Brainerd-trained mixed-blood who had gone on to the Indian school in Connecticut as editor, the *Cherokee Phoenix*'s first issue came off the press at New Echota, Georgia, on 21 February 1828. In October of the same year, John Ross took the oath of office as the first principal chief of the Cherokee Nation under a newly adopted written constitution.

These developments underscored the rapid progress the Cherokees experienced since the days of the Chickamaugas' failure to safeguard their lands by the use of the tomahawk. James Mooney emphasized their gains when he wrote, "With a constitution and national press, a well-developed system of industries and home education, and a government administered by educated Christian men, the Cherokee were now justly entitled to be considered a civilized people."[16]

But each new development only added to the crescendo of white opposition. The main body of the tribe and most of their lands at this time were within the borders of Georgia. Officials of that state for years had pressed the national authorities to remove the Indians, whom they considered as mere tenants. Georgia's growing population required the land. Moreover, some forward-looking officials seeking transportation routes to the Middle West decided that Georgia's economic future called for a road or canal to the Tennessee River which had to go through Cherokee country.

When the Cherokee written constitution went into effect, Georgia's insistence on removal intensified. The constitution highlighted a complex question of sovereign power by institutionalizing the independence of the Cherokee Nation. Which had supreme authority, the United States, the states of Georgia and Tennessee, or the Cherokee Nation? What law was valid? What authority binding? Anti-Cherokee politicians in Georgia insisted that the federal government remove the Indians; they now claimed that the United States violated the federal constitution by permitting a separate nation to be established within the boundaries of a state.

A totally unrelated event added to the storm. Cherokee youngsters had discovered "shiny pebbles"—gold nuggets. The word got abroad. Prospectors by 1828 discovered the gold fields near Dahlonega, Georgia, and several thousand whites descended on the area, none of whom had any respect for Cherokee customs or rights.

In November 1828 the removal advocates in Georgia gained new support: Andrew Jackson won the presidential election. Georgians knew Jackson could be counted on for cooperation since he showed no evidence of being a friend of the Cherokees. In fact, it was well known that the new chief executive maintained that whites and Indians could not live side by side.

The relentless pressure of about half a million Georgians against some seventeen thousand Cherokees now turned from argument to action. Georgia could engineer the removal; without waiting for the federal government to act, the state would replace Cherokee laws with Georgia laws. On 20 December 1828, the state enacted legislation annexing all Cherokee lands within its chartered limits. It also declared all Cherokee law null and void.

This new legislation went into effect 1 June 1830, along with supplementary acts. The Cherokees could no longer testify in court against whites; therefore Georgia had effectively denied the Indians the use of all courts. Contracts between Cherokees and whites were declared illegal, thereby canceling practically all debts owed the Indians. Indian assemblies for any public purpose were forbidden. Surveyors went into the Cherokee country, dividing it into 160-acre plots and "gold lots" of 40 acres. The lands became prizes in a Georgia-wide lottery to which all citizens got tickets.

As the lottery winners arrived to take over their new possessions, Georgia Indians fled into the southeastern corner of Tennessee, including Hamilton County. John Ross lost his new home at the "head of Coosa." He moved to Flint Springs near Red Clay in southern Bradley County to carry on the Cherokee opposition. The capital of the Nation moved in 1832 from New Echota to the Red Clay Council Grounds, where a rectangular council house, open on all sides, sheltered the discussions of tribal leaders who strongly denounced the tragic and crudely opportunistic acts being committed against them.

The old Ross home at Rossville owned at the time by the Scales family became the property of one James Jones, and the Scales found themselves without a home. The Reverend Mr. Scales died in the midst of making preparations for his family's departure. His wife, of the Coody clan, died shortly after while enroute west by boat with her four small children. Meanwhile Thomas Gordon and Xanders Gordon McFarland, working surveyors in the Georgia section of the Cherokee country, bought the Ross property from the lucky lottery winner and moved to Rossville.[17]

Richard Taylor, member of the Cherokee council, also lost his home and lands where he ran a profitable tavern near present-day Ringgold. He fortunately had property on the south side of the Tennessee River in the upper part of Hamilton County, where he relocated.[18]

Another mixed-blood Cherokee who became a victim of the lottery was Joseph Vann. "Rich Joe" Vann had inherited Diamond Hill from his father, James Vann. On this extensive plantation located near Spring Place, Vann had some eight hundred acres under cultivation. A fine three-story brick house stood amid surrounding kitchens, slave quarters, barns, as well as a grist mill, saw mill, blacksmith shop, trading post, and other buildings. An extensive apple and peach orchard covered the adjacent hills.

Two men claimed to have won the Vann estate in the lottery. They arrived at the same time, both heavily armed. A fight ensued. Vann and his family were spectators of the fracas in their own home. Eventually they were driven out to seek shelter beyond the state line in Tennessee. The Vanns, more fortunate than others, had a second plantation close to the mouth of Ooltewah Creek near Harrison where they lived for the next few years. In 1835 Joe Vann reported ownership of 110 slaves and thirty-five houses on his land as well as a mill, three race courses, and a ferry boat.[19]

Following the passage of Georgia's first repressive measures, the Cherokees appealed to President Jackson for relief but received none. Instead, new efforts were made to force the Indians to agree to removal; the Cherokees, with roots deep in their native soil, refused. In January 1831 Ross brought suit against Georgia in the United States Supreme Court. The Cherokees retained distinguished counsel to represent them; the state of Georgia contemptuously refused to send any defense. Although sympathetic to the Cherokees' problem, the court dismissed the suit, denying the Cherokees the right to bring suit against the state.

The next year another suit challenged Georgia. Missionaries of the Brainerd organization had been faithful and constant supporters of the Cherokees. In turn, Georgians distrusted and hated them. To eliminate the missionaries' influence, Georgia passed a law making it illegal for a white person to live in the Cherokee region without a license from the governor, which required an oath of allegiance to the state. The missionaries refused to comply. Georgia dispatched militiamen to arrest them. Harassed by threats and verbal abuse, the missionaries were chained together, tied to the back of a wagon, and forced to walk some twenty-two miles to jail.

Following their trial, the missionaries each received sentences of four years at hard labor. Some then took the oath of allegiance, but Drs. Worcester and Elizur Butler refused to compromise their beliefs and began serving their terms. The case then went to the United States Supreme Court *(Worcester* v. *the State of Georgia)*. Chief Justice John Marshall's court ruled certain Georgia laws unconstitutional in a decision that appeared to be a reversal of the first case's decision. The Cherokees rejoiced; they had triumphed by a peaceful means. President Jackson, however, refused to enforce the court's ruling and Georgia would not comply with the court's decision. The federal courts, not having fully consolidated their power within the national government by this time, were helpless to enforce their decision.

As the legal controversy lengthened over the years, conditions in the Cherokee country steadily worsened. Georgians seized the plant of the *Cherokee Phoenix*, suspending publication of the newspaper. Since the Cherokees could not testify in court against white men, they had no recourse. Suits for back rent against their own land went against them. General lawlessness prevailed. Armed bands roamed the land, ejecting occupants or assaulting those who dared to resist. Night beatings and other atrocities were commonplace. At one point, a Georgia guard actually crossed the state line into Tennessee, arresting John Ross and his house guest John Howard Payne, the nationally known composer and journalist. They carried the two men into Georgia, confining them in an outhouse at the former home of Chief Joseph Vann. After two weeks the Georgia guard released them without charges or an explanation.

The Cherokee Agency's role had changed tremendously since the days of Return Jonathan Meigs. Benevolent guidance and trustworthy assistance gave way to schemes designed to coerce the Cherokees into accepting migration. By 1834 the agency was totally inactive.[20]

Georgia urged Alabama and Tennessee, as well, to extend their authority over Cherokee lands. Tennessee could find no common agreement on such policy until 1833. Then, at the bidding of the governor, the legislature extended the jurisdiction of the state over the Cherokee lands located in its southeastern corner. Counties in this section, located north of the Tennessee River, got instructions to extend their borders southward to the state line. So, in this way, Hamilton County grew to its approximate modern proportions. However, neither the state nor the county were ever authorized to replace the sovereign rights of the Cherokee Nation with their own.

Tennessee's cautious approach to the issue had no influence on the national government. President Jackson continued to be adamant about removal. He felt the time had come to take advantage of the weariness of the Cherokees, brought on by years of chaos and deception. An agent, the Reverend J. F. Schermerhorn, was appointed to get a removal treaty signed by those who would agree to move to the West.

Word went out of a treaty meeting scheduled for New Echota in December 1835. The notice stated that all who did not attend gave assent to any agreement that might be made simply by their absence. Interestingly, the meeting was held in the old Cherokee capital deep within Georgia, where by Georgia's pronouncements it would be illegal for Cherokees to gather. Reports indicate that between three and five hundred Indians—men, women, and children—went to the talks, which resulted in the treaty of New Echota or the Removal Treaty. Only twenty Cherokees signed, none of whom were officers of the Cherokee government. The small faction willing to approve removal included only two prominent men: Major Ridge and Elias Boudinot. This minority had apparently concluded that any further resistance would be fatal to the tribe and disastrous to its individual members.

By the terms of this treaty and its supplementary sections, the Cherokees would cede all of their lands east of the Mississippi River to the United States for $5 million. In addition, the Cherokees would receive 7 million acres in the West with the privilege of purchasing additional lands. The agreement provided for the appraisal of improvements made on Cherokee lands ceded, but debts of the Indians would be paid from these reimbursements. The government would pay the cost of removal and provide subsistence for a year. Missionary organizations were to receive compensation for their establishments. Two years would be allowed for the removal of all the Cherokees.

The Cherokee government took no notice of the treaty talks. Officials circulated a petition to the effect that the New Echota treaty did not represent the will of the government or of the people. They reaffirmed their position that they did not want to cede any land at any price. Of the estimated seventeen thousand Cherokees living in the east, 15,964 signed the petition. It was clear that the treaty was a sham.

Although national attention resulting from the Supreme Court cases and the John Howard Payne incident had focused on the Cherokee question, the Senate ratified the treaty. However, humanitarians everywhere, along with the political opponents of Jackson, intensified the debates and held the ratifying majority to a single vote. The president now ceased to recognize the existence of any Cherokee government.

Throughout the Cherokee country, councils expressed their determined opposition. The treaty continued to be held null and void, and resolutions condemned the cunning and deceitful methods of the federal agents. To prevent disorder, government troops arrived in the area under General John E. Wool, supported by East Tennessee volunteers under the command of Brigadier General R. G. Dunlap. These officers soon found their duty most disagreeable. Dunlap withdrew in disgust, writing, "I gave the Cherokees all the protection in my power (the whites needed none). My course has excited the hatred of a few of the lawless rabble in Georgia who have long played the part of unfeeling petty tyrants."[21]

General Wool, relieved from duty at his request and replaced by

Colonel William Lindsay, found conditions "heart-rending." He wrote, "I would remove every Indian tomorrow beyond the reach of the white men, who, like vultures, are watching, ready to pounce upon their prey and strip them of everything they have or expect to have from the Government of the United States."[22]

The Cherokee Agency, Gunter's Landing in Alabama, and Ross's Landing became the preremoval concentration centers. One soldier in an early contingent later remembered Ross's Landing as consisting of twenty-five to thirty houses at the time. These were pole houses constructed of logs some six to ten inches in diameter. Typical frontier huts, they were one-room places about twelve by fifteen feet in size. A British-born traveler found the place "hastily built without any regard for any order or streets."[23]

Some of the first troops rendezvoused on Lookout Creek, but a more imposing camp was located on Citico Creek about two miles from the landing (near present-day Riverside High School). Later a large camp grew up about Indian Springs at the foot of Missionary Ridge (fairly close to the Brainerd Tunnel). At Citico, a fort designed to house about one hundred troops sprang up in the woods. A stockade made of split trees, sharpened and placed in the ground picket-fashion, surrounded the area. Numerous portholes in the stockade provided defensive gun positions. Inside the enclosure log cabins provided living quarters for the men while the space between the cabins and the pickets became stable areas.[24]

These typical frontier accommodations contrasted sharply with the crude lodgings thrown up for the Indians. In temporary gathering places, the Cherokees had to sleep without shelter; at the concentration centers tents or crude sheds were provided, but without thought of sanitary facilities. No privacy of any kind was available.

At Ross's Landing the soldiers and Indians soon attracted a swarm of people of mercenary motives and questionable ethics. Some people from Hamilton County moved to the southern shore of the river to establish their occupancy rights. John P. Long opened a general store, and on 22 March 1837, could call himself postmaster of Ross's Landing. Some crude cabins, through the crevices of which one could view the surrounding mountains in daylight hours, bore the dubious label, "hotel." The people who were later to become permanent residents served a transient crowd attracted by the activities of a military base: contractors who would haul goods and people, provisioners of food-stuffs, swindlers, and those who would buy Cherokee livestock, poultry, household goods, or anything the displaced families could not remove. These were the people of whom General Wool wrote.

On 3 March 1837, eleven flatboats crowded with emigrants pulled away from Ross's Landing. They numbered 466 including Major Ridge and volunteers who had come to support the treaty arrangements. In twenty-four days they reached their Arkansas destination. Although the government preferred to send the Indians west by water because it was cheaper, another band crossed the Tennessee River on the old ferry at Ross's Landing for an overland trek.[25]

But Chief Ross's policy of passive resistance had been very successful. By the expiration date of the removal treaty only about two thousand Cherokees had migrated. The government, realizing removal could not be accomplished without force, sent General Winfield Scott to the area with orders to start all the Indians west at the earliest possible time. His force of regulars, militiamen, and volunteers numbered about seven thousand. There were more soldiers than Cherokee males, who had previously been disarmed by General Wool.

On 17 May 1838, General Scott announced his plans by proclamation circulated on a handbill. There could be no further delays: "The full moon of May is already on the wane, and before another shall have passed away, every Cherokee man, woman, and child must be in motion to join their brethren in the far west." He urged them to gather instantly at one of the concentration sites where food, clothing, and provisions would be available "and thence at your ease, in comfort, be transported to your new homes according to the terms of the treaty." The Cherokees made no move to comply; General Scott instructed his men on details for a forcible roundup. While Scott's intentions were humane, the very nature of the situation precluded a merciful resolution of the problem.

With bayonet and rifle, Scott proceeded with his task. His men and hired contractors took Cherokees from their fields and from the byways; they seized them in their homes and from their midday meals. From gathering points in Georgia the Indians walked to the camp at Ross's Landing. Cattle, poultry, and pets had to be left to care for themselves, and personal possessions became the booty of the followers of every authorized move. Even the graves were robbed of buried heirlooms. By early June the army had swept the Cherokee country clean except for a few who escaped into the deep mountains. Some seventeen thousand Cherokees crowded into the three embarkation centers. Sadness, fear, misery, and utter despair overwhelmed them.

After a short stay at the concentration camp, a party left Ross's Landing on 6 June by a small steamboat and six flatboats. Because of the confusion on loading these crude craft and because many Indians refused to register their names, the exact number who embarked was not recorded. It is estimated that eight hundred weary persons left the landing; overcrowding, sultry weather, and laborious portages took a heavy toll before Arkansas was reached. A week later Ross's Landing saw another group of 875 depart aboard six flatboats. Apparently due to a lack of boats, a third contingent left this center in wagons and on foot for an overland journey.

Suffering became so acute and the mortality rate so high in the traveling parties that Chief Ross proposed that migration be suspended until fall, when the Cherokees would assume responsibility for their own removal. General Scott agreed; Andrew Jackson, although his term of office had ended, fumed furiously at the thought of delay. The overland party of 1,070 Cherokees had departed from Ross's Landing just three days before the postponement. Runners carried the news to them, but the agent in charge refused to turn back. Consequently some 300 Cherokees broke away from the wagon train and took to the woods. One runaway, it was reported, remarked, "All white men are liars and bad men. We will go home and shoot for John Ross."[26]

Apparently Ross's Landing quieted down during the summer months, for most of the Cherokees who had gathered here had departed. Nature's elements at once began their ruinous work on forts, camps, warehouses, and temporary facilities at the landing; nothing, however, could erase the shame of the American nation. At the Brainerd Mission, most of the staff members prepared to journey to the West with the Indians. On 19 August 1838, they held their last Communion there. Ainsworth Blunt remained behind because of poor health, charged with purchasing the cemetery as soon as the property went on the market to keep that plot from falling into unknown hands.

That fall the remaining thirteen thousand Cherokees assembled at Rattlesnake Springs (near Charleston, Tennessee) for the forced journey called the "Trail of Tears." They departed in thirteen detachments, each under the leadership and stoic discipline of responsible members of the Nation. They made their way over Walden Ridge and into the Sequatchie Valley near Pikeville, north of Hamilton County. The Ross and Vann families then departed by steamboat on a strenuous trip which cost Mrs. Ross, née Quatie Brown, her life before the journey's end. Only a few Cherokees remained in the east in the remote mountains.

Before marching orders sounded for the first detachment, the Indians met in council for the last time in their native land and resolved that as a lasting legacy to their descendants,[27]

> The title of the Cherokee people to their lands is the most ancient, pure, and absolute known to man; its date is beyond the reach of human record; its validity confirmed by possession and enjoyment antecedent to all pretense of claim by any portion of the human race.
>
> The free consent of the Cherokee people is indispensable to a valid transfer of the Cherokee title. The Cherokee people have neither by themselves nor their representatives given such consent. It follows that the original title and ownership of said lands still rests in the Cherokee Nation, unimpaired and absolute. The Cherokee people have existed as a distinct national community for a period extending into antiquity beyond the dates and records and memory of man. These attributes have never been relinquished by the Cherokee people, and cannot be dissolved by the expulsion of the Nation from its own territory by the power of the United States Government.

In the West the blood-revenge code of earlier days emerged; assassins immediately sought out and killed Major Ridge and Elias Boudinot.

NOTES

1. C. C. Royce, *The Cherokee Nation of Indians* (Chicago: Aldine, 1975), reprint of U.S., Bureau of American Ethnology, *Fifth Annual Report* (Washington, D.C.: Government Printing Office, 1887), pp. 84–91; J. P. Brown, *Old Frontiers: The Story of the Cherokee Indians from Earliest Times to the Date of their Removal to the West* (Kingsport, Tenn.: Southern Publishers, 1938), pp. 472–474; James Mooney, "Myths of the Cherokee," U.S., Bureau of American Ethnology, *Nineteenth Annual Report,* (Washington, D.C.: Government Printing Office, 1900), pp. 99–106.

2. Penelope Johnson Allen, "Leaves From the Family Tree," *Chattanooga Times,* 25 April 1937.

3. Robert H. White, ed., *Messages of the Governors of Tennessee* (Nashville: Tennessee Historical Commission, 1952), 1:490–497.

4. M. N. Lewis and Madeline Kneberg, *Hiwassee Island: An Archaeological Account of Four Tennessee Indian Peoples* (Knoxville: University of Tennessee Press, 1946), pp. 18–19, quotes Thomas Nuttall, *A Journal of Travels into the Arkansas Territory during the Year 1819;* see Reuben G. Thwaites, ed., *Early Western Travels,* vol. 13.

5. Royce, *Cherokee Nation*, pp. 91–93.

6. Allen, "Leaves," 8 December 1935, and 1 March 1936.

7. White, ed., *Messages*, 1:575–577.

8. Mooney, "Myths," p. 112; Robert Sparks Walker, *Torchlights to the Cherokees: The Brainerd Mission* (New York: Macmillan, 1931), p. 244.

9. Mooney, "Myths," pp. 106–107.

10. Walker, *Torchlights*, pp. 23–24.

11. Ibid., pp. 105–108, 249. On the night of 12 March 1830 the Brainerd Mission experienced a serious fire: about seventy persons had occupied the destroyed building and the school had to be closed. It was not until January 1832 that the mission could again receive scholars. Today only the cemetery marks the location of the mission.

12. Ibid., p. 57. Dr. Worcester was buried at Brainerd. In 1844 his remains were removed for burial at Salem, Massachusetts.

13. Some of the other missionaries were Ard Hoyt, Daniel Sabin Butrick, Dr. Elizur Butler, John Vail, Ainsworth Blunt, John Thompson, and Stephen Foreman.

14. The Baptists also were active but apparently had no facilities in Hamilton County. Henry T. Malone, "The Early Nineteenth Century Missionaries in the Cherokee Country," *Tennessee Historical Quarterly* 10 (June 1951): 127–139; Allen, "Leaves," 9 February 1936.

15. James W. Livingood, "Sequoyah," *The Sequoyah Review* 1 (Fall 1975): 4–5.

16. Mooney, "Myths," p. 113.

17. Allen, "Leaves," 2 February 1936. The McFarlands ran a mercantile business and the post office along with a farm until 1841 when the partnership was dissolved. X. G. McFarland moved to McFarland Gap where he lived until his death in 1887. Thomas G. McFarland lived at Rossville until 1887 and at his death the property passed to his youngest son John McNair McFarland. The house in 1962 was carefully dismantled and then restored about 150 yards from its original site.

18. Ibid., 1 March 1936.

19. Ibid., 26 July 1936.

20. After Return Jonathan Meigs's death in 1823, former Governor McMinn served as agent until his death in November 1824. He was followed by Hugh Montgomery, who held the post until it was abolished on 30 June 1834. The end of the agency, for all practical purposes, came with the appointment of Benjamin Currey to superintend the Cherokee removal.

21. Brown, *Old Frontiers*, p. 500; Royce, *Cherokee Nation*, p. 286.

22. Brown, *Old Frontiers*, p. 501; Royce, *Cherokee Nation*, p. 286.

23. Harry M. Wiltse, "History of Chattanooga", 2 vols., (Typescript, Chattanooga-Hamilton County Bicentennial Library), 1:29, 34; G. W. Feather-

stonehaugh, *A Canoe Voyage up the Minnay Sotor* (London: Richard Bentley, 1847), 2:210–220.

24. Wiltse, "Chattanooga," 1:31.
25. Brown, *Old Frontiers*, p. 504.
26. Ibid., p. 511.
27. Ibid., p. 513; Mooney, "Myths," pp. 131–132.

6

The County's Early Settlers

I N the years 1819–1838 the Tennessee River divided Hamilton County into two territories: lands open to American settlement and the Cherokee country. South of the river the history of this era, although burdened with tragedy and excitement, is enriched by the knowledge of the Cherokees' remarkable progress in building a civilization and their determined stand to retain their homeland. North of the Tennessee River these two decades produced a more prosaic story in which hewing, hauling, and plowing dominated the lives of the settlers. But beneath the daily tasks ran a thread common to virtually all America: the dramatic saga of the frontier where newcomers struggled to create a homeland and developed a social order by their own independent efforts.

The beginnings of Hamilton County hark back to the Cherokee treaty of 25 October 1805, when the United States acquired a considerable block of land. The southern boundary of this extensive acreage, lying between East Tennessee and the Cumberland Valley, ran from the mouth of the Hiwassee River westward to the headwaters of the Duck. When surveyed, this line became the Indian border south of which all white entries were illegal. To the north of the line, the Tennessee legislature detached land from Roane County and created Rhea County in November 1807 in the Tennessee Valley and Bledsoe County in the Sequatchie Valley area.

Under the same treaty by which this land was acquired, the United States obtained a reservation opposite the mouth of the Hiwassee River to which the garrison and Indian agency from Southwest Point moved in July 1807. This new complex, called the Hiwassee Garrison, housed the troops assigned to duty on the Cherokee frontier. Colonel Return Jonathan Meigs had charge of this outpost. Here the agency remained until 1817 when it moved a short distance to Agency Creek, in the present county of Meigs. From these headquarters one of Meigs's duties required him to prohibit whites from pushing across the Indian border line into the Cherokee country.

Rhea County—named for John Rhea of Sullivan County whose career included participation in the Revolutionary War, membership in the state constitutional convention, and in the Tennessee lower house and United States Congress—immediately took a salient position in the future history of Hamilton County. On 12 February 1812, a committee charged with the selection of a site for the county court decided on a spot at the head of Spring Creek, where the town of Washington developed. Here a courthouse was erected and Washington became the most important community in this part of Tennessee.

By 1833 Washington boasted a population of about four hundred residents but its significance far exceeded that of the average small village. It listed among its assets two lawyers, two doctors, one clergyman, two churches, one academy, one school, five stores, two taverns, and two cotton gins.[1] The county it served in 1830 counted 8,186 citizens.

These first settlers not only cleared land and built new homes but also immediately gained experience in organizing county government, in developing small schools, in starting church congregations, and in opening roads. Although all these activities were most modest in nature, a certain skill for organizing resulted which later spread across the county boundary when Hamilton County opened in 1819. Rhea County has been called the mother county of lower East Tennessee, with Washington the source of this accumulated experience.

Rhea County had another bearing on the development of early Hamilton County. The Indian line marking the southern boundary of Rhea County took in Sale Creek valley within the county, an area transferred in 1819 to Hamilton County. Here, pioneers settled as citizens of Rhea County, some becoming local officials. In 1819 all these folks, with the

marking of the new county boundary, became the first residents of
Hamilton County.

Numerous families, migrating from Knox County, settled in this
section. As early as 1807 Robert Patterson chose Sale Creek for his
home. Others soon followed, including Robert and Charles Gamble
and their sister Mary with her husband Joseph Brooks, William McGill,
Robert Means, Patrick Martin, James Galbreath, John Martin, Thomas
Clark, John Russell, Abner Witt, Jacob Laymon, and Thomas Allman.[2]

Some accounts place early settlers south of the Indian line, but all
evidence keeps their number to a relative few who had government
authority to reside with the Cherokees. Colonel Meigs, who struggled
to prevent illegal entry on Indian lands, had headquarters too close
to the future Hamilton County area to permit his policy to be weakened. When intruders appeared south of the line in the Sequatchie
Valley, he listed their names and ordered them out with a threat of
military removal.

An incident in the fall of 1808 shows how carefully the borders were
watched. At the time of the distribution of annuities at the agency,
Richard Green Waterhouse, trader and land speculator, planned with
some associates to do business there. They loaded a boat with green
and dried apples, potatoes, pickled beets, vinegar, whiskey, and brandy
to sell to whites, soldiers, and Indians. One night a party of soldiers
attacked the boat, pushing it off into the river's current with the expectation of retrieving it below the reservation line and claiming it as
a prize. The scheme failed but it clearly illustrates the fact that the
border was carefully patrolled. Some years later the same Waterhouse,
on a journey through the Cherokee country, lists in his diary only
Wallace Cowan as residing south of the line.[3]

When the county of Hamilton was established, the state legislature
named Robert Patterson, Charles Gamble, and William Lauderdale
as commissioners to select a site for the county seat and launch a
government. The three men—all early settlers—had had previous experience as public servants.

Patterson, probably the county's first citizen, had been one of the
leading men in the Sale Creek settlement. The Patterson family, of
Scotch-Irish descent, had moved to Tennessee from Mecklenberg
County, North Carolina, after the Revolutionary War. In Knox County
Robert married Rhoda Witt, a descendant of Huguenot forebears, be-
fore moving to Rhea County. They became the parents of nine children.
Among his numerous activities, Patterson operated a mill on Sale

Creek, served as a member of the Rhea County Court, sponsored a local school, and became a justice of the peace before Hamilton County was laid out.[4]

Charles Gamble, also of Scotch-Irish lineage, took up early residence on Sale Creek along with his brothers and sister. Like many of their neighbors, they came from Knox County. Such a short move to the frontier by a family cluster was typical in American pioneer history. Robert Gamble, a brother-in-law of Robert Patterson, built some of the buildings at the Brainerd Mission. Charles settled along Sale Creek in 1806 on a farm which on the creation of Hamilton County came into the new county.

About the time of Hamilton County's first local election its population numbered 766 white persons, 39 slaves, and 16 free persons of color. At best no more than 150 individuals had the franchise. When they voted, they selected Charles Gamble first sheriff.[5]

The Lauderdale family moved to Tennessee from Virginia following the Revolutionary War, in which William served, and by 1810 some members of the family paid taxes in Rhea County. The commissioner's wife was the daughter of Joseph Dunham. In 1809 William Lauderdale's father-in-law bought some twenty-eight hundred acres of land on Mountain Creek, within the Cherokee country, from John Hackett, who held title to the land under a North Carolina grant of Stockley Donelson. Dunham died in 1815 in Rhea County; the next year Lauderdale moved his family to the Mountain Creek area, settling on his wife's share of the estate. Here about three miles north of the Tennessee River and possibly a mile west of Red Bank the family lived on the main road from Old Washington to John Brown's Ferry. Lauderdale also rented the mill and farm on the reservation of the Cherokee David Fields "just above the suck" for a time. Later he bought from the other heirs of Joseph Dunham their inherited portion of the Mountain Creek property prior to his death in late 1827 or early 1828.[6]

According to tradition and the statements of early local historians, the commissioners decided to hold the first court at the tavern and stock stand of Hasten Poe. The two-story sturdy log structure, located at Poe's Cross Roads, now the town of Daisy, served the traffic on the busy public road. In keeping with the general practice of establishing a temporary seat of justice in a private home or facility, these decisions seem very logical. But no official records exist to testify to the fact that court actually met at Poe's, and certain evidence throws some doubt on the tradition, according to recent researchers. However, no other site can be singled out for this "first honor."[7]

By 1823 the state legislature officially changed the earlier location, stating that it would in the future be held at the residence of John Mitchell, about one mile from the place then being used "in order to alleviate the inconvenience complained of until a permanent seat of justice could be selected." Unfortunately no address is given for the Mitchell residence.[8]

Later the commissioners decided on a permanent location for the county seat. They chose the farm place of Asabel Rawlings, the first clerk of the county court, and ordered a log courthouse built. Anticipating the development of a community, they named the site "Hamilton County Courthouse." The location happened to be a part of the Fox Taylor reservation on the north bank of the Tennessee River opposite Dallas Island. Fox Taylor sold the property to his brother, Chief Richard Taylor, who owned it until 25 May 1831, when he transferred to Asabel Rawlings the deed for the "reservation of Fox Taylor for $1,200 including the mouth of Prairie creek and the seat of justice of Hamilton county." As the deed indicates, prior to the sale of the property to Rawlings, the land had been leased for almost ten years to him and the permanent county seat located on it. So the Hamilton County Courthouse stood on land leased from a Cherokee chief who was eventually forced to move west.[9]

Surveyors laid out streets and alleys for the town and planned for a school, hotel, stores, and homes, as well as the courthouse. Robert Patterson, Daniel Henderson, Jeremiah H. Jones, William McGill, James Riddle, and Cornelius Milliken served as commissioners with authorization to plat the land and sell lots.

In 1822 Asabel Rawlings became postmaster at the new office at Hamilton County Courthouse. Eleven years later the name of the village was changed to Dallas, honoring Alexander James Dallas. Dallas—lawyer, editor, politician, and financier—served as the secretary of the treasury of the United States under an appointment by President James Madison prior to Dallas's death in 1817. The next year the little town of about two hundred inhabitants proudly reported having one lawyer, two doctors, four stores, two taverns, and a blacksmith shop.[10] A century later it became a deserted village under the waters of Chickamauga Lake.

But long before its demise, Dallas fell on hard times. In 1840 by popular vote Dallas lost the courthouse. Following the negotiations of the Cherokee removal treaty in 1835, whites began to move into the region south of the Tennessee River. On the southern side the land was more fertile, the valleys broader and there was talk that Georgia would build a railroad to the river. Dallas began to lose population and prestige.

To accommodate this new situation the Tennessee legislature, on 3 January 1840, authorized a referendum on the location of the court-house: "namely, whether it shall remain at Dallas, or be removed to the south side of Tennessee, at or within one mile of the framed house lately occuped by Joseph Vann, a Cherokee Indian, in said county." A majority of twenty-five votes was required to relocate the courthouse.

The act named Henry Gotcher, George Luttrell, William Clift, Richard Price, Jonathan Wood, Alfred M. Rogers, and James A. Whiteside commissioners to determine by June a "suitable and eligible site for the seat of justice" if the vote favored a move. The commissioners were empowered to purchase land, "cause a town to be laid off," determine the number and width of the streets, sell lots, reserve certain areas for a public square and a jail, and name the new community. The proceeds from the sale of lots in this real estate venture were intended to defray all expenses including the cost of erecting public buildings. Only if construction funds were insufficient could officials levy "a county tax" for this purpose.[11]

In the election, voters marked "tickets" either Dallas or Vann. Those favoring a change won. Anticipating this result, a land company had organized earlier to develop Vanville. Among its members were James Johnson, John H. Torbett, Hugh Price, James A. Whiteside, David N. Bell, Thomas Crutchfield, Samuel M. Johnson, Joseph A. Johnson, Amos Potts, Thomas Shirley, William Gardenhire, and Samuel Williams. Price, Torbett, and James Johnson served as commissioners. They bought property from Thomas Crutchfield, Sr., which had formerly been owned by "Rich Joe" Vann where Vann had made his home just prior to his required migration in 1838. The commissioners advertised the sale of land in Vanville—some four or five hundred lots— in the February and March 1839 issues of the *Knoxville Register*.[12]

The men charged with the responsibility of selecting a site for the new courthouse chose a location adjoining Vanville which they named Harrison for General William Henry Harrison, the successful Whig presidential candidate in the "log cabin and hard cider" campaign of 1840. The new county seat was near the mouth of Ooltewah Creek (Wolftever). Here a substantial brick courthouse was constructed by

Thomas Crutchfield, Sr., who had developed a fine reputation throughout East Tennessee as a builder of public structures and fine brick
homes.

By the year Harrison became the county seat (1840) the population
of the county had grown considerably. In 1830 the aggregate number
of residents totaled 2,276, including 115 slaves and 25 free persons of
color. The largest slave owner was Hasten Poe, who had 13; only four
other owners had 8 or more slaves. The population figures show that
the Hamilton County society was very young: some sixty percent of
the whites were no more than twenty years of age and 52 of the 115
slaves are listed as under ten years of age.

Ten years later the census report gave an aggregate population of
8,175. This total comprised 584 slaves and 93 free persons of color. The
majority of the workers earned their livelihood from agriculture. Only
30 persons gave commerce as their occupation; 192 listed manufacturing and the trades, and 40 came under the official category of
"learned professions or engineering."

Representative familes of the era bore the names of John Brown,
Nimrod Pendergrass, James Cozby and his sons William and Robert,
James Varner, Gilbert Vandergriff, John McGill, Preston Gann,
Thomas Coulter, Benjamin McDonald, George Sawyers, and Nathan
Shipley. Prominent in the northernmost part of the county was the
pioneer family of McDonald, whose Irish ancestors came to America
about 1691; some members eventually got to Rhea County. Edward
McDonald bought 1,500 acres on the Tennessee River where the Cher-
okee Agency had stood, while James bought a large farm on Sale Creek
in 1831 close to the county line.[13]

The great majority of the people lived on small farms averaging
between 50 and 250 acres. Much of the best land had already been
brought under cultivation by the Cherokees, who had planted gardens
and orchards and had burned off pasture lands. Most of the first settlers
enjoyed frontier, rural abundance, but the work of clearing bottom
lands of cane roots and other areas of timber required heavy labor.

There were a few general stores and small grist mills that catered
to the people along Sale, Soddy, North Chickamauga and Mountain
creeks. Blacksmith shops served as service stations, and by 1836 John
Myers was operating a cotton gin at his plantation on Soddy Creek.
Business did suffer from a lack of circulating coins and because the
type of paper money used then had such uncertain value that merchants
feared it would not "keep over night." Many transactions and the pay-

ment of taxes depended on barter. People used as a medium of exchange such items as tallow, pelts, leathers, dry hides, bacon, and beeswax or they traded bounties earned by destroying certain predators as foxes.

Most of the first comers had Scotch-Irish backgrounds and were second- or third-generation Americans. A few of English, Irish, and German lineage added variety to the population. Some of the leaders had mastered elementary reading and writing, but most had little or no formal education, though they benefitted from ready wit and manual skills. Long hours of drudgery left little time or initiative for anything beyond the essentials of living. All subsisted in close relationship to the rhythm of the seasons; isolation had a marked effect on social life and customs. As in all frontier areas in the eastern United States, early Hamilton County developed as a "wooden country"; wood was used for houses, fences, outbuildings, furniture, and fuel. Wood dictated architectural features and homes were small, simple, and utilitarian.

Despite long distances, difficult travel, and lack of money, some settlers managed to open schools and to form church congregations. One-room schools, known as subscription schools (started by an individual or a group of neighbors), operated for a few months at a time without any governmental or tax support. The agreement between teacher Thomas K. Clingan and the school patrons of Smith's Cross Roads (now Dayton, in Rhea County) clearly illustrates the type of arrangement on which education was based throughout the area:

Articles of agreement made between Thomas K. Clingan of the one part and us the subscribers of the other part, is as follows: viz. to say if the said subscribers pays said Clingan two Dollars per scholar and one of that to be paid in good Current bank notes and the other one to be paid in trade as will be mentioned hereafter: one half bushel of corn or wheat or rye, and twenty-five cents in money per Scholar to be paid at the beginning of the School and the other part of the trade to be paid against the fifteenth of November next in corn at 2s. per bushel, or pork, or cloth, or any other good trade at the market price; and the rest of the money to be paid at the end of school; and for the same said Clingan will bind himself to teach the subscribers children to read right [sic] and Cypher to the best of his knowledge for the term above mentioned and also to keep as good order in school as possible and will make up all lost time in said term above mentioned, and the said Subscribers bind themselves to find said Clingan his boarding and lodging equil [sic] proportion to the Scholars that they subscribe During the term above mentioned and said School to be ruled by the majority and the said Clingan is to have every Saturday to himself during the said term.[14]

In Hamilton County, Robert Patterson sponsored a school for his family which was possibly the first conducted for settlers in the area as well as the first since Gideon Blackburn discontinued his work with the Cherokees. A one-room school built on the farm of Asabel Rawlings when that section had the name Hamilton County Court House gradually developed into a three-room institution as Dallas grew. By 1840, according to the census, the county residents supported five "primary and common schools," which enrolled a total of 133 students.

In one district of the county the common school commissioners made certain special arrangements in 1840–41. They found 182 scholars in the area and decided to provide for four schools, each to be in session for three months. The schools were located at James McDonald's, Robert Patterson's, Clift's stillhouse, and near Archibald McCallie's. They hired James Gasque to instruct for three months at each place, for which he was to receive $200. One half of his salary, they agreed, should be in money and "the other half in good trade." The money was to be paid quarterly and the first three quarters of the trade to be forthcoming by 1 December 1841. The commissioners further agreed

> that all those who send to either of the Schools who are not entitled to any part of the money appropriated by law for the use of common Schools shall pay the full value of their Schooling what is the customary price of schooling according to the time they shall go. one half money and the other half in goods trade at the selling price of the County all to be delivered at the schoolhouse where they shall go, at the expiration of the term and that the proceeds shall be appropriated to the use of paying the teacher for the present year. Price of schooling at the rate of ten dollars per year.[15]

The small structures which housed the classes were usually built cooperatively and generally served also as regional chapels. The first families, coming chiefly from nearby Rhea and Bledsoe counties, brought with them an association with either Presbyterian or Methodist faiths. Many early Hamiltonians, for example, had served as elders at the Monmouth Church of Washington before moving and the early Sale Creek community most likely was served by the Reverend Mathew Donald, a Presbyterian who was active in Rhea County after 1814. A Sale Creek Cumberland Presbyterian Church is recorded to have opened in 1842 with Hiram Douglas as pastor.[16]

At Soddy, Presbyterians organized the "Mount Bethel Church" with the Reverend Abel Pearson, pastor, in December 1828. Legend has it that the organization of the charter group occurred under a large oak near the Clift-McRee Spring. Until 1832 the congregation met in homes; at that time a meetinghouse was built on land donated by Colonel Clift and Major McRee. Pastor Pearson has the distinction of being the county's first author; his volume, in keeping with his profession, carries the title *An Analysis of the Principles of Divine Government.*[17]

The earliest Methodist church, first known as Prairie Springs Meeting House, was a log structure on Prairie Creek near Dallas. Asabel and Phoebe Thurman Rawlings moved to this section from Washington about 1820 when he became clerk of the court. Tradition has it that Rawlings was instrumental in founding this church about this time, although the deed for the donated property was not recorded until 1832. John Bradfield, easily recognized by the great shawl he always wore instead of a coat, served as an early minister; later a nephew of Asabel Rawlings named Asabel Jackson became minister, and the church's name was changed to Jackson's Chapel. The original name now survives only in the designation of Prairie Peninsula, where the old cemetery is located across the road from where the old chapel stood. The property of the church was increased by five acres donated by Elisha Kirklin for a camp meeting site on North Chickamauga Creek.[18]

When the Tennessee Conference of the Methodist Church was formed in 1812, a circuit rider served the Tennessee Valley Circuit, including Rhea County. In 1819 Hamilton County was made a part of this circuit, until 1824, when a reorganization placed it in the Washington Circuit of the Holston Conference. Itinerant parsons served those rural communities, preaching wherever a group gathered and officiating at belated wedding and funeral services. Camp meetings and brush arbor services became very popular during the summer months at specially designated spots.[19]

A second early Methodist group organized Hicks Chapel in 1849. The church and its adjoining graveyard were located on Morrison Springs Road near present Red Bank. The early log structure, built by the cooperative efforts of those who worshipped there, stood on land donated by Alfred Rogers and William Gray, principal real estate owners in that section. Edward E. Wylie, Thomas and John Hartman, John Walker, James C. Connor, John Brown, and Monroe Lusk worked faithfully during the early years.[20]

A few Baptist churches made early appearances as did missionaries of the Cumberland Presbyterian Church. The Baptists living near Concord organized a church in 1848, and the Salem Baptist Church near Birchwood started at an early date. Upon the organization of the

Ocoee Presbytery in 1842, several small Hamilton County churches were listed with the organization.[21]

In addition to such settlements north of the Tennessee River as those at Sale Creek, Dallas, and Mountain Creek, clusters of homes developed at Soddy, at Poe's Cross Roads, and at Hixson. Since public records for these early years are very fragmentary, one cannot list persons who held office. A few whose work is known are Jeremiah J. Jones, register, followed by James S. Yarnell; Charles Gamble and later Terrell Riddle, sheriff; Daniel Henderson, Dr. P. H. Butler, B. C. Connor, and B. B. Cannon, early circuit court clerks. Some of the early justices were Robert Patterson, Daniel Henderson, Samuel Igou, Jeremiah Jones, George Sawyer, John Bradfield, George Maguire, William McGill, Ephraim Hixson, William Rogers, John Hanna, Samuel Hamil, Jesse Sutton, and John Cornett.[22]

Land formed the basis and measure of wealth. Everyone required land with a good spring for a home, fertile soil for cultivation, land for a livestock range, and land for the family cemetery. In addition, land represented investment and offered opportunity for speculation. Consequently the county surveyor and entry taker held most essential posts. Samuel R. Russell, John Cummings, B. B.Cannon, and Robert Tunnell worked as early surveyors, and Cornelius Milliken as the first entry taker, beginning in 1824.[23]

The most desirable land lay along the river and its tributaries, but ownership was full of uncertainties because of overlapping grants, dual ownership, poor surveying, and the use of perishable boundary markers. Here early North Carolina grants had been located, here Cherokee reservations marked off, and here undefined border lines existed. Moreover, some of the large early grantees were absentee owners whose titles became clouded by a failure to pay taxes.

In 1822, for example, the sheriff sold for taxes "at public outcry" 10,000 acres, part of the original Stockley Donelson grant, to Charles McClung. The amount paid was $122.65. Richard Green Waterhouse purchased land just as cheaply. In 1826 he bought 220 acres for $2.20 (a cent an acre) which were marked off in a narrow ribbon on the north bank of the Tennessee River. The parcel was described as an acre wide and 220 acres long or extending from the Walnut Street bridge down to Moccasin Bend. Some years later, Jacob D. Garner got 5,000 acres for taxes due amounting to $5.52½.

A few other owners acquired large tracts a little later. George Williams, who came to the county from Alabama in the 1820s with his four sons, acquired rich bottomland at the foot of Walden Ridge, including Williams Island.

David Beck came to the area from Rhea County about 1822 and began entering land. He bought some tracts from the Waterhouse heirs and eventually had an estate (which comprised the present-day Chattanooga Golf and Country Club, Riverview, Dallas Heights, and most of North Chattanooga). Another pioneer from Rhea, John Foust, bought extensive acreage in the Mountain Creek area where he reared a family of twelve. In the early 1830s Samuel B. Hawkins became a major owner, while Alfred M. Rogers and William K. Gray held title to very large tracts in the Red Bank section.

Although river property was the most desirable, the state, beginning in 1823 offered mountain land for sale, usually in large tracts. Some Walden Ridge land became the property of William Clift and Robert C. McRee, brothers-in-law. In 1836 these two major real estate promoters also purchased 10,000 acres from the McClung heirs in the northern end of the county. Over the years they were associated with many real estate transactions. In addition to their partnership, they often acted independently; Colonel Clift with William Stringer, for example, in one deal acquired all of the unsold land in a major tract across the river from Chattanooga.[24]

The Walden Ridge mountain land remained unsold for years, for it was wild and inaccessible. Few families lived there before 1840 and naturally their stories are incomplete. Descendants spun exciting tales about those first days, possibly embroidering the facts. "Uncle Joe" Miles, famed as a forest distiller, claims the honor of first settler for his kinsmen. This senior Miles arrived from North Carolina to take up valley land but got into an argument with a Cherokee, whom he killed. Fearful of reprisal, Miles took to the hills with his family. Walden Ridge seemed an ideal hideout, so he loaded his family's possessions on a wagon and started up via Levi Gap. But when he reached the east brow cliffs there was no way to get a wagon through. Miles did the next best thing: he took the vehicle apart and carried it to the summit piece by piece, wheel by wheel. After reassembling it and packing his meager possessions a second time, he drove on with his family for a half day or so to a spot near Lone Oak, where he built a crude cabin. Here they lived in isolation.

Then one day a stranger appeared, leading a team of oxen pulling a covered wagon. He gave his name as Winchester; he had journeyed on top of the mountain all the way from Kentucky. Winchester and his family decided to end their wanderings; they put up a cabin just across the way from the Miles. For sometime the two families, soon closely associated by marriage, were Walden Ridge's only settlers. Then a few others slowly joined them, the Vandergriffs, the Gadds, the Hartmans, the Housers, the Becks, the Conners, and the Rogers, the Levis, and the Bob Whites.

When the state in 1823 offered mountain land for sale, some investors bought sizable tracts for very low prices ranging from $.01 to $.12½ per acre. For example, 3,000 acres on the headwaters of North Chickamauga Creek were acquired by Laton K. Smith. George R. Cannon had a 5,000-acre holding; 2,000 acres were bought by Gilbert Vandergriff, and 5,000 acres acquired by Washington and William Nixon.[25]

Few land travelers faced problems as taxing as settler Miles, but all vehicular trips were slow, tiring, and uncomfortable. The river, despite its many difficulties, provided easier access into the region from the many tributaries of the upper river system. Practically all of Hamilton County's pioneer families arrived at their new homesites by water. Upon deciding to move they simply built crude boats, loaded up their household goods, livestock, and poultry, called the dogs, and were off. Some trade craft brought supplies to the agency. Their numbers increased greatly during the Cherokee removal as ambitious farmers shipped produce for use by the army, the Cherokees, and the growing band of followers. Ross's Landing witnessed the arrival of hundreds of flatboats. In addition to farm supplies the King Salt Works of Virginia developed a thriving business in the essential product they sold. Agents of this firm worked the various landings, and one report states that 1,500 bushels of salt were sold at Ross's Landing in 1838 at eight dollars per bushel.[26]

The problems of Tennessee River travel did not go unnoticed. They received official public recognition in 1824 when Secretary of War John C. Calhoun stated that the improvement of the river was of national concern and that Muscle Shoals represented one of the most serious obstacles in the nation's waterways. Working with the state of Alabama, government agents developed plans for the building of a canal around the shoals with completion set for 1836. Meanwhile a most dramatic adventure gave vivid publicity to the river.

Early in 1828 word passed through the upper Tennessee Valley that a steamboat, the *Atlas*, was coming. Some thought it a mysterious "critter" from out of the Gulf and prepared to destroy the monster.

The fact that it carried a cannon in place of a bell added to the apprehension. By 6 February it had ascended Muscle Shoals. A Huntsville editor bade Captain S. D. Connor good luck when the little steamer left that community, saying that by press time the *Atlas* would be "wending her way through the Suck and over the Boiling Pot, a passage which has, heretofore, been deemed impossible to be performed by any being or thing except the sturgeon and the catfish."

The *Atlas* made the mountain passage: fourteen minutes at the Pot and nine at the Suck with one warp for safety. Apparently Captain Connor stopped in Hamilton County only for wood. On 3 March he tied the *Atlas* up at Knoxville, receiving the applause of that community and a purse of $640 which had been offered for the first steamboat to navigate the river to that town.

By 1831 the 100-foot-long *Knoxville* began operations. "Joy seemed to beam from every countenance" in the city for which it was named. The steamboat era on the Tennessee soon began in earnest. Although boosters bragged that their shallow-draft, flat-bottomed boats could sail on just a trace of dew, the untamed Tennessee caused a great deal of trouble. Snags, rocks, and swift currents slowed service and rivermen sought state as well as federal funds to remove obstructions.

Tennessee established a board of internal improvements and voted some funds and in 1831 and 1832 John C. Haley and his son, under a state contract, removed rock from the Suck and Boiling Pot as the first improvement in the channel for steamboat operation.

Beginning about 1835 steamboats plied regularly between Knoxville and Decatur, Alabama, through the navigable season when the river ran deep enough—November to June. As a rule they hauled anything that was brought to improvised landings, but gradually some steamboats received the designation freighters while others catered to passenger business only. The *Knoxville*, also called the *Indian Chief*, carried Cherokees and shepherded flat boats loaded with Indians going west in 1838.

The steamboat did not bring the same degree of prosperity to the area as it did on more placid western rivers. It did, however, add a new dimension to life in the valley, for it became an integral part of the economic and social fabric. When it became apparent that scheduling long voyages was impracticable because of the many snags, sucks, and whirls in the river, boatmen sought a good division point for operations. They soon realized that Ross's Landing met their needs, and the little cluster of buildings took on a new significance as a river wharf. From that time the future of Ross's Landing became closely linked with the Tennessee River.[27]

NOTES

1. Eastin Morris, *The Tennessee Gazetteer or Topographical Dictionary* (Nashville: W. H. Hunt, 1834), p. 275.

2. J. P. Brown, *Pioneers of Old Frontiers* (Chattanooga: Pioneer Bank, 1962), p. 30; Penelope Johnson Allen, "Leaves From the Family Tree," *Chattanooga Times*, 29 April 1934, and 3 December 1933.

3. Extract from journal of Richard Green Waterhouse, reprinted by Allen, "Leaves," 1 January 1935.

4. Ibid., 17 December 1933. Patterson died in 1848 and was buried in the family farm graveyard; in 1930 his remains were moved to a cemetery near Sale Creek and a monument was erected by the Judge David Campbell Chapter, Daughters of the American Revolution.

5. Ibid., 3 December 1933.

6. Ibid., 10 December 1933.

7. Among the historians who locate the first court at Poe's are John P. Long, Lewis Shepherd, Lewis Parham, Harry Wiltse, Zella Armstrong, and Penelope Johnson Allen. The extensive research of David H. Gray finds, among other things, that Poe still lived in Virginia at the time.

8. William C. McIntyre and Thomas W. Graham, comp., *Private Acts of Hamilton County, Tennessee*, 2 vols. (Nashville, County Technical Assistance Service, University of Tennessee Institute for Public Service, 1974), 1:148.

9. Allen, "Leaves," 8 December 1935. The Cherokee reservations north of the Tennessee River occupied strategic ground. In Marion County, Betsy Park deeded land for the county seat at Jasper; McMinn County's courthouse at Calhoun had been a part of Major John Walker's reservation; when the county seat moved to Athens, the site was on the Pumpkintown reservation of Major Walker's wife, Elizabeth Lowery Walker. The courthouse of Bradley County occupied part of the reservation of Andrew Taylor.

10. Morris, *Tennessee Gazetteer*, p. 141.

11. McIntyre and Graham, *Private Acts*, 1:51–53.

12. Zella Armstrong, *History of Hamilton County and Chattanooga, Tennessee*, 2 vols. (Chattanooga: Lookout, 1931), 1:112–113.

13. Allen, "Leaves," 11 November 1934.

14. Ibid., 17 June 1934; Brown, *Pioneers*, p. 31.

15. Armstrong, *Hamilton County*, 2:159; manuscript copy of eleventh civil district plan, clipping file, Chattanooga-Hamilton County Bicentennial Library.

16. Brown, *Pioneers,* p. 34; Armstrong, *Hamilton County,* 1:235.

17. Ibid., 1:114, 242–43.

18. Mary Thomas Peacock, *The Circuit Rider and Those Who Followed* (Chattanooga: Hudson Printing, 1957), pp. 54–55; Armstrong, *Hamilton County,* 1:239.

19. Peacock, *Circuit Rider,* p. 18.

20. Ibid., pp. 133–136.

21. Brown, *Pioneers,* p. 35; Armstrong, *Hamilton County,* 1:232.

22. Ibid., 1:97–98.

23. Ibid., 1:98.

24. Ibid., 1:98–108; 2:118; Allen, "Leaves," 28 February 1937.

25. Cartter Patten, *Signal Mountain and Walden's Ridge* (n.p.: author, 1962), pp. 14–19; Creed Bates, "A History of Walden's Ridge," *Hamilton County Herald,* 22 February 1974.

26. *A History of Tennessee From the Earliest Times to the Present* (Nashville: Goodspeed, 1886), p. 855.

27. T. J. Campbell, *The Upper Tennessee* . . . (Chattanooga: author, 1932), pp. 9–18, 34–38; Frank L. Teuton, *Steamboat Days on the Tennessee River* (Marlow Heights, Md.: author, 1967), pp. 21–23; J. Haden Alldredge et al., *A History of Navigation on the Tennessee River System* . . . (House Doc. 254, 75th Congress, 1st sess., Washington, D.C.: Government Printing Office, 1937), pp. 60–63, 70–73.

---- 7 ----

The Urban Frontier

O
N 18 October 1836, the Tennessee legislature created a "surveyor's district" of the Cherokee lands within the state which had been surrendered by the Treaty of New Echota. Although the national government acquired this land, arrangements had been made to transfer it to the state. During the next year John B. Tipton, surveyor general of the tract called the Ocoee District, and his staff busied themselves marking off the area. They ran out ranges six miles in width which were subdivided into townships six miles square. The surveyors then subdivided the townships into thirty-six squares of 640 acres each. The sixteenth section of each township was to be "reserved for the use of schools, in such township forever." Because of the meanderings of the Tennessee River the northern boundary line of the Ocoee District was very irregular. This irregularity naturally resulted in the formation of a number of fractional units which were generally to be treated as whole townships or sections.[1]

The general assembly took other action on 20 November 1837, when it outlined plans for disposing of this land to private ownership. An entry taker's office was to be established at Cleveland by the first Monday of November 1838, with Luke Lea designated entry taker.

102

After Lea's office began to function, whites could legally own property within the district.

The law recognized that settlers north of the Indian line had gazed across the Tennessee River, hopeful of the time this land could be occupied. They knew where the choice sites were and many of them made arrangements to move as soon as they learned of the 1835 treaty of removal. Although such occupancy violated the state law of 1833 extending county jurisdiction over the Cherokee country within the state, no one seemed to object. The state officials closed their eyes to such illegal penetration and the Cherokee Agency of the federal government had ceased to function.

The land law featured occupancy rights and a graduated sales price. Occupancy rights guaranteed squatters and all first arrivals prior purchasing privileges. Taking into account the desirability of certain soils, locations, or terrain, the sliding-scale price policy reduced the acreage price after a certain time elapsed if the land did not sell. The law specifically spelled out the following principles. Persons with occupancy rights had priority of entry for 160 acres for three months at $7.50 an acre. At the end of this period the land was open for anyone's entry for two additional months at the same price. After the expiration of this five-month period, occupants again had priority of entry for two months at $5.00 per acre; an additional two months was allowed for the purchase of the residual of land at the same $5.00 price. After this second price level expired, all remaining acreage would be sold on a two-months-plus-two-months formula at $2.00, $1.00, $.50, $.25, and $.12½ per acre. Land unsold after nineteen months was further reduced, carrying a price tag of $.01 per acre.

A few men with eyes to the future moved into the Ocoee lands within Hamilton County before the Cherokee removal treaty was negotiated. Although no complete list of persons involved is possible to obtain, the role played by these first settlers is important. Most of them gathered in the immediate vicinity of Ross's Landing where the only house seems to have been the cabin occupied by the ferryman.[2] The site was most attractive, and for about twenty years a ferry, landing, and warehouse had operated there. These facilities stood at a spot which served as a kind of avenue opening into the Cherokee country.

It was most likely in 1835 that Samuel Williams and some of his brothers moved from their father's place north of the river and opened a store near the landing. Samuel Williams prepared himself for a positive venture into real estate investments as he familiarized himself with the details of the area. He developed great faith in the future of the region by interesting and inspiring others in its potential.

Daniel Henderson, John Kenney, and a few others came about the same time. Henderson and his wife Jane Cosby Henderson had a typical Rhea County background. He had been a merchant and inn-keeper and in 1836 served as a census taker among the Cherokees. He apparently established occupancy rights on the basis of a mortgage taken out several years earlier.

Some time after taking up residency on this land, Henderson lost his life, but his widow continued to live on the property later described as being "on the south bank of the Tennessee, where the mail carriers from Dallas to Rossville formerly crossed the said river." Some consider Jane Henderson Chattanooga's first citizen; her inherited land claims at one time consisted of most of the acreage in what is now East Chattanooga. For some years Mrs. Henderson continued to operate the inn, a "curious little hostelry" made of poles and chinked, which was divided into six or seven compartments or "pens" about fourteen feet square.[3]

During the next year the Cherokee removal got under way and Ross's Landing received the designation of a military station and a point of departure for the Indians. A detail of United States troops moved in. Their presence and the activity associated with removal brought additional newcomers to the area who became permanent residents. Some of the arrivals were Aaron M. Rawlings, John P. Long, D. A. Wilds, W. M. Davis, Samuel Stewart, William Long, and Dr. Nathan Harris (a surgeon formerly stationed at the Cherokee Agency), and Isaac Baldwin.

John P. Long and his family arrived in April by flatboat from Old Washington. He immediately established a mercantile business by announcing a long list of goods for sale in the columns of the *Tennessee Journal*, published at Athens, Tennessee. His place was a typical back-woods general store which advertised that business would be conducted on "accommodating terms." According to the newspaper, his stock included bar iron, "fresh flour," nails, writing paper, "Rio coffee," Tennessee whiskey, four baskets of champagne, wine, window glass, "Eastern nails," herring and mackerel, saltpeter, tobacco, rope, axes, hoes, and brass kettles.[4]

On 22 March 1837, Long moved the newly created Ross's Landing post office into a corner of his store and assumed the duties of first postmaster. At first, not being on any established postal route, the office had an unusual status, as mail was delivered from Rossville by special contract. Some months later a triweekly line of post coaches initiated a run from Augusta, Georgia, to Murfreesboro, Tennessee, and it brought hurrahs that letters from Washington, D.C., could arrive in ten days.

In 1837 the newcomers included Reynolds A. Ramsey, who got the mail contract and operated a stage line. His optimism bubbled over immediately as he announced that the "Pleasant village of Chattanooga was soon to become the great Emporium of East Tennessee." James W. Smith put in his appearance at the same time that Albert A. Lenoir, whose daughter Elizabeth is said to have been the first child born in the village after the Cherokee removal, also moved in. Allen Kennedy, another who quit Old Washington for a new location, opened a tavern. One of his guests was the English traveler, George W. Featherstonhaugh, who stopped briefly in 1837. Of Kennedy's establishment Featherstonhaugh wrote,

> I was delighted to find that it consisted of three new log huts, built upon a high piece of ground that commanded a beautiful view of the surrounding country. The landlord was very civil, and everything was tolerably clean. I considered myself a most fortunate person, and laid down to rest with the wandering breezes of the night upon my face, that entered through the open logs. . . . On awakening I got a fine view of the country through the walls of my bedroom, which fronted that fine chain which on this side of the river is called Raccoon Mountain. The Lookout Mountain also was towering up with the numerous peaks of its extended line, that appeared wooded to the top. The rest of the landscape consisted of picturesque knolls, all densely covered with trees.

Featherstonhaugh's description of Ross's Landing was not so flattering. He called it a "small village hastily built without regard to any order or streets, everyone selecting his own site, and relying on the Legislature of Tennessee to pass a law for the permanent arrangement of their occupation."[5]

By June there were fifty-three heads of households living in the area. Most of them, like all the earlier pioneer Hamilton County settlers, arrived on the free currents of the Tennessee River. The story is that they conducted their business on the riverbank but placed their houses some distance back from the water to avoid the heavy fogs and the swarms of mosquitoes found there. Their occupancy rights rested in a quarter section and an adjoining fractional quarter section of land.

Those in each area chose three commissioners to represent them in attending to their occupancy claims and to serve as the first city fathers. The men representing the full quarter section were John P. Long, Aaron M. Rawlings, and George W. Williams; representing the fractional unit, Allen Kennedy, Albert S. Lenoir, and Reynolds A. Ramsey.

The confusion of the Cherokee removal resulted in no serious or retaliatory action against these pioneer settlers, and more newcomers continued to enter claims. The specific geographic location of Ross's Landing offered special advantages. Its good river port lay close to the Cherokee turnpike that ran southward around the southern shoulder of the Appalachian Mountains. Persons like John P. Long, anxious to settle permanently in a place that offered sound business possibilities, noted the gateway features of the region. As Ross's Landing's first postmaster expressed it, this place was a spot where the corn country of Tennessee met the cotton country. "Here is the gate—through which the history of nations must pass," he wrote prophetically. "Upon further examination I found here all the requirements necessary to build a future city." Satisfied with his decision, Long built a "log cabin in the woods and settled down for life."[6]

The significance of this gateway position received renewed attention and emphasis when the legislature of the state of Georgia on 21 December 1836 authorized the building of a railroad northward from the central part of the state. Railroads were a radically new mode of transportation, which Georgia earlier endorsed when it chartered lines from both Savannah and Augusta into the interior. Now the assembly voted to build from the future junction of these roads at Terminus (now Atlanta) to the Tennessee Valley. Georgia's willingness to invest state money in large sums to make the movement of people and goods cheaper, safer, and more dependable produced a fever of optimism. Although no northern terminal for this project, the Western and Atlantic Railroad (W & A), was definitely determined, the people at Ross's Landing hoped their village would be chosen. Their expectations mounted when they heard that the governor of Georgia had been instructed to learn if Tennessee would permit the extension of the line to some place on the Tennessee River "at or near Rossville."

The six commissioners of the people who had settled at Ross's Landing soon embarked on their duties. They hired surveyors to plat the area, which encompassed about 240 acres found within the perimeter borders of the Tennessee River on the north to Ninth Street on the South; Georgia Avenue on the east and Cameron Hill on the west.

This work, done by Josiah Paty of Roane County, resulted in town lots being marked off and streets planned. The streets extending north and south were numbered from one to nine beginning at the river; they were sixty-six feet wide. Those running north and south were given the names of forest trees, with the exception of Market Street, which in the very early days was popularly referred to as "the Road." The names selected included Cypress, Cedar, Poplar, Pine, Chestnut, Mulberry, Cherry, and Walnut. These were planned to measure 100 feet in width with the exception of Market Street, which was even wider.[7]

Four roads entered the town on the southern side of the river: the Harrison Road, the Brainerd and Shallowford Road, the Rossville Road, and the Montgomery and Valley Road. Except for a steep grade from the river's edge, most of the original town streets rested on a lower level than at present and were subject to periodic flooding. The streets were intersected by numerous "bayous," which required the construction of many wooden bridges. A natural ravine extended from around Seventh and Mulberry streets northward between Mulberry and Chestnut to the neighborhood of Third Street where it turned northwestwardly across Second Street and finally ended at the river. One estimate describes this ditch as reaching a depth of fifteen or more feet in places.

West of Market Street between Fifth and Sixth streets stood a heavy growth of oak trees; in the winter months six or more inches of water covered the ground where wild ducks frequently gathered. The low swampy area around Market and Ninth streets featured a sizable pond. To the southeast beyond the town borders was a "deadly swamp" where red gum trees grew. The tops of the "trees formed archways, the space underneath them resembling tunnels," wrote one who knew the area. Enormous numbers of waterfowl and snakes inhabited the swamplands.[8]

In addition to planning the town, the commissioners' duties required them to enter the land at the Ocoee land office, make out deeds to the occupants for the lots on which they resided, designate certain plots for use of churches, and sell the remaining land at auction to the highest bidder after which they would divide the proceeds among the "parties in interest."

The entry for the quarter section was recorded on 7 November 1838, but that of the fractional unit was delayed until 12 December because of a legal controversy. Four of the occupants attempted to enter individual claims although they were participants in the general entry presented by the commissioners. The officials of the Ocoee District, refusing to accept the individual entries, finally granted the property in the name of the commissioners. Mrs. Jane Henderson, one of the rejected individual applicants, later went to court with her case, which remained unsettled for many years.

The year 1838 had been a busy one for the founding fathers of the village as they bade a final farewell to John Ross, his family, and the last of the Cherokee emigrants, while at the same time welcoming new citizens. James W. Edwards, George D. Foster, Dr. Milo Smith, James A. Whiteside, B. Rush Montgomery, Thomas Crutchfield, Sr., James Berry, William M. Anderson, John and Samuel Martin, Major John Cowart, and Ferdinand A. Parham were among the newcomers.[9]

Dr. Milo Smith, born at neighboring Smith's Cross Roads (Dayton), arrived after receiving medical training in Philadelphia. For a time he worked in government service, making trips to the Indian territory in the West with the Cherokees. A man well informed on many topics, he not only had the largest medical practice in the area but took part in civic affairs. His fellow citizens selected him as their mayor possibly as many as seven times.

B. Rush Montgomery, a lawyer from Pikeville, Tennessee, instilled confidence in the new community by his unfailing optimism. Whiteside, also from the Bledsoe County seat of justice, at thirty-five years of age developed into a kind of one-man chamber of commerce. In the next twenty years his reputation as a successful, wealthy, and public-spirited citizen and community promoter was firmly fixed. He worked constantly for school, church, and that new method of transportation, the railroad. Tom Crutchfield, Sr., the builder who, in association with his father-in-law Samuel Cleage, taught slaves the art of making and laying brick, turned his energies to building local structures and investing in Ocoee lands.

Ferdinand Parham and his family drifted down the Tennessee River in a flatboat. In addition to household goods, heirlooms, and knick-knacks, he carried a press and type, for he was a journalist and former editor of the Maryville *Intelligencer*. Parham tied up his craft under a shade tree along the riverbank and, using the boat for living quarters and composing and press room, he published the first issue of the Hamilton *Gazette* on 19 July 1838. The county's first newspaper, published as a weekly, featured Whig political leanings until it changed hands in 1859. Parham, who was a completely self-educated man who gathered around him a circle of devoted friends, lived in Chattanooga until his death in 1862.

On a summer's day that year the people living at Ross's Landing gathered in public meeting at the request of the commissioners. They assembled in a small log building—about sixteen by twenty feet—which served as a combined schoolhouse and church building in the neighborhood of Fourth or Fifth streets near Georgia Avenue. Seated on puncheon benches without backs, they took up the intriguing subject of a new name for their community. All agreed that Ross's Landing hardly represented the prospect ahead as they optimistically envisioned it. Yet when Lookout City was recommended for a name, it was voted down as being too pretentious.

Montevideo was suggested; numerous objections were voiced. It was too farfetched, too high sounding, not American, and not local in origin. Chattanooga was then presented as "homelike" and local—the Indian name for Lookout Mountain. An objection immediately followed. That name was "too uncommon, too uncouth . . . strangers would miscall it." Still another suggestion was placed in nomination. A recent visitor to the area had commented on the white cliffs of Walden Ridge; this observation prompted the suggestion that Albion would be a fitting name.

An enthusiastic seconder jumped up and commented, "Oh yes, let us call it Albun, that would be splendid." His mispronunciation proved fatal to this recommendation, and thoughts returned to Chattanooga. Most likely it was John P. Long whose homespun philosophy clinched the debate. "The name might sound outlandish and strange to some ears," he commented, "but if our city was a success, it would become familiar and pleasant, and there would not be another name like it in the world." The ayes had it.

The post office department adopted the new name on 14 November 1838; Ferdinand Parham's newspaper became the Chattanooga *Gazette*. The final legal move to make Chattanooga the official name occurred more than a year later when on 20 December 1839 the legislature of Tennessee passed an "Act to establish the Town of Chattanooga in the County of Hamilton and to incorporate the inhabitants thereof." The law provided for an election of town officials to be held under the direction of the county's sheriff on the second Thursday in January 1840. Seven aldermen were to be elected for a one-year term of office. The seven, in turn, were to choose one of their number to serve as mayor. By this method James Berry, another former Rhea

County resident, received the honor of being the first mayor of the town of Chattanooga.

In the spring of 1839 a lively interest arose among the townspeople over the sale of town lots. The promoters of Vanville—several of whom were Chattanooga residents—advertised their sale of lots to precede the Chattanooga sale by a few weeks. Both places held out the hope to investors that their town would eventually be named the northern terminal of the Georgia railroad while Vanville also anticipated becoming the county seat.

The Chattanooga sale of lots took place on 20 April but included only the quarter section, since the fractional quarter section was still involved in litigation. Naturally, land near the river sold first, for the landing was the hub of all business activity. The auctioneer found bidding less spirited and prices lower as lots more distant from the Tennessee River came up for sale. At day's end the commissioners realized a total of approximately forty-five thousand dollars.[10]

Some buyers had received land as occupancy rights but wished to increase their holdings. Newcomers without occupancy rights also acquired property. Some investors bought lots in anticipation of moving while others who had adequate funds sought parcels for purposes of investment and speculation. One in the last category was Judge Garnet Andrews of Georgia.

By the date of the Chattanooga sale of lots, land in the Ocoee District beyond the town's limits also became available because the time allowed for the early occupancy rights had expired. Since the prices of these state lands decreased according to the formula stated by the law, they eventually became much cheaper than the land in town. Consequently the entry taker's Cleveland office did a steady business in areas close to Chattanooga.

John P. Long added Ocoee lands to his investments as did Thomas Crutchfield, Sr., whose entries comprised land around Harrison, the area around the Brainerd Mission, Chattanooga Island, and the Amnicola farm. William Lindsay, one of several military men involved in the Cherokee removal who bought land, entered a tract in his wife's name and gave his name to a later downtown street.

The state of Georgia acquired a tract south of Ninth Street for its railroad yard and various facilities. In the same area, close to the town's boundary, the Reverend Jesse James—for whom James County was named—had a large farm called James Place. After the minister's death his family moved to another site in Chattanooga Valley in the Alton

Park sector. About 1841 Thomas McCallie, merchant, arrived with his family from Old Washington. He acquired a large farm tract extending from Georgia Avenue to East End Avenue (now Central Avenue) and from Vine Street to East Eighth Street. Here he built a commodious home near the corner of McCallie and Lindsay streets and gave his name to the road to Brainerd that passed through his property.

Another who invested his career in the young community was Jesse Dugger, who had come to the Cherokee country as a lad to ride jockey for "Rich Joe" Vann. John L. Divine, a young man of Irish descent, also came, liked what he saw, stayed on, married Sam William's daughter, and prospered. Robert Hooke, brother-in-law of Thomas McCallie, had moved from Rhea County to Fort Payne, Alabama. From there he got an appointment as Alabama commissioner to assist in the removal of the Cherokees and consequently brought his family to Ross's Landing. Realizing the area's potential, he settled down in the practice of law while entering into business with his kinsman in the mercantile venture of Hooke and McCallie. From Rhea County also came David C. McMillin with his widowed mother and younger brother. David McMillin ran a mercantile business and later entered the banking field. In 1856 he served as mayor of Chattanooga. [11]

Drawn into Chattanooga's orbit during these first years were settlers who lived just across the river. An old swing ferry which crossed the stream in pendulum fashion by means of a rope fastened to the end of Chattanooga Island provided transportation. James F. Hamill lived opposite Pine Street; John Cowart, married to a Cherokee, dabbled in politics and was called "an eccentric but excellent man." David Beck owned a large acreage, as did Elisha Rogers and Rufus Tankesley. Alfred Rogers and William Gray held first place as the largest owners of real estate in the Red Bank area. In 1843 John Foust, Jr., of German ancestry, brought his family to a sizable farm which he had bought near Morrison Springs. Foust expanded his holdings to 1,500 acres in Mountain Creek Valley, counting the Morrison Springs property, and increased his family to twelve children. [12]

Samuel Williams took on the job as local representative for several syndicates investing outside capital. Williams's brother George and James A. Whiteside, a lawyer and former state legislator who had just moved to Chattanooga, also associated themselves with these investors. The nonresident members of the syndicates—the Hargrove and Hines companies—brought some very outstanding men of the southeast into the local scene. Despite the national financial panic of 1837 they boldly put money into real estate in Hamilton County. Actually, they had made some preliminary investments before the Cherokee removal.

Among the more influential members of the syndicates were Zachariah Hargrove, Dr. Tomlinson Fort, Farrish Carter, and Ker Boyce. Hargrove, a banker and lawyer, hailed from Rome, Georgia. Carter, a wealthy planter and slave owner who lived at Milledgeville, Georgia, owned plantations in the northern part of that state.

Dr. Tomlinson Fort, surgeon, banker, excongressman, and president of the Central Bank of Georgia, earned a name as an enthusiastic promoter of internal improvements. Ker Boyce, a Charleston merchant, made contacts throughout the southern hinterland and was reputed to be the wealthiest man in South Carolina. He developed an absorbing interest in railroads and gave much time to the planning and construction of the first railroad built from Charleston extending westward across the state. Williams and Whiteside (the latter entered large tracts on Lookout Mountain in his own name) encouraged the syndicates by their own private investments and faith in the Chattanooga area. But the prospect of getting the northern terminal of the Western and Atlantic Railroad located at Chattanooga gave real incentive to the investors and fostered high hopes for large profits.[13]

Just as the hamlet's strategic location attracted investors and speculators, so the magnet of opportunity drew permanent residents to the village. From the very beginning Chattanooga represented an urban frontier. Physically it had little to offer that differentiated it from other places. Except for a few brick buildings put up by Tom Crutchfield, (who, during their construction, had sat in a tree platform directing his slaves), everything was wooden. River flatboats which brought produce or immigrants to the landing sold cheaply and were a fine source of lumber. Raised wooden sidewalks kept people out of the mud, wooden bridges crossed ravines, wooden fences kept livestock either in or out. The gunwales had a special value, for they could be planted to serve as curbing.

The unique characteristics of the urban fronter stemmed largely from the manner in which village folk made their living. Chattanooga was a garden town with plenty of space to raise food, poultry, and livestock but it was unlike the rural countryside with its isolated, largely self-sufficient family units. Village dwellers practiced a degree of economic specialization. Some gathered agricultural produce for processing or shipment; others served as merchants, lawyers, doctors, teachers, ministers, millers, tanners, or distillers.

In addition, the villagers enjoyed an opportunity to cooperate socially. Living in a neighborhood, they could readily participate in government, religious, educational, and community activities as well as join in mutual aid in case of emergency. And they had the chance of exchanging ideas not only with their neighbors but also with strangers, travelers, or special visitors who stopped at the landing.

Beyond Chattanooga and its immediate environs settlement tended to follow a pattern similar to that of the early decades in Hamilton County north of the river. Although the Ocoee lands contained fertile creek valleys, settlements were scattered. A few examples indicate the general picture. George W. Gardenhire early worked a farm along Citico Creek. James Williams established occupancy rights, built a hut and planted a fair-sized orchard—to be called later Orchard Knob. Antipas Moore moved to one of the many fine springs in the Chattanooga Valley in the Ridgedale section.

In the vicinity of present Vine and Willow streets a notorious tavern, known for its dirty deck of playing cards and large pack of dogs, operated under the name Straw Tavern. A young lad who carried grain to the Brainerd mill for his widowed mother remembered years later that after he passed Straw Tavern he went by only one log cabin all the way to the mill. This cabin, occupied by a free black woman, stood on the crest of Missionary Ridge. He did pass many deer along the way and found wild turkey common.[14]

The Brainerd mill stood among other buildings on the 160-acre former mission property which had been entered at the Ocoee land office by John Vail. Vail lived there in the late 1830s as did the widow Conner with her four sons, Wes, Asbury, Sam, and Tom. Vail sold this property to Thomas Crutchfield, Sr.; Philemon Bird, who was married to a black woman, in turn bought it from him in 1852. On this site he built a larger mill known as Bird's Mill; he was popular enough to have had the road leading to Chattanooga named Bird's Mill Road. He lived until 1871 when a son, living in an old missionary house, inherited the property. Closer to Graysville the family of William Blackwell by 1834 settled among the Indians; nearby Blackwell's Methodist Chapel and a subscription school—Walnut Grove—were started.[15]

Pioneer Thomas Carroll Hawley settled east of Missionary Ridge as did Dr. Joseph Strong Gillespie, who was mayor of Chattanooga in the 1840s and whose wife was a daughter of the Whitesides. In the general region of Audubon Acres John A. Carpenter built a home about 1838 and a little later a grist mill on Chickamauga Creek.[16]

Around Birchwood the pioneer settlers were members of the Roark, Carr, Palmer, and Luttrell families. At Anderson Springs near Savannah, Colonel John Anderson, Jr., who moved from the Sequatchie Valley, built a home; he served as postmaster at Savannah for fifty years. North of Ooltewah the Cumberland Presbyterian minister, Hiram Douglas, settled early as did the Seagles, McNabbs, Poes, Roddys, and Yarnells.[17]

The Yarnell family, of English Quaker heritage, lived for a time in Knox County before moving to Hamilton. Daniel Yarnell, Jr., lived near Soddy, where he died in 1843. Aaron J. Yarnell came to the county about 1823 and is buried near Snow Hill. His son, John L. Yarnell, became a doctor with a far-flung practice. About 1835 he married Jane Brown, daughter of wealthy Cherokee chief James Brown. An influential Indian judge, Brown had a farm near Snow Hill which became the property of his son-in-law when he was forced to move west.[18]

A number of early settlers chose locations in the vicinity of the Silverdale Spring. Stories have long circulated explaining the origin of the name of this community. One, based on fancy rather than fact, ascribes it to the Cherokee Indians who worked a silver mine in the area and adorned themselves with shiny ornaments. Although many have sought the lost mine since the Cherokees departed, only the place name suggests any evidence that it ever existed. Crispian E. Shelton called his home in this area Robin's Roost. Near the spring, Methodists gathered in the fall of each year for camp meetings. Although the time for their first assembly cannot be fixed, on 3 July 1844, George Washington House deeded five acres surrounding the spring to the church "for a camp ground and houses." The trustees listed were Robert H. Guthery, George, Samuel and Marsena Julian, George P. Stephens, Charles Riley, Joshua Bush, Lewis Hall, and George W. House.[19]

When the Ocoee District opened, Lewis Shepherd, who came to East Tennessee from South Carolina, entered a large tract of land amounting to some six thousand acres. He had married Margaret Donahoo, of a leading Irish family living along the Little Tennessee River, and moved his family to Hamilton County in 1839. The Shepherds made their home on a Hickory Valley plantation. Mrs. Shepherd's sister married Colonel Jarrett Dent, who came to the area as a railroad builder. Dent bought property near Tyner called Bonny Oaks.[20]

A few other pioneer families, living in the vicinity of the home of

J. S. Tyner for whom the general community received its name, comprised those of the Reverend Henry Gotcher, the Varnells, Towreys, and Azariah Shelton. On 7 August 1839, Thomas Guthrie secured a grant of Ocoee District land of 160 acres and became one of the first to settle permanently on the south side of the Tennessee River. He raised a family of eight children on the old home place about a mile north of Harrison on the Georgetown Road now inundated by Lake Chickamauga.[21]

Still another early comer was Samuel Igou. It is claimed that the family was of French origin and after a stay in Pennsylvania moved southward. Sam's father lived in both Bledsoe and Rhea counties before his son became a major investor in Ocoee District lands and joined Samuel Williams in a number of large land transactions.

The younger Igou owned lots in Dallas, served as a commissioner for the selection of a new site for a courthouse in 1840, married Mary Ann Skillern, and raised a family of six children. From Dallas Igou moved to a farm on the north bank of the river a few miles above Harrison where a main county road crossed the Tennessee. For some time before the Cherokee removal a ferry had been operated there by James T. Gardenhire, whose wife was a Cherokee. Igou bought the ferry rights and the spot soon acquired the popular name of Igou's Ferry and the road that of the Igou Ferry Road.[22]

Some miles to the north another ferry crossed the Tennessee. William Blythe, whose wife was a daughter of the Cherokee chief Richard Fields, owned this facility. In 1828 Alexander Clingan married Blythe's daughter Martha.[23]

Downstream at Chattanooga the little village could easily have slipped into insignificance after the Cherokee removal and the departure of the military. But the river highway potential and the promise of completion of the Western and Atlantic Railroad sustained the community leaders. During the decade of the 1840s the town's future turned on the commercial activity carried on at the landing.

Flatboats and great log rafts from upper East Tennessee crowded the landing in season, but the steamboats won all the glamor. This enchantment developed an unflagging support of river navigation and the improvement of the river channel on the part of the local people.[24]

Physical obstructions in the river and the failure of the first canal at Muscle Shoals to provide effective contact with the lower Tennessee made the steamboat trade a very serious business. Boatmen, mostly men up from the ranks and without surplus funds, practiced caution and serious deliberation; they joined in no spectacular races or risky ventures. Keen competition for contracts made them willing to dock at all sorts of improvised landings for any additional business.

At first their boats came from the Ohio River, but by the 1840s East Tennessee had put many homemade steamboats on the river. Often their craft were rebuilt several times and their names changed just as often. The steamboat men of this area sold, swapped, and traded their boats in the same way horse traders exchanged animals.

Calling for wood at yards in Hamilton County or dropping anchor at Chattanooga could be seen the *Holston, Harkaway, Reliance,* and *Cassandra.* In addition there were the *Joshua Shipley,* the *Frankland,* the *Huntsman,* and the *Tennessee* which became the *Ellen White.* Others with feminine names included the *Mollie Garth, Mary McKinney,* and *Fanny Malone.* Another craft of the 1840s, the *Pickaway,* probably named in connection with navigation problems, later was rechristened the *Atlanta.*[25]

The coming and going of the steamboats riveted Chattanooga's attention upon the river, but its hopes and dreams were fixed on the Georgia railroad. From the very first the citizens of the landing bravely fought to get the northern terminal; they believed this choice would mean business opportunities and boom days for the real estate interests. They invited the Georgia governor to visit and battled the competition of other towns. John P. Long, George Williams, and A. M. Rawlings secured a charter for a railroad—the Lookout Railroad Company—to build a line from the landing to tie in with the W & A at the state line if needed.

These promotional efforts resulted in 1839 in the selection of Chattanooga as the northern end of the railroad. This decision by the state of Georgia proved to be one of the most far-reaching in the history of Hamilton County's chief town. Everyone felt certain that the prosperity of Chattanooga was assured. Georgia bought twenty acres of land just beyond the southern limits of the town for yards and other facilities. In a cooperative spirit the town government gave the Georgians railroad rights to Mulberry Street all the way to the river and proudly changed the street name to Railroad Avenue.

Everything, however, did not go forward as planned, for the boom psychology of the early 1830s gave way to an era of deep economic despair. Although construction was started on the southern end of the road in 1838, work soon slowed down under the influence of a national panic. In 1842 Georgia suspended all work. Gloom descended on

Chattanooga. One interested citizen wrote, "If Georgia fails to finish the road or make the appropriation for its completion all is flat in Chattanooga."

The nation's declaration of war against Mexico in May 1846 diverted thoughts from this local problem. Throughout Tennessee a wave of enthusiasm for the military sent men flocking to recruiting centers. By the time the news came that the state's quota amounted to only about twenty-eight hundred men, more than ten times that number had already volunteered. So the "privilege" of serving was determined by lottery, and some losers actually paid for the chance to go to war. Not all counties had recruiting stations and some recruiters attracted men from other counties, so no complete roster of Hamilton men who served is available. Some units were mustered in at Harrison. Among those who served as officers were William J. Rogers, John McCullum, Richard I. Grant, J. R. Dobbs, Lawson Guthrie, John R. Bell, John McAllen, and John Cowart.[26]

Before the Mexican War ended, a brave display of pluck broke through the local discouragement over the W & A railroad. Public meetings reaffirmed support; one man with oxen and a plow worked to clear the Tennessee River of navigational obstacles to show his concern. Others joined together to buy a little steamboat to use as a work boat to improve the channel. Lobbyists traveled to Georgia to present again the merits of the town. But of wider impact was the chartering of two railroads to connect Nashville and Memphis with Chattanooga. The success of these projects meant a much expanded market range for the W & A; Chattanooga would not be just a northern terminal but an important railroad junction. With this encouragement Georgia in 1847 voted funds to complete the last section of the road.

A difficult ridge blocked the route at Tunnel Hill in north Georgia. Construction officials decided to dig a tunnel and authorized that track be laid on both sides of the ridge before the tunnel could be pierced. They brought cars and a small locomotive from Atlanta, loaded them on wagons and hauled them across the ridge with oxen power. On 1 December 1849 this small train, loaded with special guests, made a maiden run into Chattanooga.

A gala celebration followed. Only a quarter of a century had passed since the first railroad had run as a common carrier anywhere in the world; now the iron horse had made its way to a small hamlet in the interior of North America. The new iron link bound the area with the cities of Savannah, Augusta, and Charleston, with which it had carried on business since the earliest Indian days. As the celebrants gathered by the Tennessee River, a bottle of salt water sent from Charleston and a bottle of Georgia water were poured into the stream "in token of the union and fraternity of these states."[27]

NOTES

1. The boundary of the Ocoee District followed the Tennessee River from the Alabama border upstream to the mouth of the Hiwassee River. It then followed the Hiwassee to near the present community of Delano, Tennessee. The line then took a northeasterly direction along the divide between the Tellico and Hiwassee rivers to the Little Tennessee River, which it followed to the state line. From this point it followed the North Carolina and the Georgia lines back to the original starting point.

The name Ocoee was sponsored by Senator Miles Vernon, representing the counties of Rhea, Bledsoe, Marion, and Hamilton. State of Tennessee, *Acts Passed at the First Session of the Twenty-second General Assembly, 1837–38,* pp. 5–12.

2. Harry M. Wiltse, "History of Chattanooga," 2 vols. (Typescript, Chattanooga-Hamilton County Bicentennial Library), 2:77.

3. Ibid., 1:14, 2:78; Brown, *Pioneers of Old Frontiers With Supplements: Pioneer Settlers of the Chattanooga Area* (by Penelope J. Allen) and *The Story of Another Pioneer: A Brief History of Pioneer Bank* (Chattanooga: Pioneer Bank, 1962), p. 21; L. L. Parham, *Chattanooga, Tennessee; Hamilton County, and Lookout Mountain* (Chattanooga: author, 1876), p. 18.

4. *Tennessee Journal,* 14 June 1837.

5. G. W. Featherstonhaugh, *A Canoe Voyage Up the Minnay Sotor* (London: Richard Bentley, 1847) 2:210–20; Parham, *Chattanooga,* p. 18.

6. Long paid a great deal of attention to local history and wrote frequently for the local press. Extensive quotations from him and discussions of his role are found in Wiltse, "Chattanooga," 2:132–140; C. D. McGuffey, *Standard History of Chattanooga* (Knoxville: Crew & Dorey, 1911), pp. 18–30; and J. E. MacGowan, ed., *Chattanooga: Its Past, Present and Future* (Chattanooga: Chattanooga Times Co., 1885), p. 9 ff.

7. Wiltse, "Chattanooga," 2:135. Ten years later the mayor and board of aldermen changed the width of the streets by reducing the cross streets from First to Ninth streets from 66 to 46 feet and those running north and south from 100 to 60 feet except for Market Street, which was reduced to 100 feet, and Cherry, which was cut to 48 feet.

Shortly after this decision to save money, when the Western and Atlantic

Railroad was completed, the town changed the width of Mulberry Street from 60 to 126 feet. It granted the railroad a right-of-way on the street from Ninth Street to the river and changed the name to Railroad Avenue. By ordinance passed 3 August 1880, the name was again changed to Broad Street.

8. Ibid., 1:2, 9, 10, 18, 52, 53, 69, 70.

9. Zella Armstrong, *History of Hamilton County and Chattanooga, Tennessee* (Chattanooga: Lookout, 1931), 1:127–132; McGuffey, *Chattanooga,* pp. 24–25; Parham, *Chattanooga,* p. 19.

10. Wiltse, "Chattanooga," 2:135. The sale of lots in the fractional quarter section did not take place until several years later. David Beebe, chaplain of the American Ross clan, wrote recently in regard to the change of the name from Ross's Landing to Chattanooga, "You will probably find it of interest to note that 'Ross' is an old Gaelic name meaning 'promontory' or 'jutting land.' So when our city founders changed the name of our city . . . they didn't really change the name. They just translated it from Gaelic to Creek!" *Chattanooga Times,* 22 November 1978.

11. Brown, *Pioneer,* pp. 33, 37; Penelope Johnson Allen, "Leaves From the Family Tree," *Chattanooga Times,* 1 April 1934, 27 October 1935.

12. Wiltse, "Chattanooga," 1:18, 49; Allen, "Leaves," 28 February 1837; Mary Thomas Peacock, *The Circuit Riders and Those Who Followed* (Chattanooga: Hudson Printing, 1957), p. 133.

13. Wiltse, "Chattanooga," 2:135. Wiltse says that J. Caldwell, David Turner, Ellison Smith and others from Huntsville, Alabama, participated in these syndicates.

14. Wiltse, "Chattanooga," 1:19, 20, 26, 27, 49.

15. Ibid., 1:20; *A History of Tennessee From Earliest Times to the Present* (Nashville: Goodspeed, 1886), p. 813; Robert Sparks Walker, *As the Indians Left It: The Story of the Elise Chapin Wild Life Sanctuary and the Chattanooga Audubon Society* (Chattanooga: Hudson Printing, 1955), pp. 24–25.

16. Ibid., pp. 4–5; Allen, "Leaves," 28 February 1937; *Chattanooga Times,* 30 October 1938; 16 December 1934.

17. Brown, *Pioneer,* pp. 37–38; Allen, "Leaves," 24 November 1935.

18. Ibid., 29 September 1935.

19. Ibid., 21 March 1937; Peacock, *Circuit Rider,* pp. 126–130.

20. Allen "Leaves," 4 February 1934.

21. Ibid., 31 May 1936; Brown, *Pioneer,* p. 37.

22. Allen, "Leaves," 21 October 1934. Not far away was the John McGill cabin, believed to have been built in the 1820s. Ralph McGill, editor of the *Atlanta Constitution,* once lived there. In 1978 the house was taken down to be moved to another location.

23. Ibid., 17 June 1934.

24. T. J. Campbell, *The Upper Tennessee* (Chattanooga: author, 1932), p. 32.

25. Ibid., pp. 22, 30, 31, 32, 39, 41, 44, 113, 116; Teuton, *Steamboat Days on the Tennessee River,* pp. 41–43; Alldredge, *Navigation,* pp. 61, 62, 64, 73. See chapter 6, note 27 for complete citations.

26. Armstrong, *Hamilton County,* 1:180, 190–191.

27. Gilbert E. Govan and James W. Livingood, *The Chattanooga Country,* 3rd ed. (Knoxville: University of Tennessee Press, 1977), pp. 113, 122, 126–136.

8

The Bustling Decade of the 1850s

ON 9 May 1850, the gateway connecting South Atlantic port cities with the navigable waters of the Great West was thrown open when the first through train traveled over the 137-mile railroad from Atlanta to Chattanooga. This proved to be the first rail connection between the ocean and a tributary of the Mississippi River, and marked a great day. A local newspaper called for "One thousand cheers to the State of Georgia." At the enthusiastic ceremonies in Chattanooga, according to a spectator who later described the scene, one orator happened to be so full of "hurrah juice" that two friends held him on a keg while he "hic-upped" through his remarks.

The Western & Atlantic (W&A) entered Hamilton County through the valley of South Chickamauga Creek. In order to avoid making deep cuts or costly tunnels through the numerous ridges, the builders chose a roundabout way into Chattanooga. To do so they bridged the creek at least seven times in about twenty-five miles and flirted with a potential flood problem. The result was a notoriously crooked route.

At Smith Finley's place the railroad people established a depot and post office and christened it Finley. However, the residents of the neighborhood chose the more realistic name Pulltight for the area because of the depth and stickiness of the mud. In the course of time the official name became Chickamauga, for it was near the site of the old Indian town of that name. Later when the tragedy of Chickamauga, Georgia, became so well known throughout the nation, authorities changed the small village's name to Shepherd, which is generously applied to a wide stretch of country. In the early days of the railroad, Chickamauga, Tennessee, became a major grain and country produce shipping point for the farmers of southeastern Hamilton County. In 1860 as a village of fifty people it claimed three churches, two general stores, and a grocery.[1]

From this station (now just across the highway from Lovell Field) the track continued along the creek until it could round the north end of Missionary Ridge. Here a station called Boyce served the area. Its name honored Samuel J. Boyce, who owned the farm on which it was located. In 1860 Boyce, who most likely was a kinsman of Ker Boyce (the South Carolina real estate investor of early Chattanooga), was one of the wealthiest men in the county.

Railroading, an untried form of transportation, brought criticism as well as praise from the public. One fault-finding traveler who rode the W&A into Chattanooga complained of the "miserable and disgraceful equipment: not possessing a single comfortable car as far as I have seen." The coaches, he grumbled, are "about as elastic and delightful as an ox-cart," and he went on that it is "neither pleasant nor right, that a man should pay his money for accommodations he does not receive—to be compelled to stand on the platforms in front or rear— sit on the steps outside exposed to sun and cinders—or hold on the back of seats, dangling like a pendulum from side to side."

No real comfort awaited the traveler at his destination. Chattanooga had no depot and the train stopped in the middle of a field, so noted one passenger who then had to walk to the hotel. Here at least one unfortunate person found himself stranded, for low water had halted all steamboat service. Of his experience he wrote, "I thought what a fool I am. Here I am, locked in by these mountains with no way to get out unless I take the train back. I was on my way to Alabama. The people with me agreed with me and wondered what fool had built a railroad into such a place."[2]

But the completion of the W&A infused a new spirit into the 10,075 residents of Hamilton County. Freight traffic became "immense" even before the tunnel was completed when goods had to be shuttled over the ridge. Southbound freight soon accumulated in Chattanooga faster than the limited facilities of the W&A could move it. The railroad agent adopted barbers' rules or a "ship according to turn plan" and required each shipper to keep a book in his office and register all his freight on arrival. But it was often weeks before merchandise could be moved.

Grain, bacon, flour, corn, whiskey, and other country produce from upper East Tennessee piled up on the wharf. Steamboats did an increasing business while it was estimated that as many as two hundred flatboats often were packed and wedged together at the landing. The shippers brought great quantities of cotton in season from north Alabama plantations, risking the "bad" waters in the mountain stretch of the river in order to transship it by rail. Estimates place the number of bales received yearly between forty and forty-five thousand. Rude sheds—or no shelter at all—protected the bales, barrels, and bushels of goods from the elements. Freight lined the streets; so many bales of cotton accumulated at times that the city authorities felt called upon to pass a no-smoking ordinance in the storage area. By 1853 Chattanooga boasted at least eight forwarding and commission merchants and two wholesale grocers.[3]

Other items also accumulated. Mines at Sale Creek, Soddy, and in Roane County, which had opened around 1843 and furnished fuel for blacksmiths in the area, sent coal in boxes and barrels to enter the trade. Their new activity led a writer for *De Bow's Review*, a journal seriously interested in southern economics, to comment, "Coal of East Tennessee is destined to become one of its greatest sources of wealth."[4]

Livestock also arrived for rail shipment south. A resident of this era noted, "I have seen every pen, lot, and even gardens in the fall of the year filled with horses, mules, and hogs which had been driven from Kentucky and middle Tennessee and were awaiting transportation."[5]

The W&A gave new life to the river trade and produced the bustling decade of the 1850s. In addition to the steamboats of the previous years, the *Chattanooga, Jefferson, Lady of Augusta, Lincoln, Lookout, Alabamian*, and others joined the fleet. Their function, however, differed somewhat from that in earlier times. The steamboats served as feeders to the railroad; Chattanooga became a "sort of interior export town" and by 1855 it was made a port of delivery by the federal government.

More and larger steamboats operated on the Decatur-to-Chattanooga run and "palatial" boats embarked from the Chattanooga landing every afternoon except Sunday for trips downstream carrying passengers and mail. Disaster struck on one trip when in 1851 the *Elkton* burned while trying to navigate the Suck with a load of cotton bales. Although

Tennessee had invested funds in channel improvement since 1830, the results showed the weakness of pork-barrel legislation and only spotty efforts toward improvement. The growing importance of the river led, however, in 1852 to an appropriation by the United States of $50,000 earmarked for the Tennessee River calling for a two-foot depth from Knoxville to Kelly's Ferry, some twenty-two miles below Chattanooga.

Ambitious and forward-looking local men had worked hard to get the W&A into Chattanooga, while on the river during these years the brothers James and William Williams took the leadership. Not related to other Hamilton County Williamses, they came to Chattanooga about 1850. They operated the Tennessee River Mining, Manufacturing, and Navigation Company and developed a lively interest in steamboating. For a time the brothers managed one of the largest fleets on the river; their better-known boats were the *Chattanooga*, *Mollie Garth*, *Fanny Malone*, and *Jim Williams*.

William Williams became president of the first bank in town and served as mayor in 1854. He remained in the city until ill health led to his retirement and return to Nashville. James Williams, a man of many accomplishments, not only piloted steamboats but was such an ardent spokesman for river business and stream improvement that his fellow townsmen presented him with a silver service in recognition of his leadership. His political interests led to his writing an 1856 campaign volume, *Letters of an Old Whig*. The next year President James Buchanan appointed him minister to Turkey. When the Confederate War broke out, Williams, a devout Southerner, resigned and went directly from Turkey to England. He wrote for London newspapers in defense of the Confederacy and sold bonds for the cause. These activities, having started before his letter of resignation arrived in Washington, led to treason charges which discouraged his return to the United States. He died in Austria while still under indictment.[6]

Back in Hamilton County, passenger traffic by river and rail increased annually. Along the route of the W&A, newly opened resort places offered accommodations that were especially attractive to people of the Deep South. Humid summers and epidemics sent many to the area who could afford vacation spots in the Hamilton County mountains. The railroad authorities noted that mineral springs and natural beauty "together with the bold features around Chattanooga are all objects of interest and attract summer visitors." Business people, real estate speculators, and promoters of tourism embarked on a spirited program of expansion.

The 1850 census listed a "bank agent" and a "speculator" as residents of the county. The first bank, however, did not open until 1853 with William Williams, president, and William D. Fulton, cashier. Known as the Bank of Chattanooga, it soon had a competitor in a branch of the Union Bank organized in 1857 with John G. Glass as president. Two years earlier the Lookout Savings Institute entered the field; it selected as officers Joseph Ruohs, a cabinetmaker and native of Switzerland, as president, and Jonathan P. McMillin, cashier.[7]

Before the completion of the W&A, the prospect of rail communication sparked a real estate boom on Walden Ridge. A New Yorker named Nicholas Haight, having acquired a sizable tract of mountain land, sold farms to Perez Grant, William Cunningham, Edwin Newby, Albert C. Richard (of Dutch lineage) and N. H. Gale, among others. In 1848 Haight, using letters written by these clients, prepared an extensive pamphlet entitled *Cherokee Lands on Waldens' Ridge* as a promotional prospectus. Haight reported the area as "new and unsettled country" with only fifty-two families in a twenty-mile area, but its extent and remarkable advantages had "just immerged into notice" as a result of the nearing completion of the W&A.

Whoever composed the testimonial letters certainly searched the dictionary for all of its rose-colored adjectives. One written on 12 April 1848, from "Wall'd'in Ridge" said, "This Ridge is a most heavenly place, the most easy of cultivation that I ever heard of, being mellow in the highest degree." Edwin Newby wrote,

> Aye, when I look, and in my mind's eye see the uncounted millions of bright shining dollars embowelled in the earth, ready to be brought to light by the powerful judgment of the sturdy Northern Farmer, or the brawney emigrant, it makes my head reel with the thought. The wealth and health they could obtain and keep, is beyond calculation; for health they could keep, if they have it, and if they have it not, they could obtain it here. And as for wealth, if it could not be obtained from the virgin soil of Wall'd'n Ridge, I cannot name the place it could be got by farming, to sum up the whole, it is an earthly paradise.[8]

The results of Haight's selling campaign are unknown. However, one gentleman "from the north" did acquire some four hundred acres from William and Washington Nixon in 1852. Hoping that the chalybeate waters of a large spring would prove beneficial to his ailing son, E. H. Mabbit bought the property and built a two-story log house on the site commonly called Three Oaks. Although Mabbit lived there but a few years, he left his name permanently with the spring and the area.[9]

The W&A railroad also spurred work on the Anderson Pike being built by Colonel Josiah McNair Anderson and George Williams under the authority of the state in 1839. Anderson, a prosperous Sequatchie Valley farmer and congressman, and Williams, a Hamilton County resident, finally completed their work in 1852. The Anderson Pike connected with a forerunner of the "W" road up the east side of the mountain which was partly corduroyed to give draft animals better footing. The pike gave the people of the Sequatchie Valley access to the Chattanooga railhead, and droves of cattle, hogs, sheep, and turkeys crossed the mountain on their way to market on their own power. Future mountain settlements centered on the Anderson Pike or on roads radiating from it.[10]

The "hygenic resources" and matchless panoramic scenery made Lookout Mountain another section of the county ready for development. James Whiteside had acquired a large portion of the mountaintop, and around Holman's Spring a small summer cabin settlement had sprung up. The old Indian trail up the mountain gradually was improved enough for wheeled traffic so that the McCamy, Rogers, Chandler, Glass, Morrow, and Whiteside families could seek summer comfort away from the valley, and a few scattered families even tried year-round residency.

One summer Whiteside's wife, Leonora Straw Whiteside, discovered a spring at the base of the palisades. Named Leonora Spring, it challenged her dynamic husband into developing an ingenious way to get cool, fresh water to the top of the mountain. New cabins were built and the nucleus of Summertown was started (now the 300 block of East Brow Road).[11]

Following the completion of the W&A, some of Whiteside's associates on 11 February 1852 got a charter to construct a road up the mountain with toll privileges. The old road was reconstructed and carriage service with four or six horses was furnished by a local livery stable. Tolls amounted to fifty cents per hack or twenty-five cents per horseman.

With rail and river passenger arrivals in Chattanooga increasing, Whiteside along with Benjamin Chandler, J. J. Griffin, and Joseph McCullough incorporated the Lookout Mountain Hotel. It became a real challenge to get building materials up the mountain to the site and for Joseph Ruohs, local furniture builder, to deliver all the hostelry's furnishings. A large, frame central building facing east over the valley, however, soon was surrounded by some twenty-five cottages.

During the summer of 1856 the Lookout Mountain Hotel opened with guests arriving from distant southern areas; arrangements were also possible for "Music and Dancing Parties" and conventions. An especially interesting early gathering over 4 July 1857 included bishops of the Protestant Episcopal Church from the Southern dioceses. They gathered to discuss the creation of a denominational university in the South and to select a proper location for the school. Chattanoogans were interested in having the school; the city officials entertained delegates and arranged for a local band to go to the mountaintop to entertain the guests. They received encouragement from Bishop Leonidas Polk of Louisiana, who pointed out the accessibility of Chattanooga, its central location, its mountain air, pure water, and immunity from epidemics.

No decision was made at that time and the meeting adjourned until November when delegates gathered at Montgomery, Alabama. Whiteside, Robert Cravens, and James A. Corry attended as Chattanooga's delegates with authorization to make an offer of $50,000 on behalf of the town to the university provided the school was located on nearby Lookout Mountain. However, a gift of a large tract of land at Sewanee decided the question of the location of the University of the South.

Lookout Mountain lost the college but tourism had come to Hamilton County. By 1860 a state gazetteer called Lookout Mountain a "noted summer resort" and added, "At its base is the entrance to a celebrated cave, which has been partially explored some seven or eight miles, but its dimensions have not been fully ascertained."[12]

With all the going and coming it became obvious that the small hotels and boarding houses in Chattanooga were not adequate to care for the traveling public. Although passengers continued to arrive by steamboat, the center of activity in the town had suddenly moved to the area around Ninth Street where the trains arrived. Thomas Crutchfield, Sr., builder and real estate developer, recognized the opportunity to operate a profitable hotel here. Although the exact time that he constructed the large three-story brick inn with its very ample adornment of chimneys is not known, it immediately became the social, economic, and political center of town.

The surroundings at the corner of Ninth and Chestnut streets and Railroad Avenue left much to be desired, for people had to walk from the trains to the hotel on planks raised above encircling swampy waters.

Although owned by the Crutchfields, the hotel at first was managed by others including J. J. Griffin, one-time associate of Whiteside in the Lookout Mountain Hotel. Later, sometime after the death of the senior Crutchfield, his son Tom, Jr., took over the business, giving the historic name Crutchfield House to the place formerly called "the hotel" or the "Griffin House."

Crutchfield, ably assisted by his wife, ran the hotel by choice and not necessity and developed a fine reputation as a host. His popularity and generosity led to his election as mayor. The Crutchfield House, advertised as the "Regular House for passengers on trains to take meals," contained a dry goods store and quarters for a fellow who ran a quaint place—a barber shop and oyster saloon.

The tempo of life around the hotel was measured by D. H. Strothers, a writer for *Harper's Monthly Magazine,* who visited in 1857. The journalist was obliged to walk from the river wharf to the Crutchfield House, thereby giving him a good chance to see "some pretty and substantial buildings dotted about on . . . straggling and irregular streets, which are often interrupted by stumpy fields, ponds, and patches of forest timber."

"Porte Crayon," as Strothers called himself, appreciated the natural beauty of the area but appeared much more interested in the spirit of enterprise he found at the Crutchfield House. He wrote that it

> swarmed with people arriving and departing, with the trains, east, west, north, and south . . . hurrying to and fro with eager and excited looks, as if lives, fortunes, and sacred honor hung upon the events of the next hour. All the corners and byplaces were filled with groups in earnest conversation, some were handling bundles of papers, others examining maps. Rolls of banknotes were exhibited, and net purses with red gold gleaming through their silken meshes. In the confusion of tongues the ear could catch words, Lots—Stocks—Quarter-section—Depot—Dividends—Township—Railroads—Terminus—Ten Thousands—Hundred thousands—Million. [13]

The little community showed obvious pride when it received word that the state of Tennessee on 5 November 1851 had enacted legislation "to Incorporate the City of Chattanooga . . ." Despite its many evident limitations, it was officially no longer just a town. A somewhat different form of government was prescribed: the area would be divided into at least four wards, each to be represented by two aldermen elected by the qualified voters of the ward for one-year terms. The mayor would be elected by a city-wide vote. A recorder court was established to have jurisdiction in cases of violation of city ordinances "and with concurrent jurisdiction with justices of the peace in all cases of violation of the criminal laws of the state."

In the December election Dr. Milo Smith again received the most votes for mayor of the "city." The voters chose the following aldermen: Larkin Hair, Marcellus B. Parham, John P. Long, J. J. Bryan, Robert Cravens, William Crutchfield, John A. Hooke, and David C. McMillin.

Two amendments to the charter made certain changes within the next few years. In the legislative year 1853–54 the corporate limits were extended by a half mile on the east and on the south (to Montgomery or present Main Street on the south and East End or present Central Avenue on the east). The legislature proceeded with caution regarding this annexation and agreed that residents of the area should not be liable for city taxes as long as their property remained in woodland or was used for farming.

The second amendment gave the city fathers the power "to erect a lock-up house or calaboose for the safekeeping of prisoners." This amendment continued,

> and where any person is convicted of a violation . . . and fails or refuses to pay, or secure to be paid, the fine and costs accruing thereon, the Mayor and Aldermen may provide, by ordinance for their confinement in such lock-up house, until the fine and costs are paid, or until they are regularly discharged by an oath of insolvency . . . or any person or persons so convicted . . . may be compelled to work upon the streets of the city of Chattanooga, or do any other work within said city . . . at the rate of not less than one dollar per day, until the fine and costs are paid.

In an effort to provide more effective county government, the legislature in 1856 provided for a judge for Hamilton County. John Fletcher White received this appointment, but for some unexplained reason "the county judge" act was repealed within two years and not reenacted until 1867. However, other changes did improve the legal and business climate in Chattanooga. In 1858 the legislature established a law court in the city to serve the local civil districts, thus eliminating the need for trips to Harrison. This action was soon followed by a law authorizing the holding of chancery courts in Chattanooga for the same districts. The city provided quarters for the courts and the clerk of each court kept a deputy in town to take care of business. Probate and other county court business such as the registration of deeds and other papers had to be done at the county seat.[14]

The ordinances adopted by the new city government reflect the inconsistencies and flux of the era. They blend a recognition of the industrial revolution with the age of slavery; the conscience of mid-Victorian virtue with the realism of frontier living. They illustrate the tone of an "urban hamlet" with its boisterous tendencies, its unique problems, and its moralistic facade. Extracts from the records between 1852 and 1858 tell much of the history of the county.

Recognizing the benefit of aiding progressive business, the mayor and board of aldermen ordained that "any mill or manufacturing company propelled by steam . . . shall be exempt from a corporation tax for the term of five years from the date of going into operation."

Ordinances governed conduct as well as "rude and indecent or profane discourse," and it was a misdemeanor for any person to appear in public naked or "in a dress not belonging to his or her sex, or in an indecent or lewd dress."

On 7 January 1852 the city government decreed that

> Whoever shall within this city on Sunday be engaged in any game or games whatever shall be deemed guilty of a misdemeanor. Whoever shall in this city in any street or public place or so near as to be seen by passersby, be engaged in any game of cards, whether anything is bet or not, shall be deemed guilty of a misdemeanor, and upon conviction thereof shall be fined not less than two or more than ten dollars.

A committee at this time served to contract for and supervise the building of a calaboose not to cost in excess of $200. Until this was available, the cellar of a designated building was to be used. In 1858 the plan for constructing this jail was spelled out in detail:

> First, a pen is built of hewn timber ten inches square, fitting close and notched in at the corners, to be twelve feet square and twelve feet high, with a floor of similar timbers fitting closely at the floor.
> Second, outside of the pen upright timbers of the same thickness are to surround the entire pen, extending twenty-two feet high. This pen is to be surrounded by a brick wall or house, of sufficient width to include it, and of the length of thirty feet, and two stories, and twenty-two feet high above the ground. With one wall enclosing the pen or dungeon at the same heighth—the whole to be covered with strong shingle roof, heavy rafters and joists. The jail room to be ventilated by two iron-barred windows, 12 inches by 30 inches, with one heavy iron door. . . . The room immediately over the dungeon is to be finished with . . . two iron bar windows, 2 feet by 3, with heavy iron grate door. . . . End of house intended for jailer is to be finished with two windows, good strong floors above and below, with one chimney with two fireplaces, one above and one below.

The night watch was required to cry the hour from 10 P.M. until daylight. Sunday observance was very strict: loading or unloading steamboats, keelboats, or other river craft was forbidden as well as the loading or unloading of wagons, carts, and drays. No places of business were to be kept open on Sunday except the apothecary shops; they could sell medicine "in case of absolute sickness."

Another law stated that any person who "by negligence or careless-ness" allowed a horse or mule to set foot on the sidewalks or pavement would be fined, and another ruled that no one could drive a horse or vehicle over the bridge on Chestnut Street near Water Street faster than at a walk. The penalty for these offenses was a one-dollar fine; if a slave were found guilty, five lashes constituted the punishment. In 1857 the city excluded hogs from running at large and provided for a pound, fees, and the sale of unclaimed pigs. This law, however, was repealed by unanimous vote the next year.

One of the matters requiring early attention related to slaves, free blacks, and mulattoes. All free persons of color were required to register with the city recorder within three months. All newcomers had one month to produce similar proof. Anyone without proper evidence of freedom was deemed a slave. The ordinance also stated "That if any free person of color or mulatto shall entertain or permit any slave to visit or remain in his or her home during the Sabbath day, or between sunset and sunrise, without permission from the employer or owner of said slave, he shall for such and every offense forfeit and pay the sum of five dollars." Gatherings of slaves within the city for dancing or any purpose except public worship were carefully proscribed and religious worship was subjected to council regulations. The "city watch and patrol" were required to disperse all gatherings of slaves and were authorized to inflict punishment of from five to ten lashes for any violation.

The digging of wells, street improvement, fire protection, finances, a city cemetery, and the burial of strangers received repeated attention. And, of course, there were ordinances regarding market regulations and taxes. In relation to the former, the city approved on 6 October 1853 an ordinance stating that

It shall be the duty of all butchers to exhibit the ears of such animals as they offer for sale to the clerk of the market and to give a description of the marks, brands, and color of animals so killed. No store, grocery store, provision store or any other place kept for the purchase and sale of any articles shall be allowed to sell any fresh beef in quantities less than a quarter; any fresh mutton, lamb, kid, goat, veal, or pork in less quantities than a whole carcass.

To support the various responsibilities of government the town fathers imposed a property tax on "town lots, slaves, jewelry, pianos-forte, pleasure carriages, gold and silver plate and watches of individuals or incorporated companies" chartered by Tennessee. Specifically exempt were school, church, and government property, slaves under twelve and over fifty years of age, pianos-forte used in schools, "all silver tea and table spoons," and stock exempt by the state.

Business also had to pay its share. Privilege taxes were levied on the business of slave traders in the amount of $500; amusement, circus, etc., $100; spirituous liquors, $25; ten-pin alley, $10; Jenny Lind table, $50; taverns, $10; and theaters, $10 per night. A head tax of $3 was levied on free females of color and $5 on free males of color. [15]

Neither the law nor the legal authorities had much success in giving a moral tone to the community. When a temperance wave gained ground for a few years, a deadly alcoholic compound called Pike's Magnolia was widely used and reports claim that drunkenness increased both in amount and in virulent form. Many openly rejoiced when the saloons reopened, although it was estimated that there was one such store for every thirty-four white males. Then there was the case of the bold city marshal who tried to arrest "a wagon-load of fellows" outside the city limits. The marshal announced his purpose; the gang in turn "apprehended" him and in mock baptismal ceremony tossed him into the middle of a big pond. The lawman "just waddled ashore, ejecting mud and water from his mouth as he went, scraped as much mud from his clothing as he could in haste, went to town and resigned his office as marshal." [16]

The preachers were more successful, so much so that they, in effect, turned a Tuesday into Sunday in 1857. The town had three clergymen at the time who planned a union program of evening revival services. They spent a week in each of the churches and as the Reverend David Sullins expressed it, "The Lord shook the town, and sinners cried for mercy and found it." At the end of three weeks they started a second round. The old songs were repeated again and again and the preacher proudly announced that "the revival had the right of way everywhere." Only the appearance of some ladies of questionable character disturbed the meetings.

On the fourth Monday evening a request was made that every business be closed the next day and that a day-long worship service take place. All agreed; establishments closed as on Sunday. But no one told Uncle Antipas Moore, who lived out Missionary Ridge way. Tuesday happened to be his regular day to bring beef to town. This day he found no one on the streets. Finally he learned what was going on and started home in a bad mood; his meat would not keep. When asked what had happened, the salty Antipas snorted, "That town has gone crazy; there is not a house open; nobody will talk to you about business; it's just like Sunday clean down to the river. . . . Just as well take your taters back; you can't sell anything today."[17]

While Chattanoogans labored with their conscience, workers struggled to smooth the way for more railroad tracks leading into the area. When the W&A got its charter, Nashville interests discussed the possibility of building from Middle Tennessee to meet the Georgia road. But plans remained dormant until 1845 when a Nashville campaign for internal improvements attracted much publicity. It focused attention on the importance of southern markets and especially on the potential profits awaiting the exploitation of coal fields along the road. James A. Whiteside spoke convincingly for the idea and introduced legislation to organize a company.

On 11 December 1845, the state chartered the Nashville and Chattanooga (N&C) Railroad. But financial problems delayed construction until March 1848. Vernon K. Stevenson, for whom the town in northern Alabama was named, became president and engineer. J. Edgar Thomson, famed as an experienced railroad man, selected the right-of-way. The route swung southward from Nashville into northern Alabama, crossing the Tennessee River at Bridgeport. From there it ran through Hog Jaw Valley to Shellmound and on into the Running Water Valley. It crossed and recrossed the Georgia-Tennessee boundary in avoiding Raccoon Mountain, entering Hamilton County in the sparsely populated southwestern corner. After running through Lookout Valley, the route swung around the northern end of Lookout Mountain into Chattanooga.

Construction problems became as thorny as the financial ones: the tunnel at Cowan, landslides all along the way, and a major bridge over the Tennessee River. Slaves, working for stockholders to pay for their shares, and Irish labor got the work done from Nashville to Bridgeport by May 1853 while Robert M. Hooke supervised construction on the section from Shellmound to Chattanooga. From Bridgeport, steamers carried freight and passengers until the entire route of 151 miles was opened in February 1854. Locomotives, carrying the proud emblem of the N&C, ran schedules of two trains a day each way over the spectacular road. Local interests soon began coal mining operations in the Aetna Mountain sector.

A second line to tie in with the Georgia railroad at Chattanooga carried the name Memphis and Charleston (M&C) Railroad. It developed as an outgrowth of various earlier efforts to find a way around Muscle Shoals and to connect the West with the East. Tennessee chartered the company in 1846; wrangling over the route held up organization of the company and actual work did not begin until 1852. Then under the presidency of former Governor "Lean Jimmy" Jones the company made steady progress. Since the Nashville and Chattanooga occupied the only good entrance into Chattanooga, an agreement was made with that company to use the same track from Stevenson, Alabama, into the Hamilton County town. Ceremonies marked the driving of the last spike on 28 March 1857.

This road with its misleading name (operating between Memphis and Chattanooga, it included the name Charleston since that port city could be reached by connecting lines) did not produce its expected results. This was especially true regarding the shipment of Alabama cotton, which soon began moving westward to Memphis for transfer by cheaper Mississippi River steamboat transport rather than to Charleston. As a consequence, the piles of cotton bales once visible along the streets of Chattanooga disappeared.

From a different direction—the valley of East Tennessee—Chattanooga got another railroad. This section, remote from good markets, tried desperately to enter the railroad age as early as 1836 with the Hiwassee Railroad project. A decade or more passed; much money was spent before a general reorganization of the company occurred in 1847. The project acquired a new name, the East Tennessee and Georgia Railroad (ET&Ga.), and authority to build from Knoxville to Dalton, Georgia, where it could connect with the W&A. By 1855 this new line began operation and soon a second northbound road, the East Tennessee and Virginia, made possible through connections with eastern cities.

But the passengers and freight carried by the ET&Ga., if destined for western points, had to go south to Dalton and then back north to Chattanooga. The desirability of a shortcut from Cleveland in Bradley County across Hamilton County appeared obvious to all by 1850 when a charter authorized the Chattanooga, Harrison, and Cleveland Railroad Company. The only positive result was another organization called the Chattanooga, Harrison, Georgetown, and Charleston Railroad. This company with the long name was short-lived and the ET&Ga. obtained the right to build a link to the southwest from Cleveland. The construction work, complicated and impeded by the many ridges which stood in the way, commenced in 1856. A tunnel through Missionary Ridge in 1858 admitted the thirty-mile-long road into the bowl where Chattanooga was gathering railroads.

This link, entering Hamilton County from the east, swings around the base of Grindstone Mountain through Dead Man's Gap and by the village of Ooltewah. The next station, Tynerville (later shortened to Tyner), honored Captain J. S. Tyner, who served as chief engineer of the railroad when this section was built and who had taken up residence in the area.

A fifth project, reaching into the southwest, had the support of Alabama and Mississippi. In 1853 a line from Meridian, Mississippi, to Chattanooga was chartered to build across Alabama under the name Northeast and Southwest Alabama Railroad Company. Across the southern reaches of Hamilton County and Dade County, Georgia, the route was planned as the Wills Valley Railroad Company. James A. Whiteside gave the project his wholehearted support, calling a meeting of Chattanoogans to promote the idea. While the town had not given direct aid to any other line, city authorities voted a subscription of $100,000 provided $500,000 could be secured by the sale of other bonds. They got their charter on 28 February 1854, and Whiteside's son-in-law, A. M. Johnson, who had come to the area in 1851, received an appointment to superintend construction. In 1860 about fourteen miles of track were completed from Wauhatchie to Trenton, Georgia. At Wauhatchie, a station on the N&C named for an Indian chieftain of the Lower Towns, a junction was made with the N&C and the latter's tracks were used into Chattanooga.

In town a freight and passenger depot was built by the W&A at Ninth and Market streets in 1852 but very soon increased facilities were needed. In 1856 an agreement between the W&A and the N&C provided for the erection of a joint terminal on Ninth Street west of the original depot. The M&C and the ET&Ga. later became parties to the arrangement, and in 1859 a terminal station opened for business built for "a little less than $38,000."

Chattanooga's rail connections reached south, north, east, and west, giving it a strategic position equaled by few internal towns in the country. Passengers, freight, and telegraphic service gave the area a prospect for a booming future. From a local standpoint, it is interesting to note that all the trackage in Hamilton County was south of the Tennessee River in the more recently settled section of the area.

This concentration of the most advanced transportation facilities of the day had a profound effect on the history of Hamilton County. In 1860 the census taker found a total of 13,258 persons living in the county, 2,545 of whom resided in Chattanooga. Of the aggregate, 11,647 are recorded as white, 192 free colored, and 1,419 slaves. In the two categories, free colored and slaves, more than half the total number were women.[18]

At this time, the county received postal service from, at least, the following offices: Birchwood, Chattanooga, Chickamauga, Dearing, Double Branch, Harrison, Julian's Gap, Limestone, Long Savannah, Merry Oak, Sale Creek, Snow Hill, Soddy, West View, and Zion Hill. There were twenty-two industries in the county employing 210 men and four women. The capital invested totaled $209,300 and the annual value of products $395,380.[19]

Most of the industries operated in Chattanooga. Charles E. Grenville, mayor in 1860, managed the Lookout Mills which could produce fifty barrels of flour per day. The steam flour mill of A. Bell could grind three times this amount and the distillery operated by the same firm had a daily capacity of sixty barrels of whiskey.

Bynum and Richardson ran a large tannery reputed to have been the largest steam tannery in the South. McCallie Marsh & Co., using logs floated down the river, were proprietors of a steam saw mill manufacturing sashes, doors, blinds, and furniture. Jacob Rouhs, the thirty-six-year-old Swiss who headed a local bank, advertised as a wholesale and retail dealer and manufacturer of furniture. Benjamin Chandler and Company did a $130,000 business in 1860 as a meat-packing concern employing fifty-four hands. S. R. McCamy packed pork and Rich and Hagan advertised as pork merchants.

The county received its news from three weekly newspapers. The *Chattanooga Advertiser*, edited by H. F. Cooper in 1860, offered a Southern point of view on the main issues of the day. The *Gazette*, originally started by pioneer printer F. A. Parham, supported the Union cause. The third paper, the *Southern Reflector*, was published by John W. Ford, aged sixty-one, and his sons.

The dominant industrial activity was the iron business—the smelting of ore and the manufacture of iron products. In 1860 the Chattanooga Foundry & Machine Works of Webster and Mann advertised as makers of stationary and portable engines and boilers. They employed forty-nine men and boasted an annual product valued at $75,000. Thomas Webster, the more effective partner, came to America from England at the age of nineteen. He became associated with railroading and locomotive power for the N&C Railroad. Webster moved to Chattanooga in 1857 and the census taker listed him as "master mechanic." Among the customers of Webster and Mann were the copper mines at Ducktown and the Vulcan Iron Works of S. B. Lowe, who was constructing a local rolling mill.

The leader in the iron industry was the East Tennessee Iron Manufacturing Company, incorporated on 27 November 1847. A far-seeing group of investors, including Farish Carter, Ker Boyce, and J. Edgar Thomson joined with six local men to launch the company. James A. Whiteside served as president and Robert Cravens, manager. Virginia-born Cravens was fifty-six years of age in 1860. As a young man he had lived with an uncle, George Gordon, with whom he engaged in the iron business in Greene County, Tennessee. Later he went into business for himself, moved to Roane County, and built Eagle Furnace. In 1849 he moved to Chattanooga and with his second wife acquired a large tract of land on the north end of Lookout Mountain where he built the "White House" in 1856.[20]

In 1852 the capitalization of the company was increased to $1 million; within a year operations started. The company advertised work in cast and wrought iron and brass, including railroad car wheels, freight cars, and saw and grist mill castings. But operations proceeded on a smaller scale than planned, and the persons from outside of Chattanooga associated with the concern either died or stepped aside, leaving the local men to carry on the business.

One portion of the enterprise, located at the south end of town, became the property of Webster and Mann. In addition, the company had a blast furnace near the river bluffs at the foot of Lookout Street. A company steamboat brought ore and coal from upriver; from the furnace a chute slid pig iron back to the river craft for delivery. Later the city allowed the company to build a railroad on Front Street from Railroad Avenue, which delivered coal by horse. In 1854, on completion of the N&C Railroad, some of the men in the iron business (Whiteside, Cravens, and Boyce) organized the Aetna Mining and Manufacturing Company to work the coal mines located along the railroad.

This interest in coal stimulated a progressive experiment at the bluff furnace. By 1860 the furnace had come under new management; James Henderson of New Jersey, who leased the operation, is listed in the census as proprietor. The thirty-year-old Henderson brought Giles Edwards, an experienced English iron man, to Chattanooga as manager. Needed additions and adjustments were made in the furnace to allow it to be fueled with coke. In May 1860 a trial blast produced about five hundred tons of pig iron. Again that November on presidential election day, Henderson lit the furnace for a second coke run. These experiments are believed to have been the first such operations in the South. Unfortunately, Henderson, a staunch Union man, soon found it prudent "to go North."[21]

Youth was the outstanding characteristic of Hamilton County's 1860 population. More than one-third of the people had not reached their sixteenth birthday. Only 727 individuals gave their age as being between forty-one and fifty years. The census taker listed only 16 persons over eighty years of age and only one of this group, Hardy Shadwick, had passed his ninetieth birthday.

More than one-half of the Hamiltonians were native Tennesseans. Although at least twenty-five states had sons or daughters here, neighboring southern states sent by far the largest number. Georgia had the most, followed by North Carolina, South Carolina, Virginia, Alabama, and Kentucky. Of those born in the northeastern part of the country, most lived in Chattanooga. New York counted 53 persons of whom 45 lived in town; Pennsylvania sent 47, of whom 36 lived in town; Maryland's figures were 25 and 22; Massachusetts, 19 and 14; and New Jersey, 18 and 14.

At least twelve foreign countries supplied settlers for Hamilton County. The Irish outnumbered all others with 119; Germany had 68 with Baden, Prussia, Holstein, Wartenberg, and Bavaria as identified homelands. Statistics on other birthplaces show England 40, Wales 7, Canada 5, Sweden 4, Switzerland 3, Scotland 2, Italy 2, France 2, Holland 1, Cuba 1, and 11 born in "Europe." Jobs in town attracted most of these people to Chattanooga, giving the small urban frontier quite a cosmopolitan flavor: 96 came from Ireland, 52 from Germany, 30 from England, and 10 from "Europe." Only 15 of those born outside the United States were over fifty years of age.

Few of the immigrants had much wealth and they naturally turned to such occupations with which they had some familiarity. The English came to work as mechanics and as artisans skilled in the iron industry. The Welsh were all miners. The Irish to a large extent found work on the railroads or as day laborers. There were German coopers, saddlers, shoemakers, gardeners, and teachers. A man from Canada served as telegrapher, a Swede taught music, a Swiss made furniture, and an Italian ran a confectionery.

In the county as a whole most families lived on the soil. Men listed their occupations as farmers or farm laborers and a considerable number of women were given as heads of families. The women, in many cases, are identified with "housewifery," but some are called farmers or farm laborers without any attempt to identify their legal status. Day laborers were numerous but usually they were younger men and not the heads of families. The railroads employed many but apparently were so new that jobs were not neatly classified; so one finds "railroaders," railroad "agents," "hands," "contractors," "conductors," "paymasters," "switch conductors," "Boss Yard Depot," and many more.

The law of supply and demand regulated the number of blacksmiths, millers, carpenters, tanners, coopers, wagon makers, merchants, barkeeps, cabinetmakers, hotel people, masons, wheelwrights, and bootmakers. And there were some rather unusual job classifications, listed in the census indiscriminately as ferryman, fisher, "steamboating," ditcher, grape culture, night watch, "diagerian [daguerrian] artist," speculator, "sex master," and bark grinder.

Many people must have spent the long evening hours figuring out eccentric names for their children, thereby causing spelling problems for the census taker. The enumerator in 1860 had to struggle with Hurah, Zenaby, Texious, Lutitia, Spell Monger, Parlor, Mourning, Bedvidora, Valumnia, Beneflied, Zeboder, Arrizana, Lodasky, Darthula, Virzah, Willimouth, Mahulda, Turissa, Perlimly, and Euphemisse.

Of the 192 free persons of color some seventy percent were recorded as mulattoes, six as Indians, and forty-five as blacks. The blacks earned their living as draymen, day laborers, blacksmiths, barbers, and shoemakers. All but four lived in town. The majority of the mulattoes, on the other hand, lived in the county. Most were day or farm laborers. In this group one family name, Goins, dominated the list.

The most remarkable of the free persons of color was William Lewis, blacksmith and wagon maker. Lewis came to the area before the Cherokee removal as a slave. He married an Indian and as a skilled artisan earned sufficient funds to buy his freedom and that of his family. Lewis, a man of "great force," earned the respect of the community and constantly improved his status. The census of 1850 noted that he possessed real estate valued at $1,500. A decade later when he was forty-five years of age, he is credited with real estate valued at $5,000 and personal property worth $2,000. The Lewises had eight children. In 1860 his oldest is listed as a blacksmith and his eldest daughter, Isabella, a "beautiful and accomplished" girl of seventeen, as a milliner.

By this date Isabella had attended the primary department of Oberlin College for one year. At a later date she returned to school and graduated from the college in 1865. A son, Hugh, who was thirteen in 1860, also was slated to go on to college, but he chose instead to enlist in the Union army.

According to the census records, Hamiltonians for the most part appear to have had few worldly possessions in 1860. Many apparently had no personal or real property and very few had accumulated a substantial amount of wealth. Only forty-three persons in the entire county had real estate in property and slaves valued at $15,000 or more. The largest fortune recorded was $100,000 in real estate. The ten persons owning real estate valued at $40,000 or more in increasing value were Mary A. McCallie, whose husband had recently died; Elisha Kirklen, farmer; George S. Gillespie, farmer; Philemon Bird, farmer; D. G. Cooke, farmer; William Clift, farmer and commander of the Seventh Regiment Tennessee Volunteer Militia; Samuel Williams, farmer and real estate promoter; Lewis Crutchfield, hotel man and landlord; Margaret Shepherd, listed as farmer; and Robert Cravens, ironmaster.

In the same census only thirty-two persons reported personal property valued at $15,000 or more. Twenty-one of this number had less than $25,000. Those reporting larger sums, in increasing amounts, were C. D. Luttrell, farmer; George Marsh, merchant; J. M. Dolls, farmer; H. W. Massengale, farmer; Robert Cravens; David N. Bell, farmer; George S. Gillespie; Philemon Bird; D. F. Cooke; Margaret Shepherd; and S. J. Boyce, farmer.

An asylum for the poor was operated at Harrison under Superintendent Daniel Temples apparently at public expense. The six persons living there were either paupers or insane.

The county in 1860 had a representative number of professional people although the census reveals nothing of their training or credentials. Eighteen men gave their profession as lawyer; thirteen of the group practiced out of Chattanooga. They were a surprisingly young group with only two over forty years of age. Well-known lawyers in the region were A. G. Welcker, David M. Key, F. M. Walker, John L. Hopkins, D. C. Trewhitt, and Rees B. Brabson, who had represented the area in Congress before his death in 1859.

Two men, John H. and M. L. Kennedy, served the county as druggists while T. P. Higby was the only dentist. A rather large number of doctors are recorded in the census, including eighteen-year-old

Elizabeth Kent, fifty-year-old J. A. Bury (of Swedish origin), and the senior of the group, fifty-five-year-old J. L. Yarnell. Only six practiced in Chattanooga; those most often mentioned were Dr. Milo Smith, Dr. Philander Sims, and Dr. W. E. Kennedy.

Education continued on a private, non-tax-supported basis in Tennessee in 1860. Although forty persons are listed as teachers in the census, not much can be clearly ascertained about their activities. Music teacher F. O. Winnesquist, a native of Sweden, was one of thirteen teachers living in Chattanooga at this time. For the most part, youth characterized this group with one listed as only sixteen years of age.

A Masonic Academy started in the town about 1840 on College Hill. In 1860 M. R. Warner was listed as principal of a Masonic Female Institute, which had opened four years earlier, and the Reverend J. N. Bradshaw, Presbyterian, presided as principal of the Select School. The Alpine Academy operated for a time on Walden Ridge under the aegis of Mr. and Mrs. William Mowbray, and in 1848 the Hamilton County Male Academy opened its doors at Harrison.

The legislature in 1857–58 provided a charter for a Sale Creek Academy under the direction of Lewis Patterson, J. P. Coulter, Thomas J. Coulter, A. A. Pearson, J. W. Grimsley, B. J. McDonald, and Nathan Shipley.[22]

Another interesting effort made in 1858 led to the development of the Fairmount Academy on Walden Ridge. It was built and supported by a small group which included John Fryar, Joseph Dobbs, James C. Connor, George Rogers, and John Beck. Its teacher, G. A. Gowen, received a cash monthly salary of ten dollars. Students gathered at the academy from both local areas and surrounding counties and a small year-round community grew up nearby.[23]

The experience of Professor H. W. Aldehoff, Prussian schoolmaster, possibly best illustrates the unsettled conditions in education. In 1847–48 the Tennessee legislature authorized the establishment of the Chattanooga Seminary with Aldehoff as president and resident civic leaders Robert M. Hooke, William A. Anderson, Allen Kennedy, Milo Smith, Thomas McCallie, James A. Whiteside, John P. Long, and John G. Glass as trustees. Aldehoff apparently moved from nearby Cleveland and opened the school in 1850. But he soon moved on, returning ten years later when Aldehoff's Institute for Boys opened on Lookout Mountain.[24]

Some other professional specialists offered their services. R. Hagan sold books at his shop as did occasional traveling bookmen. Dr. Thomas Jefferson Eaton, an itinerant physician, stopped in the area to practice his specialties: operations on harelip and clubfoot, the fitting of glass eyes, and the correction of crossed eyes. An artist, James Cameron, came to the county under the patronage of James A. Whiteside and settled for a time. A Scot who had studied art in Philadelphia and in Italy, Cameron filled local commissions and helped Whiteside with the planning of the Lookout Mountain Hotel. The hill west of Chattanooga on which Cameron built his house and studio became known as Cameron Hill. Cameron quit the area during the Civil War and later sold his property, leaving his name associated with a dominant landmark and some of his paintings as a reminder of his brief stay in Hamilton County.

There were at least twenty clergymen in the county in 1860 representing the Cumberland Presbyterian, Baptist, Methodist, Protestant Episcopal, New Light Presbyterian, and Catholic churches. Eight of this number appear to have lived in Chattanooga, but as in the county as a whole, early church records are sparse and gaps are numerous. Matthew Hillsman, a Baptist and one of Ross's Landing's pioneer settlers, was the first churchman to make his home there. However, he "was not there for ministerial, but for secular pursuits." Hillsman did conduct religious services at the little log community building regardless of denomination and performed wedding and funeral services.

The Baptists in Chattanooga organized in 1852 and dedicated their chapel the next year. The Cumberland Presbyterian Church had been one of the most forceful in early Hamilton County and by 1860 had churches at Chickamauga, Ooltewah, West View, Harrison, Pleasant Forest, and Chattanooga. The latter congregation was not effectively organized until 1855. In a few years this group had its own church building and counted some sixty members.

The Presbyterian Church of Chattanooga got started on 21 June 1840, when twenty-eight members organized a congregation. Two of their group had been associated with the Brainerd Mission. Meetings were held in the schoolhouse until 1845 when a church building was finished at East Third and Walnut streets. This was the first building used exclusively for religious purposes in the city. By 1854 the congregation had moved to a large new church at East Seventh and Market streets. In 1862 the Reverend Thomas Hooke McCallie became the seventh pastor of the church.[25]

This young minister had returned to Chattanooga in 1859 at the time of his father's death. A recent graduate of the Union Theological Seminary in New York City, in 1861 he received an appointment to succeed the Reverend J. N. Bradshaw as minister of the First Presbyterian Church. He assumed the pastorate on 1 January 1862 and on the same day married Ellen D. Jarnagin, daughter of United States Senator Spencer Jarnagin. McCallie, at the time, was twenty-four years of age.

The Methodists met in Chattanooga in the late 1830s as the first organized religious group in town. For some time they gathered in the small log school building used for community purposes. Not until April 1847 did they receive, as did the Baptists, Cumberland Presbyterians, and Presbyterians, a building site from the town commissioners. They built their church at the corner of Lookout and Fifth streets. Some $3,500 was raised and a frame building thirty-two by fifty-two feet was constructed. It boasted a cupola which gave it the nickname, "Pepper Box Church."[26]

The first Catholic service in Hamilton County was led by the indefatigable Reverend John Mary Jacquet in 1847. Father Jacquet's French name presented difficulties for his parishioners, who simply called him "Jacket." The priest who had traversed East Tennessee many times on horseback had the local assistance of Joseph Rouhs and Michael Harrington. In the latter's home, the Mass was occasionally celebrated. Later the Reverend Henry V. Brown, the first resident priest, built a tiny fifteen-by-thirty-foot frame building on Pine Street to serve as a church. The energetic Brown, who was something of an artist, orator, and architect, found that the arrival of many Irish railroad workers called for a larger sanctuary. He purchased a sizable tract of desirable land and sold off lots to parishioners so that they could be close to school and church along Eighth Street. The neighboring heights acquired the name "Irish hill." A church consisting of a stone basement used as a school and a wooden upper story where church was held was completed in 1857. A devout member and stone cutter, Daniel Hogan, was not satisfied, however, and gave land and wealth for a new imposing structure which was started at the time the war broke out.[27]

In 1852 another small group of worshippers gathered on the second floor of a warehouse at Fourth and Market streets under the leadership of Bishop James Hervey Otey, Bishop of Tennessee. This Episcopal service launched an organization leading to the formal beginning of St. Paul's Parish on 17 January 1853 under the Reverend John Sandels,

who had been sent by the church as a missionary. About ten families
with but seven communicants made up the group which met at the
home of James A. Whiteside. A small frame building, equipped with
a thirty-five-dollar melodeon, erected on land and with funds largely
supplied by Whiteside, served as the first church. Within a year the
parish was admitted into the diocese.

Growth was slow. Failure to win the location of the University of
the South came as a big disappointment, but plans for a large new
church went forward. Differences developed; the bishop felt that the
decision to build was ill-advised. The rector resigned and discord prevailed. In 1860 a new rector finally arrived after a time when apparently
no services were held. The parish debt stood at $2,500; the new church
was unfinished and advertised as being for sale. The new minister, the
Reverend Thomas B. Lawson, aggressively took hold of the situation.
Funds were raised and the building apparently was finished and consecrated in 1861.[28]

During the 1850s Chattanooga began to dominate the story of Hamilton County. Although architecturally crude and raw with streets variously described as "hogholes" or "frog-ponds," the small community
with its many railroads viewed the future with high hopes. The het-
erogeneous population, the business and tourism contacts with distant
places, and the instant telegraphic communication with the outside
world offered advantages which could not be denied. Some county
residents living close to the iron bonds of the railroads also enjoyed
the new modernity, but many outlying sections remained isolated and
there the life-style changed very slowly. Some of the first leaders were
gone—the Williams brothers, Sam Igou, Lewis Shepherd, James
Whiteside, Rees Brabson, and others—but the future beckoned.

NOTES

1. Lewis Shepherd, "Hamilton County Towns, Villages and Localities and
Queer Facts About Origin of Their Names," *Chattanooga Times*, 4 June 1916;
Robert Sparks Walker, *As the Indians Left It: The Story of the Elise Chapin
Wild Life Sanctuary and the Chattanooga Audubon Society* (Chattanooga:
Hudson Printing, 1955), p. 36; John L. Mitchell, *Tennessee State Gazetteer
and Business Directory for 1860–61, p. 32*.

2. *Southern Recorder*, 27 August 1850; *Chattanooga Times*, 3 November
1894.

3. J. W. Livingood, "Chattanooga: A Rail Junction of the Old South," *Tennessee Historical Quarterly* 6 (September 1947):230-250.

4. Ibid.

5. Harry W. Wiltse, "History of Chattanooga," 2 vols. (Typescript, Chattanooga-Hamilton County Bicentennial Library), 1:65.

6. Gilbert E. Govan and James W. Livingood, *The Chattanooga Country*, 3rd ed. (Knoxville: University of Tennessee Press, 1977), pp. 147–148; T. J. Campbell, *The Upper Tennessee* . . . (Chattanooga: author, 1932), pp. 32–33; Wiltse, "Chattanooga," 1:64. Wiltse lists the following local leaders instrumental in getting the W&A: J. A. Whiteside, B. Rush Montgomery, Sam Martin, Spencer Rogers, Ben Chandler, Tom Crutchfield, Sr., R. M. Hooke, Thomas McCallie, Sr., Sam Williams, Silas Williams, Sam McKamy, Matt Rawlings, Monroe Rawlings, and J. P. Long.

7. *A History of Banking in Chattanooga* (Chattanooga: Hamilton National Bank, 1925), p. 7.

8. Nicholas Haight, *Cherokee Lands on Waldens' Ridge, East Tennessee* 2nd ed. (New York: Casper C. Childs, 1848).

9. Bates, "Waldens Ridge," *Hamilton County Herald*, 22 Feb. 1974.

10. Ibid.; Cartter Patten, *Signal Mountain and Walden's Ridge* (n.p.: author; 1962), p. 19; Leonard Raulston and James W. Livingood, *Sequatchie: A Story of the Southern Cumberlands* (Knoxville: University of Tennessee Press, 1974), p. 142.

11. James A. Whiteside was born in 1803 in Kentucky. He served, while living at Pikeville, Tennessee, in the state legislature. In 1829 he married Mary Massengale, with whom he had five children. In 1843 his first wife died; later he and his second wife Harriet Leonora Straw had nine children. Whiteside again served in the state legislature in 1845–47 and was a candidate for the United States Senate. He was a leader in the organization of St. Paul's Episcopal Parish. The Whitesides lived in a large brick house on Poplar Street near the foot of Cameron Hill but began spending the summers on Lookout Mountain in the 1840s. Whiteside's interest in railroads led to his appointment as vice-president of the Nashville and Chattanooga Railroad and, while retaining his property interests here, he moved to Nashville in 1857. His interests lay with the South in the war time era; on 12 November 1861, he died of pneumonia on a trip home to Chattanooga.

12. Govan and Livingood, *Chattanooga Country*, pp. 155–156; Robert S. Walker, *Lookout: The Story of a Mountain* (Kingsport, Tenn.: Southern Publishers, 1941), pp. 211–215; John Wilson, *Lookout: The Story of an Amazing Mountain* (Chattanooga: Chattanooga News-Free Press, 1977), pp. 32–39; Mitchell, *Gazetteer*, p. 26.

13. D. H. Strothers, "A Winter in the South," *Harpers Monthly Magazine* 17 (August 1858): 297-300.

14. State of Tennessee, *Acts of the State of Tennessee Passed at the First*

Session of the Thirty-First General Assembly for the Years 1855–56 (Nashville: G.C. Torbett, 1856) pp. 230, 511–514.

15. Wiltse, "Chattanooga," 2:11 ff.; *Chattanooga News*, 9 April 1930. These sources quote directly from the 1852–1858 minute book of the city government, a record which is no longer available.

16. Wiltse, "Chattanooga," 1:57; 2:20–21; Edwin S. Lindsey, *Centennial History of St. Paul's Episcopal Church, Chattanooga, Tennessee, 1853–1953* (Chattanooga: Vestry of St. Paul's Parish, 1953), p. 4.

17. Mary Thomas Peacock, *The Circuit Rider and Those Who Followed* (Chattanooga: Hudson Printing, 1957), pp. 71–82.

18. U. S., Bureau of Census, *Eighth Census, 1860 Population Schedules Work Sheets* (Microfilm, Chattanooga-Hamilton County Bicentennial Library).

19. The list of post offices is compiled from the census worksheets for 1860 and Mitchell, *Gazetteer; Eighth Census, 1860, Manufactures*, p. 565.

20. Ruth H. McConathy, *The House of Cravens* (Charlottesville, Virginia: Michie, 1972), pp. 52-53.

21. Govan and Livingood, *Chattanooga Country*, pp. 164-169.

22. William C. McIntyre and Thomas W. Graham, comp., *Private Acts of Hamilton County, Tennessee*, 2 vols. (Nashville: County Technical Assistance Service, University of Tennessee Institute for Public Service, 1974), 1:230.

23. Patten, *Signal Mountain*, p. 20.

24. McIntyre and Graham, *Private Acts*, 1:230.

25. Zella Armstrong, *History of Hamilton County and Chattanooga, Tennessee*, 2 vols. (Chattanooga: Lookout Publishing, 1931), 1:245–246.

26. Peacock, *Circuit Rider*, pp. 61–62, 69.

27. George J. Flanigan, *The Centenary of St. Peter and St. Paul's Parish, Chattanooga, Tennessee: The Story of the First Hundred Years of the Catholic Church in Hamilton County* (Chattanooga: St. Peter and St. Paul's Parish, 1952), pp. 10–18. Hogan owned the Stone Fort and lived as a hermit nearby.

28. Lindsey, *St. Paul's*, pp. 6–10.

9

Divided Loyalties

ON 24 June 1861, Tennessee's Governor Isham Green Harris issued an official proclamation unlike any document ever to carry the great seal of the state: "Now, therefore, I, Isham G. Harris, Governor of the State of Tennessee, do make it known and declare all connection by the State of Tennessee with the Federal Union dissolved, and that Tennessee is a free, independent government, free from all obligation to or connection with the Federal Government of the United States of America."[1]

Actually the words of the zealous governor did not represent a decision but a legal formality. All of the other ten states that had broken ties with the Union had been scrupulously legal in doing so and there was no reason why the Volunteer State should not make an official proclamation of her decision, which was but the ratification of an accomplished fact. Earlier, Tennessee had provided for a military league with the Confederacy, authorized the sale of state bonds amounting to $5 million to support a military force, and energetically made preparations for war. The legislature had provided that no suits for the benefit of any citizen of any states "of the late United States of America" except Kentucky, Missouri, and Maryland (slave states) "now adhering to the government of which A. Lincoln claims to be president" should

147

be maintained in the courts of Tennessee. Payment of debts, bank dividends, and interest on state bonds to United States citizens in nonslaveholding states was suspended. Companies of volunteers were raised and camps were provided in the state, while some military units had already started for the Virginia front.

The tide of events which carried Tennessee to this crisis was channeled and directed largely by the governor. One extreme view has it that "Tennessee never seceded from the Union, but Isham G. Harris seceded and took Tennessee along with him." Others disagree and hold that secession "was but a logical reflection of the sharp and swift change in the prevailing public sentiment."

At the center of the conflict was the issue of slavery, an institution older than the state itself. While the Tennessee country was part of North Carolina, first settlers brought slaves across the mountains as well as attitudes on the legal status and social position of the chattels. The practice spread, and some Cherokees who occupied the area of later Hamilton County became owners of black slaves. At the time the county came into being, the 39 slaves made up about 5 percent of the population. With each census the number increased slowly, from 115 in 1830 to 584 in 1840. In 1850 the enumeration shows 672 slaves and in 1860 it reveals the largest increase, with slaves totaling 1,419, of whom almost one-third lived in Chattanooga.

Naturally, trading in slaves was not unusual here; some of the county's earliest records show such transactions. In 1849 F. A. Parham offered some land for sale, stating that he would take "cash or Negroes." At times the constable announced the auctioning of blacks. Such informal transactions appear to have been the general method of sale; only one firm, A. H. Johnston & Company, with offices opposite the Western & Atlantic depot on Market Street, Chattanooga, is on record as being a regular slave trader.[2]

In 1860 the proportion of slaves to whites in the town was about one to six and in Hamilton County one slave to nine whites. In East Tennessee the relationship stood at one to twelve, in Middle Tennessee one to three, and in West Tennessee three slaves to five whites. The general average for the South as a whole was one to two.

As a part of East Tennessee, Hamilton County little resembled the economy of the plantation South. Its small farms with their diversified crops operated on little capital. Where slaves were owned, they were few in number and worked in close, personal relationship with their masters. But Southern attitudes on the subject were complex and to a degree contrasting, for Hamiltonians had less in common with wealthy planters than with the freedom-loving mountain people whose views on the slave issue were anti-Negro rather than anti-slavery. Most people of the county hoped to steer a steady course between extremes, held slavery to be the only feasible solution to the race question, and above all, believed in the Union. They honored the tradition of the common man, endorsed the principle of majority rule, and paid homage to the heritage of Jefferson and Jackson.

The urban frontier found in Chattanooga included many whose backgrounds lay in East Tennessee, but the community felt the influence of other schools of thought. Its commission merchants dealt with planters of the cotton South and business houses of the port cities. Economic ties produced sympathetic understanding of secessionist ideas if not a vigorous endorsement of them. When in December 1859, for example, Charleston firms advertised in the local press, calling on all Southerners to sever commercial ties with the northern wholesale houses that helped finance the circulation of Hinton Helper's book, *The Impending Crisis*, then being used as anti-Southern propaganda, local businessmen understood.[3]

But there was no bitter political or social battle on the local scene. When the Methodist Church split in 1844 over slavery, all Hamilton County churches of that denomination silently went along with the establishment of the Southern church. Politically the county had always had a two-party system. In all presidential elections after the retirement of Andrew Jackson from the White House in 1836, the Whigs carried the elections usually by only the slimmest margins. Even in 1844 they chose Clay over native son James K. Polk; the margin was 20 votes. When the Whig party broke over the slavery question following the 1850 Compromise, its successor, the feeble American party, managed to carry the county against James Buchanan; in this case the margin was 13 votes.[4]

In gubernatorial as well as presidential balloting the local problems of the day rather than the national slavery issue tended to be dominant. In regard to slavery there were obvious inherited prejudices, but the atmosphere was not congenial to extreme views. The ghost of strife, however, never disappeared; tension might surface with any unexpected developments. In Chattanooga during the late 1850s, each side had a spokesman—moderate yet serious—in the two leading newspapers. The *Advertiser* of twenty-nine-year-old, New York–born H. F. Cooper favored the secessionist doctrine; twenty-two-year-old North

Carolina–born James R. Hood advocated the Union cause in the columns of the *Gazette*.

As the year 1860 opened, the political struggle across the nation threatened not only seriously to divide the country but also to reduce the Democratic party to shambles. The disruptive forces of sectionalism cast aside any semblance of party harmony when, in convention at Charleston, South Carolina, the Democrats rejected a platform committed to the Southern wing of the party. Delegates from the Lower South walked out; the Tennesseans remained, but in the reassembled convention in Baltimore most of the Volunteer State group withdrew with the Southern faction. The consequence was the nomination of two Democratic candidates: Stephen A. Douglas of Illinois and John C. Breckinridge of Kentucky. With hopes high the new regional Republican party chose Abraham Lincoln to carry its banner deploring disunion, recognizing each state's right to control its domestic institutions and denying the right to legalize slavery in federal territories. A fourth candidate, Tennessee's John Bell, entered the race as a representative of the Constitutional Union party. Bell, a Nashville lawyer, ironmaster, slaveholder, and speaker of the national House of Representatives and United States senator, feared that Southern ultras and the Northern abolitionists would break up the Union. His appeal was to reason, caution, and compromise; his party endorsed the constitution, the Union, and the "enforcement of the laws."

As the season moved on into late fall, the campaign across Tennessee became hotly contested. Local political conversation took on a special meaning when, on 29 October, Stephen A. Douglas came to Chattanooga. The Little Giant, on a belated campaign swing through the South, had slim prospect of gaining personal support but hoped to convince voters that whatever the November outcome, secession was not justified. His visit proved a gala occasion for the area, "possessed of two spirits—the spirit of politics and the rectified spirit of alcohol."

A large crowd, exhilarated by three brass bands and a military detachment, greeted the veteran campaigner. Douglas spoke briefly from the Crutchfield House balcony before the crowd moved to the official assembly grounds. Douglas's carriage was followed "by an immense procession, with the banners floating in the breeze and the bands playing national airs. The enthusiasm was immense! . . . . Everybody seemed to be carried away with it," commented a journalist. "Cheers for Douglas and the 'Union' and the 'Constitution' rang out, clear, loud, heartily and spontaneously all along the route, say of a quarter of a mile."

The majority of the audience appeared to be sympathetic to the point of view expressed by the Illinois senator, and the holiday mood of the crowd did not subside even after a two-hour harangue. The bands played on and after supper Douglas had to appear again on the hotel balcony.

Throughout the state the campaign grew heated and intense. Slavery, it was claimed, would be endangered by a Lincoln victory. But the desire to find some compromise solution marked the 9 November outcome across Tennessee: Bell polled 69,710 votes; Breckinridge 65,653; Douglas 11,384; and Lincoln, whose name was not on the ballot, received no votes. Hamilton County voters followed the same general pattern: Bell had 1,074, Breckinridge 820, and Douglas only 165 votes. However, voters across the nation, although giving Lincoln but 40 percent of the popular vote, gave him a winning electoral vote.

The echoes of the crucial 1860 election did not die down; an ominous cloud hovered over the land. South Carolina immediately called a convention and by 20 December, with pomp and ceremony, adopted an ordinance of secession. Within the next few weeks Georgia, Florida, Alabama, Mississippi, Louisiana, and Texas followed the Palmetto State out of the Union.

Tennesseans, however, were not ready to take such positive action; most held that Lincoln should be given a chance as president after his March inaugural and that Congress—which did not have a Republican majority—would restrain him. Many deplored the action of the Deep South states as too hasty; some even spoke of secession as "nothing short of treason." In Middle and West Tennessee many pro-Southern spokesmen did appear, while the political leaders of East Tennessee, Andrew Johnson and William G. Brownlow, denied the right of secession. Meanwhile Governor Harris, with scornful language critical of Lincoln, summoned the legislature into special session to convene on 7 January 1861, to decide the state's course of action. The lawmakers agreed to submit the question to the people and set 9 February 1861 as the date for a referendum.

As Hamilton residents prepared for the balloting, they became aware of a troubling new situation. The secession of Georgia on 19 January 1861 increased local tension and the seriousness of the issue, for now the entire southern boundary of the county touched on an independent state or nation. In theory, at least, mail service, freight or imports, the circulating medium of exchange, travel, and especially the Georgia-owned railroad (which held property in the county), would be seriously affected. Moreover, secessionist spokesmen in Georgia chided their northern neighbors for not taking similar action: perhaps Hamilton County men were abolitionists, perhaps they were not "manly," perhaps they were Black Republicans.

The resulting emotional strain widened the rifts in the county's population. Current tensions were made particularly clear when Jefferson Davis and his wife arrived to spend a night at the Crutchfield House in late January. Davis—not a radical fire-eater—had resigned from the United States Senate on the twenty-first of the month and, although ill, had delivered a lengthy swan song speech. Now he was en route home. When Chattanoogans learned of the arrival of the Davises and their party, two prominent pro-Southerners, John L. Hopkins and David M. Key, persuaded the Mississippian to address a crowd which had gathered spontaneously at the hotel.

Fatigued by his travels and the pressure of recent events, Davis spoke briefly. His audience was made up of both people of sympathetic views and those who never wavered in their devotion to the Union. As Davis and his admirers left the room, general disorder broke out. Different versions sprang up of what had happened during the chaotic situation. Some said that Davis spoke dispassionately, but when he had finished, William Crutchfield, a brother of the hotel manager, sprang upon a counter and gave a heated reply, calling Davis a traitor and denouncing his claim that states had the right to secede.

Crutchfield, well known as an "uncompromising Union man" and a rugged individualist, had served on the local board of aldermen and had a sizable political following. Davis, on learning of the rebuttal, returned to find an aroused and angry crowd. Pistols had been drawn. According to one report, the screams of some ladies, including Mrs. Davis and Mrs. Crutchfield, added to the confusion, but later Varina Davis dismissed the affair as "merely the vagary of a drunken man." Another account reported that Crutchfield stopped because the "fury of the men forced him to quit speaking." Some maintained that Tom Crutchfield pulled his brother from the counter and hurried him out of the room by a back door. A bystander claimed that Davis said he had been insulted and inquired if his assailant was "responsible and reputable" so that he could be challenged.

No duel followed; the Davis party traveled on the next day. But in Chattanooga political positions crystallized and the confrontation at the

Crutchfield House gained widespread southern attention. The town soon had a reputation as a Union stronghold and Hamilton County as a "deep dark den of Lincolnism."[5]

As the campaign to influence voting in the referendum of 9 February increased its tempo, a convention assembled on 4 February at Montgomery, Alabama, which gave birth to the Confederate States of America. The Tennessee voters, to save time, were to vote on whether or not to hold a convention to consider secession and at the same time elect delegates, should the convention be authorized. With the establishment of the Confederacy and the selection of Jefferson Davis as provisional president, the balloting now actually consisted of the question of Tennessee's joining her sister southern states in the new government.

In Chattanooga the two newspapers argued the case. The *Advertiser* stated the issue for Tennessee "to determine . . . simply whether she will go with the Southern states, or unite her destiny with those Faithless Northern States which have so flagrantly outraged the Constitution, and ruthlessly trampled right and justice under feet." The *Gazette* felt that the "perpetuity of American Freedom" was at stake. "Do the People intend to be coerced by King Cotton into submission?" the editor asked. "Is there no other interest to subserve but that of a few planters and office seekers?" He continued, "The people are for the Union and the politicians against it. Which are right, the people or the Office seekers?"[6]

On election day the people of Tennessee rejected the convention, giving a clear-cut victory to those who opposed secession by a vote of 69,675 against a convention to 57,798 for it. Even this margin was deceptive; many who voted for the convention voted to send Union delegates. In East Tennessee only two counties favored a convention. Hamilton County, upholding the position of the *Gazette*, voted 1,445 against a convention to 445 in favor of such a meeting with most of the minority votes cast in Chattanooga.[7]

The Union victory, more overwhelming than expected, led to a brief period of quietude in which postmortem explanations were issued by both sides. In March, Lincoln's inaugural address did not change minds, for men read into his words any meaning they wished. But the explosive issue repeatedly surfaced, and on 12 April at Fort Sumter words gave way to blasting guns.

All across the South the bells tolled. In Tennessee many moderate men now took firm positions favoring secession and war. On Lookout

Mountain that night, "the whole heavens were lighted with [a] bonfire" presided over by the students of Aldehoff's school. Barrels of tar burned brightly as patriotic speeches and songs aroused the emotionalism of the hour. At Chickamauga depot a Confederate flag was seen flying even before the state seceded.

President Lincoln called on loyal governors to raise troops. Governor Harris's reply rang with defiance: "Tennessee will not furnish a single man for purposes of coercion but 50,000 if necessary for the defense of our rights and those of our Southern brothers." Only in East Tennessee did a spirit of aggressive Unionism continue.

Again the governor called a special legislative session for 25 April. Now the atmosphere differed markedly from the earlier extra session. The governor's message bristled with wrath. The assembly passed an act for the submission to the voters on 8 June of a declaration of independence and an ordinance for the ratification of the provisional constitution of the Confederacy. In the referendum the voters were to approve or reject this document by voting for "Separation" or "No Separation." On this resolution, the senator from the district of which Hamilton County was a part voted aye, while the member of the lower house opposed the ratification.

Records do not disclose the reaction of Hamilton County officials to the passion of the hour, but the minute book of the mayor and board of aldermen discloses a studied calm which either must have masked the true feelings of these officials or indicated an unbelievably naive assessment of the future. They selected a watchman to guard the magazine from sunrise to 8 P.M. while the home guard detailed a patrol for night duty. The mayor at the 20 April session received authority to appoint a vigilance committee of twelve citizens "to take into consideration persons suspected of being dangerous in the community and to take such action as in their wisdom they may think expedient." An ordinance regarding slaves and free persons of color was amended, increasing punishment to thirty-nine lashes and forbidding them to go abroad in the city after 7:30 P.M. A committee of three composed of Mayor J. C. Warner, D. M. Key, and R. Henderson was named to confer with the governor about a supply of arms for the city. On 8 May a new ordinance regulated the liquor business, stipulating that "it shall not be lawful for retailers of spiritous liquors to keep their doors open during the stay of troops within the city. Nor shall any person sell any spiritous liquor or intoxicating drink to any soldiers passing through the city." This law exempted "resident volunteers" and by 6 August was repealed because the necessity for it no longer existed.[8]

East Tennessee Union men called a convention to meet in Knoxville on the eve of the referendum. They planned to assemble conservative men from all parts of the area to consider their future prospects. Delegates gathered in surprisingly large numbers. Hamilton County alone sent twenty-four men: Monroe Masterson, Wilson Hixson, A. Selser, J. G. Thomas, J. C. Rogers, J. D. Blackford, J. D. Kenner, D. C. Trewhitt, J. F. Early, F. G. Blacknall, Peter Monger, A. W. McDaniel, A. M. Cate, G. O. Cate, J. A. Matthews, John Anderson, P. L. Matthews, William Denny, A. A. Pearson, William Clift, R. C. McRee, E. M. Cleaveland, William Crutchfield, and R. Hall. "Strong and emphatic Union resolutions" were presented, permanent officers chosen, and plans for a second meeting to take place after the referendum returns were in were made to meet any new exigencies.[9]

During the heated canvass the state government continued with plans as though the state had seceded, providing for an army and entering into a military covenant with the Confederacy. Troops were raised to join the army in Virginia. The Hamilton Grays marched off carrying a flag presented by Miss Irene Sims at ceremonies at the Kennedy House. Soon the Marsh Blues followed with their flag presented by Laura Massengale.[10] Leading Confederate sympathizers included David M. Key and his brother Summerfield, Richard Watkins, Robert Berry, Frank Walker, John L. Hopkins, Peter Turney, Samuel Williams, Robert M. Hooke, and A. M. Johnson.

Finally 8 June arrived. It was a month and two days after the legislature had adopted the Ordinance of Secession and almost two months after the surrender of Fort Sumter. The result for the state stood 104,913 for secession to 47,238 against, and Tennessee became the last state to leave the Union. In East Tennessee Unionism continued to have priority over everything. Of the dissenting votes cast in the state 32,923 came from East Tennessee compared to 14,780 for separation.

In Hamilton County the tally again resulted in a sizable majority for the Union. A total vote of 2,114 was cast: 854 voted for separation and 1,260 against. Chattanooga again furnished the major portion of the secession supporters.[11]

Hamilton County and its neighbors, Bradley and Marion counties, were the southernmost counties in the United States where a hard core of Unionism showed up in 1860 and continued to exist throughout the course of the war. Following the June referendum, D. C. Trewhitt,

S. McCaleb, and William Clift journeyed to Greeneville to participate
in the reconvened Unionist Convention called for 17 June. Now part
of a dissenting minority within the Confederacy, it took great courage
and a willingness to endure personal hardship for these people to reveal
any degree of independence from the newly created government.
While trains carried Confederate volunteers within sight of the convention's meeting place, the delegates in stormy debate resolved not
to submit to the action of what they felt was an unconstitutional state
government. Included in their conclusions was a petition to the state
for its consent to allow the establishment of a separate state composed
of East Tennessee counties and any from Middle Tennessee wishing
to cooperate.[12]

In Chattanooga sentiment soon turned away from the Union. The
manager of the bluff furnace, a New Jersey man, decided it best to
quit the area. Young editor James Hood found himself isolated and
reported, "As early as June 1861, a self-appointed conclave sat in judgment upon the editor . . . and nothing but the timely interference of
Union friends enabled him to get away in safety." J. W. Wilder, who
had lived in town for eight years, also left. He wrote, "I was not driven
away but left sooner than I otherwise would had not a report been put
in circulation that I had been influancing [sic] the Union men in the
upper end of the county . . . where I have formerly resided to rebellion,
and that I was a correspondent of the *New York Herald*."[13]

In addition, there is the strange case of Father John T. Nealis, young
Dominican priest from New York who arrived in town in 1861 as pastor
of the Catholic church. While details are unknown, Father Nealis was
attacked, cruelly beaten, and shot while attending one of his missions
outside the city. One account says that the attackers were bushwhackers
and that the assault took place along the Suck Creek Road at the foot
of Walden Ridge. The genial, zealous priest lived, but suspicion points
a heavy finger at local prejudice.[14]

Tom Crutchfield found wartime conditions exasperating, but for a
different reason. Even before Tennessee joined the Confederacy, volunteers from many southern states used the railroads to reach the
Virginia front. The Confederates had no arrangements for feeding
troops in transit. In Chattanooga soldiers naturally went from the depot
to the Crutchfield House demanding meals. Crutchfield claims he soon
spent at least $10,000 personally and suffered much humilation because
of these demands. On one occasion, he wrote later, an Arkansas regiment "loaded guns & fixed bayonets and marched in front of the house

to mob me, calling me out and telling me that they had been told that I was a Lincolnite and had said that I would not feed Jeff Davis or any of his Troops and gave me five minutes to explain."[15]

Colonel James C. Nisbet of Dade County, Georgia, also stopped with his Raccoon Roughs to be fed. Nisbet says he offered to pay, but Crutchfield told him he would not feed "common soldiers." Nisbet continued,

> After Crutchfield's refusal, I went over to the depot and called my company to attention, and said that I would march over to the hotel when the gong sounded for supper; that they could take seats at the table and eat; but they must preserve order. Each man was armed with the aforesaid bowie knives, worn in leather scabbards. . . . When the gong sounded the company was marched into the dining room and a sergeant detailed to see that the cooks and waiters got a move on them. That was one time the little pot was put in the big one at the Crutchfield House! And, also, that was one time when the obsessive bowie knives were not inutile.[16]

Unable to cope with such demands and desirous of moving his family—his mother, wife, and daughter resided at the hotel—to more quiet quarters, Tom Crutchfield decided to sell the hostelry. No evidence of such negotiations has been found as to the date, but Crutchfield did move to his farm about a mile away in what is now Ferger Place area. Soon he felt that a more secluded place was needed, so he moved to a farm about five miles north of town. The house was away from any public road, hidden in a bend of the Tennessee River close to the mouth of South Chickamauga Creek. He named it Amnicola (Latin for "river inhabitant"). To satisfy Confederate conscription regulations, Tom "placed in the Rebel army a substitute" and later was exempted from service because he owned or oversaw twenty or more hands.

In Hamilton County the leading Unionists who remained included William Clift, William Crutchfield, Abel A. Pearson, Levi Trewhitt, Benjamin Chandler, D. C. Trewhitt, and E. M. Cleaveland. Of these the most remarkable was Colonel William Clift, who, at the time, was past sixty-six years of age. A well-to-do farmer, Clift lived with his family and slaves on a Soddy Creek plantation. He was one of the county's earliest settlers and for years had commanded the county militia unit. Strong-willed, tenacious, and fearless, he admired the Constitution and the Union with as strong a passion as he hated the doctrines of states' rights and secession. Any Union sympathizer could find asylum at his home; any man who wished to escape Confederate service had a friend in Clift, who would help those on their way to Kentucky to join the Federal army.

In the late summer of 1861 so many refugees congregated at the Clift place that he established a camp for them at the camp meeting grounds of the Cumberland Presbyterian Church on Sale Creek. Here he was fortifying the camp and organizing his men when the Confederate authorities decided to punish this defiant gesture. Between 300 and 400 Confederate sympathizers from Hamilton, Rhea, and Meigs counties moved against Clift's camp in the area's first brush with war. Clift's friends, realizing the amaturish nature of his effort, urged the veteran leader to disband the force. This he reluctantly did and sent his messengers to meet Colonel James W. Gillespie, assistant adjutant and inspector general of the state, and arrange a truce. Clift and Gillespie, longtime acquaintances and friends, met on 19 September at Smith's Crossroads and approved a unique document called the Crossroads Treaty. Its interesting terms reflect the seriousness of conflict between neighbors:

> Whereas the state of Tennessee has separated from the United States, by vote of a large majority of the citizens of the state, and has adopted the permanent constitution of the Confederate States of America; and we, as members of the union party, believing that it becomes necessary for us to make an election between the south and the north and that our interests and sympathies and feelings are with our countrymen of the south, that any further divisions and dissensions among us, the citizens of East Tennessee, is only calculated to produce war and strife among our homes and families, and desolation of the land, without any material influence upon the contest between the north and south:
>
> We hereby agree that we will in future conduct ourselves as peaceful and loyal citizens of the state of Tennessee; that we will oppose resistance or rebellion against the constitution and laws of the state of Tennessee, and will use our influence to prevail upon our neighbors and acquaintances to co-operate with us in this behalf; we having been assured by the military authorities of the state that no act of oppression will be allowed toward us or our families, while we continue in the peaceful pursuit of our several domestic occupations.   Sept. 19, 1861[17]

A newspaper in neighboring Cleveland spiritedly greeted the news: "Old Clift, down in Hamilton, who has been rather obstrepulous [sic] for a few weeks, we learn, has cooled down and concluded to 'ground arms' and demean himself like a loyal citizen hereafter. Sensible conclusion that, and come to just at the nick of time, because it would have been a pity to disgrace the scaffold with such an old imbecile as he has proved himself to be."[18]

The terms of the treaty were soon violated; each side accused the other of subversive tactics. Union men again assembled and called on Clift to lead them. Earthworks were thrown up at the camp; a cannon, "the most curious piece of ordnance ever devised or constructed," was made from a gum log with an eight-inch hole bored through it into which was inserted an old flue from a steamboat boiler. Blacksmiths bound the contraption together with iron bands and mounted it on the front wheels of an ox cart. For some time it stood in defiance of the Confederacy until curious gunners attempted to test its accuracy. A liberal charge of black powder was rammed in followed by a very generous amount of iron slugs. It was reported that the noise of the explosion was heard in Chattanooga and that "scarcely a splinter was left of their once splendid cannon; there was not a spoke to be found of the wheels upon which it had been mounted. The Lincolnites who were camped there were frightened out of their wits and many of them began to wish they had never joined the Clift war."[19]

Meanwhile East Tennessee leaders journeyed to Washington to seek support for their Unionist efforts. President Lincoln and his associates were most receptive; they understood the value of this long arm of Unionism that reached toward the very heart of the Confederacy. A plan developed: an army from Kentucky would invade East Tennessee through the Cumberland Gap, coordinated with civilian volunteers who would destroy nine railroad bridges in the valley, including the big Tennessee River bridge at Bridgeport, Alabama. Such plans proved too complex. The army cancelled its advance, but the civilians never got word of the change in plans. So in the early morning hours of 9 November 1861 small parties of Union men struck the widely scattered rail bridges. In some places Confederate guards drove them off; at one bridge the raiders lost their matches. Five bridges were destroyed, including two Hamilton County spans over South Chickamauga Creek just east of Missionary Ridge. One bridge demolition on the East Tennessee & Georgia railroad line cut the area off from East Tennessee and the other on the Western & Atlantic severed the region from Atlanta.

The actual physical damage was slight; bridges were soon rebuilt. But untold suffering and calamity fell on the Union people. Civilian bridge burners were defenseless and alone; Confederate fears and a spirit of revenge made any person with Unionist background suspect.

Many were arrested and imprisoned; those associated with the bridge burning were ordered "to be tried summarily by drum-head court-martial, and if found guilty, executed on the spot by hanging" for what was officially labeled the "Revolt of the Unionists of East Tennessee." In Chattanooga the city fathers reacted in haste. On 11 November, deciding that the town did not have an adequate police force, they decreed that all white males between the ages of eighteen and forty-five now constituted such a force and required a sufficient number to do duty every night. [20]

The Confederate authorities acted just as swiftly. They tried to ferret out the bridge burners and arrested Union people wherever they were found, sending them off to military prison in Tuscaloosa, Alabama. Naturally, they associated the doings of Colonel Clift with the bridge burnings. Colonel Sterling A. M. Wood was ordered to Chattanooga with his Seventh Alabama Regiment. These men, arriving on 14 November, constituted the first body of troops sent to Hamilton County. Others followed as Governor Harris, reacting nervously to these developments, ordered the capture of Clift "dead or alive."

The next day, Friday, 15 November, Wood moved troops upriver by steamboat to a point in the vicinity of Clift's camp while others from Knoxville participated. The mounted Home Guard of Rhea County also arrived in the area. All headed for the Union position, but because the various Confederate groups did not recognize each other, they opened fire on their own people, wounding several. These were the only casualties of Clift's wars. The size of the Confederate operation was much too large for his poorly equipped men, and they were dispersed before Wood's warriors arrived. Some headed for Kentucky to enroll in the Union army there while others hid out in the neighboring mountains. [21]

Colonel Wood seemed to delight in telling of his exploits to his superiors, never realizing the comic-opera aspect of his experiences. On 17 November he reported that he had moved his regiment to Tyner in order to camp closer to the Lincolnites and "to get out of the way of whiskey." He continued,

> When I arrived . . . a Tennessee regiment without arms was just arriving. All was confusion; a general panic; everybody running up and down, and adding to the general alarm. I issued an order taking command; put the town under martial law; shut up the groceries; forbade any exit, by railroad or otherwise without a permit from the provost-marshal; had every avenue guarded, arrested about twelve persons who were talking Lincolnism before I came. Arrested a

man myself on the cars as I went to Cleveland, and brought him back. Found him one of their traveling agents, going off with news of my arrival. I have relieved all our friends in this country. All were alarmed; all are now resting easy. I have run all the Lincolnites.

Colonel Wood had other concerns. A brigadier general of Tennessee troops arrived and Wood reported, "He has been drunk not less than five years. He is stupid, but easily controlled. He knows nothing, and I believe I can do with him pretty much as I please. He is going to send two pieces of artillery and 500 men to march up and down Sequatchie Valley—a useless expenditure of money." Wood advised that not so many men were needed in the area. Five hundred infantry in training here could "keep this part of the country perfectly quiet." Apparently Wood's superiors believed he had completely dispersed all troublemakers in the area, for they withdrew him and his men in December.[22]

The agitation in Hamilton County died down for a brief period only to flare up again from an entirely different quarter in totally unexpected forms. On 6 February 1862, Federal troops and gunboats captured Fort Henry on the Tennessee River and, ten days later, Fort Donelson on the Cumberland River. All of northwest Tennessee lay open to invasion. The state government hastily fled Nashville for Memphis, where a short time later the legislature adjourned *sine die*, leaving Governor Harris to run the state without a base of operations. Panic-stricken Nashvillians were preyed upon by looters as they awaited developments. Eight days after the surrender of Fort Donelson, Federal troops took possession of the state capital; on 6 March Andrew Johnson was named by President Lincoln as military governor of Tennessee.

With the fall of Nashville imminent, Nashville & Chattanooga freight trains crammed with military supplies clogged the road toward Chattanooga. The passenger trains, jammed with fleeing civilians and what little they could bring of their possessions, ran irregular schedules. The local depot overflowed with refugees and the hotels did an unusually large amount of business. No one had dreamed that one of the consequences of war would be the flight of refugees before an army, and all along the way the newly homeless left a trail of reports and rumors of the vast proportions of the disaster. Those who fled— mostly women and children—included both the well-connected and the humblest citizens. One woman, Mrs. Ben Hardin Helm, a sister-in-law of President Lincoln, was the wife of a Confederate general later killed at Chickamauga.

Amid all this confusion, Major Charles W. Anderson, quartermaster of transportation at Chattanooga, received a telegram from Nashville which read, "Prepare as best you can for the reception of some thousand or twelve hundred sick and convalescent soldiers from the Army and from the hospitals at Nashville. They will be sent forward as fast as cars can be supplied."

Anderson had no government funds nor any manpower to cope with the dilemma so casually pressed upon him. In desperation he turned to his fellow townsmen. Three buildings were commandeered and cleaned up for use as temporary hospitals. Fuel was gathered, cots prepared, bread contracts let. The first trainload of the sick and wounded carried some three hundred men packed in box and cattle cars. For eighteen hours they bumped along through a frigid winter's day without any heat and with no medical attention except that which they could offer each other. Two other trains arrived the next day carrying the same burden of wretchedness.

At least five soldiers died in transit and six others expired during the eight days while Anderson was responsible for them. Local physicians, including Drs. Milo Smith and P. D. Sims, and the humanitarian response of the community alone held down the proportions of this tragic episode. Meanwhile Confederate authorities, realizing Chattanooga was defenseless and vulnerable, sent troops to the town. On 8 March, General John B. Floyd, onetime secretary of war in the cabinet of President James Buchanan and one who had escaped from Fort Donelson, arrived with 2,500 men after a march of 250 miles.

Anderson turned over his sick and wounded men to the military, while General Floyd notified Confederate authorities about the vital site that Chattanooga occupied. His force was insufficient to protect the place, he claimed, for at least six thousand men would be required to hold it. Fearful that the Federals would attack in the near future, Floyd issued special orders to guard carefully all approaches to the city and to forward all accummulated stores to Atlanta.[23]

Following the evacuation of Middle Tennessee, the Confederates gathered their scattered forces at Corinth, Mississippi. Then, in a desperate bid to recover the initiative, they engaged the Federals in the bitter two-day battle of Shiloh. At the same time the Union command unleashed diversionary movements. On Sunday, 6 April 1862, General Ormsby B. Mitchel and some of his men became involved in what has been called the "most extraordinary and astounding adventure of the Civil War."

This scheme, apparently worked out by the imaginative general and a mysterious civilian, James J. Andrews, called for the sabotaging of the W & A railroad south of Chattanooga. Andrews, a tall, daring, theatrical-looking fellow "with a long black silken beard" who had served as a double spy, briefed the twenty-three volunteers who had changed from uniforms into civilian clothes. Alone or in small groups they would make their way from their Shelbyville camp through the enemy lines to catch a southbound train on Thursday from Chattanooga to Marietta, Georgia, where they would rendezvous. The next morning they would board the northbound train, commandeer it, destroy enough bridges to cripple the railroad, and isolate Chattanooga so that General Mitchel could readily assault the city. If stopped by anyone, their cover story was to be simply that they were Yankee-hating men from the Blue Grass State on their way to sign up with a Confederate outfit.

On the way to Chattanooga soaking rains made travel over the slippery roads difficult and slow. Some of the group crossed the Tennessee River on a ferry a few miles west of town and boldly rode a Confederate troop train into Chattanooga. Some arrived north of the city in the midst of a storm. The owner of the horse ferry did not want to make a crossing under such conditions and had to be persuaded to take his craft into the turbulent water. These raiders found every place laxly guarded; they strolled about the streets and lounged around the depot until others of their party gathered. At times they "played stupid" with strangers while with others there was much talk of war strategy and military blunders. They were able to learn that Mitchel had taken Huntsville on the railroad to the west, but the weather had made the raiders a day late.

As they boarded the southbound train, the saboteurs discovered that two of their men were missing. These two had encountered trouble at Jasper and had to sign up with a Confederate unit, hoping to desert as soon as possible. (They did and eventually got back to the Union army.) The main party made it to Marietta and then started back north the next morning. (Two did not get to the train and were later captured.) At Big Shanty on Saturday 12 April at 6:45 A.M., the train made its regular breakfast stop. Andrews' raiders uncoupled the cars and made off with the locomotive, the *General,* and three box cars—to the puzzlement of the men at the nearby Confederate training camp. Conductor William Allen Fuller and two associates pursued them first on foot, then by a pole car, later by a switch engine, and finally a regular locomotive, the *Texas*.

Andrews cut the telegraph wires, tore up track, tried unsuccessfully to burn bridges, and fled northward as fast as the wood-burner would move. However, as he knew, stops were necessary to let the scheduled southbound trains pass. To his chagrin, extra trains ran that day to carry stores and rolling stock out of reach of the threatening Union raiders in the west. As Andrews spun stories to explain the odd train and unknown crew to local railroaders at the sidings, his pursuers continued to gain on him. Finally, after a high adventure of about one hundred miles, near Graysville, just before entering Hamilton County, the raiders had to desert the weary *General*, now completely out of fuel. It became a matter of each man for himself, alone and deep in enemy country, hunted as an enemy spy.

Militia garrison at once began to hunt them down. Crossroads and country lanes had guards posted as word of the daring raid spread throughout the land. Posses with dogs, farmers with squirrel guns joined in the chase. Hamilton County had never known such Saturday night excitement. The raiders wandered aimlessly. Some made it up Lookout Mountain only to be captured in the valley to the west. Andrews got close to Bridgeport, Alabama, before his excuses wore out. Two others managed to get a boat on the Tennessee River east of Chattanooga and drifted downstream without being apprehended until they reached Stevenson, Alabama.

Eventually all twenty-two men were captured. As each was brought to army headquarters at the Crutchfield House, he was questioned, put in irons, and marched off to the jail, where he joined some runaway slaves and East Tennessee Unionists in a common cell. Andrews, in late April, was tried as a spy in Chattanooga by a military court; after reviews by the Confederate secretary of war and President Davis, a verdict of guilty was announced and Andrews was sentenced to death by hanging.

In desperation, Andrews and another raider escaped by prying a hole through the brick wall of the jail. He was seen on Williams Island, having lost his pants and shoes while swimming the river. Samuel Williams, the owner of the island and neighboring farmer, gave him clothes and fed him, but then turned him over to authorities. Andrews died on the gallows in Atlanta on 7 June 1862. Seven of the others were also hanged in Atlanta, where the men were moved when a

Federal raid threatened Chattanooga. Eight men later escaped and the remaining six were exchanged as prisoners of war. These six got to Washington by 25 March 1863 when, in a special ceremony, they received the first Congressional Medals of Honor to be issued. Later thirteen other raiders were also so honored.[24]

The story of Andrews' raid did not end for Sam Williams. According to his daughter, Mrs. Allie Williams Hampton, he had to take refuge when Union troops took Chattanooga. They threatened to execute him for turning Andrews over to the Confederates. Williams, at least for a time, hid in McLemore's Cove and occasionally slipped home. After the war he received a pardon from President Andrew Johnson and returned home despite the fact that threatening letters continued to be sent to him.[25]

The great locomotive chase failed to disrupt operations on the W & A railroad, but General Mitchel gained control of the rail lines to Memphis and to Nashville. While Chattanooga buzzed with tales of Andrews' raid, Mitchel took Huntsville, Stevenson, and Bridgeport—where defenders did manage to burn a portion of the vital Tennessee River bridge. From Bridgeport Mitchel probed in all directions; he captured Jasper and sent his troopers roaming the Sequatchie Valley.

Scattered Confederate units fell back to Chattanooga. General E. Kirby Smith in command in East Tennessee feared the loss of his entire district; Chattanooga and Cumberland Gap, the two strategic spots in his department, were 180 miles apart and he could not man both places. But reinforcements were sent to Chattanooga. General Daniel Leadbetter, in command there, was told to hold out as long as possible. Rifles were sent to help his unarmed men, but instructions directed that they were to be used only by men on the flanks while troops in the center position were expected to continue to be "armed with country weapons."

Among the reinforcements arriving in May 1863 was the Forty-third Tennessee Regiment made up of some eight hundred men with two local men serving as officers: Colonels J. W. Gillespie and David McKendree Key. Gillespie, a Mexican War veteran, lived on a county estate called Euchee. Key, a young attorney thirty-eight years old and graduate of Hiwassee College, had moved to town in 1853. The stocky Key, a spirited secessionist, had served as presidential elector on the Democratic ticket for Buchanan in 1856 and for Breckinridge in 1860. Governor Harris commissioned him a major and assistant adjutant general. With Gillespie he participated in the attack on Clift's camp;

he also raised troops, supervised drill, inspected facilities, and served as a general troubleshooter in East Tennessee. Key never felt free from worry about a possible reign of terror in the area; he had many friends who were true Union men, among them eighty-year-old Levi Trewhitt, an attorney and Hamilton County resident. After the bridge burning episode, Trewhitt fell into the Confederate net, was arrested, and shipped off in a cattle car to Tuscaloosa without a hearing of any kind. Key tried in vain to obtain clemency for the old man; failing to get any response, he wondered about the goals of the Confederacy when Trewhitt died in prison.

Hysteria filled the air when Key's men arrived at the depot in passenger coaches and cattle and freight cars. They were untested soldiers, many still dressed in country hats and wide suspenders. On orders they marched down Market Street to a bivouac area on Brabson Hill. Others arrived and rumors spread that the entire Yankee army was on the move toward Chattanooga.

Then on 7 June General James S. Negley, who served under Mitchel, appeared on the north bank of the Tennessee River opposite the town. He had crossed Walden Ridge over the Anderson Pike and began an artillery bombardment of the town that afternoon about the time Kirby Smith arrived by special train to assume command of the Confederates. Cannon played on each other until dark while sharpshooters exchanged fire across the river. The next day the general wrote his wife, "The horrors of war—could [the] experience of those who live in civil wars be extended to succeeding generations, we would not have much need or use of armies."

The shelling across the river resumed the next morning. Kirby Smith, however, led his men from the Brabson Hill camp across Market Street to Cameron Hill. Some Confederate rifle fire responded to the barrage, but their own cannon remained silent. After some three hours, Negley withdrew his men without making any effort to cross the river.

Key described his experience of that day in a letter to his wife, who had left Chattanooga for a safer spot with her parents: "They threw shells and balls all through Market Street and over the town and far beyond the Crutchfield House. . . . Several houses were hit by their balls, but no considerable damage was done. . . . They robbed and stole everything belonging to citizens on the other side of the River, took all Southern men prisoners and carried them off with them." That night the men of the Forty-third remained on Cameron Hill without baggage or tents.[26]

Kirby Smith's report was more factual: "There was considerable noise & bursting of shells," he wrote, "but little damage was done. . . . The enemy buried 8 men and abandoned one 4½-inch rifle brass gun. Our loss 3 wounded."[27]

As the men of the Union reconnaissance party withdrew, they recrossed Walden Ridge. Although hazardous and difficult, they had found a way into the Chattanooga area which others would later use. Negley especially noted in his report that "Union people are wild with joy, while the rebels are panic-stricken." The Union people, he said, met them "along the roads by the hundreds."[28]

One trooper, Benjamin Scribner, who had command of the rear guard in retiring across Walden Ridge, did not revel in his assignment. Of his experience he wrote later,

> The ascent of Waldron's ridge is steep and crooked, the road much of the way is composed of logs, one end of which rested on the side of the mountain, the other end supported in a horizontal point by props, thus forming a sort of corduroy road. At one point near the summit a stream of water ran down the mountain's side through the interstices of the logs. It was a rickety, insecure makeshift of a road and was so narrow that only in places could two teams pass each other. On looking up at the zigzag way, the wagons appeared in terraces one line above the other, and one above could look down upon the tops of huge trees which grew in great luxuriance. It was yet daylight when the train started up the ascent, and such disposition of the two regiments was made as would best protect it. The proximity of the enemy and the nature of the road increased the danger, as even a small force could inflict great damage by stampeding the mules in so precarious a situation. At length the train ceased to move, and one staff officer after another was sent forward to ascertain the cause. The wagons ahead had stalled, night and darkness came on, detail after detail from the troops was made to assist the teams until all of both regiments had gone forward for this duty, and it was midnight when I reached the summit, myself alone comprising the rear guard, for I preferred to stay behind the wagons rather than to venture upon the passage of the wagons on the verge of such a yawning abyss.[29]

NOTES

1. Robert H. White, ed., *Messages of the Governors of Tennessee, 1796–1821*, 8 vols. (Nashville: Tennessee Historical Commission, 1952), 5:303–304.

2. Gilbert E. Govan and James W. Livingood, *The Chattanooga Country,* 3rd ed. (Knoxville: University of Tennessee Press, 1977), pp. 160–161.

3. *Chattanooga Advertiser,* 22 December 1859.

4. *A History of Tennessee From the Earliest Times to the Present* (Nashville: Goodspeed, 1886), p. 358.

5. Govan and Livingood, *Chattanooga Country.* pp. 174–175.

6. Ibid., pp. 176–177.

7. Mary E. R. Campbell, *The Attitude of Tennesseans Toward the Union, 1847–1861* (New York: Vantage, 1961), pp. 288–290; C. W. Lusk, "Some Phases of Chattanooga History During the Civil War" (Typescript, Chattanooga-Hamilton County Bicentennial Library), p. 8.

8. City of Chattanooga, *Minutes of the Board of Mayor and Aldermen, 3 Jan. 1859–1 May 1863,* pp. 100–103. The members of the vigilance committee were Jesse Thompson, W. L. Dugger, James S. Edwards, R. Henderson, Jacob Kunz, Thomas Webster, D. Harrington, Foster Whiteside, P. A. Mitchell, R. M. Hooke, Thomas J. Lattner, and Robert Smith.

9. O. P. Temple, *East Tennessee and the Civil War* (Cincinnati: Robert Clarke Co., 1899), pp. 340–343; *Proceedings of the East Tennessee Convention Held at Knoxville, May 30th and 31st, 1861 and Greeneville, on the 17th day of June, 1861 and Following Days* (Knoxville: Berry's Book and Job Office, 1861).

10. Reminiscences of Mrs. Summerfield A. (Mary Divine) Key, in scrapbook of undated clippings in possession of author.

11. Campbell, *Attitude Toward Union,* pp. 291–294; White, *Messages of the Governors,* 5:304; Lusk, "Chattanooga," p. 7. The vote in Chattanooga was 421 for secession and 51 against.

12. Temple, *East Tennessee,* pp. 343–365, 573.

13. Govan and Livingood, *Chattanooga Country,* pp. 180–181.

14. George J. Flanigen, *The Centenary of St. Peter and St. Paul's Parish, Chattanooga, Tennessee: The Story of the First 100 Years of the Catholic Church in Hamilton County* (Chattanooga: St. Peter and St. Paul's Parish, 1952), pp. 15–18.

15. Thomas Crutchfield to James R. Hood, 27 Dec. 1863, Manuscript Division, Tennessee State Library, Nashville.

16. James C. Nisbet, *Four Years On the Firing Line* (Chattanooga: Imperial Press, 1914), pp. 10–11.

17. Lusk, "Chattanooga"; Lewis Shepherd, "Grotesque War Operations Known as the 'Clift Wars'" (Undated clipping, Chattanooga-Hamilton County Bicentennial Library).

18. J. S. Hurlburt, *History of the Rebellion in Bradley County, East Tennessee* (Indianapolis: n.p., 1866), pp. 66–72.

19. Shepherd, "Clift's Wars."

20. Temple, *East Tennessee,* pp. 366–387; Lusk, "Chattanooga"; City of Chattanooga, *Minutes 1859–1863,* pp. 113–114.

21. U. S., War Department, *The War of the Rebellion: A Compilation of the Official Records of the Union and Confederate Armies* (Washington, D.C.: GPO, 1884), Series 1, 4:243, 247–248 (hereafter cited as *O.R.*).

22. *O.R.,* Series 1, 4:234, 245, 248–250; Shepherd, "Clift's Wars"; Esther Sharp Sanderson, *County Scott and Its Mountain Folk* (Huntsville, TN.: author, 1958), pp. 190–191. Clift finally reached Kentucky where he received a commission as colonel of volunteers in command of the Seventh East Tennessee regiment. However, he apparently refused to obey an order to withdraw his force in one skirmish—Clift did not understand the meaning of retreat—and was arrested. There is some evidence that President Lincoln learned of this situation and, hoping East Tennessee Unionists would not be angered or humiliated, called Clift to Washington. The president convinced him his services were needed in East Tennessee, detached him from his former command, and sent him to Scott County where he was to defend that area from Confederate raiders. In June, Clift arrived at Huntsville, raised a command of some 250 men, and built a second Fort Clift. Here in August 1862 he faced men under Kirby Smith on their way to participate in the Kentucky campaign. Clift's men, badly outnumbered, managed to get out of the way of the enemy cavalry. They regrouped after the Confederates moved on and operated against guerillas and bushwhackers for over a year.

23. C. W. Anderson, "After the Fall of Fort Donelson," *Confederate Veteran* 4:289, 290; *O.R.,* Series 1, 10 (pt. 1):4.

24. William Pittenger, *The Great Locomotive Chase: A History of the Andrews Railroad Raid into Georgia in 1862* (Philadelphia: Penn Publishing, 1921); *O.R.,* Series 1, 10 (pt. 1):630–639; Stephen W. Sears, " 'The Most Extraordinary and Astonishing Adventure of the Civil War,' " *American Heritage* 29, no. 1 (Dec. 1977), pp. 34–45. Pittenger was one of the raiders. The Sears article is the best recent short interpretation.

George L. Gillespie, First Lieutenant, Corps of Engineers, who entered service at Chattanooga, received the Congressional Medal of Honor on 27 October 1897 for action near Bethesda Church, Virginia, on 31 May 1864. In the 1890s some thirty men received the same honor for deeds of valor in and around Chattanooga, including Arthur MacArthur.

25. Scrapbook of undated clippings in possession of author.

26. David M. Abshire, *The South Rejects a Prophet: The Life of Senator D. M. Key, 1824–1900* (New York: Praeger, 1967), pp. 15–37; Joseph H. Parks, *General E. Kirby Smith* (Baton Rouge: Louisiana State University Press, 1954), pp. 178–183; D. M. Key to wife, 10 June 1862, Key Collection, Chattanooga-Hamilton County Bicentennial Library.

27. *O.R.* Series 1, 10 (pt. 1):922.

28. Ibid., pp. 919–920.

29. Benjamin F. Scribner, *How Soldiers Were Made: Or the War as I Saw It Under Buell, Rosecrans, Thomas, Grant, and Sherman* (New Albany, Ind.: n.p., 1887), pp. 46–48.

Campground and Battlefield

T HE appearance of Negley's reconnaissance expedition in Hamilton County at the very gateway to the Deep South had more than local significance. By this time, ranking civilian and military officials on both sides repeated their opinions that Chattanooga was one of the most important centers in the West. Union leaders gave high priority to the occupation of the town; its strategic site could not be exaggerated, they insisted. Confederate units, on the other hand, had instructions to hold Chattanooga and to move up reenforcements with all possible haste.

Negley's raid signaled bright prospects for the Union in the western theater. Hamilton Countians and East Tennesseans generally deserved Union help, for their loyal people had sent many men into Federal regiments while others defied the 1862 Confederate conscription law demanding service in the rebel war machine. But it was the railroads that gave the place vital strategic value. Although the Civil War became the first railroad war in history, many officers failed to recognize the important military role of the iron horse. Some seized on its value: President Lincoln was one of the first. He pleaded with his leaders in northern Alabama to move rapidly to Chattanooga and gain the prize; he fretted when bold positive thrusts did not develop. Succinctly he wrote, "To take and hold the railroad at or east of Cleveland, in East Tennessee, I think fully as important as the taking and holding of Richmond."[1]

But Federal officers dispersed their strength and thereby lost a rich opportunity. They allowed great distances, made difficult by rough terrain, to undermine their strength while exposing their men to cavalry raids and guerrilla warfare.

When Negley's guns bombarded Chattanooga, they underscored for the Confederates the real vulnerability of the junction town. For months they knew that East Tennessee had to be protected against local and organized Federal forces. The critical points—Cumberland Gap and Chattanooga—both required trained soldiers, and when General E. Kirby Smith received an appointment to command the Department of East Tennessee in March 1862, he knew he had to look in all directions at once to husband his manpower.

By the end of June General Braxton Bragg replaced Pierre G. T. Beauregard as Confederate commander in the West. He soon sent the unlettered, native genius Nathan Bedford Forrest to Chattanooga to weld together the cavalry units of the area and to strike at Union supply lines—a task he performed most successfully. Other reenforcements arrived and finally Bragg, upon the prodding of Kirby Smith, decided he could best use his army by concentrating it at Chattanooga for a campaign to regain control of the provision country of Middle Tennessee or to invade Kentucky.

On 21 July 1862, Confederate wagons and artillery started from Mississippi for Chattanooga on a long, slow journey. The troops traveled by rail to Mobile, then by steamboat to Montgomery, where they again took cars. The leading elements arrived on 27 July and within a week's time four divisions detrained.

So by the end of July a new drama began to unfold; Hamilton County and Chattanooga became the headquarters of the Confederate army of the West. Not only had the railroads brought gray-clad troops to the area but also created new problems for the local people. Although delayed by the slow progress of the wheeled vehicles through the hill country of Alabama and Georgia, Bragg's aides, Generals Leonidas Polk and William J. Hardee, finally assembled more than twenty-seven thousand men. In a few short weeks more than twice as many soldiers gathered in the area as there were residents in all of Hamilton County.

The Federals maintained their nearest base, Fort McCook, at the mouth of Battle Creek in the lower Sequatchie Valley. Both sides sent foraging parties far and wide in search of food and fodder. Both toiled to protect their rail supply lines, building stockades at every bridge and trestle, and patroling vulnerable spots. Both sides used local men as couriers, guides, and informers; they scoured the mountains and kept watch over the river ferries and railroads. Confederate work teams toiled to improve the Anderson Pike where their presence disclosed something of their intended plans.

During the last days of August, Bragg's army began crossing the Tennessee River and started over Walden Ridge where Benjamin Scribner had labored in June with Negley's rear guard. No river or railroad ran in the direction Bragg decided to follow; he was off for Kentucky, using wagon trains to haul all the army's paraphernalia over mountainous and generally poor roads. After dropping down into the Sequatchie Valley, they passed through Dunlap and Pikeville where they took the mountain road to Sparta and beyond. Chattanooga served as Bragg's railhead and command headquarters during the campaign.

Although joined in Kentucky by Kirby Smith, Bragg's campaign went badly and in mid-October the Confederates began a weary, demoralizing retirement through Cumberland Gap into upper East Tennessee. From there Hardee's men rode the trains through Chattanooga and over the repaired Tennessee River bridge at Bridgeport to a rendezvous at Murfreesboro. General Polk's wagon trains and men had to make the journey by road. In Middle Tennessee the Confederates, now called the Army of Tennessee, regrouped to face their old antagonist. The Federal army, concentrated about Nashville, had a new commander, General William S. Rosecrans.

Back in Chattanooga a prominent Confederate arrived early in the morning of 4 December to establish headquarters for his command, that of all the Confederate forces in the West. General Joseph E. Johnston, recovered from wounds received at Seven Pines and reassigned to a command including everything west of the mountains, had little time to consider his new surroundings. He immediately hastened to Murfreesboro to learn at first hand about affairs in Bragg's command. He discovered there about forty-two thousand troops facing an estimated sixty-five thousand Yankees. He also found evidence of seeds of discontent over the command, generously sown during and following the failed Kentucky campaign. But before his inspection was completed, Johnston learned that President Davis planned a surprise visit to Chattanooga.

The two leaders met in town where Davis had had his unpleasant experience at the Crutchfield House early in the previous year. To-gether they went to the front, taking "an elegant new carriage" at the Union Depot. A military band struck up "The Bonnie Blue Flag" and "Dixie," "the lively strains of which fell upon the ear as the train was sweeping around the base of giant Lookout."[2]

Mrs. Johnston, who felt more at home in Washington and Richmond, did not find her restricted quarters in a small cottage in Chattanooga very satisfying as she faced the holiday season. In despondent tone, she wrote a friend, "how ill and weary I feel in this desolate land & how dreary it all looks."[3]

Davis's inspection did not change his fixed opinions. He was sure the enemy had no intention of doing anything during the winter beyond conducting limited defensive action. Consequently he ordered troops from Bragg's outnumbered force transferred to Mississippi, and by 16 December he himself was off for his home state along with General Johnston, although the latter's headquarters remained in Chattanooga.

Davis had misread Rosecrans's intentions. At the year's end he chal-lenged Bragg in the bloody contest of Murfreesboro (or Stone's River) with heavy casualties borne by both armies. After the battle the Con-federates withdrew from the field and entered winter quarters on a position through McMinnville, Manchester, Shelbyville, and Tulla-homa. Their supply line continued to be the N & C (Nashville & Chattanooga) railroad through Chattanooga.

Occasional raids and skirmishes by both sides kept the war from falling into a lull, but the Union leadership appeared very slow in seizing the initiative; Washington finally pressured Rosecrans into ac-tion when, on 24 June 1863, he launched a maneuver which dislodged the Confederates from the Cumberland Plateau. The Army of Tennessee retreated without looking back. They did not stop to estab-lish a defensive position as they crossed the Tennessee River, but continued on into Chattanooga. Only a thin patrol line stayed out to watch the river crossings. On the way back to the rail junction Bragg's men learned of the fall of Vicksburg and of Lee's Gettysburg disaster.

After about a year of optimism but no apparent achievement the Confederates were back in Chattanooga and quartered in various sec-tions of Hamilton County. During most of the preceding year only a garrison had occupied Chattanooga; however, community life was to-tally dominated by the military. Occasionally local girls rode horseback with soldiers or entertained them with picnics or trips to the mountains. Sometimes light-hearted social events were mere ruses: for instance, when bands of desperate Confederate cavalrymen passed through the area, they would serenade families in order to divert attention from other troops who were at the same time invading the stables and taking "horses, cows, everything." Occasional fund raising "tableaux" helped in the accumulating of money to aid wounded or sick soldiers. There were also formal dances where local belles provided recreation for the officers.

Early in 1863 a Walden Ridge wedding was followed by an all-night celebration to which "all parties" had been invited. It turned out to be composed of "complicated ingredients" who celebrated with abandon. One who attended claimed, "I do not suppose that the history of the world contains such a rare case of universal *concord* being the result of universal *discord*. The party was composed of 1st Rebel and Union citizens; 2d, Rebel and Union soldiers; 3rd, Rebel and Union deserters; 4th, Rebel and Union spies; 5th, Rebel and Union bushwhackers. . . . Considering the great hatred existing between the different parties," he concluded, "it is marvelous that bloodshed was not the immediate result."

The holiday season in 1862 featured the annual city election and saw Dr. Milo Smith reelected mayor. To celebrate New Year's Day Tom Crutchfield hosted an eggnog party; the beverage served was made with "pure Jamaica rum."

The minutes of the city government for this period reveal little that is unusual, possibly because the military took charge of all vital functions. The city fathers did struggle to raise wages as inflation increased and they distributed some funds to the families of volunteers. In April 1863 they found it fitting to resolve that since the well of Jacob Kunz had been of such public benefit, "in appreciation of the kindness and urbanity of Mr. Kunz" they would exempt the lot on which the well was located from corporate taxes and would excuse him from paying poll tax.

Water had become a scarce commodity and one had to wait in line at the well. There also occurred liquor droughts; once when a supply arrived, the newspaper observed that "It put a war-like spirit in everyone for we see nothing but treating and re-treating from morning till night." The provost-marshal, however, spoiled this fun by ruling that liquor could only be sold by licensed grocery and drug stores.

The soldiers stayed busy guarding rail and river facilities and handling supplies. Repair gangs including "commissioned officers and privates of the Confederate Army, Union men, Yankees, negroes and every other kind of prisoner" worked on the streets. They removed the machinery from the bluff furnace and shipped it to a small furnace in Anniston, Alabama.[4]

For a time the Crutchfield House served as a hospital (named the Ford Hospital) while the upper stories of several warehouses with some alterations became the Newsome Hospital, named for a handsome, wealthy Arkansas widow, Mrs. Ella Newsome, who was a nurse and hospital patron. Two other places, called the Bragg and the Buckner hospitals, also functioned for a time. Volunteers from the community took up church carpets and cut them into blankets. A camp across the river served as a haven for stragglers and convalescents.

With such an amount of military activity, it was inevitable that red tape would entangle the area. During Bragg's concentration there the residents' movements were restricted. For weeks few civilians, especially ladies, appeared on the streets; when the ban was lifted, the local editor noted that the normal activity "betokens a return to civilization, which many visitors to Chattanooga began to think had never existed here."

A volunteer nurse who came to Chattanooga to help with the care of the sick and wounded found herself and her associates caught in the web of regulations. In her reminiscences, she relates her experiences:

> We went to the Crutchfield House at Chattanooga, and were informed we could not procure a room without a special pass from the provost-marshal of the place. We were in a dilemma now, as we were not allowed to walk even a square without this pass, so could not get out to procure one.
>
> The clerk of the hotel kindly informed us that we could wash our hands and faces in the parlor and eat breakfast. For this gracious concession we were properly thankful. After waiting for some time for water to be brought in, I ventured to ask a white girl, who was sweeping the hall, to bring us some, as we wished to get rid of the dust by which we were covered. This *femme de chambre* informed us we could get none until the next morning, and, as if to add insult to injury, deliberately walked into the parlor and vigorously plied her broom to the carpet, enveloping us in clouds of dust.[5]

Nurse Kate Cumming knew the ardors of nursing and the drudgery that came with improvised facilities. But she found solace in the natural beauty of the area. From the third floor of the hospital she noted: "To the right was the Tennessee in its circuitous route meandering through fertile fields and meadows; facing us was quite a rise, dotted with handsome mansions, surrounded by lovely gardens of shrubbery; and to our left was Lookout Mountain, looking like a lion couchant, frowning down upon the placid waters of the Tennessee, which flows around its base. Many a time, when worn out physically and mentally, have I forgotten my trials in gazing with rapture upon this lovely scene."[6]

Other newcomers arrived. Franc M. Paul, a thirty-year-old North Carolinian by birth, had served as clerk of the Tennessee Senate. When Memphis was threatened, he was instructed to move the archives to Chattanooga. Because Chattanooga was in the war theater, he left the state records in Atlanta. He came on to Chattanooga and, being a printer by trade, saw at once the possibilities of publishing a newspaper designed to circulate in the army. Paul leased the printing office of the *Advertiser* (which like its competitor the *Gazette*, had suspended publication), found some paper, and got a small staff together. On 1 August 1862, he published the first issue of the *Chattanooga Rebel*.

With only brief interruptions the unpretentious pages of the *Rebel* appeared as a daily until April 1865, during which time it had to flee three times before Federal armies and won the name "*Rebel-on-Wheels.*" The paper allotted some of its space to local news, and carried advertisements as well as political and military orders and announcements. But its prime concern was the reporting of the war. Camp correspondents sent in news, wrote letters to the editor, and filed some poetry of very dubious quality. Some false items were planted deliberately in order to confuse Federal intelligence. Feature columns carried the by-lines of "Mint Julip," "Grapevine Telegraph," and "Bill Arp," a well-known humorist who finally "runaged" from the Yankees. Only a scarcity of paper limited the *Rebel's* circulation which, for a time, climbed to 8,000 copies.

As the *Rebel* grew, Paul brought others in to assist him. One writer, twenty-two-year-old Henry Watterson, had a reputation as a journalist with a terse, bold, forceful style. A friend of the editor's, Albert Robert, also joined the staff, contributing witty columns under the names "Kwart Keg" and "John Happy."

The two writers lived the Bohemian life in a small frame office "with a split-bottomed chair which served the double purpose of washstand and clothesrack . . ." Their bed was a "pile of exchange papers in one corner supplemented by a pooling issue of our consolidation of blankets." Newsmen, army personnel, and political figures gravitated to the office as well as "scouts" who brought in copies of Northern papers and whose arrival was "as important as would be that of an ocean liner to New York reporters before the Atlantic cable was laid." Such visits produced "high carnival in the editorial den and pine-top champagne

or equally exhilarating beverages would flow like water." When news
ran short, "inventive powers" produced copy to fill the columns.

The editors complained about speculators and turned their wrath
on East Tennessee Unionism. They gave advice about the selection of
military personnel and the planting of crops, and they pleaded for
educational privileges for conscripted soldiers and for the freedom of
the press. But the most popular piece was a column entitled "The
Situation," in which army developments (or the lack of them) were
critically discussed. General Bragg himself drew caustic criticism after
the battle of Murfreesboro, for Watterson never hesitated to hurl
thunderbolts.[7]

When word arrived that the Confederates had evacuated Middle
Tennessee, the *Rebel* cried, "The Crisis is Upon Us." As the Army of
Tennessee trooped into the city, confusion prevailed. Nurse Cumming
found turmoil everywhere as a result of "troops coming and going,
wagons hurrying past, and everything else pertaining to a large army."
Refugees came with the army, searching for shelter while waiting for
the chance of transportation farther south. Even a newspaper arrived
and sought refuge in Chattanooga. The *Huntsville Confederate* printed
a few issues there while fleeing southward.

On 21 August 1863, soldiers in blue again appeared on the river
bank opposite town. They were the brigade of mounted infantry commanded by General John T. Wilder with an artillery battery under
Captain Eli Lilly. They had forded the Sequatchie River, climbed
Walden Ridge, and descended into the valley of North Chickamauga
Creek, camping at Poe's Tavern. From there some marched to
Harrison's Landing to prevent the enemy from getting into Wilder's
rear. Others moved down the valley toward Chattanooga. On their
way one trooper wrote, "numbers of Union people came down from
the mountain sides, all dressed in their sunday clothes to watch us as
we moved by. These people had been hiding in the mts dodging the
conscript officers for two years and their greeting that 'we 'uns' mighty
glad to see 'youens' told more in the expression of their faces than their
words conveyed."

By noon the columns had reached Stringer's Ridge; scouts crossed
over this elevation and rode across the half-mile-wide bottomland to
the river. Their arrival was a complete surprise; they easily captured
some forty Confederates about to take the horse ferry into town. Meanwhile, Union artillerymen unlimbered their guns on the heights of the
ridge.

On the south side of the Tennessee River, Bragg's men had built defensive works. On Cameron Hill a fort with two James rifles stood 300 feet above the water and on a small neighboring elevation a large fort with embrasures for nine guns. Along the river nearby was a "water battery of three guns." Close by, upstream, a distillery had been "pierced for muskets" near some earthworks with placements for artillery to cover the ferry crossing. On the crown of the river bluffs an additional installation with ten embrasures stood guard. A pontoon bridge, tied up along the wharf, was readied to be swung across the river.[8]

Like Negley's raid fourteen months earlier, Wilder's surprise appearance was a feint. But this plan was designed to keep attention away from the movement of the entire Union army. On 16 August Rosecrans finally initiated his campaign out of the Cumberland Mountains. Wilder's mission across Hamilton County north and east of Chattanooga was undertaken to mislead Bragg into a belief that the main army would attempt a river crossing in this area. Rosecrans, however, crossed the Tennessee River downstream from Chattanooga at Caperton's Ferry, the rail bridge at Bridgeport, and at Shellmound and Battle Creek. Using country roads over Sand and Lookout mountains, he dispersed his men over more than forty miles in an effort to reach the W & A (Western & Atlantic) railroad south of Bragg's position either in an attempt to force the Confederates to evacuate Chattanooga or to entrap them in the town, cut off from their supplies.

Wilder's men began a noisy demonstration as soon as they arrived north of the river on Friday, 21 August. It happened to be a Confederate day of prayer. Soldiers and civilians had gathered in the Presbyterian Church to listen to a New Orleans minister, Dr. B. M. Palmer, when the first shells burst. Henry Watterson, who was in the congregation, wrote, "The man of God gave no sign that anything unusual was happening. He did not hurry. He did not vary the tones of his voice. He kept on praying. There was no panic in the congregation, which did not budge. . . . That was the longest prayer I ever heard." The young newsman's opinion that all left the church in orderly manner was disputed by a Union soldier who said, "they poured out like bees from a hive."

Lilly's gunners made targets of two river steamers, sinking one. Soon the Confederate batteries began to reply and a brisk duel across the river continued until evening. It was resumed the next day. Lilly dug his guns so deeply into emplacements on the Stringer's Ridge position that only the muzzles showed. His men settled down in a hastily constructed camp. They found surprisingly good foraging in the area, collecting "the best roasting ears, sweet potatoes, peaches, and everything that pertains to making a soldiers [sic] mouth water."

Once Lilly had his guns dug in, he began shelling the town. The depot was a favorite target; the Crutchfield House, the *Rebel* office, and some houses suffered hits. The Confederates prepared for the impending battle. Hospital patients and some civilian families moved south. Those residents, such as the Johnsons and Whitesides, who had railroad connections managed to get cars in which they set up housekeeping, moving away from trouble spots whenever a locomotive could be secured.

The machinery from the bluff furnace was shipped away and legend has it that one of the bankers carried off all the depositors' funds, which he returned at war's end. The young minister, T. H. McCallie, prepared for hard times by cutting hidden doors in the top of a wardrobe so that he could get to the attic to store food and valuables.

When it appeared that the *Rebel*'s office would be captured, a railroader moved two cars to the rear of the paper's building by night and loaded the presses, type, and other materials and moved them south. The next day some of the employees and their families joined the refugee journal. Two editors and a printer with a stand of type and an old hand press stayed behind to get out a "war bulletin." They moved into the abandoned building of the Bank of Tennessee, using its vault for a "bombproof." An eight-by-ten, single-sheet edition bragged that the *Rebel* was the only institution left in town and announced that the paper had relocated in Marietta, Georgia. The rump staff stayed on until the Confederates evacuated the town, never losing its sense of humor. On 30 August, for example, the editor wrote, "Crash came a shell over the roof, struck a Chattanooga hog in the side and sent him squealing to the happy hunting ground."9

The periodic artillery bombardment continued on through the first week of September. All this time Wilder kept up a lively activity to divert Bragg's attention from the Union river crossings to the southwest. His troopers moved over all of the county roads north of the river; they appeared at the river crossings and at night they built large fires to simulate big camp sites. Men sawed wood, dropping the end pieces into the creeks and the river to supply convincing driftwood evidence that boat building activity was furiously under way. At Poe's Tavern, rear guard activity seemed never to cease. Shots rang out at

Friar Island and cannon were placed on the riverbank at Moccasin Bend opposite Lookout Mountain. Men of Wilder's brigade demonstrated all across the county as far as Sale Creek, using the guide services of Bill Crutchfield.[10]

Crutchfield, having early secured a certificate of disability from Confederate military duty, had been ordered out of Chattanooga by General Bragg. With the help of his brother Tom, he managed to get through the picket line and across the river to Wilder's camp. Crutchfield not only had complete knowledge of local geography but also possessed information on the strength, position, and reenforcements of the Confederate army.

When Bragg's cavalry reports put together a picture of what was actually happening downriver, the commander had little choice except to abandon Chattanooga. On 9 September an advance unit of General Thomas L. Crittenden's command—the Ninety-Second Illinois Mounted Infantry—marched into the city at 9:30 A.M. Columns of dust hovering over the roads marked the withdrawal of the last Confederates. A half hour later, regimental colors floated over the Crutchfield House. "Today," a Yankee artilleryman wrote in his diary, "the Union troops entered the boasted stronghold of the West without the loss of a man." Soon Captain Lilly and colleagues under Wilder's command crossed the Tennessee River and planted a flag on the largest of the forts.[11]

The Reverend McCallie also recorded his views: "Chattanooga cavalry withdrew about 9 o'clock in the morning, and about 10 A.M. the streams of Union soldiers, the first we had seen, dressed in blue, came pouring in. Not a child was harmed, not a woman insulted, not a man killed. . . . Here was a peaceful occupation of a city without any violence or outrage of any kind."[12]

The war had scarred and battered Chattanooga. Shell holes at the depot, the Crutchfield House, and at some residences told the story. A Union soldier noted, "The town has a dirty, dreary appearance, almost deserted of citizens, very few nice houses and all old ones."[13]

But the blue-clad troops did not tarry long. Crittenden's men pushed on across the southern part of Hamilton County after the retiring men of Bragg. Other elements of the corps made their way up the south bank of the river to Friar Island where they met Wilder's troops, who had forded the stream there. They immediately moved off into Georgia toward Ringgold as the left flank of Rosecrans's army.

For the next ten days the two major forces marched and countermarched across north Georgia. The Confederates got reenforcements;

the Federals finally concentrated around Crawfish Springs. Hamilton
County, off stage to the north, watched and waited as the great drama
of Chickamauga was enacted. The roar of battle rising from the cedar
thickets, the untamed woodland, and small fields drifted northward
with its message of bravery and suffering: 4,045 men died there; 23,161
received wounds.

At about 11:00 A.M. on Sunday, 20 September, General James
Longstreet, freshly arrived with men from Virginia, tore open the
Union line, leading to a resounding Confederate victory. The right
wing crumbled. About one-third of the Union army, including two
corps commanders and the commanding general, became part of a
disorganized, shock-ridden rout. Through McFarland's Gap to Rossville and on across the state line to Chattanooga they flowed, the
wreckage and confusion of a beaten army. Charles A. Dana, a journalist
serving at the time as assistant secretary of war, was part of the mob.
He wrote that he "found the road filled all the distance with the bag-
gage-wagons, artillery, ambulances, negros [sic] on horseback, field
and company officers, wounded men limping along, Union refugees
from the country around leading their wives and children, mules running along loose, squads of cavalry—in short, every element that could
confuse the rout of a great army, not excepting a major-general commanding an army corps."[14] Reverend McCallie witnessed the disorderly
procession's entry into town, commenting that it "almost bordered on
panic."

General Rosecrans, dazed and confused, rode all the way to
Chattanooga, stopping briefly at the small Catholic Church, ever fearful
his whole army might be in ruin. Leaving General George H. Thomas
to redeem what he could on the battlefield, the Union leader seems
to have felt it his personal duty to organize affairs in the rear.[15] Word
went to Washington. Dana framed his message in curt form: "My report
today is of deplorable importance. Chickamauga is as fatal a name in
our history as Bull Run."[16]

On the field Thomas consolidated the Union troops of the left flank,
stood fast all afternoon against terrific assaults, and saved the Army of
the Cumberland from complete disaster. His tenacity and fighting
leadership qualities earned him a proper cognomen, the "Rock of
Chickamauga."

At day's end Thomas, managing to get his weary men out of the line,
fell back to Rossville via McFarland Gap. It was a journey none ever
forgot. General John Beatty captured its pathos and drama in his diary:

The march to Rossville was a melancholy one. All along the road, for miles, wounded men were lying. They had crawled or hobbled slowly away from the fury of the battle, become exhausted, and lain down by the roadside to die. Some were calling the names and numbers of their regiments, but many had become too weak to do this; by midnight the column had passed by. What must have been their agony, mental and physical, as they lay in the dreary woods, sensible that there was no one to comfort or to care for them and that in a few hours more their career on earth would be ended![17]

Thomas led his men to Rossville Gap and places along Missionary Ridge. By the next day they showed some semblance of order, but their position could easily be overrun, and so by the morning of 22 September they joined Rosecrans in Chattanooga. But the town had not been prepared defensively by the Union army; no thought had been given to an emergency. The Tennessee River was to their backs, with only the pontoon bridge and two crude ferries to offer escape. Rosecrans, for the time being, held Lookout Mountain, which controlled ways south of the river to a supply base, but the Union commander hastily pulled his forces back into town, evacuating the mountain. The Confederates moved in, and from the mountain and Missionary Ridge, sealed in their opponents. The mauled, dejected Federals worked furiously to change their temporary position into permanent works. Outlying houses and buildings were razed to clear a line of fire, rifle pits were dug, and corrals were hastily built.[18]

The Confederates now had their chance to turn Chickamauga into smashing victory. But the furious energy consumed in the last few days seemed to leave Bragg drained of the will to fight. He turned aside pleas of subordinates to press an attack—pleas that in later years often differed from immediate reactions and led to bitter controversy as southern critics unmercifully assailed Bragg for incompetence. Instead, Bragg chose the strategy of siege, relying on winter, rains, mud, and starvation as allies.

Bragg soon dominated the Union position, which was restricted to a mile-square area (now in downtown Chattanooga). Gray-clad troops anchored their lines at the base of Raccoon Mountain along the river, where sharpshooters controlled traffic on Haley's Trace on the north shore. Their position swung across Lookout Valley to Lookout Mountain and then on across Chattanooga Valley to Missionary Ridge. It followed the ridge back to the Tennessee River near the mouth of Chickamauga Creek. Although extremely long, the Confederate lines made full use of the terrain. They controlled all the railroads and all river traffic. They commanded all roads on the south side of the river in addition to the river road into Sequatchie Valley. Although Rose-crans's army was intact and alive, it had become miserably entrapped, a situation the commander's critics added to his poor performance at Chickamauga to call for his ouster.

The railhead on the N & C (Nashville & Chattanooga) railroad at Bridgeport was the Union armies' single supply base. It could be reached by only one road some sixty miles in length. This route went out of Chattanooga by a pontoon bridge, crossed Stringer's Ridge, and ascended Walden Ridge via the "W" road. It crossed the mountain, dipping down into the Sequatchie Valley by the Anderson Pike, and proceeded over more or less level country to the north Alabama town. At best it was a rough, circuitous mountain road.

Heavy traffic passed over the road immediately. The Federals had received 1,740 Chickamauga wounded and dispatched to Bridgeport "such cases as could bear transportation" in vehicles of every descrip-tion. "Walking wounded" tried the journey on foot, but ambulance wagons had to patrol the road to pick up those who fell by the wayside.[19] All artillery horses that could possibly be spared also made the trip to find pasturage.

A steady stream of wagons labored over the road in an attempt to supply the besieged army with rations, forage, medicine, and am-munition. None could deliver a full load because forage for horses and mules had to be carried for the round trip since every acre along the way had been picked clean. Prisoners did hack out a second road up the east side of Walden Ridge along Shoal Creek (where the Taft High-way now runs), but it was so primitive and steep that only empty wagons could use it.

Small units of soldiers to spy on Confederate activity and report on their own traffic worked a signal line between Chattanooga and Jasper at Bob White's, James C. Conner's place, and "View Rock." A corral off the Anderson Pike over near the little settlement of Sawyers became a kind of convalescent camp for overworked and underfed mules and horses. Corral Road still marks this special Civil War service.

The long, dry summer of 1863 came to a sudden end about 1 October when torrential rains set in. The valley portion of the road to Bridgeport became a long quagmire; mud reached the horses' bellies and it was reported that some mules died standing up because they stood so deep in mud that they could not fall over. Teams had to double up; the Sequatchie River soon was too deep to ford. Driftwood broke the pontoon bridge at Chattanooga, and the mountain slopes were covered by rushing torrents. Traffic grew utterly confused and congested, as no local forage was available for the beasts of burden. Some supplies had to be jettisoned along the way and much food spoiled, for the wet conditions and long travel time combined to ruin cargoes. Drivers, wagoneers, and guards, soaked and weary, fought and cursed the road, the weather, the army mules, and the enemy in turn or all together.[20]

The Union lifeline, strained to the breaking point, also became a target for Confederate cavalrymen. One attack along the western slopes of Walden Ridge just inside the Sequatchie County line became legend in the valley. During the last night of September, General Joseph Wheeler's horsemen forded the Tennessee River above and below Old Washington and silently slipped across the mountain into Sequatchie Valley.

In the early hours of 2 October the Confederates found a major wagon train—estimates vary from eight to fifteen hundred—toiling along the Anderson Pike. Wheeler's men quickly swept away the escort guard, some of whom cut loose their teams and fled from the scene in every direction as fast as the frightened animals could carry them. The cavalrymen salvaged what cargo and animals they could take off and destroyed everything else. A chain of fire marked the road; rations, clothes, and the trade goods of sutlers went up in flames. Ammunition wagons exploded, teams were killed, and the wreckage and debris of the canvas-covered wagons littered the roadside for miles.[21]

Starvation seemed to be the worst Union foe. Forage parties found little corn or food of any kind. Gardens were stripped and few fowls escaped. The region had been scoured numerous times for hogs and cattle. The few brought in were so poor and lean that the soldiers joked about "beef dried on the hoof." A writer for *Harper's New Monthly Magazine* drew a vivid word picture of the scene:

> After the third week of the siege the men were put on quarter rations, and only two or three articles were supplied in this meager quantity. The only meat to be had was bacon, "side bacon" or "middling," I think it is called, and a slice about the size of three large fingers of a man's hand, sandwiched between the two halves of a "Lincoln Platform," as the four inches square cake of "hard bread" was called, and washed down by a pint of coffee, served for a meal. . . . I have often seen hundreds of soldiers following behind the wagon trains which had just arrived, picking out of the mud crumbs of bread, coffee, rice, etc., which were wasted from the boxes and sacks by the rattling of the wagons over the stones. Nothing was wasted in those days, and though the inspectors would frequently condemn whole wagon loads of provisions as spoiled by

exposure during the trip, and order the contents to be thrown away, the soldiers or citizens always found some use for it.[22]

Chattanooga, described as a "town gone to pieces in a heavy sea," became strictly a military base under the orders of Chief of Engineers, General James St. Clair Morton. Soldiers dug rifle pits that extended from Brabson Hill and the river to Chattanooga Creek, ditches, and earthworks, without regard for whatever was torn up. Forest-covered Cameron Hill lost its trees to axmen and stood out naked on the horizon. Fences no longer marked the limits of lawns or gardens. Every hill or rise had military importance and was identified by such names as Fort Wood, Fort Cameron, Fort Negley, Battery Erwin, Battery Bushnell, Lunette O'Meara, and Redoubt Crutchfield.

Soldiers' shelters, including hastily built arbors, "small dog-kenneled-shaped [sic] huts," and tents of every description abounded. Homes became officers' headquarters, and hotels, churches, stores, and warehouses were turned into hospitals. The provost-marshal took over the town government and oversaw every function, military and civilian.

Residents of the area decreased in number. Some received permission to go south; others were ordered north to reduce the number who had to be cared for. Some, like the Nicklins, moved to the countryside (they found a house on what later was named McCallie Avenue, just east of the viaduct). Soon they realized that they and their neighbors, the Ruohs family, were between the two armies and had to flee to the cellar whenever skirmishes occurred. Before long they were ordered to return to town, but eventually, having relatives in New York City, they decided to make their way to them. They crossed the pontoon bridge and journeyed to Bridgeport in a wagon train. Then they rode a cattle car to Nashville before securing more comfortable transportation. They were fortunate, for they had sufficient money, much of which Mrs. Nicklin secreted in her quilted petticoat. Of the civilians who remained in town, many worked in the hospitals as volunteers and many later reported pleasant experiences with soldiers. Entrapped journalists and field artists lived in what they called the "Bohemian Club."[23]

One journalist, W. F. G. Shanks, wrote of the civilians, "They were forced to huddle together in the middle of the town as best they could, and many of the houses occupied by them . . . surpassed in filth, . . . numbers of occupants, and general destitution the worst tenement houses in New York City."[24]

Even before the Chickamauga disaster, Union officials ordered reenforcements for Rosecrans, but their instructions did not arrive until two days after the battle. Then General William T. Sherman started for Chattanooga with four veteran divisions from the Vicksburg theater. Traveling by Mississippi River steamboat to Memphis, they marched eastward along the Memphis and Charleston (M & C) railroad with instructions to repair it as they advanced.

The panicky messages sent to Washington announcing the Chickamauga defeat brought speedy action from another direction. President Lincoln was called from his bed: the holding of Chattanooga was deemed that critical. Within forty-eight hours General Joseph Hooker entrained from Virginia with twenty-three thousand men, ten batteries of field artillery, more than three thousand horses, and cars crammed with baggage. In just twelve days some of these men from the Army of the Potomac arrived at Bridgeport, where they bivouacked. They had traveled 1,157 miles in one of the most amazing rail troop movements of the time, thereby demonstrating the hidden strength of Federal management and war potential.

In yet a third development, General Ulysses S. Grant received command of all the Union armies, for the persistent criticism of Rosecrans's judgment and the continual protests of incompetency by such observers as Dana led to Rosecrans's ouster. Grant immediately put Thomas in charge in Chattanooga and started to the field himself. While awaiting his arrival, Thomas pledged that "we will hold the town till we starve." On 21 October Grant got to Bridgeport. The next day, without staff or fanfare, he set out on horseback over the supply road in the drenching rain. Still on crutches because of a riding accident, the general had to be carried over places where he could not ride. After spending a night in the Sequatchie Valley, he rode into Chattanooga over the pontoon bridge.

As the Federals marshaled new strength, they were lucky enough to find conditions in their besieged position generally quiet. The pickets of the two opposing forces early found agreement, especially those along Chattanooga Creek. They shared the stream, each staying on his own bank, but with visiting privileges to swap news, coffee, tobacco, and other tidbits. No discipline could stop this free fraternizing and one observer noted, "Right on the eve of battle Federal pickets contentedly munch biscuit that their neighbor-in-law had tossed them; and an examination of many a plug of that Indian weed in a picket's pocket would show the print of a rebel's teeth at one end and a 'Yankee's' at the other." When Grant rode the picket line to inspect his position, he found squads of Confederates across the creek at attention offering a salute.

Only rarely was the quiet punctured by artillery fire, which did practically no damage. General Beatty's men, encamped on Stringer's Ridge, witnessed some of these duels, of which the General wrote:

> While standing on the bank at the water's edge, peering through the mist to get a better view of two Confederate soldiers on the opposite shore, a heavy sound broke from the summit of Lookout Mountain, and a shell went whizzing over into Hooker's camps. Pretty soon a battery opened on what is called Moccasin Point, on the north side of the river, and replied to Lookout. Later in the day Moccasin and Lookout got into an angry discussion which lasted two hours. These two batteries have a special spite at each other, and almost every day thunder away in the most terrible manner. Lookout throws his missiles too high and Moccasin too low, so that usually the only loss sustained by either is in ammunition. Moccasin, however, makes the biggest noise. The sound of his guns goes crashing and echoing along the sides of Lookout in a way that must be particularly gratifying to Moccasin's soul. I fear, however, that both these gigantic gentlemen are deaf as adders, or they would not so delight in kicking up such a hullabaloo.[25]

Meanwhile Johnny Reb waited and watched from his elevated position. His army's chief supply depot, located along the W & A tracks, was at Chickamauga, Tennessee. Fortifications at Tyner, built by General Pat Cleburne and consisting of four large, round forts with embrasures for cannon and openings for rifles, defended the railroad. From his headquarters at the home of J. S. Tyner, the Irish-born general had guards posted at all railroad bridges to protect them from "homemade Yankees."[26]

The troops under General Bragg had plenty of time to indulge in the minor complaints common to all soldiers, but beneath the general calm an internal crisis eroded the will and strength of the Confederate army. A new series of command complaints exploded among the senior officers after Chickamauga. Faultfinding, backbiting subordinates condemned Bragg and the suspicious, quarrelsome general replied in kind. A number of officers then requested a new leader, and President Davis found the situation bad enough to make him go to Chattanooga in a reconciliation effort. Davis arrived at Chickamauga Station on 9 October and with proper escort made his way to headquarters on Missionary Ridge. A meeting followed that left many incredulous. Davis asked the assembled officers if a new commander was needed and, in Bragg's presence, had each give his reasons. The replies amounted to a chorus of no confidence, but Davis retained Bragg, nonetheless, and the anti-Bragg men received transfers. Morale in the ranks plummeted as the Confederates found out that Forrest, Polk, Hindman, D. H. Hill, and Buckner were gone.[27]

Grant, for his part, upon arrival on 23 October found plans ready for the relief of the desperate plight of his men, to whom he soon became a symbol of action. Just three nights later some eighteen hundred troops climbed into pontoons under the protective shelter of Cameron Hill and silently drifted down the Tennessee. They slipped past the Confederate position on Lookout Mountain. Another mile or so downstream, still covered by darkness, they easily gained a bridge- head on the southern shore at Brown's Ferry. Comrades, who had marched across Moccasin Bend on the north side of the Tennessee, met them and were ferried across to the bridgehead.

The next morning General Hooker at Bridgeport began his phase of the plan. He brought his men into Lookout Valley to link up with the troops at Brown's Ferry. The Confederates, surprised by a major force west of Lookout Mountain, were quickly pushed aside. Generals Longstreet and Bragg both apparently had failed to understand the strategic value of the territory they had held for weeks. Moreover, they found it virtually impossible to work together. From the summit of Lookout Mountain they viewed the Yankee activity in the valley below and finally managed to undertake a night attack, which was poorly designed and poorly executed. Hooker's twenty thousand or more men had little trouble in holding their position in what is known as the battle of Wauhatchie. They were aided by a stampede of the mules of one corps which produced quite a disturbance in the darkness. There were numerous casualties, but the attack amounted to nothing more than a skirmish.

The successful seizure of Brown's Ferry and Hooker's occupation of Lookout Valley pinched off the westernmost jaw of Bragg's siege line. Everything west of Lookout Mountain fell into Union hands and a new supply line was then able to be opened. Crossing the river at Chattanooga, a road led over Moccasin Bend to Brown's Ferry. From the ferry it continued in a southerly direction between the water and the base of Raccoon Mountain until it entered Lookout Valley. Here the way curved westward through a depression in the mountains, used also by the railroad, to Kelly's Ferry. Since this ferry was located downriver from the rough waters of the mountain stretch of the

Tennessee River, steamboat traffic to this point from Bridgeport was possible.

A third phase of the plan followed immediately. At Bridgeport a small sternwheel steamboat, named the *Chattanooga*, was improvised. In the early hours of 30 October it made its first run in the darkness with loaded barges to Kelly's Ferry. When the crude steamer tied up, forty-thousand rations and thirty-nine thousand pounds of forage were put ashore. News of the opening of the "Cracker Line" flashed like magic through the Union camps. Full rations could soon be expected; the siege had been conquered. With the help of other small boats, the *Chattanooga* took over the assignment of providing essentials for Grant's next plans. The long wagon trip became a thing of the past, but during the weeks that it served as the lifeline for the Federals, ten thousand army mules and horses had been "used up."

The Confederate weakness at Brown's Ferry had been exposed and exploited. Now only the time needed for his army to build up supplies dictated when Grant would seize the initiative. Word went out to Sherman to push on with his reenforcements.

Bragg, however, did not seem to comprehend the complete success of Grant's first maneuver nor the rising morale in the Union ranks after the "Cracker Line" became established. On President Davis's suggestion, he sent Longstreet off on 4 November with fifteen thousand men to Knoxville on an ill-advised mission. Meanwhile Union reenforcements gathered; soon there would be men from three armies— the Army of the Cumberland, the Army of the Potomac, and the Army of the Tennessee. The Union forces presently outnumbered the Confederates two to one.

All seemed serene to Bragg; on 14 November he wrote to his wife of the unique spectacle spread out before his tent: "Just underneath my HD Qtrs are the lines of the two armies, and beyond with their outposts and signal stations are the Lookout, Raccoon, and Walden mountains. At night all are brilliantly lit up in the most gorgeous manner by the miriads of camp fires. No scene in the most splendid theater ever approached it."[28]

As Bragg wrote, Sherman was riding the *Chattanooga* from Bridgeport for a briefing of his role in the forthcoming engagement. He found everyone impatient for action. Sherman examined the ground where he would fight and walked with Grant to Fort Wood. Sherman later wrote in his *Memoirs* that the fort was a prominent salient of the defenses of the place, and from its parapet we had a magnificent view of the panorama. Lookout Mountain, with its rebel flags and batteries, stood out boldly, and an occasional shot fired toward Wauhatchee or Moccasin Point gave life to the scene. . . . All along Missionary Ridge were the tents of the rebel beleaguering force; the lines of trench from Lookout up toward the Chickmauga were plainly visible; and rebel sentinels, in a continuous chain, were walking their posts in plain view, not a thousand yards off. "Why," said I, "General Grant, you are besieged"; and he said, "It is too true." Up to that moment I had no idea that things were so bad.

Sherman hurried to get his troops moving on the last leg of their long march but missed the steamboat at Kelly's Ferry. He did get a small boat manned by four soldiers and started down the river by night taking his turn at the oars. Sherman's veterans started at once from Bridgeport, but the condition of the road from Shellmound was so bad that some delay in battle plans became necessary.[29]

On Monday, 23 November, Grant called for action. He would manage his long, crescent-shaped line as a unit, but the great distances and the nature of the terrain dictated that the campaign would develop in three phases. The initial assault came from Fort Wood. Grant, fearful that the men of the Army of the Cumberland might be battle-shy after their Chickamauga experience, gave them the first assignment. Leaving their tents and huts, they marched past Fort Wood in parade precision with bands playing. About two P.M. they moved eastward toward the Confederate picket lines and outposts. Rifle fire heard by those clustered at Fort Wood told that their men had come upon the enemy. Occasionally a thirty-two-pound Parrott fired from the fort.

There was much going and coming east of town as aides galloped by and wagons hurried forward along with well-marked ambulances. Small knots of off-duty soldiers and civilians stood about at vantage points looking for smoke signs in the east. Then all became quiet. The Confederates had moved back to their rifle pits at the foot of Missionary Ridge. The strategic knoll, Orchard Knob, a little more than a mile from the ridge, was in Union hands. From Fort Wood, where Grant and Thomas watched, orders were given for the troops to hold their position. That night they slept in the rain without tents.[30]

Tuesday was "Fighting Joe" Hooker's day; his field of action was Lookout Mountain. His men, drawn from different army corps, had never worked together prior to this assignment. Fog and river mist hovered over the northern end of the mountain as the Federals crossed Lookout Creek and moved up the west side over the rock-strewn, wooded slopes. They managed to form a line reaching from the base of the craggy palisades to the bluffs at the river's edge and swept in a turning movement around the mountain point. Picking their way among the boulders, fallen trees, and undergrowth, they pushed the scattered Confederate mountain guard back to their prepared breastworks on the narrow plateau where the Confederate commander had his headquarters at the Cravens House immediately below Point Lookout.

Cannon and musket fire could be heard across the valley. At times the mists cleared enough for observers at Fort Wood and the other vantage points to watch the action with glasses. When the roar grew loudest, it was joined by the cheers of Thomas's men in the valley below.

The Confederate force which held the mountain after Longstreet's departure numbered only about two thousand men under General Carter Stevenson. Most were on the plateau; but some cannoneers had been placed on the mountaintop along with scattered sharpshooters who fired from above on Hooker's men.

By mid-afternoon the fog had thickened to such a dense blanket that only flashes of fire were now discernible in the valley below. The Federal soldiers pressed on across the open spaces near the Cravens House. Here the Confederates under General E. C. Walthall, outnumbered by about four to one, could not resist the pressure, and their prepared works fell. The fog grew heavier and by 2 P.M. it was almost impossible to see. Only sporadic firing continued.

During the night, Stevenson withdrew all Confederates from Lookout Mountain and led them to new positions on Missionary Ridge. Next morning Federal scouts climbed the "chimneys" of the palisades at Point Lookout and, finding the enemy gone, ran up the flag of the United States. The Union victory, which eliminated the left flank of the Confederate position, had come much more easily than anticipated.

The quartermaster general of the Union army was in Chattanooga on an inspection tour at the time. He watched the fight on Lookout Mountain and reported, "Much of Hooker's battle was fought above the clouds." This romantic description has stuck throughout the years, giving glamor to the action along with the erroneous idea that the engagement took place on the mountaintop.[31]

When Sherman arrived at Hooker's headquarters, his troops were strung out on the road all the way to Bridgeport. On the morning of 23 November they began crossing the pontoon bridge at Brown's Ferry in full view of the Confederates on Lookout Mountain but well beyond their artillery range. They moved back of the hills in present-day North Chattanooga to give the false impression that they planned to go on to Knoxville. In a secluded rendezvous they encamped to prepare for their role in the coming battle. Although timing had to be adjusted, all details were thoroughly planned. As General Beatty commented in his *Memoirs,* "Hitherto I have gone into battle almost without knowing it; now we are about to bring on a terrible conflict, and have abundant time for reflection."[32]

One brigade of Sherman's men moved on to North Chickamauga Creek, where a fleet of pontoons had been built and concealed. In midnight darkness with oars muffled, they drifted downriver to the South Chickamauga Creek. Men with rifles and shovels jumped ashore, easily surprising the few river pickets posted there, and began to dig in.

The boats then ferried comrades, who had silently arrived on the north river plain, across the stream from the newly won bridgehead near the north end of Missionary Ridge. As day dawned, a pontoon bridge was placed across the Tennessee and another across South Chickamauga Creek. A small steamboat assisted in the crossing, and by noon on 24 November Sherman's three divisions with their horses and artillery had reached the south bank. The Confederates on Missionary Ridge were shocked to discover their new neighbors.[33]

Much of this activity took place on the farms of Tom Crutchfield and his brother-in-law, John King. Crutchfield, seeking a quiet spot after disposing of his hotel, had chosen Amnicola. He had sent a substitute to the Confederate army and later was exempted from service under a provision of the law excusing those who supervised the work of twenty hands. When Bragg ordered Crutchfield's brother William to leave Chattanooga, Tom helped him escape across the river to Wilder's camp and he, himself, had to hide in the woods to escape rebel cavalry groups who suspected his loyalty. Then for a short time Wilder controlled the area and received mules and supplies from Crutchfield, but after Chickamauga Amnicola became an active area on Bragg's right wing. Then, as if from nowhere, came Sherman's divisions onto the Crutchfield farm. The man who sought quiet away from town now found his farm barren and in a shambles, his implements destroyed, his fences gone, and the whole acreage cut up with rifle pits.[34]

Sherman, leaving only pickets and service personnel on the farm, moved foward in a light rain, protected by low-hanging clouds. While

Hooker's men gained victory on Lookout Mountain, Sherman assaulted two isolated, unoccupied hills which faulty maps showed as the northern end of Missionary Ridge. The Confederates, given some hours of grace, busily threw up fortifications on the rise over the railroad tunnel. After a brief, spirited probing of strength, both sides dug in for the night on the narrow, wooded hills separated by a deep depression.

The Union forces were in place in accordance with Grant's master plan. At midnight Sherman got orders to attack at "day dawn." Thomas in the center, based on Orchard Knob whose Union guns were now in place, would join the battle later. Hooker's instructions called for a march across the valley from Lookout Mountain to take his place on the Union right wing near Rossville, with the possibility of working his way into the enemy's rear.

The morning of 25 November dawned clear and bright after a near-total eclipse of the moon, which was felt by some to be a bad omen. The Confederates, badly outnumbered, were all on Missionary Ridge. Their position stretched for some seven miles along the 300- to 400-foot elevation, whose steep slopes were spotted with ravines and strewn with stumps, fallen trees, and small boulders. Bragg had placed rifle pits at the bottom on the western slope, some scattered works part way up, and a line, belatedly constructed on the crest—a line which inexplicably followed the actual top rather than the military crest. Artillery in many places could not be depressed sufficiently to provide effective fire against assaulting troops.

On the Confederate left General J. C. Breckinridge's three divisions defended about two-thirds of the ridge; on the right Hardee's four divisions held the line. Not only was the Confederate position thinly manned but from their lines many could clearly see the "panorama of Yankee power." Thomas's Army of the Cumberland was in full view; Hooker's men moving across Chattanooga Valley could be discerned although their progress was slowed by the need to build a new bridge over the creek. Everyone heard Sherman launch artillery and musket fire at the north end of the ridge in the vicinity of the railroad tunnel and the Confederate's reply.

Sherman had been in the saddle since before daybreak. He soon realized his day's work was cut out for him. Not only did he need to advance up the sloping ravine, but he also found himself faced by the able General Pat Cleburne. The flow of battle, often at very close range, continued here throughout the morning. Cleburne had trouble using his artillery because of the steep nature of the ridge; some troops rolled stones down the grade while a few artillerymen tried lighting the fuses of shells and tossing them at the enemy. The Federal artillery double-teamed their pieces and, with axmen clearing the way, gained some vantage points. But Sherman grew concerned; he made little if any progress and heard nothing of cooperative action along the ridge to the south.

From his observation post at Orchard Knob, Grant realized by morning's end that Sherman had not made any progress and that Hooker had not arrived at Rossville Gap. About noon the commander instructed Thomas to prepare an attack on the rifle pits at the western foot of the ridge. Such a limited assault at the center would relieve the pressure on Sherman and restrain Bragg from sending more help to that part of the line.

Time passed. The Confederates still held Missionary Ridge and the late-fall day promised early darkness. Grant's plans seem to have faltered. Then, at about three P.M. the Army of the Cumberland moved out in a line about two miles wide. With banners flying and ranks carefully dressed they came forward *en masse* toward their objective while the Confederates on the heights watched in growing consternation. Cannon fire from the ridge and from the newly placed Union guns at Orchard Knob added to the drama.

Nearing the rifle pits, the Union veterans made a run for the Confederate works—some thought the scene resembled Pickett's charge. But now the gray defenders broke and began dashing up the ridgeside. Gunners on the top hesitated to fire as pursued and pursuer blended together amid the boulders and fallen trees. Observers in the valley saw Union flags move up the hillside beyond the rifle pits.

When Grant, watching through his field glasses at the Orchard Knob vantage point, saw the continuing charge, he was amazed and angered. He told aides to learn who gave such orders and threatened dire consequences for the officer responsible.

The headlong rush continued to propel the Union troops uphill. No general orders directed their action. It was largely a case of the privates taking charge along with the impromptu urging of junior officers fighting with their men. Units of the Army of the Cumberland reached the crest, piercing the Confederate line in several places and sending the gray defenders retreating down the eastern slope of the ridge. Hardee, on the right, held his position in spite of the breakthrough until darkness, finally withdrawing with Cleburne's men covering the retreat.

The entire battlefield resembled a vast amphitheater. The soldiers of both armies were both actors and spectators. The Confederate troops stationed on Missionary Ridge watched and measured the enemy's strength against their own thinly held line; the sight was both impressive and disturbing. One fellow wrote, "Our boys thought the whole world was marching to attack them," and others claimed they heard the Yankee command, "Attention World! By Nations, right wheel! *By States, Fire!*" When casualties were finally tallied, 4,146 Confederates were listed as captured or missing.[35]

On that Wednesday in November the campaign of Chattanooga ended; the Confederate victory at Chickamauga some two months earlier had wasted away. Union losses included 753 killed, 4,722 wounded, and 349 missing; the Confederates killed numbered 361 and the wounded 2,160.

That night members of the United States Sanitary Commission and volunteers searched the ridge for wounded and dead comrades. The night was clear and cold. Sherman's men sought out the tunnel over which the battle had been so severe; they found it vacated save for the "dead and wounded of our own and the enemy comingled." Some of Cleburne's men, whose orders to retire arrived late, searched for a road of any kind down the east slope of the ridge and a Chickamauga Creek ford in order to get out their wheeled equipment. With pine torches to light their way, they got to Chickamauga Station while pickets stayed on all night at the Glass farm at the foot of the ridge. Pursuing Yankees pushed forward for the supply depot at Chickamauga.

Their spirit gone, the defeated Confederates, described as a "howling mob," had gathered in this area. Fires from burning buildings lit up the night sky. The next day, as Sherman reported later, "The depot presented a scene of desolation that war alone exhibits—corn-meal and corn in huge burning piles, broken wagons, abandoned caissons, pieces of pontoons, balks and chesses, etc., destined doubtless for the famous invasion of Kentucky, and all manner of things, burning and broken. Still the enemy kindly left us a good supply of forage for our horses, and meal, beans, etc. for our men."[36]

The date was Thursday, 26 November; it happened to be the first national observance of Thanksgiving Day. The guns of the forts of Chattanooga fired victory salutes. The churches, functioning as hospitals, were full; outdoor "services" consisted of burying the dead and caring for the wounded. The day was "sad, solemn, grand."

NOTES

1. U. S., War Department, *The War of Rebellion: A Compilation of the Official Records of the Union and Confederate Armies* (Washington, D.C.: Government Printing Office, 1884), Series 1, 16 (pt. 2): 75.

2. Gilbert E. Govan and James W. Livingood, *A Different Valor: The Story of General Joseph E. Johnston, C.S.A.* (Indianapolis: Bobbs-Merrill, 1956), pp. 164-170.

3. Ibid., p. 169.

4. *Chattanooga Gazette*, 6 March 1864; the *Chattanooga Rebel* for this period gives a good picture of local social conditions; James M. Swank, *History of the Manufacture of Iron in All Ages* (Philadelphia: American Iron and Steel Institute, 1892), pp. 290-291.

5. Richard B. Harwell, ed., *Kate: The Journal of a Confederate Nurse* (Baton Rouge: Louisiana State University Press, 1959), pp. 60–61, 64.

6. Ibid., p. 68.

7. James W. Livingood, *"The Chattanooga Rebel,"* (East Tennessee Historical Society) *Publications* no. 39 (1967), pp. 42–55; Franc M. Paul, *"The Chattanooga Rebel," Tennessee Old and New* 2 vols. (Nashville: Tennessee State Historical Commission and Tennessee Historical Society, 1947), 2: 273–279. Henry Watterson (1840–1921) became a nationally known journalist, newspaper editor, and author. His career was closely associated with the *Louisville Courier-Journal*. The *Chattanooga Rebel* after August 1863 relocated in Marietta and Griffin, Georgia, and in Selma, Alabama; its last issue was dated 27 April 1865.

8. John W. Rowell, *Yankee Artillerymen: Through the Civil War With Eli Lilly's Indiana Battery* (Knoxville: University of Tennessee Press, 1975), pp. 94–102.

9. Livingood, *"Rebel,"* p. 51.

10. Rowell, *Artillerymen*, pp. 100–101.

11. Ibid., p. 102; *O.R.*, Series 1, 30 (pt. 1): 445, 453–455, 678, 759–760; Thomas Crutchfield to James R. Hood, 27 December 1863, Manuscript Division, Tennessee State Library, Nashville.

12. *Chattanooga Times*, 1 July 1903.

13. Rowell, *Artillerymen*, p. 102.

14. James H. Wilson, *The Life of Charles A. Dana* (New York: Harper & Bros., 1907), p. 264.

15. *O.R.*, Series 1, 30 (pt. 1): 60.

16. Ibid., p. 192.

17. John Beatty, *Memoirs of a Volunteer 1861–1863*, Harvey S. Ford, ed. (New York: Norton, 1946), pp. 252–253.

18. W. F. G. Shanks, "Chattanooga and How We Held It," *Harper's New Monthly Magazine* 36 (January 1866): 144.

19. *O. R.*, Series 1, 30 (pt. 1): 225. The Federals found two hundred bales of cotton in Chattanooga which they reserved to make mattresses. Some 150 upholsterers, tailors, and saddlers made enough of these pads "so that by the tenth day every severely wounded man was provided with a comfortable bed," reported the medical director of the Department of the Cumberland.

Joseph S. Gillespie, born in 1821 at the "Euchee Old Fields" in Rhea County and mayor of Chattanooga in the mid-1840s, was a practicing physician. During the war, because of his Southern sympathies, he spent some time in prison. Following the battle of Chickamauga he helped other local doctors in caring for wounded Confederate soldiers. For many years he lived east of Missionary Ridge on a farm named "Canachee."

20. Ibid., pp. 214–221, 830, 843, 846–847; Cartter Patten, *Signal Mountain and Walden's Ridge* (n.p.: author, 1962), pp. 1–3; 23–29.

21. *O.R.*, Series 1, 30 (pt. 1): 205; Series 1, 30 (pt. 2): 722–725.

22. Shanks, "How We Held It," p. 146; Beatty, *Memoirs*, p. 259.

23. Scrapbook of undated clippings in possession of author; this collection contains some material from diary of Mrs. John B. Nicklin, née Elizabeth Kaylor.

24. Shanks, "How We Held It," p. 146.

25. Beatty, *Memoirs*, pp. 259–260.

26. Howell Purdue and Elizabeth Purdue, *Pat Cleburne: Confederate General* (Tuscaloosa, Ala.: Portals Press, 1977), pp. 119–120.

27. Thomas L. Connelly, *Autumn of Glory: The Army of Tennessee, 1862–1865* (Baton Rouge: Louisiana State University Press, 1971), pp. 226–278.

28. Bruce Catton, *Never Call Retreat* (New York: Doubleday, 1965), p. 261, quotes a 14 November 1863 letter from General Bragg to Mrs. Bragg.

29. William T. Sherman, *Memoirs of General William T. Sherman* 2 vols. (London: Henry S. King, 1875), 1: 361–364.

30. Christopher Chancellor, ed., *An Englishman in the American Civil War: The Diaries of Henry Yates Thompson* (New York: New York University Press, 1971), pp. 150–151.

31. *O.R.*, Series 1, 31 (pt. 2): 77–80.

32. Beatty, *Memoirs*, p. 261.

33. Sherman, *Memoirs*, 1: 373–375.

34. Thomas Crutchfield to James R. Hood, 27 December 1863.

35. Govan and Livingood, *Chattanooga Country*, 248–249.

36. Chancellor, *Englishman*, pp. 162–164; Sherman, *Memoirs*, 1: 378; Nisbet, *Four Years On the Firing Line* (Chattanooga: Imperial Press, 1914), pp. 160–164; Beatty, *Memoirs*, p. 263; Purdue, *Cleburne*, p. 150.

11

A Fresh Start

ALTHOUGH the siege of the Federal army ended with the spectacular action on Missionary Ridge, the war was not over for the people of Hamilton County. The churches and all available buildings continued to be commandeered by the soldiers. Stones dressed for a new Catholic sanctuary and some grave markers were part of the hastily built fortifications. The miserable condition of the streets, the worn buildings, and the strange tents and dingy corrals of the military caused one journalist to conclude that Chattanooga was "a town gone to pieces in a heavy sea." The provost marshal still ran the town government and continued to do so until 7 October 1865.

Eighteen volumes of the county registrar's office records fell into the hands of the Union army. Since civilian government in Tennessee had, in effect, ceased to exist, local government grew steadily more confused and feeble. Both Confederate and Union army units operated throughout the area, while guerrillas and bushwhackers grew increasingly bold.

The report of a colonel of the Twenty-Fourth Illinois Infantry, filed on 24 January 1864, reflects the problems of the hour. Colonel Geza Mihalotzy's men had campaigned around Harrison and Ooltewah. They picked up Confederate deserters from Tunnel Hill and Dalton and sent to headquarters "3 citizen prisoners from the neighborhood of Harrison

(J. T. Gardenhire, J. A. Hunter, and ———— Lynn) to Provost Marshal-
General Wiles, "who charged them with having 'aided the guerrillas.'"

The Federal party encountered a squad of enemy cavalry attempting
to cut their communications and at Ooltewah arrested a Miss S. Locke
and a Miss Barnet, charging them with "carrying contraband information to the rebel army." Colonel Mihalotzy reported some three
hundred cavalrymen encamped five miles beyond Igou's Gap, who in
small groups made continuous raids on the Union villages and farms,

> committing all manner of outrages and cruelties on the local population. As an
> incident illustrative of the barbarities constantly being perpetrated by these
> outlaws, I will mention that a Mr. Tallent, a loyal citizen living near the forks
> of the road leading to Red Clay and McDaniel's Gap, recently found in his
> immediate neighborhood a young child in a perishing condition, stripped of
> all its clothing, which the rebels had left there, having attempted by that means
> to find the father of the said child, whom they proposed to hang, he being a
> loyal citizen.

The colonel continued to narrate details of the chaotic state of affairs:

> I have been reliably informed that a rebel raid on our river transportation
> at Harrison is now positively being prepared. This raiding force will have to
> pass through the mountain gaps near Ooltewah. The rebels infesting that region
> of country have been in the habit of disguising themselves in Federal uniforms,
> and have by this means often succeeded in deceiving the Union people. Messrs.
> Stone and Scroggins, Union citizens living at Julien's Gap, can give information
> of a guerrilla band commanded by a citizen of Ooltewah, who steal and plunder
> from the loyal citizens continually. They also know where a large portion of
> the spoils of this band are now secreted. A number of discharged soldiers from
> Tennessee regiments have banded together with Union citizens and organized
> themselves for self-defense. They are armed with such weapons as they have
> been able to procure, consisting of rifles, carbines, and revolvers. This band
> of loyal men, who are men of the highest sense of honor and true patriotism,
> are doing all they can to promote the success of our cause. . . . I have also
> learned that the following named citizens, [no subsequent list given] living in
> the vicinity of Ooltewah, are in the habit of harboring the guerrillas infesting
> that region, and that the rebels have signified their intention to burn the town
> of Ooltewah as soon as the families of the Misses Locke and Barnet . . . quit
> the town.

Colonel Mihalotzy recommended that a small permanent force be
stationed at Ooltewah to work with and to help protect the loyalists
who were not only intimately acquainted with the region but also "able
and willing to put in operation a most effective system of espionage."[1]

In April 1864 Federal authorities got word of unusual activity in

Rhea County. Some Hamilton County Federal soldiers, sent to arrest the participants in the disturbance, found a group of uniformed, mounted young ladies whom they accused of serving as a home guard. Although members of prominent Rhea and Hamilton County families, the girls were taken to Smith's Crossroads (Dayton) and on to Bell's Landing where they were loaded on a steamboat nicknamed the *Chicken Thief* (actually the *Chattanooga*) for a trip to headquarters in Chattanooga.

In the custody of Federal troops, the girls marched from the Chattanooga wharf up Market Street to the office of the provost marshal. Charges were heard, but the spokesperson for the girls explained that they were not in military service. Rather, their mission was to offer assistance and relief to widows and orphans of Confederate soldiers and to families whose men were in Confederate service. The commander of the post, General J. B. Steedman, dismissed all charges and ordered the arresting officers to see that the girls got home safely.

The young ladies were entertained at dinner at the Crutchfield House and spent the night at the homes of local civilian families. The next day they returned home triumphantly, their heads reeling with excitement.[2]

These were trying times for the few remaining residents of Chattanooga. The Reverend McCallie wrote of the dreary winter days. Schools did not function and the churches were all closed. No stores or markets operated and carriages did not appear on the streets. Soldiers, strangers, and freedmen made the native citizens feel lost in their own community. Food supplies dwindled and the minister noted, "We had no milk, no butter, no cheese, scarcely any fruit; but we had bacon, bread, such as could be made without milk or yeast, a little coffee, some sugar, and a barrel of pickles in brine but no vinegar to put with them."[3]

On Christmas Day a general order of Major General Thomas became a living trust for the coming ages. This soldier, at forty-seven years of age, had won fame at Chickamauga, succeeded General Rosecrans in command of the Army of the Cumberland, and played a conspicuous role in the great victory of Chattanooga. Trained at West Point, he remained loyal to the Union although a native of Virginia. At his instigation, a seventy-five-acre site beyond the Western & Atlantic Railroad was proclaimed a national cemetery "in commemoration of the battles of Chattanooga . . . and to provide a proper resting-place for the remains of the brave men who fell."

The gently sloping knoll suggested a design to Chaplain Thomas B. Van Horn, who laid out the area. He reported with satisfaction that "where nature suggested avenues they have been made, and their curves define the section." Union dead, having been hastily buried in scattered mounds throughout the area and in long trenches where battle casualties amassed in large numbers, were reinterred in the new graveyard. By 1865 more than twelve thousand bodies, almost five thousand of which were unknown, received an eternal resting place. In keeping with General Thomas's desire, none were placed by states, for he insisted on a "national cemetery."[4]

In September 1867 a group of local Confederate veterans obtained a deed for about two acres of land near the old city cemetery and dedicated a Confederate burying place. Following the battle of Stone's River, wounded men had been sent to Chattanooga and those who died along with some others who had passed away were interred in this area. After the cemetery was formally established, a man was engaged to search out scattered graves and rebury the remains. In all, some twelve hundred soldiers and their wives were buried here.[5]

Before General Thomas left this section to take his command in the Atlanta campaign, he also ordered that the various defenses of Chattanooga be given names honoring soldiers who had fallen.[6] (See Appendix O). The sites of these major works have long been obliterated by the changes of the passing years, but the cemeteries, quiet and neatly trimmed, remain consecrated ground and a perpetual reminder of the significance of what happened in Chattanooga during the fall months of 1863.

As mentioned earlier, the Union victory at Chattanooga completely nullified the significance of the Confederate achievement at Chickamauga. Immediately after Missionary Ridge the Southern commander resigned, never to take field command again. Grant, on the other hand, gained a promotion to the command of all Union armies. He received the rank of lieutenant general: only George Washington and Winfield Scott had held that position before Grant.

The network of railroads centering on eastern Tennessee had been won by the Federals as was the food supply area of the Volunteer state. Union sympathizers throughout that part of the state, including those in Hamilton County, felt liberated.

In breaking out of the siege, the Federal military organization for the first time had corps from three different armies—the Army of the Tennessee, the Potomac, and the Cumberland—fighting under a single commander. The extreme length of the battle line, the closely coordinated action at three different sections of that line, and the grandeur of the terrain, where nearly all of the fighting was in full view of both armies, made Chattanooga's campaign an impressive and unusual spectacle. So too did the remarkable concentration of Union leadership; no other battle in the war involved such a collection of first-rate generals: Grant, Sherman, Thomas, Hooker, and Sheridan.

Most important for the immediate future was the fact that the Union army stood at the southern gateway to Atlanta and the sea. A second opportunity to sever the South presented itself, the first having been the capture of the great Mississippi River route. The Federal campaign for 1864 was obvious; Chattanooga and Hamilton County now had a new role. They became the advance base for a huge army about to penetrate deep into hostile country.

Because of the length of the single-track railroad supply line, this operation would be a risky and taxing campaign for its commander, General Sherman. As soon as country roads dried and the grass of May was green enough to support the military horses and mules, everything had to be in order. As of November the rail line from Nashville to Chattanooga was in miserable condition; accidents were frequent, rolling stock and power units in short supply, spare parts lacking, and the track so bad that trains ran only eight miles per hour. All this had to be changed.

The railroads behind the Union lines were made part of the United States Military Railroad. Regularly operated hospital trains traveled northward. Engineers rebuilt bridges, erected blockhouses at major bridges, and the entire route all the way back to Louisville was put under reinforced guard. Locomotives and cars were gathered up from everywhere. To feed one hundred thousand men and thirty-five thousand animals, Sherman demanded that 130 cars, each with ten-ton capacity, be sent to Chattanooga daily. On 6 April 1864, he ordered that all trains be devoted exclusively to moving military supplies and personnel. Many troops still had to march. Beef cattle had to be driven to evenly spaced pens so that fresh meat could be had daily at the front. All this brought violent protests from sutlers, newspapers, merchants, and the loyal residents of the area. But Sherman had his way.[7]

Rebuilding and finding efficient management for the long supply rail line represented only part of Sherman's problem. Locally, Chattanooga had to be converted into a gigantic supply depot. Government sawmills appeared across the Tennessee River from the town and at the mouth of every tributary stream in Hamilton County. Forests were cut ruthlessly without much interest in ownership legalities, resulting in an enormous tangle of claims to be dealt with on some future day. But by working round the clock the loggers produced timber and lumber for buildings, boats, and bridges and fuel for locomotives and steamboats.

Huge warehouses where every imaginable bit of army gear was collected sprang up on vacant lands along Market Street. Wagon yards, artillery parks, and corrals were expanded and new ones started. To reduce the risk of fire, the government placed large water barrels on top of many structures and organized a fire company. To supply water, a reservoir was built on a spur of Cameron Hill and water pumped to it from the river. Since gravity carried the water to consumers, the government built a gristmill along the main pipeline so that its stones could be turned by the water used in town.

Down by the river, a Federal shipyard soon took shape where the steamers which opened the cracker line were kept in repair and others built. Gunboats for patroling the river were constructed. Immediately after Missionary Ridge, the small steamboats made a practice of carrying ammunition, hospital stores, and rations to soldiers stationed in East Tennessee and foodstuffs to Union supporters in northern Hamilton County and beyond. The Western Sanitary Commission planted large areas in vegetables for distribution; their efforts were supplemented by those of such charitable organizations as the Pennsylvania Relief Association for East Tennessee.

All vacant stores and town lots where tents or boxlike buildings could be erected became the business places of sutlers, those licensed merchants and service people who followed the military. Some sold clothing, others handled food, souvenirs, wine, beer, liquor, and tobacco. Certain sutlers acted as barbers, photographers, and dentists while others worked as undertakers, sending bodies home as instructed if transportation was available. Hotels, churches, and homes served as offices and hospitals. Immediately after the battles the churches supplemented hospital facilities started by the Confederates. Later they were turned to military use: the Catholic, Episcopal, and Cumberland Presbyterian structures became ordnance depots, the Methodist Church a prison, and the Presbyterian sanctuary continued to be used as a hospital for civilians, principally government people. New hospital buildings were constructed and a convalescent camp on Lookout Mountain provided for officers.

Federal construction crews also built a bridge across the Tennessee

River at the foot of Market Street to replace the pontoon bridge used so steadily during the siege. The builders used stone from the nearby bluff furnace along with ore and cinder piles to weight down the wooden cribbing of the piers. The bridge was finished in the fall of 1864 and the soldiers planned a dance as part of the ceremonial festivities, but when the bridge began to sway with the music, the commandant called a halt to the fun.

The most unusual facility built by the government dramatized Sherman's transportation problems as well as the growing importance of the railroads in the Civil War. It was a large mill for the purpose of rerolling twisted iron rails and producing bar iron. Heavy traffic had left the local lines in such a dilapidated state that accidents occurred daily. Raiding cavalry outfits and local bushwhacker gangs took sport in tearing up track: a special trick was to take up the rails, heat them over a fire, and bend them around the nearest tree.[8]

On 29 February 1864, a favorite of some of the old residents returned. In the wake of the Union successes, James Hood came back home to renew publication of the *Chattanooga Gazette*. Almost three years had passed since his "required" exodus, but now he had the entire local newspaper field to himself and was safe to flay verbally all secessionists. News of the army, of the community, and of the surrounding area filled the *Gazette*'s columns. As the 1864 campaign moved through north Georgia, the paper carried news and rumors of its progress in a column called "Late and Important from Sherman." Marauding guerrillas kept the countryside in constant turmoil; there were killings, thefts, and arson to report. Colonel Clift was captured and imprisoned during the Atlanta campaign and only the intervention of his two Confederate sons gained his release on parole.

When General John B. Hood, after the fall of Atlanta, brought his army back into Tennessee, the paper reported the mounting tension as civilians feared new battles. Emergency measures were needed and the newspaper spread the word. The *Gazette* stated that notices had been posted saying "All sutlers, traders and able-bodied men who are doing business in Chattanooga and have the interest of the Government at heart, and are willing to offer their services to the commander of the Post, in case of emergency will meet at Sharp & Downing's tent on Main Street . . . for the purpose of organizing a company, so that we may be of some service."

The *Gazette* reported on the presence of large numbers of camp followers, refugees, and freedmen who drifted into the army base.

Many were destitute. Although authorities sent them to other places as fast as possible, by November a rough census put almost four thousand at Chattanooga. Many more were never counted. Some lived in surplus army tents, others threw together crude huts, with the majority locating near the river. Eventually a large camp developed on the north bank of the Tennessee which won the name, Camp Countraband.

Editor Hood noted that some residents had to leave town under military pressure; the Reverend McCallie suffered army harassment and a threatened expulsion from town. Some citizens were arrested by soldiers and tried by the provost marshal. The *Gazette* also told of religious activities at the post chapel in the Baptist Church. It reported interments at the National Cemetery and listed the names of people who had received mail. Apparently the army provided some sort of postal service, although there appears to be no evidence that mails were ever discontinued or that a Confederate system ever existed. The busy hotels and boarding houses naturally furnished much news and gossip as a constant stream of officials, visitors, and soldiers' families poured into the community.

The heavy buildup of troops for the 1864 Atlanta campaign—Sherman started with almost one hundred thousand in May—camped all the way from Charleston, Tennessee, to Huntsville, Alabama, with central concentration in Hamilton County. General Beatty was back again; his camp was on the Tennessee-Georgia border in a dense forest. In earlier times, the general commented, the area was a rendezvous point for thieves, murderers, and outlaws of the two states. In his memoirs, Beatty confided that "the presence of large numbers of desperadoes, in this locality, at all seasons of the year, has prevented its settlement by good men, and in consequence, there are thousands of acres on which there has scarcely been a field cleared or even a tree cut."[9]

The Union soldiers camped everywhere, and later those assigned to supply duties made household words of Chattanooga and Chickamauga throughout the nation. Their letters carried a local dateline and their pictures—usually made with Lookout Mountain as a backdrop—went everywhere. When duties slackened, they found diversion from camp life in outings at Lula Falls, Rock City, Point Lookout, or Walden Ridge. Caves were explored and Indian mounds excavated. Fishing was good at the mouth of Chattanooga or Chickamauga creeks: one catch of a seventy-five-pound catfish was reported.

The military authorities used the pages of the *Gazette* to launch an unusual Civil War experiment of price control. In December 1864 they announced a schedule of prices designed to curb inflation. The order included a great variety of items—groceries, clothing, fancy goods, canned food, hardware, tobacco, and toiletries—for which maximum prices were announced. All traders and sutlers had orders to have a "copy of the list conspicuously posted." If they had items not listed in stock, they had to report them to headquarters with the bill of purchase so that a proper price could be effected. Naturally a howl of protest went up from all concerned, but it apparently went unheard. In the months following, some violaters were arrested for black marketing.[10]

After the fall of Atlanta and the battle of Franklin, Chattanooga lost its military significance, although troops, including some Negro regiments, remained there for many months. Waves of excitement passed through the camps with news of the fall of Richmond and the surrender at Appomattox. Organized cheers or wild individual war whoops undertook to compete with the "thunder tones" of the great guns. This enthusiasm gave way to deep sorrow on 15 April when word came of the assassination of President Lincoln.

Jenkin Lloyd Jones recorded in his diary the reception of the news by soldiers in Chattanooga:

'Tis night, a beautiful day has just closed. But alas! a dark pall hangs over our camp. The soldier mourns the loss of the noblest American of the day. President Abraham Lincoln has fallen by the hands of a traitorous assassin, 2 p.m. we started out to graze, each and all lighthearted and merry. But lo! while out near the foot of Mission Ridge, the stars and stripes over Fort Creighton were seen to descend to half mast, and the news reached us as if by magic of the fall of our noble president. A gloom was cast upon every one, and silently we returned to camp, still hoping for a contradiction. But it was too true. The scene that followed was one very seldom seen in the tented field. But a soldier is not, as many think, wholly void of feeling. All regarded the loss of him as of a near and dear relative. Terrible were the oaths and imprecations uttered through clenched teeth against the vile perpetrators.

Jones wrote of the following day, "The whole town was draped in mourning, flags tied with black, and white crepe exhibited in all parts of the town, while the 100-pounder Parrotts high up on Cameron Hill fired half-hour guns from 5 A.M. till 6 P.M. The gloom of yesterday still hangs over the camp."[11]

Demobilization became the daily concern of soldiers and civilians. During the winter months of 1865–66 the military dismantled the forts in the area. They shipped north some two thousand pieces of artillery and tons of ammunition. The men were mustered out as rapidly as possible and by April 1866 Chattanooga had lost practically all uniformed personnel. The civilian population of the town reported a few months earlier totalled 5,776; of this number 3,119 were listed as white and 2,657 black.

While the demobilization was in progress, the military disposed of all its holdings. Thomas Webster's iron industry had survived the war and the management salvaged tons of iron from the battlefields. They heaped the metal in the furnace yard to be recycled into peacetime goods for rebuilding the surrounding area's economy.[12]

At war's end no privately owned steamboats operated on the upper Tennessee River, but there were veteran rivermen (C. S. Peak, W. C. Henager, C. C. Spiller, Jim Johnson, John L. Doss, Joseph Glover) ready to go back to work. The government, having no further use for its boats, assembled those which had been operating out of Chattanooga and sold them at auction. Although most were bought by men who transferred them to other rivers, Jim Johnson got the *Kingston* and Captain Doss the *Resacca* at very reasonable prices. Soon other new or used boats were serving Hamilton County landings.[13]

The federal government on 15 September 1865 returned the Nashville & Chattanooga railroad to its owners. The firm, virtually penniless, found the roadbed in a deplorable condition and everything, from office supplies to heavy equipment, lacking. Gradually the railroad was brought back into shape and in 1867, as an experiment, the company tried burning as fuel coal rather than wood in a locomotive. Not long after that date sleeping cars and diners gave a new tone to the service. On 31 May 1873 the company changed its name to Nashville, Chattanooga, and St. Louis Railway in anticipation of a run to the Missouri city, which did not become a reality until seven years later.

The United States Military Railroad took over the W & A (Western & Atlantic) from 1 September 1864 to 25 September 1865. At the end of this era the Chickamauga, Tennessee, station was demolished; the roadbed from that region into Chattanooga (eight miles long) had been destroyed and had not been rebuilt because tracks of the East Tennessee and Georgia road were used. Patronage practices of reconstruction added to the company's problems and conductors at times passed black workers over the line without tickets on election days if they had "properly marked ballots" to be voted. On one occasion a Chattanooga newspaper commented that "some patriotic democrat . . . on Monday night pulled the coupling pin out and the train moved off leaving three carloads of loyal African votes behind." Finally, by 1870, two passenger trains ran daily in each direction between Atlanta and Chattanooga; the schedule called for a trip of nine hours and fifteen minutes.[14]

Hoping to aid the process of reconstruction, Christopher R. Robert, a New York City philanthropist, acquired the hospital buildings on Lookout Mountain where he established a coeducational school for white children. Seven of the old buildings were used on the 220-acre plot on the mountain, in addition to which the institution owned 400 acres on Missionary Ridge that were used as a farm. A post office, established in 1867 at the school, also served the adjoining mountain areas with the Reverend C. C. Carpenter, superintendent of the school, serving as postmaster.

About eighty students attended the Lookout Mountain Educational Institute, which offered programs in preparatory education, English, business, and classical studies along with instruction in piano, guitar, drawing, and foreign language. Sons and daughters of many local families attended the school, which operated until 1872 when Robert, in poor health, determined to invest all his resources in Robert College, in Constantinople, Turkey.[15]

The government sold the waterworks to private owners and gave the town its fire fighting equipment. This equipment, badly needed because of the many wooden buildings erected so close together, became the nucleus of a fire department for the municipality. With a great flourish the city fathers decreed that the chief engineer wear a white leather hat at fires "with intials C.E.C.F.D., and his assistants, 1st and 2nd, initials A.E.C.F.D., these hats and initials to be furnished or paid for by the city."

The warehouses and their great variety of contents—everything a horse-drawn army could use—were sold at public auction. One who witnessed the periodic sales wrote that the "dulcet tones of the sweet voice of Henry Clay Evans could often be heard crying off these sales, for he was the auctioneer."

The rolling mill, built by the government and completed in the fall of 1865, was leased to private owners and operated as the Southwestern Iron Company. Abram Hewitt, a pioneer steel manufacturer and political leader in New York, headed this organization and soon purchased the plant. Hewitt, who had refused to take wartime profits from the government, ran the business to illustrate a willingness to help Southern recovery. He drew Southerners into the organization and employed

Gustavus W. Smith, ex–major general of the Confederacy, to manage the Chattanooga operation.

For a period the business proved quite profitable. Old rails came to the mill and, combined with newly puddled metal, were made into iron to rebuild the Southern roads. By 1868 business, however, fell off, for the supply of scrap metal was used up. Two years later the company was merged with the Roane Iron Company. The latter company, incorporated in 1867, represented a group headed by two former Federal officers who had campaigned in East Tennessee: John T. Wilder and Hiram S. Chamberlain. Wilder and Chamberlain, young mid-westerners who decided to live in the South after the war, explored iron ore and coal deposits in Roane County and made plans to build a blast furnace. They got financial aid from northern acquaintances and named the small village near their project Rockwood for their chief investor, W. O. Rockwood of Indiana.

A furnace at Rockwood was smelting local ore in 1868 and producing pig iron. The availability of a rolling mill seventy miles downstream on the Tennessee where finished products could be produced seemed fortuitous. A five-mile, narrow-gauge railroad carried the iron from the furnace to Rockwood Landing, and company steamboats brought it to the Chattanooga mill after the 1870 organization began to function. This plan brought a new spirit of economic hope to the town. "From a little nest of shanties, Chattanooga is struggling forward rapidly," a visitor wrote.[16]

As a part of the demobilization program the government gave the Tennessee River bridge to Chattanooga. As early as 20 December 1865, the city officials prepared a toll schedule and other bridge regulations:

A single person on foot 3 cents or 5 cents round trip.
A man and horse 10 cents each way.
A vehicle drawn by a horse, mule, or oxen 10 cents.
A vehicle drawn by 2 horses, mules, or oxen 15 cents.
A vehicle drawn by 4 horses, mules, or oxen 25 cents.
["Horse" refers to any animal-drawing vehicle]
Each loose or lead horse, mule, or beef cattle 5 cents; other cattle 3 cents; sheep and calves 2 cents; hogs 2 cents.
Wagons hauling fuel, lumber or other building supplies, allowed one-half rate.
Any person riding or driving on the bridge faster than a walk shall forfeit and pay the sum of $5 to be recovered before any tribunal having jurisdiction.

The bridge proved to be a great headache for the town. A Mrs. Cowart claimed rent for the bank of the river on which the north end of the bridge rested. Then the bridge was leased to James R. Slayton, who asked for a release from four months' rental because of the heavy cost of keeping it in repair. This arrangement apparently was not satisfactory because in December 1866 the city government proposed selling the bridge at auction; it was "in a dangerous unsafe condition, and liable to fall at any time." The reason for this action was forthrightly given, as the city fathers wished to avoid any suit in the event the bridge collapsed. Such worries soon became academic, for the bridge was washed away in the great flood of 1867.[17]

After the flood a new swing ferry operated at the foot of Lookout Street, while two craft, powered by horses or mules, served travelers from landings at the foot of Market and Pine streets. A party crossing the Tennessee River described the experience:

> The Chattanooga ferry is very picturesque apart from the method of progression. In busy times a sort of tender accompanies the larger boat and upon this our carriage with difficulty was driven. Boat and tender were rude in construction, old and dilapidated. The main vessel had a small enclosure of a hen coop suggestiveness which was called a cabin and which at a pinch might give shelter to three or four people. The groups upon its decks were striking. There were sportsmen with a great following of dogs, horsemen with their Texas saddles and wide sombreros, vehicles and groups of cattle all mingled with the most happy contrast of color and form. On the opposite shore, as we drew near, were visible great numbers of waiting horsemen and cattle, giving evidence of the active business of the ferry and emphasizing the wonder that the bridge has not been restored.[18]

The three ferries carried on until the late 1880s when the animal-powered craft were converted to steam. They were known as the upper and lower ferries. The upper ferry, called *Myra*, was owned by Frazier interests; the lower, called *M. V. Read*, was run by Dugger and Beason.[19]

The local churches used by the military had been badly abused. After the battle of Chickamauga, the Presbyterian Church became a hospital as soon as the pews and all furnishings could be removed. St. Paul's Episcopal Church also was used as a hospital and then a warehouse; the members continued to hold services intermittently in rooms over a downtown store in the latter part of 1865, using a dry goods box covered with a tablecloth for an altar. The first service in their restored sanctuary was not held until Easter Sunday 1867. In May of that year the government allowed the parish $3,640 for damages. The contract for repairs included the following items:

> Spittoons—there will be one spitton to each pew, gothic earth ware.

Upholstering—The pews to be upholstered with Union Damask red color. The seats cuishioned [sic] loose with hair & backs upholstered to Cap of seat & kneeling stools & Bible Racks shall be upholstered to compare with the pews.[20]

The Methodist Church had lost its bell. All furnishings had been removed, doors and windows were gone, the floor broken, and much of the weatherboarding torn from the walls. For some eight years the congregation was without a church building and waited until 1918 before the government allowed a claim for war damages.[21]

The Baptist Church which had been used as the Post Chapel well illustrated the weatherbeaten condition of such structures. A newcomer's description as of the fall of 1865 tells the story most graphically:

It was not an attractive church and stood in the open; no fence enclosed it, no trees near it, and stood upon wooden pillars, and subsequently in the winter great numbers of hogs used to assemble under the floor, and when they got to fighting, which was not infrequent in cold weather, their backs would push up the floor under the feet of the worshippers, greatly to the discomfort of the latter, while their squealing, and the noise of their fighting were not especially edifying to congregation or minister.[22]

In town a new church organization appeared in 1866 with the establishment of the Hebrew Benevolent Association, which later became the Mizpah Congregation. But throughout the county, chapels had been, according to tradition, used by the military for every conceivable purpose and they suffered irreparable damage. The Methodists at Tyner worshipped for a number of years in the Cumberland Presbyterian Church. At Harrison only one church building appears to have been serviceable and was used by four denominations; each had separate Sundays for preaching but almost everyone came to each service, and the denominations operated a joint Sunday school.[23]

At Blackwell's Chapel an old log house was pressed into service. The story has been handed down that on a blustery day the circuit-riding preacher arrived on horseback. He tied his horse to a sapling, mounted the stairs, and stood by the door. He surveyed the holes and cracks in the structure and said, "Well, if the religion of the men who build this church house is as full of cracks and holes as it is, then may God have pity on their souls." Not wishing to be associated with a cold reception or indifferent faith, he jumped on his horse and galloped off, headed for a warmer climate.

Like the church houses, the human spirit everywhere in Hamilton County was badly damaged. The newspapers gave long lists of sheriff's sales. Divided families suffered in silence, and fear of retaliation hovered over the narrow valleys. General lawlessness was common; forests and mountains furnished ready hiding places for deserters, marauders, and aimless wanderers. South of Ninth Street in Chattanooga an area called Sutlertown had a reputation of being dangerous after dark. Union and Confederate guerrillas—some changed their allegiance according to the pressure of the hour—continued their reigns of terror. One, a fellow called Jackson, based his activities in the area of the Suck. In the Ooltewah-Tyner sector a man named Moss, who led a band of plunderers through the county, was murdered by Nat Taylor in a bizarre bragging contest. Joe Richey took matters into his own hands in the eastern part of Hamilton as did another desperado named Snow. Some of these robbers, it is claimed, held public auctions of their booty at a site near the Tennessee-Georgia border, where it was easy to dodge the arm of the local law.[24]

But Hamilton County was not ruled by outlaws. The courageous residents of the county began to mend their lives. An artist and journalist visiting the area in 1871 left a vivid picture of the people he met there and of that part of Hamilton County between Chattanooga and the Suck:

> Between the bluff and the river are narrow strips of arable bottom-land; and these, which sometimes are only narrow ribbons bordering the stream, and at others, wide fields, are very rich in soil and carefully cultivated. But the owners, almost without exception, live in rude log cabins. We saw but two or three houses above this condition. The occupants are sometimes negroes, but the majority are whites, who, however, as a rule, are not of the class known as "poor whites." The cabins are rude, the grounds limited, the means scanty, but the residents are a proud, intelligent set, who should be classed as hunters and woodmen rather than as husbandmen. Their delight is the woods and the mountains, and they almost live on horseback. Their needs are a gun, a dog, a horse, a cottage, a wife, and a cow—and pretty much in the order enumerated. They are semi-sportsmen, accomplished in woodcraft, who delight in all kinds of hunting, but exhibit very little energy in developing the resources of the country. It would be a mistake to accuse them of a lack of intelligence. We met many people on the road that day whose faces were refined and handsome. With their sloping sombreros, their gray shawls or army coats, their picturesque saddles, and their general air of graceful dilapidation they look like so many brigands. We noted especially two or three; and one who drove a herd of cattle along the road possessed a face that for intellectual refinement could be difficult to match.[25]

Nature's new growth did wonders for rural regions but it could not conceal a deteriorating town. Chattanooga gave the appearance of a place that a great storm had passed through. A newcomer who arrived from Ohio in August 1865 used the words "scraggy," "unkempt," "unsightly," and "sprawling" to describe what he concluded to be "anything but an attractive place." Large, irregular breastworks still crisscrossed the area and the deep gully which ran along Railroad Avenue was "capable of engulfing Pharoah and his host, with all his horses and chariots." It was a desolate place. All trees had fallen before the soldiers' ax on Cameron Hill and in town, except for those in front of a few houses that had comprised a general's headquarters.[26]

Hastily built warehouses, whose architectural contributions to the beauty of the city were all negative, stood in clusters and were a major concern to the city leaders because they were such obvious firetraps. Practically all commercial activity centered on Market Street, where wooden sidewalks kept pedestrians' feet out of the mud; sheds or covers over these walks helped keep out some of the rain or glaring sunlight. As gas street lamps had not yet come into use, anyone going out at night had to carry a lantern.

The streets worsened as the army no longer had prisoners of war to make temporary repairs; wagons sank up to their axletrees in mud. Six mule teams, mired down to their knees, at times could not move a wagon. Ruts and holes appeared everywhere because of the large number of drays that were freighting goods from the river landing to railroad depots. The numerous head of cattle driven through town to market kept the streets constantly plowed up.

Although East End Avenue (now Central Avenue) marked the eastern town limits, many farms were contained within the corporate boundaries. The older residents who had stayed on during the war had, for the most part, lost all their slaves, businesses, and liquid assets. "Their homes," according to one chronicler, "were not fit for social gatherings and they were not in the humor for society just then."

When the civilian government of the city was reestablished, it had to begin with a series of new ordinances, the first of which regulated taxes and privileges: a merchant had to pay a $10 privilege tax; retail liquor dealers $25; auctioneers $30; and butchers $10. For the use of the streets a one-horse dray paid $5 and two-horse drays double that amount while a hackney carriage paid $10. Ten-pin alleys, billiard saloons, and Jenny Lind tables were assessed at $10 each. A livery stable rated a $10 privilege tax, the same as a restaurant or second-class tavern. A first-class tavern paid $50. Circuses and menageries paid $30 for every 24-hour stand and theater performances $10 per night.[27]

By the close of the year 1865 the bulk of the area business was conducted by seventy-three merchants, three auctioneers, seven confectioners, three butchers, three livery stables, two restaurants, two first-class taverns, five boarding houses, eight peddlers, two peddlers of fresh meat, thirty-six two-horse drays, ten one-horse drays, and thirty-eight liquor dealers. An unofficial report, prepared about three years later, rounds out the picture. It comments that in all the town there were possibly twelve dwellings in good repair. Twelve doctors and fifteen lawyers practiced their professions while two dozen family groceries, four stores, one Thespian Club, one string band, and forty grog shops and saloons were doing business. Five lodges functioned— the Masons, Odd Fellows, Sons of Temperance, Knights Templars, and a Turnverein. About one-half of the white citizens, according to this account, were disenfranchised rebels and the majority of the rest Northerners.[28]

The Chattanooga *Gazette* reported 5,776 persons living in Chattanooga on 7 November 1865; that included 3,119 whites and 2,657 blacks. At Camp Contraband across. the river an estimate of 3,500 blacks was given and 3,000 soldiers were still stationed in the area. Of the adult whites there were twice as many men as women (1578 to 744).

Some prewar citizens still lived in and around the county, or had returned by the winter of 1865. Among those willing to start over were Tom and William Crutchfield, John P. Long, John and William King, Jim Dobbs, William Clift, John L. Divine, Robert Cravens, J. P. McMillin, A. Malone Johnson, Richard Henderson, Jacob Kunz, Joseph Ruohs, Daniel Hogan, James Hood, J. D. Beck, W. L. Dugger, Dr. J. S. Gillespie, Daniel Kaylor, Mrs. James A. Whiteside, the Reverend McCallie, Charles E. Lewis, David C. Carr, Dr. Milo Smith, William Lewis, Robert M. Hooke, and David M. Key.

These people and their families had played very different roles during the past five years. Some had striven to be neutral in the midst of the great holocaust. Many had consistently supported the Union, while others pledged their loyalty to the Confederacy. The latter group, uncertain of their status at war's end, faced extremely difficult decisions. The case of the D. M. Key family illustrates this dilemma, for Key had been a leading lawyer in Hamilton County, an active secessionist, a recruiter of troops, and a Confederate officer. His wife and children had fled from Chattanooga to spend most of the war years with her family. Key wished to reestablish his home in Chattanooga, but before returning, sought the advice of his former acquaintance and a staunch Unionist, Bill Crutchfield, through an intermediary. Crutchfield's reply reassured the stocky, forty-one-year old former colonel that his return home was feasible:

> Maj. Key's deportment was such as far as I have been informed to treat all men kindly, courteously & gentlemanly regardless of their political opinions—any man in the Rebel Army deporting himself thus—has nothing to fear from an honorable highminded intelligent community. As an officer in the Army, I presume he is aware of the various proclamations and the many difficulties on the path of a prominent Rebel.
>
> In this section, I can assure you, Maj. Key would be kindly treated and such help as can be rendered by me and mine and all his old friends shall be freely, frankly, & cheerfully given.[29]

The Keys, returning in November 1865, found all Crutchfield's predictions to be correct. A friend furnished a rent-free house and another supplied a milk cow. A mill owner sent breadstuffs to the family. Key's wife sold his Confederate uniform for household money. By 1870 the family was again well established, and attorney Key represented the area in the Tennessee Constitutional Convention.

In addition to Key, others who had worn "the Gray" returned or moved to Hamilton County. Counted among their number were L. T. Dickinson, Garnett Andrews, Ambrose Grant, Elbert Sevier, Amos Judd, Tomlinson Fort, Josiah Jackson Bryan, and Jonathan W. Bachman.

Some nonveteran Southerners also decided to locate in the area. In December 1870 William Thomas Walker arrived from Hawkins County, Tennessee. He had stacked his family's worldly goods into a covered wagon, tied a milk cow in back, and with a neighbor who drove a similar rig arrived at the eastern base of Missionary Ridge. Walker's wife and children, who came later by train, found him living in an abandoned log house. Two years later he bought a farm beyond Brainerd Hills (now the Audubon Acres property) and moved into another log house, one which had been built by an Indian. In this section most dwellings were log structures and, except for some cultivated fields, the whole area continued to be an untamed wilderness which supported wild turkey and passenger pigeons. Here the parents of Robert Sparks Walker cleared more land, cut wood for the locomotives that passed the place, and taught their family a respect and love for nature.[30]

In keeping with Tennessee's postwar desire to attract new citizens, Hamilton Countians welcomed northern immigrants. They insisted that no one would question a person's political or religious views and that his personal freedom would not be endangered. A newspaper advertisement succinctly summed up the qualities desired in the newcomers: "Those having capital, brains and muscle preferred."[31]

A number of young men responded to the ad, many of whom had done military duty in the area. Xenophen Wheeler, a Yale graduate from Ohio, arrived in August 1865, attracted to Hamilton County "because I thought a place so strategically important in war ought to become a large and important place in time of peace."[32] Wheeler was joined by Wilder and Chamberlain, T. H. Payne, Z. C. Patten, Frank F. Weihl, John B. Nicklin, Noah W. Wilbur, William John Trimble, Alonzo G. Sharp, J. E. MacGowan, Webster J. Colburn, Theodore Montague, Theodore Richmond, Samuel Bartow Strang, Dr. Eli Mellen Wright, Thomas J. Carlisle, G. W. Wheland, and numerous other veterans.

These men, possessing more enterprise and persistence than material assets, emerged as leading entrepreneurs in the reborn community. Since they were investing their careers in the area, they did not fit the traditional concept of carpetbaggers who schemed to skim the economic cream from a region and then leave for other parts. As businessmen they personified the concept of a diversified, balanced economy by promoting industry and commerce in relation to Southern agrarianism. Along with the loyal Unionists of the county they gave Hamilton County a reputation for Yankee ingenuity.

Flatboats piled with country produce and log rafts reappeared at the wharf as East Tennesseans desperately worked to earn cash. Some of Chattanooga's traditional businesses made fresh starts, such as grist and sawmills, cabinet shops, blacksmithies, distilleries, small foundries, and machine shops. However, the new companies launched during the latter part of the 1860s provided the chief momentum for an expanding economy. Wilder and Chamberlain brought the Roane Iron Company to town along with their personal interest in education and the church. Patten & Payne established Chattanooga's oldest present-day business as booksellers and stationers. Loomis & Bennett (later Loomis & Hart) made furniture and put down the roots of today's Cavalier Corporation. Montague & Company produced sewer and drain pipe and, in 1871, the Lookout Flour Mills of H. C. Chapman began production. Robert Scholze entered the leather business in 1872, two years after Truxal & Dunmeyer undertook to manufacture engines and machinery.

Small coal operators on Soddy Creek had taken out fuel over the years, but in 1866 the mines started up on a regular basis. Because the mines were located about four miles from the Tennessee River, a tram road had to be built to Soddy Creek in order to deliver the coal to the barges. A group of energetic Welshmen leased the postwar mines, paying one cent per bushel in royalties. Nine miles to the northeast, the Sale Creek mines got a new lease on life. Operating on a very small scale from possibly as early as 1843, these mines produced coal for area blacksmiths. In 1866 two Knoxville men, Major Thomas C. Brown and Colonel John Baxter, started shipping the Sale Creek coal. Within a few years, under lease to Welsh miners, it is reported that fifty thousand bushels of coal were shipped out monthly.[33]

In November 1865, following closely on the creation of a national banking system, the First National Bank of Chattanooga opened with a capital of $200,000. W. P. Rathburn, president, came to the city from Pomeroy, Ohio; he was the first individual to bring considerable capital into the postwar economy of the county. In addition to his banking interests, Rathburn soon developed connections with many industrial enterprises and with railroads. He served as the first president of the Chattanooga Iron & Coal Manufacturing Association and as mayor of the city in 1870 and 1871. At the bank, T. R. Stanley, an ex-Union officer, served as vice-president and Theodore C. Montague as cashier. Other directors included Charles W. Stewart and John King, who was the only member who had resided in the area before the war.

One year later the Chattanooga Discount & Deposit Bank opened under the leadership of King, Thomas Crutchfield, and Allen C. Burns. Three other banks entered the business within the next five years, including a branch of the Freedman's Savings & Trust Company under E. O. Tade. The local branch suspended operations in 1875 when the national organization went into receivership.[34]

Another partnership, that of Thomas B. Kirby and Patton L. Gamble, launched an important enterprise with the publication of the first issue of the Chattanooga *Times* on 15 December 1869. Since the war, several newspapers had been started and had failed: the *Gazette* suspended in 1866 and the *Daily American Union*, the *People's Organ*, and the *Daily Enterprise* all failed after only brief lives. The *Daily Republican*, begun in 1867, for a time claiming to be the only newspaper published within a wide area, was bought by Kirby and Gamble and immediately suspended. Certainly little in the record encouraged a prospect for long life for the *Times*, and it was not long before the editors wrote of "many vicissitudes" and "great difficulty." It lived on, however, appearing daily except on Mondays.[35]

The entire region suffered serious adversities of many kinds. Chattanooga's new civilian government sought funds and begged the army for the use of a building for a "pest house" because of an alarming outbreak of smallpox. In November 1865, because of a "large number of vicious outbreaking persons, and [because] thefts have become of such frequent occurrence, and burglary has become so common, and personal violence so frequent that the property and persons of citizens and strangers in the city are insecure," the people were requested by the government to form a voluntary police force. Four years later the city economy had sunk to such a bad state that the city issued scrip, which its city employees had to take as wages. Fire, always a serious threat, in 1867 consumed the foundry and shop of Thomas Webster and, a little later, the Crutchfield House. In 1871 a major conflagration destroyed some twenty-one establishments along Market Street.[36]

Most memorable of all such catastrophes was the record flood of 1867. Silently and with devastating power, waters from the upper valleys of the Tennessee descended on Hamilton County on the night of Friday, 8 March. River bottomlands soon disappeared under the muddy, swirling waters. Tributary streams, unable to discharge their burdens into the main river, caused the flood to pile up in every valley. Debris swiftly sailed by—corn cribs, broken rafts, boats, loose logs, boxes and barrels, hay mounds, barns, and houses. Here and there dead livestock could be spotted.

No alert went out to send citizens to high ground. The waters got deeper and deeper, the current swifter. Not till Monday did the river crest; on the present gauge it stood at 58.6 feet—the greatest recorded flood ever. Hamilton County farmers lost stock and buildings and rich bottomlands were scoured of their topsoil. In the mountain reaches of the stream, waters accumulated as high as 50 feet above the normal riverbed. Crotches of trees long held the flood's debris and served as watermarks. People fled up the mountainsides and on returning found many a homestead swept away. Area railroads seemed to have been singled out as victims of the flood, as bridges gave way and trackage was washed out.

In Chattanooga—the most vulnerable site along the entire valley— the military bridge was swept away, as were the bridges over the

Railroad Avenue gully at Fourth, Sixth, and Seventh streets. The Chattanooga Creek bridge floated away, resulting in bitter words directed at the ferryman who improvised a replacement crossing, for which he charged ten cents for each horse and rider and fifty cents for every two-horse dray.

Nearly every building along the riverbank vanished, including much of the old government shipyard and the holdings of Loomis & Bennett. Merchandise had to be moved to higher shelves, for eventually the flood measured five feet in depth at the Crutchfield House. Freight cars in the yards stood up to their very tops in water and some platform cars floated off their carriages. A popular legend of St. Paul's Church tells of men in boats who saved hymnals and prayer books. A house deposited on Chestnut Street between Sixth and Seventh streets remained unclaimed until May, when it was sold by the city fathers. Mail was brought by boat from the post office, where water stood nearly four feet deep: "The last one that left carried a large American flag at the stern in token of having surrendered with all the honors."

At the peak of the excitement a small steamboat, the *Cherokee*, sailed up Market Street. The master of the *Cherokee*, Captain Woods Wilson, made the most of this high adventure. Earlier he had cruised about in the growing flood, taking his boat up a "road" (to avoid trees and stumps) to Old Washington in Rhea County about a mile and a half from the river, where the crew had breakfast at the hotel. On Market Street in Chattanooga the mayor put a stop to the escapade, fearing that waves created by the motion of the boat would weaken building foundations. But after the captain turned back, he proceeded along Railroad Avenue to the Crutchfield House.

The famous hostelry was at that point managed by Mrs. R. A. Bishop, a "masterful business woman, strangely versatile and resourceful," whose tenure was known as a "reign" and who was addressed as "Madam." Her 250 pounds seemed to echo her vocabulary, which was "uncommonly endowed, especially in the domain of invective." During the flood the fellow who delivered milk abandoned his wagon and fashioned a milk boat, a "rakish little craft." When he stopped at the Crutchfield House, Madam Bishop asked him to take her around the first floor of the hotel in his boat. A crowd watched, encouraging the milkman to tip the boat. In a loud voice Madam Bishop warned the amateur boatman that if he tried any such tomfoolery she would drown him. When she saw the extent of the damage done by the flood, everyone's attention turned to a new subject, for she made remarks "relative to the responsible cause of it all" which were in such volume and variety of language as to shock the milkman.

Meanwhile Captain Wilson continued to ride the flood. With a complement of passengers he headed for the canyon of the Tennessee where the scenery was as spectacular as the danger. With his wheel in reverse, it is reported, the *Cherokee* made railroad time. No such record was set, however, in cleaning up the flood's wreckage or in economic recovery.[37]

The turbulent decade of the 1860s witnessed but a modest increase in the population of Hamilton County. The number of residents of 1870 totaled 17,241 compared with 13,258 in 1860, a difference of about 4,000. Of the total increase, whites accounted for 1,419 and blacks 2,572. The census of 1860 recorded 1,419 slaves and 192 free persons of color (in 1870 all blacks were listed in the category of "free colored").

Of the total population in 1870, 16,659 were persons born in this country. Those born in Tennessee naturally provided the largest number—10,594. The bulk of the remainder came from neighboring states: 2,822 from Georgia, 583 from Virginia and West Virginia, 543 from North Carolina, 405 from Alabama, and 194 from Kentucky.

Foreign-born persons numbering 582 lived in the county. Ireland furnished the most with 176, followed by 143 from England and Wales, and 143 from Germany. Scotland sent 22, France 21, British America (Canada) 17, Switzerland 16, Sweden and Norway 10, Poland 4, and Austria 4. The foreign-born group had increased by 251 since 1860. All but three of the enumerating census districts had a few foreign-born. Naturally, Chattanooga counted the largest number with 475.

Blacks also were widely dispersed throughout the county: 2,221 concentrated in Chattanooga, amounting to approximately thirty-six percent of the total population. Only the district of Fairmount reported no blacks within its precincts.

Of the total population, men outnumbered women by only 69; in Chattanooga the difference was only 47, again favoring the masculine gender. The population continued to be very young, with but 7,829 persons in the county's total of 17,241 twenty-one years of age or over.

The census gave some interesting findings relating to religion and education, although the statistics may not be complete. In Hamilton County a total of twenty-seven church organizations was counted, which included twenty edifices with a seating capacity of 3,650 and property valued at $22,600. Only three denominations are listed: Baptists with thirteen organizations and 600 sittings and Presbyterians (who most likely included Cumberland Presbyterian), having seven organizations and 1,050 sittings.

The education figures are very bleak, reflecting the fact that Tennessee did not have a tax-supported program of education in 1870. Of the total population, 1,936 attended school with no record of the length of the term or the level of training. This aggregate number represents 923 white males, 740 white females, 138 black males and 135 black females. The number of persons ten years of age and over who could not read was 4,386: over twenty-five percent of the total. The number unable to write was 5,751, or more than thirty-three percent.[38]

Although the county had noted its fiftieth birthday, the disruption created by the war years clearly required a fresh start.

NOTES

1. U.S., War Department, *The War of the Rebellion: A Compilation of the Official Records of the Union and Confederate Armies* (Washington, D.C.: Government Printing Office, 1884), Series 1, 32 (pt. 1):102–104.

2. Zella Armstrong, *History of Hamilton County and Chattanooga, Tennessee* 2 vols. (Chattanooga, Lookout Publishing, 1931), 2:54–55. The group included Mary Elizabeth McDonald, captain; Jennie Hoyal, first lieutenant; Jane Locke, second lieutenant; Rhoda Tennessee Thomison, third lieutenant; and Virginia Hoyal, Kate Hoyal, Anna Gillespie, Martha Early, Sidney McDonald, Louisa McDonald, Ann Payne, Caroline McDonald, Barbara Frances Allen, Margaret Keith, Sarah Mitchell, Rachel Howell, Mary A. Crawford, Mary Keith, and Mollie McDonald.

3. Ibid., p. 59.

4. *O.R.*, Series 1, 31 (pt. 3):487; J. T. Trowbridge, *The South: A Tour of Its Battlefields and Ruined Cities* . . . (Hartford, Conn.: L. Stebbins, 1866), pp. 260–262; *Chattanooga National Cemetery, Chattanooga, Tennessee*, Veterans Administration pamphlet, 1 May 1977, pp. 40–41.

The cemetery was not designated a national cemetery until 1867. It was under the jurisdiction of the War Department until 1933 when it was transferred with other cemeteries to the Department of the Interior. Its management was returned to the War Department from 1944 to 1973 when it was transferred to the Veterans Administration. As of 31 January 1977, the cemetery included 120.8 acres, and interments numbered 23,432; grave space is expected to be available until the year 2000.

A special monument commemorates the deeds of the men of Andrews's Raid buried there and another was placed by the Fourth Army Corps "In Memory of Their Fallen Comrades." In 1935 the German government erected a monument in honor of 78 German soldiers who died in a local prisoner of war camp; 108 World War II prisoners of war were interred in this same section.

5. Undated clippings of newspaper article written by George W. Gardenhire, files of Chattanooga-Hamilton County Bicentennial Library. Near Silverdale in an isolated cemetery are the graves of 155 unknown Confederate soldiers who died in 1862 in hospitals located near the spot.

6. *O.R.*, Series 1, 32 (pt. 3):519–520. General Order No. 63 naming the defenses was issued 27 April 1864.

7. George E. Turner, *Victory Rode the Rails* (Indianapolis: Bobbs-Merrill, 1953), pp. 319–327; William T. Sherman, *Memoirs of General William T. Sherman* (London: Henry S. King, 1875), 2:1–32.

8. Gilbert E. Govan and James W. Livingood, *The Chattanooga Country*, 3rd ed. (Knoxville: University of Tennessee Press, 1977), pp. 254–257.

9. John Beatty, *Memoirs of a Volunteer, 1861–1863*, Harvey S. Ford, ed. (New York: Norton, 1946), p. 266.

10. Govan and Livingood, *Chattanooga Country*, pp. 258–267; *Chattanooga Gazette*, 13, 16 December 1864.

11. J. L. Jones, *An Artilleryman's Diary* (Madison: Wisconsin History Commission, 1914), p. 323.

12. C. D. McGuffey, *Standard History of Chattanooga* (Knoxville: Crew and Dorey, 1911), p. 174.

13. Campbell, *Upper Tennessee*, pp. 55–58; Teuton, *Steamboating*, pp. 48–50.

14. James H. Johnston, *Western and Atlantic Railroad of the State of Georgia* (Atlanta: Georgia Public Service Commission, 1932), pp. 57–59, 62–63, 85–86.

15. Govan and Livingood, *Chattanooga Country*, p. 331; John Wilson, *Lookout: The Story of an Amazing Mountain* (Chattanooga: News-Free Press, 1977), pp. 53–55.

16. Morrow Chamberlain, *A Brief History of the Pig Iron Industry of East Tennessee* (Chattanooga: author, 1942), pp. 6–7; Robert Somers, *The Southern States Since the War* (London: Macmillan, 1871), pp. 103, 106–107.

17. City of Chattanooga, *Minutes of the Board of the Mayor and Aldermen, 1865–1868*, pp. 15, 114, 116, 139.

18. *Chattanooga Times*, 2 April 1907, reprints original article published in 1871 in *Appleton's Journal*.

19. Ibid., 19 January 1945, recollections of Jesse Gahagan.

20. Edwin S. Lindsey, *Centennial History of St. Paul's Episcopal Church, Chattanooga, Tennessee, 1853–1953* (Chattanooga: Vestry of St. Paul's Parish, 1953), pp. 11–15.

21. Mary Thomas Peacock, *The Circuit Rider and Those Who Followed* (Chattanooga: Hudson Printing, 1957), p. 84.

22. *Chattanooga Times*, 8 January 1906, based on Xenophon Wheeler's account of Chattanooga.

23. Peacock, *Circuit Rider*, pp. 126–130. Confederate smallpox cases were lodged at the Concord church; those who died, it is said, were buried in the old church cemetery. *Chattanooga Times*, 30 October 1938.

24. Ibid., 8 January 1906; 22 October 1911.

25. Ibid., 2 April 1907.

26. Ibid.

27. City of Chattanooga, *Minutes, 1865–68*, pp. 2–3.

28. Ibid., pp. 65, 201; *Chattanooga Daily Republican*, 28 November 1868.

29. Key Papers, Chattanooga-Hamilton County Bicentennial Library.

30. Robert Sparks Walker, *As the Indians Left It: The Story of the Elise Chapin Wild Life Sanctuary and the Chattanooga Audubon Society* (Chattanooga: Hudson Printing, 1955), pp. 3–6.

31. *Chattanooga Daily Republican*, 8 December 1868.

32. *Chattanooga Times*, 2 April 1907.

33. George W. Ochs, *Chattanooga and Hamilton County, Tennessee* (Chattanooga: Times Printing, 1897), pp. 16–20; *Chattanooga Daily Republican*, 7 November 1868; Joseph B. Killebrew, *Introduction to the Resources of Tennessee* (Nashville: Tavel, Eastman & Howell, 1874), p. 100.

34. *A History of Banking in Chattanooga* (Chattanooga: Hamilton National Bank, 1925), pp. 8–10. The First National Bank reorganized in 1932 and reopened on 3 January 1933 as the Chattanooga National Bank. The Discount and Deposit Bank suspended operations in 1881, paying all depositors in full. Two banks—the Second National and the City National—opened in 1870 but had short lives.

35. Gerald W. Johnson, *An Honorable Titan* (New York: Harper & Brothers, 1946), pp. 47–48.

36. City of Chattanooga, *Minutes, 1865–1868*, pp. 3, 4, 7, 10; Govan and Livingood, *Chattanooga Country*, pp. 302–303.

37. D. E. Donley, "The Flood of March, 1867, in the Tennessee River," (East Tennessee Historical Society) *Publications* 8 (1936), pp. 74–81; City of Chattanooga, *Minutes, 1865–1868*, pp. 188, 231; Harry M. Wiltse, "History of Chattanooga," 2 vols. (Typescript, Chattanooga-Hamilton County Bicentennial Library), 2: 264; *Chattanooga Times* 8 January 1906, 2 April 1907; T. J. Campbell, *Upper Tennessee*, pp. 61–66; Lindsey, *St. Paul's*, p. 14; *The Daily American Union*, 14 March 1867.

38. U. S., Bureau of the Census, *Ninth Census of Population: 1870 Population and General Statistics* (Washington, D. C.: GPO, 1872), 1:62–63, 263–264, 321, 371, 428, 554, 635, 654.

---------------------------------- 12 ----------------------------------

1870 and After

GOVERNMENT and the complex, often contradictory, forces which influenced the political affairs of Hamilton County during the war and Reconstruction era reflected the momentous changes taking place throughout the nation. National, regional, state, and local affairs were all in flux, many issues being without precedent or easy solution. A new group of citizens, the freedmen, struggled to establish a place for themselves in society while many whites, accustomed to slavery, could not accept a biracial society based on freedom.

The presence in Hamilton County after 1865 of Federal veterans and newcomers from the North who staked their careers on industrial development and future growth gave the Republican party continued strength and produced, with the support of the freedmen, a vigorous two-party rivalry. Although physical reminders of battles and military occupation were ever present, two unique local developments characterized the area, setting it apart from the common Southern experience. One emphasized a sincere spirit of reunion, which did much to repair old hurts, nourish mutual understanding, and foster a refreshing feeling of community. The other led to vigorous activity on the part of the blacks, especially in the local political arena until about 1910.

When Tennessee seceded from the Union on 24 June 1861, Mayor James C. Warner of Chattanooga and Hamilton County Sheriff J. C. Conner attempted to cooperate with the officials of the new Confederate state. The difficulty of their task, however, revealed the county's great division over the question of union—Hamilton County had voted that same month 1,200 against and 854 in favor of secession (totals which included Chattanooga's balloting of 421 to 51 in favor of secession). Neither mayor nor sheriff had the strength to cope with such developments as Clift's War or the bridge burners of November 1861, and Confederate troops moved into the area. Military rule soon overshadowed civilian authority. The local leaders had little support from the Confederate state government, which fled from Nashville after the fall of Forts Henry and Donelson and adjourned *sine die* in Memphis on 20 March 1862. At that time, for all practical purposes, the Confederate state government ceased functioning.

By this date a different state government had come into being in the portions of Tennessee occupied by Federal arms. On 3 March 1862, President Lincoln commissioned Senator Andrew Johnson as military governor of Tennessee. There was no precedent for such an office. Federal military men were not inclined to cooperate with a civilian chief. More importantly, many Tennesseans considered Johnson a traitor to the South because of his open loyalty to the Union. In Middle and West Tennessee in particular, Johnson was so hated that many assassins' plots were hatched to dispose of him. Since Hamilton County remained behind Confederate lines until November 1863, Johnson's appointment exerted little influence in the Hamilton County area until the Union victory on Missionary Ridge.

After the Union army arrived in force in September 1863, the military suspended civil government in Chattanooga—where the mayor and board of aldermen had been elected annually despite war problems. From that time until 7 October 1865, the office of the provost marshal ran the city affairs.

At the close of 1863 President Lincoln in an amnesty proclamation presented a modest plan for the reorganization of southern state governments, emphasizing the desirability of reestablishing civilian control. Johnson followed his president's lead and ordered the election of county officials on the first Saturday in March 1864. Conditions were scarcely stable enough to hope for a successful election, and voting restrictions angered many Union men as well as Confederates, who were denied the right to vote.

On 5 March 1864, Hamilton County held its first election in three years, according to the *Chattanooga Gazette*. The balloting proved orderly and quiet but, although twenty-one men received votes, only seventy-five persons exercised their right of franchise. Eight offices were filled. George W. Rider won the sheriff's post, receiving but twenty-nine votes. Others elected were R. H. Guthrie, clerk of the circuit court; W. H. Crowder, clerk of the county court; A. W. Moore, register; Joseph Yarnell, tax collector, James R. Allison, justice of the peace; and A. J. Berryhill, constable. Unopposed candidates collected only sixty-seven votes. The election was dubbed a "serious farce" by some, but the fact remains that in the midst of war a conquered country had returned to the election process.[1]

The election was a disappointment for Johnson, who did not then attempt a restoration of state government. One additional step was taken, however, to reestablish Hamilton County government. At a mass meeting in June the people discussed the desirability of appointments of a judge and a chancellor. Johnson responded at once by naming Daniel C. Trewhitt chancellor. The forty-one-year-old Trewhitt was practicing law at Harrison when the war began. An outspoken Union man, he made numerous speeches against secession. Unsuccessful in blocking disunion, Trewhitt went to Kentucky and enlisted in the Union army, serving as lieutenant colonel of the second regiment of Tennessee infantry volunteers. He had the reputation as an "excellent and upright judge," retaining the chancellorship until 1870 when the state's new constitution went into effect. Eight years later Trewhitt was elected circuit judge; he served in that post until his death in 1891.[2]

The same month as Trewhitt's appointment, politically minded residents of Hamilton County gathered to consider their function in the forthcoming national presidential election. Although Tennessee was virtually free of Confederate troops, no one had any idea of Tennessee's relationship with the United States. The local people seized the initiative and selected delegates to the National Union Convention, the wartime coalition party of President Lincoln. The Tennessee delegation gained seats at the Baltimore meeting and helped select Andrew Johnson as Lincoln's vice-presidential running mate. Since residency was a qualification for office, Tennesseans could, by inference at least, consider that the national party believed their state a part of the Union.

A Fourth of July rally at Sale Creek enthusiastically supported the ticket. Johnson's presence in the Washington administration might smoothen the area's transition from war to peace. The polls in Hamilton County opened, but the records give little information about voting in this crucial wartime election. The *Chattanooga Gazette* did report that the ticket of Lincoln and Johnson carried Chattanooga. However, Congress refused to count Tennessee's electoral votes and so denied Tennessee status as a restored state (although no such questions were asked regarding the vice-president's credentials).

The fact that Johnson would leave the office of military governor for his new position as vice-president paved the way for Tennessee Unionists to restore state civilian government. The Union Executive Committee of East Tennessee called for the selection of delegates to attend a convention on 19 December in Nashville. The invasion of the state by General John B. Hood's Confederate army and the battles of Franklin and Nashville delayed the convening of this meeting until 8 January 1865.

A large number of delegates—some officially designated, some self-appointed—poured into Nashville. From Hamilton County at least two men attended: Chancellor Trewhitt and James R. Hood, editor of the *Chattanooga Gazette*.The delegates consisted almost entirely of native Tennesseans, strong Union men, who had served in the Federal army. Although opinion was divided and debate bitter, the convention boldly proceeded with its task as it interpreted affairs. As a constitutional assembly, it submitted for popular vote an amendment to the constitution abolishing slavery. It repealed the Ordinance of Secession and nullified all acts of the Confederate state government, these actions also to be a part of the referendum. As a legislative body, it set dates for the referendum and for the election of state officials. The convention also prescribed the vital qualifications for voting. Finally, as a political nominating convention, it chose William G. Brownlow as the sole candidate for governor and nominated candidates for all seats in the General Assembly on a general legislative ticket to be voted on in all parts of the state. The voter had to decide for or against the entire slate.

Before leaving for Washington, Johnson issued a proclamation authorizing the elections of 22 February for the vote on the amendments and 4 March for the selection of state officials. All efforts were directed toward the rapid establishment of civil government. But voter turnout proved light. On Washington's birthday only 25,293 voted for the amendment to 48 against. However, by this action, slavery was legally abolished in Hamilton County and in the state.

Many counties showed no interest in the election; a number did not even open polling places. But across the state Brownlow— Methodist parson, editor of the *Knoxville Whig*, master of invective and self-declared enemy of secession—received a huge majority: one tally showed 23,222 votes for the new governor; only 35 persons voted for a write-in candidate of their own choice. Hamilton County voted 705 for the "Fighting Parson" without a single ballot cast for any other person.

On the General Assembly slate, James R. Hood was elected to the lower house and for eight ballotings was a strong contender for the speakership. Elected to the senate from the local area was A. M. Cate, a leader of the Radical political group, who came from an influential East Tennessee family and had been involved in the bridge-burning episode in 1861. Chancellor Trewhitt was on hand to give the oath of office to the new senators.[3]

On 5 April 1865, with news just arriving in Nashville of the fall of Richmond, Governor Brownlow's inaugural ceremonies took place. Tennessee reorganized civilian government. Although Brownlow was devoid of political finesse and as a leader was considered despotic, his policies did result in Tennessee's readmission to the Union in July 1866 as the first former Confederate state to return. Furthermore, under Brownlow's administration, the state escaped military occupation.

During the Brownlow regime (1865–1869) the usual political parties did not play a conspicuous part. Two schools of thought, ever shifting in membership, policy, and degree of emphasis, served instead. One, the Radicals, represented the Brownlow group; they bitterly resented former Confederates and stood in general for harsh Reconstruction terms. The Radicals especially wanted to prevent loyal Unionists from being governed by former Rebels, and used the franchise laws to keep Confederates from regaining control; when seriously pressed, they gave blacks the franchise. Although excluded from holding office or serving on juries, freedmen in Tennessee gained the right to vote in February 1867.

The Conservatives represented those persons who advocated leniency toward the followers of secession. Most had served in a military or political capacity with the Confederacy; some favored the industrialization of the area and wanted to attract capital and business. From the time of the January convention, they worked to weaken Radical rule. Some, believing they could never be heard within the law, turned to extralegal activities such as the Klu Klux Klan. By 1870 the Radicals had had their day and the Conservatives gained complete control of the state government.

In Chattanooga the Federal army turned municipal matters over to a civilian government in the fall of 1865, although the town remained a military post for some months. On 7 October a city election selected a mayor and aldermen to serve until the end of the year, at which time the traditional annual election date, the last Thursday in December, would see the selection of officers for a full year's term.

All of the interim officials had been Union soldiers or men sympathetic with the Union. The aldermen included August Bohr, A. Kesterson, J. Mann, J. D. Beck, William Crutchfield, Timothy R. Stanley, Jacob Kunz, and Daniel Hogan. J. H. Alexander was selected recorder; he was in charge of dealing with all infractions of city ordinances and tried all cases under the jurisdiction of the city authorities. The citizens elected Richard Henderson mayor. Henderson, a fifty-year-old lawyer who had come to Hamilton County in 1836, had lived in Dallas, Harrison, and later Chattanooga. He married a daughter of Daniel and Jane Cozby Henderson (apparently unrelated) and although not a member of the armed forces, strongly supported the Union cause. Mayor Henderson may have been the military's choice to head the town during these months when the government had to be entirely reconstructed. After his brief service Henderson remained a valued Republican leader and served as city attorney for a time.[4]

The problems of this first postwar government are reflected vividly in a resolution adopted by the Board of Aldermen on 4 November 1865:

> Whereas the war, which has recently terminated, has, in its progress and operations, been very disastrous to this section of the country, and more especially so in the City of Chattanooga and vicinity, it becoming necessary in the progress of events to totally destroy or render useless all the public buildings and property belonging to said City; and during the occupation of the city the civil administration of the laws of the country was suspended, and the municipal government of the city was totally disorganized and the military was for a considerable time the only power to maintain any kind of government, and during this time the municipal authorities lost all the revenue they had previously accumulated and were powerless to collect or in any way raise any revenue whatever; and whereas, the exigencies of the late war have caused to be congregated in and about the city a large concourse of people many of whom are extremely poor, being destitute of every means of procuring the ordinary

necessities of life, living in hovels in circumstances calculated to engender disease, and the smallpox is now existing among that class of residents and is rapidly assuming an alarming character and is likely to become epidemic; and whereas, also, the military authorities collected a considerable amount of money from the citizens of this place for privileges, fines, etc., in the shape of what is called a Post Fund; and the city authorities have been so recently organized that no revenue has yet or can in a short time be realized from the sources at command, and the civil government of the city is entirely powerless to do anything for the relief of the poor and destitute who are afflicted with the smallpox, or to take such precaution as may be necessary and proper to prevent the spread of said disease; and the Post Fund, referred to, is under the control and management of the military authorities.

Be it resolved by the Mayor and Aldermen of the City of Chattanooga that Major General George H. Thomas be and is hereby most respectfully yet earnestly requested to set apart or cause to be set apart so much of the Post Fund aforesaid as may be deemed sufficient to relieve such of our poor as are already afflicted with the smallpox, and to institute such measures as may be proper to prevent the spread of the disease, and that the same when so set apart, be placed at the disposal of the city authorities.[5]

The next two mayors—serving in 1866, 1867, and 1868—had resided also in the area before the war. Charles E. Lewis had entertained strong Union views. David C. Carr, who served two terms, was a prewar businessman who functioned as postmaster following his 1845 appointment. Although he did not do military service, his sympathies rested with the federal government throughout the struggle.

The year 1869 marked a new political trend as newcomers emerged as mayors. Alonzo G. Sharp won the office that year. Born in the state of New York, he enlisted in the Federal army in an Ohio outfit at the age of twenty. About 1865 he moved to Chattanooga and served in public office a number of years. In 1870 and 1871 banker W. P. Rathburn occupied the mayor's chair after a local residency of about five years. In the following year the voters favored General John T. Wilder, then engaged in the local iron industry. The ex-Union officer served only a portion of his term, resigning in April because of private business obligations. The mayor *pro tem*, Josiah Jackson Bryan, completed the soldier's term. This succession clearly demonstrates the unique social structure of the city, for Bryan, South Carolina–born, went to war from Chattanooga as a Confederate soldier.

Another Union army man was elected in 1873. Dr. Eli Mellen Wight, whose birthplace was in Maine, completed an enlistment period and then finished his medical studies. He rejoined the army as an assistant surgeon and was stationed in Chattanooga, where he stayed on after

Appomattox. Another doctor served in 1874. Dr. Philander Sims represented a new day being the first Southern sympathizer and Democrat to be elected in the postwar period.[6]

Until the time of Sim's administration all the mayors of Chatanooga had been Radicals or Republicans. All apparently were moderate in their politics and appeared to have worked well with their fellow townsmen. None should be classified as scalawags or carpetbaggers whose self-interest overshadowed their community responsibilities. No scandals developed and the major disagreement seemed to be between candidates who were old residents and newcomers who had decided to establish permanent homes in the area. The Republicans did have the support of the freedmen who had the privilege of voting by 1866 in city elections—a year prior to state enfranchisement.

A significant situation did arise in 1868 in the contest for one seat on the board of aldermen. C. P. Letcher received 440 votes from the fourth ward to 332 votes for C. C. Seigfried. Seigfried claimed his opponent was ineligible to fill the position because he was a "man of color." A three-man committee of aldermen appointed to investigate the matter filed majority and minority reports. The majority supported Letcher, citing the Declaration of Independence, the Constitution, the Civil Rights Bill, and other congressional action. The board of aldermen by a four-to-two vote accepted the majority report and seated Letcher. This action not only paved the way for numerous blacks to hold jobs in local government in the years immediately following but also was taken at a time when it was still illegal for a black to hold state office.[7]

The city ran into one major problem with the Brownlow political machine. On 14 May 1866, on the heels of racial troubles in Memphis, the general assembly enacted the Metropolitan Police Act. It provided that Shelby (Memphis), Davidson (Nashville), and Hamilton (Chattanooga) counties be made metropolitan police districts with complete authority placed in the hands of commissioners appointed by Governor Brownlow. The commissioners in turn would hire the police. The cost of the system was to be met by a special property tax, laid and collected in the respective districts by the local authorities.

William R. Tracy received the appointment as commissioner for Hamilton County and Chattanooga and on 1 June he requested that the city furnish him with a "Station House for the accomodation of the Police Force." The law immediately sparked a tremendous controversy. Some said it was passed because the area had become the rendezvous of thugs, tough gangs, loiterers, camp followers, and perpetrators of open violence. Others claimed it was passed "in order to prevent the benighted residents from voting wrong." More fundamentally, it was obvious that it represented the usurpation of local affairs by the governor and a flagrant means of creating political patronage without paying for it.

Hamilton County refused to have anything to do with the arrangement and would not impose a tax to cover costs. In disgust the city board of aldermen threatened to do away with any police force, claiming (with tongue in cheek) such protection to be unneeded. But Tracy seized the initiative. He claimed the metropolitan police law had already abolished Chattanooga's police force and the office of recorder and demanded to know at "what hour tomorrow" Chattanooga would withdraw its police from the streets and turn over "necessary papers and appurtenances from the police department."

Since the mayor was absent when this demand arrived, it became the duty of the mayor *pro tem* to respond. He happened to be none other than William Crutchfield, loyal, outspoken, and tested Unionist. Crutchfield and his colleagues had no idea of supporting such dictatorial civil government. They refused Tracy's requests and flatly stated that they neither recognized his authority nor that of the Metropolitan Police.

Chattanooga got an injunction restraining operations of the police service under the Metropolitan Police Act. This injunction was ultimately dissolved and the new policemen took over. Consequently, on 7 September the city officially disbanded its police force. But the city took the case to court; to represent the case of the Republican city government the city fathers chose the ex-secessionist, former Confederate officer, and active independent Democrat David McKendree Key. No reasons are given for this move, but it could scarcely have happened in any other Southern community.

The court decision went against the municipality but was immediately appealed while the city continued to refuse to levy any tax to cover salaries and other costs of the metropolitan police. Eventually in 1873 the state supreme court upheld the lower court's ruling and the town found itself with a burdensome debt which required the sale of bonds amounting to $18,000. An aura of fraud and corruption hung over this episode as Tracy and his successor, A. A. Pearson, both newcomers to the area, played the role of petty carpetbaggers. It was the region's worst Reconstruction experience.[8]

Attorney Key, a good-natured, modest man, received in 1870 an appointment as chancellor of the Third Chancery Division. He readily dismissed the past faults and actions of the people he dealt with and emphasized the importance of the common destiny of all residents. Dressed in a long frock coat, he rode over the mountains of East Tennessee; during these travels he had plenty of time to think over the area's complex inheritance from the recent past. Key insisted that the color line must be removed from politics and that a solid-white South meant that both economic progress and new industry would lag. His brand of Democratic thinking made it easy for northern-born Democrats, who believed in the New South concept of economic diversity, to support him.

Key received in 1872 his party's nomination for Congress, which he accepted only after making it perfectly clear he would never support Rebel animosities or sectional emotionalism. He did not endorse the banner of the lost cause, believing that the war had been a tragic mistake. Key's opponent was Bill Crutchfield. The two men had grown to be friends, sharing an interest in nature and a deep satisfaction found in the beauty and peaceful silence of the neighboring mountains. By a narrow margin, 9,950 to 8,921, Crutchfield won the seat, largely because the Democrats continued to be badly fractionalized.[9]

1870 was a landmark year in the affairs of Hamilton County. By that time the Conservatives had gained complete control of the state government. They regrouped under the aegis of the Democratic party while the term "Radical" disappeared from use as the Republican party gained most of the Brownlow followers. A constitutional convention convened and rewrote Tennessee's basic law. The new document featured universal manhood suffrage, a poll tax, limitations on the governor's authority, and a check on the easy granting of the state's credit. Chancellor Key represented Hamilton and adjoining counties in this vital work which the voters overwhelmingly approved on 26 March 1870.

Just prior to this time a change in the county government's structure again created the office of county judge. One of the judge's duties was to preside over the county court which replaced the quorum court on which justices of the peace acted collectively. A. G. W. Puckett, a Republican, filled the new position for a term of eight years when Judge R. C. McRee, a Confederate veteran and industrious Democrat, succeeded him.[10]

Alterations were also made in the charter of Chattanooga. The corporate limits were enlarged to the south and five wards created, to be represented by two aldermen elected from each. The office of recorder was reestablished as was that of the marshal. In 1872 an amendment extended the mayor's term to two years.[11]

Despite the obvious physical limitations, Chattanooga clearly had become the commercial, manufacturing, and financial center of Hamilton County. Traffic on the river and by rail made it a major transportation hub. To facilitate common legal transactions, the Tennessee General Assembly approved a private act on 24 June 1870, providing for a referendum on the removal of the county seat from Harrison to Chattanooga. The balloting that fall gave the necessary two-thirds of the votes in favor of removal. On 5 December Judge Key presided over the last court held at Harrison and a two-horse vehicle loaded with books and records finalized the transfer as it made its formal trek from the old to the new courthouse. The Law Court of Chattanooga merged into the Circuit Court of Hamilton County and the Chancery Court of Chattanooga in similar manner became the Chancery Court of Hamilton County.[12]

When the county seat moved, all offices occupied space in James Hall at the northeast corner of Market and Sixth streets. The county later bought and fitted up for a jail and courthouse property at Fourth and Market streets which was used until 1879. This prewar structure, designed originally as a business block by Hooke and McCallie, had been used by the wartime government as a military prison. It then became Chattanooga's municipal building until acquired by the county.

Judge Shepherd relates a story of an arsonist's attempt to burn the building in a scheme to destroy the county books in the register's office. These essential records had been seized by the Federal army but with the exception of "Book I" had been restored to the register. With the courthouse at Harrison, Jason S. Wiltse and Colonel J.E. MacGowan had made abstract records of land titles to facilitate title investigations without having to travel to the county seat. The private owners of the abstracts gave an option for their purchase to the incendiary, who saw their value mount if the register's books were destroyed. Some of the records were so badly scorched in the fire that they had to be transcribed and many deeds had to be reregistered. The culprit, caught and sentenced to fifteen years in the penitentiary, had his sentence reversed by the supreme court on the grounds of insanity and finally prosecution was dropped.

When the courthouse at Fourth and Market streets became inadequate, plans for a new building took shape under the supervision of

Judge McRee. A beautiful eminence in the very heart of the city was acquired (present Courthouse Square), bounded by Sixth, Walnut, and Seventh streets, Georgia Avenue and Lookout Street. A courthouse costing $100,325 was erected and in addition to county offices and courtrooms for a time housed the United States Circuit and District courts. In 1881 a $33,500 jail was built across Walnut Street. The courthouse was enlarged and remodeled in 1891 for about $50,000 during which time court was held in "Turner hall," over the saloon bearing that name. A fire started by lightning totally destroyed the courthouse on the night of 7 May 1910.[13]

The folks in the eastern portion of Hamilton County did not welcome the removal of the courthouse from Harrison. They cried fraud; they accused Chattanoogans of cheating in the election. Some sought an injunction to prevent the move; however, nothing came of this effort. But emotions ran high and another scheme was concocted. On 30 January 1871, its supporters succeeded in getting a law passed to create a new county out of the eastern part of Hamilton and a section of Bradley County. It consisted of 285 square miles and a rural white Republican population. The new county created in peevish reaction to the loss of the Hamilton County seat, was named James for the Reverend Jesse J. James, father of the Hamilton County legislator who sponsored the legislation.

James, Methodist clergyman and merchant, had moved from Blountville, Sullivan County, to Chattanooga about 1854 and died there some two years later. He was the father of four sons, all of whom became favorably known. The eldest, George, entered the banking field in Oregon. John W. served as alderman and in 1875 as mayor of Chattanooga. Elbert A. became a lawyer and state legislator. The youngest, Charles E., was a successful Hamilton County industrialist, financier, builder, and community booster.[14]

The creation of James County reduced the size of Hamilton by almost one-third and explains the relatively slow population growth in the county in the decade of the 1870s. Within the new county, deep differences soon surfaced over the location of the county seat. This very common type of disagreement was settled by a customary referendum and Harrison, on the river, lost out to the small railroad hamlet of Ooltewah. Completely frustrated, some Harrison people managed to get their property relocated in Hamilton County.

The most significant development of the period was the establishment of a system of tax-supported public schools. In early years

Tennessee had made a feeble, abortive effort to finance some schools from land moneys which was tinged with fraud and corruption. Where schools operated, they were regarded as "pauper schools." After the war the first Hamilton County school was the federally supported post school. Several private or church-related schools and the Lookout Mountain Educational Institute took pupils. In 1867 the Radical Brownlow regime enacted state legislation to initiate a genuine public school program administered by a state superintendent and county superintendents. Financed by tax money, the Hamilton County unit included the city of Chattanooga in its nineteen local districts. It was a bold idea.

Hamilton County's first superintendent was Reverend E. O. Tade, a black who came to the area about 1865 from Memphis under the auspices of the American Missionary Association to establish a school for freedmen. With funds from the association, Tade completed the construction of a school building at Georgia Avenue and Ninth Street at a cost of upwards of ten thousand dollars to start classes in 1871. The school, known as the Howard School, honored General Oliver Otis Howard, soldier and able commissioner of the Freedmen's Bureau.

In addition to his work with the Howard School, Tade established the First Congregational Church, served as cashier of the Freedmen's Saving and Trust Company, a national organization with numerous offices throughout the South, and as county school superintendent. Describing the demanding nature of the latter job, he wrote, "Up at 3:30 A.M., traveled fifteen miles on railroad; walked six miles; made up Civil District Clerk's report; visited three schools, examined one teacher; traveled nine miles further and reached home by cars at 8 P.M., eating one meal."

When the Conservatives gained political control of Tennessee, they revoked all Radical legislation in July 1870—the good with the bad. One casualty was the burgeoning educational program. With it went Tade's position, although as Tade wrote of Chattanooga, "The Union sentiment here is the ruling sentiment of the place. The postmaster recognizes me as Supt. of Education." Tade stayed on with the Howard School, where in 1869 a staff of six teachers is reported to have worked with 855 part-time and full-time students of all ages.[15]

In Chattanooga a few private schools financed through tuition payments continued. Under the leadership of H. Clay Evans the city government on 18 July 1872 passed an ordinance authorizing a fresh attempt at launching publicly supported schools. A board of education consisting of two representatives from each of the five wards managed the program and appointed Henry D. Wyatt superintendent. Wyatt, a New Englander, had graduated from Dartmouth College with a master's degree after completing his tour of duty with the Federal army.

Much of the early progress of the school system resulted from Wyatt's able leadership. He early gained the respect of the community which appreciated his special interest in the classics and fine arts. The versatile Wyatt played the organ at the First Presbyterian Church, directed a large chorus, and conducted music classes in the schools.[16] On 1 January 1873, the first graded schools for whites opened in Chattanooga.

On the state level, the Democrats rekindled interest in tax-supported schools. Prodded by the governor, who reminded the legislature that Tennessee would be "third in ignorance" among the states if nothing were done, the lawmakers adopted a program in 1873 which provided for a system of management as well as financial support very similar to the 1867 plan.

The school program of the city, like that of the state, faced troubled days. The economic conditions in the postwar South grew much worse with the swift developing national panic of 1873. In Chattanooga, for example, the board of education members signed a $1,000 note pledging their personal credit to get the program through the first year. The scanty funds had to assume the burden of a required provision for separate but equal facilities for the races. Moreover, without a tradition of free education, some public indifference and even hostility confronted these early efforts.

Chattanooga acquired the old Masonic Hall and worked out an agreement with the American Missionary Association to use their building rent-free with the AMA appointing the teachers. In 1873 school property was valued at $5,000; classes remained in session five months. Teachers' salaries ranged from $35 to $45 per month. The total expenditures for the first year were $8,824.80. Two years later the anuual budget was $25,000 and salaries were reported to range from $25 to $55 for teachers. In 1878 twenty-one teachers received total salaries of $11,222, while reports as late as 1885 indicated that teacher earnings averaged $55.64 per month.[17]

During the first years of the school system, only primary classes were offered. Superintendent Wyatt began teaching a few boys informally in his office, especially in the classics, in an endeavor to arouse public interest in a high school. In December 1874 Chattanooga High School was organized with a student body of thirty-five pupils; the first graduating class, numbering five young ladies, completed studies in 1879. The Howard School, incorporated into the city system, moved to a building at East Eighth and Douglas streets and in 1883 a high school curriculum led to the creation of Howard High School.[18]

During Superintendent Tade's administration of the county schools, the county outside of Chattanooga owned three tracts of land but no schoolhouse. In 1871 Tade was succeeded by J. H. Hardie, who in turn was followed by W. M. Beene. During Beene's term four school buildings were erected and efforts were launched to provide primary classes for all students. This was a major undertaking requiring raw pioneer courage. In addition to the problems found in town, all of which were even more critical when seen in the rural areas, were the difficulties of travel and the necessity to provide for the small, scattered black population which was by law entitled to separate but equal educational opportunity.

The county schools consisted of one-room, one-teacher institutions; they were of log or frame construction and as rudimentary in equipment as were the subjects taught. The county superintendent was elected biannually by the county court and the electorate chose their school directors annually in each school district. The superintendent's job description reveals the weakness of these early efforts; this important official by law was specified to be a "person of literary and scientific attainments, and, when practicable, of skill and experience in the art of teaching." Professionalism only gradually crept into the program, which was lengthened by 1885 to five months and one extra day per year. The census of 1890 shows that Hamilton County had 164 teachers (115 white, 49 black) of whom Chattanooga had 74 (45 white, 29 black). The number of pupils totaled 10,160 for the county (7,106 white, 3,054 black) of whom Chattanooga claimed 4,541 (2,578 white, 1,963 black).[19]

After the state made provisions to extend tax-supported school programs to secondary education in 1891, Hamilton County slowly accepted the challenge to start high schools about 1902. Hixson, Sale Creek, Soddy, and Ridgedale (later known as Central) high schools, were started about that time and were soon joined by Birchwood High School. In 1907 the unit for school administration became the county, and a county board of education replaced the numerous district school directors.[20]

During these years students walked many miles to school or drove their own buggies or wagons. Barns built at each schoolhouse sheltered the horses and mules. Horsedrawn buses—the drivers had to stay at the schools all day—later furnished needed transportation. During times of high water it is reported that in the Hixson area pupils were rowed from one hill to another to attend classes. Many did not or could not make the effort to attend. The census shows in 1900 that 2,571 males over twenty-one years of age were classified as illiterate and that the total illiterate population ten years of age and over was 7,331.[21]

The experiences of two students vividly depict the early high school days. Professor S. H. Proffitt of Sale Creek tells this story:

Sam Cunningham, valedictorian of the first graduating class of Sale Creek High, had to walk five miles to school and five miles back, making a total of 10 miles a day, but he was never absent a day. I recall early one spring morning we had a downpour of rain which flooded all the small creeks and bottoms around Sale Creek. When Sam reached the footlog where he usually crossed the stream, he found that it had been washed away. Not to be outdone, he walked about two miles to another crossing, but it, too, was flooded. Every avenue of reaching the school was cut off, but that did not stop Sam Cunningham. He waded into that swirling water up to his armpits, but he got across. He arrived at school soaked to the skin, but soon dried by the boiler in the basement.[22]

Adela Haenseler told her own story of school days:

I had finished the eighth grade at King's Point in the spring of 1907. Our own one-room school at Jersey was closed that year, but because my father believed in education, I walked to King's Point, a distance of about 2½ miles, so I could graduate.

I well remember that one day during that summer my mother and I were out under the peach tree doing the family laundry when a stranger came and told us about a new high school that was going to be opened at Tyner the next fall.

This was Mr. Abel, and he was out scouting over the county looking for pupils to go to school. I still remember how thrilled he was to find someone ready and anxious to go.

My brother and I drove to school the next August, using our horse and buggy and sharing the ride with a neighbor girl.

We met in the two churches, Baptist and Methodist, because the building was not ready for occupation.

There were two teachers—Mr. Abel teaching Latin, English, history and allied subjects and also acting as principal, and Mr. Bright teaching agriculture, algebra, zoology, botany and other subjects.

How proud we were when the brick building was finished and we moved in. We had outdoor water supply and outdoor plumbing, but everyone was happy. They built a good barn for the horses, and the pupils gathered in for miles around.

Most of the pupils were well beyond regular high school age, and some were too young and had not completed the eighth grade. These latter were put into a preparatory class. It took all of these to make enough to justify starting a high school.

Later in the year we had a home economics room equipped and Miss Helen Buguo was added to the faculty.[23]

For students not so enthusiastic in attending school or who got into serious trouble Judge M. M. Hope in 1893 came up with a progressive idea. He established a whipping post system which allowed parents under police supervision to administer punishment in place of a fine or jail sentence.

Since many of the education leaders were elected, it was only natural that the public school program frequently became a subject of local political interest. When Hamiltonians went to the polls to decide such matters, they generally were influenced by personalities and local concerns rather than by political affiliation. They campaigned vigorously because the margin of victory was traditionally narrow, but they seldom allowed results to nourish lasting animosity.

In state and national elections, party commitments held firmly and Chattanooga, jokingly called "that swollen village," as well as Hamilton County usually rang up Republican victories. Grant, Hayes, Garfield, Blaine, and Harrison won majorities. Then in 1892 both county and town gave the Democrats a victory—the first time both had given that party a majority in a national election. To make it possible for the victors to celebrate, "the Republicans loaned their torches and stood as spectators and really enjoyed the glorious, good time." In gubernatorial elections the same pattern generally held true, but because the state after 1870 usually returned Democratic leaders, Hamilton County suffered as a minority area.[24]

After a decade of divided loyalties and the uncertainties of Reconstruction, the people of the area found it best to turn to the future and not to dwell on the past. At first a few strident voices would not let bygones alone. A Radical Republican newspaper, the *Unconditional*, was published at Harrison by Dr. C. A. Gowin. Later he published *The Tennessee Republican*. Contemporaries found him radical but personally and politically honest, although eccentric and caustic. They also found Metropolitan Police Chief W. R. Tracy and his successor, A. A. Pearson, to be men of radical views. At times petty social differences surfaced from old wartime opinions, but on the whole a spirit of community overshadowed differences. The neighborliness of a small town and the cooperation demanded by such adversities as fire, flood, and disease brought folks together. A tolerance of diverse views and backgrounds placed the residents on the road to reunion.

Ex-Federals and ex-Confederates met jointly in political sessions at an early date and voiced approval of a lenient, national Reconstruction policy. Local editors wrote frequently of the longing for harmony. In 1868 the *American Union* claimed that "[we] desire to have peace and an honest and friendly Union . . . [with] those we contended [with] so long and well for a cause which we must do them the justice to say they believed to be right, whatever we may think about it."[25] All newspapers denounced political adventurers and discouraged any from residing in the area.

Individual community leaders like D. M. Key, the self-styled Independent Democrat, helped direct the local course. General Wilder bragged of his adopted home to visitors, "This is the freest town on the map. All join together here for the general good and strive, to a man, for the upbuilding of the city."[26] The Reverend Thomas McCallie, who had lived through the local holocaust, preached faith and harmony. In 1873 he was joined by Reverend Jonathan Waverly Bachman. Bachman came from a divided family and as a Confederate veteran understood the agony of the lost cause. But as the minister of the First Presbyterian Church and honorary "Pastor of Chattanooga" he rendered service to the entire county as a liberal advocate of a genuine belief in a reunited country. He was known as an unselfish, noble, compassionate human being.

Yet another voice carried much influence. It belonged to Colonel J. E. MacGowan, white officer in the First United States Colored Artillery, who was mustered out of service in Chattanooga on 31 March 1866, and stayed on in the community as lawyer and journalist. In February 1872 he became associate editor of the *Chattanooga Times* and under publisher Adolph S. Ochs he worked as chief editorial writer beginning on 1 July 1878. MacGowan had a strong paternalistic attitude toward blacks. He advocated support for their education and condemned those who would use the freedmen as political pawns. Publicly he deplored "the white man who maltreats a decent colored man merely to exploit his superiority or display his brutal prejudice."[27]

The gala Fourth of July celebration commemorating the nation's centennial offered an opportunity to display publicly this fraternal spirit. The master of ceremonies presented veterans from both armies to the crowds, and the *Chattanooga Times* noted,

> The perfect harmony that has been apparent throughout, the energy with which the ex-Confederates and the ex-Federals took hold of the work assigned them, and worked side by side, was the pleasing feature of the occasion, and one particularly characteristic of Chattanooga. Chattanooga knows no North, no South, no East, no West, and but one indivisible country.[28]

The next year another occasion provided an opportunity for dramatic action. On Decoration Day (May 10) the Confederate Memorial Association laid the cornerstone of the Confederate monument in the cemetery. Among the participants in the "grand procession" that marked the occasion were "boys in blue" from the local veterans' post.

The very next day prominent former Confederates met to plan some return of this courtesy by taking part in the Memorial Day (May 30) services at the National Cemetery. They said it was their wish to show their Union neighbors and "the people of the United States that we cherish none of the bad feelings engendered by the late war." Their desire was to march to the National Cemetery and return with the planned procession without uniforms, banners, badges, or flags. Their request received warm endorsements, and invitations to attend were sent to the president of the United States, key federal officials, and the former generals of the opposing armies of the recent war.

Again the *Times* editorialized about "The Harmony": "The hearts of the people of this community had no room for hypocrisy on these two glorious days. There was no time, no need of it,—sincerity was the guiding star of our actions."[29]

The political fortunes of Chancellor Key conveyed this community spirit of harmony to the national scene. In 1875 Key unexpectedly received an appointment as United States senator to fill the seat of Andrew Johnson, who had died in office. His fellow townsmen, with blazing torches, serenaded the new senator at his home while a neighboring newspaper commented, "The village of Chattanooga is as proud of her new Senator as 'a negro with a new shirt.' " In Washington Key gained attention through his eulogy of the former president.[30]

Within the year the famous disputed presidential election of 1876 occupied all thinking persons; the result of the Hayes-Tilden controversy hung in the balance for months. Many feared a new civil war; others worked for a compromise solution. Conservative Southerners eventually agreed to support the Republican Hayes if national Reconstruction were ended, Federal troops removed from Southern states, and a Southerner placed in the cabinet. Hayes agreed and won the office. He then selected David M. Key to be postmaster general. Key was the first Southerner, first Democrat, and first Confederate officer to receive such an appointment following the war.

All of this was very unorthodox. From many parts of the country complaining voices deplored the "deal." Some of Key's Hamilton County neighbors were puzzled and divided in their views. Was Key a man of expediency, rather than principle? Had he joined the enemy camp? Was he a mere political opportunist? How could a Democrat sit in a Republican administration? Most, however, knew the man and praised his courage and willingness to make personal sacrifices for the South.

To dispel Southern doubts, Hayes planned a fall tour, which included Key's hometown, and became the first president to visit Hamilton County since James Monroe stopped at Brainerd Mission. Speeches, toasts, and messages of reunion highlighted the day. The president in his remarks cited a morning editorial which he found most fitting:

> For a long while our faces were turned away from each other; the light of brotherly love and kindness had faded; a common sorrow, deep and dark, lay like a fragment of night between us. It is part of our mission, and the best part, to join hands with you, and take all these sad and hurtful things up by the roots and destroy forever the last vestige of reproductive power that they have. We ask you to give us your hands in this matter in all sincerity, that the early days of a united brotherhood may break once more and all hearts rejoice that the night has passed forever.[31]

Four years later the same spirit found expression before another national audience. In the fall of 1881 the Society of the Army of the Cumberland, a veterans' organization, planned a Chattanooga reunion. It marked the first time Federal veterans agreed to meet south of the Ohio River and one of its leading members, who had been General Rosecrans's chief of staff at Chickamauga, was president of the United States.

Excitement mounted as the anniversary days of the battle approached. Local committees composed of ex-Confederates as well as Union veterans worked to decorate the streets and prepare for the guests. The visitors came in large numbers, but just as the reunion was about to begin word arrived that President James A. Garfield had died of a gunshot wound inflicted by an assassin some eighty days earlier. The planned program gave way to a memorial service. A huge flagpole was planted on the highest crown of Cameron Hill and a flag hoisted by the joint pull of four Federal veterans and four Confederate veterans. The flag was immediately run down to half-staff after which two men addressed the hushed audience: Captain Summerfield Key on behalf of the Confederates and the governor of Ohio for the Union men.[32]

The local population increased steadily during the postwar decades. Hamilton County grew from 17,241 in 1870 to 53,482 twenty years later. In 1890 the total included, as in the early years of the area's history, a vast preponderance of native-born persons; they numbered 51,386 as compared to 2,096 foreign born. The largest number of foreign born (526) came from Germany. England had sent 336, Wales 324, Ireland 321, Scotland 94, and Canada 170. Other European countries represented included Switzerland 58, Sweden 35, Russia 76, Hungary 25, France 42, and Italy 17. From Asia had come 10 Chinese, 2 Japanese, and 6 "civilized" Indians.

In 1890 more than one-half of the residents of Hamilton County lived within the limits of Chattanooga. They numbered 29,100 of whom approximately 4.4% were foreign born. The county's Negro population that year totaled 17,717, or about 33%. Most of them, 12,563, were concentrated in Chattanooga. Within the city the percentage of blacks in the aggregate population grew from 36.5% in 1870 to 39% in 1880. In 1890 it reached 43%.[33]

During the war years, blacks living in the vicinity secured jobs either with the Confederate or Union armies, usually in the commissary departments. Following the decisive military activity of 1863 many freedmen collected around the Union camps. Some established homes in the area, working as barbers, hotel employees, railroad or steamboat hands, draymen, tailors, and moulders. They were joined by professional persons whose interests rested with the church, the law, medicine, and teaching. Among their leaders were E. O. Tade, banker and schoolman; R. Emerson Andrews, druggist; Thomas William Haigler, physician, surgeon, and minister; George W. Franklin, Jr., undertaker; Dr. Edmond W. Rogers, and Dr. O. L. Davis. Dr. Davis graduated from the Meharry Medical College's dental department in 1902 and is credited with being the first colored woman dentist to graduate in the South. She was born on Lookout Mountain and returned to practice in Chattanooga. Representative black newspaper men were the Reverend G. W. Hayes, H. C. Smith, and Randolph Miller; among the lawyers, William C. Hodge, Styles L. Hutchins, and J. W. White.

Almost immediately after Appomattox blacks became eligible to vote in Chattanooga elections and to hold public office. In 1868 C. P. Letcher gained a seat on the board of aldermen and he was soon followed by Reverend Clem Shaw, George Shaw, and D. Medow. Most of the blacks were associated with the Republican party although in the 1880s Henry C. Smith, who had received a federal clerkship under President Grover Cleveland, campaigned for the Democrats.

In Chattanooga conditions favored black participation in politics. Community leaders, always interested in attracting capital, railroads, and industry to the city, wished to prevent any trouble or signs of radicalism. They demonstrated a strong feeling of responsibility for blacks and worked for the kind of environment where paternalistic racial attitudes would be possible. Furthermore, there was a sufficiently large proportion of blacks in the small city to be a decisive force at election time, for the major parties were well balanced numerically.

The freedmen, naturally, suffered many disadvantages. Politically they had little expertise, practically no money, and their church or fraternal organizations had little strength. With limited political power the local blacks found their opportunities to run for office on the Republican ticket limited. But with astute leadership they entered the political arena as bargainers; they became active participants in the election process and were not merely spectators.

Blacks in Chattanooga were more effective than those of other Tennessee communities in gaining minor offices and in winning patronage jobs. Blacks served with fire companies, on the police force, and on the board of education. Others held positions as justices of the peace, constables, poor commissioners, deputy sheriffs, and jurors. The Republicans grew more and more dependent on the black vote and blacks grew increasingly dissatisfied with their meager rewards. Occasionally Democrats bid for black votes or attacked their opposition for using the blacks as pawns. Editor MacGowan fumed in 1880 when, on a police force of ten, four were blacks, hired, he wrote, by the "Republican party machine." A year later seven blacks worked on a twelve man police force.[34]

On the state level the Democrats were badly split into a number of bickering groups with white supremacy interests serving as the only glue. Some Democrats of the "New South" economic point of view could work with blacks, but one element, the "Bourbons"—who like the French monarchs never learned a thing from past experience—deplored black activism. In the spring of 1883 a great storm broke, raised by Democrats who called themselves "three-fourths of the businessmen of Chattanooga" representing both the city and Hamilton County. They had introduced into the Tennessee General Assembly a bill to repeal the city charter and change the political status of Chattanooga into a taxing district. Local authority would then rest in a council made up of members of the fire and police commission and a public works commission, most of whom would be appointed by the governor. Those officers to be elected would have to run on a city-wide ticket, thereby eliminating ward politics and black officeholders.

The sponsors of the repeal claimed that Chattanooga's government was a complete failure. They insisted that the white Republicans who controlled it were a radical, unscrupulous gang who manipulated a group of subservient blacks; that the whites willingly made any concession necessary to retain power; that one of the worst was the appointment of blacks to the board of education. The supporters of repeal claimed that the history being taught in the schools was prostituted and stressed a radical view. Furthermore, they recited a story that a black commissioner of education on a school visit had offended the children in the town's most important white school and humiliated the white teachers. "If the legislature did not grant relief," they cried, "we will soon have negro teachers over our children. . . . We have no prejudice against the Negroes, but dislike to be ruled and ruined by them." One advocate before a senate hearing bluntly announced, "If any of you gentlemen will come over to Chattanooga and get on a little bender we will furnish a nigger to arrest you, a nigger to lock you up and a nigger to take care of you after you get into jail."

Mayor H. Clay Evans and the local Republicans denied the charges. J. W. Adams, president of the school board, revealed that the history text so bitterly denounced had been in use ever since the schools were organized. He further reported that the principal of the school where the incident had occurred said that the black commissioner had visited the school at the request of and with white commissioners. He had not made any comments or asked any questions. The independent Democratic *Times* joined in the exposé, characterizing the episode as a "Proposed Municipal Reform." Editor MacGowan revealed the demogogic, fraudulent nature of the original petition. Although he basically felt most blacks were unprepared to exercise the rights of citizenship, he did not want charter repeal. It would destroy home rule and also turn the city government over to the Bourbon wing of the state Democratic hierarchy. Money, time, worry, and energy were consumed in large amounts during the struggle.

A compromise bill was finally worked out and passed in March 1883. It was clearly aimed at reducing the political influence of the local blacks. It called for registration procedures and a poll tax and provided for a police commission appointed by the governor. The number of aldermen was reduced to six and a $10,000 bond required of each.[35]

The effect of this charter change never became as clear or positive as its supporters hoped. The Republicans continued to work with the blacks, who at times even threatened members of their own race, lest they cast Democratic votes. The blacks sponsored registration drives and launched a large number of newspapers which were highly political in nature. Although most of their journals lasted but a few months, they revealed an energetic and able leadership. By remaining loyal to the Republicans under these circumstances the blacks did gain political clout.[36]

Within the following decade blacks continued to hold many patronage positions and to win elections as aldermen, justices of the peace, school commissioners, jailors, deputy sheriffs, and city councilmen. Then in 1886 John James Irvine was elected circuit court clerk by a large majority of 1,400 votes; the newspaper reported that he was a "man of intelligence and acknowledged honesty" and that he was the first of his race to occupy a county office. Irvine, born a slave in Virginia, had attended night school and worked as an engineer and machinist. In Chattanooga he had previously been elected constable and was an effective member of the Knights of Labor.[37]

The local legislative district sent two Hamilton County blacks to the lower house of the General Assembly. William C. Hodge gained a seat just one year after the charter-repeal struggle, challenging his Republican colleagues to nominate and elect a black. Hodge had been active politically for some years and had been a member of the Chattanooga city council since 1878. The second black legislator, outspoken, Georgia-born Styles L. Hutchins, had a college education and had studied law. In 1881 he had moved to Chattanooga and immediately went into politics and in the newspaper field served as an editor of *The Independent Age*, a journal "independent in politics and somewhat arrogant of expression." In 1886 Hutchins won a seat in the General Assembly.[38]

Hodge and Hutchins comprised two of the twelve Negroes who were elected to the Tennessee General Assembly in the 1880s. Nine of the number came from western Tennessee counties where the blacks outnumbered the white residents and one represented Davidson County. After 1887 no black was elected until 1965.[39]

This revival of Republican interest in blacks did not mean that others discontinued their efforts to find methods of restricting their political activity. New attempts at charter repeal, restrictive voting regulations, or ward gerrymandering continued to be made locally through the turn of the century. Emerging Jim Crow laws on a state level and a nationwide municipal reform movement all had the effect of diluting the political influence of the blacks. The secret ballot, a much-desired reform, suggested that uneducated blacks would find voting more difficult while municipal reform to establish more efficient government would eliminate manipulation, graft, and fraud. On the whole, all such efforts expressed a desire for structural changes in government rather than any appeal to social justice.

Although conditions permitted less flexibility for Chattanooga blacks than earlier, they did not have the rigid impact experienced in other areas. Blacks continued to gain positions in minor offices and to sit on the board of aldermen. Dr. T. Edinburg was elected school commissioner in 1904 for a four-year term. Eugene L. Reid and Charles Grigsby served on the city council along with Hiram Tyree. Tyree came to Chattanooga in 1867 and by the end of the century was the foremost black political leader in the community. Tyree served as school commissioner for ten years, as alderman for fourteen years, and as a member of the city council for seven years. Grigsby and Tyree continued on the council until the commission form of city government went into effect in 1911.[40] By the 1890s some blacks held that the "debt of gratitude" philosophy referring to their obligations to the Republicans was a "ghost of the past" and that blacks should vote independently.

The cohesiveness of the black community resulted partly from the influence of the *Blade*, a journal characterized by its picturesque and forceful style of writing which circulated for about twelve years. Its editorials were composed, its type set, and its presses managed by Randolph Miller, whose personal trademark was a high silk hat worn always at a rakish angle. Miller, a former slave, arrived in Chattanooga in 1864 with Sherman's army. He later took work with the *Times* and learned the printer's craft. In 1898 he launched the *Blade* with, most likely, the patronage and quiet encouragement of Adolph S. Ochs. Miller possessed a rugged standard of values as well as strong opinions as to how people ought to conduct their lives. He never hesitated to tell his white fellow townsmen of their shortcomings; they, in turn, appreciated his flamboyant style, his character, and his "unique bits of philosophy."[41]

This era of black activity in politics, having endured since 1867, came to a close on the twenty-fifth day of April 1911, when the city electorate voted for the first mayor and commissioners under a new charter calling for city-wide elections.[42] The keen political jousting during these years not only produced a strong local two-party system but was in part responsible for the development of two outstanding Republican leaders who attained state and national recognition.

Newell Sanders moved to Chattanooga in 1878 from his native Indiana, where he had graduated from the state university. At the suggestion of General John T. Wilder he acquired a small, modestly equipped factory and entered into the manufacture of plows. Sanders, skillful and inventive, designed a plow especially suited for southern soil; he became a very successful industrialist and president of the National Association of Agricultural Implements and Vehicle Manufacturers. As a relative newcomer he sat on the Chattanooga board of aldermen and school board. In 1894, as campaign manager, he aided his fellow townsman H. Clay Evans in his race for governorship.

Evans, a Pennsylvanian of Quaker ancestry, moved as an infant with his parents to Wisconsin. He served in the Union army and in 1870 settled in Chattanooga where he engaged in the manufacture of freight cars. Evans spent a good deal of time involving himself in civil and political affairs. He is credited with the establishment of the public school system and was appointed the first school commissioner. After four years as an alderman he served two terms as mayor and in 1889 entered Congress, but was an unsuccessful candidate for reelection two years later. In 1891–93 he held office as the first assistant postmaster general of the United States.

The next year Evans, with Sanders working as his manager, ran for governor against Democratic incumbent Peter Turney. Evans ran a spirited campaign and the balloting proved so close that official returns were not made public until five weeks after the election. The returns showed a small Republican majority. The Democrats cried foul and a Democrat-controlled investigation followed. Evans and the Republicans were counted out and finally on 9 May Governor Turney took the oath of office for the second time.

Evans and Sanders emerged as party martyrs and as heroes. Sanders became chairman of the Republican state executive committee and a delegate to six national Republican conventions. In 1912 he was appointed to the United States Senate to fill out the term of Robert L. Taylor, who had died while in office. Sanders was the first Republican senator from Tennessee in forty years. Evans enjoyed a vice-presidential boom in 1896. He was appointed commissioner of pensions by McKinley and consul general in London by Theodore Roosevelt. He concluded his political career with his election in 1911 as Chattanooga's commissioner of health and education.[43]

NOTES

1. *Chattanooga Gazette*, 5 March 1864.

2. Penelope Johnson Allen, "Leaves From the Family Tree,"*Chattanooga Times*, 24 June 1934.

3. Robert H. White, *Messages of the Governors of Tennessee, 1796–1821*, 8 vols.(Nashville: Tennessee Historical Commission, 1952), 5:379–401; Thomas B. Alexander, *Political Reconstruction in Tennessee* (Nashville: Vanderbilt University Press, 1950), pp. 18–32. Hood remained active in politics only a short time. In 1866 he suspended publication of the *Gazette* and died shortly afterward. *Chattanogga Times*, 8 December 1892.

4. Harry M. Wiltse, "History of Chattanooga," 2 vols. (Typescript, Chattanooga-Hamilton County Bicentennial Library), 2:270; Zella Armstrong, *History of Hamilton County and Chattanooga, Tennessee*, 2 vols. (Chattanooga: Lookout Publishing, 1931), 2:62, 201.

5. Wiltse, "Chattanooga," 2:71.

6. Armstrong, *Hamilton County*, 2:202–203; City of Chattanooga, *Minutes of the Board of the Mayor and Aldermen, 1865–1868*, pp.145–156, 315, 319–322.

7. Wiltse, "Chattanooga," 2:67.

8. Ibid., 2:74–75; City of Chattanooga, *Minutes, 1865–1868*, pp. 87, 90–93, 101–105, 113, 119, 203. *Chattanooga Times*, 20 April 1873, 8 December 1892; Alexander, *Reconstruction* , p. 172.

9. David M. Abshire, *The South Rejects a Prophet: The Life of Senator D. M. Key, 1824–1900* (New York: Praeger, 1967), pp. 63–67.

10. William C. McIntyre and Thomas W. Graham, *Private Acts of Hamilton County, Tennessee, 1867–1868* (Nashville: County Technical Assistance Service, University of Tennessee Institute for Public Service, 1974), 1:156–57; *Chattanooga Times*, 18 September 1938.

11. Ibid., 8 December 1892.

12. McIntyre and Graham, *Private Acts*, 1:54–55.; undated clipping of an address by Judge Lewis Sheperd on the dedication of the courthouse in 1913.

13. Ibid.

14. Robert M. McBride, "The Search for Jesse James," *Tennessee Historical Quarterly* 24, no. 3 (Fall, 1965): 241–244; Robert M. McBride, "Lost Counties of Tennessee," (East Tennessee Historical Society) *Publications* 38 (1966), pp. 3–15.

15. Clarence Scaife, "Howard's Hundred Years Helped Mold Community," *Chattanooga Times*, 5 May 1974; *Chattanooga Times*, 29 August 1971.

16. Wyatt was with the school system from 1872 to 1917. He served as superintendent from 1872 to 1893 and then had no connection with schools for two years. Between 1895 and 1910 he was principal of Chattanooga High School, relinquishing this post to serve as musical director for the city system until his death in 1917. Elizabeth K. Wade, *History of Chattanooga High School* (Chattanooga: Adams Lithographing, 1974), p. 21.

17. *A History of Tennessee From Earliest Times to the Present* (Nashville: Goodspeed, 1886), pp. 843–844; *Chattanooga Times*, 16 January 1887, 8 December 1892.

18. Wade, *Chattanooga High*, pp. 21–23; *Chattanooga Times*, 4 February 1896. Members of the first high school faculty were W. D. Underhill and Miss Hattie Ackerman. The first graduates were Minnie C. Bryson, Clara E. Carpenter, Belle McClure, Emily McClure, and Nellie Miller. The first graduate of Howard High School was Belle G. Washington.

Actually it was not until 1885 that state law authorized municipalities to levy additional taxes for "graded high schools"; the right to tax extended throughout the state in 1891.

19. U.S., Eleventh Bureau of the Census, *Population of the U.S. at the Eleventh Census, 1890; Population*, pt. 1 (Washington: G. P. O., 1895), pp. 91, 139.

20. *Chattanooga Times*, 7 July 1912, 25 February 1945, 10 April 1959; Goodspeed, *Tennessee*, pp. 841–842. The principals of the first four high schools were S. H. Proffitt, Sale Creek; J. A. Roberts, Soddy; J. W. Abel, Tyner; and G. M. Swingley, Hixson. The first principal of Central was A. E. Darrah. Central was established in 1906, graduating nineteen students that year.

21. U.S. Bureau of the Census, *Population, 12th Census: 1900*, part 1, 489, 998.

22. *Chattanooga Times*, 20 Feb. 1960.

23. *Ibid.*, 26 Feb. 1960.

24. *Ibid.*, 12 Nov. 1892; Goodspeed, *Tennessee*, pp. 830–831; Wiltse, "Chattanooga," 2:111. The torches or flambeaux used in parades were fed by a coal-oil attachment.

25. *Chattanooga American Union*, 5 March 1868.

26. *Chattanooga Times*, 11 January 1884.

27. *Ibid.*, 8 December 1892.

28. *Ibid.*, 6 July, 1876.

29. *Ibid.*, May, 31 12 June 1877.

30. Abshire,*Key*, pp. 71–77.

31. *Ibid.*, pp. 188–191; *Chattanooga Times*, 20–22 Sept. 1877.

32. *Ibid.*, 8 Dec. 1892.

33. U.S., Bureau of the Census, *Population, 1890*, pt. 1, 40, 429, 440, 481, 656.

34. Joseph H. Cartwright, *The Triumph of Jim Crow: Tennessee Race Relations in the 1880s* (Knoxville: University of Tennessee Press, 1976), pp. 147–149.

35. *Ibid.*, pp. 150–155; *Chattanooga Times*, 8 Dec. 1892; Wiltse, "Chattanooga," 2:130–131.

36. *Ibid.*, 2: 163–164. Some of these journals were *The Enterprise, The Agitator, Justice, The Observer, The Age, The Liberator, The Freeman, The Searchlight,* and *The Blade.*

37. *Chattanooga Times*, 7 Aug. 1886.

38. Cartwright, *Jim Crow*, pp. 79–80, 86, 104, 106, 114, 117, 149, 154, 155; J. Bliss White, comp.,*Biography and Achievments of the Colored Citizens of Chattanooga* (n.p., 1904), p. 63.

39. Joseph H. Cartwright, "Black Legislators in Tennessee in the 1880's: A Case Study in Black Political Leadership," *Tennessee Historical Quarterly* 32, no. 3 (Fall 1973): 265–284.

40. White, *Colored Citizens of Chattanooga*, p. 31; *Chattanooga Times*, 27 April 1896; Lester C. Lamon, *Black Tennesseans, 1900–1930* (Knoxville: University of Tennessee Press, 1977), pp. 38–39.

41. *Ibid.*, pp. 29–30; Wiltse, "Chattanooga," 2: 163–165.

42. *Chattanooga Times*, 26 April 1911.

43. U.S. Congress, Sixty-ninth Congress, Second Session, House Document no. 783; *Biographical Dictionary of the American Congress, 1774–1927* (Washington, D.C.: G. P. O., 1928), pp. 950, 1492; Rufus Terral, *Newell Sanders: A Biography* (Kingsport, Tenn.: author, 1935). Sanders gave much effort to the promotion of Tennessee River traffic. In May 1919 he sold his plow industry to the International Harvester Company.

13

Utilities and Real Estate

THE local committee—Adolph S. Ochs, Chairman, Mayor I. B. Merriam, Tomlinson Fort, J. R. Shipp, and C. E. James—worried about the fickle weather of March and about the long guest list for the complimentary dinner to be sponsored by the chamber of commerce. On 12 March 1891, the leading officials of the Southern Iron Company were to be honored at a dinner at the Read House celebrating the successful manufacture of basic steel by their company. The firm had been in operation since September. The success of their business experiment, it was maintained, marked the beginning of the most important epoch not only in the history of Hamilton County but in the entire South.

The honorees, all Tennesseans and former cavalrymen under General Forrest, had been associated with the iron and coal business in the Cumberland Mountains and had ventured into the developing Birmingham, Alabama, industrial complex. Alfred M. Shook, widely known as "the best looking young fellow on Big Mountain," had grown up with the company. Nathaniel Baxter, Jr., of Nashville joined the company at the time of one of its reorganizations, and John H. Inman, who made a fortune as a postwar cotton broker in New York—and was called a "carpetbagger on Wall Street"—was a heavy investor. In 1889

254

these three, along with others, acquired the Chattanooga properties of the Roane Iron Company and renamed it the Southern Iron Company. In preparation for the introduction of a new steel-making process Captain Hiram Chamberlain, one of the company directors, and Shook journeyed to England to learn the new technique and to engage a skilled manager for their plant.

"Statesmen and Soldiers, Financiers and Railroad Kings, All Unite to do Honor to the Great Benefactors of the South" screamed the headlines of the *Times* the morning following the banquet. Nineteen members of Congress, including William McKinley, Joseph G. Cannon, Joseph Wheeler, and at least six generals rounded out a guest list of some two hundred national figures and local leaders. They dined, sipped wine, gave toasts, and listened to speeches from 10:15 to 3:00 A.M. Part of the meal was served on tin plates made from Chattanooga steel. It was a regal affair. A hundred waiters "dressed in black, with dress coats, and each wearing white gloves" served the many courses.

Witty and serious speeches told of a new era, for the successful local steel story was related to the importance of a diversified southern economy. Much, too, was said about Chattanooga's reputation for harmony. In good humor, former Mayor Tomlinson Fort, who had been a staunch Confederate, joked about Shook, Baxter, and Inman as rebel soldiers. He was sure they would be forgiven. "No one," he claimed, "who believes in the justice of God will believe that He will punish any of His creatures for the same offense, and anyone who served in the Rebel army for four years and four months and was whipped by the Yankees, has been in hell once, and I don't believe God will ever put any of those fellows in hell a second time."[1]

The source of this interest in steel went back to the days of the government rolling mill and to the coming of General Wilder and Captain Chamberlain to the area after they established the Roane Iron Company. In addition to this firm, the Chattanooga Furnace Company was organized in 1874 to operate a small, twenty-five-ton blast furnace which four years later employed twenty-six men. That year the public acclaimed the iron industry in a graphic way: banners on floats in the 4 July 1878 parade read, "Cotton Was King," "Iron Is King Now," "Coal Is Prime Minister." About this time a not-too-optimistic journalist warned, "One cannot repress a fear that some day all [Chattanooga's] natural beauty will be hidden by the smoke from the five hundred chimneys which will be erected in honor of the god Iron. For it is to be a town of rolling-mills and furnaces, giant in its traffic."[2]

At the Roane mill the open-hearth process proved to be uneconomical and unsatisfactory because it could not produce a high-quality product from the inferior local ores. Nevertheless, Chamberlain, J. F. Loomis, D. P. Montague, and others, building on the eastern town limits, started the Citico furnace in 1883 to produce pig iron. With accompanying ceremonies the blast furnace of 125 tons' daily capacity was blown in the following April. It used local coke, some of which came from Soddy, red ores barged downriver from Roane and Rhea counties, and brown ore from northern Georgia and Alabama. After a decade or so of no profits, Citico achieved satisfactory earnings until the business was discontinued in 1911.[3]

Meanwhile the Roane Iron Company was experiencing great difficulty with its steel production. Rather than abandon its effort, the company under the leadership of Chamberlain undertook another experiment—the manufacture of steel by the Bessemer method. On 7 May 1887, Chattanooga celebrated the making of rails by this process; this was the first time in any of the old Confederate states that Bessemer steel was produced. For a brief period the company's success appeared to be assured, but then the market price fell, and by 1889 the Chattanooga properties of the Roane Iron Company were sold to the Southern Iron Company.[4]

For two decades or more Chattanooga served as a center for the East Tennessee iron and steel business. Prospectors, investors, and speculators combed the mountains and valleys from city hotel headquarters. Pig iron blast furnaces sprang up at Dayton, Rockwood, Cowan, and South Pittsburg, giving life to all the neighboring coal mining interests. Locally the Chattanooga and Citico furnaces sold most of their output to such neighboring establishments as the Vulcan Iron and Nail Works, South Tredegar Iron and Nail Company, Wesson Car Foundry Company, Chattanooga Boiler Factory, Wheland Machine Works, Chattanooga Plow Company, Cahill Iron Company, Ross-Meehan Malleable Iron, and the Casey & Hedges Manufacturing Company. In 1910 some forty factories employing 5,290 hands used iron for at least a part of their finished product.[5]

These small plants, most of which required cast iron, were spin-offs from the defunct steel business and represented a healthy diversification. As for the production of steel, the banquet for the Southern Iron Company proved premature. Just as the Bessemer process experiment had failed a few years earlier, the Southern Iron Company's undertaking later had to be abandoned. In little more than a year the plant closed permanently and Chattanooga's dream of becoming a regional Pittsburgh vanished. Local iron ores occurred in unprofitably thin veins and their high phosphorous content made it impossible to produce a quality product profitably. Moreover, an efficient new competitor entered the field: Birmingham, Alabama. Despite heavy investments and boastful local acclaim, natural advantages gave the victory to the Alabama city.

For a time the furnace business helped restore interest in the Tennessee River as navigation slowly recovered from the paralysis of the 1860s. For some fifteen years the *J. T. Wilder* carried pig iron and miscellaneous freight between the Roane Iron Company's Rockwood and Chattanooga plants. The *R. M. Bishop* and the *Rockwood* performed similar duties, often guiding ore and coal barges. The Soddy Coal Company used the *M. H. Clift,* usually under Captain John C. Haley, to keep open needed transportation lines with the Soddy area and to help gain better freight rates from the railroad. The *Dayton* was another; built out of the "remains" of the *James Hobson,* it served the iron interests of Dayton. The *R. C. Jackson,* the *W. L. Dugger,* and other vessels also acted as mine servants.[6]

During the last decades of the century rivermen continued to buy, sell, trade, and rebuild steamboats as in the years before the war. The river, too, remained as before; for all practical purposes it was two rivers, one ending at Chattanooga and the second beginning there. On the lower river there were some 95 landings enroute to Decatur, while between Chattanooga and Kingston there were 126.

The river business reached its zenith during these years, supporting (though often meagerly) a host of craft with colorful traditions and interesting names. Some were the *May Bell, Emory City, Water Lily, Tellico, Dixie, City of Knoxville, Josh V. Throop, City of Chattanooga, Last Chance, General Joe Wheeler, Pinhook, Plucky City, R. C. Gunter, Emory City, Bill Tate, Pickaway, N. B. Forrest, Omega, Avalon,* and the *John A. Patten.*

Some of these packets were quite commodious. The *Gunter,* for example, built in 1886 and rebuilt in 1893, was 153 feet long, drew forty-two inches of water, and boasted three boilers. Most had some twenty staterooms along with kitchens, dining rooms, offices, and bar on the "boiler deck" (just above the boilers). Crews consisted of the captain, a mate, two pilots, two engineers, a cabin boy, chambermaid, cook, and eight or ten roustabouts. The *Gunter* in 1894 left Chattanooga every Monday and Friday at 10 A.M. for Guntersville, arriving at midnight. The fare, including meals and berth, was $3 to $5 for a round trip. Travel upstream averaged about eight to ten miles per hour.

Freight was the principal business with a steady, silent rivalry existing between boats, most of which operated independently and without fixed schedules. In January 1881 the three boats owned by Kendrick Brothers delivered to the Chattanooga wharf 23,473 sacks of corn, 162 of wheat, 260 of oats, 2,067 of peas, 127 bales of hay, and 31 barges of ore totaling 3,400 tons. In 1880 there were 553 steamboat arrivals at Chattanooga.

The people of Hamilton County who lived near the river knew each of the packets by the tone of its deepthroated blasts or by its musical whistle. They felt a close kinship with the veteran rivermen. Such men as Captains J. P. Kendrick or his brother W. E., Charles W. Coker, W. C. Wiley, John L. Doss, C. S. Peak, Jacob Fritts, Joe Glover, W. L. Dugger, the Gunter brothers (Cue, J. M., and Cal), C. C. Spiller, and John C. Haley.

The riverside dwellers came on board at times for parties, music, chicken dinners, and dancing, or to go on excursions. Captains served as calico matchers for housewives up and down the river. Residents stood in silence as river funeral processions passed. When Captain Doss died, nearly every boat on the Chattanooga-Knoxville run joined the sad caravan, with crepe streaming from every flagstaff. The valley people waited for the mail boat and for the store boat. A young fellow by the name of Dobbs operated one of the latter for a time. He would pay a dollar for a tow northward to the mouth of the Hiwassee River and then would drift downstream. With a shining six-foot trumpet he announced his arrival at each landing, selling his wares or swapping goods for chickens.

Well into the 1890s farmers brought their produce downstream to the Hamilton County port in homemade flatboats. The number of arrivals of these bulky craft (measuring sixty to seventy-five feet long and twenty feet wide) depended both on the current corn market and favorable "tides." Practically all stopped at Chattanooga, loaded with as much as one thousand sacks containing corn, apples, hay, and other country products. In 1880 one report mentioned 308 flatboat landings at the wharf.[7]

Flatboats often had to compete with giant rafts for loading space. Until about the time of World War I, millions of board feet of lumber annually floated down from the upper tributaries when the "tides" ran high. An average raft contained up to twenty thousand feet of poplar and twelve thousand feet of oak; often in the 1890s the newspapers reported the arrival in Chattanooga of three hundred to seven hundred rafts. Four men rode each raft and often as many as one thousand hardy mountaineers swarmed into the city at a time. Their logs lined the banks near the headquarters of Loomis & Hart, Snodgrass & Field, and Blair and Taliaferro, who paid out thousands of dollars for the lumber.

These large sums of money were practically all carried homeward by the raftsmen, at least as far as Knoxville. The raftsmen often caught the train at Chattanooga for the return journey. An observer noted that they were "a little green about railways" and when the trains pulled in, they often took over the mail, baggage, and express cars. When the conductors tried to get them into the passenger cars, they refused to move, for "no city chap could boss them if they did wear blue coats and brass buttons." Since the rivermen carried arms, the trainmen had to exercise caution. The fact that the raftsmen left the city carrying most of their cash disturbed some Chattanoogans because "They are worth twice as much to the town as a convention and yet few people seem to know when they arrive."[8]

Business concerns dominated the river scene; although generally a quiet place, occasionally some trouble occurred. The *Mary Byrd* in 1871 sank at the Suck on her way to Chattanooga after striking a submerged log. All passengers and crew got off as the steamboat fast took on water; they scrambled up the mountainside, hiding behind trees and rocks, fearful that the boilers would explode. Four years later the boilers on the *Hugh Martin* did explode. Captain Jake Fritz and two other persons were killed and a number of others injured; the steamboat was "a perfect wreck." In 1891 the Suck brought about an economic catastrophe for a boat operated by the Cincinnati Southern Railroad. In September it went downriver and loaded on bales of cotton to be transferred at Chattanooga. It started upstream on 1 October from Decatur, got to the Suck, and had to tie up because of low water. It stayed tied up for two months while the price of cotton tumbled. The railroad made up the losses to the shippers but was cured for all time of "the river fever."

In January 1893 the dangerous mountain waters struck again. Severe cold produced solid ice from bank to bank. While the *J. C. Warner* was attempting to plow through the ice at the Skillet, the flues in the boilers collapsed. Two deckhands were blown into the river and drowned; fifteen others were badly scalded. "A portion of the *Warner's* cargo consisted of a bull tied about three feet from the boiler. A hot stream from one of the flues struck a dead center in the bull's eye and left the poor animal an unsightly, half-skinned and tortured mass of mangled beef."9

Tennessee River traffic continued to suffer because of the natural hazards found in the stream, and agitation for channel improvements started in the valley immediately after the close of the war. In the very wake of the states' rights struggle, citizens of Chattanooga in an 1867 mass meeting resolved that improvement to the mouth of the river was vital and turned to the federal government for aid. Congress responded by directing a survey of the stream from Chattanooga to Paducah, Kentucky. Colonel William B. Gaw, a Union veteran who had settled in Chattanooga after the war, was appointed to direct the project.

Gaw noted that the obstruction of the Chattanooga mountains and Muscle Shoals "sealed" the area so definitely that it appeared that the Tennessee "had no outlet to the Mississippi valley." But he was most enthusiastic about improvements which would help a stricken area recover from war, give employment to "deserving people," have military value, and strengthen the bonds of union between the North and the South through commerce.

The idea of improving the national welfare became a theme at a river convention attended by 143 delegates at Chattanooga in 1868. A Tennessee River Improvement Committee was appointed with the chairmanship going to Colonel Timothy R. Stanley. The colonel was another Union veteran residing in Chattanooga; he had commanded the pontoon flotilla which had slipped down the river by night in the October 1863 assault on Brown's Ferry. Stanley's committee helped in getting a Congressional appropriation for open-channel improvement in 1868, and Colonel Gaw supervised the work on the Suck from a suboffice of the Army Engineers in Chattanooga, only to encounter harassing Reconstruction politics.

River conventions, with Chattanoogans stirring up interest throughout the valley, continued to be held. Between such assemblies the press exerted pressure and finally, in 1875, the national government undertook the construction of a major project—a second Muscle Shoals canal. For fifteen years the river promoters watched the frustratingly slow progress of the engineers before the canal was completed. Meanwhile, enthusiastic supporters insisted that the canal would open trade with the booming Middle West and that all who lived in the Tennessee Valley would enjoy a new and flourishing prosperity.

Hamilton County river interests seized the opportunity to organize packet companies which would not only give them the economic advantage of size but also open up business with the Ohio and Mississippi rivers. Moreover, they strove to make Chattanooga a "water competitive point" to use as a lever to get reductions in railroad freight rates, thought to discriminate against the area.[10]

Leaders in the initial efforts included Adolph Ochs, S. D. Webster, C. E. Stivers, J. P. Kendrick, Z. C. Patten, H. Clay Evans, H. S. Chamberlain, J. N. Trigg, and Newell Sanders. In 1892 they chartered the Chattanooga Steamboat Company. Their plan consisted in operating towboat-type steamboats with barges through Muscle Shoals canal to St. Louis. They bought the *Herbert* and rebuilt it as the *City of Chattanooga* . But the canal, not designed for this type of equipment, actually proved to be totally unsatisfactory and the venture had to be canceled.

One by one other companies started up, reorganized, and failed. But the river promoters refused to acknowledge defeat. John A. Patten, J. N. Trigg, and T. H. Payne were three men who seemed to be associated with every effort, and the majority of the steamboats on the Tennessee at the turn of the century had their headquarters in Chattanooga, including the *N. B. Forrest, Joe Wheeler, Avalon, J. N. Trigg, Chattanooga, John A. Patten, Sam Davis* , and *John Ross* .

The Tennessee River Transportation Company carried on business for eight or nine years. It ran on both the upper and lower river sections, using nine steamboats, two of which were towboats used to move barges of iron ore, tanbark, sand, lumber, and coal. Competitors appeared in the Chattanooga and Tennessee Packet Company and the Tennessee River Navigation Company. These outfits and others frequently reorganized, thus eliminating some debts in the process. Serving several as manager was the veteran riverman, Captain Walter C. Wilkey, who had followed the river since his youth, working in every capacity except that of cook. He reportedly had no peer in the entire valley and in his rugged, honest way made a gallant stand for the survival of the river trade until his death in 1918.[11]

The lure of the river, for the most part, drew men who had grown up along its banks while others from outside the region reactivated interest in postwar railroading. Brothers from Boston, Massachusetts, John C. and Daniel N. Stanton, appeared on the scene shortly after the guns grew silent. They conceived the idea of consolidating the old Wills Valley line with the Northeast and Southwest Alabama Railroad and building on through to Meridian, Mississsippi, a distance of 295 miles from Chattanooga. In a daring, carpetbagging railroad venture these "capitalists," who possessed little but bold plans and ingenious financial schemes, organized the Alabama and Chattanooga Railroad in 1868. By sheer legerdemain they received commitments of millions of dollars from the Alabama state Reconstruction government in order to support this project.

With a vigorous display of energy they began construction using the labor of both local farmers and Chinese railroad workers. The line, thrown together by these jerrybuilders, was hastily completed. But fraudulent bond endorsements brought on trouble. In June 1871 the United States District Court of Alabama placed the company in receivership. The project was in a shambles. The southern end could not operate, unpaid workers took possession of it and hid vital locomotive parts. As more money was lost, no one seemed to care if the trains ran or not. [12]

Only a few miles of the company's track reached into Hamilton County and its construction and operational problems had only slight influence on the area. But the activities of John Stanton had a profound effect. A man of limitless energy, supreme self-confidence and charismatic personality, he promised everything and then accomplished what he could. With Alabama funds he acquired (mostly on credit, however) a large tract of land to the south of Ninth Street. He subdivided the acreage and sold lots in a development called the Stanton Addition, or Stanton Town. Where the Chattanooga Choo-Choo now stands he built an elaborate hotel called the Stanton House.

Stanton's Chattanooga era was referred to as the "Stanton times." Everyone had confidence in this man who sent minstrels through the streets to encourage folks to work for him. They were lively, expansive times, but all rested on borrowed money, Alabama and Chattanooga Railway paper, or the easy promises of Stanton. So he gave the county its first big postwar boom as suppliers accepted his word, draymen took his credit, and merchants wrote him credit slips. Then everything exploded in the "most extensive crop of litigation which Chattanooga ever harvested," offering plenty of work for all the lawyers. Bankruptcy, it was said, "stalked into almost every door." Stanton stayed on in town for some time and somehow managed to retain his popularity; he ran for mayor but failed to win by only a narrow margin before he quit the area about 1880. [13] The Stanton House continued to be the city's social center and tourist headquarters for years.

The A & C Railroad experienced a long receivership; in January 1877 it was sold to the account of Emile Erlanger and Company of London and was renamed the Alabama Great Southern. Erlanger, an Austrian who was a successful Paris banker, married the daughter of Confederate diplomat John Slidell. He headed a financial syndicate which invested in American industry and transportation. On a visit to examine the A & C properties, Baron Erlanger made a donation of $5,000 for a local hospital whose name honors his wife, the baroness, and pledged a similar amount from each of the railroads in which his syndicate had an interest.

While Stanton skated on credit's thin ice, another group, more prudent and pragmatic, decided to build a railroad to Chattanooga from an entirely different direction. Cincinnati merchants had found that Louisville fast threatened to capture the role of chief distributor of northern merchandise to southern customers. The Ohio River was not a sufficient highway to keep the "Queen City" in the race for markets. The required legislation was passed to finance and build a railroad and approval was obtained from Tennessee and Kentucky to acquire a right-of-way. Before all these arrangements were completed, Chattanooga was chosen as the southern terminus. On 7 June 1869, when the Hamilton County town learned the news, a mass meeting of citizens gathered at the city hall to celebrate with booming cannon and "a gorgeous display of fireworks."

Work started on the 338-mile road in December 1873, which happened to be the beginning of a panic year. Financing therefore proved to be a major problem. Engineering was equally difficult, for the road originally required twenty-seven tunnels and 105 bridges and viaducts. Nevertheless at the end of 1879 the way was completed. "Go, ring your bell and fire your gun, shout glory, for the 'Boom' has come," shouted the *Times*. The town rejoiced when the first freight train, three sections of twenty cars each, arrived and repeated its outbursts of joy when the first passenger train pulled into the station.

Plans for celebrations waited until great banquets could be prepared. On 17 March 1880, special trains left Chattanooga for Cincinatti "adequately equipped with 15 kegs of beer and numberless square wicker baskets and provisions." More than two thousand diners celebrated the fact that the city of Cincinnati had leveled a smooth path southward over which men and goods could easily pass. Chattanooga then returned the courtesy; 312 guests detrained and every conceivable vehicle carried them on a sight-seeing tour. At the Stanton House all enjoyed a dinner and "lawn dance." Everyone cheered the Ohio River city which, however, soon thereafter leased the railroad to the Cincinnati, New Orleans, and Texas Pacific Railway Company for the Erlanger syndicate.

This new rail line had a special significance for Hamilton County, for it ran close to the very center of the county. The area served, located north of the Tennessee River, had had no rail transportation up to this time and had been forced to depend on river travel or rough country roads. The people living near the right-of-way of the Cincinnati Southern now had a chance to enjoy the economic and social benefits of modern travel just as those in the southern portion of the county had since 1850.

Entering the county from the north, the railroad left Graysville and Rhea County, running by the McDonald Cemetery and passing the oldest settled area of Hamilton County. On or near Sale Creek the railroad people built a depot named Coulterville in honor of T. J. Coulter, an old and respected citizen who lived nearby and who had served as Governor Harris' appointee to head the county militia at the outbreak of the Civil War.

This community some thirty-one miles from Chattanooga had gained a certain notoriety back in 1869 when William Beene and his brother conducted a school. Beene, a tough disciplinarian, inflicted corporal punishment on one of the students. The boy's father took out a warrant against the teacher for assault, which the constable with the aid of one Frank M. Smith undertook to serve. Beene, as the officials anticipated, resisted arrest, and a gun battle followed. Both the constable and the student were killed while Beene and Smith received serious wounds. Smith stood a much discussed trial and won acquittal.

A few miles south of Coulterville the railroad passed close to the village of Sale Creek. Nearby coal mines, reopened in 1867, had attracted a group of Welsh miners. Among the dozen or more families were those of David R. Griffiths, Daniel Thomas, William Richards, Thomas Price, Daniel Reese, John M. Jones, David Thomas, Rees Rees, John D. Jones, David Miles, and Phillip Jones. These industrious, thrifty, and intelligent citizens immediately were accepted by the older residents.

Under the leadership of Griffiths the Sale Creek Coal and Coke Company began mining operations and Sale Creek took on new life. A tram road to the river with mule-drawn cars carried the coal to barges over sawed oak rails. With the opening of the railroad the coal taken from the Pearson's or Rocky Creek diggings or from Jack's Bank found a better way to market and the tram was abandoned. The company reorganized as the Waldens Ridge Mining Company with William R. Lloyd, superintendent. Griffiths, in addition to other activities, ran a sizable mercantile business which served as a commissary for the miners and general store for the surrounding area.

On to the south the Cincinnati railroad came to a station bearing an odd name: Retro. A local property owner had donated a plot of ground to the railroad where a depot was to be built. The station was constructed according to plan but the deed for the land had not even been transferred before the land became a subject of litigation. Those responsible refused to turn over the property unless they received payment. The railroad attorney, educated in the classics, named the station Retro after a Latin term meaning "back or backward." Years later the name was changed to Bakewell.

Through Back Valley the road passed the Hickman and Varner cemeteries and Pilgrim Rest Church and swept onward to Soddy past nearby Posey and Clemmons points of the Cumberland escarpment. Here, in the home country of Colonel William Clift and Major R. C. McRee, the railroad people named the station Rathburn. They had in mind honoring an enthusiastic supporter of the railroad, Chattanooga's former mayor who had close business connections with both the Roane Iron Company and the First National Bank. But the local people would have none of this; they refused to retire the old name Soddy. So for a time the two names were used interchangeably until that of Rathburn disappeared.

In the Soddy area the veterans Clift and McRee pioneered in the mining industry but were often inclined to sell mining rights on their property to such operators as the Welshman Abram Lloyd and the Soddy Coal Company. They began to "wound" the mountain and to establish much more extensive and elaborate operations than existed farther up the valley. Associated with Lloyd were other Welshmen— some from the old country, some who had come via Ohio or Pennsylvania—including James T. Williams and John Jenkins. As at Sale Creek, their enterprise had a tram road to the river. Locks built in Big Soddy Creek made it possible to bring barges about halfway from the river to the mines. A little locomotive furnished power on the tramway and a tipple dumped the coal into barges.

Unlike the Sale Creek miners, those at Soddy did not stop shipping their coal by water with the coming of the railroad. For years barges were poled up and down Soddy Creek and loaded ores were carried on to Chattanooga. In the early 1870s the Coker brothers, in addition to their steamboat business, ran a market yard for Soddy coal in Chattanooga. With the railroad, Soddy expanded its mining activity and chutes were constructed along a siding for coal delivery into the cars.

When the Welsh arrived, the village of Soddy consisted of only a few scattered houses. Hastily built homes and tents sheltered the newcomers at first. In 1871 a hurricane set back their initial efforts at permanence: tents disappeared, houses were unroofed, and destruction was rampant. Two years later the Welsh established a church with the Reverend Thomas Thomas as pastor.

When the locomotive arrived, all the people in the neighborhood went down to the water's edge to watch it being hoisted out of the barge and to hop a ride back to town if there was room to climb aboard. Somehow it got the name "Nance" and became a local institution as it made its runs from mine to barge tipple. Then one day a carload of powder ignited and blew everything, including Nance and her engineer Billy Lloyd, to pieces.

The Soddy mine reorganized in the early 1880s and also took in operations at Sale Creek. Abram Lloyd continued as general manager at Soddy and his brother, William R., held a similar post at Sale Creek. The company established an office in Chattanooga with James T. Williams in charge, built the steamboat *M. H. Clift* to tow barges, and worked the river for many years until the boat burned.

Southward from Soddy the railroad passed close to Hineman Spring, the old burial plot of the Lovelady family, and the cluster of homes which in 1881 took the name Daisy to honor Daisy Parks, the daughter of Thomas Parks. Parks was an officer of the Tabler and Crudup Coal Company which opened a mine on the mountain opposite the village. For a time this activity was under the management of the Soddy Company.

Some Chattanoogans maintained summer homes on the mountainside near Daisy. When the railroad came that way, Mel Adams donated five acres of land on which to locate a station. The railroad people, in appreciation, named the place Melville. Since that day Melville has been absorbed by Daisy, which also reached out to claim the old Poe's Crossroads. A small depot fourteen miles from Chattanooga was called Cave Springs, so named for the spring with its cool waters by the side of the track. The station was about a half mile from the hamlet of

Falling Water, where the stream by that name tumbles over the side of Walden Ridge.

At this point the Cincinnati Southern turned into the valley of North Chickamauga Creek. It continued on to Lakeside, once the site of a large lake which had receded to the size of a pond. The railroaders changed this name to Lookout because the surveyors, it is said, first sighted Lookout Mountain from this point. However, on account of the wide use of the name Lookout, the railroad people two years later rechristened the stop Hixson since it was close to the home of Ephraim F. Hixson, patriarch of the numerous Hixson clan living in the neighborhood. Beyond Hixson the tracks crossed the Tennessee River via the first river bridge built in the county after the military structure disappeared in the 1867 flood waters, went on to King's Point (just west of the present Chickamauga Dam), and continued on into Chattanooga.[14]

With the Cincinnati market open, Hamilton County people along the railroad right-of-way planted new cash crops. Local berries, grapes, fruits, and vegetables presented an excellent business opportunity. For some years grapes and strawberries had been commercially grown on the slopes of Missionary Ridge. In 1885 the Lookout Mountain and Mission Ridge Horticultural Society counted 130 members who reported the cultivation of 685 acres in strawberries, 300 in vegetables, and 1,012 in fruits.

Prospectors roamed the northern section of the county for good slopes which created a down draft of air so that the moving currents would reduce the possibility of early or late frosts. Stark Brothers nurserymen planted peach orchards on leased sites or for resident growers. Newcomers with experience in the business moved in. R. C. and M. Corbly, for example, came by wagon on a thirteen-day trip from southern Ohio and got land across the river from Cameron Hill to start strawberry culture and the production of early vegetables.

The Cincinnati Southern for some years ran special daily trains during harvest times. By 1895, estimates claim that truck vegetables and fruit produced within ten miles of Chattanooga alone had a value of a half-million dollars; two years later there were predictions of a hundred-thousand-crate strawberry crop.[15]

The Cincinnati railroad had the unusual feature of being sponsored, financed, and owned by the city of Cincinnati. After Chattanooga had been designated the southern terminal, the city was urged to appropriate $100,000 as a token of interest in the project. The city government authorized funds, but years passed and the city fathers never made any actual appropriation until after the trains began running. When they finally allocated the money, city officials gave it to a Cincinnati representative who took a Chattanoogan with him as a body-guard. The two entrained for the Ohio city well armed and prepared to sit up all night, fearing a robbery attempt at one of the dark, isolated tunnels, but they made the trip safely.

Although outside interests constructed most of the railroads into Hamilton County, there were significant local efforts to promote the economic welfare of the area. A Board of Trade, started in 1870, re-organized as the Iron, Coal and Manufacturers Association six years later, with W. P. Rathburn and J. T. Wilder as the early presidents. In 1887 this organization expanded to include commercial members and took the name Chattanooga Chamber of Commerce, with David B. Loveman as president.

Loveman, born in Hungary, spent his boyhood in Michigan. He came to Chattanooga in 1875 at the age of thirty-one and with his brother Herman purchased the dry goods business of D. & E. Rich at the corner of Eighth and Market streets, then known as the New Orleans Store. In 1876 they employed the first woman clerk in Chat-tanooga; this experiment failed, for the lady proved to be "over shy of masculine patrons." They also introduced such progressive ideas as the position of cashier and a checking and wrapping system while discon-tinuing the habit of "throwing in" hooks, eyes, and thread.[16]

Chattanooga businessmen and newspapers never seemed to tire of railroad building. Although but a few miles of track lay within Hamilton County, the city in an unusual cooperative move voted a bond issue of $100,000 to assist the Chattanooga, Rome, and Columbus Railroad which began building a 157-mile road in 1887. By 1890 this railroad was operating as far as Carrollton, Georgia, and later was made a section of the Central Railroad of Georgia. At the ground-breaking exercises in 1887 a young attorney, William Gibbs McAdoo, made the address. McAdoo had moved to the city in 1882 where he remained for a decade before leaving for New York as a promoter of the building of the Hudson Tunnel. Political leadership eventually carried him to the post of secretary of the treasury.

There was much talk of the need for another rail line along the base of Lookout Mountain to Gadsden, Alabama, before construction started on the Chattanooga Southern Railway. A half-mile-long tunnel through Pigeon Mountain held up the completion of this line. There were high hopes that the iron ore, coal, timber, wood, and agricultural products of the area, along with passenger service, would make the railroad profitable. One of the moving spirits was Charles E. James, who soon took over the presidency of the line.

This road, like several others, had little mileage in Hamilton County. Its passenger trains used the Chattanooga depot at 910 Georgia Avenue, which was the station and starting point of the Chattanooga Union Railway, better known as the belt line. James, the busy promoter of the Gadsden road, was also the builder and owner of the belt line and worked out arrangements to use the station and some six miles of the track of the latter.

The Chattanooga Southern opened for business on 23 June 1891, but immediately ran into financial problems. It fell into the hands of receivers and was sold by 1895. Difficulties continued; in 1911 a new corporation acquired the property known as the Tennessee, Alabama, and Georgia Railway (TAG). The railroad's money worries actually never went away, and in 1922 C. E. James again acquired control.[17]

James, brought to Chattanooga in his infancy, grew up in the area, developing a passion for machines, real estate, buildings, railroads, and blueprints. Like the James A. Whiteside of an earlier generation, his energy and love for the decision-making process of a businessman made him a most enthusiastic promoter. His persuasive manner and his contacts with New York City financiers won support for his many projects while his marriage to Kate Webster, daughter of ironmaster Thomas Webster, planted his roots even deeper in Hamilton County. Never interested in public acclaim, Charlie James devoted his boundless ambition to cement, iron, railroads, real estate, banking, and the brokerage business.[18]

The belt line was only one of his projects. It was designed to move freight between various industries and the many railroad yards in the area. Officially known as the Union Railway Company, it was started in early April 1884 and in three years practically encircled the city. The idea soon occurred to James that the road should also cater to passenger business. He began running coaches to Ridgedale with seven daily round trips and continued to expand this valuable service. By 1889 the belt line operated about 128 round-trip passenger schedules. With the belt line began the story of the development of the Chattanooga outskirts—Ridgedale, Highland Park, East Lake, St. Elmo, Sherman Heights or East Chattanooga, Orchard Knob, Oak Hills, Alton Park, Avondale, and Stanleyville. Corn fields were prime sites for suburban growth and residences appeared where only orchards or vineyards had once been.

James, however, soon faced a competitor. The Chattanooga Electric Street Railroad Company was reaching out in many directions, using the new electrical energy. James at first had no faith in such power; he was sure it was a passing fad. Rather than modernize his line, he invested in the new Georgia Avenue depot, which served for nine years after its opening in January 1890. But the belt line passed from Charlie James' ownership the year after the depot opened. By that date he was carrying four thousand passengers daily, operating fifty-two freight and twenty-one passenger cars, and serving the public at thirty-seven passenger depots.[19]

The electric line was a descendant of a horse-drawn rapid transit system designed to give Chattanooga a mass transportation service. The horse-powered line made its maiden run on the route from the river to Montgomery Avenue (Main Street) along Market Street on 4 September 1875. The cars of the Chattanooga Street Railroad Company which traveled the fifteen-block line were not big enough for the four-hundred-pound owner, A. J. "Fatty" Harris, to board. The company's only actual assets were an old four-windowed secondhand car, a mule which wore a tinkling bell, and the track. Nevertheless, the horse cars were something to brag about; one could avoid the mud or dust which covered the street as well as the wrecks of ox carts or stranded vehicles.

It was not surprising that the company changed ownership. Joshua Warner assumed control of the infant company and planned various extensions. Tracks reached out to White Street (now Twenty-Third Street), nearly three miles in length from the river, which was close to the southern limits of the city near Chattanooga Creek. Warner's goal was Lookout Mountain, but this required county approval; the special problem was the use of the road bridge over Chattanooga Creek which was rickety at best. It was not until October 1885 that the St. Elmo horsecar line reached the foot of the mountain.

Other extensive plans came and went; competitors loomed up to crowd the business. Passengers complained that they could walk faster than the cars could run; some residents took out injunctions to stop certain construction and to enjoin the company from tearing up McCallie Avenue, "the city's only pleasure drive." One case went to the state supreme court. But new routes opened and by 1887 the company had a twelve-mile system in operation.

One of the most bizarre of the speculative new routes called for a bundle of developments, most of which were to be located on Cameron Hill. This area, close to downtown Chattanooga, had grown into a fashionable residential district. In 1888 ambitious planners talked of an in-town horsecar line, an incline railroad up the steep slope of Cameron Hill, a real estate development, pagoda, park, big hotel, water company, and "a first class beer garden and concert hall." The promoters immediately met with financial reverses, suits and countersuits, and internal company squabbles. By 1890, however, the incline, pagoda, and water company standpipe were in use and the beer garden nearly ready to open as a fashionable summer evening rendezvous. A company advertisement puffed that the hill was "the most attractive point in and about Chattanooga." For ten cents and a five-minute ride from Market Street one was promised "elegant surroundings on the Hill, spacious park buildings, music hall, verandas, restaurant, cooling breezes, etc." Seven years later the bubble burst; the incline, pagoda, and standpipe were dismantled and a little later the beer parlor was destroyed by fire.[20]

Progressive entrepreneurs challenged the old horsepowered system. In 1888 some local enthusiasts talked about the electric cars which a few American cities were using. Without wasting much time, they developed plans to build an electrical power plant, erect poles, string wires, and buy cars which could move at thirty miles per hour. Although most of the townspeople registered fright at the very mention of electricity, the installation work progressed without any interference. But just as the big day inaugurating the service approached, the East Tennessee Telephone Company got an injunction against putting the cars in operation. Electrical leakage "a thousand times more powerful than the electricity used in the phone company's wires would do irreparable harm to its operation," it was claimed.

The case, heard on 22 June 1889, was dismissed. That same day a trial run of streetcar No. 1 of the Chattanooga Electric Street Railroad Company drew a curious, applauding crowd as it tackled the Seventh Street grade to Georgia Avenue and went on to the foot of Missionary Ridge. Horses shied and bystanders groaned when the car jumped the track. But by 1 July the company headed by Joshua Warner, one-time head of a horsecar company and president of the Fourth National Bank, was ready for the public. Some 4,550 persons rode that day, a day that signified the drawing of the curtain on horse- and mulecar service. Just two weeks later the line's first extension opened; it was authorized and regulated by the county, for it reached from East End Avenue to the top of Missionary Ridge, using an ingenious switchback system to mount the steep slope.

A whole crop of streetcar companies sprang up. Many were short lines and soon reorganized, combined, or merged. Fights, suits, and injunctions were the order of the day; big problems arose over which would be allowed to use the Walnut Street bridge. A quarrel with the city over street paving proved difficult. The question of educating the public "to enter and leave cars safely" required a major campaign, and ways had to be found to meet public wrath when a rule required that cars no longer would stop at a passenger's signal but hereafter designated stops would be at "far sides of the squares and railroad crossings— except in Highland Park and places where there are no stepping stones."[21]

During these years the great advances in science and technology exerted a tremendous impact on urban life. In Chattanooga the fragmentary waterworks of the wartime occupation became the property of the Lookout Water Company in 1869. With A. M. Johnson as president, this firm operated several miles of pipe from the reservoir on the lower spur of Cameron Hill. In 1886 ownership passed to the City Water Company with C. E. James as one of the chief promoters. At this time water was pumped directly from the river into the reservoir and mains. This "raw water," often turbid and rich in organic matter, was hardly fit to use and probably contributed to such epidemics as the cholera contagion of 1873 and the yellow fever epidemic of 1878. The new company undertook to experiment with newly developed scientific water treatment methods. It moved the pumping station to the mouth of Citico Creek and built a filtration plant. This method, however, soon proved to be inadequate and was replaced in 1891 with coagulating basins.[22]

A gas company initiated customer service in 1870. With only two miles of mains and with gas used only for lighting, the new fuel did replace candles and kerosene in some homes and stores, which took pride in installing clusters of jets.

Some outside lights on Market Street showed pedestrians where to step and possibly made the work of the burglar a bit more difficult. A man on horseback using a blowtorch made his rounds every evening lighting the lamps, but complaints arose over the fact that some people felt the lamps were not cleaned or properly cared for. Gradually rates declined as the production of gas became more efficient, and about 1882 people started to use it as a fuel in the newly invented gas range;

some seventeen years later gas came into use for automatic water heating. In 1906 the local company merged with the United Light and Power Company.[23]

Alexander Graham Bell's telephone was still largely a plaything when on 3 July 1878, a message went over a wire connecting two instruments in Chattanooga. The Stanton House possessed one; the other had been installed at the Wisdom and Owen livery stable just a short distance away. It gave the hotel the right to brag that vehicles could be easily and quickly ordered. Two years passed before an exchange opened by the East Tennessee Telephone Company installed service for fifty-two subscribers. All had low numbers with the fashionable outdoor ice cream and cake parlor called Tshopik's Garden honored with the number "1." By August a few more customers joined the list, including four subscibers on faraway Lookout Mountain. But growth proved to be slow; some church groups solemnly discussed the moral aspect of using the phones on Sunday. After a decade records show only 450 phones in service; practically all were business customers.

Early in 1899 progress had been made in long-distance connections and it was now possible to say hello to people in St. Louis and Chicago, as well as Nashville. The next year the original company sold out to the Cumberland Telephone Company.[24]

Another infant utility celebrated its birth on 6 May 1882, and crowds of interested citizens "surged through the streets." Civic excitement mounted as the hour of 8 P.M. approached, when twenty-five electric lights would be turned on. The first electric company, the Brush Electrical Company, was sponsored by these leading citizens: H. Clay Evans, H. S. Chamberlain, S. A. Key, W. S. Marshall, and George C. Conner. A generator was installed which could produce energy in the amount of 125 horsepower and was powered by a steam engine.

On that first night Loveman's store had three globes; the *Times* sported one on a flag pole, the "highest light on Market Street," and the Read House boasted of three lights. All for a considerable time were at places of business, for no one would dare to install such a dangerous genie in his own home.

A second plant started up under the name Hauss Electric and in 1886 the two groups merged as the Chattanooga Electric Light Company. About two hundred commercial users had lights about this time. Service was furnished from dusk until midnight; a company man usually made rounds of all stores and industries to check if the lights were burning and to replace burned-out sockets.[25]

As forward-looking businessmen, daring and resourceful, ventured into pioneering utilities, the city fathers and members of the county court struggled with less glamorous matters. In 1867 Chattanooga decided to do away with the W & A (Western & Atlantic) Railroad's right-of-way on Railroad Avenue. This area, apparently, was being used as a place to park freight cars and clutter created, along with the nuisance of switching freight cars, was very offensive. Workers, following the instructions of a city ordinance, commenced tearing up the track only to be arrested on behalf of the railroad for "maliciously tearing up the rails." Once bound over to court, they returned to their jobs. A second arrest netted the mayor and city marshal along with the laborers, whereupon the whole affair went into court. Georgia lost: the tracks came up and Railroad Avenue was renamed Broad Street. But both parties by this time claimed credit for taking the initiative to "beautify" that corner of town.

Hogs continued to run at large and cows "despoiled the court-house lawn." A prison force, including women, labored on the rock pile and repaired streets. Most streets remained in poor condition or worsened, and in 1881 when the federal government built a road to the national cemetery, it was reported to be the only stretch of good road near or in the town.

The downtown section (from Cherry to Pine streets and from Ninth Street to the river) was still characterized by low, swampy stretches and by the deep gully which meandered down Railroad Avenue. In haphazard fashion some sites received fill dirt to raise them above ordinary high water, while others were overlooked. Then the major flood of 1886 crippled the town and reminded everyone of tales of disaster nineteen years earlier. City boosters then demanded a comprehensive plan to raise all street levels.

The *Times* on 10 April stated,

> Unless the project to raise the grade on the streets . . . is promptly made effective the tendency of mercantile men to locate on higher ground will go on with an accelerated speed and in larger volume, until the flat will become a secondary consideration if not quite abandoned. . . . The danger is we shall go on as in the past. . . . We have hitched up a corner here, a block there and part of a block yonder, each hitch bringing with it a lawsuit for damage . . . and all this time we have been putting the streets in the most absurd and unattractive shape, confusing builders so they cannot tell what height to put their first floors, and still leaving the grade too low by at least three feet on the average.

Carts loaded with fill dirt presently appeared on this amateur flood control project. By 1890 it was reported that Market Street and nearly all cross and parallel streets in the business center of town had been raised two feet. At a later date evidence of this work tells an interesting story, water mains were found covered with as much as six feet of "made- earth" and in 1906 timbers of Ross's Landing days were found while excavating for the car barns on Market Street near Third. Here twenty-one massive beams had been buried six feet underground. In 1888 paving of Market Street with asphalt began and about ten years later the city was improved by 16.9 miles of better streets.[26]

The Tennessee River presented other problems in addition to rampaging floods. One simple difficulty was getting to the other side. Except for the brief era of the military bridge the most modern crossing method scarcely differed from John Ross's original ferry. Horse ferries, steam ferries, and swing ferries operated at different times; service was slow, cumbersome, and often dangerous. Sam Thatcher, a lad of ten, for example, was killed when family cattle stampeded on being driven onto a barge for a river crossing.

Beginning in the early 1880s there was much discussion about the need for a bridge. The residents of both Chattanooga and Hill City on the north shore campaigned for a county-financed span: people in the north end of the county opposed the project. They threatened to secede rather than have tax dollars invested in construction which would be of little direct benefit to them. The county court, buffeted under pressure, finally voted to build the Walnut Street bridge largely as a result of the continuous efforts of R. M. Barton. In July 1889 contracts were let; Hill City contributed $25,000 to the $241,388 project, for years called "the county bridge."

This span, a high-level structure one hundred feet above low water and twenty-four hundred feet long, was constructed as a free highway bridge for foot passengers, wagon traffic, and electric car service. It opened to the public on 18 February 1891, with a festive celebration headed by the civic-minded Captain H. S. Chamberlain. A military parade and program at the bridge site gave prominence to six children who "put on the finishing touches" by driving the last nails into the superstructure. After the ceremonies a streetcar pulled by mules crossed over and made a maiden trip to the top of Stringer's Ridge at Dry Valley Road (now Dayton Boulevard). The city of Chattanooga inherited the bridge in 1929 with the annexation of Hill City.[27]

The county had been pressured for some years to improve the rural roads. By the mid-1890s roughly 150 miles of macadam and graveled roads had been completed. The first road radiating from Chattanooga was the Rossville Pike, which connected at Rossville with the way to Chickamauga Park. To the east, McCallie Avenue and Montgomery Avenue (now Main Street) connected with the government boulevard along the crest of Missionary Ridge while Harrison Pike took a northeasterly direction. North of the Tennessee River the Washington Road was improved to Sale Creek, and the Dallas Road, leaving it to the east, was finished two miles east of Hixson. Branching to the left from the Washington Road, the Anderson Pike climbed Walden Ridge from Mountain Creek and at Daisy another mountain road was being improved. Local promoters spoke proudly of the great progress. They were almost ecstatic in describing the road up Lookout Mountain; it "offers its graveled boulevard, rivaling the famous shell roads of Mobile and New Orleans, to the tourist who would explore the wonders of Rock City, or visit the sylvan shades of Lula Lake."

Into the robust life of Hamilton County, whose leaders had an almost religious enthusiasm for iron, railroads, and utilities came a youth who quickly absorbed the gusto and vitality of the place to mature as its leading spokesman and promoter. Adolph S. Ochs, not quite nineteen years of age, arrived in town with the ambition to become a newsman. The slender youth, son of Bertha Levy and Julius Ochs, Bavarian immigrants who had married in the United States and represented the two opposing sides of the late war, had abandoned school early. Quiet, hard-working, and somewhat naive, he grew into an idealist, striving for perfection and humanitarian justice for others while content with the simple pleasures of life for himself. He also apparently had an inborn talent for making money, although financial success never became a driving factor in his life.

In Chattanooga, Ochs associated with Colonel J. E. MacGowan and Franc Paul, the newsman who ran the wartime *Rebel*, in publishing the *Dispatch*. Like so many local newssheets, it failed. Ochs stayed on in town; with David B. Harris he got out a city directory for 1878 and in the process formed close ties with the community. Then came an opportunity to buy the *Chattanooga Times* .

The *Times*, first issued on 15 December 1869, appeared as a four-page, six-column sheet. Its history had been one of financial reverses, new management, new hope, and more of the same old problems. In the summer of 1878 S. A. Cunningham of Nashville owned the paper although it was under lien to Z. C. Patten, who had started a business in medicines in preference to one in the press. Cunningham offered the *Times*, with its dilapidated plant and circulation of 250, to Ochs for $800. Ochs did not have that much cash and found that he could not borrow it. Another offer followed and for $250 Ochs bought half-interest, including complete control of the paper with the option to buy the remaining portion at the end of two years for a negotiated sum.

The First National Bank loaned $300 to the twenty-year-old news-paperman. He had $50 left, but an outstanding bill of $25 to the Associated Press required payment. Now he had only $25 to meet his first payroll and operating expenses. On the other side of the ledger Ochs knew the newspaper business and he had the good fortune to engage Colonel John E. MacGowan as editor. MacGowan had stayed on after his service with the Union army and soon proved to be a source of fatherly advice to young Ochs. On 2 July 1878, they published the first issue of the Ochs-owned *Chattanooga Times*.

From the outset Ochs inaugurated a policy of honest, sound, searching journalism devoid of emotional or sensational flavor. He insisted on professionalism; Ochs became a spokesman for a diverse southern economy and a constant trumpet blower for Hamilton County and Chattanooga. Politically he took an independent Democratic posture. In addition to the demands of his business, Ochs early had his hands in every civic and cultural activity in the area. He was a young man in a young town and reacted with enthusiasm to the challenge of community.[28]

In the late summer days of 1878 the *Times* and, in fact, the entire southern region faced a dread crisis. From out of the Deep South, up through the valley of the Mississippi an epidemic of yellow fever spread. The people of Hamilton County seemed safe, for they felt that the fever could not infect a mountainous area. Some did not advocate more careful regard for sanitary regulations. They made contributions to people in contaminated areas and invited refugees to come to the safety of the highlands.

Then suddenly "Yellow Jack," as the illness was commonly called, struck some of the refugees; fear overcame the residents as they learned of a growing list of deaths. Some moved their families to Walden Ridge as they had in the cholera scare five years earlier; some arranged temporary quarters on Lookout. Others embarked on a steamboat and pitched camp some miles upriver. Railroad cars made temporary mobile homes and the city board of health set up a camp at Blowing

Spring at the base of Lookout Mountain. Chattanooga's population dwindled to an estimated eighteen hundred persons.

Passenger trains that stopped at the depot were quarantined by neighboring communties. The *Times* shrank to a single sheet without advertising and quickly lost money. A relief committee supervised the disposition of funds and property of deceased persons and carried fever patients to nursing stations such as Camp Bell near Orchard Knob.

Silent heroes aided doctors and nurses; whites and blacks labored side by side in a frantic effort to deal with the unknown killer, referred to in lighter vein as Bronze John. Mayor Thomas J. Carlyle, Father Patrick Ryan, teacher Hattie Ackerman, and one Henry Savage, described as a local gambler with a big heart and no fear, died while helping others.

Local county residents sent in chickens and other food supplies and tried to disinfect newspapers before reading them at arm's length. Help came from Atlanta and Memphis; donations arrived from New York and even Paris. As October gave way to November, the fever's daily toll finally abated. On the first day of November the W & A, (Western & Atlantic) restored regular train service and people began to return home. A frost ended the horror but not before 366 persons had died.[29]

As the epidemic waned, the spirit of the "Plucky City" returned; confidence in the future could not be quashed. Among those who led the cheering was Adolph Ochs. His paper gloried in every materialistic advance; some claimed it overreacted every time a new peanut stand opened. It likewise encouraged civic pride and cultural activities. Then, before long, came the opportunity to promote a great real estate boom.

Exactly when the boom started no one can safely say, but there were clear traces of it by the time the Cincinnati Southern Railway was completed in 1880. Seven years later it ran at full tide. Buying and selling, swapping and trading property became a fascinating game. Everyone tried to convince others that there was a sound basis for unusual prices.

Actually the boom was not an isolated frenzy; a speculative mania swept the southeast and every little community in southeastern Tennessee sought out eastern investors and speculators who came by the trainload. In Chattanooga town lots attracted attention and prices soared, but it was in the surrounding countryside that the boom reached its greatest proportions. Charlie James's belt line railroad had opened new suburban opportunities. Lots carved from old fields stimulated buyers to subdivide tracts, lay out streets, and begin construction of homes. Orchard Knob, Highland Park, East Lake, Ridgedale, St. Elmo, and Hill City each had their promoters. Expansionists also dreamed of potential profits from mountain investments.

Every enterprising fellow seemed to enter the real estate business or joined a syndicate. The more aggressive bought out merchants, removed their merchandise, and rented out desk space to the new realtors. Barbecues attracted buyers; wagons and horses toured the streets carrying elaborate signs; bands drummed up trade. Curbstone operators had a busy time; the livery stable business became so brisk that it had to expand.

Anyone with a little money joined in. "Refined ladies," wrote the chronicler H. M. Wiltse, "took a hand and some of them showed no little skill in the scramble for wealth." Even the flood of 1886 did not faze the salesmen; they simply rowed prospective buyers over the land. Advertisements in the *Times* multiplied, requiring additional pages, and Ochs responded by lining up with the boom's most optimistic sponsors.

In June of 1889 the *Times* announced it would give away some thousand "town lots" to subscribers. Ochs had acquired a large tract on Walden Ridge, which was surveyed and laid out as "Timesville." Every subscriber to the newspaper had an equal chance to win a lot and eventually a large number were awarded.

Along the belt line or trolley routes the transformation from farmland or woodlot to city plots extended in every direction. Charlie James was active in his encouragement. The area called Tunnel, near where Sherman and Cleburne had fought, was renamed Sherman Heights and later East Chattanooga. Mayor E. M. Dodson, a confederate veteran, along with the ex-Union industrialist Hiram Chamberlain and others, bought the Glass farm there and carved it into the first subdivision. Ridgedale, Fort Cheatham, and East Lake experienced the same kind of growth. The Mission Ridge Land Company, in which James was one of the chief developers, did business here and on behalf of the company James gave the lake in East Lake to Chattanooga on 4 July 1896. Feverish land sales boomed also in St. Elmo where the Forest Hills Cemetery had been dedicated on 24 September 1880.

The fury of the speculation continued; prices rose, property changed hands, and mortgage terms were arranged. Investment groups such as the New England Improvement Association and the Boston and Chattanooga Syndicate represented distant investors, but many negotiations involved local money, promises, and loans. Business and social organizations sprang to life: the Highland Park Improvement Company, the Chattanooga Association for the Encouragement of New Business, the Chattanooga and Hamilton County Development Association, the Real Estate Exchange, the Driving Association, the Young Men's Prohibition Club, and many more.

The most elaborate scheme, outlined in a glowing prospectus, was that of the Chattanooga Land, Coal, Iron and Railway Company— popularly called the "Over-the-River-Company." It enthusiastically promised to make Chattanooga "the largest city of its size in the world." Active in the original promotion were J. W. Adams, T. D. Young, H. C. Beck, and Adolph Ochs; they were later joined by Charles E. James. Eventually ownership passed to Boston capitalists and then to Scottish investors, who changed the name to the Chattanooga Company, Ltd. Later the company transferred its bonds to the Chattanooga Estates Company, organized by James, from which a future Signal Mountain development materialized.

The "Over-the-River-Company" claimed control of about twenty-five thousand acres of land, one-fifth or more in Hill City and about the same amount on Walden Ridge. This company held title or options to some ten miles of the north bank of the river, stretching from the Suck to North Chickamauga Creek, making such early land speculators as the Hargrove Company or Richard Waterhouse seem to shrink to pygmy proportions. Blast furnaces, coke ovens, mines, railroads, river bridges, and even oil wells gained high priority in future plans.

As the frenzied pace of the boom slackened, people began to wonder how they could meet their outstanding notes. The building spree that followed the speculation in lots produced additional debts. The 1890s brought more burdens and the panic of 1893 delivered the final blow to speculative hopes. But the real estate mania had laid the foundations for the suburbs and some realtors received solid training—often at high cost—in the fundamentals of business, including J. Fred Ferger, whose 1887 beginnings grew into today's successful company.[30]

Many newcomers, attracted by the stepped-up pace of the local economy, came to town to settle permanently. Fred Ferger was in part responsible for one, a young lawyer from Covington, Kentucky, who had known the Chattanoogan at school. Edward Young Chapin visited the area in December 1886, returned home, closed out his affairs, and moved south by mid-February of the next year. In the early part of these hectic boom days Chapin became an active director in a dozen or more businesses and gave his time and talent to educational, cultural, and welfare activities. No richer dividend of the boom could have been paid than the presence of this excellent citizen.[31]

The county, however, lost one person who had suffered financial reverses but rose from the debris of the boom to find national distinction. Adolph Ochs, realizing that he needed a greater income to meet his obligations, in 1896 purchased the *New York Times*. Although this venture naturally necessitated a change of residence, Ochs left his heart in the community where he had found his first opportunity, and he never lost contact with the area.

NOTES

1. *Chattanooga Times*, 1, 8, 12–14 March 1891.

2. Edward King, *The Southern States of North America* (London: Blackie & Son, 1875), p. 532; Morrow Chamberlain, *A Brief History of the Pig Iron Industry of East Tennessee* (Chattanooga: author, 1942), pp. 15–16. The Chattanooga furnace operated intermittently until 1919.

3. Ibid., pp. 20–21. In 1911 Chamberlain and Montague bought the New Soddy Coal Company from which the furnace had obtained coke.

4. Ibid., p. 8; *Chattanooga Times*, 8 May 1887.

5. C. D. McGuffey, *Standard History of Chattanooga* (Knoxville: Crew and Dorey, 1911), p. 174.

6. T. J. Campbell, *The Upper Tennessee* . . . (Chattanooga: author, 1932), pp. 82–84.

7. Ibid., pp. 71–76, 91–95; J. Haden Alldredge et al., *A History of Navigation on the Tennessee River System* . . . (House Document 254, 75th Congress, First Session, Washington, D.C: Government Printing Office, 1937), p. 102; *Chattanooga Times*, 1 February 1881; 25 January 1894; 19 February 1896; 19 May 1899.

8. Ibid, 1 April 1892; 21 September 1894; 3 August 1895; 12 January, 24, 29; March 1896; 13–17 February 1897.

9. Ibid., 16 October 1891; 14, 17 January 1893; Campbell, *Upper Tennessee*, pp. 71, 74, 85; Frank L. Teuton, *Steamboat Days on the Tennessee River* (Marlow Heights, Md.: author, 1967), pp. 53–54; Harry M. Wiltse, "History of Chattanooga," 2 vols. (Typescript, Chattanooga-Hamilton County Bicentennial Library), 2:73.

10. *Chattanooga Times*, 4 February 1900; Nashville District, Corps of Engineers, *Engineers on the Twin Rivers: A History of the Nashville District Corps of Engineers, U.S. Army* (n.p., 1979), pp. 103–108, 121–135.

11. Ibid., 22 September 1893; 3 June 1934; Campbell *Upper Tennessee*, pp. 96-107; Teuton, *Steamboating*, pp. 58, 62–64.

12. John F. Stover, *Railroads of the South, 1865–1900* (Chapel Hill: University of North Carolina Press, 1955), pp. 89–94.

13. Lewis Shepherd, "John C. Stanton's Contribution to Local History and Some Other Sketches," *Chattanooga Times*, 29 October 1911; Chattanooga *News Free-Press*, 14 June 1970; Wiltse; "Chattanooga," *1:90*.

14. Lewis Shepherd, "Hamilton County Towns, Villages and Localities and Queer Facts about Origin of Their Names," *Chattanooga Times*, 4 June 1916; T. J. Campbell, "Welsh Settlements in Tennessee: Sale Creek and Soddy," *Chattanooga Times*, 1 February 1930; Ibid., 9 May 1900; 18 March 1923; 30 July 1962.

15. Ibid., 14 November 1880; 11 December 1895; 24 March, 25 April 1896; *City Directory 1885*, 63, *Chattanooga Weekly Commercial*, 21 December 1879.

16. Wiltse, "Chattanooga," 2:90–91. The three policies of the New Orleans store were "fair and square," "one price," and "one cent change."

17. David Steinberg, "TAG: The Pigeon Mountain Route" (Unpublished paper, Chattanooga-Hamilton County Bicentennial Library).

18. Ibid., 8 December 1892; George M. James, *A Remarkable Man* (n.p. author, 1977).

19. David H. Steinberg, *And to Think It Only Cost a Nickel! The Development of Public Transportation in the Chattanooga Area* (Chattanooga: author, 1975), pp. 52–57.

20. Ibid., pp. 5–16, 69–72.

21. Ibid., pp. 18–36, *Chattanooga Times*, 20 October 1891; 8 December 1892.

22. Ibid., 21 May 1916; 18 September 1938.

23. Ibid., 7 May, 22 October 1879; 8 December 1892; 18 September 1938.

24. Undated clipping, files of Chattanooga-Hamilton County Bicentennial Library. It was about 1926 when the Cumberland Company was succeeded by the Southern Bell Telephone and Telegraph Company. *Chattanooga Times*, 16 April 1899; Wiltse, "Chattanooga," 2:112.

25. *Chattanooga Times.*, 20 October 1929; 18 September 1938.

26. Ibid., 10 April 1886; L. M. Pindell, *A Paper on the Tennessee River and Flood System* (Chattanooga: George M. Bradt Printing, 1896), p. 10; Wiltse "Chattanooga," 2:94, 98, 119.

27. *Chattanooga Times*, 18, 19 February 1891; 5 June 1938; *Engineering News*, 16 May 1891, pp. 462–463. (copy in clipping file, Chattanooga-Hamilton County Bicentennial Library). The Walnut Street bridge was the only highway bridge in the county until the Market Street or Chief John Ross Bridge was finished in 1917.

28. Gilbert E. Govan and James W. Livingood, *The Chattanooga Country*, 3d ed. (Knoxville: University of Tennessee Press, 1977), pp. 314–321; Gerald W. Johnson, *An Honorable Titan* (New York: Harper & Brothers, 1946), pp. 13–59. A board of arbitrators at the end of the two-year period awarded

Cunningham $5,500 for the remaining second half interest in the paper. So instead of paying $800, Ochs eventually paid $5,750.

29. Ibid., pp. 59–61; Govan and Livingood, *Chattanooga Country*, pp. 321–325.

30. Wiltse, "Chattanooga," 2:105–106; *Chattanooga Times*, 8 December 1892; 14 March 1920; 14 February 1937; Govan and Livingood, *Chattanooga Country*, pp. 344–350.

31. *Chattanooga Times*, 14 February 1937.

14

The Park and the Fort

CONGRESSMAN H. Clay Evans hurried along the streets of the District of Columbia between the Capitol and the White House on the summer evening of 19 August 1890. He carried a bill which Congress had just endorsed to President Benjamin Harrison for his signature. That night marked the official creation of the Chickamauga and Chattanooga National Military Park, which was destined to have a tremendous impact on Hamilton County as well as on her neighbor to the south, Walker County, Georgia. With it was established the concept of an outdoor historical laboratory, for it represented the first of our nation's military parks and, today it is still the largest such reservation.

This idea, supported by veterans of both armies, moved rapidly through Congress without sectional or partisan protest. The House took only twenty-three minutes to approve the bill. The Senate was even more expeditious:

> the Senate clerk being a more rapid reader, and a deeply interested and most efficient friend of the measure, namely, Gen. Anson G. McCook, of the "fighting McCooks," one of the most brilliant officers of the Army of the Cumberland, a participator in the storming of Lookout Mountain, beat the record of the House clerk, and the bill passed the Senate in twenty minutes.

Prior to this speedy action went months of planning. The notion first occurred to Henry V. Boynton and a friend on a June day in 1888 as they rode over the battlefield of Chickamauga. Boynton, a Federal regimental commander in the battle, was now a Washington correspondent for the *Cincinnati Commercial Gazette* and a well-known figure in veterans' circles. He brought his thoughts together in news stories advocating the need to preserve and mark the battlefield before tangled growth and cultivation devoured all significant landmarks. Beginning with the plan of marking Union lines only, the idea broadened to record positions of both sides. Veterans of the Army of the Cumberland then appointed a committee to inaugurate the movement for a private memorial association. These men, joined by a group of Confederate veterans, obtained a charter from the state of Georgia.

By good fortune the Society of the Army of the Cumberland planned its 1889 reunion in Chattanooga; Confederate veterans received invitations to meet with the Unionists to discuss the park. In a great tent festooned with the national colors the ex-Confederate "Pastor of Chattanooga" led the prayer and Adolph Ochs, chairman of the local committee, welcomed the guests. A former Confederate moved that General Rosecrans be selected chairman by acclamation. The Union general caught the spirit of the hour when he remarked, "It is very difficult to find in history an instance where contending parties in after years meet together in perfect amity. It took great men to win that battle, but it takes greater men still, I will say morally great, to wipe away all the ill feeling which naturally grows out of such a contest."

The leaders in the park movement met at Crawfish Springs, Georgia, with their veteran colleagues to effect an organization on the site. They chose General John T. Wilder as president of what later became the Chickamauga Memorial Association, concluding their gathering with a barbecue supper. But before long the plans broadened again; by unanimous consent the sponsors decided to seek the participation of the federal government.

The act passed by Congress not only provided funds and managerial guidelines for the Chickamauga and Chattanooga National Military Park but also gave birth to the idea of setting aside land for other national historical parks. Specifically the legislation placed responsibility for the enterprise in the hands of three commissioners responsible to the secretary of war. In addition, there was to be an official historian, a post immediately assigned to Boynton.

The commissioners' main tasks comprised the acquisition of land, marking the area in keeping with the facts of 1863, approving the erection of federal markers, and supervising the planning of state monuments and markers. The park was not to be thought of as a pleasure ground or picnic area and no expenditures for beautification were anticipated. Fundamentally it was to be preserved as it was at the time of the conflict.

The principal area consisted of some 7,600 acres within Georgia where the bloody struggle of Chickamauga occurred. Titles to the approach roads were transferred by the states of Georgia and Tennessee to the United States. Within Hamilton County these highways included Missionary Ridge Crest Road from Sherman Heights to the Georgia state boundary and the road from the crossing of Lookout Creek across the northern slope of Lookout Mountain to the ridge where General Hooker had commanded. Some vital park acreage within Hamilton County became a part of the project during its formative years: 6 acres at Orchard Knob, 3 acres at Bragg's Missionary Ridge headquarters, a 5½-acre spur on the northern sector of the ridge called De Long's reservation, and 45 acres at the far northern end of the ridge, including Tunnel Hill, commonly called Sherman's Reservation.

The commission began the slow, complicated task of buying the land and of gathering the exact truth about the military operations now twenty-seven years past. Tablets containing historical information about the engagements were financed by federal funds; the participating states in turn received authorization to put up suitable markers for their men. The places where general officers or persons exercising such command had been killed or mortally wounded were marked by triangular pyramids of eight-inch shells. Four hundred cannon of the type used in the action, mounted on cast-iron carriages and realistically painted, recorded the position of batteries. Five observation towers made it possible for visitors to get a proper idea of the terrain. To mark the field, twenty-five state commissions worked with the national group; although they attempted to follow the roads and landmarks of the 1860s, their decisions naturally provoked some disagreements among the veterans.

The momentum, funding, and planning of the park became a national effort in which the people of Hamilton County took great interest. When work had progressed sufficiently, Congress authorized $20,000 to finance proper dedicatory exercises for 18–20 September 1895. Vice-President Adlai E. Stevenson was chosen as master of ceremonies.[1]

The opening of the park could not have come at a more propitious time for the area. Every major economic venture since 1865 had turned sour. The Muscle Shoals canal with all its hopes of converting the Tennessee River into a profitable highway had failed, and the freight rates on the railroads continued to be discriminatory. The real estate boom of the 1880s had come to nothing. The Southern Iron Company, within about a year of the great tin-plate dinner, had failed and taken with it any dreams of a great steel industry for the area. Then the national panic of 1893 took its toll.

As in other American urban centers, money grew scarce: several weak Chattanooga banks suspended operations—the Merchants Bank, The Phoenix Bank and Trust Company, the Penny Savings Bank, and the City Savings Bank. The streetcar company was only one of many firms that had difficulties in meeting interest payments; it drastically cut schedules and then drifted into receivership in 1894. Many shops closed. The city experienced a wave of robberies and other crimes associated with hard times, and because of stringent financial conditions the community issued labor tickets as a form of charity. These tickets gave holders the privilege of working at fifty cents a day for single men and a dime more for those who were married.[2]

During these years the people of Hamilton County watched the progress of the park's development. It represented a real source of new hope. Judge Hugh Whiteside speaking for the county observed, "The idea of establishing such a park is one of the grandest ever conceived and the advantages that will accrue to Chattanooga as a result of it are simply incalculable."[3]

Some noted the new federal roads within the county and thought of them as models for local contractors to use in building additional highways. Others spoke of the steady stream of visitors and students expected in the years to come; no greater boost could be given the tourist business. The editor of the *Times* claimed that the real benefit came from the fact that the area was nationally known and that people everywhere would "talk of Chattanooga." The dedication was the first of many celebrations; the town folk had to prove their ability as good hosts, since the press and people of America would all turn their eyes their way.

The three days of September 1895 marked the thirty-second anniversary of that darkest period in the area's history. The Hamilton County Court voted $2,500 as its contribution and set up a dedication committee composed of five county court members, five men from the N. B. Forrest Post and five veterans of the Grand Army of the Republic

Post. The town of Chattanooga also appointed a committee and allocated a matching sum. In an effort to make the most of the situation the two groups consolidated with a citizens' committee, pooling their funds and assuming tasks under Chairman Adolph Ochs.[4]

Ochs used the pages of his newspaper to lecture, cajole, and admonish his readers; he shamed them into improving shabby residences, seedy lawns, and walks crowded by dog fennel, grass, and weeds. He badgered them to become tidy and courteous. Ochs also let authorities know how to deal with undesirables: "Pound the thieves into insensity when they are caught plying their trade and try them later," he advised. "Hit the fellow's head, it will do him good; it will be better for society if he is killed. The idea is to render these vermin as harmless as possible; and a professional thief is 'no good' until he is very dead."

For weeks virtually everyone was involved in frantic preparations. Groceries, restaurants, and hotels filled their shelves with special supplies and great quantities of staples. Residents prepared white badges to be worn so that visitors could identify their hosts. Bright-colored bunting and waving flags, along with special street decorations, gave the town a holiday air. A huge tent capable of seating fifteen thousand people was pitched in the Newby-King street area.

Steamboat owners announced excursions to Brown's Ferry and the area of Sherman's crossing. Barracks where guests could secure bunks appeared at several sites: Camp Grant at Seventh and Chestnut streets and Camp Grayson near the Stanton House. Camp Lamont at Chickamauga took care of certain military units. The railroads ran special trains at reduced fares and arranged for some hundred sleeping cars to stay in the yards. Hotels enjoyed capacity advance bookings and residents offered to house guests in their homes.

Several rail and trolley lines joined together to provide a "loop" to Chickamauga to speed service to that portion of the park. The city temporarily repealed its hack ordinance requiring licenses and invited rural folk from James, Bradley, Marion, Hamilton, Walker, Dade, and Catoosa counties to

burnish up their vehicles and come to Chattanooga on Sept. 18, 19, 20, when they will not only see the grandest dedication ceremony in the world's history but will get well paid for hauling passengers to the park and return, a distance of only 18 miles the round trip; a journey which any ordinary horse or team should make without turning a hair as the route is over the most perfect roads that skill and money can make. . . . Another thing to be noted by the farmers is that varnished rigs with velvet cushions and silver mounted harness are not expected; any safe vehicle with comfortable seats will suit and appearances won't count.

As the time approached, the tempo of preparation accelerated. Then the crowds began to gather. They came by seventy-four special trains from the north and south as well as by river boats. At least one group traveled in a covered wagon cavalcade and some journeyed on horseback. There were numerous military units with their bands—all in splendid dress. And there were veterans of the Chickamauga and Chattanooga campaigns, some wearing their old uniforms. Special delegations included "governors galore": fifteen were counted. Four cabinet officers and some twenty congressmen represented the federal government. Conservative estimates place the total attendance at forty thousand; the vice-president guessed sixty thousand. The number of visitors approximately equaled the total population of Hamilton County.

The week's billing at the opera house featured a "galaxy of good things" including the Mozart Opera Company's *Pirates of Penzance* and Al. G. Fields's minstrels. A cyclorama presenting a giant war canvas and a war museum competed for business. Band music and a war song concert were planned. At the old market house visitors could see exhibits of the natural and manufactured products of the area.

Jostling, scrambling crowds filled the depot night and day. They jammed the streets downtown; all were in good humor and little trouble developed. A few visiting pickpockets were ordered to leave town and many folks had to wait in line at hotels and restaurants for service. The most discussed mishap involved the superintendent of police of Detroit. While riding the incline he pulled off his new shoes and accidentally let one fall overboard. With one shoe on and one shoe missing, he sheepishly made his way back to his hotel.

The first day's festivities highlighted the dedication of state monuments. By that time, representatives from Michigan, Ohio, Illinois, Indiana, Massachusetts, and Wisconsin had all placed markers on the field. In the evening the Society of the Army of the Cumberland, with some ten thousand members and guests present, held its annual reunion. The next day was reserved for Chickamauga. A forty-four-gun salute at noon called the assembly to attention for the formal dedicatory service after which orations were given by Governor John B. Gordon of Georgia and Senator John M. Palmer of Illinois, followed by generals James Longstreet and John M. Schofield.

On 20 September the exercises opened with a great military parade in Chattanooga. Units of United States military men and national guardsmen marched to vigorous band music. Crowds lined the route and gathered at the reviewing stand on the campus of Grant University. A commanding figure on his spirited mount, Governor William McKinley of Ohio, later president of the United States, caught the attention of the onlookers as he received "tremendous cheers"; he was not allowed to proceed "until he had saluted the crowd again and again." The hot weather which caused pitch to ooze from the flooring of the reviewing stand did not lessen the patriotic zest of the day.

As the crowds dispersed to go home, many praised the local people for their hospitality and for the spirit of brotherhood that dominated the dedication. Some carried under their arms a special edition of the *Times* containing more than one hundred pages of the saga of war and the record of Chattanooga. This edition, of which over one hundred thousand copies were printed, brought high praise from the *New Orleans Picayune*, which hailed it as "one of the biggest things in American journalism."

In appreciation for his work in establishing the park, the citizens of the community presented a 225-piece chest of sterling silver to Henry V. Boynton.

Many of the dedication guests found special satisfaction and pleasure in the hotel accommodations and transportation facilities in the Hamilton County section of Lookout Mountain. Although no part of the mountain was included in the original park, its historic role and striking panoramic scenery attracted visitors. Naturally the owners and proprietors of the mountain facilities saw in the military park an added incentive to tourism and closely followed its development.

At the close of the Civil War, life for those people who chose to live on Lookout was little different from that in any rural part of the county. Hard-surfaced roads were nonexistent; houses were crudely built, without running water, basements, or insulation against the winter cold. The only road to the summit was the Whiteside Turnpike, which was constructed by the builder of the area's first hotel and owner of much of the land on the mountaintop.

The Whiteside interests, managed by Harriet Straw Whiteside since her husband's death in 1861, produced scant income during the war years. Both armies used Whiteside property and, to add to the difficulties, the hotel burned to the ground. Mrs Whiteside struggled to keep her large family together, but in 1864 she was ordered north by Union officials and actually spent some time in prison before returning to her home about a year later. Then she had a steady income only from the turnpike up Lookout Mountain although she still owned much of the mountaintop.

Following the peace in 1865 several efforts were made by small operators to restore summer hotel service on Lookout Mountain. The Lookout Mountain House stood where the turnpike reached the mountaintop (a spot on which modern condominium apartments have now been built). This "family-style" hostelry for a time in the 1880s was run by the downtown Read House; it continued to serve visitors until destroyed by fire in 1921. A second small summer place was the Hermitage, and at the site of the old Aldehoff School the Natural Bridge Hotel with forty-five rooms advertised health-restoring springs.

The latter establishment stood amid strange rock formations named Natural Bridge, Old Man of the Mountain, Chinese Grin, and Telephone Rock. In 1884 the hotel and its grounds were sold to the Southern Association of Spiritualists. The grounds, arranged for outdoor services, formed the setting for summer lectures on the faith, and seances were conducted by nationally known mediums until 1890 when interest in spiritualism waned and the property changed hands.[5]

Refugees fleeing from the 1878 yellow fever epidemic found haven on Lookout Mountain and their experiences emphasized the need for a better road up the mountain. The next year a stock company surveyed and built a second route, the St. Elmo Turnpike, named for the small village nestled at the foot of the mountain. Later the road acquired the name Johnson Turnpike for Colonel A. M. Johnson, founder of St. Elmo. This road, completed in 1879, turned up the mountain a short distance south of the Whiteside road.

Travelers immediately took advantage of the new and cheaper toll road, which cut into the earnings of the Whitesides, who continued to own the valuable Point area of Lookout. On the bluff the Whitesides rented out a little house for a photographer's gallery. The founder of the establishment, Robert M. Linn, came to Lookout after the battle of Missionary Ridge in 1863 from Marion, Ohio; later his brother, J. B., joined him in the business.[6]

With two roads up the mountainside a lively competition began, which history has named the "Turnpike War." To meet their losses the Whitesides began charging persons who reached the mountaintop for the privilege of seeing the majestic view from the Point. A fence to keep out nonpayers blocked the way, and when it did not prove a sufficient barrier, armed guards with shotguns patrolled the area. Then the Whitesides arranged a contract with a Chattanooga livery stable, the Owens Livery Company, for which they received an annual fee of $5,000 for granting this firm the exclusive right to haul passengers to the Point via the Whiteside Turnpike. Only Owen and Company passengers could get to the Point; St. Elmo Turnpike travelers, after making the three-hour drive from Chattanooga, could not get in even if they agreed to pay admission. A competing livery stable brought suit only to lose, for the judge reasoned that the area was private property which the Whitesides could use as they wished.

Soon after this time the Whitesides negotiated a sale of their Lookout Mountain lands to E. W. Cole of Nashville, who boldly announced a grandiose plan to build a great hotel, a college, and a railroad up the mountain. Real estate prices immediately inflated; the builder of the Mount Washington railroad in New England received a hurried summons to come to make a survey. Optimism gushed from Lookout Mountain when suddenly the bubble burst; the contracting parties disagreed over the acreage covered by their contract and Cole dropped the whole venture.[7]

Promoters' dreams for Lookout Mountain, however, did not disappear. For a decade or more imposing ventures sprouted in unbelievable form as more and more people risked their capital to transform the mountain into a resort and to wrestle with its craggy slopes in an effort to find comfortable and swift transportation to the summit. Much of this activity coincided with the real estate boom in the valley below.

The very next day after Cole made his flamboyant announcement a group of investors headed by Major W. P. King, United States engineer in charge of navigation improvement of the Tennessee River, entered the scene. They planned to build a cable car line from St. Elmo to the northern end of the mountain directly below the rocky palisade at the Point where the Whiteside ownership ended. Here a hotel would be built tall enough to reach the elevation of the mountaintop in order to match the view from the Whiteside land.[8]

In August 1885 this group, the Lookout Incline Railway Company, began construction on what was to be known as Incline No. 1. This spectacular line started in St. Elmo on what is now property of Chattem (Thirty-Eighth and Church streets). It measured 4,360 feet in length with a peak grade of thirty-three degrees and numerous high trestles. Two cable cars capable of carrying twenty-four passengers each were manufactured by the Wasson Car Company for the mountain firm. They were open-air contraptions with handrails for safety and side canvas curtains to keep out wind and rain. A mule-drawn streetcar brought passengers from Chattanooga to the station at the foot of the mountain.

Incline No. 1 opened on 21 March 1887; a round-trip ticket cost fifty cents. In 1890 over 150,000 persons took the breathtaking ride. More than a year passed before the Point Hotel, the mountaintop terminal of the incline, opened on 28 May 1888. Called a "palace set upon a hill," the hotel featured great balconies on all sides from which guests could take advantage of the striking scenery. In the basement the clientele could use a barber shop, billiard room, and bathhouse. The lobby, office, dining room, and narrow-gauge railroad tracks occupied the first floor. The upper stories contained a parlor and fifty-eight guest rooms. The fabled location of the resort brought guests from near and far, but, following years of service, the hotel was eventually razed after it and the land surrounding were acquired by the national park.

While the incline railroad was under construction, plans developed to build about one and one-half miles of narrow-gauge track from the hotel around the west side of the mountain to Sunset Rock. Much of the route, blasted from solid rock, ran on the brink of space at the base of the bluffs. An eleven-ton engine pulled the cars along this precarious way. Later the Narrow Gauge, as it was popularly called, extended its tracks to the Natural Bridge, giving the company a means of getting visitors and prospective real estate buyers onto mountain lands south of the Whiteside property. At the Natural Bridge, the company erected a train shed, souvenir stand, and a building to house the Lookout Mountain post office. Another extension of service carried the narrow-gauge trains to the Lookout Inn. In 1900 the route was electrified and the tracks extended to the east brow.

The "Turnpike War" flared up anew after the Tennessee legislature technically designated the Point a park or public resort. Several new court suits followed, but schemes to get visitors and tourists to the mountaintop did not end. Even before Incline No. 1 started regular service, another band of entrepreneurs organized the Chattanooga and Lookout Mountain Railway Company. Among the chartered group were R. L. and Ed Watkins and the busy C. E. James. Their plan called for a steam-powered railroad up the mountain to the neighborhood of the Point. Commonly called the Broad Gauge, this project featured the idea of taking freight or Pullman cars to the summit without transferring in Chattanooga; tourists from New York or Atlanta could ride directly to their hotels.

Like other routes the Broad Gauge track started in St. Elmo. It wound over the northern end of the mountain just below the Cravens House and trestled over Incline No. 1. About halfway up the grade a switchback allowed the mountain-climbing locomotives and cars to double back in front of the Cravens House, go under the incline track, and make their way to the summit at the rear of the old Lookout Mountain House. On 19 May 1888, the Broad Gauge made its maiden run; six thousand passengers rode that first day in the five cars decorated in a wine color with gold stripes.

The promoters of this line also hoped to profit from the sale of some five thousand acres of land they had acquired on the mountaintop from the Whitesides. An elaborate auction with all the typical trappings— cornet band, free refreshments and barbecue—planned for late May 1888 showed how capricious real estate speculations could be. Crowds ascended the mountain. The auction started and then the rains came. The next day it poured. A landslide along the Broad Gauge prevented the train from descending, and the soaked potential investors had to walk in the downpour to the rival line—the Narrow Gauge and Incline—to get back to Chattanooga. The real estate venture dissolved in the spring torrent.

On 19 January 1889, the Broad Gauge completed its line to within a few blocks of the Point. The daughter of Ed Watkins, president, drove a silver spike to complete the opening festivities. By midsummer the company began construction of its hotel, located just across the way from the present-day Incline station. It was a "massive structure of stone and wood," 365 feet long with 365 rooms. A contest with a $10 gold piece for a prize was held to find an appropriate name for the hostelry. Wisely they chose H. M. Wiltse's play on words, Lookout Inn, in preference to such entries as Alaska House, Eagle Nest, or Dreamland Home.

Lookout Inn opened for business in June 1890 and became one of the very popular southern resorts. Its balls and germans, coaching parties, and musicals gained a wide reputation; advertisements quoted such guests as H. M. Stanley, the African adventurer, who claimed that "the view from Lookout Mountain is one of the most magnificent to be seen in the world." Presidents Cleveland, McKinley, and Roosevelt sat at its dining tables. But the huge hotel, never free from financial pressures, changed hands a number of times. Boston investors operated it for a while; then for a few years it opened only in the summer season. Periodically it closed and opened until 17 November 1908, when a disastrous fire, visible for many miles in the valley below, totally destroyed the inn.

Nor did the Broad Gauge enjoy prosperous days. Even when the hotel served numerous guests, the income from the railroad never proved adequate. It too changed hands and in 1899 finally suspended all schedules. Later a streetcar line ran on the Broad Gauge tracks from 1913 to 1920.

There appeared to be an irresistible challenge in scaling the mountain. But despite the fiscal problems that all before them had experienced, another group planned to enter the competition with a shorter, faster, and more direct incline route which would attack the steepest part of Lookout. On 1 June 1895, John T. Crass, Jesse Cravens, Linn White, Josephus Guild (an engineer who had moved to the area a decade earlier), and members of the Whiteside family got a charter for the Lookout Incline & Lula Lake Railway Company, more popularly known as Incline No. 2, which is the present incline operated by Chattanooga Area Regional Transportation Authority (CARTA) since 28 January 1973.

Their goal was completion before the September park dedication date. Despite feverish efforts, plans went awry; mid-November came before Incline No. 2 started service from its St. Elmo station to the mountaintop just across the way from Lookout Inn. The steep section of the track rose at a 72.7-degree rate and was as exciting as the inn was magnificent. Incline No. 2 frightened many travelers, but earned it the name "America's Most Amazing Mile."

As in 1863, Lookout Mountain brought national attention to the area. Bold engineering schemes and elaborate architectural renditions that never left the drawing board added new interest to the natural beauty and historic significance of the mountain. B. B. Floyd's exaggerated drawing which he called "Romp Frolique" gave a carnival-like atmosphere to the area: he crowned his blueprint of the mountain with banner-waving hostelries, crisscrossed it with inclines and railways, honeycombed it with tunnels, and threw in some horse-drawn contraptions to boot.

The days of the "Turnpike War" were forgotten as two Inclines, a narrow-gauge and a broad-gauge railway, and two hotels competed for business. The acres of Point Lookout, still owned by the Whitesides, lay directly between Incline No. 1 with its Point Hotel and the Lookout Inn and Incline No. 2, in which the Whitesides had investments and of which Vernon Whiteside served as vice-president. So a new phase of the struggle for tourists turned into an "incline war"; the feud went on.

At one time prior to the completion of Incline No. 2, stone steps were built from the Point Hotel up to and across the Point leading to the Lookout Inn only about four blocks away. But just as soon as Incline No. 2 opened, Vernon Whiteside and a work crew tore out the steps. In addition, the Whiteside interests withdrew the right of the Narrow Gauge Railway to use the broad-gauge route beyond the Natural Bridge to the Lookout Inn. The Whitesides again fenced off the Point and announced that only people with tickets for Incline No. 2 would be given access to that area.

Incline No. 1 responded by reducing fares to twenty-five cents round trip, including passage over the narrow-gauge, and by increasing its daily schedule. In addition, it put an observation car on the scenic but roundabout route.

Incline No. 2 also had its money worries; the 1890s were difficult years. The closing of Lookout Inn for a time in 1896 crippled Incline business, and a fire (there were rumors of arson) on 13 December 1896 destroyed the power machinery near the mountain terminal, the waiting room, and one of the cars which, while burning, broke loose, hurtled down the mountainside, jumped the track, and smashed among some trees.

Business conditions worsened to the point where the competitors finally made a truce: they would both charge the same fares, use interchangeable tickets, and all passengers would have access to the Point. But mutual distrust ended this suspension of hostilities in a month's time and a bitter new round of controversy began.

By this time the federal government became interested in adding the area to the Chickamauga and Chattanooga National Military Park. During negotiations the Whitesides leased the Point to the Lookout Mountain Land Company. Before long a sublease was in the hands of the proprietors of Incline No. 1, who had been victims of the Whitesides' operations. Retaliation followed. The stone steps from the Point Hotel were rebuilt and on 26 July 1898, a newspaper advertisement carried an unmistakable hint of revenge: "Lookout Mountain Visitors—Take Note: Only passengers holding round trip tickets over the Incline No. 1 are allowed into Point Park."

The commercial showdown, however, did not materialize. Mrs. Whiteside fumed, but instead of undergoing another round of suits and recriminations, the Whitesides sold the Point. Fortunately, far-sighted citizens of the area, tired of the commercial wars, interested the federal government in expanding its park system.

The first expansion of the park on Lookout Mountain encompassed the shelflike ledge below the Point where the 1863 battle had taken place. Robert Cravens and his family returned to their home, "the White House" (or "Cravens House") at war's end. He repaired and rebuilt the house with profits made from the purchase and resale of army wagons. Following the death of Cravens and his wife, the home and surrounding eighty-five acres were sold on 4 September 1896, to the federal government under terms of legislation passed three years earlier.[9]

The citizens active in acquiring the Point as part of the national park were headed by Adolph S. Ochs and Alexander W. Chambliss. Chambliss, a South Carolinian, came to the area as a young lawyer. He grew increasingly interested in local history and politics, serving as mayor of Chattanooga from 1901 until 1905 and as chief justice of the Supreme Court of Tennessee. Ochs and Chambliss had enthusiastic public support for their plan, and on 23 August 1898 announcements reported the purchase of sixteen and a half acres for $35,000, which included the Point Hotel. The purchase agreement of the Point guaranteed that it would be open to all.

A wall of native sandstone running from east to west on the brow of the mountain defined the southern limits of this new addition to the park, and in 1905 a massive gateway in the form of the insignia of the Army Corps of Engineers marked the entrance. Five years later the ninety-five-foot-high New York State Peace Monument made of Tennessee marble and Massachusetts pink granite was dedicated as a memorial to New York veterans and as a symbol of national unity.

The legacy of commercial bitterness over the Point left a deep impression on Ochs. With the coming of the automobile, Lookout Mountain's summer community developed into a prosperous suburban area which brought with it a cluster of enterprises and a growing danger that the mountainsides would be cluttered with cheap, gaudy commercialism. Ochs never ceased to think of the mountain with its distinctive geographic features and natural beauty as one of the area's great assets. Putting aside a rather naive dream of cascades and hanging gardens, he organized a movement to save the area for public use in 1921.

Four years later on one of his many trips from New York, Ochs discussed a specific plan. A corporation to acquire the mountainside was formed: many acres were donated and others were bought with the $117,000 subscribed. Ochs and his family contributed $24,000; his brother Colonel Milton Ochs handled most of the details. Altogether, 2,700 acres of wild forest land were acquired and presented as a gift to the federal government on 22 June 1935. Ochs also advanced to the county $150,000 to rebuild the old St. Elmo Turnpike, which was renamed the Ochs Highway to honor the publisher and his brother.

On 12 November 1940, the people of the area paid their respects to Ochs, who had died on a visit home on 8 April 1935, only a few months before the Lookout Mountain lands were turned over to the park authority for perpetual preservation. Through public subscription Ochs's friends raised funds for the erection of an observatory museum on the point of Lookout Mountain. Hewn from native stone, the building blends into the landscape close to nature's unusual formation, Umbrella Rock. Beyond is the panorama of the valleys below. The mountain lands remain in their natural state because of the foresight and determination of Ochs.

From time to time other strategic sites were added to the park. In 1899 property owners along the crest of Missionary Ridge generously gave a 20-foot strip along the front of their holdings for a distance of some eight miles to facilitate a plan to widen the Crest Road from thirty to fifty feet. Years later, in 1932, the town of Signal Mountain made a gift of Signal Point, from which messages had flashed during the siege days of 1863. When it was learned that the government could not accept less than a five-acre plot, the Signal Mountain Garden Club accepted the challenge. It eventually increased the grant from two to seven acres and on 1 May 1948, in fitting ceremonies in which Mrs. E. Y. Chapin unveiled a marker, the club turned over the historical area to the park. In 1966 a $10,000 improvement in the form of a circular observation shelter overlooking the canyon of the Tennessee River was added through the continuing leadership of the garden club.

On Lookout Mountain the inspiring spot known as Sunset Rock near which the old Narrow Gauge Railroad passed and where many a visitor had his picture made also was added to the Chickamauga and Chattanooga National Military Park. In 1949 the town of Lookout Mountain quitclaimed this plot on the western brow to the park as a memorial to Adolph and Milton Ochs for their unselfish efforts in acquiring the "historic, scenic, and natural arboretum of the Slopes of Lookout Mountain." A variety of problems delayed official acceptance of the area until 1977.[10]

Through the years the Moccasin Bend at the foot of Lookout, a recognized hallmark of Chattanooga, was discussed as a park site. Here Yankee guns once challenged Confederate mountain positions and across its level reaches the route of the "Cracker Line" had passed. On 5 August 1950, President Harry Truman signed enabling legislation to make this a possible park area, but Tennessee failed to conclude the necessary land purchase. Later the bend became the property of Hamilton County and Chattanooga and was jointly dedicated to public use on 20 June 1961. In one corner of this reservation the state of Tennessee located the Moccasin Bend Psychiatric Hospital, where innovative treatment practices widen medical horizons.

Cameron Hill, the historic Civil War site closest to the heart of Chattanooga, never was made a part of the park system. However, when Hamilton County friends learned of the death of Henry Boynton on 4 June 1905, they determined to honor this man by creating a park on the summit of the hill in his name. Although greatly altered as a residential area through the years, this eminence continues to recognize the soldier who not only played an important role in the creation of the national park but who also served as park historian and later as chairman of the park commission. Also, Henry Boynton was largely instrumental in having the park serve as a military base in the Spanish-American War.[11]

When the country suddenly found itself on the brink of a foreign war in 1898, the small United States Army was serving in widely scattered western frontier posts. Campsites where troops could be concentrated and from which they could readily be dispatched to such points of embarkation as Tampa, Florida, had to be arranged. The government, recognizing the strategic position of Chattanooga along with its major rail facilities, decided early in April to use park lands at Chickamauga. They named the new facility Camp George H. Thomas for the "Rock of Chickamauga."

The first regular troops arrived on 15 April; five days later General J. R. Brooke with his staff took command. Five additional days passed before the declaration of war. Volunteers and state militia units joined the regulars and by the end of May forty-five thousand men were in camp; by mid-September when troops were demobilized it was estimated that some seventy-two thousand men had been at Camp Thomas.

Local militiamen under Major James Perry Fyffe who had drilled over many of Chattanooga's streets went into temporary quarters at the old Driving Park, Chattanooga's race course (now Warner Park). They received orders to report to Nashville at the time when plans were fast developing for the city's big spring festival. The occasion featured a parade of military units and floats on which festival queens from suburban centers and neighboring towns rode, attended by their courts. The queen in this flower parade whose float was judged the best reigned over the festivities. But in 1898 the military organization left early. It marched in uniform in the rear of the parade and moved on from the dispersal grounds directly to the Union Depot. The station, packed with well-wishers, rocked to the martial music as the men boarded the cars and went off to war. Before long, however, they were back at Camp Thomas as trainees.

The camp, although located in north Georgia, had a tremendous economic impact on Hamilton County; the summer months of 1898 witnessed the end of the long depression of the 1890s in the region. The hotels in town and on Lookout Mountain were crowded with newsmen, salesmen, people looking for employment, and the curious. Spectators and family members of trainees visited the camp to watch reviews and sham battles. In June paymasters distributed upward of $3½ million to the soldiers, who at infrequent intervals got leave to come to town where they shopped and spent money freely. Camp bakeries, for a time at least controlled by local enterprise, turned out thirty thousand or more eight-ounce loaves a day. Local social life in early summer was enlivened by balls, parties, picnics, lawn fetes, and "romps."

The camp, hastily constructed without regard for precautionary health requirements or proper sanitation, was extremely crude. Men lived in tents; hospitals, small and inadequate, met no standards. Kitchens and mess halls were unscreened. Drinking water was hauled from springs and cooking water was pumped from the creek. Many trainees had no uniforms and drilled with sticks. A dingy cluster of buildings down by the railroad named Lytle furnished the only spot for amusement, legal or otherwise.

The inevitable happened: typhoid fever broke out. Doctors and nurses could not cope with the disease, and a total of 425 men died. The number killed in action or who died of wounds during the entire war was 379. In addition, hundreds suffered from a variety of fevers. The townspeople rallied to help in the crisis. They contributed money and arranged to get milk and ice to the hospitals and clothing for the ill and convalescent, as it was no mean feat to make the trip over the dusty roads in the heat of summer.

The camp hospitals could only be regarded as disgraceful. Some arrangements were made to care for men in town. The Knights of Pythias furnished a home on East Fifth Street and made it into a small hospital. The Christian Endeavor Society established a temporary hospital in Concordia Hall and the Baptist Church fitted up quarters in the old armory at Fourth and Market streets. There may have been other institutional efforts in addition to those of private citizens who opened their homes to care for the sick, despite the fact that some townspeople had contracted the fever.

The war came to an end on 12 August, but the discontentment with camp life did not improve the morale of the camp so depressed by illness. Five days later the last review at Camp Thomas found forty-four thousand soldiers on parade and some twenty-five thousand spectators lining the crest of Snodgrass Hill. But by mid-September only a few troops were left to dismantle the camp.[12]

Although critics carped about the unhealthy conditions at Chickamauga, Hamilton Countians praised the location of the camp, insisting that the area itself had not caused the fever epidemic. They campaigned to have Camp George H. Thomas made a permanent military base. This idea was not new; since the passage of the law in 1890 creating the park, individuals had pressed for an installation and the Chattanooga Chamber of Commerce had at different times recommended it. Only a few days before the dedication exercises in 1895 when Secretary of War Daniel Lamont was slated to be present, the chamber appointed a special committee to call on him and urge his recommendation of a garrison and instruction camp.[13]

These continuing efforts overcame the criticism of the camp's Spanish-American War record, and in 1902 construction of permanent barracks was undertaken; in December 1904 the base was designated Fort Oglethorpe in honor of the British founder of the colony of Georgia. Businesspeople rejoiced as they envisioned the soldiers freely spending their ready cash. Others emphasized the stimulus the post would give the tourist business. They realized the broader value of the Chickamauga and Chattanooga National Military Park in attracting the location of the fort and gained a greater regard for the local railroads which made the selection possible.

Before the war the rail lines through Chattanooga changed markedly in character as, in keeping with national trends, they merged into

major trunk lines. What had been small, independent companies became links in major networks. The old Nashville and Chattanooga had
early extended its service into Missouri and took the name Nashville,
Chattanooga, and St. Louis Railroad. In 1890 this company gained a
lease on the Western and Atlantic from the state of Georgia, giving
the road control of a great north-south rail corridor.

In and around Richmond, Virginia, plans formulated in 1887 pointed
to the development of another major southern network, but the panic
of 1893 delayed consolidation. Foreclosures, reorganizations, and sales
brought the banking house of Drexel, Morgan & Company into the
endeavor and finally, on 1 July 1894, the Southern Railroad Company
was born. Locally the East Tennessee, Virginia & Georgia line, the
Alabama Great Southern, the Cincinnati Southern, and finally the
Memphis and Charleston came into the new system with Chattanooga
a major junction.[14]

NOTES

1. William T. Alderson and Robert M. McBride, eds., *Landmarks of Tennessee History*, 2 vols. (Nashville: Tennessee Historical Society and Tennessee
Historical Commission, 1965). 1:91–111, reprints article by James W. Living-
good, "Chickamauga and Chattanooga National Military Park," *Tennessee Historical Quarterly* 23 (1964): 2–23. The observation towers were later removed.

2. *A History of Banking in Chattanooga* (Chattanooga: Hamilton National
Bank, 1925), pp. 11, 17; Harry M. Wiltse, "History of Chattanooga" 2 vols.
(Typescript, Chattanooga-Hamilton County Bicentennial Library), 2:111.

3. *Chattanooga Times*, 21 August 1890.

4. The story of the dedication is based on the *Chattanooga Times*; H. V.
Boynton, *The National Military Park Chickamauga-Chattanooga* (Cincinnati:
Robert Clarke, 1895), and H. V. Boynton, comp., *Dedication of the Chicka-
mauga and Chattanooga National Military Park, September 18–20, 1895*
(Washington, D. C.: GPO, 1896).

5. John Wilson, *Lookout: The Story of an Amazing Mountain* (Chattanooga:
News-Free Press, 1977), pp. 55–60. The Natural Bridge area was completely
changed with the construction of the Green Street Bridge on Scenic Highway
and the opening of Bragg Avenue. The property belongs to the town of Lookout
Mountain, Tennessee.

6. Robert Sparks Walker, *Lookout: The Story of a Mountain* (Kingsport,
Tenn.: Southern, 1941), p. 241. J. B. Linn carried on the business after his

brother's death until 1886. Hardie Brothers of Michigan then rented the place and kept it open until after the Spanish American War. James Gaston leased it after the government took over the property. George, a son of R. M. Linn, entered business with his uncle in 1880. When the Hardies took possession, George Linn moved to Sunset Rock; he returned to the studio at the Point in 1900 where he operated the business until 1939 when the building was razed to allow space for the Ochs Museum.

7. Wilson, *Lookout Mountain*, pp. 66–70; Walker, *Lookout*, pp. 196–198.

8. David H. Steinberg, *And to Think It Only Cost a Nickel! The Development of Public Transportation in the Chattanooga Area* (Chattanooga: author, 1975), pp. 78–96.

9. Alderson and McBride, *Landmarks*, 1:157–175. This is a reprint of an article by Eugene J. Lewis, "Cravens House: Landmark of Lookout Mountain," *Tennessee Historical Quarterly* 20 (1961):203–221.

10. *Chattanooga Times*, 25 December 1899; 2 May 1948; 15 October 1949; 14 July 1966; *Chattanooga News-Free Press*, 3 May 1948; 7 July 1966; conversation with Edward Tinney, historian, Chickamauga-Chattanooga National Military Park.

11. Alderson and McBride, *Landmarks*, 1:109–110.

12. Constructed from the newspapers of the period and Wiltse, "Chattanooga," 2:114.

13. *Chattanooga Times*, 25 December 1899; 20 July 1902. The 1895 committee consisted of Foster V. Brown, Captain H. S. Chamberlain, Dr. J. W. Bachman, W. B. Swaney, Captain J. P. Smartt, H. Clay Evans, Dr. Wm. M. Pettis, Colonel Garnett Andrews, and Adolph S. Ochs.

14. Gilbert E. Govan and James W. Livingood, *The Chattanooga Country*, 3d ed. (Knoxville: University of Tennessee Press, 1977), pp. 360–362.

The Dynamo of Dixie

ALTHOUGH business remained listless and many residents of Hamilton continued to live under the heavy shadow of depressed times, in 1897 a cogent observer noted that "day is breaking" for the economy. The panic of 1893 had only reluctantly released its hold on the area, but the change somewhat enlivened the drab decade as the twentieth century found its way to the calendar.

Old residents had passed away: John P. Long, a founding father; William Lewis, free black; Joseph Ruohs, the Swiss man of business; S. B. Lowe, early manufacturer; Judge D. C. Trewhitt; William P. Rathburn, banker; and others. New leaders emerged, among them Judge John A. Moon, Henry Scott Probasco, Josephus C. Guild, Jerome B. Pound, John H. Race, John L. Hutcheson, Sr., Thomas Maclellan, E. Y. Chapin, Benjamin F. Thomas, John T. Lupton, and Garnett Andrews, Jr. Others who had struggled to carve out their careers in the stringent postwar days continued to provide community leadership. Abraham M. Johnson, Charles James, Dr. J. W. Bachman, Captain Hiram S. Chamberlain, Reverend Thomas H. McCallie, Henry Clay Evans, Z. C. Patten, Sr., D. P. Montague, and Xenophen Wheeler formed the backbone of this group.

As the new century was ushered in, the sound and smell of horses told of the still constant use of animal power for work and pleasure, but the number of animals present slowly declined. An interurban transportation network hauling freight and passengers and the widening use of a contraption called a bicycle made many people less dependent on dobbin. Furthermore, the fascinating possibilities of a horseless carriage occasionally sparked the discussions of progressive persons.

In 1900 Hamilton County's population numbered 61,695: 42,187 white, 19,490 black, and 18 Indian. The eighty-year predominance of native-born residents persisted: 60,110 fell into this classification, completely overshadowing the 1,585 foreign-born. Chattanooga at the time counted 30,154 persons: 17,032 white and 13,122 black.

In the decade of the 1890s the county added 8,213 citizens but Chattanooga gained only 1,054. This demographic development came about because the city boundaries had not been enlarged but the streetcars and the belt line had made suburban living comfortable and a necklace of small villages surrounded Chattanooga, all within easy commuting distance.[1]

The city directory of 1900 claims that the residents of these new communities numbered about fifteen thousand. All lived in the county beyond the corporate limits best described as the Tennessee River, East End Avenue (now Central Avenue), and a line just north of Chattanooga Creek (Twenty-Eighth Street). This satellite population included:

Alton Park	415	Highland Park	1,690
Avondale	842	Hill City	1,748
Bushtown	584	Indian Springs	34
Cedar Grove	109	New England Park	101
Churchville	614	North Chattanooga	314
East Chattanooga	636	Orchard Knob	254
East End	985	Ridgedale	980
East Lake	544	Rosstown	145
Eden Park	117	St. Elmo	2,305
End Line	419	Sherman Heights	1,190
Fort Cheatham	466	Suburba	52

This list omits the residents scattered along Missionary Ridge, who numbered a possible 400, and the 452 persons living in the incorporated village of Lookout Mountain.[2]

Elsewhere in the county the population remained widely separated with only a few villages identified in the census. In 1890 Daisy village

had 370 people; Sale Creek numbered 486, and Soddy village 1,173.
The rural sections were brought into closer relationship with other
parts of the county when in May 1901 rural free delivery of the mail
was inaugurated.[3]

In 1900 the number of Hamilton County families totaled 13,486;
they lived in 12,140 dwellings. The illiterate portion of the population
continued to be extremely high: those ten years of age and over who
could not read numbered 7,331. The average number of wage earners
reported in the census was 5,472.[4].

Most employees worked in small establishments; by 1897 only sixteen firms hired one hundred or more hands. The largest, the Chattanooga Foundry and Pipe Company and the New Soddy Coal
Company, employed three hundred men each. About 1881 the union
movement organized some workers in the national organization bearing
the name Noble Order of the Knights of Labor. Designed as an industrial union with members all associated with one large organization,
the Knights' aim was to secure for the worker the full share of the
wealth he created but with leisure for the laborers' intellectual, moral,
and social activities. Specifically they agitated against Tennessee's con-
vict lease system, which competed against free labor. The first local
assembly, the Lookout Assembly, at one time claimed twelve hundred
members. By 1886 the Knights had five local assemblies, including the
Eureka Assembly for blacks. The district organizer opposed unionizing
women. He did not sympathize with the new bloomer-clad woman and
felt that she was "not calculated to elevate the morals of the nation."[5]

The first unions were referred to as "secret societies" and little can
be learned of their activities. In a short time, craft unions organizing
around one skill came into existence. In 1887 the local scene saw the
beginnings of two such groups, the Typographical Union and the Iron
Molders' Union. The trend toward multiple organizations along craft
lines gained in popularity and the Knights of Labor disappeared. In
1897 the American Federation of Labor chartered the local Central
Labor Union. By 1900 seventeen different craft groups held regularly
scheduled meetings in Chattanooga. This variety not only reflects the
increasing union membership but also the growing diversification of
local industry. Memberships were held by the following groups: blacksmiths, boilermakers, brewers, bricklayers, carpenters and joiners,
cigarmakers, ironmolders, machinists, plumbers, pressmen, topogra-
phers, locomotive engineers, railway trainmen, locomotive firemen,

and railway conductors; the Dixie Division No. 48 Ladies' Auxiliary of Order of Railroad Conductors of America was also formed.[6]

In 1900 the county listed 332 manufacturing concerns with a capitalization of more than $8 million. Small firms produced such diverse items as native wines, carriages, carbonated drinks, cigars, black powder, slate pencils, patent medicines, and cedar pencil slats. The principal fields consisted of lumber and iron and their cognate industries; ores, clay and building stone; coal mining and coke making; and leather working.[7] In addition to these activities the railroads, the national military park, the post at Fort Oglethorpe, and tourism enriched the economic opportunities of the area.

Three new types of business emerged about the turn of the century, laying the foundation for today's growth. One of these was the textile industry. A few abortive efforts had been made to launch textile mills in the past—for example, Joseph Ruohs's 1873 cotton mill and the Chattanooga Cotton Factory in 1880. In 1885 the city of Chattanooga sent representatives to New England to try to persuade established firms there to relocate in Hamilton County.

Two years earlier, with John L. Hutcheson serving as company secretary and treasurer, the small Park Woolen Mills began manufacturing Kentucky jeans. In 1906 Hutcheson went into business for himself, opening the Peerless Woolen Mills in nearby Rossville, Georgia.

In the cotton textile line, local pioneers Garnett Andrews, Jr., and Edward Gould Richmond took the lead. Richmond, born in Utica, New York, and educated at Racine College, was a son of the president of the New York Central Railroad. At the time he moved to Hamilton County he had already acquired a good deal of business expertise as well as a considerable inheritance. Although his religious interests centered on St. Paul's Episcopal Church and his civic service in work at the hospital and at the Carnegie Library as a trustee, his primary concern was the cotton business.

Andrews had come to the area as a lad with his parents in 1881. The senior Garnett Andrews, a lawyer and mayor of Chattanooga in 1891–93, had risen to the rank of colonel in the Confederate army. In 1896 young Andrews organized the Chattanooga Knitting Mills which soon employed thirty people, had a capitalization of $12,000 and a $30,000 estimated value for its annual product, cotton hosiery. In March 1898 Andrews, along with Richmond and others, reorganized this firm under the name Richmond Hosiery Mills. Like Hutcheson, they located in Rossville. One year later Richmond, David Giles, and

Morgan Llewellyn started the Richmond Spinning Company in East Lake with a $200,000 capitalization.[8]

A second new industry, the insurance business, was brought into existence in 1887 when a local group organized the Mutual Medical Aid and Accident Insurance Company of Tennessee. The next year the name was changed to Provident Life and Accident Insurance Company. The region had nothing else like it; in the first years the company limited its business to accident insurance sold to the employees of Chattanooga industry.[9] In 1892 a New Brunswick, Canada, Scot joined the concern and rapidly rose to the post of chief officer. The association of this man, Thomas Maclellan, marked the broadening of the scope of the business from local to regional, and on to national, prominence.

About 1900, sickness coverage was added to the accident policy, making the company a pioneer in each of these fields; soon the business was expanded into the coal fields of East Tennessee and Kentucky and later into the lumber industry. In 1905 Maclellan's son, Robert J., joined the firm and succeeded his father as president in 1916. His long tenure as president contributed much to the company's expansion and growth. He organized a department specializing in the insurance needs for the nation's railroad employees. In 1916 and 1917 he took steps to develop a life insurance program. By the time Robert J. Maclellan passed the presidency on to his son in 1952, the Provident had topped the billion-dollar mark in life insurance in force. The company continued to lead the way in the field of disability insurance and in 1929 it became the first private company to offer hospital-surgical insurance to the public.[10]

On Columbus Day 1903, a second major insurance company held a charter-signing ceremony which brought the Volunteer State Life Insurance Company into being. Among those participating were Z. C. Patten, E. B. Craig, Theo F. King, A. S. Caldwell, and R. H. Caldwell. With Patten, a prosperous and respected leader in the community, as president the group ventured into a pioneering phase of the insurance business for this region. The life insurance business had been quite active for some years, but southerners had to purchase policies from northern or eastern concerns, thereby creating a steady flow of premium money out of the area. So Volunteer set out to capture the life insurance business of the South. Patten's two-score years as head of the company saw its home office grow into a vital local institution.[11]

About six years after the Volunteer started business, a third company initiated an insurance program. On 16 August 1909, a charter granted the Interstate Life and Accident Insurance Company the right to do business. The company with a $100,000 capitalization wrote policies covering accidents, health, and other casualty lines. As someone said jokingly, "Interstate's first policies insured against window breakage and underwriters cautiously took a chance that policy owners would not get trampled by a horse."

Hugh D. Huffaker, an educational and civic leader and a specialist in accident underwriting, served as president from 1910 to 1920 and Dr. Joseph W. Johnson as medical director. By 1911 they had a fifty-man field force and nine thousand policy owners and the next year adopted a program of weekly premium insurance. Dr. Johnson later acquired stock control of the company and in 1922 became president; H. Clay Evans Johnson succeeded his father in the leadership of the company in 1946.[12]

Another newborn business was first announced in an advertisement tucked away in an unpretentious column of the 12 November 1899 issue of the *Chattanooga Times:* "Drink a bottle of Coca-Cola, five cents at all stands, grocers, and saloons." At least three small bottlers were producing carbonated drinks in Chattanooga by 1897, but this ad proclaimed something quite novel. The Chattanooga Coca-Cola Bottling Company, located at 23 Patten Parkway and owned by J. F. Johnston and Ben F. Thomas, was not only the first franchised bottler of the drink but also one of an expanding number whose headquarters were located here.

Ben F. Thomas moved to this area as a struggling young lawyer with hopes for a successful business career. While in Cuba as a soldier in the Spanish American War, he was impressed with the extensive sales of bottled carbonated beverages. As he considered the idea, he began to understand the success of the business: a cheap product with imbibers ready for repeat consumption. The first crucial step meant finding a beverage with a distinctive flavor and name.

Back home, Thomas shared his idea with a lawyer friend, Joseph B. Whitehead, who enthusiastically concurred, and the two decided to try to get the bottling rights for a popular fountain drink which claimed medicinal value called Coca-Cola®. It was the property at this time of Asa G. Candler, who had incorporated the Atlanta-based business in 1892.

Candler, at first reluctant to expand his operation beyond a fountain syrup supply service, finally agreed to give without compensation the bottling rights to Thomas and Whitehead. Candler would supply the syrup at a stated price. On 12 July 1899, they signed a contract which gave the Chattanoogans the right to bottle Coca-Cola throughout the United States with but a few specifically stated territorial exceptions. Actually this agreement was the foundation on which a worldwide bottling business eventually grew.

The two novice bottlers, needing additional capital, found a third partner in a young fellow townsman, John Thomas Lupton, a Virginian who had left his native state in 1887. Trained in the law at the University of Virginia, he, however, turned to business when he took the post as treasurer of the newly founded Chattanooga Medicine Company. As the three involved themselves in the widening scope of the managerial and financial problems of their burgeoning enterprise, they made several major policy decisions.

First, they agreed to split the bottling territory: Thomas received the populous eastern portion of the United States while Whitehead and Lupton controlled most of the vast remaining area of the country. The second policy determined the structure of the operational organization which both groups planned to use. It consisted of a franchise system for the bottling and distribution of Coca-Cola which planned to seek individuals in all parts of the country who could establish and manage plants in their home communities. These local bottling companies would get syrup from the parent company, benefit from its promotional assistance, and operate on standards and business ethics approved by it. As a local bottler in the franchise plan, the Chattanooga Coca-Cola Bottling Company of Thomas and Johnston opened for business in 1899.

Marketing developed slowly. Only a two-mule wagon was needed to make deliveries; ten cases a day seemed to be a fair sale. By 1909 the local plant ran four teams and wagons for city and suburban routes. Various anti-Coke campaigns, sharp competition, and lawsuits growing out of attempts at trademark infringement plagued the management.

In 1904 Ben Thomas brought a seventeen-year-old nephew, George Hunter, to Chattanooga to train as his eventual successor in the Coca-Cola business. Thomas by this time had sold his share of the local bottling plant and was concentrating his attention on the parent company. Ten years after Hunter arrived, Thomas's death thrust the young man into the top position of the company, which in 1909 had 379 bottling franchises in operation. Ever alert to the importance of attractive marketing techniques, the company advertised widely and in

1915 created the "hobble-skirt" bottle designed to be recognized full, empty, or broken.

Fundamental changes were made later on. So that Ben Thomas would not be forgotten, the name Coca-Cola Bottling Company was renamed in 1929 the Coca-Cola Bottling Co. (Thomas), Inc., and in the 1930s Lupton and Whitehead sold their organization and the entire territory it served to the mother company in Atlanta.

Coca-Cola had greater meaning for Hamilton County than that of the usual successful local business. Persons from the area took bottling franchises and either moved to their territory or placed others in managerial positions. Three men, for example, who had been connected with the incline railway left town and set up Coca-Cola plants: John Carson in Evansville, Luther Carson in Paducah, and James E. Crass in Richmond. Earnings from Coca-Cola investments brought funds to the Chattanooga area, some of which went into other industries or retail outlets. Moreover, independently owned local businesses associated with the industry got an early and strong start: the Chattanooga Glass Company has sold bottles since 1901; Temple-Chattanooga has made beverage cases since 1917; and the Cavalier Corporation has manufactured coolers since the 1930s. [13]

In addition to textile, insurance, and Coca-Cola interests, around the turn of the century Chattanooga gained a second strong newspaper. Since the Civil War a host of journals had appeared with great initial fanfare only to suspend operations after a short run. On 1 July 1888, the *Evening News* published its first edition under the masthead of Jerome B. Pound, a young Georgian who had gained some experience in journalism in Macon. On his arrival in Chattanooga this ambitious, self-made twenty-one-year-old boldly announced the start of his daily, which would be Democratic in its political views. The fact that the *Times* was Democratic and that the vigorous local Republican party had no mouthpiece did not influence Pound. As an exponent of municipal progress and civic pride he was a genuine community booster. Although the *News* endured lean times, Pound published regularly until 1909, when he sold the newspaper to George Fort Milton, Sr., Curtis B. Johnson, and Walter C. Johnson. [14]

The real estate boom helped breed many small banking institutions, but, like the newspaper record, most had very little capital and very short lives. However, some, either by absorption or merger, evolved as solid institutions in the years following the 1893 panic.

To facilitate local transactions the Chattanooga Clearing House Association organized in January 1890 with T. G. Montague as president. Representatives of the six member banks met at stated times and placed "all the checks each bank had against the others, drawing out the amount the checks entitled them to." All this was done informally and no records existed until 1901 when "it was voted that the secretary buy a minute book for the association, and charge each bank with its share of the expense." Ten years later Frank A. Nelson was elected manager of the Clearing House and provisions were made for office space and a stenographer.

In 1905 associates of Thomas Ross Preston organized the Hamilton National Bank. Preston moved to Chattanooga from the small town of Woodbury, Tennessee, in 1889 and at first worked as a messenger for the South Chattanooga Savings Bank. He advanced rapidly to the position of cashier and later president. The Hamilton started with a $250,000 capitalization; Preston was president, H. T. Olmstead and G. H. Miller vice-presidents. Six years later the bank moved into a fifteen- story building at Seventh and Market streets. In 1920 the bank stockholders purchased the stock of the Hamilton Trust and Savings Bank (formerly the South Chattanooga Savings Bank); nine years later the two institutions merged, creating the largest bank in East Tennessee.

The American Trust and Banking Company opened for business in 1912 with Harry Scott Probasco as president. Associated with Probasco were E. Y. Chapin, vice-president and trust officer; Scott L. Probasco, vice-president; and D. H. Griswold, cashier. Harry S. Probasco, moving from his native Ohio, decided in 1885 to make Chattanooga his home. He represented the seventh generation of an American family which had emigrated from Madrid, Spain. Starting in the brokerage business, in partnership with F. F. Wiehl, he set up a private banking concern. The business prospered and in 1900 the bank was chartered under the name Bank of Chattanooga, with Probasco as president and Z. C. Patten, Sr., vice-president. Later this institution's banking business was taken over by the American National Bank which in turn was absorbed by the First National Bank in 1911. Probasco then moved to the newly organized American Trust and Banking Company as president; in 1948 the company became a national bank, using the name American National Bank and Trust Company. Probasco's son, Scott L. Probasco, joined his father in the bank while also making a place for himself as a cultural and civic leader in the community.

A third major bank received its charter on 9 February 1916, the

Morris Plan Bank, which developed a brisk business under Gaston C. Raoul. After more than twenty years the bank underwent a major change; on 5 November 1938 it became the Pioneer Bank and instituted regular commercial banking business under George M. Clark.[15]

The most visible sign of the more prosperous days at the turn of the century appeared in many physical changes. The fortifications at Fort Wood and the last of the old wartime hospitals that once dotted College Hill were razed. The removal of the Stone Fort from the center of Chattanooga took place in January 1905. The first McCallie Avenue viaduct, finished in 1903, eliminated the dangerous railroad crossing just east of town and the name Rouhs Crossing gave way as a place name to Highland Park.

Work on the Stringer's Ridge tunnel was finished in 1910 and spoke volumes, it was claimed, "for the alertness of the public mind to grasp opportunities for general betterment." Judge S. M. Walker promoted the project on which most of the work was done by workhouse convicts without the aid of "a single expert tunnel builder." It opened the door to the north for farmers and truckers and attracted much attention from the traveling public. Many people made a special trip when the approaches were completed that spring "just to see what it would feel like going underneath instead of over the ridge." As the people north of the river cheered, those who watched the slow work on the Missionary Ridge tunnel had to wait another three years before the hard pull over the ridge was eliminated.[16] Another major development was the opening of the Market Street bridge in 1917.

The Fireman's Fountain, dedicated 9 June 1888 in honor of heroes Henry Iler and W. M. Peck who died in the disastrous Bee Hive store fire at Fourth and Market streets the previous year, gave a new appearance to the courthouse block. Fine new homes crowned the river bluff, made a neighborhood of the Fort Wood section, and appeared in scattered areas in Riverview and on Missionary Ridge.

The one building (Old Main) of Chattanooga University built in 1886 dominated the heights along McCallie Avenue. Commanding another vista, the Times Building (1892) was a landmark easily recognized by its domed corner bay. A city auditorium (1897), a Romanesque Revival post office (1895), a city hall of Classic Revival lines (1907), and Central High School in Ridgedale (1908) gave new character to the area along with the buildings of Erlanger Hospital (1899).

The hospital created the city's foundation for modern health care. After a twelve-year struggle to found it, the facility opened on 17 July

1899 with a capability of caring for seventy-two patients. Drs. G. A. Baxter and Hiram Chamberlain led the effort to build this hospital with a $5,000 gift from Baron Erlanger. Citizens contributed funds to an association which acquired a four-acre tract on the edge of the city. But the panic years made satisfactory financing impossible. So the structure, consisting of two four-story buildings or wings connected by a covered walkway, stood empty for nearly ten years. The buildings were purchased at a trustee sale by the city and county, but additional funds were needed to furnish the hospital and carry on repairs. Finally a four-man board of trustees (C. D. Mitchell, president; Dr. G. A. Baxter, E. G. Richmond, and W. B. Swaney), with appropriations from Hamilton County and Chattanooga, completed one wing. By 1899 some $50,000 had been spent and one section was still unfinished. At that time it was announced that patients would be charged "according to their station in life and the service they received"; Dr. Baxter estimated that charges would range from fifty cents to two dollars a day.[17]

A strikingly beautiful new building, the Hamilton County Courthouse, was dedicated in 1913. It stands where the earlier structure had been struck by lightning in the violent storm of 7 May 1910. The new building, designed by Reuben H. Hunt, who began his architectural career in the area in the 1880s, cost $350,000. It featured Tennessee gray marble, a glazed tile roof, and a colored-glass dome. On the courthouse grounds were placed statues honoring Confederate General A. P. Stewart of Tennessee, who campaigned in the area in 1863, and John Ross, "Indian Chief, Loyal Cherokee, Great American."

Among the larger new buildings for worship were the Old Stone Church of the Methodist Episcopal congregation (1885), St. Paul's Episcopal Church with its brickwork and arches (1888), and the Victorian Gothic brick of Sts. Peter and Paul Catholic Church (1889). Sanctuaries for the black community included the First Baptist (Shiloh) Church (1885) and the Wiley Memorial United Methodist Church (1887). Facing each other across McCallie Avenue rose the First Presbyterian Church (1910), designed by the famed architects McKim, Meade, and White, and Christ Episcopal Church (1908), which in 1929 had its interior remodeled according to the plans of the celebrated church architect, Ralph Adams Cram.

Scattered throughout the area a number of professional and business structures gave the city a new profile: the Pound Building (1906); the Hotel Patten (1908); the Southern Railway Terminal Station (1909), now the Chattanooga Choo-Choo; the James Building (1908), claimed as the town's first skyscraper; a City Hall (1908); the Signal Mountain Inn (1913); the Volunteer Building (1917); and the Carnegie Library (1905).

Efforts to establish a library had been repeatedly undertaken by interested individuals. As early as 1867 a library association maintained rooms and a small book collection. This little library, however, apparently was not continued. Twenty years later the only source of books of which there is record was a circulating library run from a drugstore, with the proprietor giving his time and store space to support it. In December 1887 another library association encouraged by the chamber of commerce was organized; its financial support came only from individual contributions and funds raised by public entertainments. Xenophen Wheeler as president headed a group of 353 members with an annual income of two thousand dollars. At a gathering in 1889 more than one thousand persons expressed an interest in the project, but the panic of 1893 almost snuffed out this enthusiasm as business fell prostrate.

Around 1900 a group of lawyers demonstrated how to develop a "working" book collection. In the destruction of the Richardson Building by fire in 1897 many of the privately owned law book collections in the area were burned. Since these volumes, some rare and all expensive, had been accumulated over the years, few if any of the attorneys were in a position to replace them, but their work required the reference books. So the lawyers incorporated a Bar and Law Library Association by buying a collection of books with money from stock subscriptions and annual dues.

The small library association of 1887 weathered the economic storm of 1893 only because of the enthusiasm of certain of its supporters and the appropriation of $50 per month by the city of Chattanooga. But much more was needed. In 1900 the chamber of commerce sent Fred Ferger and John H. Race to call on Andrew Carnegie, who had generously given money to found libraries across the country. Carnegie promised a gift of $50,000 to construct a library building; the city in 1902 agreed to acquire a site for the structure and to appropriate at least $5,000 annually for its maintenance. City officials bought land at the corner of East Eighth Street and Georgia Avenue and held cornerstone ceremonies on 15 April 1904. The library opened the following year in July as a free reading room and reference library, adding a circulating department by year's end. In 1906 Mrs. Caroline E. Richmond endowed and furnished a children's room as a memorial to her late husband, E. G. Richmond, textile executive and library trustee.

A desire to expand service to county residents resulted in enactment of needed legislation empowering the Hamilton County Court to appropriate adequate money to the library; in the fall of 1909 Hamilton County made funds available to help support the library.[18]

The earliest library committee also promoted dramatics, and later amateur groups such as the Concordia Club and the Phoenix Club sponsored theatricals. In so doing, they carried on a tradition begun during the Civil War when a large tent sheltered performers on the north side of Sixth Street between Cherry and Market Streets. Crowds gathered through 1866 to witness performances which, it must be added, were not noted for their especially high standards.

The first building regularly used for dramatics was Kaylor Hall, where a second-story room was cleared out in August 1869. It served as an amusement center and at times was called a theater, although it had no stage. Edwin Forrest, booked here for a three-night stand, looked over the place and "became wroth to the profanity pitch" and refused to go on. It so happened that at Sixth and Market streets there was a new building, James Hall, which had not been completed on the interior. On the third floor a carpenter finished a temporary stage, others collected chairs, and someone put up stage wings and screens of white domestic. Forrest put on his show; Chattanoogans paid $1.50 for what was held to be "a mighty event theatrical." The year was 1870.

This third-floor theater or "showhouse," as it was commonly called, staged a variety of performances until a skating fad made it more profitable for the management to use it as a rink. Then when enthusiasm for this type of entertainment waned, operas, musicals, plays, and minstrel shows returned. As a railroad junction town, Chattanooga had an advantage in booking such stars as Edwin Booth, Joseph Jefferson, Julia Marlowe Taber, and John McCullough.

As the real estate boom days neared, the people, more affluent, grew dissatisfied with the James Hall accommodations and, under the aegis of Adolph Ochs, founded the New Opera House Company. Forty men formed a stock company and raised $40,000 with which to renovate the old theater.

On 4 October 1886, the New Opera House opened its first season. The entrance from Market Street was "inclosed by gates of filigree iron"; the box office was at the foot "of the grand staircase leading up to the theater proper, which had been dropped from the third to the second floor." The theater, heated by steam and lighted by gas, had acoustics which were "guaranteed," and the entire building was declared to be "almost absolutely fireproof." The house, which could accommodate more than one thousand patrons, had a gallery and one balcony reserved for blacks. On occasions, the theater could be converted into a ballroom or "grand" supper room. The Opera House, later called the Lyric, was the cultural center of Hamilton County for a number of years.

The Bijou Opera Company ushered in "Opera Festival Week," consisting of six night performances and one matinee. The community outdid itself in making preparations. "The dressmakers of the city," it was reported, "have been busy all week, and it is said that there will be the finest display of fashionable and elegant toilets on the opening night, ever seen in Chattanooga. . . . A number of gentlemen will attend in full dress suits. It will be a magnificent display of Chattanooga's fashion and wealth and an occasion long to be remembered."

The newspapers carried lists of the scheduled engagements for Opera Festival Week, accompanied by a suggestion of appropriate neckwear for the gentlemen to wear at each show:

The Princess of Trebizonde	a Teck Scarf
The Mikado	a four-in-hand
The Bohemian Girl	a Windsor tie
The Bridal Trap	a sailor knot
Fra Diavolo	a Claudent Scarf
The Chimes of Normandy	a Dude Tie

When Sarah Bernhardt came to perform in *Camille* in the spring of 1906, she was invited to lay the cornerstone for a new theater, the Shubert, on Eleventh Street. Crowds of people anxious to see the great French star waded through mud and water and stood in the cold, blustery March weather. But the famed actress never stirred from her hotel. After a long delay and an unsuccessful effort on the part of the management to arrange a belated ceremony the crowd reluctantly dispersed. Bernhardt had sent a message to the mayor, who had planned to serve as master of ceremonies, but because it was written in French, which neither the city's chief executive nor his aides could read, the prima donna's apology was never understood.[19]

When James Hall was razed in 1913 to make room for a commercial enterprise, a reporter noted, "There is probably no building in all of Chattanooga which is dearer to old residents."

Changes were just as pronounced in formal education during this period. County high schools were established, while parochial and private schools broadened their educational opportunities. In 1886 the Catholics dedicated a new brick school building at the corner of Eighth and Lindsay streets. They reported 250 students in attendance and a faculty of twelve. This parochial school, named Notre Dame, actually had originated ten years earlier when its first classes met in the basement of the church then in use. Four sisters of the Third Order of St. Dominic coming from the motherhouse at St. Cecilia in Nashville pioneered the movement and set the standards for the sisters who served the school in the days ahead.

Baylor School, in early days referred to as University School, opened in 1893 under the guidance of J. Roy Baylor, a graduate of the University of Virginia. Beginnings were modest for this first male "pay school" (tuition, $100) and enrollment was limited to day students. In 1900 Baylor moved the school from the corner of McCallie and Lindsay Streets to 611 Palmetto Street. A growing student body soon produced fundamental changes; the school was incorporated in 1914 and a board of trustees, with J. T. Lupton as its first president, became the policy-making body of the nonprofit institution. Plans were already under way to move in 1915 to a new campus. The new facility would be located on the Tennessee River at the base of Walden Ridge some four miles from the city, where both day and boarding students could be accommodated.

A second private school for boys was started on a site donated by Reverend Thomas Hooke McCallie on the slope of Missionary Ridge, which had been a part of his old family homestead. The initiative came from McCallie's sons, Professor Spencer J. McCallie and Dr. J. Park McCallie. With their brother, Ed, and Lem White as fellow teachers they opened the school in 1905 with fifty-eight students. The officials of this school, which was located three miles outside the city, advised the parents of early students that the site enjoyed a special advantage: "The boys are cut aloof from the temptations incident to the city school." Through the years the program of McCallie School has been expanded and in 1937 it became a nonprofit institution under a board of trustees.

A year after the launching of McCallie School, three Chattanooga teachers, Grace McCallie, Tommy Payne Duffy, and Eula Lea Jarnagin, laid the groundwork for a private school for girls. Named the Girls' Preparatory School (GPS), its purpose was to offer a program designed to fulfill requirements for college admission. The first classes in 1906 met at 106 Oak Street; fifty students made up the student body. Having outgrown these limited facilities, the school moved in 1915 to the building then just recently vacated by Baylor School. In 1947 GPS moved to a campus in North Chattanooga; it had been incorporated two years earlier.

In the area of higher education, the administration of John H. Race (1897–1913) marks the modern beginning of the University of Tennessee at Chattanooga. Race, at thirty-five years of age, came south from his native Pennsylvania to Athens, Tennessee; he held both a bachelor's and a master's degree from Princeton University and was an ordained Methodist minister. His acceptance of the position as chancellor of the local institution testified to his energy and dedication, for the job description was anything but inviting. It read, "The Chancellor is certainly the President. He would be expected to teach and to meet the necessities of the school and Faculty. . . . [He also] ought every Sunday to be in a pulpit [and visit] all the patronizing territory, drumming up students, preaching, raising money, etc."

Twenty-five years had passed since members of the Methodist Episcopal Church in Chattanooga had discussed the creation of a university. They enlisted town support as well as that of the national church organization, emphasizing the desirability of establishing a central university for the south. Administrators of a church school at Athens, Tennessee, the East Tennessee Wesleyan College of the Holston Conference (also affiliated with the northern Methodist Church), had aspirations of their institution becoming the central university, and an unavoidable rivalry developed between the towns of Athens and Chattanooga.

The national church was interested. Its educational program administered by the Freedmen's Aid Society, provided "for the education and special aid of Freedmen and others." Under this policy the church supported both a black and a white college in Little Rock, Arkansas. In Chattanooga, although there was some talk about racial coeducation at the time the church's site committee selected Chattanooga for the university, no one actually foresaw a challenge to the traditional separation of the races.

The charter for Chattanooga University, granted on 8 July 1886, established a board of trustees to manage the institution, of which sixteen were local men. Strong figures in this group were General Wilder, David M. Key, Captain H. S. Chamberlain, and Dr. John J. Manker.[20] Classes first met in the fall of 1886 under the strict control of the faculty, which passed regulations forbidding "unnecessary noise, coarse or profane language, and the use of tobacco . . ."

The total enrollment numbered 240 students: of this group, only 26 were in the collegiate curriculum, 29 in the school of theology, and, as a significant index of the condition of public education at the time, all others were registered in the preparatory department or were special students. At the end of the session three persons graduated from the college and four from the preparatory school. All were out-of-town boarding students.

Much of the enthusiasm of the planning years vanished as troubled days early descended on the inexperienced administrators of the new institution. By matriculation time two written applications for admission and three verbal ones had been filed by blacks. The next term, two Athens blacks sought admission. From the local point of view the acceptance of black students was impossible, while spokesmen for the church seemed to disagree. Many aspects of the issue indicate a relationship between the applicants and the Athens college rivalry.

The situation took on greater proportions as word of an unfortunate incident in a downtown church bookstore reached every ear. A university professor visiting the store either refused or failed to acknowledge an introduction to a black minister. Several versions of this incident, some certainly distorted, found their way into the national press. The local board of trustee members took a different position regarding the matter than did the church authorities, and there was some possibility that the professor's contract might be terminated. He eventually was relieved of his position and local enthusiasm for the school markedly declined. This unfortunate affair created more tension than did the much more fundamental issue of the matriculation of blacks. Enrollment in the fall of 1887 dropped to 104, with an obvious decline in Hamilton County and other Tennessee students.

The final solution to the troubles, effected in 1889, provided for a merger of the Athens and Chattanooga schools under the name U. S. Grant University. Administrative offices were located in Athens and collegiate work discontinued at Chattanooga, where only the professional schools of medicine, theology, and law functioned. With the appointment of Dr. Race as president, a series of changes resulted in the rehabilitation of the Chattanooga campus.

President Race first changed his residence to Chattanooga and in 1904 reopened the undergraduate college. Three years later, by charter amendment, the school's name was changed to the University of

Chattanooga. The first regular football schedule was begun in 1905 and in the fall of 1908 playing fields were graded, small stands erected, and the facility dedicated to Captain Hiram Chamberlain. On 21 May 1909, the Methodist Episcopal Church deeded all its local property to a self-perpetuating board of trustees. One year later all the professional schools, whose standards had been marginal at best, were discontinued so that all possible resources could be channeled toward accredited undergraduate instruction.

Dr. Race's emphasis on a harmonious "town-gown" relationship, coupled with his successful restoration of confidence in the university, led citizens of the area to build a presidential residence on the campus for him and Mrs. Race. In recognition of the institution's improved academic standards, the Association of Colleges and Secondary Schools for the southern states invited the University of Chattanooga to become its twenty-first collegiate member. Shortly after the Race administration ended in 1913, ground was broken for a gymnasium, classroom buildings, administrative quarters, and the John A. Patten Memorial Chapel. On 16 November 1917, classes met for the first time in the new buildings; Old Main was razed.[21]

Hamilton County just missed having a second college during these years. For some time appeals had been made to establish a state college for blacks; by 1896 all former Confederate states except Tennessee had, with federal support, formed land-grant colleges for blacks. After much delay and politically motivated postponements some state money was provided in 1911 to establish the Tennessee Agricultural & Industrial State Normal School (A & I). Communities competing for the school were expected to make financial commitments.

Towns and cities across Tennessee shied away from the project; only Nashville and Chattanooga made efforts to attract the institution. But Nashville voters defeated a bond issue and enthusiasm waned in the Middle Tennessee city. Meanwhile Chattanoogans made a positive effort to get the school, spearheaded by William Jasper Hale. Hale, a young black teacher and elementary school principal, raised more than $10,000 among local blacks and got a promise of $60,000 from the Hamilton County Court. This apparent success was short-lived, for Nashville then reconsidered, offered an attractive fund, and won the votes of the State Board of Education.

Although Hamilton County failed to get the school, Hale's devoted interest in the project caught the serious attention of the authorities, despite his lack of much formal education, and he was selected to head the new school. Politically astute and counting on a number of white friends, he followed a conservative educational philosophy and under spartan conditions guided Tennessee A & I from 1912 until his retirement in 1943. In the early years of his tenure Hale enjoyed the support of his Hamilton County colleagues, who sent more students to the college than any other county except Davidson, for at least the first fifteen years.[22]

Education occupied much of the attention of John A. Patten, recognized by all as the area's leader in civic and religious affairs. Throughout his adult career he was an aggressive and generous member of the board of trustees of the University of Chattanooga, a one-time member of the Hamilton County Board of Education, and a member of the General Board of Education of the Methodist Episcopal Church.

Patten, brought to Chattanooga as a lad, first worked as an office boy for the Chattanooga Medicine Company owned by his uncle Z. C. Patten and his father George Patten. As time passed, the young man was appointed managing director and then president of the firm. In addition to his catholic interests, Patten served as head of three river packet lines during the declining years of the steamboat era. His interest in the Tennessee River and its navigation problems readily earned him distinction as the "dominating river spirit of the whole Tennessee Valley."

A valley group on which Patten's impact was keenly felt organized in 1898 as the Tennessee River Improvement Association. While the principal concern of Chattanoogans centered on navigation improvements, they also hoped that river traffic would help bring about reduced railroad freight rates. Recognizing the limitations of piecemeal river improvements and the failure of pork-barrel legislation to effect major betterment, the association called for "complete improvements of the Tennessee River" to regulate its flow and conserve its volume.[23]

The association's members received solid support from local congressman John Austin Moon. Born in Virginia in 1855, Moon entered the practice of law in Hamilton County when he was nineteen years old. He later served as circuit court judge until his election to the House of Representatives in 1897. For the next twenty-four years he repeatedly won this seat until his death in 1921.[24]

Moon advocated river improvement, insisting that it be based on systematic planning for the entire stream rather than a continuation of appropriations to separate states or districts. His thinking was in harmony with the growing conservation movement of this era. Moreover, developing national interest in hydroelectric power turned the attention of engineers and scientists to river planning. This desire to develop a new source of energy led to a major new issue for Congress: should potential hydropower sites be awarded to any individual or company willing to develop them for profit, or should they be managed as a public resource and developed by one of society's political institutions?

The congressman's views on this latter subject corresponded with those of President Theodore Roosevelt: Moon maintained that waterpower sites used to generate electricity should be granted to municipalities. In 1902 he introduced legislation calling for the construction of a dam below the Suck with power rights awarded to Chattanooga, but the measure was not heartily supported by local businessmen and was consequently dropped.

Two years later Moon introduced a second bill calling for the construction of a dam in Marion County below the rough mountain waters where the natural fall of the river was a great advantage. The dam, to be built according to the design of the U.S. Army Engineers, provided for navigation improvements and the generation of electricity. The cost of the dam was to be borne by the recipient of the power franchise, which was to continue for ninety-nine years; the locks were to be provided by the government, which would hold title to the dam. The city of Chattanooga would have the option on the generating rights. This measure became law on 27 April 1904.

The city made a hasty study of the project, estimated to cost some $3 million, and declined the option. At this point the franchise went to Josephus C. Guild, an engineer who had had an interest in the Lookout Mountain Incline No. 2 and who was a supporter of the developing electrical business, and Charles E. James, Chattanooga's well-known promoter and financier. These two men made a vigorous team and soon gained the financial support of Anthony W. Brady, New York utility financier.

The three organized the Chattanooga and Tennessee River Power Company and began work in 1905 after the dam site had been relocated at Hales Bar, thirty-three miles downriver from the city. Progress was discouragingly slow because of a limestone foundation. Guild passed away and his son, Jo Conn Guild, took his place. The cost of the 1,200-foot structure more than tripled by the time it was completed. Before the task was finished, hydroelectric power was made available in Chattanooga from dams on the Ocoee River. This competitive venture, promoted by local contractor J. W. Adams, was constructed by E. W. Clark & Company of Philadelphia and financially supported by Drexel & Company.

A dinner preceded the formal ribbon cutting at the Hales Bar Lock and Dam, scheduled for 13 November 1913. The dual purpose of the dam was readily realized by the crowd of onlookers who sailed the *James N. Trigg* and the *Joe Wheeler* downriver to the dedication the next day. They rode over the Suck, the Pot, the Skillet, and all the rough waters of the valley of the Whirlpool Rapids. John A. Patten, speaking for the Tennessee River Improvement Association, praised the slack-water pool which reached back to Chattanooga; submergence was the way to overcome navigation obstacles. "Some of us yesterday," Patten commented in his annual address to the Association, "sailed over and past drowned farms, good rich bottom land. And none of us, not even the men who owned the farms, is the worse for it."

Two little girls threw the switch at the dam; a surge of energy raced along the wires to Chattanooga. It lighted a large sign on the James Building and touched off one of the biggest celebrations in the area's history. All the power generated at the dam was under contract to be delivered to Chattanooga and the restless waters of the Tennessee were under harness. The city boosters developed a proud slogan: "the dynamo of Dixie."[25]

This slogan seemed to forecast coming technological developments. By 1920 the Clark-Drexel interests, owners of the Ocoee River facilities and of streetcar projects in Chattanooga and Nashville, held merger talks with the Guild-Brady people and as a consequence in early June 1922 the negotiations ended in a consolidation under the name, the Tennessee Electric Power Company. A year later, energy demands necessitated adding to the power facilities at Hales Bar, where a steam plant was built. The energy from the flowing waters and the fossil fuel of the mountains pushed Hamilton County into the modern age.

There were some who believed Hales Bar Dam generated another "power," that of reducing floods. Nature tested this theory as early as 1917. As in 1867, March rains and melting snows in the mountains caught the people by surprise. They had paid little heed to notices because twelve times in the last seventeen years the danger point had been reached without serious damage. On 3 March the mayor of Chattanooga saw the need to appoint a relief committee; four days later the river crested at 47.7 feet in the gorge. All of South Chattanooga was covered with muddy water. An extreme wave of cold weather inten-

sified the suffering. The black school at Orchard Knob served an unusual purpose; its furnace room was turned into temporary quarters
for the neighborhood chickens. One dairyman who had to drive his
herd to Missionary Ridge gave his entire milk supply to the relief
committee, which had raised over $25,000 and helped man two public
soup kitchens. There was some looting in the form of boat stealing and
a few "boat pirates" used the flood to their advantage. Hales Bar Dam
did nothing to reduce the flood damage, but two rather new inventions
were put to good use during the floodtide: the telephone and the
automobile.[26]

Nothing did more to change the life-style of Hamilton Countians in
the first decades of the new century than the motorcar. It shortened
the traveler's day, cut marketing costs, broadened the scope of school,
church, and health services, made neighbors out of strangers, helped
criminals escape the law, sharpened Cupid's arrow, demanded engineered roads, and created new business opportunities. It was too novel
a device to be accepted in a short time, and it also had to face the
challenge of the competing livery stable people, the horse and mule
trader, and the carriage and harness interests.

The first Chattanooga listing of auto sales and service was found in
the 1903 city directory. The Chattanooga Automobile Company, established two years later, advertised as the "only garage." The Wallace
Buggy Company, sellers of buggies, wagons, and harness, and agents
for the Cartercar, Stoddard-Dayton, and Maxwell, by its very name
tells what was happening. In addition to the models offered by the
buggy company, Cadillacs, Stearns, Marmons, Franklins, or Stanley
Steamers could be purchased in Chattanooga. One seller reported that
he took a bicycle as down payment on a car and that he drove the car
to the customer and rode the wheel back.

By 1906 a journalist wrote that autos were a common sight in the
area and some fifty to sixty were owned locally. In three years this
number increased to 250 owners, with some possessing more than one
machine. An estimate in 1909 placed the number owned in the county
at 350.[27]

That year the automobile got a tremendous local boost and Chattanooga found itself in the national spotlight. Under the sponsorship
of the Lookout Mountain Automobile Club of Chattanooga, one of the
biggest sporting events in Hamilton County's history took place on
22 April. A thrilling motor race up the winding Lookout Mountain road
attracted wide publicity. On this bright spring day, a crowd estimated

at fifty thousand people lined the route from St. Elmo to the very mountaintop. They came with picnic baskets to shady spots or as guests of cottage owners to witness a sport that involved speed, danger, daring, and skill.

Big-name drivers representing the Buick national racing team dominated the field: Lewis Strang, Bob Burman, and the flashy Frenchman Louis Chevrolet. The course, 4.9 miles of winding road, had sixty-three turns and hairpin curves and demanded all their skill. Some entrants who drove big cars had to drop out of the competition because they could not get them around such spots as "Moccasin Bend," "Undertaker's Delight," or the "Spine Scratcher." Chevrolet made the record time of 6 minutes, 30.4 seconds, but his run was unofficial because he had made several starts to get past the first mile.

Little boys dashed from one turn to another so that they would not miss any accidents (Creed Bates was one) or sold spring water for a nickel from a common cup. The race route was patrolled by the state militia to keep the way clear, but an enterprising insurance firm nevertheless advised, "Invest 25 cents for an accident policy before going to the races. The mountain roads are narrow and dangerous, the crowd will be large and in spite of the military protection, you are liable to be injured."

The mountain race stimulated fresh popular interest in the automobile. Sales of all models increased and businesses began to use delivery trucks. Coca-Cola used a delivery car by 1912 and some buses came into use about 1915. By 1920 an auto truck carried pupils to the Soddy High School while a wagon continued to be used for grammar school students. At Tyner, four motor trucks transported students to high school; younger pupils continued to walk to neighborhood schools despite the growing trend toward consolidation. In 1920 trucks finally replaced horses for mail service and the last horse of the Chattanooga police force was retired to permanent pasture. That same year an ordinance prohibited horse-drawn vehicles on Market Street.[28]

Another result of the automobile race was renewed discussion of the need for an additional Tennessee River bridge. The press revealed not only the desirability of a second structure but also the suggestion of a route from Georgia Avenue crossing Chattanooga Island to Riverview; one rumor described stairs down to the island which would be converted into a "summer garden" or a "sort of Coney Island on a small scale." After years of discussion, engineers finally designed a new concrete span called simply the Market Street Bridge, later officially named the Chief John Ross Bridge.

Construction proved to be slow; costs doubled during building and reached the million-dollar mark. The biggest problem encountered came from the untamed river, which in 1915 challenged the builder's intrusion on its free spirit. A journalist's report tells that "Span No.3 on the Market Street bridge went out yesterday morning Dec. 19, 1915, at 8:30 in a 38-foot stage flood. Falsework and forms reinforced ready for pouring of concrete were swept 10 miles down the river."

For hours men had battled to dislodge brush and logs which kept building up pressure against the forms. The temperature dropped, ice formed, and cracking timbers broke. The forty workmen finally had to climb away from the danger.

> The framework had buckled and twisted under the strain until we knew that it couldn't last much longer. Cracking of the timber was like the noise of a lot of fire crackers and then came a report like a cannon. The whole thing had burst. The south end collapsed first and then the north end and the entire 180 feet of it toppled like a house of cards. It was all away in a minute.

When the bridge was finally completed, the engineers not only gained a significant victory over the river but they had built one of the longest concrete bridges in the South. Most remarkable was its lifting apparatus called a bascule or balanced drawbridge. At the time, it was claimed to be the longest spanned, movable bridge in the world. "Like a huge monster of primeval days," a journalist wrote, "the big steel girders and beams . . . at a given signal and without apparent assistance of human craft, began to slowly leave their resting place."

At 3:18 P.M. on 16 November 1917 the bridge was formally opened. By nightfall it was reported that "practically everybody had availed themselves of the new passageway." The notion of building this bridge, the political struggle required to gain approval, and the patience needed to see it through construction were all the work of Judge Will Cummings. [29]

The new bridge was encouraging to automobile drivers but it further pointed up the additional need for good roads. Anyone who ventured out of town was indeed a hardy soul; mud holes, ruts, roots, rickety bridges, and steep grades often made it necessary to call on the mule of a nearby farmer to come to the motorist's rescue. A trip to Dalton, Georgia, by four members of the automobile club in 1916 took from 9 A.M. until 2:30 P.M. In 1917 "good road" promoters started out for Cincinnati; it took five days to get there and on one fourteen-mile stretch of a Kentucky road they spent thirteen hours. Another motor-cade in 1915 reported its experience; the drivers left Tullahoma in the morning, motored all day and all night, arriving in Chattanooga at 5 A.M.

In the fall of 1914 a group of local drivers organized the Chattanooga Automobile Club to promote improved roads. At that time there were no federal or state programs and no organized system to finance roads. Members of the club joined some midwestern enthusiasts to press for a north-south highway to Miami and soon took the lead in the campaign. In 1915 the governors of seven concerned states and others attended a large meeting in Chattanooga to introduce the proposal. They organized the Dixie Highway Association and elected as president Judge Michael M. Allison, a son of the Sequatchie Valley, who had moved to Chattanooga to serve as circuit judge.

In planning a great national highway, the first major problem was the designation of the route. Financing depended on local funds and some counties and communities refused to participate. As a consequence the final route was not the shortest or most direct but the most practicable under the circumstances. In the local area it descended from the Cumberland Mountains, crossed the Sequatchie Valley and wound its way over Suck Creek Mountain into Chattanooga; from there it turned toward Atlanta. On the top of Suck Creek Mountain, the highway's highest point, a marker to Allison reads:

In Appreciation
This memorial is erected by the people of the United States to mark their appreciation of the great service rendered our country by Judge M. M. Allison, president of the Dixie Highway Association, since its organization in 1915. The Dixie Highway was founded upon his faith, his hope, and his far vision; his indefatigable labor throughout the states wherein it winds its useful way made possible its realization.

By 1927 the Dixie Highway was almost completed. Most of the road had been graded and much of it paved from Detroit to the Florida city of Miami.[30]

Years before this, the sportsmen of the county found special activities in which to participate or to encourage as fans. When the Southern Baseball League organized in 1885, Chattanooga fielded a team as a charter member. The team dressed in a downtown storeroom and rode on a dray to the field back of the Stanton House. Some time later after the Southern franchise had lapsed, promoter O. B. Andrews had a Sally League team which by 1909 played under the name Lookouts.

For years the legendary Joe Engel brought baseball fame and promotional high jinks to the area while Doc and Jimmy Johnston represented the best of the local crop of major-league professional players.

Beginning about 1890 Olympia Park became a center for athletic activity. On a large tract of more than forty acres one of the streetcar companies sponsored this commercial venture. The park boasted a baseball diamond, racetrack, bandstand, skating rink, zoo, and other facilities; it featured harness races until the bicycle, motorcycle, and automobile brought more daring and thrilling events. In 1912 when the Electric Railway Company of Chattanooga changed hands, the city of Chattanooga bought the property, renaming it Warner Park, to honor J. H. Warner, the city commissioner responsible for its development as a public park.[31]

NOTES

1. U.S., Department of Commerce, Bureau of the Census, *Twelfth Census . . . 1900, Population*, pt. 1 (Washington, D.C.: Government Printing Office, 1901), pp. 39, 475, 520, 556.

2. *City Directory of Chattanooga and Suburbs, 1900* (Chattanooga, G.M. Connelly, 1900), 21:4.

3. U.S., Department of Commerce, Bureau of the Census, *Eleventh Census . . . 1890, Population*, pt. 1:320; Harry M. Wiltse, "History of Chattanooga" (Typescript, Chattanooga-Hamilton County Bicentennial Library), 2:115.

4. U.S., Department of Commerce, Bureau of the Census, *Twelfth Census . . . 1900, Population*, pt. 2:484, 636.

5. George W. Ochs, *Chattanooga and Hamilton County, Tennessee* (Chattanooga: Times Printing, 1897), pp. 16–20; *City Directory, 1886–1887*, 8:xxiv; Wiltse, "Chattanooga," 2:94; *Chattanooga Times*, 6 January 1896.

6. *City Directory, 1900*, 21:49–50.

7. Ochs, *Chattanooga and Hamilton County*, pp. 12, 16–20.

8. *City Directory, 1900*, 21:5, 35–36; Zella Armstrong, *History of Hamilton County and Chattanooga, Tennessee*, 2 vols. (Chattanooga: Lookout Publishing, 1931), 2:272.

9. The early accident insurance policies were sold on a "pay order" basis. The sale to employees of industries was a forerunner of modern group insurance and the "pay order" of payroll deduction. *Chattanooga Times*, 7 December 1960, carries a twenty-page advertising supplement tracing the firm's history from 1887 to 1960.

10. Ibid.

11. *City Directory, 1904*, xxiv, 447, 834.

12. Clipping file, Chattanooga-Hamilton County Bicentennial Library.

13. DeSales Harrison, *"Footprints on the Sands of Time": A History of Two Men and the Fulfillment of a Dream* (New York: Newcomen Society, 1969): *Chattanooga News-Free Press*, 9 June 1974 (Special supplement on seventy-fifth anniversary of the company); *Chattanooga Times*, 16 September 1971.

14. J. B. Pound, *Memoirs of Jerome B. Pound* (n.p.: author, 1949), pp. 37–43, 44–46; *Chattanooga News*, 26 July 1938, an anniversary edition with an article on the history of the paper by Walter Johnson.

15. *A History of Banking in Chattanooga* (Chattanooga: Hamilton National Bank, 1925), pp. 16–19, 22–23.

16. *Chattanooga Times*, 11, 20 March 1910. It was claimed that farmers coming to Chattanooga could carry loads twice as heavy as those that had to be wagoned over the steep ridge. Work on this tunnel began in 1908.

The McCallie Avenue tunnel encountered financial, legal, and engineering problems and, although begun in 1907, was not completed until 1913. This tunnel was rebuilt 1952–1955. The Bachman tubes were started in 1927 and the Avondale, or Wilcox, tunnel in 1930.

17. *Chattanooga Times*, 16 July 1899; 9 May 1900; 16, 18 February 1913. The medical staff at first consisted of G. A. Baxter, chief of staff; and Drs. H. Berlin, George R. West, W. G. Bogart, J. R. Rathmell, F. B. Stapp, D. E. Nelson, B. S. West, E. A. Cobleigh, S. T. Rucker, Cooper Holtzclaw, physicians; Drs. N. C. Steele and B. F. Travis, oculists; Dr. E. C. Anderson, pathologist and bacteriologist; and Mrs. Adelaide Hicks, head nurse.

18. C. D. McGuffey, *Standard History of Chattanooga* (Knoxville: Crew & Dorey, 1911) pp. 274–283. The first directors of the Carnegie Library were A. N. Sloan, John H. Race, Z. W. Wheland, R. W. Healy, L. M. Coleman, H. Schwartz, E. G. Richmond, P. S. Poindexter, and M. Freeman.

19. Ibid., 295–296; *Chattanooga Times*, 17 March 1906; 17 March 1913; Marion P. Jones, "Some Notes for a History of the Chattanooga Theater, 1877–88" (Thesis, Duke University, 1942, typescript in Chattanooga-Hamilton County Bicentennial Library). Over the years the name of the building changed from James Hall to the Opera House, to the New Opera House, to the Lyric Theater, and to the Grand Theater.

20. Other local board members were J. W. Adams, architect; D. E. Reese, banker; J. F. Loomis and A. J. Gahagan, lumbermen; H. C. Beck, county official; Creed Bates, attorney; Samuel D. Wester, commission merchant; Drs. Joseph Van Deman and John R. Rathmell; and David Woodworth, tanner. Captain Chamberlain headed the board from 1890 to 1897 and from 1898 to 1916.

21. Gilbert E. Govan and James W. Livingood, *The University of Chattanooga: Sixty Years* (Chattanooga, University of Chattanooga, 1947), pp. 3–133.

22. Lester C. Lamon, *Black Tennesseans , 1900–1930* (Knoxville: University of Tennessee Press, 1977), pp. 88–109.

23. Gilbert E. Govan and James W. Livingood, *The Chattanooga Country*, 3rd ed. (Knoxville: University of Tennessee Press, 1977), pp. 442–443; *Chattanooga Times*, 27 April 1941.

24. A. M. Moon and J. Phillips, *John A. Moon, Father of the Parcel Post* (Chattanooga, Chattanooga Printing and Engraving, 1941), pp. 20–34.

25. Govan and Livingood, *Chattanooga Country*, pp. 445–448; *Chattanooga Times*, 28 April 1904, 14 November 1913; Nashville District, Corps of Engineers, *Engineers on the Twin Rivers: A History of the Nashville District Corps of Engineers, U. S. Army* (n.p., 1979), pp. 163–168.

26. *Chattanooga Times*, 3–8 March 1917.

27. Wiltse, "Chattanooga," 2:120; *Chattanooga Times*, 22 April 1899; *Chattanooga News-Free Press*, 8 June 1975.

28. Wiltse, "Chattanooga," 2:97; *Chattanooga Times*, 14 March, 22, 23 April 1909; *Chattanooga News-Free Press*, 16 April 1966; Charles A. McMurray, *Chattanooga: Its History and Geography* (Morristown: Globe, 1923), p. 191.

29. *Chattanooga Times*, 20 December 1915; 4 August, 17 November 1917; 27 August 1978.

30. Ibid., 16 August 1925; Govan and Livingood, *Chattanooga Country*, pp. 468–469.

31. *Chattanooga Times*, 7, 8, 15 February 1912; 12 April 1918; 4 May 1952; 18 September 1938. The East Lake Park is Chattanooga's oldest and for a time, beginning in 1906, it featured the Oxley Zoo. Boynton Park was created in 1903 and Lincoln Park in 1918. Some others were Houston Park, Jackson, Park, and Montague Park. Warner Park was dedicated 4 July 1912; later a rose garden, largely the work of Jack Brizzie, was made a park attraction.

16

Social and Cultural Debits and Credits

T HE life-style of the people of Hamilton County in large measure reflected their particular frontier surroundings as was the case in almost every part of the nation. In many of the less accessible regions this pioneering process lasted longer than in other areas of the country, leaving a persistent stamp on the local culture. It fashioned a heritage of self-reliance, independence of mind, and explosive passion. It molded a people with a certain strain of toughness; many were more handy with their fists and guns than with words. An old Tennessee adage, still in current usage, underscores this traditional attitude: "That lawsuit may be settled at the courthouse but it's not been settled up the holler yet."

The people of early generations, well acquainted with privation, misery, drudgery, and loneliness, lived close to the rhythm of a demanding wilderness, and society's civilizing process often appeared to be too weak or immature to restrain excess and violence. In addition, certain historical episodes left their marks on the local residents: the tragedy of the Cherokee removal and, a little more than a generation later, the brutality of civil war made indelible impressions. And life in a land infested with bushwhackers and guerrillas and burdened with poverty did little to encourage even a minimum respect for law.

Enforcement of the law, when it was accomplished, was often carried out with a savage intensity. For years Hamilton County, in keeping with long-established custom, announced public hangings which brought together a morbid and ruthless crowd of onlookers. "Public executions," the *Chattanooga Times* commented on 3 September 1881, "are barbarizing and disgraceful to our pretenses of refinement."

Hangings, not always public, continued in the county until 1908; three years later state law required that the gallows be destroyed and that all executions be carried out at the state penitentiary. Although there was crime aplenty during this era, Attorney General M. N. Whitaker, who held his position some sixteen years, summed up the local experience by saying that only six men were executed during his tenure; of this number only one was a black.[1]

Tragedy and violence often sprang from this rough pioneer heritage. Convivial, smart young Mat Taylor, for example, was involved in many Chattanooga brawls, shootings, and cuttings. A terror to the police, he never hesitated to fire on the city marshal on Market Street.

From 1879 to the present, twelve city police officers have been shot to death in line of duty. Possibly the most celebrated case of wanton murder of a lawman involved the death of the sheriff of Hamilton County. In 1881 as result of a personal quarrel John Taylor shot and killed John W. Fletcher on board the steamboat *Tellico*, tied up at the Chattanooga wharf. Although the two had worked together as rivermen, they fell into an argument over the installation of machinery on the packet or about the payment for work done.

Taylor fled the scene, seeking a haven among familiar haunts in Roane County. Sheriff H. J. "Jack" Springfield, a determined man, took up the fugitive's trail which led to the home of a friend of Taylor. The sheriff, working with a posse, surrounded the place, demanding the surrender of the suspect. Although he was told Taylor was not there, Springfield refused to be diverted. Further negotiations, however, proved fruitless until the sheriff threatened to burn down the house. Only then did Taylor surrender; he was placed in the Hamilton County jail to await trial.

A citizen's group headed by Hiram Chamberlain collected funds to engage lawyers to assist the attorney general in prosecuting Taylor. The case dragged on and on, bitterly fought at every turn. Eventually Taylor was pronounced guilty of voluntary manslaughter and sentenced to ten years' imprisonment. Taylor's supporters appealed the decision to the state supreme court, which had scheduled its fall session to be set in Knoxville. Under the law it was required that, in the hearing of an appeal of this sort, the prisoner be present in the court.

During the interval before the court sat, Hamilton County held its regular election. Sheriff Springfield, ineligible to succeed himself, gave up his office to W. T. Cate. Springfield, experienced and cautious, noticed that the prisoner had frequent jail visits from two brothers; he sensed trouble. He advised Cate not to let anyone know when he planned to take Taylor to Knoxville and to make the trip in a box car, not on a regular passenger train.

When the time came for the journey, however, Sheriff Cate and Deputy Sheriff John J. Conway took Taylor and several other prisoners, manacled together, on a regularly scheduled train. At Sweetwater, two men boarded and took seats in the coach with the group from Chattanooga, who did not appear to recognize them. They were Taylor's brothers, Bob and Andy. At a stop at the small hamlet of Philadelphia the Taylors found the opportunity to shoot Conway and Cate dead; John Taylor, according to one account, was wounded. As soon as his handcuffs were removed, the brothers went to the engine and at an appropriate spot ordered the engineer to stop the train so that they could strike out on foot.

Bloodhounds sought their trail without success. Posses organized, military companies were called to duty, and sheriffs' forces from several counties scoured the region. Excitement spread, reaching a fever pitch in Hamilton County. The funerals of Cate and Conway attracted a large crowd of mourners. The county court immediately reinstalled Jack Springfield to office and voted a reward of $2,500 for each of the Taylors dead or alive. Tennessee added another $5,000 for the capture of the three or one-third of that amount for each man. Posters announced that John, Bob, and Andy Taylor each had a handsome price of $4,166.67 on his head.

John Taylor's wound, unattended during his long trek toward freedom in the West, developed gangrene and he was forced to stop for medical treatment. He died a few days later in New Madrid, Missouri. Sheriff Springfield investigated the report of Taylor's funeral, had the body exhumed, and established the identity of the deceased.

A Missouri sheriff recognized Bob Taylor on a train and without a word or warning shot and killed him. He brought the body to Hamilton County "packed in ice" and collected his reward. According to attorney Lewis Shepherd, the corpse lay "in state in the outer porch or vestibule of the courthouse next to Walnut Street. The people went to see the body in such great numbers that they broke down the solid sleepers on which the vestibule rested."

Andy Taylor, a young fellow, became homesick and gave himself away. He was arrested and brought back to Loudon County, where the murder of Cate and Conway had taken place, and was tried and executed.

There is a sequel to the tale of the Taylors. The prisoner shackled to John Taylor at the time of the murders on the train was one Jake Carter. One night at a Moccasin Bend corn shucking two fellows named England and Gholston killed another man. The two escaped, but Carter, arrested as an accomplice for encouraging the crime, was convicted and sentenced to seven years in prison. He appealed the judgment and while being taken to Knoxville for a supreme court hearing with Taylor, Carter saw an opportunity to escape with the three Taylors when his manacles were removed. However, he deliberately gave up such a chance. Instead he journeyed on to Knoxville and, unaccompanied by a law officer, delivered himself and the other two prisoners in the original party to the Knox County jail. Carter's exemplary conduct gained him a hero's fame in the newspapers. The court remanded his case for a new trial and he was later acquitted. Only Jake Carter gained from this sordid tragedy.[2]

Desperados such as the Taylors symbolized a blatant disregard for law, but at times even law officers themselves proved unworthy of their responsibilities. In 1885 a disgraceful situation developed in Chattanooga: it was reliably reported that the entire police force was arrested for carrying concealed weapons. Several of the officers were also charged with burglary.[3]

The practices and beliefs of the frontier, handed down to succeeding generations, naturally were influenced by racial problems. In the years immediately following Appomattox no hard-and-fast system of segregation, except in the area of education, existed by law. Local mores and prejudices set the code of relationship between white and black; this condition was more flexible and less harsh in Hamilton County than in most parts of the Deep South. Here the major concentration of blacks was in Chattanooga, where there were more job opportunities, practical paternalism, and more political participation by blacks than in other Tennessee cities. Most blacks, often so encouraged by their own leadership, showed an inclination to accommodate silently to the trend of the times.

Beginning in about the 1890s, a definite change manifested itself across the South, which led to an age of legalized segregation. Calculated and deliberate means to limit all interracial contact led to "Jim Crow" legislation. This produced, in turn, much more political talk about "Lily Whites" and "Lamp Blacks"; more newspaper columns were written about the general subject of the black, and fear of black crime resulted in a contagion of violence, extralegal organizations, and lynchings.

Hamilton County naturally reacted to this tension and frustration but without the same intensity as in some other areas. The experience of the past thirty years had done much to establish a good sense of community. There were, however, protesters who spoke out with each extension of Jim Crow legislation and an abortive boycott when the streetcars were segregated. Upon occasion, outbreaks of lawlessness occurred in which the majority—black and white—felt only shame and regret that law had failed.

The Jim Crow laws drawing the greatest attention related to public transportation. As early as 1881, the state of Tennessee required that railroads furnish "separate cars, or portions of cars cut off by partitioned walls" for the races; this policy was broadened by interpretation in 1903 to cover all forms of railroad travel. The railroads, however, pleading financial constraints, never provided equal service; blacks with first-class tickets had to use second-class, desegregated cars, since no first-class "separate" accommodations were available. Occasionally a black made public issue of this situation. One determined citizen, Mrs. Georgia Edwards of Chattanooga, brought charges against the Nashville, Chattanooga & St. Louis Railway in 1907. She charged that although she had bought a first-class ticket she had to occupy unequal facilities without lavatory, towels, or a smoking compartment.

Since bringers of suits of this type, heard before southern state courts, got little satisfaction and because other complaints were rejected or ignored, Mrs. Edwards took her cause to the Interstate Commerce Commission, which ruled in her favor. Although this body reaffirmed the idea of the "reasonableness" of segregation, it stated that it did not follow "that carriers may discriminate between white and colored passengers in the accommodations which they furnish to each." It ordered, therefore, that the facilities lacking be provided in the cars designated for blacks or that they be removed from the cars for the whites.

Mrs. Edwards's victory resulted in some personal recognition from the black community but little if any change in travel conditions. The railroad appealed the right of the commission to interfere with its methods of operation. Although the appeal was rejected four years later, the decision remained largely ignored.[4]

In 1905 Tennessee extended segregation to streetcars, which not only touched many commuters, but also resulted in personal indignities. Across the state opposition mounted, and the blacks undertook vigorous methods to resist. On 5 July 1905, Chattanooga blacks launched a streetcar boycott; they declared the new law "an insult to the negro race." The boycott only slowly gained momentum, for the black civic and religious leaders did not support it openly. The chief advocate of the move to refuse to ride the cars was the newspaper, the *Blade,* and its provocative editor, Randolph M. Miller.

To accommodate the blacks who refused to use the public transportation, Miller and associates organized hack lines on 16 July, at which time "three vehicles of sorry appearance" started handling passengers. Within a few weeks, nine black businessmen sought a charter from the state for the Transfer Omnibus Motor Car Company. With a capitalization of $10,000 they planned to use the newly developed motor bus to replace the hacks. Their plans failed; some people believed their interest was in the bus business rather than in the boycott. Furthermore, there were few blacks with funds to invest and little public support for the black political leaders.

Some revenue from the hack lines could go into the bus enterprise, but the city humane officer stopped this, for he threatened to prosecute the operators for "working old worn-out animals from early morning until late at night . . . only half feeding them." Both the boycott and the bus line failed, but editor Miller continued to rail. On October 1905 he stormed,

> They have taken our part of the library; they have moved our school to the frog pond; they have passed the Jim Crow law; they have knocked us out of the jury box; they have played the devil generally, and what in thunder more will they do no one knows.[5]

Miller was incorrect in his sweeping charge against the whites. This was clearly demonstrated in a terrifying episode in 1892. One May day Frank Weims, a black, attempted to assault a white woman in a wooded area in Hill City. He was caught immediately and brought to the county jail. Indignation ran high, reflecting the bitter racial feelings throughout the South at the time. Sheriff John Skillern, without even a preliminary examination of the accused, immediately sent the prisoner out of town.

That night a mob stormed the jail only to learn that Weims was else-where. The *Times* and the *Observer*, a black journal, both praised the sheriff for his bold decision; both papers called for a speedy trial strictly under the law.

Jailer Holt and Deputy Frank Selcer now began a memorable jour-ney with the accused man as they hustled him from jail to jail. They were severely handicapped on all sides, especially by telegraph op-erators who, acting contrary to all company rules, wired ahead, thus keeping Chattanooga rioters and those along the route posted as to their movements. At many stations jeering, howling troublemakers demanded that Weims be turned over to them and threatened the officers. Wherever rumors led the rioters, a close search was made for the accused. In addition, Holt and Selcer found many of the jails in the state closed to them, and legally they could not go out of Tennessee. A local newspaper stated in Middle Tennessee that the jails had "stand-ing room only" cards out and that Memphis shook a red rag even at the suggestion that Weims might be brought there.

In Nashville where Weims was imprisoned for a time, a large gath-ering of extremists threatened to lynch him. Several officers received wounds in the melee. Every kind of subterfuge imaginable was used to attempt to take the prisoner away. Finally the lawmen spirited him out unobserved by giving him a market basket and instructions to walk up the street smoking a cigarette with a self-possessed air. An officer walked ahead of him, one followed, and a third casually rode horseback at his side.

After attempts to use several other jails, the two officers started out with their prisoner for East Tennessee via Chattanooga. A howling, well-organized mob met them at every turn. At a way stop called Hooker Station, they received a warning that an ugly throng awaited them at Wauhatchie. The officers made a hasty and bold decision. In a sparsely populated area they threw Weims from the train and then jumped after him. They crossed Raccoon and Lookout mountains on foot, avoiding houses and all passing travelers. Exhausted, they got back to Chattanooga only to slip away on the train to Knoxville. Finding no room in the jail there, they went on to Morristown, often called a "law abiding community."

Meanwhile a hostile uneasiness hung over Chattanooga as crowds gathered at the jail. At the request of Sheriff Skillern, a committee of Hill City people examined the prison, going through every cranny to prove that Weims was not there. Skillern finally persuaded the crowds to disperse. A public meeting called for noon at the courthouse on 26 May was announced to "reverse the apparent order of the day by putting the law above the wild and wooly mob."

A throng of a thousand citizens congregated; the Reverend T. H. McCallie, who served as chairman of the meeting, addressed those assembled on the harm that lawlessness could bring the community. A committee of leading residents drew up a list of resolutions endorsing law and order which was eagerly approved by those assembled. The citizens applauded Sheriff Skillern and his aides for the way they had handled the case so far.

One more matter had to be attended to: Weims had to be returned for trial. Again the sheriff took no chances. He brought the accused man back in broad daylight but placed at the depot a guard of seventy-five "trusty, determined, well-armed citizens." The sheriff marched the prisoner and guards up the middle of the street to the jail. Weims pleaded guilty to assault with intent to rape and received a twenty-one-year sentence. The sheriff got him away immediately, again calling on the community for help. "Many of the leading citizens of the city and the county," the morning newspaper stated, "appeared gun in hand, as guards to prevent any violence or unlawful demonstration."

The Weims episode brought acclaim to the sheriff and his staff as well as to Judge John A. Moon for the way he had conducted the trial. All across Tennessee Hamilton County gained praise for its fervent desire and strenuous effort to follow the law.[6] However, the region within a year failed to maintain this standard of conduct and turned to the use of the "lynch law."

On 14 February 1893, a black described as slightly built, assaulted an "aged woman" in her home in the very heart of town at about nine A.M. The woman fainted while sturggling with the assailant and remained in a thoroughly frightened state for some days. Neighbors called the police and Sheriff Skillern had his entire force out on horses searching for the man. Confusion and excitement enveloped the community. On McCallie Avenue the police picked up a suspect and took him to the home of the victim for identification. From her bed the woman gave a confused and tentative identification. The suspect, one Alfred Blount, was marched off to jail.

A crowd of more than 150 loitered around the area all day. Several people from time to time insisted in short speeches that the accused had not been definitely identified. Later a dodger was circulated with the information that the arresting officer, the sheriff, and the mayor

stressed that identification had not been satisfactory. They also pleaded
that any extreme reaction at least be postponed awaiting more information.

As night fell the crowd grew in size and boisterousness. The sheriff
and a squad of deputies barred the jail door and stood behind it all
heavily armed. By eight P.M. the throng numbered a thousand or more;
the majority occupied the courthouse yard and held secure positions
of safety close to the big trees growing there. The hard core of the mob
packed the jail yard nearby. The shouts and din of the crowd could be
heard two blocks away where an audience had assembled at the Opera
House.

The mob surged toward the jail door and broke it down. A deputy
fired a shot into the air. The crowd pushed back; those on the outskirts,
onlookers whose curiosity had brought them there, took flight in all
directions.

An hour or so later the unorganized, leaderless gang jammed forward
again, shrieking as if possessed. They battered down a jail door, pushed
aside the sheriff's men, broke the steel locks and bolts of the prison
door, and dragged the cowering Blount to the street. The 100 to 150
hard-core rioters took their man to the "county bridge" (Walnut Street)
where he was promptly lynched.

The morning newspaper carried the full story, embellished with
melodramatic detail and opinion. That day a "curious kind of quiet"
hung over the community. Many repeated that there was no positive
evidence that the right man had died; some deplored the violence of
the mob; others criticized the sheriff for dereliction of duty. A strange
kind of contradiction prevailed. The *Times* illustrated this clearly. Although editorially deploring the event as an insult to the law and to
the courts and decrying the injury to the community's reputation, some
of its headlines seemed to tell another story. "The Ghastly Work of
Last Night Accomplished by Cool and Deliberate Men Who, When
their Work had been Accomplished, Quietly Dispersed," read one
headline.[7]

This same type of frenzy struck in Soddy four years later in a section
of the county with a relatively small black population. Charles Brown,
a young, husky black, assaulted a white girl in a wooded area near
Soddy Landing. Her screams brought assistance and the attacker fled
but was closely followed by men attracted by the commotion. On
reaching the village of Soddy, Brown took refuge in the loft of a house.

The people living there notified the constable and a posse at the time who were out searching for the fugitive.

They surrounded the house and ordered Brown out but got no response. Then Constable Saddler entered the house, climbed up toward the loft and put his head through the opening. Brown shot him, putting a ball through the officer's neck. He fell to the floor seriously wounded. The enraged crowd of about forty surrounding the house were now determined to lynch Brown. Many shots were fired into the loft; all missed. Brown refused to budge until he was told that the men were about to blow the house up with dynamite. On his surrender, a majority of the crowd favored killing him at once, but cooler heads argued that he first had to be properly identified.

They went off to the girl's home where she definitely identified Brown. A deputy sheriff appeared and took charge after deputizing six men to assist him. They used the store of W. H. Card as headquarters. The armed lawmen locked the store door, planning to spend the night there before starting with the prisoner to Chattanooga and the county jail.

About eleven P.M. a band of some sixty armed and mounted men rode up, all wearing disguises, and demanded admittance. The lawmen refused but the mob quickly battered down the door with a heavy piece of timber. They dragged Brown, paralyzed with terror, to the Chickamauga Creek bridge and tried to hang him. When the rope broke, they simply turned their guns on the victim.

The next morning Card had the body brought to his store. A jury was empaneled and an inquest held. The conclusion simply stated that Brown "had come to his death at the hands of unknown parties."

Without any thought of the deeper meaning of this incident the *Times* reported that "without any ado, delay, or circumlocation [*sic*] he is duly executed in quite an orderly manner." The report continued, "From all that can be learned Brown's execution was a good riddance."[8]

On the night of Tuesday, 19 March 1906, a Chattanooga mob lynched another black, Ed Johnson, on the Walnut Street bridge. This extralegal action took place only after the U.S. Supreme Court had agreed to review the Johnson case; the prisoner was therefore being held in jail for the federal authorities. The lynching created a furor in Washington and brought humiliation to all local residents who represented law and order.

The story all began in St. Elmo near the Forest Hills Cemetery on the evening of 23 January when Johnson assaulted a young white woman. The sheriff, at the head of his deputies and working with posses, arrested several men; a witness identified Johnson, who was at once taken to the county jail. Fearing a lynching attempt, Judge Sam McReynolds ordered the man taken to Knoxville. The sheriff and a deputy started out on this mission but encountered such a fired-up gang at Harrison Junction that they changed their destination to Nashville.

That night (25 January) a mob of upward of fifteen hundred stormed the jail, wrecked the front of the building, and got as far as steel doors that separated the waiting room from the cells. At that point two deputies barred the way, refusing to surrender their keys. Judge McReynolds, H. Clay Evans, and others finally quieted the crowd, which then agreed to have a committee search the jail to ascertain if the prisoner was there. When these men reported that he was not there, the mob dispersed. Meanwhile the militia, drilling just a few blocks away, was ordered to the scene. They set up a gatling gun and, according to one who was there, "This enraged the mobsters who promptly took the gun away from the soldier boys."

On the following Saturday, Judge McReynolds called a special session of the grand jury, which returned a true bill against Johnson. It was decided that he be tried at once. Only police vigilance kept a second mob from forming. One week after the crime was committed Sheriff Joseph Shipp slipped the accused back into town and the tense trial began. The jury brought in a verdict of guilty and the judge set 13 March as the date of execution. Johnson was taken immediately to Knoxville and jailed there.

At this point Styles L. Hutchins, the former state legislator, and attorney Noah W. Parden entered the picture. These two black attorneys, engaged by Johnson's family, asked the judge for a new trial; otherwise they would appeal the case to the state supreme court. Judge McReynolds refused.

The state supreme court decided that there was no error in the trial and the attorneys for Johnson petitioned a federal judge, alleging that their client's constitutional rights had been violated. It was maintained that the indicting grand jury was improperly drawn and that court officials had manipulated the jury lists to exclude all blacks. In addition, it was held that Johnson had not been tried by a jury of his peers "in an open and public manner" and that he had been compelled to testify against himself.

The application for an appeal to the federal court was denied, but the judge granted a stay of execution until 23 March to give the defendant time to appeal to the U.S. Supreme Court. In and around Chattanooga there was much speculation as to how Johnson had raised enough money to appeal; reports of black gatherings to raise funds described them as "large and rather violent." A black church group moved its worship services to the jail. The prisoner was baptized in a prison bathtub and received into the church amid shouts of religious zealots while some "became prostrate on the floor as in a trance." The crowd was packed into the lobby to such an extent that the jailers could control the situation only with difficulty.

Although no one actually believed the attorneys could gain the attention of the United States Supreme Court, there was unrest over the scheduled execution. The newspaper did not help matters with its headline, "Day of Doom is very near." In Washington, Parden and Hutchins submitted their case to Justice John M. Harlan, who allowed an appeal pending action by the full bench. On 19 March the Supreme Court ordered a stay of execution awaiting an appeal, so informing state and county officials in Chattanooga and succinctly ordering the "custody of the accused retained pending appeal here." The time of Johnson's execution now was uncertain.

That very night a mob lynched the prisoner. About 8:30 P.M. a small, well-organized gang, consisting mostly of young fellows from the suburbs, attacked the jail. Only the night jailer was present; Sheriff Shipp arrived an hour later, but no police or deputies were in evidence as the men broke down the jail doors and barriers. No precautions had been taken that evening to protect Johnson, and some even hinted that a certain degree of internal complicity existed. After about two hours the mob, which numbered no more than one hundred, took Johnson to the bridge and, failing to hang him, riddled his body with bullets.

The morning press virtually shouted its headlines detailing the event. "Mandate of the Supreme Court of the United States Disregarded and Red Riot Rampant," read one. " 'God Bless You All—I Am Innocent,' Ed Johnson's Last Words Before Being Shot to Death by a Mob Like a Dog," the front-page story was headlined. There was apprehension in the city all the next day. Plants were idled as workers stayed home. Rumors spread that blacks were plotting to "get" Judge McReynolds and Attorney General Matt Whitaker. Friends then organized an armed guard which patrolled the streets around the judge's McCallie Avenue home all night.

Investigators from the United States Department of Justice arrived in Chattanooga and spent several weeks gathering facts about the case. Eventually twenty-eight men were cited to answer charges of contempt of the United States Supreme Court. In May 1908 the court dismissed all but six of the defendants, but not until July 1909 was a judgment of guilt handed down. More time passed until 15 November when sentences were pronounced.

In a five-to-three decision, the Court held Sheriff Shipp and jailor Jeremiah Gibson guilty of contempt as a result of negligence in not protecting Johnson, and sentenced the other four for taking part in the lynching. Terms to be served in the jail of the District of Columbia varied from sixty to ninety days.

The unusual circumstances of the case attracted national attention. Earlier, when the accused group left Chattanooga for Washington for sentencing, a large crowd applauded them. Since both Shipp and Gibson were Confederate veterans, they drew special attention. People gathered at all the way stations along the railroad to cheer them.

It was maintained that their case was the first example in American history of men being imprisoned "for contempt of the supreme court of the United States, and the first time, too, the federal government has placed men behind bars as an outcome of the lynching of a negro."

The imprisonment of the six was soon over, but for the black attorneys, Parden and Hutchins, the result of the episode was more lasting. They found the climate so unfavorable in Chattanooga that both left the city to start new careers in Oklahoma.[9]

Spontaneous outbursts of lawlessness with considerable destruction of property occurred in 1917 as a result of entirely different circumstances. Directly or indirectly, the disturbances grew out of a labor dispute: the attempt of streetcar employees to organize a union. The differences between company and employees simmered for a long period before they erupted in unrestrained madness. All of the ingredients for trouble were present—outside organizers, strikebreakers, sympathetic union colleagues, and the fact that the strike was brought directly to busy downtown streets. Moreover, the traveling public had a direct interest in the dispute.

Back in 1909 a new company, the Chattanooga Railway and Light Company, combined the streetcar business with the commercial supplier of electrical power into one organization and undertook to expand and improve trolley service provided by 109 cars over some sixty-nine miles of track. Two years later, in early April this firm discharged several motormen, accusing them of driving while drunk and of operating their cars in a reckless manner. The men contacted the Amalgamated Association of Street & Electric Railway Employees of America which lost no time in sending in a representative. An abortive strike followed; the employees were weakly organized, the company adamant in its opposition.

In 1916 some motormen and conductors again tried to unionize. They were discharged. Again the national group sent in a representative who was determined to organize a union. On 21 August a union mass meeting ended with a march accompanied by a brass band to Sixth and Market streets where a strike was slated to start. At the arranged time, along came motorman W. M. Eaves in his car; he stopped and let the crowd know he was on strike. His conductor, however, did not agree with him and attempted to wrest control of the car from the motorman until someone pulled the trolley rope from the wire.

Other cars had to stop; congestion grew. Company personnel tried to pilot the stranded cars to the barns amid a crescendo of catcalls from the assembled crowd.

The mob milled about, smashing some car windows, but damage and injuries were slight in this comic opera performance. At first the few policemen in the area did nothing to control the crowd, but as the evening wore on it became clear that the situation might get out of hand. The fire department arrived and hosed down some of the crowd; heavily armed police began making arrests, which finally totaled thirty-seven. For some three hours the tussle continued, spreading to Tenth Street and breaking out in a few outlying spots.

For several days only a few cars operated a skeleton schedule; passengers were few and many people had to walk to work. More and more men joined the union and before long managed a total strike. Under heavy pressure, the company agreed to recognize the union and arbitrate differences. This honeymoon period did not last and was marred by frequent misunderstandings and suspicion. By the late summer of 1917 the company again took a hard line in ceasing to recognize the union as a bargaining agent. Each employee had to sign an individual contract or be fired. In anticipation of union resistance, the company brought in strikebreakers to man the trolleys. On 6 September 1917, a new strike started.

At 6 P.M. the next day rioting broke out after a union mass meeting. Union men at that hour quit their cars wherever they happened to be. When company personnel or nonunion men tried to get the cars through, the mob barred the way. At Ninth and Market streets the melee continued without a break for at least twenty minutes. The rioters pulled nonstrikers from the cars and beat several severely. They also took stools from the car vestibules and, tearing out the legs, used them as clubs; others used metal knuckles or swung pieces of broken glass. A barrage of rocks shattered car windows; knives flashed; and trolley poles were jerked down. Rumor spread that the car barns would be burned. Only after firemen arrived with hoses and police reserves appeared in numbers did the unrestrained terror abate.

Violence spread all over the streetcar network, complicating matters since both city and county peace officers were involved. Four cars were crashed together in St. Elmo when deserted cars were turned loose to make a wild downhill run. Abandoned and crippled cars were eventually brought in, but tension did not lessen, nonetheless. Frequent rumors of impending acts of destruction, what the city and county officials regarded as "seditious talk," and "critical riotous conditions" resulted in a public call for help. At 2 A.M. 11 September the federal government responded. Two troops of cavalry and a machine gun company arrived from Fort Oglethorpe on orders of the secretary of war. It was the opinion of the city and county fathers that the situation had passed beyond the point of being a dispute between labor and management, but the question had become whether Chattanooga and Hamilton County would be ruled by constituted authority or by rioters.

A federal labor mediator also was sent in, but the relative calm was punctured by outbursts of trouble. On 16 September a car, on which company guards rode, crossed into Tennessee from Chickamauga, Georgia. It was met by mobs who threw a volley of rocks at the car, breaking windows and sending passengers to seek safety under their seats. The conductor had to stop the car to remove a pile of rocks placed on the track. Another shower of stones fell on the workers. The guards fired; a bystander inside a store was hit. Strangely, the victim happened to be a former motorman, the very same W. M. Eaves who had staged the one-man strike in 1916.

Negotiations wavered from predicted settlement to gloomy prospects. The third week of the strike opened. At 3 P.M. on Sunday, 24 September, a mass union demonstration called to show support for the striking streetcar workers had just ended in midtown. A streetcar manned by strikebreakers happened along and had to stop, for the street was jammed with autos, sightseers, and the disbanded paraders. The crowd jeered and hooted the trolley men; all were burning with enthusiasm for the union cause. A few rushed the car, seized the strikebreaking crew, and began beating them up. Others took out their fury on the car itself, breaking doors and windows, as well as the seats. Other cars came along; all received the same treatment at the hands of about two thousand people crowded into the street from Sixth to Ninth streets. The shoving mass of humanity screamed, cursed, and howled out defiance.

A company guard fired his riot gun and William Massengale, a brewery worker, fell dead. A boy and a soldier were also wounded. The crowd's fury rose and fell, but police and soldiers did not restore order until 6:30 P.M. and then only because no more cars or strikebreakers appeared.

The irrational and destructive rioters of that Sunday afternoon finally calmed down, and the two groups of adversaries turned to the conference room. But scars remained, and the basic dissension did not disappear. The days of tension dampened the union men's spirit; except for brief strike efforts they lost their zeal and the streetcar workers' union movement collapsed. The Chattanooga Railway & Light Company, so opposed to union recognition, also lost out, for in 1919 the company was forced into receivership.[10]

Such periodic outbursts of violence have long been forgotten by Hamiltonians. They sprang from attitudes passed down from the days of frontier existence and post-Civil War race relations when many lived on the narrow margin of poverty. The same eruptions, present in varying manifestations across the nation, came to be interpreted by many as expected incidents or, at best, as examples of sin or virtue, depending on one's station. In Hamilton County these excesses were never as numerous as in many other areas of the South, and they did eventually give way to a policy of tolerance and a leadership dedicated to equality for all before the law.

The social and cultural heritage found within the county had a positive effect on other residents. They, like the persons of violent mood, were few in number and their contributions are no longer known by many. But there were Hamiltonians who possessed native talent and the required discipline to cultivate creative activity. From all walks of life they emerged as spokespersons for art, music, literature, and history.

From the beginning a number of citizens without fanfare or pretense recorded the happenings in which the people of the region were involved, including John P. Long, Louis L. Parham, Rev. T. H. McCallie,

George W. Ochs, Harry M. Wiltse, E. Y. Chapin, Lewis Shepherd, Xenophen Wheeler, and Charles D. McGuffey. In the early days Thomas Crutchfield, Sr., displayed his talent as a practical builder and years later the county enjoyed the services of the imaginative architect, R. H. Hunt, who planned many local structures including the impressive present-day courthouse and the federal building.

In the early 1850s James A. Whiteside persuaded an artist, James Cameron, to relocate in Chattanooga. With Whiteside's patronage this transplanted Scot, who had studied in Philadelphia and Rome, earned numerous commissions. He established his home and studio near the center of town on the scenic hill which still bears his name. His best-known work, "View of Moccasin Bend," a panoramic landscape completed in 1857, currently hangs in the Hunter Museum. This painting shows a Whiteside family group against a background of Umbrella Rock on Lookout Mountain and the sweeping valley below.

Cameron went back to Philadelphia during the war years. After hostilities ended, on returning to Chattanooga, he found Cameron Hill naked of trees and his patron deceased. Discouraged, he gave up his artistic interests and in 1870 moved to California as a minister of the gospel.[11]

Two men who moved to the county as adults developed outstanding careers, one in literature, another in music. Francis Lynde began his literary work as he neared middle age. Born in a small New York town, he spent his boyhood in Kansas City, traveled widely through the West, and had extensive experience as a railroad official. On moving to Hamilton County this modest man, who lacked formal education, bought a small section of the Cravens farm on Lookout Mountain and embarked on a writing career. The historic setting of his new home stirred his imagination and, drawing on his earlier experiences, Lynde wrote nearly three hundred articles, stories, and novels. Contemporaries spoke of him as the "dean of local letters." Among his best works were *A Question of Courage*, *The Taming of Red Butte Western*, *Master of Appleby*, and *The Grafters*, novels of romance and adventure.[12]

The second newcomer first visited the area as a musician at the Lookout Inn in 1893. A gifted violinist, Joseph Cadek, was born in Prague, Bohemia, and schooled at that city's renowned conservatory. In 1892 he migrated to America, leaving a promising European career and shortly thereafter by chance spent some time in Chattanooga. The surrounding mountains reminded him of his homeland; opportunities in music were strong enough to influence his decision to make the area his permanent residence. Cadek returned to Prague, married, and brought his bride to his new home.

In addition to performing, Cadek became a teacher and an active musical promoter, bringing many visiting artists to the area. In 1901 he and his associates opened the Southern Conservatory of Music. Three years later he founded the Cadek Conservatory. In 1920 a suggestion was made that a curriculum be arranged to offer a joint program with the University of Chattanooga. The implementation of this idea was postponed in part by the death of Cadek in 1927, but in 1935 the Cadek Conservatory of the University of Chattanooga was launched with three of Joseph O. Cadek's children, Ottokar, Harold, and Lillian Dame, as key faculty personnel.[13]

Two young blacks, raised in poverty, resided in Hamilton County until promising opportunities carried them to national and international success. Bessie Smith, born probably in 1898, lost both parents at a very early age. She possessed remarkable native talent as a singer and attracted crowds along the streets to hear her as a brother accompanied her on the guitar. While still a young girl, she joined a touring minstrel group and came under the tutelage of Gertrude (Ma) Rainey, popularly known as the mother of all blues singers.

Large, strong, quick-tempered Bessie Smith reached the pinnacle of her career in the 1920s and earned the distinction of being the "greatest blues singer of all time." She worked from Beale Street to Broadway and was probably the first black artist to make phonograph recordings. Columbia Records billed her "Empress of the Blues." Bessie Smith's career ended abruptly in 1937 when she was killed in a Mississippi highway accident.[14]

Roland Hayes also rose from impoverished surroundings to become an internationally renowned concert artist. Born to former slaves on 3 June 1887, in the small north Georgia village of Curryville, young Hayes lost his father when he was a small child. His mother kept the family together but, finding no opportunity to educate her three sons, moved to Chattanooga when Roland was fifteen. The boys took turns working and going to school. Hayes had a job at an iron foundry and began singing at the Monumental Baptist Church. A music lover, Colonel William M. Stone, encouraged him to develop his talent and to further his education. Hayes eventually entered the Preparatory School of Fisk University in the sixth grade when he was about twenty years old. Before long he joined the school's famed Fisk Jubilee Singers; later he studied in Boston.

Since the American concert stage was not ready to receive a black artist, Hayes turned to Europe. His renditions of Afro-American spirituals and German lieder won him high praise. He successfully integrated the European stage and in 1925 received an invitation to sing for British royalty at Buckingham Palace. Concert tours in America followed; Hayes appeared with the Boston, Philadelphia, Detroit, and New York symphony orchestras. At Carnegie Hall, on his seventy-fifth birthday, the audience rose and sang "Happy Birthday" as a token of affection and appreciation. Throughout his long career Hayes not only cultivated his talents as a lyric tenor to the highest point of perfection but also gained recognition for black artists in the field of serious music throughout the western world. In 1968 Hayes returned to Chattanooga to receive an honorary degree from the University of Chattanooga. The following year, at his request, he gave a free concert at the Tivoli Theater as a gesture of love in memory of the friends of his youth.[15]

Like Hayes, Alice MacGowan came to Hamilton County as a young person; she was the daughter of a Union soldier who stayed on after being mustered out of service and who was hired as editor of Adolph Ochs's newspaper in 1878. Alice lived most of her life in Chattanooga and on Missionary Ridge, spending the long summers on Walden Ridge or in the Sequatchie Valley. She wrote both short stories and novels.

Beginning with western romances Miss MacGowan switched later to Tennessee mountain stories featuring a people of deep prejudices and warm hospitality. Under the G. P. Putnam's Sons imprint she brought out *Judith of the Cumberlands* and the *Wiving of Lance Cleaverage*. In 1910 after moving to California she completed *The Sword in the Mountains*, a Civil War tale centered on the Hamilton County area and its surrounding highlands.

While Alice MacGowan was writing about the mountain folk she had come to know, Emma Bell Miles, a contemporary, was herself of the mountains and became a sort of legend of the highlands. She was born in 1879 in Evansville, Indiana, to parents who were both teachers. Very soon after her birth they moved to Rabbit Hash, an isolated community in the mountains of Kentucky. When Emma was about nine years old, the family, traveling on horseback, came to Hamilton County and before long settled on Walden Ridge. Here the young girl spent her adolescent years, ever awake to the wonders of nature around her and constantly touched by the beauty and freedom of the mountains. A prodigious reader, she was largely self-taught and early recognized in herself a talent for painting and writing.

Splendid little sketches of everyday mountain scenes attracted the eyes of the summer residents of Walden Ridge. They not only revealed Emma Bell's promising native ability but also an extraordinary skill in interpreting the curious world around her. Admiring patrons sent her off to the St. Louis School of Design at an early age. She made steady progress but eventually the call of the mountains became too over-whelming and in a bout of homesickness she left the city and the school behind.

On returning home she married the local hack driver, G. Frank Miles, a descendant of mountain pioneers, who proved incapable of steady employment. With a growing family to provide for, they found it necessary to move from cabin to cabin; increasing poverty forced Emma to find a market for her poems and stories. She was successful in selling her literary efforts to several journals, *Harper's Monthly*, *Century*, *Lippincott's*, *Putnam's*, and others whose editors readily spot-ted their high quality.

Humiliation, pain, and want at times embittered this high-spirited sensitive woman; a strong will and solid character, however, offset such trials. In 1905 she published *The Spirit of the Mountains*, a sympathetic evaluation of life in the southern mountains. Illustrated with her own paintings of mountain scenes and people, it develops a perceptive interpretation of the religion, customs, music, superstitions, and spe-cial traits of the mountain people. Emma Bell Miles, with her contacts in the urban world of Chattanooga and with the summer residents of Walden Ridge, had a dual insight into mountain life. She concluded that mountaineers should avoid becoming "poor imitation city people" but should work to be "better mountaineers."

Much of Emma Bell Miles's later life was a struggle between fleeting glimpses of success and hope and a dreary, shabby existence made ever more difficult by failing health. She published a second book, *Our Southern Birds*, and started another, *Our Southern Wild Flowers*, but died on 20 March 1919 before the latter was completed. Another volume published after her death under the title *Strains From a Dul-cimer* contains many of her poems. Today some of her bird pictures can be seen in the library of Harvard University and a facsimile edition of *The Spirit of the Mountains* carries the 1975 date of the University of Tennessee Press. This book, which contains none of the despair of the author's personal life, retains the fresh quality of a gifted and unique woman who knew both the rural acres of Hamilton County and the changing world of a modern community.[16]

NOTES

1. *Chattanooga Times*, 11 April 1926, contains reminiscences of Attorney General Matt N. Whitaker.

2. T. J. Campbell, *The Upper Tennessee* . . . (Chattanooga: author, 1932), pp. 87–90; *Chattanooga Times*, 22 October, 3 December 1911; 15 August 1977.

3. Harry M. Wiltse, "History of Chattanooga," 2 vols. (Typescript, Chattanooga-Hamilton County Bicentennial Library), 2:105.

4. Lester C. Lamon, *Black Tennesseans, 1900–1930* (Knoxville: University of Tennessee Press, 1977), pp. 7–8.

5. Ibid., pp. 8, 29–31.

6. *Chattanooga Times*, 20–21, 22, 24, 26, 27 May, 14 June 1892.

7. Ibid., 15, 16 February, 18 September 1893.

8. Ibid., 26, 27 February 1897.

9. Ibid., 24–31 January, 10–22 March, 25 May, 16 November 1909; 11 April 1926; 4 February 1964; J.P. Brown to Alfred D. Mynders, 22 March 1950, Chattanooga-Hamilton County Bicentennial Library; Lamon, *Black Tennesseans*, p. 10; Wiltse, "Chattanooga," 2:164.

10. *Chattanooga Times*, 19–26 August 1916, 4–30 September, 1–22 October 1917; David H. Steinberg, *And to Think It Only Cost a Nickel! The Development of Public Transportation in the Chattanooga Area* (Chattanooga: author, 1975), pp. 36–41.

11. Budd H. Bishop, "Art in Tennessee: The Early Nineteenth Century," *Tennessee Historical Quarterly* 29, no. 4 (Winter 1970–71): 387-88.

12. Clipping file, Local History Section, Chattanooga-Hamilton County Bicentennial Library.

13. *Chattanooga Times*, 10 November 1927; *Chattanooga News-Free Press*, 26 September 1956.

14. *Chattanooga Times*, 2 October 1973; *Time*, 3 August 1970, p. 40.

15. *Chattanooga Times*, 27 September 1925; 7 November 1976; 2 January 1977. Hinton D. Alexander was a member of Fisk Jubilee Singers some years before Hayes.

16. Cartter Patten, *Signal Mountain and Walden's Ridge* (n.p.: author, 1962), pp. 41–45; Adelaide Rowell, "Emma Bell Miles, Artist, Author, and Poet of the Tennessee Mountains," *Tennessee Historical Quarterly*, 25, no. 1 (Spring 1966): 77–89; Emma Bell Miles, *The Spirit of the Mountains* (Knoxville: University of Tennessee Press, 1975). Kay Baker Gaston, "Emma Bell Miles and the 'Fountain Square Conversations,'" *Tennessee Historical Quarterly*, 37, no. 4 (Winter 1978): 416–429.

17

The Teens and Twenties

W HEN word flashed to Hamilton County that the United States on 6 April 1917 had entered the war against Germany, the local people immediately demonstrated their approval. Blasts from whistles in Chattanooga and its suburbs blended "in a wild exultation with the ringing of church bells and scattered cheers from the people downtown." Like the rest of the nation, the county released a patriotic display of energy and unrestrained emotion which marked the emergence of the country as a world power at an hour when international rivalry had reached an intense crisis.

In 1914 European affairs seemed remote to Hamiltonians. They read of the Sarajevo assasinations and the explosive diplomatic talks that ensued, but these topics vanished almost immediately from the local newspapers. However, as August came bringing general war, county opinion makers grew apprehensive. The local business barometer reflected the situation: prices of imported goods soared and the European demand for American items fell drastically. This sudden slump led to a stagnation in manufacturing until the Western allies turned to the United States for war materials. Chattanooga's iron industry, in particular, recovered rapidly and with the coming of 1915 the local economy boomed.

Since few county residents had come from Central Europe, ties with the Germans and their allies were minimal. And because information reaching them about the causes of the spreading conflict was superficial at best, people in the area gradually took sides on the basis of blood, race, economic ties, political affinity, or cultural interests.

Public and private points of view on the degree of American involvement in the European war varied from internationalist to isolationist. In November 1916, running true to historical trends, Hamilton County and Chattanooga endorsed Woodrow Wilson's war policy by voting for his reelection. The majority of area citizens at this time continued to encourage a program of neutrality despite such provocations as the sinking of the *Lusitania*, in which tragedy a local couple, Reginold Purse and his wife, were listed as dead.

Most local people supported some degree of military preparedness, but their ardor was limited by the fact that the leading national advocates of preparedness were also actively in favor of intervention in the war. This attitude changed rapidly after the election, as Germany unleashed unrestricted submarine warfare and when other infringements of traditional neutrality became bold proof of her intentions. Congressman Moon, representing Hamilton's district, voted for participation in war as did all other Tennesseans in Congress.

The nation seemed emotionally ready for the conflict, but for all practical purposes, was totally unprepared. Estimates called for one million trained men overseas within the year and three million more for later service; these calculations meant a twenty-fold increase in the number of military personnel would be necessary. Selecting and training officers would be a much more troublesome task; in 1916 only about nine thousand officers were in federal service; two hundred thousand would be needed.

A few Hamilton men joined foreign forces before the United States entered the war; the first local casualty was Charles William Loaring-Clark, who was with the British Army. Others rushed to enlist immediately after the declaration of war. A number of county men volunteered for reserve officers' training, because direct commissions in World War I were granted only to specialists such as doctors and those qualified for duty in supply and technical services. An encampment for these trainees was set up at Snodgrass Field in the Chickamauga and Chattanooga National Military Park (Camp Warden McLean) and received its first contingent on 8 May 1917. Three months later, a large group winning shoulder straps there included more than 150 from

Hamilton County. Other local men who were members of the National Guard were inducted into federal service and, late in the war (1 October 1918), another group of young men donned uniforms. They formed a unit of the Students' Army Training Corps organized at the University of Chattanooga.

The great majority of the future soldiers entered service under the Selective Service Act of 19 May 1917. Remembering the unpopular features of Civil War conscription, the government placed the draft machinery in the hands of civilian boards who served in their local districts; 5 June 1917 was designated the day for all men between the ages of twenty-one and thirty to register. In Hamilton County factory and locomotive whistles greeted the arrival of this memorable dawn "with the whole-souled blast of jubilation." The day featured perfect June weather and because all males of the designated age bracket had to come forth, some prophetic soul designed a sign that read: "Today is equality day for men of all races in the United States."

Registration, handled informally by neighbors, developed no serious problems. In addition to booths in Chattanooga, numerous rural and suburban registration places were located in virtually every neighborhood.[1]

By the day's end some 11,000 men had completed registration at these county centers, including 6,811 from Chattanooga. By the third week in July the county received its quota of first draftees—a requirement of 828 men. This group represented the second largest number to be called from a county in the state, surpassed only by Shelby County. There were some indications that the number registered in Hamilton was inflated by persons from outside its borders, but no serious issue resulted. Those in authority expressed great pleasure at the surprisingly large number of blacks who registered.

To meet the first quota—423 from the county and 405 from Chattanooga—twice this total received orders to have physical examinations. By September all paperwork was in order and the specified number of recruits entered service at Camp Gordon, Georgia. At the time of departure the new soldiers entrained amid great outbursts of patriotism. Parading family members and well-wishers accompanied them to the depot as sirens screamed, military bands played, and whistles blew. When the first contingent left, veterans from Confederate and Union battle days marched arm in arm with the draftees to display again the national unity they had discovered after Reconstruction.[2]

Hamilton County continued to provide manpower for the armed

services throughout the conflict. Its experience in this role was similar to that of countless American communities reflecting the same intense outpouring of loyalty and emotional support. The "home front" experience of Hamilton County, on the other hand, differed markedly from that in most sections because Fort Oglethorpe and the Chickamauga and Chattanooga National Military Park were near by.

Although the fort and the bulk of the concentrated park acreage were located across the state line in North Georgia, their orientation was toward Chattanooga. Here a speedy construction program suddenly created as if by magic a great military base. By October 1917 it was reported that there were 1,326 buildings with a floorspace of more than fifty-two acres. Of this number 546 barracks provided sleeping quarters for 43,000 men and 762 officers; 207 mess halls could seat 29,000 at a serving; and 110 stables sheltered about eight thousand animals. Many local contractors and suppliers and Hamilton County craftsmen worked with the government on this project, which cost approximately $2,137,000 by this date.[3]

Besides the troops stationed at Fort Oglethorpe, which had been a permanent installation since 1904, other regiments arrived at the park by May for training at Camp Nathan Bedford Forrest, which operated separately until combined with Fort Oglethorpe in January 1919. Both engineer and infantry units were given basic training at this camp. The officers' training center, unofficially called Camp Warden McLean, was also located on park lands.

Another phase of the training program at the park was carried on at Camp Greenleaf, where medical and sanitary units developed one of the chief centers in the country for this vital branch. At maximum strength it numbered some three thousand officers and more than twenty-three thousand who used the facilities at Central High School and the University of Chattanooga for technical instruction. Another part of the Fort Oglethorpe complex was the sprawling War Prison Barracks where both prisoners of war and civilian enemy aliens were incarcerated.

In Chattanooga uniformed men filled the depots, streets, shops, hotels, and amusement centers. They monopolized the growing jitney service and participated in every local celebration and parade. At times, as in the case of the streetcar strike, soldiers responded to the urgent call to preserve law and order. Eating places and retail shops did a thriving business and, in response to a pressing need, the city fathers made the unusual concession of granting the movie theaters the privilege of opening for Sunday shows during the war.

The large number of young men freshly removed from home and friends presented a great challenge to the civic and patriotic-minded people of Hamilton County. Virtually the entire adult population was mobilized to help. The National League of Women's Service organized a local chapter on the very eve of the war and gave yeoman service by coordinating the efforts of thirty-five patriotic societies, churches, and civic clubs under the leadership of Mrs. D. P. Montague.

Eighteen churches helped with the management of the Soldiers' Recreational Rest Rooms on Broad Street. The YMCA, Knights of Columbus, and Jewish Welfare each manned huts at Fort Oglethorpe. The chamber of commerce, the newly organized Red Cross with its county branches, the Chaplains' Aid Society, YWCA, Salvation Army, the Godmothers, the Canteen Workers, the Colored Women's Service League, and other groups offered aid, entertainment, and solace.

Such charitable tasks were endless. Some people rolled bandages, made surgical items, or knitted socks, mufflers, sweaters, and other garments. The League of Patriotic Demonstration, through short talks to civilians, taught respect for the flag, how to meet strangers, and to show reverence for funeral corteges. One busy committee sent Christmas boxes overseas while hundreds of local families entertained men in their homes for Sunday or holiday dinners. Dances, teas, receptions, lectures, and recreational activities were organized for officers and men of the ranks. A music committee reported that it provided over thirteen hundred Sunday programs.

One group sponsored sidewalk speakers and another provided travelers' aid. Hostess houses and hospital work kept other volunteers busy. A convalescent committee visited the sick wards, bringing reading matter, snacks, jams, and other goodies. A memorial committee sent representatives to all funerals; they attended 1,370 and persuaded the mayor to assign two mounted officers to lead all funeral processions.

Still another phase of volunteer work concerned the production and conservation of food. Throughout the county "Victory Gardens" received special attention. Forty rural and fourteen suburban groups were organized, using the schoolhouses as meeting centers. The farm and home demonstration agents directed much of the work with the assistance of teachers and volunteers. Several businessmen raised money to buy tin cans by the carload which were sold in small lots at the courthouse. In 1918 five carloads of cans were used. A similar plan was adopted in acquiring canning equipment, which was generally installed at the schools, and, in season, at least two days a week people of the section gathered to put up surplus vegetables. This food was used at home or sold with proceeds going to the Red Cross.

Numerous volunteer groups aided in the sale of War Savings Stamps and Liberty Bonds. The direct money cost of the war to the United States was over one million dollars an hour and loans to allies added another half million. All across the land people paid new and higher taxes, including the relatively new income tax, and made government investments. For the first time in their history, the people of Hamilton County began to talk in terms of millions of dollars.

Different areas of the county had bond quotas and consequently many high-pressure methods came into use. Gaudy signs carried such messages as "Stop! Look! Loosen!" On one side of Market Street, a platform was erected across the sidewalk requiring an "able-bodied though not difficult step"; close by was the sign reminding everyone, "We must go over the top."

One aggressive ten-minute drive to meet a certain quota represented solicitation methods carried to an extreme:

> At 11:50 a bomb exploded high above the Hamilton National Bank. This was the signal, and the city awoke to feverish activity. One hundred buglers sounded the assembly, sections of Camp Greenleaf's band played on street corners; sirens, whistles and bells sounded above the bomb, while scores of automobiles, each carrying a bugler, a mail clerk, and members of the Service League, or the men's committee raced through the cleared streets and collected pledges.

In the sale of bonds, quotas were not only assigned to an area but also to individuals. These quotas often reflected little if any regard for one's personal financial situation and were at times blatantly used to shame, humiliate, or intimidate people into making pledges. The new term, "slacker," along with "spy" and "traitor," began to be loosely thrown about. This false patriotism which boiled up in all corners of the country also surfaced in Hamilton County. One observer noted that it was a "feverish, hysterical, erotic and neurotic, not to say tommyrotic mental state which the victims mistook for patriotism." One example involved a Spanish-American War veteran, currently a munitions worker, who was known only to his solicitor as number so-and-so. He was informed that his bond purchasing record was not up to the quota set for him. When he tried to explain his situation, he was summarily told that the committeeman did not have time to listen to excuses. The solicitor advised, "Make up your mind what you are going to do right quick." The veteran bought bonds which he could not afford and like others who had bought under pressure sold them immediately at a big discount.

In other manifestations of patriotism, scare tactics and threats were used, and actual court charges were brought against people who were rumored to have made indiscreet remarks, who spoke with an accent, or who merely looked capable of espionage. A retired tailor of some means was accused of violation of the Espionage Act and was imprisoned because he protested a bond purchase. Another case reported by a chronicler of that day shows the extreme behavior of some:

> A woman lawyer saw a man at the movies and did not like his looks. He seemed to her excessively German and she jumped to the conclusion that he was a German, pro-German, of sinister intentions relating to war affairs, and in all probability a spy. She raised an outcry against him, invoked the aid of a policeman and demanded the fellow's immediate arrest. The policeman, upon investigation, was unable to adopt her point of view and refused to make the arrest. She denounced him in the newspaper as a "bonehead," but he was allowed to remain in service.

While episodes of this type marred the genuine war record of the county, they did not deter the majority from willingly putting up with gasless Sundays, heatless Mondays, meatless days, and numerous shortages as well as wartime inflation.

But most discouraging and frightening was the epidemic of influenza in the fall of 1918. The disease struck in late September and lasted some six weeks, reaching crisis proportions in Chattanooga as well as at the military base. In Chattanooga and its suburbs schools and theaters closed; attendants at the markethouse and barbers wore masks. A sign at the public library well expressed the attitude at the time. It simply commanded, "Please get your book and hurry away."

The widespread sickness at the camp presented a new challenge to the weary, overworked medical staff and the volunteer workers as muffled drums sounded a constant reminder of the new enemy. One unofficial report dated the end of October stated that 175 deaths had occurred in Chattanooga by that time and 517 at the army base. The total number of cases of influenza was estimated to be between seven and eight thousand.[4]

Just as the epidemic began to wane, news of the armistice sent everyone into ecstasy. Bombs were fired from the Times Building and the Patten Hotel launched a celebration which started in the small hours of the night and continued unrestrained. As various units arrived for demobilization at Fort Oglethorpe, enthusiasm again soared when the returning heroes paraded down the streets in full military garb. These veterans drew crowds of cheering people from all the neighboring towns, who lined the parade route decorated with bright-colored bunting. Finally on 4 July a great peace pageant to welcome home "the boys" was staged at Warner Park before some fifteen thousand citizens.[5]

Upward of ten thousand men from Hamilton County had served their country, of whom slightly more than two hundred lost their lives. The first battle casualty among the local men in American service was David King Summers, for whom the Chattanooga American Legion Post was named. James Craig Lodor, who was among the officers from the area commissioned at the first training camp at Chickamauga Park, was killed in action in France; his name is honored by the St. Elmo American Legion Post. Black veterans under the presidency of William M. Hixson also effected a permanent organization.

The government singled out at least thirteen Hamilton County men for special recognition and allied countries cited five. The United States awarded the Distinguished Service Cross to Major Julius Adler, Sergeant Luther F. Davis, Sergeant Marshall B. Duderar, First Lieutenant R. E. Gilliam, Sergeant Paul Igou, Lieutenant Colonel John W. Leonard, Second Lieutenant James Craig Lodor, Private Sewell K. Roberts, First Lieutenant Charles Seagraves, Second Lieutenant R. E. Sharp, Sergeant Fred B. Shannon, First Lieutenant Joe Wheeler Starkey, and Private Thomas J. Wilson.

Sergeant Davis also received the British military medal and four men earned the Croix de Guerre from France. They were Marshall Lasley, Mike Cohen, S. K. Roberts, and Joe Wheeler Starkey who won the Croix de Guerre with two palms.[6]

As a memorial for all who had served in the war, the voters of Chattanooga on 11 March 1919 approved a bond issue for the construction of the Soldiers and Sailors Memorial Auditorium. Land on McCallie Avenue was acquired and on 11 November 1922, the cornerstone laid for the five thousand-seat auditorium.

The war work record of women gave tremendous impetus to the suffrage movement, resulting in the ratification of the Nineteenth Amendment to the Constitution in 1920. In Hamilton County, active campaigning for women's rights developed much later than in some parts of the country and its pace was much slower. Two young ladies, cousins, were responsible for the first efforts and jokingly were known as the "local synonyms" for the movement. Catherine J. Wester moved to Chattanooga from Roane County and studied drafting with a local architect. Margaret Ervin, a graduate of Chattanooga High School and student at the local university, worked as a teacher, real estate agent, and advertising representative before training for the law.

In the fall of 1911 these two ladies decided to attend a national suffrage convention and emerged as devotees of the movement. That December they held the first local meeting, from which grew the Chattanooga Equal Rights Association, which boasted a membership at one time of 207, over one-third of whom were men. But growth proved to be very slow.

Wester and Ervin, however, did not lose their enthusiasm. They talked and planned on the local level, helped organize a state body in 1912, and marched in suffrage parades in the nation's capital. Miss Wester represented Tennessee on the national council while Miss Ervin at one time appeared before a congressional committee on matters relating to equal rights.

The first legislative success for women in Tennessee came in 1915 when the general assembly made them eligible for the office of notary public. In 1917 a municipal enfranchisement act passed by the general assembly allowed the town of Lookout Mountain to permit women to vote in municipal elections and to hold positions on the school board. This, except for a small Florida town, is claimed to have been the first community in the South where women gained such recognition.

Under the provisions of this law, Mrs. Newell Sanders became the first woman in Tennessee to cast a ballot when she voted in the April 1918 election. Mrs. Sanders, wife of the Republican United States senator, graduated in 1873 from Indiana State University before moving south five years later. A resident of Lookout Mountain, she gave much time to civic, religious, and educational work. In the 1918 election her daughter, Mrs. James (Norinne) Anderson, won a seat on the Lookout Mountain school board, the first woman nominated and elected to such an office.

In 1919 the state suffragettes managed to have this law broadened so that women could vote in all municipal and presidential elections. Consequently, in June, Chattanooga women voted for the first time in the primary election. Of the approximately 2,700 registered, 2,047 voted, including an impressive proportion of blacks.

In that same year the Congress adopted the Nineteenth Amendment and the states began the ratification process. In August 1920 the spotlight turned on Tennessee, where a special legislative session convened to consider the volatile issue; an affirmative vote by Tennessee would make the amendment a part of the nation's basic law. Lobbying had been growing in intensity for months. The "Suffs," as the headline writers called the supporters of ratification, brought in their national leadership; the "Antis" did likewise. These impassioned spokeswomen besieged Nashville and held meetings all across the state. In Hamilton County readers of the *Times* found the opposition view upheld while those who read George Fort Milton's *News* got the Suffs' point of view. Abby Crawford Milton, wife of the publisher, was a busy, energetic, staunch suffragist who headed the newly organized state body of the League of Women Voters. The lady orators and lobbyists used all their wiles on the legislators; the lawmakers vacillated but eventually ratified the amendment.

With the right to vote assured, the women gradually gained the privilege of holding more public offices. Sadie Watson on 1 February 1922 assumed her duties as county register, becoming the first woman to hold elective office in Hamilton County government. Four years later Sarah Frazier entered on a very active legislative career as a member of the Sixty-Fifth General Assembly, the third woman to win election to Tennessee's representative body.[7]

The war had exerted a major influence on another and entirely different development. The conflict propelled prewar aviation away from its cratelike planes and the popular notion that flyers were "birdmen" into an era of great practical development. On 5 December 1919 area citizens dedicated a flying field in East Chattanooga (near Roanoke Avenue and Glass Street), naming it Marr Field to honor Walter S. Marr, supporter of aviation. Marr had been a designer for the Buick Motor Company and had built automobiles himself before moving to Signal Mountain for health reasons. A spirited crowd of some three thousand gathered for this novel occasion; a few planes flew over the city to announce their presence; some did circus tricks to thrill the crowd and others took daring passengers aloft for $15 to $25 a ride.

Local pioneers had experimented with planes for some time before Marr Field opened; they generally had much more pluck than skill. George B. David built a bamboo-and-canvas "glider-like" motorless monoplane in 1904. Expecting to launch it with a tow car, he and an associate pulled it to Olympia Park on a wagon. The associate who attempted to pilot the contraption did not get off the ground. He smashed the plane, broke both of his arms, and found the machine so badly battered that the men simply gathered up the remains and burned them on the spot.

By 1910 two planes visited Olympia Park to demonstrate the miracle of flight. As barnstormers, they did a fair business entertaining school children dismissed from classes to witness powered flying. Soon a local man joined the new clan of aviators; Johnny Green learned to fly by trial and error, or "by the seat of his pants," as some described it. His airplane, made under the direction of Carl Morefield, who had worked for the Glenn Curtis people, was actually built at the Chattanooga Automobile Company's garage. Green flew from an improvised field off Rossville Boulevard and sometimes took along in his fragile craft John E. Lovell, a newcomer to the area.

Lovell, a Giles County, Tennessee, native, came to Chattanooga in 1910. He worked at the Patten Hotel where he later was promoted to general manager. An ardent promoter of improved highways, he at one time or another had offices with the Dixie, the Henry W. Grady, and the Lee highway associations. In 1917 he entered on a long tenure as chairman of the chamber of commerce's aeronautics committee; four years later he organized the Chattanooga Chapter of the National Aeronautical Association.

John Lovell had a hand in the establishment of Marr Field where, in due time, passenger and airmail planes began to land. The Interstate Air Lines Company, flying from Chicago to Atlanta, used the field. Since a flight from Chicago could not always be completed in daylight and no beacon lights marked the route to Atlanta, planes often stopped at Marr Field overnight. Flying was, at best, not very safe at the time and tricky air currents at the field, caused by its proximity to Missionary Ridge, gave the airport a poor reputation. At any rate, Interstate had several bad accidents here and after four men riding an airmail plane died in a crash, the field was condemned.

The need for a new airport could not have been made more clear. Lovell urged Chattanooga to float a loan to purchase a field and finally got the approval of the voters for a $250,000 bond issue. Land near the Chickamauga, Tennessee, railroad station, where the Confederate army had had its supply base in the fall of 1863, was acquired. The 130 acres there became the nucleus of Lovell Field, which opened in 1930.

There was nothing pretentious about the unpaved field, the small administration building, and one hangar. A twenty-four-inch rotating beacon and only a few lights aided nighttime landings. Moreover, aviation received a major setback when Tarbell Patten, Sr., a leading local promoter and head of Southern Flyers Incorporated, died in an air accident on 24 February 1930. Nevertheless, the momentum generated by World War I brought steady and rapid progress to aviation; local passengers and airmail traffic grew increasingly during the coming years, necessitating constant improvements and new facilities at the municipal field and terminal.

Some years earlier, in 1921, aviation had faced a new challenge. Major Harold C. Fiske of the Army Corps of Engineers, working out of the Chattanooga District office, had orders to prepare a comprehensive study of the Tennessee Valley for multipurpose planning. This assignment required very detailed maps, but the officer did not have funds to cover the cost of traditional mapping. Fiske turned to the Army Air Service with a request to experiment with aerial photography as a method of developing topographical maps. Two aviators in a De Haviland plane took some four thousand pictures of the area between Knoxville and Chattanooga. Never before had this method been used on such a large scale and the success of the experiment led to recommendations that it be used on similar surveys across the country.[8]

Another postwar innovation was the radio. Hamilton County had its first broadcasting station when WDOD dedicated its facilities in the Hotel Patten on 13 August 1925. Earl W. Winger served as president and Norman A. Thomas as vice-president and general manager.

As the postwar economy stabilized, the building tempo regained its earlier twentieth-century momentum. Children's Hospital, later renamed the T. C. Thompson Children's Hospital, opened on 15 July 1929 as a joint Chattanooga and Hamilton County project. Thompson, the Civitan Club, and the Junior League strongly supported this cooperative venture, which in recent years moved from its original Glenwood location to the Erlanger Hospital complex after having merged with the latter facility in 1952.

Several major new religious structures were completed, including the John A. Patten Memorial Chapel at the University of Chattanooga where dedication services were held on 30 May 1919. Centenary Methodist Church, having purchased the old home site of Thomas McCallie, held its first service in the new sanctuary on 26 March 1922. The Julius and Bertha Ochs Memorial Temple, home of the Mizpah Congregation, built by Adolph Ochs in memory of his parents, was dedicated 23 March 1928.

More commercial houses dotted the landscape: the Tennessee Power Company building at the corner of Sixth and Market streets (1924), the Maclellan building (1924), the new Read House (1926), the Chattanooga Bank building (1928), and the American National Bank building (1928). Most impressive was the Tivoli Theater, which opened on 19 March 1921. This "movie palace," featuring "grand interiors and unique space" seats eighteen hundred and contained the first commercial air-conditioning unit installed in the county. An unusually fine setting for the performing arts, it has long outlasted its original purpose and is presently the property of the city.

Throughout the county, construction monies went mainly for schools and roads with the credit for these important programs going chiefly to Judge Will Cummings. Cummings, born on his family's farm at Wauhatchie in 1872, started his political career in Hamilton County government at an early age. Educated in the county schools, the Winchester Normal School, and the University of Tennessee, he acquired a seat on the County Court in 1894. He was elected judge from 1912 to 1918 and again for the long tenure of 1926 to 1942.

As pleasure cars, trucks, and buses came into wider use, the county built chert roads which, according to one observer, made travel "easy." Such construction was responsible for a growing trend toward school consolidation and the gradual abandonment of one-room schools, for "auto trucks" could carry pupils to larger high schools. Among the new and rebuilt roads the county constructed was Riverside Drive in 1918, which unfortunately was built without regard for the preservation of Indian artifacts found in the great mound leveled at the time. On 24 July 1918 the new Wauhatchie Pike was dedicated, but because it measured only twenty feet wide around the base of Lookout Mountain, an additional contract in 1930 called for widening this busy thoroughfare. An eleven-mile stretch of concrete paving from Soddy to the county line in 1920, the first such construction in the area, proved novel enough to attract a large crowd of specatators at the first pouring. In 1928 "Brainerd Boulevard" was concreted as a part of Lee Highway, thus making it possible to drive to Cleveland in less than one hour.

In appreciation for the judge's work, the state named the highway from Chattanooga to Jasper the Will Cummings Highway; the citizens erected a marker which reads, in part,

> In recognition of the rare vision, the indomitable courage and capacity for achievement of Will Cummings, County Judge of Hamilton County, the pioneer of permanent road building and public improvements in East Tennessee and the Chattanooga District, the 1931 session of the State Legislature of

Tennessee by joint resolution designated this Highway as the Will Cummings Highway.

Here is one of the most picturesque highways of the State. It extends from Chattanooga to Jasper, under the historic Point of Lookout Mountain—site of the Battle Above the Clouds—above Moccasin Bend, winds through Wauhatchie Valley and skirts the beautiful Tennessee River. Every foot of the scenic route was bitterly contested and fought for by the Federal and Confederate armies during the War Between the States.

An obstruction to ready transportation flow handicapped downtown Chattanooga where Broad Street came to an abrupt end at Ninth Street. On the south side of the latter street the state of Georgia owned the land from the early days of the W & A (Western & Atlantic) railroad and had a row of small shops blocking the way to St. Elmo and Lookout Mountain. The city of Chattanooga wanted to open the street; the state of Georgia, not impressed by the city's appeal, went to the courts to prevent any change.

On the night of 6 May 1926, between injunctions, the commissioner of streets, Edward D. Bass, prepared to act. He gave the shopkeepers notice that afternoon so that they could protect their merchandise if they would keep his secret. Under cover of night Bass swung an ax, striking the first blow as a signal to a crew of workers who shortly demolished the structures in order to allow automobiles to drive through. The noise attracted citizens. A band practicing nearby stopped to go and see what was going on and soon struck up the tune, "Marching through Georgia."

Commissioner Bass had established the city's use of the passage through Georgia lands which later was recognized in a contract effective in January 1927 between Georgia, the lessee of the railroad, the N C & St. L, and the city. But Chattanooga's daring action did not sit well with some Georgia officials, who sought to reawaken the old issue that the state boundary line was in the wrong place—that it was too far south and that parts of Hamilton County actually belonged to Georgia.

Although the opening of Broad Street greatly facilitated travel from Chattanooga to Lookout Mountain, some hardy souls had endured the trip by horse-drawn conveyance for years by a longer route. In January 1867 a post office opened to serve the Lookout Mountain Educational Institute and the few year-round residents. Their number grew with the construction of the Inclines and on 3 March 1890 the village of Lookout Mountain was incorporated, although a municipal government was not organized until March of 1899. Then, J. B. Ragon, a Hamilton

County farm boy who read law with Judge D. C. Trewhitt before working in the county government, was elected the first mayor.

By 18 October 1892, there were enough citizens to organize services on a regular basis at the Lookout Mountain Presbyterian Church. Services had been held at the home of the Alexander Hunts (near the site of the present triangular park) up to this time. The Hunts had moved to the mountain in the 1880s from New York State and operated a farm and orchard, selling fresh peaches to eastern markets after the Broad Gauge Railroad was completed. A gift of land to the church from the Lookout Mountain Land Company made it possible to build a sanctuary, which came into use on 14 October 1894.

The growing use of the automobile in the 1920s did much to make comfortable living on the top of the mountain practicable, and the three-mile stretch north of the Georgia state line was quickly filled with fine homes. On 3 August 1926, the people selected Jerome Pound as mayor. He had just acquired property on the mountain and took the lead in advocating a variety of improvements sponsored by the Lookout Mountain Improvement League. Among the goals of this group were paved roads, improved schools, better sanitary conditions, and fire protection.

The dirt road up the north end of the mountain was closed for paving in September 1926 and a detour routed over the unused St. Elmo turnpike. Recommendations soon were made that this road also be improved, and with the financial aid of Adolph S. Ochs the project was begun in 1930.

The booming economy of the 1920s stimulated real estate developments, and in the fall of 1924 a business group headed by O. B. Andrews and Garnet Carter acquired a large tract of land which spread out beyond the state line. Carter came to the area with his family from Sweetwater, Tennessee. Andrews, son of a former Chattanooga mayor, had been a fervent promoter of professional baseball and the construction of Engel Stadium in 1929. The developers called the area Fairyland. They sold many building lots and in June 1925 formally opened the Fairyland Inn. Andrews soon sold his interest to Carter, who worked out details for the Fairyland Golf Club, which opened in 1927. At this time the inn was converted into a clubhouse and operated privately.

While awaiting the completion of the golf course, Carter by chance developed the idea of a miniature game called "Tom Thumb" golf which caught on like wildfire all across the country. Carter's patent and manufacturing plants made a fine profit until he sold his interests in 1930. That year he sponsored the first National Tom Thumb Tournament at the Fairyland course where such celebrities as Bobby Jones and Babe Ruth also putted the ball through hollow logs and around native rock.

Just south of the Hamilton County border, where Georgia begins, more building activity enlivened the area. Garnet Carter's brother, Paul, Jerome Pound, and others built a new Lookout Mountain Hotel, which marked its opening on 23 June 1928. (The hotel, like earlier Lookout Mountain ventures projected on a grand scale, suffered financial reverses and in 1964 was sold and became the home of Covenant College.) Four years later, on 8 May 1932 Garnet Carter and his wife opened the Rock City Gardens; This enterprise has done much to make Lookout Mountain a remembered name among visitors who come by the thousands to Hamilton County.

Another mountain tourist attraction featuring geological wonders—this one within Hamilton County—grew out of an accidental discovery. The mountain, honeycombed with caverns, has fascinated the amateur explorer ever since the days of the Brainerd missionaries. One large cave with an entrance on the north end of the mountain overlooking Moccasin Bend especially attracted spelunkers. But in 1908 the Southern Railway built a double-tracked tunnel through Lookout at this spot, striking the entrance to the old cave. This subterranean space, wellhidden deep in the tunnel, was a hideout for bootleggers until the railroad company permanently sealed it.

A young spelunker named Leo Lambert, who had moved to the area from Indiana, had crawled through miles of local underground passageways. The idea came to him of developing the cave commercially. His plan was to acquire land on the side of the mountain and to drill a hole down to the passage. A company backed mostly by Indiana money began the drilling on 1 November 1928. When they had gone about 260 feet, their shaft broke clear of the rock into an unknown opening. Lambert and friends immediately climbed down to explore the area and to their great surprise discovered a waterfall with a 100-foot plunge within the mountain. Lambert named the falls for his wife Ruby.

The shaft was continued to the lower-level cavern some 420 feet below the surface. Six months later, during the week of 16-22 June 1930, the Ruby Falls project was open to the public. A Cavern Castle gateway made of mountain sandstone marked the entrance from which elevators carried the public into the lighted passages. Unfortunately

Lambert's success coincided with the national depression; his company lost money and went into receivership. In 1932 Claude Brown bought Ruby Falls for $25,000. Today hundreds of tourists visit the intriguing rock formations and marvel at the large underground waterfall.[9]

Another nearby mountain also attracted both tourists and local residents. Its development resulted from the perseverance of Hamilton County's biggest promoter, Charles E. James. Back in the boom years of the 1880s "Charlie," or "Cholly," James along with his many other enterprises projected the Chattanooga Western Railroad, designed to cross Walden Ridge on its way to Evansville, Indiana. In the highlands a town called Signal Point City was slated to be developed. Grading operations, however, were halted with the coming of the depressed economic conditions of the 1890s. Undaunted, James switched to the idea of building a fine hunting club for wealthy sportsmen, but it too failed after a number of prospective members, including Theodore Roosevelt, had been secured.

By 1911 James was ready to start again. He owned some forty-four hundred acres on the mountaintop overlooking the canyon of the Tennessee to the south and Chattanooga to the east. He now proposed to erect a hotel in this dramatic, eye-catching setting and at the same time tie the area to Chattanooga by an almost thirteen-mile electric streetcar line to be chartered as the Chattanooga Traction Company.

James undertook both projects at the same time. Work crews from a camp at Glendale graded the interurban line on a zigzag route and leveled a twenty-four-foot parallel roadbed for vehicular traffic. A road was also cleared from the top of the "W" road to the hotel site so that building materials could be delivered. Sawmills cut cross ties, timbers, and lumber from the neighboring forests. Charles B. Adams, storekeeper and postmaster at Albion View, supervised much of the work.

By June 1913 the sumptuous inn opened for the public and by fall the streetcars ran to the crest of the mountain. James kept his sawmills working, building cottages near the inn and a number of permanent residences close at hand. As one wit put it, Charley James ran the "catamount from his hiding place on Walden Ridge and founded there a city."

Although the number of permanent residents did not exceed two hundred, James expanded his plans with a large addition to the inn in 1916 (later to become the Alexian Brothers Rest Home). A casino and riding stable were added, and a golf course in 1918. Later a town hall and fire station were built, all in the vicinity of the inn. James lived on Signal Mountain, commuting each day by trolley to his office in the James Building in Chattanooga.

Surrounded largely by uninhabited forest, the community faced a novel problem after the golf course was completed. As there were no fence laws, farmers from the valleys continued to drive cattle to the mountaintop to forage for themselves during the summer. The roving bovines found the greens of the golf course to be especially good grazing areas and did not mind feeding on people's lawns. In order to deal with this problem, a charter for the town of Signal Mountain was obtained on 4 April 1919. James served as its first mayor until his death in 1925. The first act of the new government dealt with the cattle problem by making it illegal to run cattle within the town limits. A ranger was hired and a pound provided. Gradually the "cattle war" ceased, but then a new problem arose. Grass and weeds grew in abundance on all the vacant lands, and the city fathers in 1926 finally decreed that no weed should be allowed to grow over ten inches tall anywhere within the corporate limits. Anything higher would result in a fine for the owner. A half-century later, with the ordinance still in effect, trim lawns carpet the ever expanding populated parts of the mountain.

In 1934 streetcars gave way to buses. After World War II Signal Mountain expanded rapidly, but preserved the natural beauty of the terrain and forestland amid the modern, growing residential community.[10]

While Lookout and Signal mountains prospered, the people of the county of James immediately to the east of Hamilton faced only dreary prospects. This rural county, established in 1871, had problems from the time it was created, and on several occasions there was talk of abolishing it. This point of view drew more supporters when in 1913 the county courthouse at Ooltewah burned. Although a new seat of justice was built, from that time until December 1919 arguments for annexation to Hamilton County grew increasingly persuasive.

James County simply did not have the tax base to meet the demand for school and highway budgets. One merchant who favored annexation stated his position thus:

> I have several reasons for wanting to join Hamilton County. First, and most important, is because of their better schools. Their term is for nine months, ours but five. Another reason is the prospect for good roads. Hamilton's cross-country roads are better than our main roads.

Because of James County's bankrupt condition, Tennessee authorized the county to hold a referendum on annexation to Hamilton

County. By a twelve-to-one margin (953 to 78) the voters endorsed the idea on 11 December 1919 with only a few officeholders and persons desirous of becoming officeholders voting against it. Hamilton County was receptive of the result and assumed the indebtedness of her old neighbor, which became a civil district. The annexed territory of 285 square miles held a population of about fifty-three hundred, most of whom lived on farms. The small villages in the area outside of Ooltewah comprised White Oak Mills, Birchwood, Harrison, Work, Salem, White Oak, Snow Hill, Apison, Howardville, Tallant, and Maddox.[11]

Ooltewah, the largest settlement in James County, claimed a possible five hundred persons. It had grown up along the tracks of the East Tennessee and Georgia Railroad, beginning in 1857. The village, called a "citadel of temperance," in addition to serving as the county seat, also supported a powder plant. Following the demise of James County, Ooltewah ceased being the hub of political activity and gradually slipped into a very quiet existence. The old courthouse served as a school for a time, a headquarters for a fraternal order, and later a civic center. In the latter capacity, it came to life especially on election days and at times when people brought in their dogs for rabies shots. In 1977 the old courthouse became the North Hamilton County Police Station.[12]

In 1881 the railroad had built a branch line from Ooltewah across the county to Cohutta, Georgia. One of the way stations was Thatcher's Switch, where Jim Thatcher owned lime pits and several kilns, along with a commissary. By 1916 business fell off and Thatcher sold his property. The new owner was the Southern Junior College; in due time Thatcher's Switch was know as Collegedale and the school Southern Missionary College.

This school was started in 1892 by the Seventh Day Adventist Church as an elementary and high school at Graysville, Tennessee, and was located in one room over a grocery store. After a fire in the Graysville quarters, the school was moved to a new location on a large tract nestled at the foot of White Oak Mountain. Shortly after the annexation of the area to Hamilton County, the school enrolled some 250 students ranging from elementary school to junior-college age. Practically all of legal age earned their way in industries carried on by the school, which included a dairy, bakery, furniture factory, broom factory, bookshop, and silk mill, and by gardening and farming on their 750 acres. With steady growth, by 1944 the institution changed to a four-year accredited college; in 1978 it enrolled 2,000 students.[13]

On down the branch railroad which later became the property of the Southern Railway, the trains passed the early settlement of Jacob and Mary Plowman. A depot established here acquired the name O'Brian, honoring a railroad official, but it had to be changed because another Tennessee town had already used the name. According to tradition Jim Roberts, a local merchant and businessman who had some acquaintance with geology, called attention to the local shale that was unusual and known as Apison Shale. Thus O'Brian became Apison. The village supported a grist mill, broom shop, cotton gin, wagon shop, and smithy before a 1924 cooperative cheese factory was started. That same year a bauxite mine opened on the ridge between Collegedale and Apison. Although it did not prosper, the mine gave the ridge its present name, Bauxite Ridge, and hastened the arrival of electric power lines into the southeastern corner of Hamilton County.[14]

Some time before Hamilton County began wrestling with the annexation of James County, Chattanooga had already awakened to the advantages of growth by annexation of neighboring settled areas. Until the twentieth century the original limits of the town—the river, Ninth Street, and Georgia Avenue—had been changed but once. This expansion occurred in 1854 when the corporate limits were extended from the winding Tennessee River to East End Avenue on the east (Central Avenue) to Twenty-Eighth Street on the south close by Chattanooga Creek. The vast stretch of land eastward toward Missionary Ridge and southward to the base of Lookout Mountain remained largely a forested area with a sparse population. The land boom in the late 1880s and the building of the belt line railroad and the electric streetcar lines, however, caused a number of satellite villages to spring up.

The first area, annexed in May 1905, consisted of parts of Highland Park and Orchard Knob, following affirmative voting by both the annexed area and the city. During the same year some additional adjacent lands were annexed by legislative act without a vote. Before the real estate boom, the area claimed only scattered dwellings until the Chamberlain Avenue Land Company, composed of local and New Orleans investors, laid out streets and promoted the building of the street railway. The area, the promoters said, was "all above overflow" from floods and contained heights so "commanding and desirable" as to give it its name, Highland Park.

Orchard Knob, along with Pine Knob and Bald Knob (or Indian Hill), developed as a project of the McCallie Avenue Land and Improvement Company in 1887. It centered on the historic hill from which General Grant directed the battle of Missionary Ridge and got new attention when the battle site was incorporated into Chickamauga and Chattanooga National Military Park. This section and Highland Park were both strictly residential areas.[15]

In 1913 another major territory was annexed and an estimated ten thousand Hamilton County citizens found themselves residents of Chattanooga. This area comprised Orange Grove, Ferger Place, Oak Grove Park, Ridgedale, and a small detached area referred to as the Gardenhire tract, where the city water company operated its station by Citico Creek.

Orange Grove came into the city without a ballot, for ninety percent of the voters had signed petitions in favor of annexation. Before the Civil War, brothers from England living here had planted Osage orange trees along the road (later Main Street) giving this area its atypical name. The citizens of the remaining territory voted on 8 April 1913 and although few citizens bothered to vote, annexation was carried by a margin of 174 to 98.

The main subdivision in the group, Ridgedale, located at the eastern base of Missionary Ridge, as late as 1885 consisted of a tangled woodland except for the 350-acre farm of John L. Divine. When Montgomery Avenue, later called Main Street, was extended to the ridge and interurban transportation was available, the real estate market opened up. D. L. Dodds of Illinois bought a tract of the Divine land and established his home near the corner of Dodds and Main streets near a refreshing spring located in a shady grove.

Ridgedale began to grow as Dodds sold off lots. The construction of Central High School and the McCallie School attracted residents as did such industries as a coffin factory, the Converse Bridge Company, and a canning plant. According to plan, Central High School remained county property after annexation, and the new McCallie Avenue tunnel was not considered to be within the new city limits either.[16]

The fact that the 1920 census gave Chattanooga a population of less than fifty-eight thousand disturbed many local businessmen who felt the statistics misrepresented the area and were a deterrent to industrial growth. Friends of annexation also noted that the city contained only about seven and a half square miles and that annexation would bring economies of administration for all. The chamber of commerce planned a campaign to change this; George Fort Milton headed its efforts until his death, when his son continued the crusade. Their newspaper, the

News, constantly pointed out the advantages that would accrue from a larger population credit.

In 1921 the suburbs participated in a referendum on the subject which lost by a scant twenty-odd votes. This election focused on a blanket plan with the total vote of all districts being the deciding factor. Paradoxically two suburbs, East Chattanooga and East Lake, cast enough negative votes to defeat the annexation movement but became the first areas to join the city in the coming years.[17]

East Chattanooga along with Avondale, Churchville, and contiguous areas joined the city in formal exercises on 8 January 1925. Actually East Chattanooga voted by a margin of 391 to 371 to be annexed in 1923, but some citizens contested the election, thus postponing admission for two years. The area comprised a large section which in the past had been known in part or on the whole under a variety of names: Amnicola, Tunnel, Sherman Heights, Avondale, Boyce. It contained many fine springs, all the railroads coming into the area from the south and east as well as the belt line, and roughly sixteen thousand citizens. Not until 1884 did the first store, schoolhouse, and post office open, the latter located at the residence of W. J. Johnson.

The East Chattanooga Land Company developed this section during the boom and, before long, small industries grew up: a butter-dish factory, curtain pole factory, stove foundries, wheelbarrow works, sawmill, hosiery mill, and shoe factory. Here, too, Marr Field served aviation after 1919.

To the east of East Chattanooga along Third Street were found the two black hamlets of Bushtown (sometimes called Stanleyville) and Churchville, both of which simultaneously approved of annexation.

Later, in 1925, East Lake with its smaller neighbors, Cedar Hill and Fort Cheatham, changed views and voted for annexation. The referendum campaign grew very heated; out of a total vote of 1,009 the margin of victory for those who would join Chattanooga was only 29. The East Lake section located south of Ridgedale included a beautiful lake and was the home of the Richmond Spinning Company and the Chickamauga Knitting Mill.

East Lake voters long opposed annexation by echoing the opinions of the industrialists who did not want any change which might disturb the tax base. In 1921 and again in 1923 they defeated moves to join the city, but on 4 August 1925, with the "pros" thoroughly organized, East Lake approved annexation with a margin in this community exclusive of Cedar Hill and Fort Cheatham of only four votes.[18]

The long annexation campaign conducted by the Chattanooga Chamber of Commerce and numerous civic clubs climaxed in a big celebration party on 30 September 1929. At midnight the annexation of Alton Park, Brainerd, Missionary Ridge, North Chattanooga, Riverview, and St. Elmo became a reality. Only Ridgeside (Shepherd Hills) turned down the chance to join Greater Chattanooga. The six suburbs that approved annexation contained an estimated ten square miles and thirty-five thousand people.

A large crowd gathered for the festivities highlighted by a pageant, "The Crowning of Greater Chattanooga," and the naming of Mary Turner as queen. The mayor told the audience that "tomorrow marks the consummation of the most progressive step in Chattanooga's history." Speakers praised A. F. Porzelius, president of the chamber of commerce, and presented a silver cup to George Fort Milton, Jr., for his leadership as chairman of the chamber's annexation committee.[19]

Each of the districts had its own story. Alton Park to the south of Chattanooga occupied lands that were once the homesite of Daniel Ross. Later the Kirklin and James farms were located here, and after C. E. James acquired them the general area was referred to as Oak Hill until about 1890. With the coming of the belt line and other modern transportation the small village emerged as an industrial and residential suburb. Its economic interests centered around the shops of the Chattanooga and Southern Railroad, a glass factory, and a cotton oil company. In 1929 Alton Park had an organized government with a bonded indebtedness of half a million dollars, about seventy-five hundred citizens, and a property valuation figured at about five and a quarter million dollars. That May, Alton Park turned down annexation by a margin of 119 votes, but after reconsideration approved it in a 20 June balloting of 287 to 187. This switch resulted largely from the willingness of the city to construct a highway where the Alton Park people suggested, thereby linking the two areas. The pledge to extend Market Street from Twenty-eighth Street brought Alton Park into the city.[20]

A mile or so to the west, the town of St. Elmo with about five thousand residents voted in May in favor of annexation. This, the oldest suburb, nestled against the evening side of Lookout Mountain where long, sunless summer evenings produced cool comfort. Only the Chattanooga Medicine Company (now Chattem) provided employment there for any sizable group of workers.

Part of St. Elmo was located on the old Elisha Kirklin farm. At the place where Hooker Road and the Wauhatchie Pike crossed, a settlement grew up called simply Crossroads, Midway House, or Kirklin; boisterous times earned it a rather unsavory reputation. After the war Kirklin had a post office that served a wide area. Nearby, Colonel Abraham Malone Johnson owned large holdings which his wife had inherited from her family, the Whitesides. Johnson built the second turnpike up the mountain, laid out the Forest Hills Cemetery in 1880, and opened up a real estate subdivision. About 1885 he changed the name of the area to St. Elmo. This name was the title of a novel published by Augusta Jane Evans Wilson in 1866. The story opens with scenes from the area at the base of the mountain which the author had visited in 1853 and again during the war when she came to visit her brother, a wounded Confederate soldier.

The real estate boom years and the construction of the Lookout Mountain Inclines and railways brought rapid growth to St. Elmo and by 1892 three schools and four churches were built. In 1905 the town incorporated primarily to provide more support for public schools. Annexation in 1929, favored by the mayor and the town commissioners, was readily approved [21]

On the north side of the river both North Chattanooga and Riverview voted in May 1929 to enter the city. The early landowners in the area— the Divines, Beesons, Cowarts, Ruoffs, Clauses, Carrolls, and Becks— used the rich bottomlands for agriculture. In 1884 a new steam ferry dates the first organized attempt to build a residential community, with Captain S. J. A. Frazier as its godfather. The subdivision developed by the North Side Land Company profited by the euphoria of the general real estate boom of the late 1880s and the prospects of a span across the Tennessee River.

When the Walnut Street bridge opened, two streetcar lines served the north side—one to Riverview and one to Vallombrosa and Stringer's Ridge. Property values rose although certain accommodations had to be made to meet the problems of the new day. The county court ordered that a mule be hitched to every car crossing the bridge so that the new contraption would not frighten passing teams. After some time the mule got so accustomed to his task that he moved in front of the cars and guided them across without being harnessed. Jokesters began to call the mule "County Court," a practice which finally led that august body to rescind the mule ordinance.

As residences sprang up in this hill country, many of the area's wealthiest and most prominent citizens moved there. Streets with sweeping curves fit into the terrain and created attractive homesites. At least three communities—North Chattanooga, Hill City, and Riverview—organized governments, and a recreation center, the Golf and Country Club, added to the property values. In 1925 the residents of Hill City voted to become a part of North Chattanooga; this move led many to believe the latter would soon join Chattanooga. In the May 1929 election North Chattanooga's population of some sixteen thousand did approve annexation, 591 to 516, and in a surprising result Riverview voted the annexation of its estimated six hundred citizens by a margin of 49 to 42.[22]

Another suburb taking part in the 1929 voting was Missionary Ridge, a strictly residential community with only two small commercial businesses. The settlement began as a group of sparsely populated farm units, grew into a taxing district, and in 1925 incorporated to secure fire protection. A unique feature of the area was the fact that it was 4½ miles long and only 1,100 feet wide. Dividing the width of this town was the Crest Road, owned and maintained by the federal government as part of the Chickamauga and Chattanooga National Military Park; the city limits extended 600 feet west and 500 feet east of the thoroughfare. At the time of the annexation vote, the mayor reported that practically all available building sites in the town had been used.

The ridge voters in March decided against annexation, 184 to 139, but because Brainerd had approved, many ridge residents were immediately open to reconsideration. The state legislature, in session at the time, approved another election for 16 April in which the opposing sides virtually exchanged majorities, 181 to 133. It was claimed that the March election had gone against annexation because of a careless comment of an annexation worker. The ridge residents, having already taken care of pressing service needs, requested beautification work from the city if annexed, which led to the remark that the Missionary Ridge ladies "wanted gold-plated fire plugs."[23]

Like the ridge, Brainerd took its name from the Brainerd Mission, although it was not until the spirited campaign of the Community League in 1926 that the matter of a name was settled. The area was quite extensive and only gradually did farmlands become formally developed residential sites. Comprising this section were Sunnyside, home of Judge R. B. Cooke and the site of a school by that name, and Dutchtown, a prosperous Swiss and German settlement in which Jacob Kellerhals was a key figure. Here also lived Colonel William Riley Crabtree, former Chattanooga mayor, state senator, and candidate for governor. Crabtree had chosen the name Belvoir for his estate, which contemporaries described as "one of the most splendid farms in this section."

The development of the Brainerd community depended to a degree on the construction of a tunnel through Missionary Ridge which the county undertook in 1907. For rural residents taking produce to the Chattanooga market, the matter of crossing the steep ridge was slow, wearing on their teams, and a definite factor that limited their loads. But the stubborn ridge resisted all attempts to bore through it; construction, legal, and financial troubles held up tunnel completion until 1913, after which commercial establishments clustered near the eastern portal.

By 1929 the more than seven thousand people in the Brainerd district were among the first citizens to encourage annexation. Mass meetings and circulars helped get a wide margin of victory in the 11 March referendum, 467 to 167. To demonstrate its support of annexation, Brainerd held an independent, festive celebration after the more staid ceremony at the auditorium. From nine P.M. until midnight on 30 September the young people danced in the street by the east end of the tunnel and cheered the arrival of Mayor Bass when he took over the government of the ward at midnight. Some jestingly referred to the merrymaking as Brainerd's last hour of independence; others claimed it marked the first moments of cityhood.[24]

NOTES

1. *Chattanoga Times*, 9 May 1915; 3 June 1917; 6 April 1918; Edwin S. Lindsey, *Centennial History of St. Paul's Episcopal Church, Chattanooga, Tennessee, 1853–1953* (Chattanooga: Vestry of St. Paul's, 1953), pp. 48–49.

2. *Chattanooga Times*, 6,7 June; 21, 22 July; 6, 19 September 1917.

3. Ibid., 6 October 1917.

4. Ibid., material gleaned from scattered references throughout war years; Harry M. Wiltse, "History of Chattanooga" (Typescript, Chattanooga-Hamilton County Bicentennial Library), 2:122–128.

5. *Chattanooga Times*, 11–13 November 1918; 3, 9 April 1919.

6. Ibid, 8 August 1920; Mrs. D.P. Montague, chairperson of the Women's Service League, compiled this material along with the available citations. Her list is more complete than that found in Philip M. Hamer, ed., *Tennessee: A History, 1673-1932*, 4 vols. (New York: American Historical Society, 1933), 2:917–920.

7. Ibid., pp. 717–730; Zella Armstrong, *History of Hamilton County and Chattanooga, Tennessee*, 2 vols. (Chattanooga: Lookout Publishing, 1931), 2:188; John Wilson, *Lookout Mountain: The Story of an Amazing Mountain* (Chattanooga: News-Free Press, 1977), p. 62; *Chattanooga Times*, 29 March, 1912; 18 January 1914; 7 May 1915; 11 June 1919; 2 February 1922.

8. *Chattanooga Times*, 12 September 1912; 5, 6, December 1919; 1 July, 25 December 1928; 22 July 1941; *Chattanooga News-Free Press*, 14 July 1964; Nashville District, Corps of Engineers, *Engineers on the Twin Rivers: A History of the Nashville District Corps of Engineers, U.S. Army* (n.p., 1979), p. 181.

9. Robert S. Walker, *Lookout: The Story of a Mountain* (Kingsport, Tenn.: Southern Publishing, 1941), pp. 13–21, 23–26, 179–184, 215–216, 255–256; Wilson, *Lookout*, pp. 60–61, 107–112, 118–129. Some of Lookout's early mayors were J. B. Ragon, W. B. Mitchell, Frank Caldwell, Richard Watkins, P. F. Jones, S. B. Lowe, and Hollis Caldwell.

10. Cartter Patten, *Signal Mountain and Walden's Ridge* (n.p.: author, 1962), pp. 46–57; George M. James, *A Remarkable Man* (n.p.: author, 1977); David H. Steinberg, *And to Think It Only Cost a Nickel! The Development of Public Transportation in the Chattanooga Area* (Chattanooga: author, 1975), pp. 73–78. Albion View was Walden Ridge's first post office. Early mayors of Signal Mountain were C. E. James, Webster T. James, Frank M. Robbins, Burton Franklin, and Joe Richardson.

11. *Chattanooga Times*, 26 February, 10 March 1913; 29 March 1915; 12, 17 December 1919; 11 October 1956; 13 October 1958; 25 September 1961. Hamilton County retired the last James County road bonds in 1956.

12. J. P. Brown to Zella Armstrong, 26 September 1959, Chattanooga-Hamilton County Bicentennial Library.

13. Ray Hefferlin, "Glimpses into the Tri-Area Past," (Photocopy, Chattanooga-Hamilton County Bicentennial Library); *Chattanooga Times*, 15 May 1920.

14. *Chattanooga Times*, 24 February 1971; Hefferlin, "Glimpses into the Tri-Area Past."

15. *Chattanooga Times*, 8 December 1892; 21, 22, February 1899; 9 May 1913; *Chattanooga News*, 2 July 1890; 14 December 1915. The name East End Avenue was changed to Central Avenue on 24 April 1911.

16. *Chattanooga Times*, 12 February 1911; 9 May 1913; *Chattanooga News*, 2 July 1890; 14 December 1915; *Chattanooga News-Free Press*, 8 December 1955.

17. *Chattanooga News*, 30 September 1929.

18. *Chattanooga Times*, 8 December 1892; 11 April 1923; 31 December 1924; 1 January, 5 August 1925.

19. Ibid., 1 October 1929; *Chattanooga News*, 30 September 1929.

20. *Chattanooga Times*, 11, 12 March, 4 May, 21 June, 1 October 1929; *Chattanooga News*, 29 November 1901; 30 September 1929.

21. Wilson, *Lookout*, pp. 66-68; Walker, *Lookout*, pp. 227–235; *Chattanooga Times*, 8 December 1892; 4 June 1916; 21 January 1917; 1 October 1929; *Chattanooga News-Free Press*, 21 September 1938; 7 May 1978. A. M. Johnson (1830-1903) married Thankful Anderson Whiteside in 1857. He served in the transportation department of the Confederacy holding the rank of colonel. He returned to Chattanooga after the conflict, rebuilt his destroyed home, and became cashier of the Lookout Savings Institute. For seventeen years beginning in 1869 he supervised the development of the water company. His brick home built on the side of Lookout Mountain, known simply as "The House," was a social center of St. Elmo.

22. *Chattanooga Times*, 8 December 1892; 15, 16 May 1925; 24 January 1926; 4 May, 1 October 1929; *Chattanooga News*, 2 July 1890; 30 September 1929.

23. *Chattanooga Times*, 7 May, 1 October 1929; *Chattanooga News*, 30 September 1929; *Chattanooga News-Free Press* , 28 November 1964. Chiefly responsible for the final decision of the Missionary Ridge voters was T. C. Betterton; the mayor at the time was J. F. Holbert.

24. *Chattanooga Times*, 4 June 1916; 13 November 1926; 1 October 1929; *Chattanooga News*, 30 September 1929.

A New Use for the Old River

SHORTLY after three o'clock on the afternoon of 18 May 1933, President Franklin D. Roosevelt put his signature to legislation creating a vast undertaking in the highlands and valleys of the Tennessee River's watershed. Federal interest in the yellow-colored river carrying heavy burdens of soil to the sea dated from 1824. Surveys and projects on the main stream by 1918 numbered some seventeen with an additional ten on the tributaries. Practically every project had comprised a waste of energy and money squandered on unplanned, porkbarrel schemes. Down at Muscle Shoals stood Wilson Dam and the nitrate plant, eroding in idleness—ghosts of World War I's preparedness efforts. They served only as political footballs kicked about by the advocates of private and public electric utility development.[1]

A buoyant group, including Senator George W. Norris and the Tennessee congressional delegation, stood by the president at the birth of the authority designed to represent the newly-elected administration's "three-r's" program of relief, recovery, and reform. The bill had passed through Congress in a very brief time; the Senate approved it without debate or roll call while the House of Representatives approved it, 259 to 112. To the people of Hamilton County and of the valley as a whole it represented an influx of money, national recognition, and an assurance of better days ahead.

During the time that the legislation was taking shape, the name Tennessee Valley Authority emerged and "TVA" became a symbol for a complex, many-faceted program. Its statement of long-term objectives called for control of the Tennessee River so that the flow of water would do maximum good and minimum harm. As a multipurpose plan it was intended to maintain navigable depths at all times, provide storage of floodwaters, and generate the maximum amount of electric energy consistent with the first objectives. To these goals Roosevelt added the important notion of proper land usage—reclamation of marginal lands, reforestation, wildlife management, and improved agricultural practices. As a pledge to the future, the act called for "the economic and social well-being of the people living in said river basin."

The valley of the Tennessee River conforms to no state boundary lines but embraces lands in the seven states of Tennessee, Virginia, North Carolina, Kentucky, Georgia, Alabama, and Mississippi. In size the valley is about equal to England and Scotland combined; in shape it resembles on the watershed map, a huge butterfly with wings widely spread and with slender body positioned at Hamilton County.

Throughout its history the county had experienced numerous decisions crucial to its destiny made by federal solons. The central government had created western states such as Tennessee set up on an equal basis with the thirteen original ones. It had formulated the Cherokee removal policy and conducted military campaigns during the troubled days of disunion. From Washington had come Reconstruction policy and in 1890 the government created the Chickamauga and Chattanooga National Military Park. Since 1871 Chattanooga had been the district engineer's headquarters, where federal representatives translated certain river improvement plans into action.

But at no time in the past did a national project embrace such bold and extensive ramifications for the area. In addition to the long-range design to harness the river, the TVA legislation meant jobs and wages to a depression-ridden people. When word came from Senator Nathan Bachman that Congress had passed the bill shortly after noon on 17 May 1933, Chattanooga's whistles sounded a "bedlam of noise" and the county people joined in the celebration, sensing that the event contained an omen of good things to come.

The very rapid evolution of the TVA legislation was the indirect product of studies by the Army Engineers. In the 1920s, surveys of the Tennessee and other valleys were authorized by Congress. Locally the task fell to Major Harold C. Fiske, district engineer at Chattanooga, who had used aerial pictures to help prepare the necessary maps. The surveys, designed to be comprehensive and multipurpose in nature, drew both hearty approval and caustic criticism, for they went far beyond the traditional Engineers' mission of improving river navigation. Fiske's reports were not only exhaustive but were supported by his enthusiastic advocacy for multipurpose developments. The idea advocated high, main-river dams designed to aid navigation and flood control and provide hydropower. Such facilities, however, could not be developed by traditional federal policy; the alternative would be thirty-two low dams to improve navigation only. The debate over these alternatives ended with President Roosevelt's endorsement of the TVA﹒ concept.[2]

The Hamilton County people who welcomed TVA numbered 159,497, according to the census of 1930, which showed a population increase of some 43,000 over the previous decade. Of this number 22.7 percent were blacks (36,155). As all through Hamilton's history, the population was almost totally native American; only 1 percent were foreign-born. Those who were born abroad included some from southern and eastern Europe, a trend which was found in immigration in the United States as a whole. Representative of this group were 412 from Russia, 48 from Lithuania, 61 from Greece, 41 from Italy, and 149 from Poland.

As a result of Chattanooga's comprehensive annexation program in the 1920s, the population of the city jumped from 57,895 to 119,798 in ten years. Of this number 33,289 were black. The percentage of blacks in 1930 was 27.8 percent as compared to 32.6 percent in 1920 when they numbered 18,800. In 1930 the black population outside Chattanooga was less than 3,000 with certain concentrations at Turkey Foot, a belt along the road between Tyner and Harrison, and the Bakewell black community.[3]

By the end of the third decade of the twentieth century Hamilton County's population still retained its native purity. This was a source of family and regional pride and featured the retention of old ballads, traditions, songs, and folkways. At the same time this homogeneity fostered provincialism.

Religious worship followed an orthodox pattern and deviated only slightly from fundamentalist interpretation while black churches assumed a growing importance with a better-trained clergy and more durable and comfortable church buildings. A promise of "old-fashioned preaching," a call for periodic revivals (or "protracted meetings") with visiting evangelists, and the appeal of the old gospel hymns kept faith with the conservative theology. But as older denominations grew more formal and departed from the emotionalism of camp meeting days, other groups appeared, some using "unknown tongues" and healing seances.

Among the new groups of worshippers were the Church of God (Tomlinson), Church of God, and the (Original) Church of God. Another smaller group, started about 1909 near the Grasshopper community, was the Church of God with Signs Following After. The members believed in handling poisonous snakes in their religious service; after 1947 when Tennessee prohibited snake handling, they refused to obey the law, which they claimed interfered with their religious freedom.

Fundamentalism often expressed itself through the state legislature as in the case of blue laws regulating Sabbath commerce. The state government also prohibited the teaching of evolution, a "forbidden doctrine," with the approval of a large portion of the population. Many Hamilton Countians applauded the efforts of William Jennings Bryan in the 1925 Dayton Trial, while some expressed their disapproval that Chattanooga had not thought to bring such a court suit before their Rhea County neighbors had.

Paralleling the antiscience crusade was a campaign against the sale and use of alcoholic drink, which still continues in some sections today. Through the years this policy produced inconsistencies, many of which the people seemed to enjoy rather than to take very seriously. With state prohibition established in 1909, the paradox of voting "dry" and drinking "wet" often became a laughing matter. A heavy traffic in home-made potions kept the law of supply and demand functioning. It also kept the sheriff's men reasonably busy searching the coves and mountains for the lair of the moonshine artist with his prize copper still or ordinary Alabama blackpot. Sometimes moonshiners operated in the city itself and on one occasion a working still was found on a truck touring the streets and byways of Chattanooga. So remarkably fine was the quality of some of the illicit corn liquor that local political leaders had to make frequent trips home from Washington to keep their Congressional friends in the proper "spirit."[4]

Naturally the census takers made no notes of employment in this *sub rosa* profession, but in 1930 they did report that 65,948 persons, including 18,139 women, engaged in gainful occupations in Hamilton

County. The number of blacks employed was approximately the same as the number of women. According to the classifications used, the largest number of persons worked in wholesale and retail trades, textiles, the iron and steel industry, construction work, steam and street railways, and agriculture.[5]

During the 1920s the county slipped into a decade of economic growth placing it more in the mainstream of the American economy. Some fifty years earlier northern men had moved to the area; they came as individuals and entrepreneurs who were successful in becoming leading members of the local community. By the 1920s a new situation emerged, with newcomers arriving as agents, retainers, commission merchants, or managers of outside investments such as the electric company, the street railroad company, chain retail outlets which brought national names to Market Street, and firms like International Harvester and Combustion Engineering which bought out local companies. New industries, many of which had outside ties— radio, motion pictures, auto accessories, chemicals, building supplies, etc.—attracted new capital and technological skill.

During these years Hamilton County's agriculture, in which 3,838 were engaged in 1930, slid into the doldrums. Farming no longer dominated the region's economy, and its weakened condition adversely influenced business and industrial activities at the time of the 1929 crash. As the depression's hard times settled in, the saying, "too poor to paint and too proud to whitewash," describes the county's rural condition.

Marginal economic activities such as mining, textile manufacturing, and real estate soon felt the pinch. In Chattanooga the 1930 census reported 3,639 persons either unemployed or on layoff without pay.[6] High school and college graduates found few jobs and were lucky to get gas station or grocery store work. Men walked to and from work as far as from Avondale to Alton Park to save a few cents' carfare. The lavish Lookout Mountain Hotel sold for a fraction of its value; Ruby Falls changed hands, and the Signal Mountain Inn became the property of a religious order.

There was banking trouble too. On 3 January 1933, the Chattanooga National Bank opened as the successor of the old First National Bank (the 1865 chartered institution of W. P. Rathburn and Theodore G. Montague), which had just undergone reorganization. Following the March bank holiday, the Chattanooga National Bank did not reopen and was liquidated under the direction of the comptroller of the currency. In due time, after much concern, the depositors were refunded the full amounts of their deposits.[7]

In 1933 many Chattanooga teachers were paid less than $90 per month and before the year's end protests arose about pay cuts up to one-third of the teachers' salaries. Barter again became a way of business. Attendants at mass meetings demanded reduction of bus fares. Vacant houses, it was claimed, were carried away for firewood by the unemployed. The Salvation Army canned surplus peaches to give out in winter, and "old clothes days" were common. Bankruptcy sales increased, and in the early winter of 1932 a newspaper story reported that the city fed as many as four thousand persons daily while refusing handouts to drifters. At Onion Bottom, Blue Goose Hollow, Hell's Half Acre, and Hayne's Flats people lived in abject poverty amid filth and squalor. The old Eleventh Street school became a "Hobo Paradise" for derelicts, and along the railroad tracks and under the viaducts hobo camps grew up where wanderers clustered. From one of these depression camps the Scottsboro boys began their freight train ride that carried them to a tragic ending.[8]

Against this dispirited background the county people watched and waited for news about the projected plans for the river. As early as 6 January 1933, they heard of the proposed visit of the president-elect to Muscle Shoals, where he could learn about the many problems before his inaugural. An upsurge of optimism swept over the area, but after its first flash, people lost interest. Gradually they learned of later developments: the president presented a plan to Congress and House and Senate bills were offered.

As the nature of the legislation unfolded, its very comprehensive nature and huge proportions made a deep impression on the citizens; businessmen began to express caution or outright criticism when they learned that the government might build transmission lines, sell electric power, and produce fertilizer. They questioned the "yardstick" idea to measure private enterprise efficiency and critically pondered Roosevelt's formula of a "corporation clothed with the power of government, but possessed of the flexibility and initiative of a private enterprise."

George Fort Milton, on the other hand, gave the projected plan his full backing in the columns of his paper, the *Chattanooga News*. "There is in prospect the greatest plan for social as well as economic reconstruction of a region ever undertaken," he wrote. "The Tennessee Valley will be Exhibit A of the new America." The editor of the *Times* constantly chided the local businessmen for burying their heads in the sand and ignoring the great opportunities that could be developed for the area. Are we "cowed by the depression?" he asked. "Why does the city slumber?" He saw the proposed plans as being the opportunity of a lifetime but grew cautious when discussing government activity beyond the areas of flood control and navigation. The day following the signing of the TVA act, his editorial carried the caption, "In This Valley 'the Old Order Changeth.'" Now faced with a specific law he wrote, "There will . . . be present in this valley a distinctly socialistic order promoted and directed by the government at Washington." For the immediate future, the *Times* opposed TVA.

The man who did most to rally early support for river legislation was former Senator William E. Brock. A North Carolinian by birth, Brock had come to the area in 1909 when he organized the Brock Candy Company. He enjoyed such success in his business that he was elected president of the National Confectioners Association. Long devoted to public welfare service, church work, and education, he commanded high respect in the community. On his appointment to the United States Senate, Brock worked for the improvement of the Tennessee River and now, in the early months of 1933, he repeatedly spoke out in support of the TVA legislation. He challenged all to fight for every advantage which could come to Hamilton County. "Let's declare a moratorium at least on fault finding and criticism," he said publicly in early May, "and all stand together for President Roosevelt's plan."

Taking the initiative because of the lack of community leadership, a group of citizens held a mass meeting in Chatanooga and organized the Tennessee Valley Club. Among their plans were efforts to win TVA offices to Chattanooga and to get a commitment for a dam near Chickamauga Creek, which someone at first inappropriately called Sherman Dam. They arranged to send a delegation to a giant rally scheduled in Nashville which called special attention to the split in the local business community.

At the Nashville meeting some two thousand representatives from seven states shouted their support for the valley development. In organizing for future activities they adopted bylaws barring employees, representatives, and stockholders of public service corporations from holding office and adopted the name Tennessee Valley Association. They selected Brock chairman pro tem of their initial board of directors.

The local disagreement over the impending TVA legislation, at times harsh, bitter, and personal, left many scars. Mercer Reynolds for twelve years chairman of the river committee of the chamber of commerce, resigned the day the TVA act was signed; he could not approve government operations at Muscle Shoals or the planned Cove Creek (Norris) Dam. Other businessmen, power officials, security holders, and utility employees supported his stand.

The deepening split in Chattanooga was not unexpected, for the city was the home base of the Tennessee Electric Power Company, which served most of the Tennessee Valley. Negotiations had begun in 1920 between two groups which led to the birth of this company two years later. The E. W. Clark group of Philadelphia, which controlled the Chattanooga Railway and Light Company, joined with the Anthony Brady interests, which were represented by the Chattanooga & Tennessee River Power Company operating the Hales Bar hydroelectric facility. On 16 June 1922 the new company, the Tennessee Electric Power Company (commonly known as TEPCO), opened for business. Eleven years later Jo Conn Guild, Jr., was elected president.

Guild, a native Chattanoogan, had studied engineering at Vanderbilt University and had begun his career in the construction of the Hales Bar Dam. He rose step by step in TEPCO and in 1927 became vice-president and general manager. When Guild assumed the presidency, Wendell Willkie was elected a director of the company.

Willkie was also president of the Commonwealth and Southern Company, a holding company recently chartered and known as one of the best-organized utility consolidations in the country. TEPCO was one of the thirteen major subsidiaries of Commonwealth and Southern, which in 1933 controlled assets valued at over one billion dollars. Willkie brought to this giant firm a strong, positive leadership. A shrewd lawyer and skilled public relations man, he was quick of mind and confident in his manner. His Hoosier twang and rumpled suit gave him the misleading image of a rustic. But Willkie was an effective and passionate defender of the private enterprise system. In testifying before a Congressional committee on the TVA bill he firmly held that Commonwealth and Southern securities would be destroyed if the program were implemented. Many local people believed their TEPCO stocks would also lose all their value; they regarded "the socialistic element of the undertaking" as most repugnant.

Another entirely different concern added to Chattanooga's disillusionment about TVA. The establishment of the Authority removed the Army Engineers from responsibility for work in the Tennessee Valley except for the operation of dam locks. This fact struck like a powerful concussion not only the engineers assigned to the Chattanooga district office but also their many friends and supporters in the city. Since 1867 improvement on the Tennessee River had been directed from this office, which was to close forever on 1 August 1933. To many Chattanoogans, it was like losing an old friend without gaining anything in return. Moreover, the man who headed the office at the time was one of the most popular who had served here during the sixty-six years. He was dynamic, energetic General Robert R. Neyland, who not only commanded the office but also taught military science at the University of Tennessee and coached the "Vol" football team, leading the squad of the Big Orange to national recognition.[9]

From across the nation a barrage of criticism and propaganda provided Hamilton Countians with other arguments. Coal and ice interests insisted they should be protected from the competition of government in business. Power companies, holding conglomerates, banks, and other powerful organizations joined in the chorus. The "yard-stick" idea drew wrath as did the building of transmission lines. Fertilizer production was off limits, too, and a strong point was made that the Tennessee Valley could not possibly use all the hydroelectric power generated. Some disapproved of the concept of a "titanic laboratory of civilization." An ex-Tennessee governor fumed, "The TVA has in Knoxville two buildings filled with sociological experts who are making blue prints of the East Tennessee mountain people with a view to scientific reconstruction of their character, habits, and mode of life."

But, as George Fort Milton put it, Chattanooga was "really the Hindenburg line of private power." In the city and county no agressive TVA leadership appeared; a resident commented that "Chattanooga is the center of the Tennessee Valley, is in the center of the TVA storm and like the center of the storm it is dead center." The Citizens' Council of Chattanooga and Hamilton County, headed by L. J. Wilhoite, accelerated activities but it tended to act as a warring faction rather than offering constructive leadership. It did challenge the chamber of commerce, stating that "Chattanooga continues to pay homage to the god of private power, while other communities are setting about the serious business of catching the vision of a new valley of the Nile."

The citizens' council, drawing its membership from the general public through mass meetings, worked with such groups as the Kiwanis Club in pressing for what they believed to be Chattanooga's and Hamilton County's interests. They pushed for the early construction of Chickamauga Dam, as did the county council, and for municipal ownership of the power distribution system so as to enjoy TVA rates. They campaigned for the location of TVA offices and were pleased to win the headquarters of the Electric Home and Farm Authority in May 1933. This TVA organization granted low-interest loans for electrical appliance purchases and worked with manufacturers to get low-cost appliances put on the market.

More importantly, TVA announced the location in Chattanooga of its Maps and Surveys Division, the General Engineering and Geology Department, and the Electric Division. The latter unit was destined to make the area the very heart of the greatest public utility in the nation.

But there were many other matters in addition to power issues in this period and some created deep misunderstanding. Hamilton County people, as others throughout the valley, tended to fasten their attention on limited, specific items rather than on the comprehensive, long-term objectives of the Authority. Still hampered badly by depression conditions, they failed to comprehend that considerable time was required to plan and design dams before work crews would be hired. They impatiently accused TVA officials of inactivity and of delaying construction; they talked of empty stomachs and hunger while the Authority spun "fanciful schemes."

To relieve unemployment they called for the construction of a Chickamauga dam at once. Such a structure did not have a high TVA priority at the time because the TVA directors believed tributary storage dams to control floods were more vital. Many of the political leaders from the area seemed to "sour" on TVA for these reasons; also the officials of the Authority had taken a strong position against political patronage, which some legislators especially desired.

There was still another issue: East Tennesseans resented the "idealistic engineers" who "invaded" the areas armed with long questionnaires. Critics talked of "sociological straight-jackets." They poked fun at hiring practices, saying that TVA would positively not have "any dumb ditch diggers digging ditches." When a long, "confidential" questionnaire about home life in the valley was circulated in 1934, the *Chattanooga Times* complained that the survey "opens the door of every bed room, bath room, clothes closet, refrigerator, food storage place, kitchen, living room, stable, barn, chicken house, silo, garage, linen cabinet, china closet, coal bin and pig sty in the valley of the Tennessee."[10]

But the biggest controversies arose over electric power. When TVA started building a transmission line between Muscle Shoals and Norris, valley towns and cities began planning to participate in the Authority's low-rate program. Everywhere the inevitable conflict between public and private ownership arose. Chattanooga, as one of the best industrial power markets in the state and as home of TEPCO—where some fifteen-hundred, or about half, of the company's stockholders lived— naturally experienced a long and bitter contest. Men honestly concerned about the future of the area argued their convictions with utter sincerity, but prejudice, self-interest, and rumor brought the level of the campaign to acrimony.

The city commission, divided on the issue, engaged the Scofield Engineering Company of Philadelphia to prepare a study on the cost and feasibility of developing a publicly owned electrical distribution system. Then the state government authorized a city referendum for 12 March 1935 that provided for the sale of $8 million in general obligation bonds to finance the acquisition of a municipal power distribution system which would sell TVA current. A special feature of this authorization provided that poll tax receipts would not be a requirement for voting.

In January the advocates of public power organized the Public Power League and began an extensive campaign based on civic enthusiasm and little money. Hayes Clark, Dr. T. B. Cowan, Humphrey Colvard, Will Chamlee, L. J. Willhoite, and Phil Whitaker emerged as leading spokesmen of this group. Private power supporters countered with the Citizens and Taxpayers Association; in addition to TEPCO officials, Fred Frazier, Paul Mathis, John Brizzie, Clarence Avery, and E. Y. Chapin and others worked for this cause. Later they got the support of the Chattanooga Manufacturers Association and of a youth group called the Future Taxpayers Association. The Manufacturers Association, in a straw vote of its eighty-eight members, stood sixty against the bond issue, three for it, while twenty-five abstained.

For weeks civic clubs heard the opposing spokesmen, and rival broadcasts sponsored the debate. Town meetings were held in all parts of the area while newspapers devoted long columns to the subject. Some carried full-page advertisements advocating antibond votes. The news journals, not content with simple reporting, joined sides and became the major mouthpieces for the contending forces. The *Times* did its best to defeat public power and did not refrain from vigorous assaults on the opposition organization, press, or individuals. Also upholding private ownership was the newly founded *Free Press*, begun by Roy McDonald as a handout news sheet advertising a local chain of grocery stores in 1933. The *Hamilton County Herald* of Will Shepherd also used its influence to try to defeat the bond issue.

George Fort Milton's *News* vigorously supported both the TVA and the local public power people with hard-hitting liberal reporting. The position of the *News* cost heavily in advertising losses and it later was alleged that the struggle led to the demise of the newspaper. During the referendum campaign Milton was supported by the *Labor World*, a weekly voice of local organized labor.[11]

Those favoring public power held that a victory for a municipal distribution system delivering cheap TVA power would "give every home an opportunity for a higher level of living." They believed in TVA's formula for cheap energy and criticized the power company for attempting "to loot the public of Muscle Shoals" and for encouraging those who searched for court cases to harass the TVA. They also accused TEPCO of excessive rates, of watered stock, and high managerial costs. They further implied that a vote for the bond issue indicated that the voter stood by the president of the United States and endorsed the TVA program. So frequent was this latter reference made that the referendum was commonly called "the TVA election."

The private power group stated that President Roosevelt and the TVA had nothing to do with the election, which was strictly a local affair about bonds and the city ownership of a utility. To this group TVA represented socialism rather than "good old Americanism," and the crux of the matter was whether Chattanooga "shall be an upstanding municipality or a suckling of the Federal Government."

If a bond issue of $8 million were approved, they argued, the city would become bankrupt under the staggering interest burden. Moreover, a city-owned and managed enterprise would not only be inefficient but also a colossal political machine subject to the manipulation of greedy public servants. Taxes would have to go up and electricity customers would have to pay large surcharges. Graft, inefficiency, and high electric bills would surely drive industry away. TEPCO stockholders were constantly told they would ultimately lose their investments and employees their jobs. Spokesmen for private power ridiculed the promises of their opponents as far too glowing and unattainable, while holding up the past record of the then present company as most satisfactory.

Exaggerated rumors added spice to the debate. One story had it that if the public operated the electrical distribution system, all homes would have to be rewired because private power wiring was not suitable for public power. Another bit of gossip claimed public power made meters run faster, while a third tidbit of hearsay circulating just before election day claimed that the buses and streetcars—all operated by TEPCO—would stop operating the day after the bond issue was approved.

And charges of fraud and countercharges muddied the waters. Both sides cried foul at the time of the registration of voters for the referendum. The private power supporters, noting no poll taxes had to be paid, claimed "herds of transients and hitch hikers" registered to swell the ranks of the public power group. While TVA made pointed statements, it took no part in the election contest; private power advocates noted that surveyors had begun work at Chickamauga Dam. While they carefully asserted that the dam would be built even if public power were defeated in Chattanooga, they also feared that the local unemployed people would all vote for bonds to prove that they stood behind TVA.

On the other hand TEPCO left itself open for considerable criticism. It lent personnel to the Citizens and Taxpayers Association to produce private power propaganda while other employees allegedly sought votes with offers of drink and dole. Since corporations registered in Tennessee could not contribute funds to such campaigns, the Commonwealth and Southern Company provided some $20,000 for this purpose from out-of-state offices. In addition, a number of TEPCO employees, possibly working independently of the company, used an unusual Chattanooga law to their advantage. This law allowed property owners within the city to vote although they might be nonresidents. So 162 persons jointly bought a $50 lot in East Lake for the purpose of qualifying to vote at a cost of about $.33 each.

Although the twelfth day of March brought snow and rain, the polls were crowded. When the final tally of votes was compiled, public power bonds were approved by 19,056 to 8,096. Of the thirty-three voting precincts, only three had antibond majorities. A heavy vote by workers and blacks assured this decisive margin, which was large enough to relegate all charges of corruption to insignificance. A rhymester of the day expressed the feeling of many of his fellow townsmen in a poem entitled "After the Battle":

> There is calm upon the mountain, in
> the valley there is peace.
> There's a blessed soothing silence and

a feeling of release.
As upon some bloody battlefield when
all the volleys cease.
The municipal election now is over.

On 15 April the state legislature amended the city charter to permit the creation of the Electric Power Board of Chattanooga, which officially began business two days later. The board, consisting of five citizens, was headed by Colonel Harold C. Fiske, who had been responsible for the exhaustive survey of the Tennessee Valley. Following retirement from the Engineers, Fiske worked in New York City before returning to Chattanooga to take up his new duties. The legislature's selection was an admirable one; at the time of Fiske's death in 1942, the Chattanooga *Times* noted, "in a large sense the Tennessee Valley program and public power in the region are monuments to his foresight."

The board assumed the responsibility of acquiring and operating a power distribution system to market TVA electricity. The appointments were carefully made to protect the board members from direct or indirect political pressure, with the result that this board has functioned smoothly through the years.[13]

Several years passed before the board actually rendered service; its logical starting point would have been the acquisition of TEPCO's lines and equipment. But immediately after the bond referendum, TEPCO's Guild and Commonwealth and Southern's Willkie eliminated this possibility. They would not sell to the city, to TVA, or to anybody. They would fight to the finish, for a sale of the Chattanooga service area would be like taking the hub out of the entire TEPCO network.

An impasse resulted; numerous lengthy court tests followed. The board challenged the legality of the franchise under which TEPCO operated; TEPCO, in turn, tried to prevent the board from receiving and using WPA (Works Progress Administration) funds to help finance a costly, duplicated distribution system. Residents and owners of Chattanooga city bonds compounded the problem of the board by attempting to block the sale of bonds approved in the referendum, maintaining that their holdings would depreciate in value. Others worked to get a new referendum to cancel the bond victory in the first one and gathered some five thousand signatures from a booth set up in town.

A contract between Commonwealth and Southern and the TVA also delayed any contractual agreement between the board and TVA regarding a source of power for Chattanooga. The board did get a WPA grant and loan and turned to its only remaining alternative: the construction of a costly competing distribution system. All realized that duplicate substations, lines, poles, and other equipment were both uneconomical and undesirable, but the board was under contract with the WPA to start operations within a given time.

The board consequently began preparing blueprints for a second electrical distribution system for the area. In April 1938 work was finally begun and on 25 January the Electric Power Board of Chattanooga made its first customer connection. About fifty other homes soon received service; TEPCO still generated power and dominated the local market. [14]

These early customers of the board were, however, not the first* residents of Hamilton County to use TVA current. In late July 1936 people in the Birchwood area in the northeastern part of the county received TVA power from Meigs County lines through a rural electrification program. This service represented the first use of TVA current in any section of Hamilton County. [15]

During the period when Chattanooga was working on building a duplicate system, TVA survived countless lawsuits and gradually gained constitutional strength. The position of Willkie grew more restricted. In Chattanooga it became clear that the Power Board's program would eventually reduce the value of the TEPCO properties. Willkie concluded that a sale was inevitable, and the local issue gradually merged into a broader plan for TEPCO to sell all its electrical properties. Again, time was required to settle all the delicate negotiations and legal arrangements.

On 15 August 1939, formal transfer ceremonies in New York City noted the sale of all TEPCO holdings for $78,425,095, with numerous valley communities in cooperative participation with TVA. This sum represented a negotiated price which meant no loss to bondholders or preferred TEPCO stockholders. The Electric Power Board acquired title to and took over the operation of the so-called Chattanooga District for $10,850,000. Not a cent from the city's general taxing income was used in the acquisition of the private utility's facilities nor did the city lose any tax income as a result of the purchase. At midnight on 15 August 1939 the board took over the distribution stytem, incorporating in it the facilities it had completed as part of the contemplated duplicate system.

This purchase eliminated the prospect of competing systems; the board could now concentrate on serving the people of its market area. Under contract with TVA the board would buy power at wholesale rates and sell it to consumers according to an agreed price schedule based on a low-rate philosophy designed to cultivate a large demand—a TVA formula largely drawn up by one employee, Llewellyn Evans, a newcomer to Chattanooga from the West Coast. The Power Board was designed to be self-supporting and, if a financial surplus showed up, consumer rates were to be reduced.

The board in 1963 retired the last of its outstanding bonds, accordingly making it the largest debt-free publicly owned electric utility in the country.[16]

Actually the board's service lines reached out not only beyond the city limits but also beyond the boundaries of Hamilton County. They extended from the small community of Graysville on the north to Flintstone, Georgia, on the south, and from beyond Ooltewah on the east to the area of Hales Bar Dam on the southwest border. About fifty percent of the early customers lived outside of Chattanooga. Moreover, the board was obligated to extend its service as rapidly as possible to all, however remote, who desired current. World War II delayed this expansion, but by 1950 the board estimated that ninety-five percent of the people in the 500-square-mile area had access to electricity.

As a part of the TEPCO sale, TVA acquired the Hales Bar Lock and Dam, completed in 1913, along with a nearby steam plant TEPCO had built during the 1920s to supplement its generation of hydroelectricity. With this Marion County facility TVA immediately increased its generating capacity, while the dam—the work of Charlie James and the Guilds (father and son)—became one of the main units in TVA's river engineering plans. To meet required specifications, the dam was raised to provide a nine-foot channel across Hamilton County to Chickamauga Dam. Moreover, the authority TVA got from Congress to purchase the private utility system, including a steam plant, implied for the future the right to build and operate generating facilities other than hydrogenerators.[16]

When the board took over TEPCO's network, the community schism of referendum days, now more than four years past, was still a factor to be reckoned with. The *News* noted the event as "the true signal for the community's—and the region's—forward march." The *Free Press* did not agree: "Today," the editor wrote, "the tragedy of personal loss to ourselves and to our community in the passing of the old order overwhelms all other emotions." The *Times*, with a new editor, was more friendly to municipal ownership; on 16 August 1939, it advised, "The dead past ought to bury all the arguments pro and con which have been settled by the established fact." TEPCO, in a farewell advertisement, offered reminders of the values of pioneer days, rugged individualism, private ownership, and frontier independence.[17]

No interruption of service marked the change of ownership; at the time, the peak demand was only fifty-five thousand kilowatts. The change did signal the beginning of remarkable growth which has been entirely free of political intervention or dominance. At the time of the board's first annual report, it counted 39,942 customers and 397 employees, over ninety-three percent of whom had been former power company workers. At the end of 1978 the employees numbered 546 and the total number of customers had grown to 118,662.

In 1978-79 residential customers paid about seventy-five percent of the national average per kilowatt-hour, using 18,172 kilowatt hours compared to 8,900 for the entire United States. Of the board's operating expenses, approximately eighty-two percent went for the purchase of TVA power, amounting to $123,733,000. Throughout its history the board paid, in lieu of taxes, large sums to both Chattanooga and Hamilton County and continues to be the largest payer of *ad valorem* taxes to both governments. In 1978 these tax payments amounted to $4,454,322. Of this amount $1,745,404 went to Chattanooga and $2,505,819 to Hamilton County.[18]

The availability of cheap power resulted in unprecedented changes throughout Hamilton County. New industry moved in while, at the same time, lights were turned on in homes in isolated coves and in mountainside cabins. Many of the day's ordinary chores were now done by electrical "servants"; as drudgery was reduced and comfort increased, the amount of available human energy increased, along with an expanding sense of pride in person and property. Moreover, by 1976 approximately seventy-five percent of the board's residential customers used electricity to heat their homes. As people discontinued the use of bituminous coal in stoves and fireplaces, and commercial and public buildings switched to cleaner heat, the black storms of winter soot gradually diminished.

But this new dependence on the electrical genie did sometimes present problems that were revealed most dynamically in early March 1960. A cruel ice storm struck with war-like fury on the higher elevations—Lookout, Signal, and Mowbray mountains, Walden Ridge, and the crest of Missionary Ridge. Telephone and electric power poles snapped; giant trees twisted and fell, bringing down service lines every-where. Some ten thousand homes had no heat as frigid temperatures descended. A state of emergency brought the National Guard to the hardest-hit areas and for some ten days only residents were allowed to go to and fro. Rural folk with wood stoves and fireplaces managed the crisis far better than their suburban neighbors, whose world had been totally disrupted.

During the years when the Power Board struggled to obtain a distribution system, two related but very different TVA developments occurred within Hamilton County. One placed Chattanooga in the national spotlight while the other brought a main river dam and one of the great lakes of the South to the county.

TVA's initial years produced a huge crop of litigation. On 29 May 1936 a suit (variously known as the "nineteen companies" or "eighteen companies", after one withdrew, or the TEPCO case), based on broad constitutional allegations, challenged the very existence of the Authority. The plaintiffs claimed that TVA under the false guise of flood control, navigation, and national defense was nothing more than a vast plan to produce salable power, which they were sure was its principal and not its secondary aim. They were successful in the district court and the decision was appealed by TVA.

For seven weeks during the winter of 1937-38 the court of appeals headed by Judge Florence Allen sat in Chattanooga. Batteries of nationally known attorneys represented the opposing interests while experts testified in their special fields. Local citizens watched with interest as national newsmen reported the unfolding drama. The three-judge court decided every issue in favor of TVA. Judge Allen's concluding statement held that TVA's hydroelectric facilities were the best kind of navigation dams and that power was not the chief and hidden primary purpose of the Authority. This opinion completely sustained the good faith of TVA. On appeal, the supreme court denied the companies' standing to sue and the Chattanooga ruling remained the highest constitutional judgment rendered on TVA.

While the lawyers fought over legal questions, others struggled over engineering priorities and timetables. In Hamilton County, interest groups began promoting a TVA dam project. Judge Will Cummings, one of the first and most loyal supporters of the idea, got the Hamilton County Court squarely behind a dam project by midsummer 1933. Backed by the Kiwanis Club and others, the proposal called for the county to build the dam using federal aid from the WPA. TVA vetoed this idea, assuming the responsibility of the total development of the entire valley.

TVA's first construction program, however, was limited in nature and gave the impression that Hamilton County would go without any major benefit for another generation. Judge Cummings and his associates did not give up; they now trained their political guns on Washington with the cooperative support of Senators Kenneth McKeller and Nathan L. Bachman and Representative Sam McReynolds. In the 1934 elections, the judge and the congressman both made repeated proclamations in the best oratorical style that Chickamauga Dam would be built. On their reelection, Cummings and McReynolds carried their case directly to President Roosevelt.

The judge and the congressman used two potent arguments: Chattanooga's great need for flood control and the dire depression conditions in Hamilton County, where at one time there were some eight thousand registered unemployed. Roosevelt was interested and suggested they try to get funds for a dam in the next appropriation bill. Meanwhile Chattanooga had its referendum, at which time it was pointed out that the Chickamauga dam project provided a good reason for voter support of public power. The bond victory on 12 March 1935 strengthened the hand of those who wanted the dam started, and Senator McKeller and Representative McReynolds got it "in the pot" and effectively managed the needed legislation through Congress. By August 1935 the Chickamauga dam project was assured and Chattanooga whistles again blasted a victory chorus. Judge Cummings was elated. An economic boom was possible; former Senator Brock immediately called for efforts to attract new industry.[19]

When Chattanoogans literally pushed Chickamauga Dam into TVA's lap, some leaders in the Authority began to change their thinking about construction priorities. The court cases challenging the constitutionality of TVA, they believed, required some bolstering of the Authority's power program; moves were made to emphasize navigation work as "a more immediate thing." Congress in 1935 approved a nine-foot channel all the way from Paducah to Knoxville and the dam at Chickamauga fit perfectly into this changing concept.

By the summer of 1935 engineers and geologists made surveys to find a satisfactory site for the massive structure. Archaeologists worked rapidly to explore chosen areas for Indian artifacts. By 13 January 1936 construction started and Hamilton County's unemployment rate dropped drastically.

Approximately sixty-thousand acres of land were purchased. Some families resisted removal and deplored the thought of having their good bottomlands flooded. In all, nine hundred families had to vacate, including the residents of the old county seat of Harrison; 425 graves from twenty-four small cemeteries were also moved. Telephone, telegraph, and electric lines had to relocated and some eighty-one miles of roads rerouted or raised. Wolftever, Soddy, Sale, and Oppossum creeks would become embayments, with water pushed up to the town of Soddy. The old Indian site of Dallas would be nearly covered over to appear only as a small island.

The work, all done by TVA crews, drew many visitors after the area was opened to the public in March 1936. Local residents and tourists were joined by numerous foreign visitors to whom TVA told its story in a booklet in five languages. A colony of buildings and a jungle of coffer dams marked the central area; in addition, the entire lake bed had to be freed of obstructions, buildings torn down, brush cleared, and timber cut. The cost came to about $39 million.

When construction was finished (water impounding began on 15 January 1940 and the first electricity was produced on 4 March) three generating units had a capacity of 81,000 kilowatts. These hydroelectric facilities produced approximately the maximum Chattanooga demand of 82,769 kilowatts. By 1952 an additional generator raised the capacity to 108,000 kilowatts, but by this time Chattanooga's demand had risen to approximately three times that amount. The solid, simple lines of the dam, locks, and powerhouse had the "honest beauty of a fine tool." The dam's vital statistics were as follows:

Length of dam	5,800 feet
Height	129 feet
Volume of concrete	506,400 cubic yards
Earth and rock fill	2,793,500 cubic yards
Lock	360 x 60 feet
Normal lock lift	51 feet
Area of Lake	35,400 acres
Length of lake	58.9 miles
Maximum width of lake	1.7 miles[20]

Soon after the dam was authorized, the name Chickamauga was threatened when admirers of Congressman McReynolds sought federal legislation to name it in his honor. Speedy and effective opposition arose from a variety of sources, notably patriotic societies. The Indian word so long associated with the area, they insisted, represented a heritage that should be preserved despite the fact that engineers had altered the landscape. Representative McReynolds understood the message and graciously had his name withdrawn from further consideration.

President Roosevelt kept in close touch with the progress of TVA. On Labor Day 1940 he came to Hamilton County to dedicate Chickamauga Dam. His appearance was part of a three-day celebration highlighted by a coloful parade, Cotton Ball, and dance honoring "The Lady of the Lake," Mrs. John L. Hutcheson, Jr. From a vantage point near the dam—not many miles from where President Monroe stopped at the Brainerd Mission in 1819 and within sight of the place where some of General Sherman's troopers took boats to flank Confederate forces on Missionary Ridge—the president spoke under a scorching sun to a crowd of perhaps eighty thousand and to a national radio audience.

Roosevelt noted that the dam gave the people "human control of the watershed of the Tennessee River in order that it may serve in full the purposes of men." He pointed out that it stood as a "monument to a productive partnership between management and labor, between citizens of all kinds working in the public weal." He further made this astute observation: "the only note of sorrow that can properly be sounded on a great day like this is in the misplaced emphasis which so many people have put on the objectives of the government in building up this great Tennessee Valley project." The president made brief references to the European crisis and to the role of the TVA and the great lakes of the South in national defense before concluding,

> I, therefore, today on this very happy occasion dedicate this dam and these lakes to the benefit of all the people, the prosperity they have stimulated, the faith they have justified, the hope they have inspired, the hearts they encourage—the total defense of the United States of America.[21]

No one could foresee the great change that Chickamauga Lake would make. Steamboats, rafts, and commercial fishermen had disappeared from the old river, but within a short time after the dedication of the dam a new life developed along the 810 miles of shoreline which reached across Hamilton County and beyond to Watts Bar Dam. Rolling hills with their hardwoods and evergreens reached to the waterline in irregular patterns and created desirable home sites. Although delayed by World War II, TVA auctioned off these acres. Rustic homes, club facilities, park lands, private and public boat docking facilities, and campsites appeared where little development had previously occurred. Water recreational activities with their supporting businesses fashioned a new life-style.

Two state parks and one county park have been provided for public use. In 1940 Harrison Bay State Park and the Booker T. Washington State Park for Negroes were developed by the combined efforts of TVA, the Civilian Conservation Corps, National Park Service, and the Tennessee Department of Conservation. Harrison Bay Park, about fifteen miles from Chattanooga, at first contained some nine hundred acres; Booker T. Washington Park (approximately four hundred acres) is only eight miles from the city. Development at both parks was halted during World War II and their dedication did not take place until 2 July 1950, when TVA transferred deeds to the state, which continued to expand cabins, shelters, camp-sites, swimming pools, boat slips, picnic areas, and marina facilities. In 1958 an improvement at Harrison Bay opened; it included a drinking fountain, shelter, and rest rooms and bore the name of John A. Patten. This memorial to the former civic leader and staunch advocate of river improvement stands on a knoll overlooking Patten Memorial Island and Harrison Bay.[22]

Near the dam TVA maintains recreational facilities and across the lake on the north shore Hamilton County has developed a park on Gold Point Road about two miles off Hixson Pike. The county government accepted an offer of TVA in 1959 of 223 acres with the understanding that a park would be developed. This tract extends along the shoreline in the old Jackson Chapel area and includes two islands, one of which was the site of the old Hamilton County courthouse prior to 1840. A sand beach, shelters, and extensive camping facilities attract summer crowds to the area, named Chester Frost Park. In 1978 TVA made available 205 adjacent acres for additional recreational usage.[23]

Downstream from Chickamauga Dam in the very heart of Chattanooga is an 18.8-acre island which in October 1954 Robert Maclellan gave to the Chattanooga Audubon Society as a wildlife refuge. The society, founded by Robert Sparks Walker, Mrs. Sarah Key Patten, Mr. and Mrs. E. Y. Chapin, and others in 1944, converted the old Walker farm in the valley of South Chickamauga Creek into the Elise Chapin Wildlife Sanctuary (now called Audubon Acres). The old cabin of the Cherokee, Spring Frog, the village of Little Owl of the era of Dragging Canoe, marked trails, bird walks, wild flower patches, and large trees distinguish these acres preserved in their rugged beauty.

West of Lookout Mountain along the banks of Lookout Creek another privately developed open area called Reflection Riding stands watch over more of nature's wonders. Here one can walk at leisure through the well-kept park-lands or drive the winding roads. The vision and labor of John A. Chambliss in the 1940s made this sanctuary a reality; today a foundation and the support of many friends maintain the area where a natural history educational complex (Chattanooga Nature Center) has been erected.

Across the Tennessee River on the north shore the city and county acquired on 20 June 1961 Moccasin Bend, dedicating it to public use. A few miles beyond, the state in 1943 had procured some thirty-five thousand acres of undeveloped land along the Marion-Hamilton county border, taking in much of Suck Creek Mountain. Private citizens added gift tracts to this wilderness reserve called the Prentice Cooper State Forest and Wildlife Management Area. In this game and forest management tract but a few minutes from urban traffic, deer and turkey thrive and occasionally the eagle soars.[24]

Hamilton County people had not grown accustomed to the "new geography" created by TVA before a harsh and distant world crisis brought a new challenge to the valley. Even before the dedication of Chickamauga Dam the Electric Power Board recognized that the country's national defense program would affect the economy of the area and established a liaison in Washington to get information for local industrialists about defense contracts. As the United States became directly involved in World War II, Hamilton County workers produced army and navy woolen cloth, blankets, alloys for steel products, shells, artillery parts, textiles, tanks, liquid containers, cement, boilers, and many other items. The Chattanooga Medicine Company (now Chattem) retooled to package "K" rations. Throughout the area old plants remodeled and new ones appeared. In 1945 there were 446 manufacturing plants within a twenty-five-mile radius of Chattanooga employing approximately fifty-five thousand workers and producing some fifteen hundred different products.

The most important of the new producers was the Volunteer Ordnance Works (VOW), constructed in 1941-42 on a tract of 7,500 acres near Tyner. During the war years VOW, operated by the Hercules Powder Company, made about 823.3 million pounds of TNT before it ceased production in August 1945.[25]

TVA played a major role in the war effort by quickly completing construction of dams and power facilities in various parts of the valley. The electrical hub of the network functioning in Chattanooga expanded so that by 1945 the Authority claimed it "produced one-tenth of the power produced for war purposes by all the public and private power systems in the United States"; the system had trebled in size in five years. It was this source of energy which brought many new industries to Tennessee, including the Oak Ridge installation, and Hamilton County workers frequently commuted great distances to work on these pressing projects. In Chattanooga the most impressive TVA war work fell to its Maps and Surveys Division: from aerial photographs they mapped more than a half-million square miles of enemy country from Italy and France to never-before-heard-of islands of the Pacific.[26]

In Hamilton County, as throughout the nation, World War II generated no gaudy displays of patriotism or public emotionalism. The keynote was privation, hardship, and heartache; the war was a great crusade. Hamilton County men began leaving for the service shortly after the Selective Service Act of September 1940 was passed. In all, 25,258 local men and women joined the armed forces through the draft or as volunteers.[27]

One soldier, Technical Sergeant Charles H. Coolidge of Signal Mountain, earned the highest commendation, the Medal of Honor, for his deeds of 24-28 October 1944. His citation reads,

> With a handful of new reinforcements he directed a 4-day battle against a superior German force during which time he dueled two tanks with his carbine, advanced alone to stop a German attack with two cases of grenades and frustrated an attempt to turn the flank of his battalion.[28]

On 22 February 1950 the people of the area honored the 695 from Hamilton County who died in service in a dedicatory ceremony of a memorial in the Patten Parkway.

On the home front Hamilton Countians experienced the same trials as their fellow citizens across the land. Early reverses in the war made it evident that virtually every phase of life would be influenced. It was clear to the national leadership that the absence of price control in World War I had been perhaps the greatest failure of that era. So the Office of Price Control regulated local wages and prices while rationing boards carried out the government's policies regarding tires, gasoline, sugar, meat, coffee, and other items. Although employment demands were rigid, people managed to do volunteer work with the Red Cross, civilian defense, salvage programs, bond sales, and also raised victory gardens.

As in past conflicts, uniforms dominated the Chattanooga scene. Air cadets trained at the university. At Fort Oglethorpe, where cavalry units had long been stationed, training turned to mechanical conflict weaponry while the area also operated an induction center. Fort Oglethorpe personnel were joined by visitors from Camp Forrest at Tullahoma, Tennessee, in seeking entertainment and relaxation in Chattanooga. But by January 1943 a great change had taken place at the North Georgia center which altered the characteristic look of the military: it was designated the Third Women's Army Auxiliary Corps Training Center.

By summer's end Fort Oglethorpe housed a female army except for the induction center, and by April 1944 the commander of the post was Lieutenant Colonel Elizabeth Strayhorn. Uniformed women crowded Chattanooga's streets, theaters, hotels, and shops, and totally different inventories had to be stocked by local merchants.

At war's end there were no great hurrahs in Chattanooga; only an expression of relief came with the armistice and with demobilization. Uniforms soon disappeared from the streets; Fort Oglethorpe was designated an Army Redistribution and Specialty School. GI's came home and many immediately took advantage of the splendid educational opportunities offered them. Industry and business folded and stored their well-deserved Army and Navy "E" for outstanding service or "M" from the Marine Commission and prepared to adjust to peacetime markets.

Then on 31 December 1946, taps sounded for the last time at Fort Oglethorpe as that installation closed permanently. For Hamilton County it was the end of an era.

NOTES

1. Wilson Dam and the nitrate plant were not finished until after World War I was over. For the next fourteen years they were the center of a controversy between those who wished to sell or lease the properties and those, led by Senator George W. Norris, who believed it better for the government to operate them. The issue was at a stalemate in 1933.

2. Nashville District, Corps of Engineers, *Engineers on the Twin Rivers: A History of the Nashville District Corps of Engineers* (n.p.: 1979), pp. 181–186; *Chattanooga Times*, 18 May 1933. Senator Bachman, a heavily built man, was the son of the Reverend J. W. Bachman. A Phi Beta Kappa graduate from the University of Virginia, he was appointed senator when Cordell Hull resigned his seat to become secretary of state.

3. U.S., Department of Commerce, *Fifteenth Census of the United States: 1930, Population* Vol. 3, pt. 2 (Washington, D.C.: Government Printing Office, 1932), pp. 884, 890, 893, 899, 903, 905; *Chattanooga Times*, 4 June 1916; 28 October 1939. Other foreign-born citizens came from Germany (221), England (202), Canada (144), Scotland (65), Irish Free State (44), Switzerland (38), Wales (37), Sweden (22), France (20), Austria (19), Hungary (13), Czechoslovakia (12), Northern Ireland (11), Palestine and Syria (9), Denmark (8), China (6), Norway (5), Mexico (4), Netherlands (4), and India (3). Of the 1,667 foreign-born in the county, 1,464 lived in Chattanooga.

4. "Uncle Joe" Miles of Walden Ridge was the most famous producer of illicit liquor.

5. U.S., Department of Commerce, Bureau of the Census, *1930 Census, Population*, vol. 3, pt 2, p. 912.

6. U.S., Department of Commerce, Bureau of the Census, *Fifteenth Census of the United States; 1930, Unemployment*, , pt. 1 (Washington, D.C.: Government Printing Office, 1931), pp. 926, 932, 936.

7. *A History of Banking in Chattanooga* (Chattanooga: Hamilton National Bank, 1925), pp. 8, 26–27.

8. *Chattanooga Times*, 13 July 1930; 15 January, 24 March, 13 July 1931; 13, 15 February, 24 May 1932; 17 April, 23, 28 August 1933.

9. Thomas K. McGraw, *TVA and the Power Fight* (Philadelphia: J. B. Lippincott, 1971), pp. 51, 52; Nashville District, Corps of Engineers, *Engineers on the Twin Rivers* (Nashville, 1978), pp. 186–187.

10. *Chattanooga Times*, 15 January 1934.

11. Ibid., 11 March 1935, contains a summary statement of the campaign.

12. Ibid., 12, 13 March, 12 April 1935. The poet was John A. Patten. A Hamilton County grand jury found no fraud or corruption in the referendum. It found that the Citizens Taxpayers League spent almost $24,000 and that $20,000 came from outside the state. The Public Power League was reported to have spent $1,540.

13. Electric Power Board of Chattanooga, *First Annual Report, 30 June 1940*: Corps of Engineers, *Engineers on the Twin Rivers*, p. 184; *Chattanooga Times*, 9 January 1942.

14. *Chattanooga Times*, 20, 21 February, 28 August, 19 September, 2, 11, 13, 25, October, 6, 10 November 1936; Electric Power Board of Chattanooga, *Tenth Annual Report*, 30 June 1949.

15. *Chattanooga Times*, 22 July 1936.

16. Electric Power Board of Chattanooga, *Twenty-fifth Annual Report*, 30 June 1964, pp. 58-59. A new dam six and a half miles downstream from Hales Bar was built by TVA to replace the old structure which was leaky and had very small locks. In December 1967 engineers closed the gates to impound water on the $71-million project called Nickajack Dam.

17. *Chattanooga Free-Press*, 16 August 1939; *Chattanooga News*, 16 August 1939; *Chattanooga Times*, 16 August 1939.

18. Electric Power Board of Chattanooga, *1978 Report; Second Annual Report*, 30 June 1941; *Thirty-ninth Annual Report*, 30 June 1978; *Fortieth Annual Report*, 30 June 1979. The second annual report was used in this comparison because the first one covered only ten and a half months. During fiscal 1978–79 residential consumption declined by 8.5%, reflecting at least in part the conservation efforts of the area.

Additional statistics help to complete the story:

	Fiscal 1940–41	*Fiscal 1977–78*
Sale in kilowatt hours	431,914,000	5,305,054,000
Revenues	$4,067,000	$132,298,000
Revenues: residential	$1,339,000	$53,983,000
Maximum kilowatt demand	87,341	1,248,195
Purchase from TVA: kilowatt hours	471,300,000	5,564,350,000
Property tax payments	$279,000	$4,452,000

The members of the board at the time of the TEPCO sale were L. J. Wilhoite, chairman, J. Courtney Twinam, Roy McKenzie, E. J. Walsh, and T. R. Cuthbert. "States Rights" Finley was general superintendent. The first board, sworn in on 30 April 1935, consisted of Colonel H. C. Fiske, Wilhoite, Twinam, Stanton Smith, and George H. Patten.

19. Fred Hixson, *History of the Beginning of Chickamauga Dam: A Story of a Dream That Came True* (Chattanooga: author, 1940), pp. 1–36; Robert S. Walker, *The Chickamauga Dam and Its Environs* (Chattanooga: Andrews Printing, 1949); *Chattanooga Times*, 8 August, 18 September 1935.

20. Ibid., 30 December 1935; 1 January, 16 August, 6, 31 December 1936; *TVA Handbook*, rev. ed. (n.p.: TVA Information Office, 1976), pp. 46–49.

21. *Chattanooga Times*, 11 November 1938; 3 September 1940; 29 August 1963.

22. Ibid., 30 August 1939; 7 March 1948; 8 September 1948; 5 May 1950; 22 June 1958; 1 January, 12 May, 8 July 1959.

23. Ibid., 8 July 1959; 5 April 1979. Frost served as county judge at the time the park was established and worked for its improvement. The present state park system dates only from 1937.

24. Cartter Patten and Burkett Miller made land gifts to the state. Ibid., 19 November 1944. The Junior League gave generous support to the nature center; Mrs. James Irvine serves as president of the three-hundred-acre arboretum.

25. *The Atlas Family*, 28, No. 3 (Fall 1966): 10. After the installation was shut down, it was maintained in standby condition by the Atlas Chemical Industries until the close of 1964. Later Atlas reactivated the plant for the Vietnam conflict.

26. TVA, *Annual Report of the Tennessee Valley Authority, 1945*, pp. 2–57; *1946*, pp. 1–3.

27. *Chattanooga News-Free Press*, 27 June 1946; *Chattanooga Times*, 4 September 1945.

28. U.S. Department of the Army, *The Medal of Honor of the United States Army* (Washington, D.C.: Government Printing Office, 1948), p. 61.

Yesterday and Today: Part I

HAMILTON County's history has always been colored by the unexpected events for which no one could chart consequences or plan to meet resulting changes. For more than a century, the gateway site in southeastern Tennessee gloried in a railroad tradition; virtually the entire world heard Glenn Miller's orchestra bring the Chattanooga Choo-Choo into the station on Track 29. Then at 11:35 P.M. Tuesday, 4 August 1970, a porter called all aboard as the Birmingham Special left the Southern Railway's Terminal Station on its last trip.

The station, a structure of elegance and civic pride, then stood as a deserted relic. Railroad officials vacated the area in which passenger trains had stopped for more than six decades. They boarded up the doors and windows of the station; dust and grime sullied the waiting rooms where travelers had congregated since 1 December 1909, when the massive building was dedicated.

In the Victorian fashion the Terminal Station by its one-level complex eliminated the usual long stairs to trainside. The design of the station came about in an interesting way. In 1900 the Beaux Arts Institute of Paris held a student contest for the best architectural drawing of a rail depot; the prize went to one Don Barber of New York City. Four years later, when the Southern Railway officials decided to build a "grand" station in Chattanooga, one person offering a drawing was the same Don Barber. His design appealed to the company people, but they requested that he alter the interior along the lines used in the then popular National Park Bank of New York. The $1.5-million station that stood idle for three years after 1970 had combined the Paris Institute's prize design and first-rate interior architecture.

On 30 May 1973, the Terminal Station reopened: a group of local businessmen had bought the property and undertaken an ambitious historical preservation project. Where tracks had once been they placed gardens, fountains, statues, and gas torchlights, leaving some room for parked sleeping cars where one could spend a nostalgic night. A street-car now chugs through the old railyard and treats tourists to some of yesteryear's experiences.

In the station, the high-standing dome some eighty-five feet above the floor of the old waiting room (hidden by a false ceiling to cut heating costs) got a thorough cleaning and four chandeliers were refurbished. The large depot was transformed into dining space for some thirteen hundred guests while adjacent structures house shops and entertain-ment places. Restored for the pleasure of residents and tourists, the new Chattanooga Choo-Choo, proudly claiming a spot on the National Register of Historic Places, blends the hustle of the past with the commercial pace of today.

The end also came to north-south passenger service when the L & N's (Louisville & Nashville) famed Georgian paid its last call on 1 May 1971. Unused baggage carts and echoes of the past cluttered the old Union Station on the following lonely nights. Since 1858 its sheds had sheltered the traveling public and endured the confusion and wear of wartime use. Located in the heart of Chattanooga on land owned by the state of Georgia, the old depot represented an age gone by.

For 120 years or more the people of Hamilton County had traveled the Georgia railway and had fought with the state over its landlord rights to prime land in the center of their county seat. With the pas-senger business ended, Georgia sold the parcel of property around the station in 1972 to the local Stone Fort Land Company, which promptly razed the old structure—to the chagrin of many historically minded residents. Gradually Georgia sold off the rest of its "city empire" which had been created in pioneer rail days when yards and terminal facilities, located beyond Chattanooga's city limits, brought the outside world to the small community by the river.[1]

Even before the retirement of the *Georgian* and the *Birmingham Special* a comic-opera episode marked the passing of rail passenger service and the local railway tradition. Since 1891 in a corner of the Union Station the Civil War locomotive, the *General*, had stood on exhibit—a Chattanooga link to the past, a symbol of heroic deeds and the chosen symbol of the city. Saved from the scrap heap as an historic relic, the old engine was legally a possession by lease right of the L & N Railroad from the state of Georgia. Occasionally it was let out of the shed to the Chicago World Fair or to reenact its role in a Disney film, but it was unquestionably thought of as a Chattanooga heirloom.

One night in 1961 under suspicious circumstances, L & N officials spirited the *General* away; to still a local clamor of protest, L & N officials implied that it would be returned. The train's removal, reports announced, was but a patriotic gesture to refurbish the locomotive for its proper role in the Civil War centennial.

Following a spectacular trek across America as a "living" emblem of the past, word went out that the *General* would not return to Chattanooga after all but instead would be permanently placed at Kennesaw Mountain, Georgia. Dedicatory ceremonies were announced; Georgia planned to celebrate the occasion. The old engine, however, would have to pass through Chattanooga on an L & N freight train on its way to its new home.

Around city hall, farfetched schemes turned into firm plans when this news arrived. Mayor Ralph H. Kelley, trained as an attorney, would "play the part" of James J. Andrews and with a cadre of volunteer raiders would "liberate" the *General*. Air observers relayed the time when freight No. 51 on its southbound journey arrived at the Wauhatchie Yards. In the postmidnight darkness of 12 September 1967, Kelley's men struck—city commissioners, a city police chief, the county sheriff, and sheriff's aides. They carried papers authorizing them to attach the engine as well as an injunction to prevent its removal from the yard.

The yardmaster and railroad men were not cooperative; they indicated they would defy all orders and proceed southward. The raiders climbed aboard the freight while others sent out radio messages to block all Chattanooga crossings with police cars so that No. 51 could not get out of Tennessee. Two hours of haggling took place before L & N officials agreed to leave the *General* on a sidetrack in the yards; the freight rolled across Hamilton County bereft of its valuable cargo. A long court struggle followed with final judgment in favor of Georgia, but before it was over the entire nation knew of the twentieth-century raid which reaffirmed Chattanooga's railroad heritage. Supporters in White Plains, New York, wired Kelley, "Even if you lose, you got class."

While the *General's* latest escapade was taking place, other local rail fans led by energetic Paul Merriman organized the Tennessee Valley Railroad Museum. On an abandoned section of trackage leading to the old tunnel through Missionary Ridge where Generals Sherman and Cleburne had fought one November day in 1863, the museum was dedicated on another November day in 1970. Here has been accumulated "one of the finest collections of operating railroadiana in the Southeast," restored to original appearance and operating condition. At the museum the spirit of a century of rail service is maintained, and from its wooded setting excursion trains hauled by "fire-breathing steam locomotives" carry passengers through the old historic tunnel or on journeys into the surrounding countryside.[2]

Desirous of moving "into a railroad environment" the National Model Railroad Association, composed of thirty thousand members, announced in 1979 plans to relocate its world headquarters in Chattanooga. On a fifteen-acre tract next to the Tennessee Valley Railroad Museum this group hopes to make Chattanooga a "mecca for the study of rail history."

During the declining years of rail passenger service modern diesel engines drew longer and longer freight trains into and through the area past many small, rural, deserted stations. Newly designed cars and piggyback facilities carrying an ever-increasing variety of commercial products reflect this vital but less romantic phase of railroading. In Chattanooga, car loadings rose from slightly less than 100,000 in 1941 to more than 148,000 in 1976.[3] Within the city a vexing, long-accumulating problem of traffic jams at downtown grade crossings finally resulted in a major rerouting compact between the L & N, the Southern Railway, the Tennessee State Highway Department, Hamilton County and Chattanooga. Programmed into sequences involving more than a decade of teamwork, the plan called for a reduction or elimination of downtown trackage and traffic, a relocation of main rail lines, a rechanneling of Chattanooga Creek, and bridges to carry the rails over certain principal streets.

A fundamental feature of the plan was the L & N's abandonment of the intown Cravens Yard and the construction of a completely modern facility in the valley of Lookout Creek, some seven miles from downtown. Close to the site of the battle of Wauhatchie, some 180 acres of rough land were leveled; twenty-five miles of track in the yard proper, to accommodate 1,430 standard-sized freight cars, were built and placed in service in April 1961. Although designing the yard as a freight car classification facility, the L & N respected the inspiring natural beauty of the area enough to screen the yard from Reflection Riding by a cleverly landscaped strip more than a mile long.

This complex relocation project labeled the "Chattanooga Runaround" officially opened on 22 November 1972. By this date the state of Georgia had sold the Union Station and surrounding acres and released the former Cravens Yard for modern usage.[4]

The Southern Railway, likewise, brought its De Butts Yard by Amnicola Highway up to standards of modern efficiency, making it one of the six most sophisticated computerized classification yards in the Southern system. As a junction of several heavily used lines in the southeast, the yard provides direct service to virtually every major southern city and through connections with all parts of the United States. Computers, triggered by monitors along the way, detect mechanical problems; other computer networks keep track of car locations. Trains entering the yard are filmed by closed-circuit television for bookkeeping purposes.

Associated with the area throughout its history, the Southern Railway in 1977 employed 1,077 Hamilton County people. Its technological wonders are a curious contrast to the nearby railroad museum where reconditioned old equipment represents the direct ancestry of the powerful modern diesel locomotives.

Southern Railway property holdings edge up to the Tennessee River where altered geography and changing times also have combined to disguise the past. The old romantic packets disappeared in the late 1920s with the sad demise of the *Chattanooga* and the *Joe Wheeler*. The once splendid *Chattanooga*, tied up opposite the city wharf awaiting her end, quietly slipped to the river bottom one night. The *Wheeler*, too, had grievous last days serving as a "galley slave among boats"; her cabin was reduced to a shack to house a small crew on a homemade river tug.[5]

The new Tennessee River of TVA with its 650-mile, nine-foot channel created by locks and dams brought to Hamilton County the benefits of a port on the nation's inland waterway. Boats on the Tennessee no longer had to wait for the "tide"; trips could be scheduled the year round. But the route to the Ohio River is still long and meandering, and as of this writing, boatmen now look forward to the completion of the Tennessee-Tombigbee Waterway. Begun in 1972, this cutoff will give local shippers the choice of two ocean ports—New Orleans and Mobile—with the distance to the Gulf at the latter city reduced by as much as 850 miles.

The influences bearing on navigation, however, have changed. As on the railroads, passenger service has disappeared and the nostalgia for days past alone recalls their many pleasures. Industrial work boats, built for power and profit, carry no excursion crowds nor brag of sumptuous meals. What utilitarian beauty they possess is usually hidden behind the cargo of their giant barges.

In 1933 river commerce, reaching almost one million tons, consisted chiefly of local shipments; forty years later it amounted to more than 29 million tons, mostly of an interregional nature. Chattanooga, as an industrial and distributing center, continues its close ties with the Tennessee River. Two public terminals, owned and operated by private corporations, serve local shippers along with many private docks. Grain, soybeans, sand and gravel, fuel oil, asphalt, and iron-steel products make up the bulk of the tonnage. Annual statistics record some 2.6 million tons received locally and two hundred thousand tons shipped out from the wharves. Most interesting from time to time have been the massive shipments of nuclear power components from the Combustion Engineering loading platforms by oceangoing barges.[6]

With declining rail and river passenger service, many travelers changed to flying as upgraded schedules helped to better connect Hamilton County to the rest of the nation. On 1 July 1934, an Eastern Airlines plane landed at Lovell Field with seven passengers as a celebrating group of local officials welcomed this pioneer commercial air flight to the area. Thirty-one years later Eastern brought the first jet to Lovell Field, which was no longer just a grassy meadow.

During the 1960s United Airlines, Delta Air Lines, and Southern Airways joined Eastern, giving the region wide connections across the nation on a relatively equal competitive basis. Total boardings rose from 179,419 in 1961 to 514,892 in 1976. This municipal field also had operators providing aircraft, instruction, charter service, sales, maintenance, and tie-down space for private planes. In addition, Dallas Bay Skypark, a privately owned facility, and the Collegedale Airpark serve private operators.

A fundamental change has occurred in local commercial passenger service in recent years as the "hub" theory of flight patterns has gained wide popularity. According to this scheme, feeder flights from smaller cities into "hub" centers at regular intervals provide the most efficient service. Delta, a strong advocate of this arrangement, has gained the bulk of Chattanooga business, transforming Lovell Field into an Atlanta satellite. Consequently in 1978 Eastern, the local pioneer, ended its Chattanooga service as did United Airlines in 1979.[7]

The major transformation in Hamilton County's life-style came earlier with the popular use of the automobile and hard-surfaced roads. After World War I the Federal Highway Act helped provide budgets while Tennessee funded its Highway Commission created in 1915 and floated bonds to help pull the state out of the mud, so to speak. The mobility provided by flexible transportation made industrial commuters of former farmers, allowed schools to consolidate, churches to band together, and suburbs to grow. It brought the doctor to his patients, or vice versa, and put law enforcement on wheels. In town, by 1947, riders said good-bye to streetcars for buses. Motorcar and truck registrations in Hamilton County jumped from 52,493 in 1950 to 184,756 in 1978 while on the farms gasoline-powered equipment replaced the horse and mule in a few short years.

Two interstate bus lines making almost one hundred daily departures and forty regular common carrier truck lines now provide service across the nation. Locally the Chattanooga Area Regional Transportation Authority (CARTA) manages mass transportation for the city and some neighboring communities.[8]

The Dixie and Lee highways, the Taft Highway over Signal Mountain, the Cummings Highway around Lookout Mountain, and the Dayton and Hixson pikes were among the popular roads, but these original routes became worn and incapable of dealing with traffic demands. The gateway position of Hamilton County made it a natural junction point for the new thoroughfares or interstate roads which in large measure followed the old buffalo paths and Indian trails of the past where grades were less steep and stream crossings easiest.

In the late 1950s the local interestate highways began to materialize. Routes from Knoxville, Atlanta, Nashville, and Birmingham converged in Hamilton County; they bear the colorless names I-24, I-59, I-75, and I-124. The engineers took advantage of the natural scenery while struggling with rugged and costly construction problems. They arranged a panoramic introduction to the lands of Hamilton from White Oak Mountain on the east, opened a matchless view of Chattanooga from a cut through Missionary Ridge, and built up a river-level stretch around the base of Lookout Mountain by nudging the Tennessee River to the north to make enough room for the roadbed. Older villages and crossroads were bypassed and new commercial oases with their clutter of advertising "palm-trees" sprang up at the interchanges.

Over these great highways the traffic rolls by in a constant stream—giant trucks, tankers, air-cooled buses, vans, campers, and a variety of motorcars large and small—resembling a gypsy caravan. In summer the tourists pass through Hamilton County on their way to and from the southern mountains; in the winter months they quit the Midwest and Canada for treks to Florida. More than one-half of the nation's population lives within one day's drive of Chattanooga. Many of the travelers stop in Hamilton County en route, for the area possesses the three primary interests of tourists—scenery, history, and natural attractions—which make it one of the prime tourist centers in Tennessee. In the year 1976 it was claimed that this "transient travel market" moving through the state made up about seven percent of the state's population.

Today there are almost enough motel and hotel rooms in Hamilton County to sleep all the Confederate troops General Bragg assembled in 1862 for his Kentucky campaign. Since 1958 growth has been steady and the tourist business in Hamilton County is said to have multiplied by 528 percent. In 1978 alone, visitors spent in the county a total of $188 million.[9]

One recently organized attraction brings guests to the area who are at times called the sons of Icarus (the legendary Greek who flew too close to the sun). These mid-twentieth-century soarers are hang gliders who have found ideal conditions for launch sites on Lookout and Raccoon mountains. This sport, promoted locally by the Tennessee Tree Toppers, draws participants from states ranging from Florida to Michigan, who call this area "their home hill."

In the fall of 1978 more than ten thousand gliding fans converged on Hamilton County for two very special events: the third annual Great Race and the American Cup competition, an international meet with teams from Great Britain, Canada, Japan, and the United States. Professionals and amateurs gliding from the mountain bluffs give a new if not especially practical dimension to travel.[10]

Just as modern transportation media changed the geographic relationship of Hamilton County to the rest of the nation, so maturing programs and the growth of power requirements of TVA caused the Authority to go to methods never dreamed of in 1933. Two such changes have had a major influence in Hamilton County, which not only is the seat of TVA's entire power operation but also the headquarters of the agency's Office of Health and Environmental Sciences.

From an annual production of about 1.5 billion kilowatt hours in 1933, the TVA has become the nation's largest power utility, selling 122 billion kilowatt hours in 1977. The steadily increasing demand from old customers, new industry, and such government installations as the Oak Ridge National Laboratory required a shift from water power generation to steam turbines by the 1950s.

Although none of TVA's giant fossil fuel plants were built in Hamilton County, their output was and still is managed from local headquarters and local people became involved in the renewed argument over government in the business of running coal-fueled steam plants. A threat that the United States might consider selling TVA surfaced during the Eisenhower administration. The Authority had the support not only of Hamilton Countians in this but also gained the spirited backing of progressive Senator Estes Kefauver. Kefauver, Lookout Mountain resident and Chattanooga lawyer, entered Congress in 1939 and the Senate nine years later where he gave consistent support to TVA.

The idea of selling TVA never gained popular favor, but as a consequence of this threat the power program of the Authority after 1959 was financed on a plan whereby TVA raised capital for expansion through bond sales. This development stressed the fact that power operations are now financed separately from all other TVA programs. From that time, power has had to pay its own way through revenue income and bond and note issues while paying about $80 million per year to the United States treasury for repayment of earlier appropriations.

In addition to coal-burning plants, TVA turned to nuclear generation of electrical energy and to a uniquely designed project called by the clumsy name Raccoon Mountain Pumped-Storage Hydro Plant. Located on the mountain by Nickajack Lake on the Hamilton-Marion county boundary, it is planned to produce "peaking" power to help satisfy maximum fluctuations in demand at different times of the day since electrical current cannot be stored.

Work began in 1970, but completion was held up by heavy equipment deficiencies. Now finished, the project includes a 528-acre storage reservoir on the mountaintop some one thousand feet above the lake. In a large chamber carved from solid rock deep inside the mountain are four reversible pump-turbine units. During hours when power demands are lowest (usually at night) pumps draw water from Nickajack

Lake to the mountaintop. Then when peak power demands exist, the pump-motor units reverse and operate as turbine-generators (up to half-million horsepower each), driven by the force of the falling water.[11]

The same year that work began at Raccoon Mountain, TVA started full-scale construction on the Sequoyah Nuclear plant in the north end of Hamilton County. Although delayed by changing design regulations, this project, estimated to cost about $1 billion, nears its fully operational date. Planned to produce nearly 2.5 million kilowatts, it will develop energy comparable to twenty Chickamauga Dams. At peak construction times an estimated twenty-seven-hundred worked at Sequoyah. Like Raccoon, it is being developed by TVA work crews and the two projects have done much to keep the county's unemployment rate low during the 1970s.

The national energy crisis of the 1970s pointed up a second condition affecting TVA and Hamiltonians. The Authority from earliest days based its rate structure on the theory of low costs and a correspondingly large sales volume. Rates as a consequence went down as more units of energy were used; consumers were encouraged to acquire all kinds of appliances, install electric home heating, and use power on farms and in industry in place of other types of energy. Electric bills far below the national average became a tradition.

In 1970 the specter of fuel shortages crept into the picture. In the 1974 winter season TVA coal stockpiles dwindled to crisis levels; Hamilton County as well as other places experienced a Christmas season brownout. Later the world oil situation and bitter local weather intensified the problem; rising costs of fuel, labor, and environmental protection equipment caused power bills to escalate. The forty-year-old pricing philosophy was challenged at every turn although in 1977 the average residential rate continued to be about one-third less than the national average.

The government naturally turned to TVA to develop a model to deal with the energy crisis as well as pollution and environmental issues. But local customers' rising power bills brought forth bitter cries that TVA had deserted its people: the Authority's apparent departure from the tradition of a promotional rate structure resulted in misunderstanding and caustic public criticism. Faced with this dilemma, TVA appears in a weak role in advising such undramatic measures as conservation, elimination of waste, and new standards of home weatherization.

Since power remains the glamour portion of TVA's total multipurpose program, this energy crisis exerts a crucial influence on the Authority's total program. Moreover, many of the veteran members of its staff who joined the experiment in the 1930s have retired, having given TVA both heart and spirit. At the crossroads in 1978, TVA found all three of its directorships vacant.

Realizing the consequential role of the Authority, President Jimmy Carter instructed TVA to lead national experimentation in the energy struggle. He sought out the newly appointed chairman of the board of the Authority, S. David Freeman, with this challenge. Freeman, Chattanooga-reared, is the son of a poor Russian immigrant who came to the United States in 1906. Freeman knows the valley well, has had previous experience as a TVA employee, and is living proof that the American dream continues to live.

As public discussion of power problems goes on, TVA and the city of Chattanooga quietly work on an entirely different matter—the South Chickamauga Creek Flood Control Project. Flood control advocates for years pointed out the vulnerable position of the city and the potential destruction it could suffer: they recalled the record waters of 1867, 1875, 1886, 1917, and 1920. Then in March 1973 the value of the unified resource development of TVA was clearly demonstrated. An intense storm dumped from five to ten inches of rain in less than three days on the mountains of eastern Tennessee and neighboring North Carolina. Tributary dams impounded a share of the resulting flood and the upper main-river dams flattened the crest so that at Chattanooga the level reached only seven feet above flood stage. It was the worst flood in the area's post-TVA history. Engineers reading the situation claimed that, if uncontrolled, the flood would have covered roughly half of the city and would have caused a half-billion dollars' worth of damage. Even so local property losses amounted to some $12 million with havoc concentrated along South Chickamauga Creek.

To attempt to eliminate or at least reduce the possibility of any repeat submergence of this area, the city and TVA pushed a flood control project based on an agreement already developed on paper whose price tag was $15 million. It consisted of a widening and relocation of portions of South Chickamauga Creek, the building of a levee about four miles long between the Eastgate Shopping Center and Shallowford Road, and the construction of three pumping stations to take water away from the wrong side of the levee. The hope is that it will protect some fifteen hundred homes and about 150 businesses on the south side of the creek.[12]

Although Hamilton County was saved from a disastrous flood in

1973, officially the size of the county shrank as a result of the building of TVA. In 1964 the Bureau of the Census changed its figures for the water area of the county from eleven square miles to 36.6 square miles. Two years later this decision showed up in the land measurements when the county's actual size was given as 550.4 square miles instead of 576; Chickamauga Lake covered the missing acreage.

The population of the county, on the other hand, did not shrink. In 1970 the census reported 254,236 county residents of whom 119,082 lived in Chattanooga and 135,154 outside the city limits. In the county totals, 46,397 or 18.2 percent were black; within Chattanooga the 42,610 blacks made up 35.8 percent of the population. The blacks living in the county beyond the city limits made up only 2.8 percent of the total population.

The majority of Hamiltonians stayed in the native-born category; 1,548 foreign-born lived in the county in 1970 and 641 of these resided in Chattanooga. The countries sending the largest number to the area included Germany, with 837; the United Kingdom, 736; the USSR, 596; Canada, 433; Italy, 253; and Poland, 236. Many of the county families had serious financial problems; the census reports 13.3 percent were below the poverty level. In Chattanooga the total was 19.8 percent and for the balance of the county 7.9 percent.[13]

Continued growth and Chattanooga annexation efforts have changed the totals since 1970. In 1980 Chattanooga reported 169,565 citizens, while the census gave Hamilton County's population as 287,740.

Hamilton County, beyond the limits of Chattanooga, has generally been dependent on agriculture. Its great variety of soil from rich bottomlands to chert banks promoted diversified farms with stock, cereals, fruit, and truck the principal commercial products. A "crop of suburban lots" took over the vineyards and fruitlands on Missionary Ridge in the early part of the twentieth century. Since then, residences, commercial centers, shopping areas, highways, and TVA installations have removed other areas from cultivation.

Under the direction of Samuel E. Mullins, county extension agent for thirty-five years until retirement in 1973, great changes have taken place in the county's farm story. While most farms remained family units, a few incorporated as commercial ventures; the total number decreased while the average size increased. In 1970 about twenty-six percent of the acreage was cultivated on the 679 farms reported in the census. Over twenty-four thousand acres of waste and idle cropland by 1972 have been planted in forest trees since the time farmers first participated in the planting programs.

About seventy-five percent of the farm income derived from poultry, milk, and livestock production and the remaining twenty-five percent from crop sales. In 1970 Hamilton County ranked as the third-largest egg-producing and seventh-largest broiler-producing county in the state with about three hundred farms producing poultry commercially. Today pasture and soybeans take up many of the fields, but truck farmers continue to have a steady market for their vegetables and fruits. In season "You Pick" signs indicate a scarcity of field labor while the ritual of sorgham making in the fall recalls pioneer days before most Hamilton farmers commuted to an industrial job in town for a second income.[14]

As in the 1880s, clusters of suburban residences mushroomed around Chattanooga, now encouraged to grow by the increased use of the automobile and the extension of bus lines. These new developments, architecturally the product of modernism, preserved no distinctly regional characteristics. Beyond the reach of city planners and desirous of remaining free of the city tax gatherer, the residents faced three possible alternatives: to remain independent communities, to seek annexation by Chattanooga, or to work for countywide metropolitan government.

The largest and most rapidly growing area, East Ridge, claimed a population of 21,799 in 1970 and an estimated 23,352 five years later. According to tradition, Pressley Ruth Lomenick was the first settler in the area around 1850. Along the stage road to Ringgold, Georgia, other pioneer families grouped: the Boyds, Beans, Lerches, Clines, Stumps, Harrises, McBriens, and other members of the Lomenick clan. For a time, they called portions of the district Smoky Row, Nickle Street, Penny Row, or Dutchtown (where Jacob Kellerhals had his large dairy). Later the general region was referred to as East Side before it finally acquired the name East Ridge about 1921. In that year the approximately three hundred residents incorporated under Mayor J. M. Hudlow.

In 1928 the Bachman tubes through Missionary Ridge opened East Ridge for more convenient settlement, but the area was still considered so remote that some thought the tunnel should be used for barn dances since there was so little traffic. By 1930 only 2,152 persons lived in the town. Then a surge of development was ushered in by the builder Weldon F. Osborne. Ringgold Road changed from a narrow tar-and-gravel path in 1928 to a four-lane highway in the mid-thirties. Later the Osborne Shopping Center brought a new business concept to East Ridge,

This residential town, it is said, "obviously desires to stay small." It prides itself on its low taxes, independence in politics—political campaigns there are often hotter than the weather—and no industry. The building of the neighboring interstate highway system, however, has resulted in the concentration of around two thousand motel rooms within the community.

With this heavy tourist trade has come a plethora of special problems. The community has defeated referendums on the sale of liquor, largely splitting the city along the lines of a place with a big tourist income and a residential city with a large number of churches. In addition, the East Ridge police department is burdened with a major responsibility in dealing with the mobile, interstate, criminal element which temporarily stops within its jurisdiction. [15]

North of the Tennessee River another satellite town, Red Bank, has grown up along a busy highway. The general area, called Hamilton or Dry Valley, early attracted settlers—James Elisha Rogers, James C. Conner, the Hartman brothers Martin, John, and George, Jacob Foust, William K. Gray, and others. The Methodists of the group built a log church and school called Hicks Chapel.

The Civil War years damaged the unity of the region and difficult days ensued. By 1870 a union church where all denominations could worship was constructed. Here for the next fifty-three years Methodists, Baptists, and Cumberland Presbyterians shared the building, using Reed Lake for baptismal ceremonies. They named the section Pleasant Hill.

When Pleasant Hill applied for a post office in 1881, the postmaster, George S. Hartman, got word that another Tennessee hamlet was already using that name. A different name had to be found. Hartman and his wife pondered the problem until Mrs. Hartman on glancing out the window at a red clay ridge suggested the town be called Red Bank.

For years the area remained rural and, as one resident put it, there were "practically no houses" in the village until after World War I. In 1917 the interurban streetcar line was completed, linking Red Bank with Chattanooga; the community soon had a reputation as a good place to live because it was "high, dry, and close in," but all the way to Daisy the land was used for truck farming with only a few modest homes dotting the landscape.

The trolley line passed through Valdeau, White Oak, Flora, Morrison, Ford, and on to the tiny commercial center of Red Bank. Homes sprang up along the way and the different church groups now could support their own chapels. Red Bank blossomed with a few new stores and the people there began to consider a new name; for a time they toyed with "Daytonia" as a designation which would better suit their prospects, but eventually they stayed with the Hartmans' choice.

In 1942 a six-lane highway through the section was finished and community leaders spoke of incorporation. The first effort matured four years later, but the residents vetoed the idea. Finally on 21 June 1955, Red Bank and neighboring White Oak voted to unite as a town, comprising 6.4 square miles, to be called Red Bank-White Oak Township.

The census takers counted 10,777 residents in 1960; a decade later they listed 12,715 or an eighteen percent increase. The subject of the name of the community again became a topic of public discussion. The hyphenated name was both long and clumsy and in January 1967 it officially was changed simply to Red Bank. That same year a modern city hall opened. Steady growth continues, especially marked by the erection of duplexes and apartment complexes, and population estimates in 1975 climbed to 14,677.[16] Today Red Bank is completely surrounded by the city of Chattanooga.

A third town located close to Chattanooga was incorporated as Lookout Mountain, Tennessee, as early as the 1890s. Tightly restricted in land area, it retained a constant population growth of only 4.2 percent between 1960 and 1970 when the census reported 1,741 residents. Although its highways and byways are crowded with tourists, this splendid residential site—many properties have unmatched panoramic views—affords quiet retreats, As available homesites in the Hamilton County section of the mountain were occupied, the settled area pushed southward into Georgia.

Lookout Mountain sent out to the nation several persons who made unusual contributions. Estes Kefauver (1903-1963) as a young lawyer fresh from Yale University, moved there in 1927. A big man known for his friendliness, strength, and rugged independence, he entered Congress in 1939, serving on until his sudden death. His reputation for eliminating boss rule in Tennessee, for exposing crime syndicates, for supporting TVA, and for fighting monopoly overshadow the fact that he was chosen by the Democratic party as the vice-presidential candidate in 1956. As a maverick politician, Kefauver did not have the constant support of his local constituents, but all respected what his coonskin cap symbolized: that the raccoon's rings are in its tail and not in its nose.

Not far from the Kefauver home lives William Brock III, a Washington and Lee University graduate and navy veteran. Attracted to the growing Republican strength in the South, Brock left the party of his grandfather who had served in the United States Senate. He won the Third Congressional District seat four consecutive times, beginning in 1962. His conservative economic views won national attention and in 1970 he successfully ran for the Senate, defeating incumbent Albert Gore. Brock, however, lost in the contest for reelection, after which he took the position of chairman of the national Republican party.

The town of Signal Mountain, in contrast to Brock's home community of Lookout Mountain, grew by leaps and bounds after World War II. The population jumped from 3,413 in 1960 to 4,839 in 1970, showing an increase of 41.8 percent, and has continued to expand at about the same rate. In 1975 it reported an estimated 5,187 residents. As a popular middle-class suburb, it supports no industry but does include orchid growers' establishments and the Alexian Brothers Rest Home, which occupies the old Signal Mountain Inn. Since 1954 dogwood festivals have become the pride of the mountain residents; all are encouraged to plant these beautiful trees, thus continuing a practice begun more than a half-century ago.

Late in April 1937 the town officials declared a thirty-day period of mourning following the untimely death of one of Signal Mountain's most popular residents. Nathan L. Bachman loved his mountain home, his orchards and gardens, his kennels of hunting dogs, and the "old settlers" of the area. This son of Dr. Jonathan W. Bachman practiced law. He was elected circuit court judge and later selected associate justice of the Tennessee Supreme Court. Early in 1933 when Cordell Hull resigned his Senate seat to become secretary of state, Bachman received an appointment to complete Hull's term. Elected to a full term in the next general election, Bachman, a gentle, warm person, was hailed as one of the "best beloved members" of the Senate. His death at the age of fifty-eight was a great shock to his mountain friends and to all of Hamilton County. They agreed with Joseph T. Tumulty's assessment of him penned to Bachman's widow, "He made the world brighter."[17]

In 1961 a newcomer to Hamilton County took up residency on Signal Mountain. Frank W. Wilson, newly appointed United States district judge who succeeded retiring Judge Leslie R. Darr (1939-1961), was a forty-three-year-old Tennessean trained at the state university and recent resident of Oak Ridge. Through the years Judge Wilson has demonstrated his deep faith in the American judicial system in dealing with the routine cases of his office while displaying remarkable poise and "judicial temperament" in such cases as the 1964 jury-tampering trial of Teamsters Union President James R. Hoffa when federal marshals guarded his residence, the long Chattanooga school desegregation case, and the suit over the teaching of Bible in the public schools. As a citizen of the county Judge Wilson has gained the spontaneous trust and respect of his neighbors.

In another corner of the county the community of Collegedale listed 3,031 citizens in 1970. Some seven years before that time public discussion was first heard about the advantages of incorporation. This eventually led to a referendum in November 1968 when supporters of municipal government won 216 to 74; Fred Fuller became the first mayor. The new town included some twenty-nine hundred acres and a population of around three thousand, most of whom were students at Southern Missionary College. Economically the community's chief support came from the college and the McKee Baking Company which produces Little Debbie® cakes and pies for a national market.

The reason for Collegedale's incorporation is unique. The great majority of the people are Seventh Day Adventists who worship on Saturday, and work or study on Sunday. Incorporation gained favor in order to eliminate any possibility of annexation by Chattanooga, which would have meant an extension of that city's Sunday ordinances. Such Sunday regulations had caused the Adventists serious trouble in the past. In 1895 their academy was closed by the state when Sunday laws were invoked and again in 1916 an effort was made to take action against the school officials for "desecration" of the Sabbath. So the history of blue laws helped create a little city.[18]

In the northern end of the county near the villages of Soddy and Daisy the eerie night glare from coke ovens and ceramic kilns, after years of operation, was permanently extinguished. Even before the Civil War mining was an important way of life in the Soddy area of Walden Ridge. At the turn of the century some 450 miners, many of them members of the United Mine Workers, were employed by the New Soddy Company, which also operated a battery of coke ovens. Later controlled by the Durham Coal and Iron Company, this operation was joined by a competitor, the Montlake Coal Company, located in the North Chickamauga gulch in Walden Ridge. In the early 1920s 2,500 tons of coal were mined daily in this district.

Walden Ridge also contained shale which was profitably used to produce pottery, fireplace tile, floor tile, and roofing tile. Before 1900 the Herty Shale Brick and Manufacturing Company made "little brown jugs" and hollow tile for a national market; in 1916 the B. Mifflin Hood Brick Company started operations. Steam shovels and cable conveyors carried the shale to the plants where as many as three hundred people worked the shale and operated the ovens and kilns. During World War I millions of condensation rings manufactured for the chemical industry in making explosives and poison gas were produced at Daisy for domestic firms or shipped to Norway, Canada, Cuba, or Mexico.

A rich lore of these busy times lingered on after depression days' adverse winds swept away tile, coke, and coal profits. But motor traffic soon brought new life to the area and eventually new citizens helped the older residents recoup their economic losses.

A desire for political independance and self-rule led to a vote for incorporation by the residents of Soddy and Daisy in April 1969. By a margin of fifty-five votes the twin city was created, covering some twenty-three square miles stretched out along the highway. In June the people elected their officials and Mayor Malcolm Luther Orr took charge of this new governmental venture.

All the needed services had to be arranged; street paving had high priority as a major undertaking, and construction was started on a community park at the Soddy Creek Embayment. The Sequoyah Health Center, begun as a primary medical facility for the northern part of the county, gave "doctor office" service to a rural area which lacked doctors. Public interest in all these matters has kept the Soddy-Daisy political kettle boiling.

In 1970 the town's population numbered 7,569. The construction of TVA's Sequoyah Nuclear Plant nearby brought jobs and good wages to the area. Branch banks, franchise food outlets, and new business encouraged an air of prosperity noted by some local leaders by the fact that the brow lots on Flat Top Mountain overlooking the area have been sold for future residences. Construction of a limited-access highway around the community, it is hoped, will relieve Soddy-Daisy's vexing traffic problem but will not cause business to depart from the downtown area.

North Hamilton County's most acclaimed son, Ralph McGill, returned some years ago to address the Soddy-Daisy High School commencement. Before his death, this talented writer and editor of the *Atlanta Constitution* had established a national reputation for his progressive and liberal views. On returning home, McGill found everything had changed since his youth; he recalled for the students the "unpainted general store that smelled of tobacco, of calico, and dry goods, of cheese, kerosene and bananas." At that time no one in Soddy-Daisy even dreamed of a great nuclear power plant—Sequoyah's latest namesake—that would rise along the shores of Lake Chickamauga.[19]

Three other small and strictly residential areas also organized as independent municipalities. Ridgeside, or Shepherd Hills, in 1929 voted against annexation by Chattanooga, thirty-eight to fourteen. Since that time it organized a town government as a small island surrounded by the city; its population increased by only ten people in the decade of the 1960s, reaching 458.

In the rapidly growing residential district along the shores of Lake Chickamauga, Lakesite decided on an independent course in 1972 when the people numbering about three hundred voted to incorporate, seventy-five to fifteen; Ray Dodson became first mayor. The expenses of developing services and maintaining roads led to a movement in 1978 to reconsider their status. However, in a second referendum in May the Lakesite community decided to retain its city charter, voting 106 to 64.[20]

The third minicity is Walden. Located north of Signal Mountain on Walden Ridge, this wooded residential area's citizens voted on 30 July 1975 to incorporate, 253 to 68. This fledgling town had an estimated eight hundred citizens when Fred Hetzler was elected mayor. Walden undertook no elaborate program to provide common services but concentrated much of its attention on the restoration of the Conner Toll House along the old Anderson Pike. This 1858 structure of oak and poplar logs, rebuilt on strategic ground, has a deserved place in the National Register of Historic Places. The Waldenites also are working closely with the Tennessee Department of Conservation regarding the Falling Water Natural Area nearby.[21]

The creation of new Hamilton County municipalities was, at least in part, related to Chattanooga's effort to solve a serious problem common to all American cities. In the mid-century the population within the corporate limits shrank in relation to the total county population—from seventy-one percent in 1940 to sixty-three percent in 1950 and to fifty-five percent ten years later. Businesses as well as citizens moved from the downtown districts to suburban subdivisions beyond the town's borders. Chattanooga political leaders began calling attention to the "hardening of traffic arteries" in and out of town, to the new bedroom communities beyond the city's power to tax, and to the "daylight citizens" who used Chattanooga services without contributing to their payment.

Following the major annexation era of the late 1920s, Chattanooga took in only one small factory area along Manufacturers Road north of the Tennessee River during the next twenty-five years.[22] Prior to the "home rule" constitutional amendment in 1953 municipal boundaries were set by the state legislature in local acts. This method was capable of adjustment to local desires which for years had been unfriendly to annexation. Consequently, annexation virtually ceased, for the legislators did not wish to alienate the suburban voters.

After the 1953 amendment, the legislature in 1955 acted to pave the way for city growth by setting up a uniform standard for all cities of the state. Very different from the old method, it simply permitted Tennessee cities to extend their borders without any referendum in the areas affected: annexation became lawful on the passage of a city ordinance without the consent of the parties involved and without a public hearing. Furthermore, the burden of proving that annexation was unreasonable rested on the private citizens affected who had to pay court costs. Not until 1974 was this changed, and the burden of proof of "reasonableness" was placed then on the annexing municipality.

The 1955 law created controversy which raged for years; it was declared authoritarian and undemocratic. As Chattanooga proceeded to use this law, neighboring Hamilton County communities, fearing annexation, initiated their own plans to incorporate. Red Bank (1955), Collegedale (1968), Soddy-Daisy (1969), Lakesite (1972), and Walden (1975) became independent governing units. Eastdale, however, decided by a vote of 379 to 306 that it could not support itself as a municipality while, after some discussion, Ooltewah and Apison gave up the idea.

Ridgeside (Shepherd Hills), surrounded by the city, clung to its independence, deciding to live with its inadequate fire protection and sewers rather than join the city. East Ridge, wedged in between Chattanooga and the Georgia state line, voted in 1957 and again in 1959 in heated contests not to become a part of Chattanooga. East Ridge, however, did not oppose annexation in principle; it helped to create a new complication by moves to annex two areas, Crestwood and the Frawley Road-Harris Hills sections, which Chattanooga also was at that time in the process of annexing.[23]

As debate, often spirited, exaggerated, and self-centered, grew heated across the county, Chattanooga proceeded with plans to take in a number of neighboring subdivisions. Antiannexation leaders accused the city of ramming citizenship down the throats of their suburban neighbors. But the city moved ahead, annexing three small areas and four larger ones. The small sections were Hampton Heights, contiguous to North Chattanooga, Chevoit Hills, a tiny area of two hundred residents, and Crestwood at the south end of Missionary Ridge. The larger settled areas were Eastdale, Sequoia-Woodmore, Spring Creek, and East Brainerd. These seven added some twelve thousand people to the city's population and 8.23 square miles.

Eastdale, an older community, grew from a rural hamlet just east of Missionary Ridge named Hornville. In 1909 with the prospect of the completion of the McCallie Avenue tunnel and improved public transportation, the citizens experienced steady growth and discarded the earlier name. To the southeast of Eastdale, the newer residential division of Sequoia-Woodmore brought 3,157 new residents to the city while East Brainerd, the largest area annexed since 1929, added 2,500 persons. Spring Creek's total population was 924.

This spate of annexation brought on a crop of new lawsuits because the county sought compensation for several schools turned over to the city. Chattanooga did profit from the transfer not only as a result of additional property taxes but also from state allowances. It is estimated, for example, that the city would receive from the state about $11.50 per person in annexed areas for sales tax and street maintenance allowances.[24]

There were other areas beyond the corporate limits attractive to city annexation advocates, and in the fall of 1959 the chamber of commerce embarked on an educational campaign to promote a further drive. That December the city commission voted to take in the Riverside and Stuart Heights-Rivermont areas. This move, greeted by the usual lawsuits, provoked the opposition of major industry, which took the lead in contesting the action. E. I. du Pont de Nemours & Co. (whose multimillion dollar plant was located on the northern edge of Rivermont), Central Soya, Dixie Mercerizing, Quaker Oats, the Georgia

Industrial Realty Company (a subsidiary of the Southern Railway Company), along with other businesses and individuals challenged Chattanooga. Finally after years of frustration and the incoming of a set of new officials, the city repealed this annexation ordinance in 1963. [25]

In the following months a few municipal leaders still insisted on annexing "growth" areas, and the entire matter became a tough and exciting political issue. As infighting intensified, the residents of areas subject to annexation persisted in defending the status quo; they wanted no one to tamper with property taxes. City officials were divided over the issue as annexation politics entered the picture. During this era some people switched to another solution: they advocated metropolitan government with consolidation of all political institutions. Now and then some small contiguous areas were annexed, such as the section from Moccasin Bend up Mountain Creek Valley to Reeds Lake Road. This loosed a new feud, for the town of Red Bank also wanted these people. [26]

Finally in 1968 after a careful investigation produced a "Fringe Area Study," the city commission launched a new series of annexations. The localities involved comprised Airport, Amnicola and Stuart Heights, Tyner-Hawkinsville, Lake Hills, Murray Hills, and East Brainerd. Included also were residential areas around Lake Chickamauga, the "deannexed" regions which had earlier contested inclusion in the city, and the industrial lands below the dam. In their move the commission proceeded under the 1955 law, but except for the Airport area which came under the city unbrella in April 1968, litigation and delays held up official annexation of the other areas.

Opposition persisted until a more palatable plan than that of 1955 was approved by the legislature. This provided for a pledge by the city that partial service would be provided by the city to newly annexed areas but that the new city residents would pay only corresponding partial taxes instead of taxes equal to all other Chattanoogans. But this plan was immediately challenged and the variable tax idea was declared unconstitutional. Annexed areas were then virtually deannexed; the legal battle accelerated. Many Chattanooga blacks, viewing the matter from a practical standpoint, joined the opposition to annexation because new suburban white residents would dilute the political strength of the central city blacks.

After about five years the Tennessee Supreme Court ruled in favor of the city, and the concerned areas became an integral part of Chattanooga. Tyner, Murray Hills, Lake Hills, and East Brainerd added some nine thousand acres and between eighteen and twenty thousand people to the city.[27]

Meanwhile the city commission on 2 February 1972 passed on final readings ordinances annexing ten large contiguous areas estimated to contain thirty-two thousand residents. The areas comprised North Hixson (including Du Pont), Signal Hills, Middle Valley, Gold Point, King's Point-McCarty, East Brainerd, Tyner-Hawkinsville, Wauhatchie-Williams Island, North Mountain Creek, Union Springs, and Tiftonia. The King's Point-McCarty and Tyner-Hawkinsville sections entered the city at once but all the others filed suits to block annexation. Hamilton County took legal steps to support the county residents in their struggle against the city. Antiannexation committees again functioned; mass meetings decried the pending change; antibusing groups who opposed desegregation joined in seeking financial aid and legal support.

While the legal struggle ground slowly on, a judge set aside the annexation of Wauhatchie (the old battleground of Lookout Valley) and the community of Tiftonia nearby. Tiftonia, a real estate development of in-laws of the Jerome Pound family named Tift from Tifton, Georgia, grew up along the Cummings Highway west of Lookout Mountain. The ruling in these two cases differed from all others; they were declared to be self-contained communities without ties to Chattanooga because they were west of the city, whose natural growth was to the east and north.

Not until July 1974 was the legal process for the mass annexation exhausted. Then the Supreme Court of Tennessee upheld Chattanooga's annexation of a total of 39.4 square miles containing 25,137 persons. The territory included the tremendous growth area along Highway 58 and the bustling Northgate Shopping Center. It embraced the veteran communities of Tyner well over one hundred years old, and Hixson with its shopping plazas, Lakeshore Lodge, and Valleybrook Golf and Country Club with its proud tradition for gracious living. Annexed also were the new Du Pont plant and the older model village of Lupton City which was provided by the Dixie Mercerizing Company in the 1920s as a company town. A changed ruling relating to Wauhatchie and Tiftonia brought these western areas into the city at the same time that fine lake properties came under municipal jurisdiction.

According to Mayor Robert Kirk Walker, a strong advocate of annexation, the city of Chattanooga in mid-1974 had a population of

166,200; the size of the community had jumped to 118.6 square miles. These statistics represented an increase since 1970 of 46,277 persons and 62.3 square miles. A few small, contiguous sections became part of the city in the following years and in June 1977 Chattanooga claimed a population of 170,046 and a territory of 126.9 square miles.[28]

The active advocates of annexation rejoiced, but the antiannexation people found new sources of complaints. Many now awaited city services with growing impatience. The city fathers did receive additional state and federal funds in programs dependent on population statistics, but they likewise found expenses soaring.

As Chattanooga reached out to add new territory, it became apparent at least to some people that urban planning could not be limited to downtown and that inadequate housing and slum districts were not found only in the core city. The transfer of school property from the county to the city and the countless complex problems of providing convenient schools and reasonable busing policies became virtually an endless process.

Within the new city limits blackberry and honeysuckle tangles still grow along fence rows, and bare, eroding chert cliffs show where machines have scratched away fill dirt. Kudzu vines festoon the trees in places and roadside ditches fill up with summer weeds and winter trash. "City beautiful" committees have faced a new challenge and much discouragement. In the town's early history, visitors noted how vast spaces and little planning characterized Chattanooga; today's tourist who passes roadway signs that read "city limits" may have exactly the same reaction.

While the incorporation wars were in progress, some citizens challenged the old political structures of both the city and the county. They put forth a popular new concept of local government by proposing the establishment of a metropolitan government to replace both the city commission and the county court. There had been cooperation between the two units for some years in such departments as health care and police work but nothing resembling the elimination of the old structures in favor of one government.

State law under a 1953 constitutional amendment did make such experimentation legally feasible and in December 1962 a movement to promote metropolitan government got under way in Hamilton County. By that time Shelby and Knox counties had each held referendums on metropolitan charters—both rejected by the voters. In

Nashville and Davidson County the issue was approved in 1962 after the rejection of a similar proposal four years earlier.

A charter commission of ten members chosen by the city commission and the county court began work on a frame of government. The group of three city residents and seven from the county was carefully selected. As volunteers who had little political experience, they held regular public meetings in order to hear expressions from people from all parts of the area and all walks of life. Visiting experts in political science furnished technical advice and practical guidance. The local press gave exhaustive coverage to each new proposal and development.

Finally in January 1964 a lengthy, detailed charter, unanimously approved by the charter commission, was readied for public consideration. To gain acceptance it would have to receive concurrent majorities within the city and within the remaining county area in a special referendum.

A salient feature of the consolidation charter was the recommendation for general service and urban service districts. The general service district contained the total area of the county; the urban service zone was comprised of the city of Chattanooga. This arrangement permitted tax differentials between districts receiving or not receiving the more extensive urban services. Provisions were, of course, included for an orderly expansion of the urban services to sections beyond the city corporate borders when such services were desired.

The charter provided for a mayor-council form of government. The metropolitan legislative council, of eighteen members, consisted of six elected at large and twelve chosen by districts. Judicial authority was to be vested in a metropolitan court of four judges.

On 28 April 1964, Hamilton County voted on the issue. The campaign had been spirited for weeks with "pro" and "anti" groups gathering in public meetings and soliciting support through radio and television programs. The press gave coverage to every point of view. The antimetropolitan people saw a clique at work who would impose city dictatorship over the rural areas; others stressed the well-worn tax bugaboo. Labor objected to the proposed new form of government while old officeholders and their adherents in both city and county offered only minimal acceptance. Stormy weather greeted election day, but 51,619 people went to the polls. They defeated the referendum decisively both inside and outside the city; the majority seemed content with the two existing governments.

Those who worked hard for "metro," however, were not discour-

aged. By 1970 they were ready for a second try. This time an elected
charter commission spent seven months drafting an instrument. Its
research convinced the members that the document should be briefer
and more flexible than the 1964 version. The mayor of Chattanooga,
three of the four city commissioners, the county judge, the county
school superintendent, both Chattanooga newspapers, and about fifty
civic and business associations endorsed it.

But the referendum debate preceding the voting of 6 August 1970
again was heated and in many instances the issues distorted. In addition
to concern about police power and taxes, the county people, now aware
of the school busing problem, read this new dimension into the metro
issue. The black population of Chattanooga also voiced its opposition;
they envisioned metro as diluting their political potential. In addition
to these fundamental differences, the prometropolitan government
supporters gave zest to the campaign by their enthusiasm while the
antis spiced up the contest with half truths and distortions of the dire
consequences of changing to a new form of government.

The number of people who went to the polls was fewer than that
six years earlier, and metropolitan government again failed to get their
endorsement. Chattanoogans—despite the position taken by many
blacks—approved of consolidation 10,846 to 9,577. The approval, however, of the people living beyond the corporate limits was also required,
and they turned down any change by 13,967 to 11,687.[29]

Although memories of this vote have begun to fade in the public
mind, diverse groups keep the metropolitan government idea alive.
They emphasize the various anachronisms which exist in the old government forms as the region becomes more urbanized. Although rural
politics change but slowly, they hope to plant new seeds which will
have plenty of time to germinate before a third referendum is attempted. [30]

NOTES

1. In June 1978 Chattanooga acquired for $460,000 the downtown block,
consisting of Ninth, Market, Tenth and Broad streets, from Georgia. On 4
April 1979, the remaining three acres (between Market and Broad streets, just
south of Eleventh Street) were acquired for $425,000. These purchases, made
with Office of Community Development funds, are a part of a program of land

assemblage by the city which, it is planned, will lead to major redevelopment projects.

2. "TVRM Revisited," *L & N Magazine* (March 1971), pp. 18–19.

3. *Chattanooga Business Trends* (Chattanooga: Greater Chattanooga Area Chamber of Commerce, 1977); *Chattanooga Times*, 10 April 1979.

4. "A Yard-to-Be Nearly Is," *L & N Magazine* (October 1960), pp. 8–10; "Wauhatchie Yard Activated," Ibid. (May 1961), pp. 12-13; "Chattanooga Run-around," Ibid. (January 1973), pp. 8–10.

5. T.J. Campbell, *The Upper Tennessee* . . . (Chattanooga: author, 1932), p. 124

6. TVA, *Annual Report, 1977*, p. 37; *Chattanooga Times*, 18 February 1979; *Business Trends*. Technology did not completely remove the old navigation problems at the site of the Suck. In the fall of 1973, two tugs sank there in very deep water. Since no explanation of the cause of these accidents makes clear what happened, it may be plausible to link them to the Indian gambler, Untsaiyi, of Cherokee mythology.

7. Ibid., 11 February 1979; *Forward Chattanooga*, (Chattanooga: Greater Chattanooga Chamber of Commerce, 23 June 1977).

8. Ibid.; Lee S. Greene, David H. Grubbs, and Victor C. Hobday, *Government in Tennessee*, 3rd ed. (Knoxville: University of Tennessee Press, 1975), pp. 332–326.

9. Material on tourism furnished by Robert Elmore, Director, Chattanooga Area Convention and Visitors Bureau: *Chattanooga News-Free Press*, 6 August 1978; 4 February 1979. In 1977 convention delegates numbered 118,266.

10. *Chattanooga News-Free Press*, 15 October 1978; *Chattanooga Times*, 25, 29 September 1978.

11. *Raccoon Mountain Pumped-Storage Hydro-Plant* (TVA); TVA, *Annual Report, 1977*.

12. *Chattanooga News-Free Press*, 23 October 1976; 7 January 1979; "Reducing Chattanooga Floods," *TVA Today* (April 1977): 4–51.

13. U.S., Department of Commerce, Bureau of the Census, *1970 Census of Population and Housing, Chattanooga, Tennessee–Georgia, Standard Metropolitan Statistical Area* (Washington, D.C.: Government Printing Office, 1972), pp. 1, 8, 15, 22.

14. *Chattanooga News-Free Press*, 27 January 1970; 29 February 1972; 24 July, 25 September 1977; 19 May, 22 October 1978; *Chattanooga Times*, 8 December 1960; 12 May 1962; 6 July 1973. Mullins was succeeded in 1973 by Henry B. Ford.

15. *Chattanooga News-Free Press*, 2-4 April 1971; *Chattanooga Times*, 2 May 1954; 13 March 1966; 6 November 1968; 15 January 1978.

16. *Chattanooga News-Free Press*, 15 February, 10 December 1972; 25 September 1977; *Chattanooga Times*,9 August 1919; 13 July 1924; 30 Novem-

ber 1928; 13 November 1942; 15 April 1946; 21 June 1955; 21 October 1967; 15 January 1978.

17. *Chattanooga Times*, 24-27 April 1937.

18. Ray Hefferlin, "Glimpses into the Tri-Area Past" (Photocopy, Chattanooga-Hamilton County Bicentennial Library); *Chattanooga Times*, 23 October, 27 November 1968; 17 February 1971.

19. *Chattanooga Times*, 12 July 1899; 6 June 1903; 14 February 1926; 18 May 1929; 23 April 1969; 23 April 1972; 15 January 1978.

20. Ibid., 23 March 1972; 2-5 March 1978.

21. Ibid., 30 July 1975; *Chattanooga News-Free Press*, 1 February 1977.

22. *Chattanooga Times*, 11, 15–17 February, 13 March 1945.

23. Ibid., 29 June 1955; 24 April 1957; 10 September, 9 December 1959; *Chattanooga News-Free Press*, 4, 20 April 1957.

24. *Chattanooga News-Free Press*, 4 January 1957; *Chattanooga Times*, 3 October 1909; 5 August 1955; 13 January, 9 June 1956; 1 July 1957.

25. *Chattanooga Times*, 1 July, 10 September, 9 December 1959; 18, 25 July 1961; 22 March 1962; 9 October 1963.

26. Ibid., 29 June 1966.

27. Ibid., 28 November 1967; 1 October, 14 December 1972; 6 November 1973; *Chattanooga News-Free Press*, 24 August 1967; 11 November 1973.

28. Ibid., 3 February 1972; 30 July 1974; *Chattanooga Times*, 1 April 1973; 8 January, 28 February, 30 July, 10 August 1974; 10 October 1976; *Forward Chattanooga* (Chattanooga: Greater Chattanooga Area Chamber of Commerce, 23 June 1977).

29. A suit seeking to void the vote was dismissed by chancery court on 27 October 1970, ending all efforts to establish "metro" government. The suit claimed that, because the referendum was held in conjunction with a regular primary and general election and listed at the bottom of the voting machine, it lost "the dignity" of a special election. Frank W. Prescott, "Chattanooga Area to Vote on Charter," *National Civic Review*, 53, no. 3 (March 1964): 149–50; ibid.; "Chattanooga Area Defeats Charter," *National Civic Review*, 59, no. 11 (December 1970); 595–96; *Chattanooga Times*, 17, 18 November 1964; 5–7 August 1970.

30. Ibid., 16 May 1978.

——————————— 20 ———————————

Yesterday and Today: Part 2

AT the close of World War II, the city of Chattanooga met its monthly obligations with some three thousand hand-written checks. The finance department was reported to own three adding machines, two typewriters, a cash register, a machine to punch out the amount of a check and a pencil sharpener.[1] In large measure this obsolescence in both equipment and office practice mirrored the situation in other departments. At the county courthouse methods and furnishings were also of depression standards.

The postwar world, however, soon jolted the Hamilton County people out of their former habits and patterns of life, and the county, like the entire country, rapidly passed over a divide into a new era. The region was now closer to the mainstream of the national economy but was aware that its best efforts to achieve national norms were frustrated by the simple fact that such standards constituted a moving target. The area was drawn into a season of momentous adjustments produced by new federal laws and judicial decisions in civil rights, economic opportunity, and political reapportionment cases. As society itself underwent disruptive changes, so too did its physical surroundings as the "bulldozer revolution" gained momentum.

County and community leaders continue to wrestle with the issues of this new age but have found no final solutions. Progress has been made in many areas, but what seems like a satisfactory answer often produces spin-offs of totally unanticipated proportions. Moreover, social problems, crime, and violence remain a part of community life and chicanery still lingers in the local political thickets.

In Hamilton County the emerging industrial South, the presence of TVA, and the historic advantages the region offers manufacturing led to solid economic growth in the years after 1945. By 1977 Chattanooga had become the home base for two of the largest financial corporations in Tennessee: the Provident Life and Accident Insurance Company ranked third and Ancorp ranked ninth in size.[2]

In 1978 thirteen local companies reported employing more than one thousand workers, the largest being Combustion Engineering, Inc. and the Du Pont Textile Fibers Plant. Combustion grew out of local plants known as the Walsh-Weidner Boiler Company and the Casey-Hedges Boiler Company; its locally owned predecessors date back to 1888. The two companies were consolidated in June 1928 and six months later sold their interests to the Connecticut-based engineering company. With greatly expanded facilities the company manufactures fossil- and nuclear-fueled steam supply system components. The company gained extensive experience in making nuclear equipment as a result of the navy's nuclear submarine program and in 1956 shipped the nation's first commercial nuclear reactor. Twenty years later Combustion sent from Chattanooga on a single oceangoing barge 2,040 tons of one-system components.

The Du Pont plant, constructed in 1948, has become a thriving member of the industrial community. It claims an amazing record as the world's safest manufacturing plant. This facility manufactures from manmade fibers such fabrics as Qiana®, used for women's blouses and dresses, men's ties and shirts; nylon textiles for pantyhose, sportswear, and other goods; industrial nylon for tractor tires and other durable items; and Dacron® for general apparel.

The most noticeable trend in the business community has been the growing number of concerns with nonlocal headquarters and the consequent transfer of new people to the area. This development was apparent in the 1920s but spread rapidly by mid-century.

Of the county's manufacturers in 1977 employing two hundred or more persons, thirty-one were controlled by parent companies located elsewhere and sixteen were home-based. Some of the larger firms in the first group in addition to Combustion and Du Pont are the U.S.

Pipe and Foundry, Cavalier Corporation, Central Soya, Chattanooga Glass, Cutter Laboratories, Ernest Holmes; the Koehring, 3M, Mueller, and Rockwell International companies.

A number of locally owned concerns, some more than a hundred years old, hire over two hundred workers. Representative of this category are the American Manufacturing Company, Boaz Spinning Company, Brock Candy, Chattanooga Boiler and Tank, Chattem, Cumberland Corporation, Dixie Yarns, Gilman Paint & Varnish, Jackson Manufacturing, Nation Hosiery, North American Royalties, Pro-Group, Ross-Meehan Foundries, Skyland International Corporation, Standard Coosa Thatcher, Tuftco, McKee Baking Company, and the Times Printing Company.[3]

These manufacturing concerns draw employees from all parts of Hamilton County and beyond. More than one-third of those employed in the city are in manufacturing; this fact gives Chattanooga the distinction of claiming ninth position in the United States in the number of manufacturing employees in relation to the percentage of nonagricultural workers.

One of the new industries of the era, broadcast television, spawned numerous supporting activities including retail marketing of sets, servicing businesses, and cable TV. Interest in this medium emerged in the fall of 1948 when an Atlanta station pioneered as the southeast's first broadcasting facility. Despite the fact that "snow" and uncontrolled "fading" marred reception, this development was hailed as good news by people on Lookout and Signal mountains and other high spots in the county. The few who owned home sets entertained crowds of guests invited to view the marvels of TV, and by February 1950 it was estimated that 175 sets were in use in the city and some 400 in the area.[4]

Chattanooga finally got its own station when WDEF's Channel 12 "signed on the air" on 25 April 1954. The successful promoter of the business and the station's first president was Carter Parham. Parham's family represented continuous ties with the area, for it was his great uncle, Ferdinand A. Parham, who published the *Hamilton County Gazette* from a flatboat on the river back in the Ross's Landing days. The men associated with Parham in the TV activity included Jac Chambliss, Alex Guerry, Cartter Patten, and Moses Lebowitz. At a later date the station affiliated with CBS.

A second station, Channel 3, began telecasts in May 1956 under the direction of Mountain City Television, Inc. with Ramon Patterson, Judge Will Cummings, and their wives, as officers. This organization offered NBC network programs. Two years later, on 11 Februry 1958, Channel 9, an affiliate of ABC, went on the air. It was originally owned by the Martin Theaters of Georgia and managed by Reeve Owen. After a very long delay Chattanooga's quest for an educational channel gained success with regular telecasts offered by Channel 45 in 1970 from studios on Amnicola Highway operated under the auspices of the Tennessee State Board of Education.[5]

Television not only offered recreational and educational programs for city dwellers and isolated rural people but also provided regular newscasts. In this latter capacity it competed with radio broadcasting for news coverage and with such personalities as commentator Luther Masingill, a veteran voice on local affairs, disasters, charitable needs, and good causes.

In the field of printed news the *Chattanooga Times*, celebrating its centennial in 1969, carries on in the Adolph A. Ochs tradition with Mrs. Ruth Holmberg, granddaughter of the journalist, as publisher. A new newspaper entered journalistic competition with its first daily edition printed on an ancient press on 31 August 1936, under the direction of Roy McDonald. The *Chattanooga Free Press* actually began without plan or prospects about three years earlier when depression conditions caused McDonald to try to cut advertising costs for his local chain of food outlets, the Home Stores. It all started as a weekly "throwaway" carrying a little news. Then a furniture store took out an ad; before long the unpretentious sheet became a weekly newspaper published every Thursday. A Sunday issue followed from headquarters in a remodeled warehouse.

In 1939 McDonald acquired the *Chattanooga News* and renamed his journal the *Chattanooga News-Free Press*, continuing publication in both the evening and Sunday fields. George Fort Milton's *News* ended a liberal career with its final edition on 16 December 1939, and shortly afterward the McDonald staff moved to the 117 East Tenth Street address which had been the home of the *News*. The expanded journal followed its initial policy—of and for Chattanooga—while adhering to a conservative philosophy editorially. A lively competition with the *Times* ensued and the *Times* company entered the evening market in October 1940 with the publication of the *Evening Times*.

With materials and manpower growing short in the early part of World War II, the two newspapers concluded a joint publication agreement on 10 May 1942, a plan not uncommon in American cities. The two organizations retained separate and independent ownership, editorial policy, and circulation management while combining their advertising and business departments as well as the mechanical plant. A new organization, the Chattanooga Publishing Company, was formed in order to conduct all common business. The *Times* stopped publication of its evening paper and the *News-Free Press* discontinued its Sunday edition. The *Times* moved from its old home in the Dome Building to the Tenth Street building where the *News-Free Press* had been located.

This arrangement continued until 18 May 1966, when it was announced that the joint operation would shortly be terminated. The Chattanooga Publishing Company was dissolved and McDonald moved his operations to the old Davenport Hosiery building on East Eleventh Street. On 28 August 1966 he resumed separate publication of six evening papers and a Sunday edition. The *Times* at the same time in an abortive effort added an evening edition, the Chattanooga *Post* for a short period.

So competition returned to the printed medium until 1980, when a generally similar arrangement was renewed after receipt of a grant of immunity from antitrust suits by the government. According to this agreement, the *Times* discontinued its Sunday paper.[6]

In the local business community, however, many adjustments reflected the general drift toward consolidation. Some of the area's oldest concerns illustrate what was happening. The Volunteer State Life Insurance Company in 1968 merged with the Monumental Corporation, a Maryland-based company. The Interstate Life and Accident Insurance Company became a unit in the Jacksonville, Florida, Gulf Life Holding Company. The Coca-Cola Bottling Company (Thomas), Inc., in August 1975 discontinued its Chattanooga operations completely after the company's business was sold to Coca-Cola of Atlanta and the last of the original parent bottlers of the beverage dating back to 1899 disappeared from the scene.

The idea of merger also affected higher education, involving the University of Chattanooga and Chattanooga City College. After a decision had been made to establish a state college in Chattanooga under the aegis of the University of Tennessee, plans emerged to bring the local private institutions into the state organization. The Board of Trustees of the University of Chattanooga approved merger arrangements which provided for the establishment of the University of Chattanooga Foundation where all endowment funds of the private college would be placed for enrichment programs on the local campus. Chattanooga

City College, formerly Zion College, also joined the merger which became effective on 1 July 1969. The new state campus, organized under the administration of the University of Tennessee, took the name University of Tennessee at Chattanooga.

In the midst of economic growth, Hamilton County was unprepared on 16 February 1976 for the shocking news that one of its veteran fiscal institutions was experiencing trouble. For more than seventy-five years the Hamilton National Bank had served the area; in 1971 it became associated with a holding company which used the name Hamilton Bancshares, Inc. The public was taken by surprise by the announcement that the bank was insolvent. The Federal Deposit Insurance Corporation was named the receiver and immediately sold the Hamilton Bank to the First Tennessee National Corporation of Memphis. By the twentieth of the month Hamilton Bancshares filed a voluntary petition in bankruptcy court and was also declared insolvent.

The failure, reported to be the third largest in the history of the nation, resulted from heavy real estate loans made by a nonbanking subsidiary and an unexpected collapse of that market. Although the depositors did not lose any of their investments, a suit of almost $155 million was filed against former bank officials and the auditing company with final solutions still pending as of 1979.

The business community during these years found it necessary to make numerous adjustments as environmental deficiencies revealed a demand for air and water pollution control. For more than fifty years individuals and small groups had protested what people were doing to Hamilton County's streams and air. Attention centered on the noxious condition of Chattanooga and Citico creeks and the "thickened and discolored" Tennessee River. Protestors also called attention to heavy industrial smog and soft-coal filth. Although Chattanooga in 1924 adopted a Boiler Inspection and Smoke Control Ordinance, all solutions to the problem were lost in rhetoric. The term pollution was not then in common use; technology was not sophisticated enough to make legal controls practicable. Furthermore, jobs and industrial interests crowded out any effective environmental safeguards.

After World War II, public apathy turned to action as the national government assumed leadership. Studies confirmed that Greater Chattanooga was one of the most heavily polluted areas in the nation. The county tuberculosis association, noting the high mortality rate from the disease, became involved by 1963 in sponsoring educational efforts relating to health and air pollution. Chamber of commerce committees encouraged positive action although some industrialists lent their support very grudgingly.

After frustrating efforts, a tough new law was adopted in 1969 to control air pollution in both the city and county; eventually each municipality in the county endorsed this measure. The law created an expanded Air Pollution Control Board of nine volunteers appointed by the mayor and county judge along with one ex-officio member representing the Chattanooga-Hamilton County Health Department. Standards allowed open burning only by permit, set a two-percent limit on sulfur content in fuel, regulated odors and dust, restricted sulfur oxides, and outlawed visible automobile emissions. They established a compliance deadline for old plants of October 1972, while new plants had to meet more stringent requirements set for 1974.

The board was fortunate that users of residential heating were already discontinuing the use of soft coal in favor of electricity, but even so, found its task far from easy. State and federal standards constantly grew more stringent while more sensitive technological equipment strengthened the board's position as watchdog. The cost of compliance for industry mounted and naturally caused vigorous complaints. And the situation was constantly compounded by the concentration of heavy industry in downtown Chattanooga and by the unique topographical and meteorological features of the region. Atmospheric temperature inversions commonly occur and the heavy air cover holds great quantities of suspended matter over the county.

But progress was made. On 13 October 1972, Clean Air Day was celebrated and the National Air Pollution Control Association awarded its first place to Chattanooga in its annual ceremonies. Wide attention focused on the success noted in Hamilton County in the early 1970s. Among the kudos, an article appeared in *U.S. News & World Report*, stating, "This city was known as the most polluted city in the nation. Now Chattanooga is rated as one of the cleanest cities." Governor Tom McCall of Oregon, noted for his concern for the environment, commented during a visit there, "When a city of which industry is polluting such a great part can turn things around, as Chattanooga apparently has done in the past five years, it does represent a truly Herculean effort."

The governor did not overstate the magnitude of the achievement, but higher state and federal standards, such as those in the Tennessee Water Control Act of 1977, demanded more. Large pockets of suspended particulate are still found and occasional pollution alerts are sounded. The region still faces the question: Can it regulate itself, or will state and federal direction prevail?

While Chattanooga struggled with its environmental problems, the American trend of creating suburban shopping centers showed up in Hamilton County. Cheap outlying lands encouraged the development of these "horizontal department stores" where merchants could offer free parking and enjoy lower taxes. The first planned was Brainerd Village, located near the spot where John McDonald had his early trading station and where Brainerd missionaries instructed the Cherokee youth. When ceremonial ribbons were cut on 18 August 1960, the shopping center occupied over twenty acres with thirty-two stores. A neighboring second shopping complex named Eastgate followed immediately in 1961. Begun as an open walkway, it rapidly expanded to more than seventy-five acres with ninety-two retail outlets and a fully enclosed climate-controlled mall.

To accommodate the fast-growing Hixson suburban market, a huge complex called Northgate opened for business in 1972; six years later an estimated thirty thousand persons visited this mall daily.[8] Numerous smaller centers—Highland Plaza, Lake Hills Shopping Center, Signal Mountain Plaza, the Osborne Center, and others—added to the migration of convenience and department stores and specialty shops from the inner city.

As businesses joined residents in their move to outlying areas, the need for adequate highways and streets naturally was felt. By the time Chickamauga Dam was completed, some recognized the mistake that had been made in not building a bridge over the structure. A decade went by before definite plans for such a span were made, and finally on 17 October 1954, appropriate festivities marked the opening of the bridge, named for Judge Wilkes T. Thrasher, who was the prime supporter of this project.

This span made possible a major, limited-access highway from Interstate 75 on the south to Route 27 which carries a large flow of traffic east of Chattanooga and which opened up large tracts of land for industrial and commercial enterprises. By the 1970s, however, the two-lane Thrasher Bridge proved to be totally inadequate. Four lanes were deemed essential to handle the traffic, but at this writing an entirely new span (the Amnicola Bridge) must be completed to carry the detour traffic while the bridge over the dam is being widened.

When construction of interstate highways involved Chattanooga, Mayor Peter Rudolph Olgiati worked determinedly to achieve early completion in the area. He also resolved to win a spur route through the downtown section and across the Tennessee River, which would give Chattanooga an additional downtown river bridge.

Mayor Olgiati took office in 1951. Born at Gruetli in Grundy County, Tennessee, of Swiss ancestry, he grew up in Hamilton County. He joined a labor union, fought in World War II, and returned home as a major in the Corps of Engineers. "Rudy" Olgiati as mayor, it was said, planted projects the way Johnny Appleseed planted fruit orchards; he "altered the face and heart" of Chattanooga.

Forceful, stubborn, and progressive, the mayor combined administrative talent with the traits of a hard-nosed politician. His $7-million "footlog" across the Tennessee River started amid the traditional wrangles over specific location, but all disagreements had vanished by 20 November 1959, when the bridge opened. Few people at the time argued with newsman Springer Gibson's words that the Olgiati Bridge forged an important "link in Chattanooga's chain of progress and [was] an appropriate monument of concrete and steel to the city's master builder."

At the dedication of the bridge, persons who had been present at the 1891 opening of the Walnut Street bridge were introduced to the public. The old span still carried a heavy traffic flow, but suddenly in May 1978 it was declared unsafe and was hastily closed. At this writing, replacement is in the planning stages and Hamiltonians are again going through the tribal ritual of deciding where to put it.[9]

During the depression years and World War II few arguments about expensive projects disturbed people. No one wanted the city to spend money, let alone increase taxes. During this entire time span, Edward Davidson Bass, who preached and practiced economy, served as a city official. A native Chattanoogan, he had little opportunity for formal education. He was the son of a Confederate army captain who had moved to the city from Alabama shortly after the hostilities ended. Young Bass operated a small neighborhood grocery before entering politics; he ran for the post of justice of the peace and won. Next he became a state senator and in 1911 played a part in getting legislation approved to change Chattanooga's government from the mayor-city-council form to a mayor-commission structure. Four years later he gained a seat on the newly established commission, whereupon he aggressively directed the opening of Broad Street where Georgia land ownership had created a traffic bottleneck. After his election in 1915

Bass served on every commission until 1947, the last twenty years of which he was mayor—a record for tenure in that office.

Mayor Bass felt a sense of pride about the fact that he had guided Chattanooga through the Great Depression without issuing scrip. He met all payrolls and refused to resort to new taxes but he did cut services and had to disregard many pressing needs. His very nature led him to resist all the "extravagant trends of the times." Bass's aim was to follow the wishes of the people and to protect the taxpayer. Even after the financial crisis lifted, he never gave up this ingrained fiscal conservatism. [10]

During the Bass administration the Chattanooga Housing Authority was established on 15 June 1938, three years after the state authorized such municipal action. It was composed of five volunteer commissioners appointed by the mayor who assumed the task of "development, management, and maintenance of the city's low-rent public housing and the execution of the urban renewal program." Early efforts, with the aid of the United States Housing Authority, produced the College Hill Courts and East Lake Courts projects.

Housing in the central city was in a deplorable state. Census reports for 1950 show that 37% of all units had no inside plumbing or were in a dilapidated condition. In a district bounded roughly by the Union Station to Central Avenue and by Main and East Eighth streets, 76% of the housing was substandard; the Citico-Bushtown-Churchville area was close behind with 63.8 percent in the same rundown state. [11]

The housing situation presented a thorny problem when Mayor Olgiati took office in 1951; its solution required local initiative. Tennessee's larger cities had already undertaken some renewal programs and Olgiati had an opportunity to point to their efforts in gaining popular support. Urban renewal, the mayor reasoned, was everybody's business and he proposed a major blueprint for change. It was not a simple matter, and much more than housing was involved. Revitalization meant railroad relocation, freeways, a river bridge, annexation services, an interceptor sewer system, and slum clearance. It required the support of every sector of the population.

Central to all of this was the Golden Gateway Redevelopment Project taking in some 403 acres of the dying west side of the city, just a stone's throw from the middle downtown area. Preliminary talks led in 1958 to a contract for a grant and loan from the federal government to cover the estimated $20-million project. Included in the tract to be cleared was the once-prominent residential section of East Terrace, the famed

Civil War promontory Cameron Hill, and two other elevations called Boynton Terrace and Reservoir Hill. From this area some fourteen hundred families had to find other residences. This necessity set off a chain reaction movement of people across the city and beyond into the county. The relocation of blacks was especially pronounced; critics called it "Negro removal" rather than "urban renewal," and it caused new overcrowding in low-rent areas.

The buildings to be razed numbered 1,170. Everything was to be swept clean, the terrain contoured, and the land presented for sale to private parties subject to compliance with a master plan for land usage. So the bulldozer revolution came to Chattanooga; a few pre–Civil War homes came down along with the hovels. Not a tree was left standing; the historic hills looked again as they had in 1863 when war struck down all of the pines, oaks, poplars, and hickories.

The din of critics was almost as loud as the grading machines. There were those who did not think slum clearance was public business and some who wanted growth and opportunity without change. Patriotic organizations and history-conscious individuals sounded a different complaint. The gateway project was directly related to the construction of the freeway system and called for the removal of millions of cubic yards of dirt from the crown of Cameron Hill to be used in building the highways. The protestors insisted that the planners did not understand or appreciate the role of these summits in the colorful heritage of the area. Their efforts continued, but in vain. Cameron Hill in particular shrank in size and a nasty mudslide continues to bleed as a reminder of its decapitation.[12]

After the land was cleared and new streets planned, tracts in the Golden Gateway were gradually purchased by private interests. Businesses moving into the west side were joined by such new buildings as the YMCA (1969), the First Baptist Church (1967), the St. Barnabas Nursing Home and Apartment complex (1965–66), and the Jaycee Towers I (1970) and II (1975), which were designed as medium-priced housing facilities for elderly tenants.

Careful planning, controlled land usage, and modern buildings combined to give the west side an expansive, fresh aspect. By December 1976 the project was completed; by this time the Golden Gateway had contributed greatly to changing the physical appearance of the central part of Chattanooga.

West-side renewal exerted an invigorating influence on the core city. The timing coincided with railroad relocation and the availability of

Georgia-owned land in the heart of downtown. Furthermore, the wide main streets laid out by the first Chattanoogans and retained through the years gave planners a rare opportunity to work with space. The new John Ross's Landing Park by the river's edge at the foot of Broad Street; Miller Park (named in honor of White B. and Mary Miller, parents of the park's benefactor, Burkett Miller); and a miniature Boynton Park, dedicated to Henry Boynton, and replacing the larger area add to the attractiveness of the city with trees, grass, walkways, flower beds, and fountains.

The latest effort to dress up the downtown area saw the transformation of three blocks of Market Street into "Market Center." Street parking disappeared from this area; a straight street was changed to one of graceful curves while plazas, brick sidewalks, and concrete planters made it a shoppers' street. This new tone, "snappy, crisp, and clean" and the growing use of space as a medium of pleasure reemphasize the values of renewal.[13]

New buildings added to the revival. Some, scattered through the heart of Chattanooga, include the Hamilton County Justice Building (1976), the Civic Forum (1979), the Chattanooga-Hamilton County Bicentennial Library (1976), the Krystal Building (1978), the enlarged Provident (1976), Blue Cross-Blue Shield of Tennessee (1971), the First Centenary Methodist Church (1972), the Commerce Union Bank office towers (1974 and 1978), the First Federal Savings and Loan (1978), the TVA Federal Credit Union (1978), and the IBM Building (1969).

Old buildings blend with the new on the city's skyline. Some of an older vintage have been rescued from the effects of age and neglect. The Tivoli Theater, owned and managed by the city, and the Choo-Choo, developed by private enterprise, demonstrate the very satisfying results obtained from careful preservation. To these examples must be added the tasteful restoration efforts of North American Royalties, Inc., under the direction of the company's board chairman, Gordon P. Street.

Street discovered, to his personal satisfaction, a businesslike manner of coupling the best of the past with the promise of tomorrow. His father had moved to Hamilton County from Ohio after the Civil War and the son found ready opportunity in the area as an industrialist. In 1969 he acquired the old Carnegie Library building and restored it for his company headquarters. Later he preserved the unique steeple marking the site of the Methodists' Old Stone Church where his family had long worshipped. In May 1978 he completed work on restoring the neighboring Dome Building, an eye-catching landmark with its distinctive bay.[14]

The legacy of past years has also been preserved in the Patten Towers, a low-rent home for elderly tenants rebuilt from the Patten Hotel, and the Park Plaza Building. Some of the streetcar barns have been saved to be transformed into an athletic center while the old clock at the corner of Market and Eighth streets which has announced the time to passersby since 1883 has also been restored and refurbished.

The physical renaissance of the inner city is not yet finished. Deteriorating buildings and a few burned eyesores line some streets and a glance at the upper stories reveals a vintage of years gone by atop first-floor false fronts. Paved parking areas and old walls exposed after the razing of neighboring structures do not add to the architectural appeal. But the spirit of the city and the quality of the street environment do point to a steady comeback of downtown, while the new skyline and open spaces help produce a modern metropolitan air. People seem to appreciate that the inner city is the basic marketplace of the county, the center of convention business and tourism, the civic pivot point, the hub of city and county government, as well as of the printed and electronic news media. Prospects of vast additional expenditures, including a TVA comprehensive office complex (which is a proposed "showcase" for the nation's utilities on the use of solar energy), as well as private investments, give exciting promise for the future downtown.

The core-city revival has also generated the upgrading of various contiguous neighborhoods, mainly residential in nature. Federal and local funds in 1966 made the Highland Park Neighborhood Improvement Program a reality with public improvements—new sidewalks, curbs, gutters, repaved streets, sewer work, and street lighting—coordinated with private undertakings. Similar projects involve Orchard Knob, East Lake, the Third Street sector, and Fort Wood. The latter area of aging but splendid residences and the Fountain Square region close to the county courthouse were placed on the National Register of Historic Places in 1979.

Structures of a bygone day, preserved and protected, serve as historic evidence of early rural Hamilton County, many of which are also listed on the National Register (see Appendix E for complete list). At Audubon Acres stands one of the oldest, dated 1754, the cabin of Cherokee naturalist Too-an-tuh, commonly known as Spring Frog. To the west on Brown's Ferry Road is the sturdy two-story log house of John Brown, once used as a tavern for early travelers. Built in 1803 and currently the home of Judge and Mrs. Herschel Franks, it is a model of preservation.

Lookout and Signal mountains have Civil War homes restored and open for public inspection. The Cravens House, oldest surviving structure on Lookout Mountain, was restored by the Chattanooga Chapter of the Association for the Preservation of Tennessee Antiquities under the leadership of Mrs. Z. Cartter (Elizabeth) Patten in 1956. The house, occupied by both Confederate and Union forces and virtually destroyed during the battle, stands on lands of the national military park. In 1974 the park service assumed complete responsibility of the property. On Signal Mountain the restoration of the log tollhouse, where travelers' fees on the Anderson Pike were collected and where the Union army had a relay station during the siege days of 1863, sparked a community-wide effort spearheaded by the Walden's Ridge Historical Association.

Another landmark of antebellum days is the old Colonel Jarrett Dent home, Bonny Oaks. Dent, a railroad contractor, sympathized with the Confederacy and, it is reported, had to leave his home because of strong local Union feelings. Bushwhackers used the Dent house as a wartime rendezvous. The colonel did not return after the conflict ended. In 1898 under the aegis of Dr. Jonathan W. Bachman this property was acquired by the county court to become the Bonny Oaks School for indigent and wayward youths. Equipment and buildings were gradually increased; Z. C. Patten donated the girls' department, and long and faithful aid was rendered by the Civitan Club. In May 1957 the school was rechartered with its role defined as the care of "dependent, neglected, abandoned youthful persons." For many years Dr. and Mrs. William S. Keese supervised the school as a joint city-county project.[15]

Buildings old and new stand as tributes to the persons who constructed them but it is the use they are put to under the guidance of Superintendent Keese which truly contributes to the well-being of society. Just as revolutionary physical and technological changes have altered Hamilton County in recent decades, so have the expansion and vitality of education, health care, and cultural activities.

Public education as a result of annexation has witnessed an exchange of facilities and responsibilities as Hamilton County gave over jurisdiction in many areas to Chattanooga. In 1977–78 the city operated thirty-eight elementary, thirteen junior high, and nine senior high schools; the county system comprised twenty-four elementary, six junior, and six senior high schools. The modern era has seen the establishment of numerous parochial and private schools and, on the secondary level, the ongoing success of Girls' Preparatory School, Baylor, McCallie, and Notre Dame.

The two older institutions of higher learning in the county continue to flourish. Southern Missionary College operated by the Southern Union Conference of the Seventh-Day Adventists enrolls almost 2,000 students, about sixty percent of whom come from the southeastern states. The University of Tennessee at Chattanooga since the 1969 merger has grown as of 1977–78 to a student body of 6,621 and has enjoyed a vigorous campus expansion program.

New institutions include the Chattanooga Area Vocational-Technical School on Amnicola Highway where classes opened on 16 March 1970. This state facility reported 580 students for the year 1977–78, enrolled in such "marketable skills" courses as food preparation, data processing, and mechanical repair.

A second state institution welcomed students in September 1965 under the name Chattanooga State Technical Institute, with a two-year, college-level program. It moved from downtown Chattanooga in 1967 to a campus on Amnicola Highway close by Chickamauga Dam. Effective 1 July 1973, the state changed the name of the institute to Chattanooga State Technical Community College, which shortly developed a vigorous continuing education program along with its community college credit work. In 1978–79 it reported about five thousand students enrolled.

Another post–World War II college, Tennessee Temple University, is a "Baptist school both in belief and practice." On 3 July 1946, the Highland Park Baptist Church of Chattanooga voted to sponsor a bible school and junior college. Seminary-level work was added in 1948, a senior college division in 1950, and graduate studies in 1975. The name was changed from Tennessee Temple Schools to Tennessee Temple University in 1979, but the purpose remains constant, to train Christian leaders and workers both spiritually and academically. In 1977–78 it enrolled over thirty-seven hundred students.

Across a small embayment from the Sequoyah Nuclear Plant, the TVA runs its Power Production Training Center. Classes first met in the large modernistic building in October 1976; the students earn no college credit but are paid to study in the two-year program designed to train operators, technicians, and instrument mechanics who will run TVA's nuclear plants and some fossil-fuel operations. Mammoth computers operate nuclear plant control-room simulators that can program malfunctions. This sophisticated instruction, testifying to TVA's commitment to nuclear power as well as its primary concern for safety, represents an $18-million investment which, according to a May 1979 announcement, will eventually be doubled in size.[16]

Health care in the early twentieth century presented a dismal picture; shocking sanitary conditions contributed to an especially bad local record of tuberculosis cases. To treat and arrest the "white plague," citizens, clubs, and the city and county governments joined in 1909 in chartering the Pine Breeze Sanitarium. Hamilton County donated land among the hills of North Chattanooga, and in June 1913 the first patient was admitted. The hospital developed into a fine example of community cooperative effort, serving thousands of people until 1 July 1968 when, after tuberculosis was conquered, the Pine Breeze complex was donated to the state to be used for emotionally disturbed adolescents.[17]

To strengthen public health service the governments of Hamilton County and Chattanooga consolidated their health units in 1941 under Dr. F. O. Pearson; this merger is reported to be the first consolidation of a large city unit with a county unit in the state of Tennessee and one of the first in the South. Although the two governments had previously cooperated in supporting three hospitals and a venereal disease clinic, this union pointed to greatly improved, uniform service and led on to the opening of the Chattanooga-Hamilton County Health Department building on 16 April 1961 and to constantly expanding branch offices and mobile services.[18]

The area also developed a fine reputation for its medical education program, sponsored by the Tennessee Valley Medical Assembly. Erlanger Medical Center also has become a major center of medical education, as well as a rapidly expanding modern facility serving the tristate area. Among its latest additions are the wings housing the T. C. Thompson Children's Hospital Medical Center and the Willie D. Miller Eye Center. Even more significant was public approval of the establishment of the Hospital Authority, which would manage the sprawling complex, sell bonds, and plan systematic expansion and modernization programs. In 1979 Hamilton County and Chattanooga turned over the hospital responsibility to the Authority, headed by Dr. David McCallie.

Within recent decades several major hospitals have been opened. In 1961 Moccasin Bend Psychiatric Hospital, built on land made available by the city and the county and founded with the ardent support of Dr. Joseph W. Johnson, Jr., was opened by the state. This facility, acclaimed for its modern and innovative treatment, has grown into one of the South's largest hospitals for the treatment of mental disorders. The handsome yet functional original buildings and always-expanding additions are sometimes referred to as the "beads on the Indian moccasin."

Memorial Hospital, operated by the Sisters of Charity of Nazareth, Kentucky, first received patients in 1952. The Downtown General Hospital (originally Newell Hospital, started in 1908) was sold in May 1969 to Health Care, Inc., and has been completely renovated to meet modern medical standards. Parkridge, operated by Hospital Affiliates, Inc., of Nashville, opened in February 1971 and has since never ceased to expand. In 1974 the East Ridge Community Hospital, with 128 beds, was dedicated and in 1977 the Red Bank Community Hospital began comprehensive service. Numerous other smaller facilities and clinics render personalized treatment. However, in contrast to this concentration of professional, modern medical service in the Chattanooga area and its suburbs, the rural parts of Hamilton County continue to experience medical deficiencies. In 1979, for example, Soddy-Daisy proudly announced that the community was finally "getting a doctor" on terms which provided for a guaranteed monthly salary, rental space, and salary assistance for one employee.[19]

Two special programs embracing treatment and training of the physically and mentally handicapped deserve special recognition. The Rehabilitation Center of the Siskin Memorial Foundation, specializing in dental and physical therapy clinics as well as speech and hearing programs, was created with the foundation in 1950.

This foundation, established by the late Mose and Garrison Siskin in memory of their Russian immigrant parents, supports a building complex used for community cultural, civic, and charitable activities in addition to the rehabilitation center. Beginning in 1961, through the 365 Club, the public has participated in supporting this venture, which has brought recognition (including the President's Distinguished Service Award) from national and international organizations to the Siskins.

More than twenty-five years ago another humanitarian effort led to the establishment of the Orange Grove Center for the Retarded. The founding of the center resulted from an advertisement placed in 1952 by the Isadore Tyber family. Other parents rallied to the challenge; an abandoned city school building, Orange Grove, was leased for $1 a year and twenty-seven students enrolled there in September 1953. Area support, industrial gifts, and the strong arm of the Chattanooga Jaycees saw the venture improve the caliber of its programs and care. Federal and state funds and an allocation from the United Fund encouraged the parent-sponsored group. In 1971 a modern center with self-contained classrooms forming a village cluster and a sheltered workshop was opened at the base of Missionary Ridge. Here more than seven hundred retarded students from the tristate area attend school and participate in a day-care program or workshop.

The close association of community and university so carefully nourished under University of Chattanooga President Alexander Guerry resulted in organizations which matured into dependable cultural leadership. An early art association fell heir to the George Hunter home overlooking the Tennessee River from Bluff View. This handsome property, renovated and greatly enlarged in 1975, is the home of the Hunter Museum of Art where traveling exhibits and the work of local artists are shown. Skilled in the use of palette and brush or in three-dimensional art, Frank Baisden, George Cress, Gail Hammond, Lillian Feinstein, Elizabeth Shumacker, Hubert Shuptrine, Harold Cash, James Collins, and Earl Counts represent an ever-growing group of local artists.

Directly across the river from Hunter Museum the Little Theater—second oldest in the South—moved into a new home in 1962 constructed for the specific needs of its programs. Scores of talented local amateurs, too numerous to mention, entertained appreciative audiences for years. On the national scene, native born Dorothy Patten appeared there in regular seasons, summer stock, and tours between 1929 and 1964. In addition to on-and-off-Broadway productions she performed on all the major television networks as well as on radio and in films.

The Chattanooga Symphony Orchestra (with continuous seasons since 1934) and the Opera Association (since 1943) are both spin-offs from university beginnings. Today they enjoy the excellent facilities provided by the city-owned Tivoli Theater. Dorothy Hackett Ward, Werner and Emmy Wolfe, Milton Allen, Arthur Plettner, Joseph Hawthorne, Richard Cormier, Harold Cadek, Oscar Miller, and Ann Lee Patton have given these organizations professional skill and enduring strength.

Youngest of the local cultural troupes are ballet and dinner-theater groups, the Chattanooga Boys' Choir, and the Festival Players. Treasures of the past are housed at the Houston Antique Museum, the Tennessee Valley Railroad Museum, and the Chattanooga Museum of Regional History.[20]

The area's most celebrated singer in recent years was Grace Moore. Called the "daughter of the hills of Tennessee," she became associated with Hamilton County when her parents, Colonel and Mrs. Richard L. Moore, moved to Riverview from Jellico, Tennessee, in 1932 after her father purchased the Loveman department store. Known for her friendly personality, golden voice, and captivating beauty, Miss Moore excelled as a radio singer, screen star, Broadway actress, and operatic prima donna. On 26 January 1947, the community received the shocking news of her tragic death in an air accident near Copenhagen and joined in services prior to her burial in Forest Hills Cemetery.[21]

Many Hamiltonians have found satisfaction in historical writing. Some of the contributors in past decades include: Zella Armstrong, Penelope Allen, George Fort Milton, John Fort, John P. Brown, Robert Sparks Walker, Lou Williams, E. Y. Chapin, Sr., Gilbert E. Govan, Elizabeth Bryan Patten, Cartter Patten, Adelaide Rowell, Joan Franks, Fred Hixson, Charles Lusk, Lee Anderson, John Wilson, Mary Thomas Peacock, William Masterson, Culver H. Smith, Frank W. Prescott, Nathaniel C. Hughes, Jr., James A. Ward, Albert Bowman, David Lockmiller, Leonard Raulston, George J. Flanigan, Edwin Lindsey, Elizabeth Dalton, David H. Steinberg, Rufus Terral, Elizabeth Wade, Kay Gaston, Stanley Lewis, James W. Livingood, and Robert Adams.

The most prolific family of authors, Christine Noble Govan, her daughter Mary Q. Steele and son-in-law the late William O. Steele, and another daughter Emmy West, while specializing in children's literature, have also published mysteries, historical novels, and nature essays. Paul Ramsey, well-known professor, is the county's leading published poet, and Ellis K. Meacham, former city judge, has gained wide acclaim for his sea adventure novels.

Through the years cultural organizations as well as groups interested in health care, education, city beautification, and welfare work have been encouraged by the generous assistance from local foundations. In addition to the Siskin Foundation launched in 1950, the Benwood Foundation is deeply committed to philanthropic work. It was created by the will of George T. Hunter to honor his uncle, Ben F. Thomas, who had brought the young Hunter into the local Coca-Cola organization.

A third foundation with allegiance to the Hamilton County area is the Maclellan Foundation, which has a strong commitment to health, education, and especially religious support. Another large endowed philanthropic agency is the Lyndhurst Foundation, which was established after the death in 1977 of Thomas Cartter Lupton, pioneer in the Coca-Cola bottling industry. This foundation grew out of his Memorial Welfare Foundation, handling his personal giving since 1938. Another local foundation, the Tonya Memorial Foundation, was established by Burkett Miller primarily to promote the free enterprise system. The Hamico Foundation (1956), whose name is derived from "Hamilton County," is identified with Chattem, Inc., and honors Dorothy Patten, daughter of a former company president. Closely associated with the insurance firm formerly known as the Interstate Life & Accident Company is the Evans Foundation, which stresses assistance to persons pursuing an education and those striving to improve the local quality of life.

Another agency, somewhat different in structure and objectives, is the Community Foundation of Greater Chattanooga. Incorporated in 1964, it provides administration for large and small gifts and bequests designated as general funds or special-purpose endowments. [22]

The generous giving of Hamilton County residents complementing foundation grants can be appraised in the record of the United Fund of Greater Chattanooga, officially begun in January 1954. In 1978 almost sixty-three thousand contributors raised $4,150,463. In the twenty-three years of annual fund raising the organization has never failed to meet its goal, which has grown annually; if the work of its predecessor, the Community Chest, is included the achievement is fifty-seven-years long—a national record. The Greater Chattanooga area has a $15.20 per capita giving record, which is "tops" in the South and sixth nationally among cities raising $2 million or more.

In the years after World War II the whole fabric of southern life was caught up in a great web of revolt against the past. In a quest for equality the revolution struck out at the old order in the form of civil rights activities, social adjustments, and political activism. The unsettling pace of events challenged the inferior citizenship role of the blacks and the political power of rural state leaders. This urge for change spilled into Hamilton County, producing scattered incidents of confusion, uncertainty, and violence, and change which carried signs of being permanent.

Since the black population of Hamilton County has always been concentrated in the city of Chattanooga, the quest for social equity was mainly an urban matter. A major change in Chattanooga's government in 1911, however, had eliminated blacks as potential officeholders.

From the time of the first city charter in 1840 until 1911, except for the Civil War years, Chattanooga had a government directed by a mayor and a board of aldermen. Beginning in 1867 blacks had won seats on the board. In the late nineteenth century, numerous efforts to modify the government finally led to the creation of a second body, a city council. A number of special, appointed boards were also created, some of the members being selected by the governor without any consideration of the principle of "home rule." This complex and cumbersome machinery brought on protests against political rings and boss rule; petty politics and maneuvering seemed to be the prime sport of those who held office. The various calls for reform added a second concept: the growing desire to reduce the role of the blacks, who continued to hold city jobs because elected posts were based on ward voting.

About 1907 a concerted effort by civic leaders was directed at changing the nature of Chattanooga's government. They sought out the local legislative delegation to ask for prompt action for a commission form to be approved by the state assembly without voter participation. The delegation refused. Consequently the next election stressed this issue as the sole campaign platform and those supporting a new government won a rousing victory.

The legislature immediately approved the commission form of government for Chattanooga on 3 February 1911. The act provided for a mayor and four commissioners elected at-large to four-year terms. Each commissioner would serve as administrative head of a defined department and would sit with the commission in policy making. This measure, denounced by some as a "ripper bill" because it ousted all city officials and abolished all standing boards of the incumbent city government, thoroughly aroused the public.

In a stormy election the old-order candidates lost to the reform supporters. The winners, however, immediately faced an injunction prohibiting them from assuming office. Finally on 8 May the state supreme court announced it held the act creating the Chattanooga commission form of government constitutional and at 11 A.M. the same day the new officials were sworn in with T. C. Thompson as mayor, and Commissioners J. H. Warner, for public utilities and buildings; T. C. Betterton, fire and police; H. Clay Evans, education; and A. U. Sloan, streets and sewers.

Under this new system things did not change very much. Republicans and Democrats both won seats, personalities vied with issues at election time, and petty squabbles frequently took attention away from serious policy making. Since commissioners had to stand citywide elections, no blacks won commission posts until 1971, when John P. Franklin became commissioner for education. This former schoolman, who earned an undergraduate degree at Fisk University and a master's degree at the University of Indiana, continues to hold office in 1979 and at this writing is vice-mayor.[23]

Only two basic changes have been made in the city government since 1911. Prior to 1957 commissioners did not seek election for specific positions; the four winners simply drew lots for their administrative assignments. In that year a change was made requiring candidates to run for and win a specific commission post.

A second alteration resulted from a 1953 "home rule" amendment to Tennessee's constitution. Until that time the state legislature by general legislation or local private acts controlled Tennessee cities; there was no constitutional restriction on this authority. The amendment changed this; the general effort of home rule prevented the General Assembly from passing local laws which affected cities adopting home rule. In 1972 Chattanooga joined about twelve other communities in approving home rule.

During these years the local social system did not differ fundamentally from conventional Southern custom. Segregation was the established way of life, legalized by Jim Crow legislation. In Hamilton County an attitude of understanding developed after Appomattox which helped bridge the gulf between the races. The step from slavery to freedom had been gigantic; many blacks continued to live on the margin of economic survival. Housing and health care were deplorable, but some satisfaction was found in comparing the local situation with other places in the South.

After the end of World War I a group of local citizens, realizing the value of the interracial movement started in Atlanta, organized and established, under former Mayor T. C. Thompson, a large biracial committee to consider ways to alleviate unjust social conditions. About the same time the city, joined by the county, purchased land for Lincoln Park for blacks; the importance of this recreational area was greatly enhanced about twenty years later when a swimming pool and lights for night baseball were added. Black leadership noted that this gave a new spirit to their civic and fraternal clubs which had declined during the depression and that a greatly improved civic feeling had come about.

The black community found pride in the role of James A. Henry, the first black school principal, for whom the YMCA branch was named. The Reverend Joseph E. Smith, Congregational minister, civic leader, and member of the school board, was recognized when his name also was given to a black school. Blacks particularly admired the work of Dr. E. R. Wheeler, a physician and graduate of Meharry Medical College who started the Walden Hospital for Negroes about 1918. Under her direction it afforded facilities for nineteen black doctors of the Mountain City Medical Society. Blacks also applauded the city's move to provide a black city physician and its 1938 decision to permit black doctors to treat patients of their race at Erlanger Hospital. This was the first time, it is claimed, that black medical men were afforded such an opportunity in a municipal hospital in the South. Chattanoogans were also gratified that Howard High School was one of the three accredited schools for blacks in the state. [24]

Although blacks elected none of their race to city office, they were not without a political voice. They continued active participation in local affairs under the leadership of Walter C. Robinson. From 1933 until his death in 1968 this Howard High School alumnus edited the *Chattanooga Observer* and became a strong figure in Republican circles. Generally considered the most influential black political leader in the city's history, he organized the Voters League of Greater Chattanooga to encourage fellow blacks to vote—a move which naturally laid him open to the criticism of the opposing party. [25]

In county affairs blacks had little clout; not only were they few in number and scattered, but village life and the frontierlike environment reinforced currents of tradition. For more than seven decades county government had been directed by the county quarterly court chaired by the county judge, who dominated the government, for his responsibilities were in fact administrative rather than judicial.

The form of Hamilton County's government underwent a fundamental change on 10 February 1941 when the governor of the state signed a bill creating a council-manager system. Hamilton was the first Tennessee county to adopt this modernized structure. The legislation— long sought by certain citizens' groups—went into effect immediately, for the members of the first council were named in the act itself. The creation of this new county government represented a direct assault on the power of the quarterly court which, although retained, lost practically all of its authority.

All of the legislative and policy-making functions of the county government went to the council, composed of the county judge and four part-time members who would be elected for four-year terms. Although the designation "judge" continued to be used, the county judge continued to be the chief administrative official with the responsibility of running the day-to-day business of the county. His duties, however, changed with the new arrangement providing for a county manager who would handle routine and detailed work. The judge, as chairman of the council meetings and its fifth member, did need the constant support of at least two members in order to operate effectively. The job required the type of strong leadership given by Judges Will Cummings, Wiley O. Couch, and Wilkes T. Thrasher, Sr.

The duties of the county court became almost negligible; it did, however, appoint the county school superintendent and members of the school board. It also filled vacancies in all elective offices created by death, resignation, or ouster, including that of the county judge.

At the time this change in county government occurred, Judge Will Cummings, a staunch Democrat of some seventy years of age, was serving one of his several terms; in the act, he was designated the first judge under the council-manager plan. The colleagues of this colorful veteran politician on the council were Wiley O. Couch, James Pitts, V. N. Hallmark, and R. E. Holbert.

Tenacious political struggles and political cronyism did not end in Hamilton County after 1941. A clamor immediately arose over the appointment of the first manager. Then, before a year had elapsed, Councilman Couch, a big, handsome man with many friends, challenged Cummings and won the judgeship. Couch held the position as a kind of personal fief for about eight years, dominating political affairs in Chattanooga as well as in Hamilton County.

Disagreements between the members of the county council and the court reverberated across the area. Their struggle was largely one over authority and political influence. The squires, offended by the fact that the court was little more than a ceremonial body, struggled to entrench themselves even though their authority had been badly eroded. They especially drew critics' fire for appointing their own members to fill choice vacancies in the county government.[26]

Hamilton County, because of constitutional requirements, still elected the fifteen-member court. Although Democratic Chattanooga controlled four of the seats, county Republicans began to make a serious effort to control the court and in 1972 gained a ten-to-five victory. That same year the question of neglected reapportionment arose. There was no doubt about the need for reform, but the matter at once degenerated into a spirited political feud. As the two parties attempted to redraw district lines, racial gerrymandering drew most attention. When this controversy was finally compromised and a new election held in November 1972, the Republicans again controlled the court. The makeup of the county court, however, was different; two blacks won seats and so did two women.[27]

The political turmoil over the court helped to becloud the major sociological-political issues of the era. A national revolution generated by U.S. Supreme Court decisions, federal and state civil rights legislation, and protest demonstrations across America naturally had a major impact on Hamilton County but with special local modifications.

Through the years the local record revealed no blatant intimidation of black voters or public harassment. Certain efforts, as in the case of the building of a new Howard School building, helped to equalize the physical facilities for education. Moreover in 1947 when the National Urban League, supported by funds from the Rockefeller Foundation, surveyed in a 340-page report blacks' place in Chattanooga society, the compilers found that despite numerous shortcomings there did exist a real cooperative effort on the part of whites and blacks.

On the heels of this report the local Council of Community Forces and the Interracial Commission selected a group of about fifteen from each race to work with S. Bartow Strang, chairman, to put some of the league's recommendations into effect.

This type of gradual change, however, scarcely touched the fundamental questions created by Jim Crow legislation. Here the central issue was the terminating of segregation in public education, and on 17 May 1954, the U.S. Supreme Court announced its decision in *Brown* v. *Board of Education* which would affect all Americans. Henceforth, in the field of public education the doctrine of "separate but equal" had no place. The Court did not call for precipitate action; it did imply a period of grace for solving the complex and serious problems involved in compliance with "all deliberate speed."

The Chattanooga Board of Education announced its intention to comply with the Court's decree in 1955. Then, at the first meeting of an advisory citizens' committee appointed to help prepare the city for compliance, someone dropped a tear-gas vial. Alarmed that this incident signaled a prelude to violence, the board decided to suspend planning for integration. Disturbances at Clinton and Nashville seemed to confirm the wisdom of this decision.

In the next dozen or more years the city experienced periods of civil turmoil, hoodlumism, and fear, reflecting current national tensions. In hours of crisis, however, the necessary local leadership did emerge on the side of reason and order.

A brawl at the city auditorium in early February 1958 shocked the community. A crowd of some five thousand (including about one thousand whites who had purchased spectator tickets to a black dance) got into a race-inspired free-for-all. It required hours of police duty to restrain fists and bottle throwing and days of intense dialogue to banish the bitter words spoken by representatives of both races.

Similar to a pattern set elsewhere, Howard High School students in February 1960 staged "sit-down" demonstrations at lunch counters in downtown variety stores. Their quiet protests eventually ended in fighting in one store. Curious crowds gathered as the street scene grew tense. Police and firemen with hoses prevented an ugly situation from becoming explosive and again the community rallied to prevent a major confrontation. The next year echoes of other regional protests promoted "stand-in" demonstrations at movie theaters where blacks had not been admitted.

From the brink of trouble in the early 1960s Chattanooga recovered its poise under the calm direction of citizens' committees working earnestly to remove peacefully the social barriers created by segregation legislation and custom. Interracial and interdenominational groups of ministers, members of civic clubs, public-spirited citizens, and city county government officials never retreated from the most complex issues. All also paid tribute to the thoughtful, restrained, and dedicated leadership of the late William E. Brock, Jr., whose humanitarian spirit was contagious in the community.

The work of the citizens' groups was largely completed by 24 September 1963 when the Chattanooga city commission passed a landmark ordinance announcing that "all facilities of the city of Chattanooga are open to all citizens." This presaged a formal farewell to Jim Crow.[28]

This resolution actually reaffirmed earlier decisions to open the public library, parks, auditorium, and golf courses to all citizens. In addition, private facilities were largely desegregated by this date. Seating rules for buses disappeared in January 1959; most restaurants and food counters were opened by August 1960. Hotels, motels, movie houses agreed to cater to all. Although black patronage remained light in these establishments for some time and many businesses complied reluctantly, the "right" was, however, approved and accepted. Citizens' committees continued to labor on segregation problems, being especially concerned in limiting the influence of militant "outside" forces.

After the 1954 school decision, local implementation of the decree developed slowly. Dismayed by the early threat of violence, the board of education deferred all its desegregation planning. Eventually the blacks sought action; three petitioned the board to permit their children to register at white schools. Denial of their request resulted in a suit in the United States District Court charging Chattanooga with operating a "compulsory biracial school system." This charge was filed by James R. Mapp and others representing the local branch of the NAACP. Mapp, as a student in 1941, took up the cause of civil rights as á member of the Orchard Knob Junior High School NAACP Youth Council. In 1954 he was elected president of the Chattanooga branch and in 1977 named chairman of the Southeast Region of the NAACP.[29]

After in-depth planning, the board of education announced that limited desegregation would begin on 5 September 1962. The arrangements called for the admission of black students in the first three grades in sixteen schools with an annual broadening of the scope of the plan, a process the courts ordered to be speeded up so that desegregation of all grades could be completed in 1966. That first year forty-four blacks attended six formerly all-white city schools.

When Chattanooga desegregated its first classes under the court order, Hamilton County voluntarily announced a similar program commencing in the fall of 1962. Fourteen black students were enrolled at that time. The University of Chattanooga opened its summer graduate programs to qualified black students in 1963 and to all classes in the fall term of 1965. The private secondary schools followed suit within a short time. Although some outspoken objectors threatened violent resistance to every move, calm prevailed at the time of implementation.

In the fall of 1966 city and county schools had legally ended the practice of separate schools, but the "mix" did not, by the very nature of living patterns, provide maximum integration. In 1971 the U.S. Supreme Court ordered that "all vestiges of state imposed segregation must be removed" and approved busing as a means to accomplish this goal. Before this opinion was handed down, a general malaise concerning the race issue had overcome the nation. The strong 1964 civil rights legislation had produced a violent reaction. The idea of "black power" grew and spread; militancy threatened to overwhelm earlier nonviolence. Ghetto upheavals produced defiance and destruction and the assassination of Martin Luther King, Jr., vastly heightened emotions. Hamilton County did not escape the contagion.

In 1969 trouble broke out at Brainerd and Central high schools in scuffles between black and white youth. The hostilities at Brainerd revolved around school symbols: the nickname "Rebels," the song "Dixie," and the use of the Confederate flag. Incidents of rock throwing and fisticuffs spread into the community; adults in flag-covered cars circulated as "night riders." The school closed for a number of days when attitudes hardened. Trouble flared up several times, and when school authorities suspended a white student for persisting in wearing a Confederate flag on his clothing, the youth's parents took the case to the federal courts. When district and circuit courts ruled against them, the case went to the U.S. Supreme Court which in 1973 denied a review of the appeal.

In May 1971 when the Chattanooga Board of Education was under court order to establish a "unitary school system" to accomplish maximum integration, violence again erupted . Mob fights opened the way for sniping, window smashings, fire bombings, and burnings. Wild rumors intensified community and county-wide anxieties. Even night curfews banning movement of all persons save medical personnel and law enforcement officers did not restore order. The mayor called for National Guard service and the two battalions numbering upward of two thousand men assumed the responsibility for law and order—reminiscent of the troubled times in 1917. Airlines canceled night flights into the city and industry adjusted its shifts to fit the curfew. Tragedy stalked the area for about a week before the tension eased, and one man died of gunshot wounds.

That fall apprehension continued to torment the local people; schools were to start the new term under plans based on pairing and clustering of schools and busing. A great emotional storm seemed to be brewing. Crowds congregated on the opening days, but no major demonstrations developed. At this time Chattanooga had some blacks in key positions who worked very closely with community groups. One was a city judge; another, John P. Franklin, had just won his post as commissioner of education, and a third was schoolman Claude C. Bond, who had come to Hamilton County from west Tennessee armed with a bachelor's degree from Lane College and a master's from Fisk. In 1956 he was appointed principal of the Howard School and in 1967 assistant superintendent of the city schools.

The relationship between the races, aggravated by the slow implementation of school desegregation and by the precipitous course of social change, was not made any easier by the unpopular war in Vietnam. Men from Hamilton County were among the more than half-million Americans in the war zone at the peak of operations. At home demonstrations reminded the local people of the serious objections to the conflict although public protests were not as prevalent as elsewhere. But Hamilton County well knew the cost of the war and by May 1971 when the Military Family Club unveiled a monument at Lovell Field to those who gave their lives, the number of dead from the area came to 162.[30]

The impact of the social changes of the past twenty-five years was accompanied by political alterations equally weighty. Again the impetus came from a decision of the U.S. Supreme Court; legally it was referred to as *Baker* v. *Carr* but popularly as "one man, one vote."

The case had its origins in Tennessee. Despite a constitutional requirement for legislative reapportionment every ten years based on the census, no changes had been made since 1901. Rural Democrats in Middle and West Tennessee held the balance of power over both the East Tennessee Republicans and the major urban centers. The four major cities, after sixty years without adjustment, held barely half of the legislative seats to which they should have been entitled. In 1950 Hamilton County had only three of the six members of the lower house to which its population entitled it. The voting population for one Hamilton County state senator was 131,971 compared to 16,892 in 1900.[31]

The Court's ruling, handed down on 20 March 1962, represented an unprecedented use of federal power in requiring states to change their practices. It altered the composition of virtually every state government in the United States; shortly after, congressional as well as state legislative districts had to undergo change to make all as equal as possible.

Tennessee's rural politicians, who still controlled the machinery of government, delayed complying with the decree as long as possible. When submitted, their plan required a system of single-district elections in place of county-at-large voting in the metropolitan counties; this ruse gave the rural politicians a chance to work deals with more friendly suburban delegates, instead of being confronted only by urban or central city delegations.

With reapportionment, the four major centers of the state together received fourteen of the thirty-three senate seats and forty-two of the ninety-nine house seats. Single-district elections meant that Republicans and blacks had much greater chances of winning elections. No black sat in the legislature between 1887 and 1965, but with reapportionment blacks gained places not only in the lower house but also, for the first time, in the senate. In 1974 Hamilton County sent Clarence B. Robinson as one member of its delegation to Nashville; he was the first black to serve since the days of Hodge and Hutchins. Robinson, who had been employed for thirty-nine years in the city school system as a teacher and principal, continues at this writing to hold his seat.[32] In state elections, reapportionment meant progress toward a two-party system, and in the first decade the Hamilton County delegations contained more Republicans than Democrats.

In national elections since the mid-century the Republicans have been especially successful. The county's vote after 1948 went to their presidential candidate every time except in 1968 when George Wallace's American party carried the area. Even Estes Kefauver's vice-presidential candidacy failed to result in a local Democratic win in 1956.

In 1962 the Republicans gained success in the third Congressional District race when they elected Bill Brock. After continuous success, Brock in 1970 moved to the U.S. Senate, defeating incumbent Albert Gore. After serving one term, Brock did lose his bid for a second, but even in defeat, Hamilton County leaned heavily toward the Republican nominee.

At the time Brock became a senator, LaMar Baker ran as his Republican successor in the Third District and was victorious. Four years later Baker faced Democratic candidate Mort Lloyd, who died in a plane crash on 20 August 1974 while campaigning. After this tragedy the Democrats chose his widow, Marilyn Lloyd, as their standard-bearer. Her victory that November ended a twelve-year Republican dominance in the House of Representatives and was one of the biggest political upsets in Hamilton County's history.

Mrs. Lloyd was the first woman elected to Congress to represent Hamilton County. She successfully defended her post in the elections of 1976, 1978, and 1980 and, having remarried, is now serving under the name Marilyn Lloyd Bouchard.

On the local level, reapportionment had created quite a stir in relation to the county court in 1972, but in an unexpected turn of events, the court soon disappeared from the political scene. As the result of a state constitutional convention's revision of the county government act and its subsequent ratification by the voters on 7 May 1978, an entirely new form of government was authorized for Hamilton County. At the time of the referendum the measure was described only in general terms; few details had been worked out. The Hamilton County electorate voted against the new arrangement, but it received statewide approval. So Hamiltonians got a brand-new government which they themselves had refused to approve.

The legislature hastily fleshed out the plan between the time of the referendum and the impending election, when new officials were to be selected. It provided for a board of county commissioners to replace both the county court and the county council. Nine part-time commissioners elected to represent the districts from which they were elected were designated a legislative body. A county executive replaced the county judge in his administrative role although the incumbent retained his post as county judge until the expiration of his term in 1982, serving in a strictly judicial capacity.

The principle on which the new structure was based was that of three divisions of government—executive, legislative, and judicial— and a definite separation of powers. The county executive now has no vote on the board of commissioners as the old county judge had on the council, but he does possess veto power over its actions.

On 1 September 1978, the new model government assumed power with the swearing-in of officials elected the previous month. The county executive's post went to Dalton Roberts, a former teacher and school administrator, county manager under Judge Chester Frost, and country musician. His election was a victory for the Democratic party.

Both new and old political faces appeared on the board of commissioners; its membership included one woman and two blacks. The Democrats held a majority of eight to one in the first legislative group.[33] The new county government, launched in an era of sociological and political change without precedent or blueprint, has not had time to plow its first true furrow as of this writing.

NOTES

1. *Chattanooga Times*, 4 June 1961.

2. *Nashville!*, July 1978. In 1977, Hamilton County had nine of the fifty largest companies in the state based on sales: Dorsey ranked 10, Dixie Yarns, 13; Red Food Stores, 16; Standard Coosa Thatcher, 17; North American Royalties, 22; Wayne-Gossard (Signal Knitting Mills), 24; Chattem, 32; Pro-Group, 39; and Heritage Quilts, 42.

3. Industrial Committee of One Hundred, *1977 Manufacturers Directory: Chattanooga and Tri-State Area: Major Employers in the Chattanooga Area*, rev. ed. (Chattanooga: Greater Chattanooga Chamber of Commerce, 1978): *Chattanooga Times*, 13 February 1977; 12, 18 February, 17 July, 8 August 1978; 18 February 1979; *Chattanooga News-Free Press*, 1 February 1977; 4, 6 August 1978.

4. *Chattanooga Times*, 28 September 1948; 26 February 1950.

5. Ibid., 26 April 1954; 24 March 1956; 15 December 1966; 27 December 1968; *Chattanooga News-Free Press*, 13 April 1977; 29 December 1978.

6. Ibid., 31 August 1951; 31 August 1956; 31 August 1961; 18 May 1966; *Chattanooga Times*, 19 May 1966; 1 January 1967.

7. Chattanooga-Hamilton County Air Pollution Control Bureau, *A History of Air Pollution Control in Chattanooga and Hamilton County (1977)*, pp. 1–18; *U.S. News & World Report*, 17 June 1974; *Chattanooga Times*, 12 February, 15 October 1978; 4 February 1979; *Chattanooga News-Free Press*, 1 February 1977.

8. Ibid., 6 August 1978; *Chattanooga Times*, 23 July 1959; 6 August 1960.

9. Ibid., 18 October, 18 November 1954; 21 November 1959; 28 January 1963; *Chattanooga News-Free Press*, 17 October 1954; 3 March, 19, 20 November 1959. A Kiwanis Club study in 1939 led to the establishment of the Convention and Visitors Bureau.

10. Mayor Bass retired in 1947, only a few months before his fifth term expired; he died at eighty-seven years of age in 1960. *Chattanooga Times*, 13–15 March 1960; *Chattanooga News-Free Press*, 13–15 March 1960.

11. Ibid., 3 August 1961. A study by the National Urban League in 1947 stated that "over 76 percent of the total dwelling units occupied by Negroes here are substandard." *Chattanooga Times*, 7 December 1948.

12. Ibid., 2 December 1955; 21 November 1959; 5 June 1961; *Chattanooga News-Free Press*, 17 January 1962; 13 December 1976.

13. Miller Park was dedicated on 8 December 1976. Another city park in the planning stage is an eight-acre tract at the intersection of Suck Creek and Signal Mountain roads. This property was donated in 1974 by the General Portland Cement Co.

14. *Chattanooga Times*, 8 May 1978.

15. Ibid., 19 June 1932; 17 January 1934; 24 March 1965.

16. Ibid., 24 May 1979; TVA, "Going to School at 'TVA College'," *TVA Today* (April 1977).

17. The persons who signed the charter for the Chattanooga Anti-tuberculosis

Sanitarium (its original name) were E. Y. Chapin, H. S. Probasco, D. B. Loveman, Dr. E. B. Wise, and Dr. Y. L. Abernathy. Generous contributors through the years include J. T. Lupton, John Stagmaier, J. A. Caldwell, Charles W. Cox, George Scholze, Charles F. Milburn, W. J. Dobbs, W. R. Long, W. L. Brown, and Adolph S. Ochs.

18. *Chattanooga Times,* 26 June 1944; 17 April 1961. Branches are located at Eastside Health Center on Main Street, Mid-Central Health Center at Ooltewah, and the Sequoyah Medical Center at Soddy-Daisy.

19. In 1978, county hospitals had the following number of beds: Baroness Erlanger, 652; Downtown General, 54; East Ridge Community, 128; Memorial, 308; Moccasin Bend Mental Health Center, 330; Parkridge, 223; Red Bank Community, 57; and T. C. Thompson Children's, 110;

20. A great variety of programs are available sponsored by the Adult Education Council, the colleges, the Chattanooga Area Historical Association, the Audubon Society, the Association for the Study of Afro-American Life and History, Landmarks Chattanooga, Inc., Senior Neighbors, the Civil War Roundtable, the Afro-American Heritage Council, the Kiwanis Club, the Clarence T. Jones Observatory, to name but a few.

21. Miss Moore made her Metropolitan Opera debut on 7 February 1928, as Mimi in *La Bohème;* in 1934 she brought grand opera to the moving-picture screen in *One Night of Love,* for which she received the Medal of the American Academy of Arts and Sciences as the first motion-picture star to receive this honor.

22. Among the special funds managed by the Community Foundation are the Pine Breeze Fund, a Health Education Fund, the Leah James Fund, the Robert Wright Fund, the City Beautification Fund, the Z. C. Patten Fund, and the Carter-Chapin Memorial Fund. *Chattanooga News-Free Press,* 19 August 1979.

23. *Chattanooga Times,* 12 May 1911; 11 October 1931; 3 May 1936; 11 July 1937; 18 September 1938.

24. Ibid., 12 April 1918; 2 February, 18 September 1938.

25. Ibid., 13 September 1968; *Chattanooga News-Free Press,* 28 March 1960.

26. *Chattanooga Times,* 11 February 1941; 15 August 1965; 9 January 1966. The George McInturff tapes in the Chattanooga-Hamilton County Bicentennial Library. D. S. Etheridge was named first county manager.

27. *Chattanooga News-Free Press,* 9 March, 2 December 1972; *Chattanooga Times,* 21 July, 5, 11 August, 2 December 1972. First women members were Mrs. Mary Gardenhire and Mrs. Alma Lewis.

28. The resolution was printed in full in the *Chattanooga Times,* 25 September 1963.

29. Ibid., 31 August 1977. Mapp served as Chattanooga branch president 1956–67 and 1969–77. He was named state president in 1976 and regional

chairman the following year. George A. Key, Sr., took the local presidency in 1977.

30. Ibid., 8 May 1971; *Chattanooga News-Free Press*, 10 May 1968.

31. Richard C. Cortner, *The Apportionment Cases* (Knoxville: University of Tennessee Press, 1970), pp. 268, 270.

32. *Chattanooga Times*, 24 May 1974; 9 December 1975.

33. Ibid., 10 March, 1, 12 May, 17 August, 2 September 1978; *Chattanooga News-Free Press*, 8 March, 11, 12 May, 1 September 1978.

Hamilton County Measurements

Size

Hamilton County land area	550.4 square miles
Hamilton County water area	36.6 square miles
Chattanooga land area	126.9 square miles
Chickamauga Lake	35,400 acres

Altitude

Chattanooga	665 feet above sea level
Signal Mountain	2,080 feet above sea level
Lookout Mountain	2,391 feet above sea level
Missionary Ridge	1,100 feet above sea level

Climate[a]

Average annual precipitation	51.92 inches
Average annual snowfall	4.1 inches
Average annual temperature	59.8°F
Monthly average temperature, January	40.2°F
Monthly average temperature, July	68.1°F
Average growing season	228 days
Hottest temperature on record	106°F, 1952
Coldest temperature on record	−10°F, 1966
Maximum monthly snowfall	15.8 inches, January 1893

[a]On 19 January 1879, the Army Signal Service established the local weather service. Renamed the Weather Bureau in 1891, it came under the U.S. Department of Agriculture and in 1940 was moved to the Department of Commerce. Later it officially became the National Weather Service. Since 1930 the local office has been at Lovell Field; earlier weathermen had measuring instruments at the corner of Ninth and Market streets, the U.S. Customs House, the James Building, and the Federal Building.

APPENDIX B

Population

Year	Hamilton County				Chattanooga		
	Total	White	Black		Total	White	Black
			Slave	Free			
1820	821	766	39	16			
1830	2,276	2,136	115	25			
1840	8,175	7,498	584	93			
1850	10,075	9,216	672	187			
1860	13,258	11,647	1,419	192	2,545		
1870	17,241	13,053[a]	4,188		6,903	3,872[a]	2,221
1880	23,642	16,243	7,399		12,892	7,807	5,032
1890	53,482	35,765	17,717		29,100	16,525	12,563
1900	61,695	42,187	19,490		30,154	17,032	13,122
1910[b]	94,477	67,957	26,518		44,604	26,660	17,942
1920	115,954	88,829	27,120		57,895	39,001	18,894
1930	159,497	123,342	36,155		119,798	86,509	33,289
1940	180,478	140,845	39,633		128,163	91,712	36,404
1950	208,255	165,699	42,556		131,041	90,617	39,276
1960	237,905	190,618	47,287		130,009	86,783	42,141
1970	254,236	207,236	46,397		119,082	76,216	42,610
1980[c]	287,740				169,565		

[a]Beginning this year, there are some discrepancies as "other nonwhites" are not included.
[b]Includes James County.

APPENDIX C

Hamilton County Municipalities Other Than Chattanooga

Municipality	Date of Incorporation	Population in 1970
Collegedale	1968	3,031
East Ridge	1921	21,799
Lakesite	1972	300[a]
Lookout Mountain	1890	1,741
Red Bank	1955	12,715
Ridgeside	1931	458
Signal Mountain	1919	4,839
Soddy-Daisy	1969	7,569
Walden	1975	800[a]

[a]Approximation.

APPENDIX D

Counties Bordering On Hamilton County

1. Bledsoe County, Tennessee—Established 30 November 1807. Named for Anthony Bledsoe, early Tennessee settler and major in the Revolutionary Army, killed by Indians in 1789. County seat, Pikeville. Population: 1850, 5,959, including 96 free blacks and 827 slaves; 1900, 6,626; 1970, 7,643.

2. Rhea County, Tennessee—Established 3 December 1807. Named for John Rhea, veteran of battle of King's Mountain and prominent political leader who served in first Tennessee Constitutional Convention and as U.S. Congressman for terms 1803–1815 and 1817–1823. County seat, Dayton. Population: 1850, 4,415, including 28 free blacks and 436 slaves; 1900, 14,318; 1970, 17,202.

3. Marion County, Tennessee—Established 20 November 1817. Named for Francis Marion, "the Swamp Fox," South-Carolina Revolutionary War hero. County seat, Jasper. Population: 1850, 6,314, including 45 free blacks and 551 slaves; 1900, 17,281; 1970, 20,577.

4. Walker County, Georgia—Created 18 December 1833. Named for Major Freeman Walker, lawyer, Georgia legislator, mayor of Augusta and U.S. senator, 1819–1821. County seat, LaFayette. Population: 1850, 13,109, including 1,701 blacks; 1900, 15,661; 1970, 50,691.

5. Meigs County, Tennessee—Established 21 January 1836. Named for Return Jonathan Meigs, Cherokee Indian agent, 1801–1823. County seat, Decatur. Population: 1850, 4,879, including 4 free blacks and 395 slaves; 1900, 7,491; 1970, 5,219.

6. Bradley County, Tennessee—Created 10 February 1836. Named for Colonel Edward Bradley of Shelby County, renowned for military activities in War of 1812. County seat, Cleveland. Population: 1850, 12,259, including 37 free blacks and 744 slaves; 1900, 15,759; 1970, 50,686.

7. Dade County, Georgia—Created 25 December 1837. Named for Major Francis L. Dade, veteran of War of 1812 killed in the Florida Indian wars, December 1835. County seat, Trenton. Population: 1850, 2,680, including 148 blacks; 1900, 4,578; 1970, 9,910.

8. Catoosa County, Georgia—Created 5 December 1853. Indian name meaning "mountain," according to John P. Brown, a local Cherokee Indian historian. County seat, Ringgold. Population: 1860, 5,082, including 714 blacks; 1900, 26,575; 1970, 28,271.

9. Sequatchie County, Tennessee—Created 25 February 1856. Named after Sequatchie Valley which, in turn, was named in honor of an Indian chieftain by that name. County seat, Dunlap. Population 1870, 2,335; 1900, 3,326; 1970, 6,331.

APPENDIX E

Hamilton County Properties On the National Register of Historic Places

"The National Register is a list of properties 'significant in American history, architecture, archaeology, and culture—a comprehensive index of the significant physical evidences of our national patrimony.' Properties listed thereon deserve to be preserved by their owners as a part of the cultural heritage of our nation."

The Brabson House, 407 East Fifth Street

Brown's Ferry Tavern, 703 Browns Ferry Road

James Brown House, Georgetown Road, vicinity of Ooltewah

Civil War Fortifications, Volunteer Army Ammunition Plant, Tyner

Chickamauga and Chattanooga National Military Park (includes the Cravens House, Lookout Mountain)

Connor Toll House, Taft Highway at old Fairmount Pike, Signal Mountain

Hiram Douglas House, Snow Hill Road, vicinity of Ooltewah

James County Courthouse, Ooltewah

The Lookout Mountain Incline, St. Elmo to top of Lookout Mountain

The Pleasant L. Matthews House, Georgetown Road, vicinity of Ooltewah

Saints Peter and Paul Catholic Church and Buildings, 214 East Eighth Street

Gaskill House, 427 East Fifth Street

Brainerd Mission Cemetery, Eastgate

The Newton Chevrolet Building, 329 Market Street

Old (Carnegie) Library Building, 200 East Eighth Street

The Old Post Office, East Eleventh and Lindsay streets

The Read House, West Ninth and Broad streets

Ross's Landing, foot of Market Street

Terminal Station (Chattanooga Choo-Choo), 1434 Market Street

Tivoli Theater, 709 Broad Street

Topside (summer home of Judge D.M. Key), Wilson Avenue, Signal Mountain

Williams Island, on the Tennessee River seven miles downstream from Market Street Bridge

Fountain Square, Georgia Avenue

The Mikado Locomotive No. 4501, Tennessee Valley Railroad Museum

Fort Wood Historic District

Shiloh Baptist (First Baptist) Church, 506 East Eighth Street

The Ochs Building (Times or Dome Building), Georgia Avenue and East Eighth Street

The Hutcheson House, South Crest and Old Ringgold roads
Hamilton County Courthouse, block of West Sixth Street and Georgia Avenue
St. Paul's Episcopal Church, Pine and West Seventh streets
Missionary Ridge railroad tunnel, Tennessee Valley Railroad Museum
Chattanooga Car Barns, West Third Street, Broad to Market streets
Wiley United Methodist Church, Lookout at East Fifth Street
Union Station, Ninth and Broad streets, razed in 1973
Bonny Oaks Plantation House at Bonny Oaks School, 5114 Bonny Oaks Drive
Park Hotel, 177 East Seventh Street
Judge Will Cummings House, west of Chattanooga on State Road
Ferger Place Historic District, between Eveningside and Morningside drives
Patten Parkway Historic District
Asbury United Methodist Church, 1901 Bailey Avenue
Frances Willard Building, 615 Lindsay Street
James Building, 735 Broad Street
Second Presbyterian Church, Seventh and Pine streets
Tucker Baptist Church, 860 McCallie Avenue
U.S. Federal Building, Georgia Avenue between Ninth and Tenth streets
Kelley House, 1903 McCallie Avenue
Benjamin F. Thomas House, McCallie Avenue at Central Avenue
East Tennessee Iron Manufacturing Company Blast Furnace ruins, adjacent to Walnut Street bridge
Reuben H. Hunt Buildings in Hamilton County Thematic District
Faxon-Thomas Mansion, (Hunter Museum of Art), 10 Bluff View

NOTE: Sites are located in Chattanooga, except where otherwise noted.

APPENDIX F

Chief County Officials

County Judges

1856–1858[a]	John Fletcher White	1918–1926	Sam A. Conner
1867–1876	A.G.W. Puckett	1926–1942	Will Cummings
1876–1886	Robert C. McRee, Jr.	1942–1947	Wiley O. Couch
1886–1894	Hugh Whiteside	1947–1960	Wilkes T. Thrasher
1894–1910	Seth M. Walker	1960	Wilkes T. Thrasher, Jr.
1911–1912	Joe V. Williams	1960–1974	Chester Frost
1912–1918	Will Cummings	1974–1982[b]	Don Moore

County Executive

1978–	Dalton Roberts

[a]Until 1856 the chairman of the county court acted as judge. The office created that year was abolished two years later.

[b]The county judge lost all administrative and executive duties when the structure of government was changed in 1978 to the County Executive-Commission form.

APPENDIX G

Chattanooga Mayors

Under the provisions of the 1839 incorporation of Chattanooga as a Tennessee town, the voters elected seven aldermen who chose one of their number to be mayor. The term of office then was but one year:

1840	James Berry	1842–43	Dr. Milo Smith
1841	Dr. Beriah Frazier	1844–45	Dr. Joseph S. Gillespie

Official documents for the next few years do not exist; it is believed the following mayors served:

1846–48	Henry White Massengale
1849	Thomas Crutchfield
1850–51	Dr. Milo Smith

Under the 1851 city charter the mayor was elected directly by the voters, as were the eight aldermen. Mayors continued to serve terms of one year:

1852	Dr. Milo Smith	1857	W. D. Fulton
1853	Henry White Massengale	1858	Dr. W. S. Bell
1854	William Williams (resigned July 1)	1859	Thomas Crutchfield
		1860	Charles E. Grenville
1854	William F. Ragsdale	1861	James C. Warner
1855	E. G. Pearl	1862–63	Dr. Milo Smith
1856	D. C. McMillin		

From 9 September 1863 until 7 October 1865 a federal provost marshal ran the city for the Union Army. Following the suspension of civil government, the first mayor served only from 7 October until the end of the year; elections were again held on the last Thursday in December:

1865	Richard Henderson (7 October–31 December)	1867–68	David C. Carr
		1869	Alonzo G. Sharp
1866	Charles E. Lewis	1870–fall 1871	W. P. Rathburn

A new city charter in 1871 specified fall elections, which continued to be held until 1911:

1872	John T. Wilder (resigned in May)	1878	Thomas J. Carlisle (died 29 October)
1872	Josiah Jackson Bryan	1878	A. J. Gahagan
1873	Dr. E. M. Wight	1879	J. T. Hill
1874	Dr. P. D. Sims	1880	H. F. Temple
1875	John W. James	1881	John A. Hart
1876	Tomlinson Fort	1882–83	H. Clay Evans
1877	Dr. E. M. Wight		

In 1883, the term of office became two years:

1883–85	Hugh Whiteside	1893–97	George W. Ochs
1885–87	A. G. Sharp	1897–99	Edmund Watkins
1887–89	John B. Nicklin	1899–1901	Joseph Wassman
1889–91	James A. Hart (died 15 January)	1901–05	Alexander W. Chambliss
		1905–07	W. L. Frierson
1891	Isaac B. Merriam	1907–09	W. R. Crabtree
1891–93	Garnett Andrews	1909–11	T. C. Thompson

In April 1911 the commission form of government began; the mayor's term became four years:

1911–15	T. C. Thompson	1951–63	P. R. Olgiati
1915–19	Jesse M. Littleton	1963–69 (resigned)	Ralph H. Kelley
1919–23 (resigned)	A. W. Chambliss	1969–71	A. L. Bender
1923–27	Richard Hardy	1971– (acting)	S. Dean Peterson
1927–47 (resigned)	E. D. Bass	1971–75	Robert Kirk Walker
1947–51	Hugh P. Wasson	1975–	Charles A. Rose

NOTE: Material for the early years based on Zella Armstrong, *History of Hamilton County and Chattanooga, Tennessee* (Chattanooga: Lookout Publishing, 1931).

APPENDIX H

County School Superintendents

1867–70	E.O. Tade	1917–19	J. White Abel
1873–75	J. H. Hardee	1919–24	J. A. Roberts
1875–77	W. M. Beene	1925	J. L. Hair
1877–79	H. F. Rogers	1925–31	J. A. Walker
1879–83	A. Shelton	1931–39	Arthur L. Rankin
1883–87	H. B. Heywood	1939–41	Marshall Clark
1887–96	H. D. Huffaker	1941–42	Arthur L. Rankin
1896–1902	Samuel Hixson	1942–52	Marshall Clark
1902	J. B. Brown	1952–55	Roy C. Smith
1902–07	R. L. Jones	1955–74	Sam P. McConnell
1907	Nita Cowart	1974–80	Dale Carter
1907–13	J. B. Brown	1980–	Don Loftis
1913–17	J. L. Hair		

APPENDIX I

Chattanooga School Superintendents

1872–92	H. D. Wyatt	1942–56	Lawrence G. Derthick
1892–03	A. T. Barrett	1948–49	Creed F. Bates (acting)
1903–09	S. G. Gilreath	1957–59	John W. Letson
1909–14	D. A. Graves	1960–66	Benjamin E. Carmichael
1914–19	C. H. Winder	1967–69	Charles E. Martin
1919–21	R. L. Jones	1969–70	Jack D. Lawrie
1921–27	J. S. Ziegler	1970–78	James W. Henry
1927–42	W. T. Robinson	1978–	James D. McCullough

APPENDIX J

County Councilmen, 1941–1978

1941–42	Wiley O. Couch	1946–50	James Pitts
	James Pitts		W. C. Smith
	V.W. Hallmark		R. N. Logan (1946–47)
	R. E. Holbert		Fred Robinson (1948–49)
1942–46	R. W. Logan		Tom Brown (1949–50)
	W. C. Smith		Scott Z. McBryant
	George McInturff		(1946–48)
	(1942–44, 1945–46)		Herbert Barks (1947–48)
	Helen McInturff (1944–45)		Hugh Abercrombie
	James Pitts		(1948–50)

1950–54	Ernest Cushman		Raulston Schoolfield
	Carrie Robinson Wells[a]		(1964–66)
	Herbert Dunlap	1966–70	Jack Hixson, Jr. (1966–69)
	Dr. Joseph Killebrew		Richard Winningham
1954–58	Dave Eldridge		J. Howard Callaway
	Paul Wilbanks		(1969–70)
	Phil Osborne		Jack Mayfield
	Carrie R. Wells		Z. Cartter Patten
1958–62	Dave Eldridge	1970–74	Robert Long
	Carrie Robinson Wells		Luke Wilson
	Phil Osborne		Jack Mayfield
	James Turner		Frank Newell
1962–66	Dave Eldridge	1974–78	Floyd Fuller
	Arthur Vieth		James Penley
	Jack Mayfield		Robert Long
	James Turner (1962–63)		Jack Mayfield
	Phil Osborne (1963–64)		Coyle Ricketts

In 1978 the government structure was changed to the county executive-commission form. The first commissioners were:

Claude Ramsey, resigned, replaced by William C. Bennett | Jack Mayfield[d]
Sam Robinson, Jr. | Howard Sompayrac
Brenda Hundley Bailey | Rheubin McGhee Taylor
Rev. Paul McDaniel[b] | Robert Long
| Floyd Fuller[c]

[a]Carrie Robinson Wells replaced her husband, Fred Robinson, at his death in 1949; in 1956 she remarried.
[b]Chairman, 1979–80.
[c]Chairman, 1978–79.
[d]Chairman, 1980–

APPENDIX K

Chattanooga City Commissioners

Health and Education

1911–15	H. Clay Evans	1943–45	R. M. Cooke[a]
1915–19	H. D. Huffaker	1945–54	F. H. Trotter
1919–27	Fred B. Frazier	1954–56	Henry Allen
1927–33	H. D. Huffaker[a]	1956–59	F. H. Trotter
1933–35	W. E. Wilkerson	1959–71	S. Dean Peterson
1935–43	T. H. McMillan	1971–	John P. Franklin

Fire and Police

1911–19	T. C. Betterton	1956–63	H. P. Dunlap
1919–27	E. D. Herron	1963–71	James. B. Turner
1927–41	Eugene J. Bryan	1971–78	Gene Roberts[b]
1941–47	E. R. Betterton	1978	H. P. Dunlap, acting
1947–56	Roy Hyatt	1979–	Walter Smart

Public Works, Streets, and Airports

1911–15	A. M. Sloan	1941–46	F. L. Brown
1915–27	E. D. Bass	1946–51	P. R. Olgiati
1927–30	R. H. Crox	1951–62	Patrick Wilcox[a]
1930	C. A. Betts	1962–69	A. L. Bender
1931–34	G. H. Taylor	1969–75	Charles A. Rose
1934–41	E. R. Betterton	1975–	Paul Clark

Public Utilities, Parks, and Playgrounds[c]

1911–15	J. H. Warner	1943–44	E. J. Self
1915–19	E. D. Herron	1945–46	J. T. Mahoney[b]
1919–24	Emil Wassman	1946–67	G. C. McInturff
1924–27	E. J. Bryan	1967–75	Steven Conrad
1927–34	J. A. Cash	1975–	James Eberle
1934–43	R. M. Cooke		

[a]Died in office.
[b]Resigned.
[c]Name of department changed as functions of the office changed.

APPENDIX L

Presidents of the Greater Chattanooga Area Chamber of Commerce

The city Chamber of Commerce began as the Coal, Iron & Manufacturers Association, established 22 October 1876. The Association's presidents were:

1876	W. P. Rathburn	1882	D. E. Rees
1877	J. T. Wilder	1883	H. Clay Evans
1878	H. S. Chamberlain	1884	M. J. O'Brien
1879	W. D. Van Dyke	1885	Marcus Grant
1880	John C. Griffiss	1886	C. C. Conner
1881	S. B. Lowe		

Chattanooga Chamber of Commerce

1887–88	D. B. Loveman	1901	George W. Ochs
1889	M. J. O'Brien	1902–03	Newell Sanders
1890	J. B. Merriam, Sr.	1904	C. A. Lyerly
1891	Tomlinson Fort	1905	C. W. Olson
1892	H. T. Olmsted	1906	G. F. Meehan
1893	W. O. Peeples	1907	G. G. Fletcher
1894	Andrew J. Gahagan	1908	N. H. Grady
1895	John W. Faxon	1909	J. B. Pound
1896	D. M. Steward	1910	John A. Patten
1897	Joseph F. Voigt	1911–12	W. E. Brock
1898	C. V. Brown	1913	Frank E. Mahoney
1899	W. B. Swaney	1914	P. J. Kruesi
1900	A. S. Glover	1915	M. M. Allison

1916	Claudius H. Huston	1951	Alf J. Law, Jr.
1917	J. Read Voigt	1952	R. L. Moore, Jr.
1918	R. C. Jones, Sr.	1953	J. Garnett Andrews
1919	F. H. Cantrell	1954	Mark K. Wilson, Jr.
1920	F. C. Bickers	1955	H. Clay Evans Johnson
1921	S. L. Probasco, Sr.	1956	J. Polk Smartt
1922	Paul Campbell, Sr.	1957	J. Gilbert Stein
1923	Mark K. Wilson, Sr.	1958	Scott N. Brown
1924–25	S. R. Read	1959	F. R. Kollmansperger
1926	R. H. Kimball	1960	Lou J. Williams
1927	Mercer Reynolds	1961	E. Y. Chapin III
1928–29	A. F. Porzelius	1962	De Sales Harrison
1930	Sanford Bennett	1963	Floyd C. Delaney
1931	E. J. Walsh	1964	Carter M. Parham
1832	Mark H. Senter	1965	Scott L. Probasco, Jr.
1933	John Lovell	1966	T. A. Lupton, Jr.
1934	I. B. Merriam	1967	T. O. Duff, Jr.
1935	R. W. Williams	1968	John C. Stophel
1936–37	Harry Miller	1969	Blackwell Smith, Jr.
1938	John B. Crimmins	1970	Harry R. White
1939	Emmett S. Newton	1971	David F. S. Johnson
1940	T. O. Duff, Sr.	1972	Edward M. Cooper, Jr.
1941	Harry C. Carbaugh	1973	John P. Guerry
1942	R. E. Biggers	1974	Elgin Smith
1943	H. W. Hirsheimer	1975	Gordon L. Smith, Jr.
1943–44	S. J. McCallie	1976	Richard W. Cardin
1944–45	E. E. Brown, Sr.	1977	Herbert F. McQueen
1946	J. V. McLaughlin	1978	Ira Trivers
1947	Roy McDonald	1979	Henry Unruh
1948	Earl P. Carter	1980	John F. Germ
1949	P. H. Wood	1981	James D. Kennedy, Jr.
1950	Everett Allen		

APPENDIX M

Chattanooga's First Citizens

In June 1837 the people living in the Ross's Landing area organized themselves by selecting commissioners to represent them and to enter their land claims at the Ocoee Land Office.

Those in the northeast quarter-section chose John P. Long, Aaron M. Rawlings, and George W. Williams as commissioners. These men represented the following:

Isaac Baldwin	Thomas Edmondson
George W. Cherry	Joseph Ellis
Arsley Cope	Andrew Evans
Samuel H. Davis	Samuel Fitzgerald
William M. Davis	Matthew Frazier

E. H. Freeman
Charles Griggsby
George B. Gwathney
Berry Jones
John Keeney
John P. Long
Thomas W. Munsey
Abram Perry
Ezekiel Price

Aaron M. Rawlings
Joseph Rice
Eliza Russell
James Woods Smith
Wiley Starling
Rachel Webb
George W. Williams
Samuel Williams
Abner Witt

Allen Kennedy, Albert S. Lenoir, and Reynolds A. Ramsey were the commissioners chosen for those in the southeast fractional quarter-section. They represented:

John C. Cathey
S. S. M. Doak
William B. Gilliland
Nathan Harris
Jane Henderson
William Hill
Matthew Hillsman
Benjamin K. Hudgins
Cary A. Jones
Allen Kennedy
M. W. Legg
Albert S. Lenoir

William Long
John T. Mathis
Thomas Antipas Moore
David G. Perry
John A. Porter
Reynolds A. Ramsey
William G. Sparks
William Thrailkill
William Thurman
James W. Tunnell
Jane White
Matthew Williams
Darlen A. Wilds

NOTE: Zella Armstrong, *History of Hamilton County and Chattanooga, Tennessee*. 2 vols (Chattanooga: Lookout Publishing, 1931), 1: 128-129.

APPENDIX N

Civil War Defenses of the Union Army

1. Fort Creighton—Better known as Fort Wood, name used before official names were assigned by General Thomas's order of 27 April 1864, in honor of General Thomas J. Wood. This work with high walls and deep ditches covering a city block was on a hill east of the town (later between East Fourth and Vine streets east of Palmetto Street). Official name, Fort Creighton, honored Colonel William R. Creighton, Seventh Ohio Infantry, killed in action at Ringgold, Georgia, 26 November 1863. Fort was leveled in 1888.

2. Fort Phelps—Better known as Fort Negley. Detached work on the plain in the vicinity of Main Street and Rossville Avenue and Mitchell and Read streets. Named in honor of Colonel E. H. Phelps,, Thirty-Eighth Ohio Infantry, killed in charge at Missionary Ridge, 25 November 1863.

3. Fort Sherman—Main interior line on east side of town from the intersection of East Fifth and Walnut streets east of and around Brabson's Hill to

Bluff View. Contained huge walls of earth and stone and deep, wide ditch. Named for Major-General W. T. Sherman.

4. Battery Bushnell—Battery of Fort Sherman north of East Fourth Street and west of Lindsay Street, now called Battery Place. Named in honor of Major Douglass Bushnell, Thirteenth Illinois Infantry, killed 25 November 1863 at Chattanooga.

5. Lunette O'Meara—Field work in main line of Fort Sherman on crest of Brabson Hill, vicinity of East Fifth and Houston streets. Named in honor of Lieutenant Colonel Timothy O'Meara, Nineteenth Illinois Infantry, killed in front of Chattanooga, 25 November 1863.

6. Redoubt Putnam—Redoubt of Fort Sherman on Signal Point overlooking river bluff at north end of High Street (Hunter Art Gallery), named in honor of Colonel Holden Putnam, Ninety-Third Regiment of Illinois Volunteers, killed in battle of Chattanooga, 25 November 1863.

7. Battery McAloon—Battery in front of Battery Bushnell on rise overlooking lowlands near mouth of Citico Creek. Named for Lieutenant Colonel P. A. McAloon, Twenty-Seventh Regiment of Pennsylvania Volunteers, killed in battle of Chattanooga, 25 November 1863.

8. The Star Fort, later officially Fort Lytle—Large work, star-shaped with twenty-foot walls and deep ditches located on spur southwest of railroad depot on College Street, at south end of Academy Hill. Named for Brigadier-General William H. Lytle, killed at battle of Chickamauga, 20 September 1863.

9. Redoubt Crutchfield—Redoubt and indented line west of Fort Lytle on Terrace Hill, extension south of Cameron Hill (137 East Terrace Street). Named for local Union supporter William Crutchfield, who had his home at this site.

10. Fort Mihalotzy—On Cameron Hill south of Sixth Street, named for Colonel Geza Mihalotzy, Twenty-Fourth Regiment of Illinois Volunteers, killed before Dalton, Georgia, 25 February 1864.

11. Battery Coolidge—On Cameron Hill west of and near Fort Mihalotzy not far from Tennessee River on west side of Terrace Hill. Named in honor of Major Sidney Coolidge, Sixteenth U.S. Infantry, killed 19 September 1863, at Chickamauga.

12. Fort Cameron—Citadel on hill named for James Cameron who had home here in years just prior to war. Battery of 100-pound Parrott guns was located about two hundred yards south of the crown of the hill.

13. Redoubt Carpenter—A redoubt on northeastern spur of Cameron Hill named for Major Stephen D. Carpenter, who died in battle of Stone's River, 31 December 1862. Earthworks enclosed crest of spur where military waterworks were built.

14. Redoubt Jones—On rocky knob east of railroad depot, also known as Stone Fort. On elevation south of Tenth Street and east of Market Street where Patten Hotel and old municipal building stood. Named for Captain William G. Jones, Tenth Regiment of U.S. Infantry, acting colonel of Thirty-Sixth

Regiment of Volunteers, killed at Chickamauga, 19 September 1863.

15. Battery Taft—First embrasure battery of field guns in line running from Lunette O'Meara to Redoubt Jones. Located on the west side of East Ninth Street between Lindsay and Houston streets. Named to honor Colonel J. B. Taft, Seventy-Third Regiment of Pennsylvania Infantry, killed at Chattanooga, 25 November 1863.

16. Battery Ervin—Second embrasure battery of field guns in same line south of Battery Taft. Occupied highest part of knoll south of East Ninth Street and west of Peeples Street (corner of Eighth and Mabel streets). Named for Major S. C. Ervin, Sixth Regiment of Ohio Volunteer Infantry, killed at Chattanooga, 25 November 1863.

Military prisons were located at 912 Market Street and at Swim's jail at the northwest corner of East Fifth and Lookout streets.

The Federal Army used the town hall and market house on East Sixth Street for their general headquarters.

The post chapel was the First Baptist Church between Walnut and Lookout streets.

NOTE: The defenses of Chattanooga received their official names by the orders of General Thomas dated 27 April 1864. See U.S. War Department, *The War of the Rebellion: A Compilation of the Official Records of the Union and Confederate Armies*, (Washington, D.C.: Government Printing Office, 1884), Series 1, 32 (pt. 3), 519-520.

APPENDIX O

Act Establishing the County of Hamilton
(From Private Acts, 1819, Chapter No. 113)

An act to establish a new county south west of Rhea and south and east of Bledsoe and Marion Counties.

SECTION 1. That the territory lying southwest of Rhea and south and east of Bledsoe and Marion counties, shall constitute a county by the name of Hamilton, in honor and to perpetuate the memory of the late Alexander Hamilton, secretary of the treasury of the United States.

SECTION 2. That the said county of Hamilton shall be bounded as follows, to wit: Beginning at a point at the foot of Walden's Ridge of Cumberland mountain on the east side thereof; thence running to a point on the Tennessee river two and one half miles below the lower end of Jolly's island, so as to include Patrick Martin in the County of Hamilton; thence south thirty-five degrees east to the southern limits of this state; thence west to the point where Marion county line intersects said western boundary; thence north eastwardly with Marion County line to Bledsoe County line; thence with Bledsoe County line to a point opposite the beginning and thence to the beginning.

SECTION 3. That for the due administration of justice, the court of pleas and quarter sessions and the circuit court of the county of Hamilton shall be holden at such place as shall be designated by Charles Gamble, Robert Patterson, and William Lauderdale until otherwise provided for by law; under the same rules, regulations and restrictions, and shall possess and exercise the same power and jurisdiction of said courts in other counties in this state.

SECTION 4. That the Sheriff of Hamilton County shall hold an election at the place for holding courts in said county, on the first Thursday and Friday in March next, for the purpose of electing field officers for the said county of Hamilton under the same rules, regulations, and restrictions as are prescribed by law in similar cases; and the militia of said county shall compose the 64th regiment, and shall be attached to, and become a part of the 7th brigade.

SECTION 5. That it shall be the duty of the commandant of said regiment having been first commissioned and sworn to lay off said regiment into companies of convenient size, and to issue writs of election for company officers in said companies, giving the notice prescribed by law in each company, which election shall be holden and conducted under the same rules and in the same manner as in other cases for company offiicers.

SECTION 6. That the county of Hamilton shall be part of the district for electing governor, members of the General Assembly, representatives to congress, and elections to elect a President and Vice-President of the United States to which the county of Rhea belongs; and that the elections shall be held at the place of holding courts in said county at the time and in the manner by law directed; and the sheriff or returning officer of said county shall make return of the polls of said election to the sheriff of Rhea county in the town of Washington on the day next succeeding each election and comparing the votes, the sheriff of Rhea county shall declare the candidate for the representative of the counties of Rhea and Hamilton, who may have the greatest number of votes, duly elected representative for said counties, and give him a certificate accordingly; and it shall be the duty of the sheriff of Rhea county to make return of the votes for senators of Rhea and Hamilton, members to congress, governor, etc. as heretofore for Rhea county.

SECTION 7. That it shall be lawful for any justice of the peace of Rhea county to attend at the place appointed by said commissioners for holding courts in Hamilton county, at the first court of pleas and quarter sessions for said county, for the purpose of administering to the justices of said county the necessary oaths.

Passed: 25 October 1819.

Index

487

Index 491

Hamilton Co. Courthouse; community of, 90, 94
Hamilton Co. Herald, 392
Hamilton Indians, 35–36
Hamilton National Bank, 312
Hardee, William J., 172, 173, 194
Harris, Isham G., 147, 148, 151, 154, 160, 161, 165
Harrison, community of, 12, 13, 77, 91, 110, 115, 129, 140, 199, 212, 227, 230, 235, 236, 371, 383, 400
Harrison Bay State parks, 402
Hayes, Roland, 349–350
Hayes, Rutherford B., 243, 244
Health care and hospitals, 140–141, 162, 176, 184, 230–231, 277–278, 300–301, 313–314, 330, 364, 452–454, 459, 468–469
Henderson, Daniel, 90, 104, 230
Henderson, James, 137–138, 156
Henderson, Jane, 104, 230
Henry, Patrick, 47
Highland Park, community of, 269, 272, 279, 305, 372, 373
Hill City, community of, 275, 279, 280, 305, 337, 338, 377
Hiwassee Garrison, 58, 61, 87
Hiwassee Island, 35, 36, 37, 38, 40, 41, 66
Hiwassee River, 6, 7, 55, 58, 66, 67, 70, 86, 87, 258
Hixson, community of, 96, 239, 267, 276
Hixson, Ephraim, 96, 267
Hodge, William C., 245, 248, 466
Hood, James R., 150, 156, 205, 206, 215, 228, 229, 251
Hooke, Robert, 111, 133, 141, 145, 155, 215
Hooker, Joseph, 187, 189, 191, 192, 194, 195, 203, 286
Howard School, 237, 239, 459
Huffaker, Hugh D., 309
Hunt, Rueben H., 314, 348
Hunter, George T., 310, 454, 455
Hunter Museum of Art, 348, 454
Hutcheson, John L., 304, 307
Hutchins, Styles L., 245, 248, 342, 343, 344, 466

Igou's Ferry, 115
Igou, Samuel, 115, 144
Incline 1 (Lookout Mountain Railway Co.), 292–293, 295, 296
Incline #2 (Lookout Incline & Lula Lake Railway Co.), 295, 296

Indians, prehistoric, 32–40
Industry, 136–138, 176, 180, 203–205, 208, 209–210, 250, 254–257, 307–311, 386, 425, 426, 429, 437–442, 468
Interstate Life and Accident Insurance Co., 309, 441
Irvine, John James, 248

Jackson, Andrew, 5, 50, 64, 69, 75, 77, 78, 79, 82, 149
Jackson, Rachel, 50
James County, 12–14, 236, 370–371
James Hall, 235, 316, 317, 330
James, Charles E., 236, 254, 269, 270, 272, 278, 279, 280, 293, 304, 323, 369, 370, 375, 396
James, Jesse, 12, 110, 122, 236
Jim Crow legislation, 335–337
Johnson, A. M., 135, 155, 180, 215, 272, 291, 307, 376, 380
Johnson, Andrew, 161, 226, 227, 228
Johnson, H. Clay Evans, 309
Johnson, Joseph W., 309
Johnston, Joseph E., 173, 174
Johnston, J. F., 309, 310
Jolly, John, 66

Kefauver, Estes, 417, 423, 424, 466
Kelley, Ralph H., 411
Kelly's Ferry, 189, 190, 191
Kennedy, Allen, 105, 106, 141
Key, David M., 12, 140, 152, 154, 155, 165, 166, 215, 216, 233, 234, 235, 242, 243, 244, 319
Kingsbury, Cyrus, 70, 72
Kingston, community of, 7, 58, 257
Knights of Labor, 306
Knox County, 7, 9, 88, 432
Knoxville, TN, 26, 55, 59, 99, 134, 155, 190, 193, 218, 258, 259, 334, 335, 338, 342, 415

Lakesite, community of, 427, 428, 472
Lauderback Ridge, 16
Lauderdale, William, 4, 67, 88
Lenoir, Albert S., 106
Letcher, C. P., 232, 246
Lewis, William, 139–140, 304
Lincoln, Abraham, 150, 151, 154, 171, 187, 207, 226, 227, 228
Lindsay, William, 80, 110
Linn, Robert M., 291, 302–303
Little Owl, 45, 402
Little Theater, 454